108

MICROCOMPUTERS AND MICROPROCESSORS

The 8080, 8085, and Z-80 Programming, Interfacing, and Troubleshooting

Third Edition

John Uffenbeck

Wisconsin Indianhead Technical College

Prentice Hall
Upper Saddle River, New Jersey
Columbus, Ohio

Library of Congress Cataloging-in-Publication Data

Uffenbeck, John E.
    Microcomputers and microprocessors : the 8080, 8085, and Z-80
    programming, interfacing, and troubleshooting / John Uffenbeck. —
    3rd ed.
        p.   cm.
    Includes index.
    ISBN 0-13-209198-4
    1. Microcomputers.   2. Intel 8080 (Microprocessor)   3. Intel 8085
(Microprocessor)   4. Zilog Z-80 (Microprocessor)   I. Title.
    QA76.5.U35   2000
    004.165—dc21   98-50972
                                                              CIP

Cover art/photo: FPG International
Publisher: Charles E. Stewart, Jr.
Associate Editor: Kate Linsner
Production Editor: Alexandrina Benedicto Wolf
Cover Design Coordinator: Karrie Converse-Jones
Cover Designer: Tanya Burgess
Production Manager: Deidra M. Schwartz
Editorial/Production Supervision: Tally Morgan, WordCrafters Editorial Services, Inc.
Marketing Manager: Ben Leonard

This book was set in Times New Roman by The Clarinda Company and was printed and bound by Courier Westford. The cover was printed by Phoenix Color Corporation.

© 2000, 1991, 1985 by Prentice-Hall, Inc.
Pearson Education
Upper Saddle River, New Jersey 07458

Printed in the United States of America

10 9 8 7 6 5 4 3 2 1

ISBN 0-13-209198-4

Prentice-Hall International (UK) Limited, *London*
Prentice-Hall of Australia Pty. Limited, *Sydney*
Prentice-Hall of Canada, Inc., *Toronto*
Prentice-Hall Hispanoamericana, S.A., *Mexico*
Prentice-Hall of India Private Limited, *New Delhi*
Prentice-Hall of Japan, Inc., *Tokyo*
Prentice-Hall (Singapore) Pte. Ltd., *Singapore*
Editora Prentice-Hall do Brasil, Ltda., *Rio de Janeiro*

PREFACE

This is a book about microcomputer technology. It is appropriate for use in a one-semester introductory course on microprocessors and microcomputers. The primary emphasis is on developing an understanding of the hardware components of a microcomputer system and the role of software in controlling that hardware.

HANDS-ON APPROACH

In this book, we examine three compatible 8-bit microprocessor chips: the Intel 8080 and 8085 processors and the Zilog Z-80. A hands-on approach takes the reader through the steps involved in building a microcomputer. For example, after introducing the stored-program computer model in Chapter 1, we proceed to "construct" CPU modules for each of the microprocessors. The emphasis is on developing a three-bus architecture to which the memory and I/O devices can be interfaced in later chapters. Chapter 4 deals specifically with these buses and explains topics such as noise immunity, bus loading, reflections, and tristate and bidirectional buffers.

TROUBLESHOOTING

Practical troubleshooting hints regarding problems with circuits are provided, including methods for resetting and single-stepping each of the processors. Chapter 11 explains how a test ROM can be used to boot up a computer for the first time. The end-of-chapter questions and problems marked with an asterisk deal specifically with hardware and software troubleshooting issues.

SUGGESTED BACKGROUND

You will get maximum benefit from this book if you have a good understanding of DC and AC circuits. In addition, you should be familiar with digital logic circuits, such as gates, flip-flops, decoders, and counters. The hexadecimal number system is used throughout, and a brief review of this topic is presented in Chapter 1.

IMPORTANT FEATURES

Several unique features are associated with this book:

1. Chapter 1 provides a "mini-history" of computing from ENIAC to the Pentium II. It compares the general-purpose microprocessor with other computers, including microcontrollers, digital signal processors, minicomputers, supercomputers, and mainframe computers.
2. Software for each of the three processors is presented using a *learn-by-doing* approach. Fourteen detailed examples are used to help illustrate common programming techniques. The examples culminate with the development of an assembly language game program called NIM.
3. New components are presented using the manufacturer's data sheets, which are included throughout the text and the appendices.
4. Detailed descriptions and examples help illustrate the peripheral controller chips associated with each processor. Included are the 8255A PPI, 8245 PIT, 8259 PIC, 8237 DMAC, 8251 USART, Z-80 PIO, Z-80 CTC, Z-80 DMA, and Z-80 SIO and DART.
5. Chapter 12 provides an introduction to the 16-bit 8086 and 8088 processors. Examples of 8086 memory and I/O interfaces and several programming examples are presented.
6. More than 70 laboratory projects are described. These should give you ideas on how to test and demonstrate the concepts discussed in the chapters.

CHANGES IN THIS EDITION

Many changes have been incorporated into this third edition:

1. Each chapter now begins with an outline, an overview, and a list of learning objectives. In addition, each subsection begins with a brief introduction and repeats the learning objectives associated with that section.

2. Self-review questions and answers have been added to the end of each subsection.

3. The chapter summaries have been rewritten in question-and-answer format to make them more interesting to the reader.

4. More than 50 new diagrams and tables are interspersed throughout the book.

5. Chapter 1 now includes a section on the history of computing and the various types of computers in use.

6. Chapter 5 has been updated to include information on the latest memory technologies, including flash memory and synchronous DRAMs.

7. In Chapter 9, the section on the RS-232 has been rewritten and updated. Also, information on the latest modem standards is provided, including V.34 28.8K and V.90 56K modems. Examples using the AT command set are shown in this chapter as well.

8. Chapter 10 has been updated to reflect changes in floppy and hard-disk technologies. IDE and SCSI controllers are presented.

9. Chapter 12 now includes a detailed description of each of the 80x86 processor family members, through the Pentium II.

THE THREE-MICROPROCESSOR APPROACH

I believe that a first course in microprocessors should provide a solid foundation in the technology of microcomputers. This means learning the difference between RAM and ROM and how these two types of memory are interfaced to the microprocessor. It also means learning how an input or output port works and how to construct a serial interface. None of these concepts depends on a particular microprocessor chip. In this book, we have chosen the 8080, 8085, and Z-80 processors because we need something "real" to work with. In that respect, the Z-80 works as well as a Pentium (maybe even better—the Z-80 is a lot easier to understand!).

Because the 8080, 8085, and Z-80 are all software compatible, it seems logical to cover all three of these at once. And once the CPU modules have been constructed (in Chapter 4), even the hardware differences are minimal. When the differences are significant, the sections are clearly marked as pertaining to the Z-80, 8085, or 8080.

ACKNOWLEDGMENTS

Once again I extend my thanks to both Zilog and Intel Corporations for their permission to use the large number of data sheets you will find throughout this book. I would also like to thank all you readers, students, and teachers who have used the book over the years. Finally, a special thanks is extended to Charles Stewart and Kate Linsner at Prentice Hall for their encouragement and help with this latest edition.

CONTENTS

4 BUILDING THE MICROCOMPUTER, PART 1: THE BUSES   149

Contents

Contents

1

INTRODUCTION TO THE MICROPROCESSOR

OBJECTIVES

After completing this chapter, you should be able to:

- List the three main units of a stored-program computer.
- Identify the function of the address, data, and control buses in a stored-program computer.
- Trace the evolution of the computer from the vacuum tube machine to the microprocessor.
- Identify significant computers that have been built over the years.

- Explain the difference between a microprocessor, a microcomputer, and a microcontroller.
- Explain how to convert decimal numbers to binary and hexadecimal and vice versa.
- Show how the ASCII code is used to represent letters of the alphabet, numbers, punctuation symbols, and control codes.
- Compare machine language programming with assembly language programming.
- Explain what is meant by a high-level computer language.
- Compare signal levels for TTL and CMOS digital systems.
- Draw a memory map for a processor with 64 KB of memory space.
- Sketch a machine-cycle timing diagram, showing the address, data, and control bus signals.
- Sketch processor timing diagrams for memory read and write and I/O read and write bus cycles.

OVERVIEW

In this chapter, we present the basic principles of digital computers. We begin with the *stored-program model* for a computer first proposed by Dr. John Von Neumann in the 1940s. Although more than 50 years old, the model still applies to nearly all computers made today.

With this model as background, we trace the evolution of the computer from the early vacuum tube machines through the transistor and integrated circuit eras and the modern microprocessor. Studying this material, you will learn that there are several different types of computers, ranging from desktop PCs to "hidden" microcontrollers, supercomputers, RISC processors, and digital signal processors. Also included is a brief review of the binary and hexadecimal number systems, the ASCII code, and a comparison of several different computer programming methods.

The chapter concludes by looking at the processor as a complex timer with a carefully orchestrated set of signals on its address, data, and control buses. In later chapters, you will learn how to connect memory and I/O devices to these buses to build a complete microcomputer system.

1.1 DIGITAL COMPUTERS: SOME BASICS

Introduction

One of the first digital computers was a machine called the Electronic Numerical Integrator and Computer (ENIAC). It was designed and built at the Moore School of Electrical Engineering at the University of Pennsylvania in 1946. ENIAC measured over 18 feet high and was 80 feet long. It contained nearly 18,000 vacuum tubes, weighed more than 30 tons, and required 1500 square feet of floor space. More than 200,000 man-hours went into its construction. (Half a million solder connections alone were required.) The machine was programmed by setting up to 6000 switches and connecting cables between its various units.

While ENIAC was under construction, Dr. John Von Neumann, also of the Moore School of Electrical Engineering, wrote a paper in collaboration with A. W. Burks and H. H. Goldstein that would define the architecture to be used by nearly all computers from that day on. Von Neumann suggested that, rather than rewire the computer for each new task, the program instructions should be stored in a memory unit just like the data. The resulting computer would then be software programmable rather than hardware programmable. Von Neumann's proposal is now called the *stored-program concept.*

In this section, we:

- List the three main units of a stored-program computer.
- Identify the function of the address, data, and control buses in a stored-program computer.

The Stored-Program Computer

Figure 1.1 is a block diagram of a typical digital computer. The *central-processing unit,* or CPU, shown on the far left, is often likened to the human brain because it is in the CPU that all decisions are made and the system timing is generated. The arithmetic–logic unit, or ALU, is contained within the CPU, and all the mathematical operations are performed there. The results of these calculations are left in a special register in the ALU called the *accumulator.*

The memory unit shown in Fig. 1.1 is used to store the specific sequence of commands that will be used to instruct the CPU to perform some task. These instructions are called the computer *program* (hence the name *stored-program* computer).

Finally, no useful task can be performed by the computer without the input/output devices—the *I/O* in "computerese." It is with the keyboard that we input the instructions or commands about the task to be accomplished. The results are then viewed on the printer or cathode-ray tube (CRT) screen.

Note that each cell in the memory has its own unique identifying number, or *address,* and that the total capacity of the particular memory unit shown is 25 cells. If we were to examine the contents of these memory cells, we would see a strange collection of numbers having no particular meaning to us. Yet, to the CPU, these numbers would represent a concise set of commands instructing it to carry out some sequence of operations. The numbers represent the operation codes (*op codes*) for the various instructions in the CPU's instruction set.

Fetch and Execute

Note in Fig. 1.1 that the CPU has been designed to follow repeatedly four simple steps:

1. Fetch data from the memory cell whose address is currently in the program counter register. Put the data into the instruction register.
2. Add 1 to the address in the program counter.
3. Decode the command currently in the instruction register, and do what it tells you.
4. Go to step 1.

All figures and tables by Zilog were "Reproduced by permission © 1977, 1978, 1981, 1999 Zilog, Inc. This material shall not be reproduced without the written consent of Zilog, Inc." "Zilog Z-80® is a trademark of Zilog, Inc., with whom Prentice Hall is not associated."

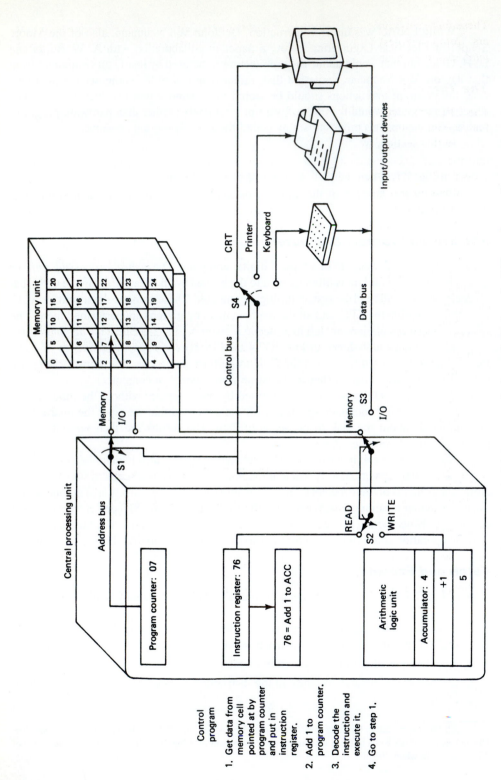

Figure 1.1 Block diagram of a digital computer. The three main blocks are the CPU central-processing unit (CPU), the memory unit, and the input–output (I/O) devices.

These four steps constitute the principle of operation of all stored-program digital computers, from the largest IBM mainframe to the tiniest microcomputer. The principle is called *fetch and execute* and is the key to understanding the activities of a microprocessor.

The Three-Bus Architecture

The CPU, memory unit, and I/O devices must be able to communicate with each other. For example, the CPU must be able to specify which memory cell is to be selected and whether the contents of that cell should be read or whether new data should be written into the cell. Such communication is the purpose of the address, data, and control buses shown in Fig. 1.1. When the CPU is required to read the contents of a particular memory cell, it first outputs the proper address on its *address bus*. This address is actually the contents of the program counter. Next, the *control bus* causes switches S1 and S3 to switch to the MEMORY position and switch S2 to the READ position. The *data bus* now carries the contents of the selected memory cell back to the CPU and into the instruction register.

As a further example of the three-bus architecture, let us assume that the command in the instruction register specifies that the contents of the accumulator are to be output to the printer. The execution of this command requires the CPU to output the address of the printer on its address bus. Switch S4 will examine this address and, seeing that it is for the printer, switch to the printer position. Next, the control bus will switch S1 and S3 to the I/O position and S2 to the WRITE position. The data to be output can now be placed on the data bus and routed to the printer.

In sum, the CPU begins each command cycle with an instruction fetch from the memory unit. The program counter is then incremented in preparation for the next fetch cycle. Finally the op code for the instruction is decoded and executed during the execution phase of the cycle.

From the standpoint of the three-bus architecture, there are only four unique instruction cycles possible. These are listed in Table 1.1, with the contents of the three buses specified for each case. When we study microprocessor programming in Chapters 2 and 3, it will be interesting to note that all microprocessor instructions are made up of combinations of these four cycles. (Later in the chapter, we will call them *machine cycles*.)

Computer Programming

From the preceding discussion, you can begin to see how the CPU controls the flow of data between itself, memory, and the I/O devices. The instruction set of a computer can be thought of as a list of commands that cause unique sequences to occur on the three buses.

TABLE 1.1 Instruction Cycles of a Digital Computer

Instruction type	Address bus	Control bus	Data bus
Memory read	Memory cell address	Select memory and read	Contents of selected memory cell
Memory write	Memory cell address	Select memory and write	Data to be written to memory
I/O read	I/O device address	Select I/O and read	Data from selected I/O device
I/O write	I/O device address	Select I/O and write	Data to be written to I/O device

As an example, the command LD A,(10)—load the accumulator with the contents of memory cell 10—would cause the address bus to output address 10, the control bus to establish a memory read cycle, and the data bus to input data from memory cell 10 and store the data in the accumulator of the CPU.

Writing a computer program requires assembling the proper instructions and storing them sequentially in the memory unit of the computer. In Chapters 2 and 3, we will study the instruction sets of the 8080, 8085, and Z-80 microprocessors and learn in detail how to program these processors.

SELF-REVIEW 1.1*

1.1.1 What are the three main parts of a stored-program computer?

1.1.2 List the three buses used by the CPU to communicate with its memory and I/O devices.

1.1.3 The stored-program computer can perform four different types of instruction cycles. List these.

1.2 TYPES OF COMPUTERS

Introduction

The first generation of computers was described in terms of hundreds of feet of floor space, tons of weight, and thousands of vacuum tubes. Reliability was often measured in hours or even minutes. Loading a new program required tens of man-hours to rewire the computer and could only be done by trained engineers and technicians. Today we have desktop computers, laptop computers, and even notebook computers. We describe the processor in terms of submicron line spacing, millions of transistors, and onboard floating-point processors. Indeed, the evolution of the computer has occurred so rapidly that it is sometimes called a revolution.

In this section, we:

- Trace the evolution of the computer from the vacuum tube machine to the microprocessor.
- Identify significant computers that have been built over the years.
- Explain the difference between a microprocessor, a microcomputer, and a microcontroller.

The Vacuum Tube Era

First-generation computers were massive machines based on vacuum tube technology. They occupied entire rooms and required an air-conditioned environment to operate reliably. In fact, because the average life of a vacuum tube was 3000 hours, and several thousand tubes were required to build a machine, some predicted that the machine would

---

*Answers at the end of the chapter.

never do any useful work—technicians would constantly be tracking down and replacing bad tubes! Nevertheless, in 1951, Remington-Rand delivered the first Universal Automatic Computer (Univac I) to the Bureau of the Census. In 1952, CBS used a Univac I to predict the defeat of Adlai E. Stevenson by Dwight D. Eisenhower in the presidential election.

International Business Machines (IBM) reluctantly entered the computer field in 1952 with its Model 701 Data Processing System. IBM's founder, Thomas Watson, Sr., had to be convinced by his son, Thomas Watson, Jr., of the importance of these machines. Indeed, Watson, Sr., is reported to have said that he could imagine a need for no more than 8 to 10 of the large "brains" for the entire scientific and business community!

The Transistor Is Born

In 1956, three Bell Laboratory scientists—Drs. William Schockley, John Bardeen, and Walter H. Brattain—received the Nobel Physics award for their 1948 invention of the bipolar transistor. In 1954, another Bell Labs team demonstrated the significance of this invention with the first all-transistorized computer, TRADIC. The 800-transistor machine generated much less heat than its vacuum tube counterpart, making it more reliable and less costly.

IBM's first transistorized computer was the 7070/7090, announced in 1958. It was followed by another all-transistorized computer, the business-oriented 1401, in 1959. Computers of this era were called *second-generation machines,* and because of their re-duced size and cost, they became popular with business and industry. These machines were built on circuit boards mounted into rack panels or frames. The term *mainframe* was applied to describe the central-processing unit (the *main* frame) of such computers. Today we think of a mainframe computer as a computer designed to handle large volumes of data while serving hundreds of users simultaneously.

Integrated Circuits

Certainly one of the most significant scientific developments of the 20th century was the invention of the integrated circuit (IC) in 1959, by Dr. Robert Noyce of Fairchild Semi-conductor Corporation and Jack Kilby of Texas Instruments. Their invention was more a triumph of creative thinking than it was a technological breakthrough. After all, the in-vention of the transistor at Bell Laboratories had ushered in the solid-state era 21 years previously. In fact, the concept of a solid-logic module (a module with all circuit compo-nents fabricated from one piece of semiconductor material) was well known. What was not known, however, was how to realize the concept. The following, quoting Noyce, voices this frustration:

> With the advent of diffusion, the industry was able to make hundreds of transistors in a slice of silicon. But then people cut these beautifully arranged things into little pieces and had girls hunt for them with tweezers in order to put leads on and wire them all back together again; then we would sell them to our customers, who would plug all these separate packages into a printed circuit board.

Kilby's invention, patented early in 1959, involved fabricating resistors, capacitors, and transistors on a germanium wafer and then connecting these parts with fine gold wires.

Later that year, Noyce, working independently of Kilby, suggested isolating the individual components with reverse-biased diodes and depositing an adherent metal film over the circuit, thus connecting the components (and avoiding the connecting wires in Kilby's design). Noyce filed his patent six months after Kilby's.

Third-Generation Computers

The first integrated circuit contained only a handful of components, enough to construct a simple two-transistor multivibrator (oscillator). However, manufacturers were soon producing ICs with several hundred components, and by the mid 1960s, memory chips with 1000 components were common. In 1964, IBM announced one of the most famous computers ever to be built and the first to use integrated circuit (third-generation) technology, the 32-bit 360 series. The IBM 360 was actually a family of six compatible computers with 40 different input/output and auxiliary storage devices. The machine's memory capacity varied from 16K words to over 1M. Internally, the processor contained 16 32-bit registers, a 24-bit address bus, and a 128-bit data bus. The IBM 360 could perform 375,000 computations per second.[1] IBM reportedly spent nearly $5 billion developing this computer, and its success gave them a lead in the (mainframe) computer business that the company has yet to relinquish.

Minicomputers

With the advent of the transistor and integrated circuit, the electronics industry began to boom in the 1960s. The United States was engaged in a "space race" with the Soviet Union, and President John F. Kennedy had challenged the nation to put a man on the moon by the end of the decade. Accordingly scientists and engineers demanded an inexpensive computer that they could operate themselves. A young engineer named Edson de Castro, working for Digital Equipment Corporation (DEC), was put in charge of designing such a computer. The result, in 1965, was a landmark machine called the Programmed Data Processor (PDP-8). Using integrated circuits, de Castro's group constructed a low-cost ($25,000) *minicomputer* (scaled-down mainframe). The 12-bit (data bus width) PDP-8 became an immediate hit and was soon followed by the 16-bit PDP-11.

Today, the distinction between minicomputer and mainframe computer (or even microcomputer) is not so clear. The so-called *supermini* has capabilities rivaling those of the mainframe. And top-of-the-line microcomputers (discussed in the next section) are challenging minicomputers. Nowadays, minicomputers are used primarily by small organizations in a timed-shared environment with 50–100 users.[2] With the advent of local and wide-area microcomputer networks, even this distinction is fading.

Microprocessors

In 1968, Robert Noyce and Gordon Moore, two of the original founders of Fairchild, started a new company called INTEL (Integrated Electronics). Their intention was to exploit the then-expanding semiconductor memory market. However, in 1969, the Japanese

---

[1] A 100-MHz Pentium can perform 150 million instructions per second!

[2] For a fascinating insider's view of the minicomputer world in the 1970s, read Tracy Kidder, *The Soul of a New Machine* (New York: Avon Books, 1982).

calculator company Busicom approached them to fabricate a custom set of ICs for a new calculator design. Two engineers, Ted Hoff and Stan Mazor, were assigned to the project and came up with the idea of fabricating a 4-bit central-processing unit on a single chip, supported by separate read-only memory (ROM) and random access memory (RAM) chips. Fredrico Faggin, a process engineer for Intel, took these ideas and converted them into a chip set that became known as the *4000 family,* consisting of four chips:

1. The 4001, a 2K ROM with 4-bit I/O port.
2. The 4002, a 320-bit RAM with 4-bit output port.
3. The 4003, a 10-bit serial-in, parallel-out shift register.
4. The 4004, a 4-bit processor.

Never before had the entire central-processing unit of a computer been constructed on a single piece of silicon. The trade journals soon began describing this processor on a chip as a *microprocessor.* The 4004 was followed by the 8-bit 8008 in 1972 and an improved version called the 8080 in 1974. At this same time, several other companies began to introduce competitive microprocessor chips. Motorola had the MC6800, MOS Technology (a spin-off of Motorola) the 6502, and Zilog (a spin-off of Intel) the Z-80. These chips all had 8-bit data bus widths and 16-bit address buses. The addressable memory space was 64K bytes.

In the late 1970s, several 16-bit microprocessors began to appear. The two most popular were Intel's 8086 and Motorola's MC68000. These processors introduced new 16-bit instructions, including hardware multiplication and division, and, with 20-bit address buses, could access up to 1 MB of memory.

The evolution continues to this day with 32-bit (the 80386, 80486, MC68020, and MC68030) and 64-bit (Pentium and Pentium II) CPUs.[3] Table 1.2 charts the astonishing growth of microprocessors from the 2250-transistor 4004 to the 7.5 million-transistor Pentium II. Considering Fig. 1.2, that's quite an achievement for a little man with a jack-hammer!

The Personal Computer

Once the microprocessor became a reality, microcomputer *systems* began to appear—complete computers based on a particular microprocessor chip. One of the first was the MITS Altair 8800. Announced in 1975, it cost $399 in kit form and featured the 8-bit Intel 8080 microprocessor. Figure 1.3 shows an ad for the Altair taken from the October 1976 issue of *BYTE* magazine. In its simplest form, the Altair was programmed by depositing 1's and 0's into memory via a set of front-panel switches. LED indicators provided a view of the contents of memory.

New microcomputer companies began to spring up almost overnight, each based on a particular microprocessor chip. Using Intel's 8080 were MITS, Imsai, HAL Communications, E&L Instruments, and Processor Technology. Motorola's 6800 was utilized in Southwest Technical Products SWTPC 6800 computer, and the Z-80 was used by North Star Computers, Cromemco, and Radio Shack/Tandy. (The latter in its TRS-80 computer.)

---

[3]Externally, the Pentium has a 64-bit data bus. Internally, the data bus is 32 bits wide.

TABLE 1.2 The Evolution of Intel Microprocessors[1]

Microprocessor	Year introduced	Number of transistors	Minimum feature size (microns)	External data bus width	Internal register widths	Address bus width/ memory space	Estimated processing rate (MIPs)[2]	Onboard coprocessor	Internal cache memory	V_{CC} (volts)	PD (watts)
4004	1971	2,250	10.0	4	4	10/1KB	.06 (.108MHz)	no	no	±5, 12	1.2
8080	1974	6,000	6.0	8	8	16/64KB	.2 (2 MHz)	no	no	5	1.7
8086	1978	29,000	3.0	16	16	20/1 MB	.47 (4.77 MHz)	no	no	5	1.7
8088	1979	29,000	3.0	8	16	20/1 MB	.33 (4.77 MHz)	no	no	5	3
80286	1982	134,000	1.5	16	16	24/16 MB	2 (8 MHz)	no	no	5	1.95
80386DX	1985	275,000	1.5	32	32	32/4 GB	5.5 (16 MHz)	no	no	5	1.9
80386SX	1988	275,000	1.5	16	32	24/16 MB	3.9 (16 MHz)	no	no	5	5
80486DX	1989	1.2 million	0.8	32	32	32/4 GB	20 (25 MHz)	yes	8K	5	3.4
80486SX	1991	1.2 million	0.8	32	32	32/4 GB	13 (16 MHz)	no	8K	5	4.8
80486DX2	1992	1.2 million	0.6	32	32	32/4 GB	41 (50 MHz)	yes	8K	5	
80486DX4	1994	1.2 million	0.8	32	32	32/4 GB	60 (75 MHz)	yes	16K	3.3	
Pentium P60	1993	3.1 million	0.8	64	32	32/4 GB	100 (60 MHz)	yes	16K	5	14.6
Pentium P100	1994	3.1 million	0.6	64	32	32/4 GB	150 (100 MHz)	yes	16K	3.3	10.1
Pentium P120	1995	3.1 million	0.35	64	32	32/4 GB	185 (120 MHz)	yes	16K	3.3	12.8
Pentium Pro 150	1995	5.5 million[3]	0.6	64	32	36/64 GB	350 (150 MHz)	yes	16K/256K[4]	3.3V	29.2
Pentium Pro 200	1996	5.5 million	0.35	64	32	36/64 GB	475 (200 MHz)	yes	16K/512K	3.3V	35
Pentium II	1997	7.5 million	0.25	64	32	36/64 GB	950 (400 MHz)	yes	32K/512K	2.0V	24

[1] Specifications shown are for initial introduction of part.

[2] Millions of instructions per second (internal clock rate shown in parentheses).

[3] 256K-level two cache (separate die in same package) has 15.5 million transistors.

[4] 16KB data/code level-one cache, plus 256KB-level two cache.

At about this same time, two college dropouts, Steve Jobs and Steve Wozniak, began showing off a new computer they had designed called the Apple I. It was based on the MOS Technology 6502 microprocessor, featured 8K of memory, and could be programmed in BASIC. The rest of the story, as they say is history, as Jobs and Wozniak went on to become multimillionaires, and Apple became the fastest growing computer company of all time.

Figure 1.2 Microprocessor chips began to flourish in the late 1970s. The January 1979 issue of *BYTE* magazine illustrates one point of view on how these chips are made. (Reprinted courtesy of Robert Tinney Graphics and BYTE Publications, Peterborough, N.H.)

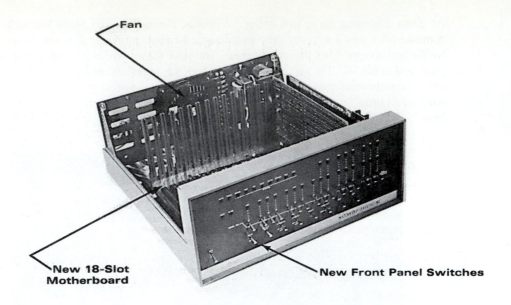

Fan

New 18-Slot
Motherboard

New Front Panel Switches

The four boards, along with the power supply, mount
in an 18" deep x 17" wide x 7" high (45.7 x 43.2 x
17.7-cm) metal cabinet.

SPECIFICATIONS

Number of Boards	Up to 18
Microprocessor	
Model	8080A
Technology	NMOS
Data Word Size, Bits	8
Instruction Word Size, Bits	8
Clock Frequency,	2MHz
Add Time, Register to Register, Microsec.	
Per Data Word	2
Number of Instructions	78
Input/Output Control	
I/O Word Size, Bits	8
Number of I/O Channels	256
Direct Memory Access	Optional
Interrupt Capability	Std. one level
Vectored Interrupt (8 priority levels)	Optional
Software	
Resident Assembler	Yes
Cross Assembler	No
Simulator	No
Higher-level Language	BASIC
Monitor or Executive	Sys. mon.; text edit.
Software Separately Priced	Yes

2450 Alamo S.E. Albuquerque, New Mexico 87106

Figure 1.3 The MITS Altair is often credited with starting the microcomputer revolution. This ad ran in the October 1976 issue of *BYTE* magazine. (Reprinted courtesy of BYTE Publications, Peterborough, N.H.)

Many of the early microcomputers were offered in kit form and required expertise in machine language programming to do useful work. (Thus, they were hardly machines for the masses.) In 1982, IBM began selling the idea of a *personal computer.* (See Fig. 1.4.)[4] It featured a system board designed around the Intel 8088 8-bit microprocessor, 16 KB of memory, and five expansion slots. The latter feature was probably the most significant, as it opened the door for third-party vendors to supply video, printer, modem, disk drive, and RS-232 serial adapter cards. Indeed, the open architecture of the original IBM PC led to the development of the *generic PC,* a computer with interchangeable components manufactured by a variety of companies.

Today, most users describe their computer in terms of its microprocessor chip. For example, one might say, "What kind of computer do you have?" to which the reply might be "I've got a 16-MB Pentium 166 with a 1.6-GB SCSI drive." Translated into layperson's language, the latter statement says that the user has a computer based on the 64-bit 166-MHz Pentium microprocessor chip, with 16 million bytes of user memory and a 1.6-gigabyte hard drive with a SCSI (Small Computer Systems Interface) controller.

Microcontrollers

Microcomputers get all of the headlines, but *microcontrollers* are far more popular. Dataquest, a semiconductor market research firm out of San Jose, California, reports that microcontrollers outsell microprocessors by as much as 10 to 1. But little is heard of these workhorse chips. Study Fig. 1.5, and see if you can spot the 14 microcontrollers in the scene shown.

A microcontroller is an entire computer on a chip—that is, a microprocessor with on-chip memory and input–output (I/O). Typically, these parts are designed into (embedded within) a product and run a "canned" program that never changes. For example, an electronic thermostat is controlled by a microcontroller that inputs an analog temperature signal, converts this to digital form via an internal analog-to-digital converter (ADC), reads the time and date from an internal clock, compares the value read with preprogrammed limits, and activates a furnace or air conditioner via an output control signal.

As Fig. 1.5 suggests, there are numerous applications for embedded controllers. In addition to applications in the home, there are industrial applications (e.g., machine tools and programmable logic controllers), telecommunications applications (e.g., modems), and automotive applications. Indeed, the modern automobile has several "hidden" controllers used for engine control, antilock braking systems (ABSs), heat, venting, and air-conditioning control (HVAC), navigation systems, and multiplex wiring control (several devices connected via a single wire).

Microcontrollers have evolved somewhat differently from microprocessors. While the latter are continually being upgraded to higher speeds and greater bus widths, the newer microcontrollers have greater I/O capabilities. Intel's MCS-51 family, for example, is based on an 8-bit processor, but features up to 32K bytes of onboard ROM, 32 individually programmable digital input–output lines, a serial communications channel, and

---

[4]IBM's apparent strategy was to get people thinking about owning their own computers (count the number of times the phrase "Personal Computer" appears in this ad). The strategy apparently worked: to this day we speak of a microcomputer as a *"PC."*

"My own IBM computer. Imagine that."

One nice thing about having your own IBM Personal Computer is that it's *yours*. For your business, your project, your department, your class, your family and, indeed, for yourself.

Of course, you might have thought owning a computer was too expensive. But now you can relax.

The IBM Personal Computer starts at less than $1,600[†] for a system that, with the addition of one simple device, hooks up to your home TV and uses your audio cassette recorder.

You might also have thought running a computer was too difficult. But you can relax again.

Getting started is easier than you might think, because IBM has structured the learning process for you. Our literature is in *your* language, not in "computerese." Our software *involves* you, the system *interacts* with you as if it was made to—and it was.

That's why you can be running programs in just one day. Maybe even writing your *own* programs in a matter of weeks.

For ease of use, flexibility and performance, no other personal computer offers as many advanced capabilities. (See the box.)

But what makes the IBM Personal Computer a truly useful tool are software programs selected by IBM's Personal Computer Software Publishing Department. You can have programs in business, professional, word processing, computer language, personal and entertainment categories.

You can see the system and the software in action at any ComputerLand® store or Sears Business Systems Center. Or try it out at one of our IBM Product Centers. The IBM Data Processing Division will serve those customers who want to purchase in quantity.

Your IBM Personal Computer. Once you start working with it, you'll discover more than the answers and solutions you seek: you'll discover that getting there is half the fun. Imagine that. **IBM**®

IBM PERSONAL COMPUTER SPECIFICATIONS
*ADVANCED FEATURES FOR PERSONAL COMPUTERS

User Memory 16K - 256K bytes*	**Display Screen** High-resolution (720h x 350v)*	**Color/Graphics** *Text mode:* 16 colors*
Permanent Memory (ROM) 40K bytes*	80 characters x 25 lines Upper and lower case	256 characters and symbols in ROM*
Microprocessor High speed, 8088*	Green phosphor screen*	*Graphics mode:* 4-color resolution: 320h x 200v*
Auxiliary Memory 2 optional internal diskette drives, 5¼", 160K bytes per diskette	**Diagnostics** Power-on self testing* Parity checking* **Languages** BASIC, Pascal	Black & white resolution: 640h x 200v* Simultaneous graphics & text capability*
Keyboard 83 keys, 6 ft. cord attaches to system unit* 10 function keys* 10-key numeric pad Tactile feedback*	**Printer** Bidirectional* 80 characters/second 12 character styles, up to 132 characters/line* 9 x 9 character matrix*	**Communications** RS-232-C interface Asynchronous (start/stop) protocol Up to 9600 bits per second

The IBM Personal Computer and me.

†This price applies to IBM Product Centers. Prices may vary at other stores.

For the IBM Personal Computer dealer nearest you, call (800) 447-4700. In Illinois, (800) 322-4400. In Alaska or Hawaii, (800) 447-0890.

Figure 1.4 In 1982, using ads such as this, IBM began selling the idea of a *personal computer* or *PC*. (Reprinted courtesy of BYTE Publications, Peterborough, N.H.)

Figure 1.5 Microcontrollers are often called "hidden computers." In this picture there are 14 different microcontrollers. (Reprinted courtesy of Intel Corporation and Microcomputer Solutions.)

three 16-bit timers. The MCS-96 family is similar, but is based on a 16-bit processor and includes an onboard 10-bit ADC.

Supercomputers

One definition of a *supercomputer* is, simply, "the most powerful computer available at any given time." These machines are used to solve a complex problem such as the design of a supersonic aircraft, the modeling of global climates, the structure of oil-bearing formations within the earth, the molecular design of new drugs, or the prediction of complex financial behavior in securities markets. Two of the first supercomputers were the Control Data Corporation CDC 6600 and CDC 7600. Both were developed by Seymour Cray, one of the founders of CDC. In 1972, Cray left to found Cray Research, Inc., and in 1976 he developed the Cray-1, generally acknowledged to be the first supercomputer.

The Cray-1 used high-speed emitter-coupled logic (ECL), the fastest (and most power-hungry) logic circuits available at the time. The computer was packaged as a 6.5-ft-high cylinder surrounded by a circular seat. (See Fig. 1.6.) Each circuit board was mounted on a copper heat exchanger through which liquid freon was circulated. The total

Figure 1.6 The CRAY-1 supercomputer. (Photo courtesy of Smithsonian)

power consumption of the computer was 128 KW! The processing speed was 130 million floating-point operations per second (MFLOPS).[5] In all, 63 Cray-1 computers were sold (at a cost of $5.1 million each), and many are still in operation today.

Parallel Processors

Computers like the Cray-1 were single-processor, sequential machines. This type of processor handles one instruction at a time, in sequence. In the 1980s, the performance of such machines (measured in MFLOPS) began to level off, due to the finite length of time required for an electrical signal to propagate through a piece of wire. Researchers began looking for a new computer architecture that could achieve performance levels measured in the tens of *gigaflops* (billions of floating-point operations per second, or GFLOPS).

One of the answers was *parallel processing,* a scheme in which multiple processors are wired together via a common bus, with each processor given a portion of the problem to solve. The *hypercube,* shown in Figure 1.7, was initially thought to provide the optimum architecture for supercomputers. The hypercube consists of a set of interconnected

---

[5]A 100-MHz Pentium can achieve 150 MFLOPS.

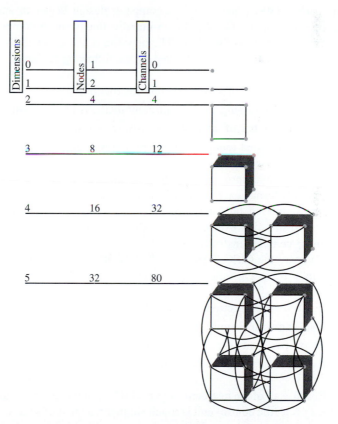

Figure 1.7   A hypercube is an arrangement of processors in the form of an *n*-dimensional cube each connected by a high-speed data channel.

processors called *nodes;* the figure shows examples of 1-, 2-, 4-, 8-, 16-, and 32-node hypercubes. The first hypercube computer was the Cosmic Cube developed at the California Institute of Technology in the early 1980s. The Supercomputer division of Intel Corp. (now called the Scaled Systems Division, or SSD) developed the iPSC hypercube, based on the i860 (RISC) microprocessor.

More recently, supercomputer designers have opted for a two-dimensional rectangular mesh architecture with multiple processors at each connecting node. Nodes communicate over a high-speed internal interconnect network. Intel, for example, is developing a *teraflops* (1000 GFLOPS) computer with 4500 nodes. Each node will be powered by two 200-MHz Pentium II processors. The total memory of the machine is expected to exceed 600 gigabytes, with over two trillion bytes of disk storage! The projected processing performance is 1.8 teraflops.

Cray Research is offering a similar computer called the T3E. With liquid cooling, it supports up to 2048 DEC Alpha EV5 RISC processors, has 1 to 4 terabytes of memory, and a processing rate as high as 1.2 teraflops.

RISC Processors

In the early 1980s, a new trend in computer design began to appear—the reduced instruction set computer (RISC). Taken literally, this means a computer with a small number of instructions (less than 128). The opposite of RISC is CISC—a complex instruction set computer. A CISC is characterized by the following features:

1. A large number of variable-length instructions.
2. Multiple addressing modes (different methods of specifying the memory address).
3. A small number of internal processor registers.
4. Instructions that require multiple numbers of clock cycles for their execution.

The Z-80 microprocessor fits the definition of a CISC exactly, with over 600 different instruction forms, each requiring anywhere from 1 to 4 bytes. Six different addressing modes are supported, but internally, the processor has only eight general-purpose registers (two sets). Instruction execution times vary from 4 clock cycles to 23 cycles for several of the more complex instructions.

Compare the CISC Z-80 to Intel's i860 RISC processor (sometimes called a "Cray on a Chip"). It has the following features:

1. Eighty-two instructions, each 32 bits in length.
2. Four addressing modes.
3. Thirty-two general-purpose registers.
4. Execution of all instructions in one clock cycle.

Because all of the instructions in a RISC are of the same length and require only a single clock cycle, the control unit is much simpler than that of a CISC. This simplicity allows the instructions to be executed faster with less total on-chip logic. In fact, studies have shown that in a CISC, the control unit accounts for 50% of the chip area, compared with only 10%

in a RISC. This means that there is more area available in a RISC processor for other features, such as an expanded register file, data and instruction caches (onboard memory for storing the most recent instructions and data), and a floating-point unit, or coprocessor.[6]

In 1993, the industry alliance of IBM, Apple, and Motorola announced a new 32-bit RISC processor called the PowerPC. Designed to combat Intel's 80x86 family of processors, the PowerPC supports several different operating systems, including MS-DOS (via emulation), IBM's OS/2, Apple's System 7 and 8, Windows NT, and Unix.[7] The advantage to users is the ability to run and exchange data between programs that were theretofore limited to a specific processor. (For example, Apple programs required a Motorola 680x0 processor, MS-DOS programs an 80x86 processor.)

Digital Signal Processors

As the microprocessor has continued to evolve, many application-specific processors have been developed. We have already seen the example of the *microcontroller*, which includes onboard memory and I/O functions. Other examples are video and graphics processors, printer coprocessors, local area network (LAN) coprocessors, and communications processors.

Note that each of the computers in the above list is designed for processing digital (on-and-off) signals. Analog signals, which can take on an infinite set of values over time, are processed with discrete circuits. Typically, this means operational amplifiers (op amps), supported by capacitors, inductors, and resistors to form filters, amplifiers, and other frequency-selective circuits. However, as IC technology has advanced, low-cost analog-to-digital and digital-to-analog converters have become available. This in-turn has led to the development of the *digital signal-processing system*. As shown in Fig. 1.8, this is a specialized computer system that inputs an analog signal, converts it to digital form, performs specialized arithmetic operations on the data, and then converts the data back to analog form via a digital-to-analog converter (DAC).

The key element in this system is a new type of microprocessor called the *digital signal processor* (DSP). DSPs are used to perform complex mathematical computations on the converted analog data. For example, a digital filter can be constructed by sampling the input data and then transforming each of the resulting data points according to a math-

---

[6]Typically, the coprocessor "watches" the instruction stream of the CPU, looking for special floating-point instructions. These instructions might be transcendental functions like the tangent, sine, and cosine, basic mathematical operations such as addition, subtraction, multiplication, and division, or more complex operations such as computing the logarithm of a number. When such an instruction is spotted, the floating-point unit takes over for the main CPU and generates the result.

[7]An operating system is a control program that manages the resources of the computer. Chapter 2 discusses operating systems in more detail.

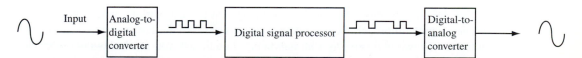

Figure 1.8 In a digital signal processing system, analog input signals are converted to digital form, processed by the DSP, and then converted back to analog form.

ematical formula. In this operation, one computation can require as many as 500,000 add–multiply operations. To enhance the process, the architecture of a DSP is made to differ from that of a conventional microprocessor in several ways:

1. The data and program instructions are stored in two different memory areas, each with its own bus. This is called the *Harvard Architecture*.
2. Hardware multipliers and adders are built into the processor and are optimized to perform a calculation in a single clock cycle.
3. Arithmetic pipelining is used so that several instructions can be operated on at once. For example, two numbers may be multiplied in one part of the processor while two other numbers are being added in another part.
4. Hardware DO loops are provided to speed up repetitive operations.
5. Multiple (serial) I/O ports are provided for communication with other processors.

DSPs are in widespread use today. Multimedia sound cards, for example, typically employ DSPs to compress speech and music signals so that they can be stored as (reasonably sized) data files. Because the DSP can be reprogrammed, some sound cards can be altered to also function as modems, thereby combining the functions of two typical microcomputer peripherals on one adapter card.[8] Other applications include cellular phones, speech and image compression, optical character recognition, and video conferencing.

SELF-REVIEW 1.2

1.2.1 The first and second generation of computers are generally associated with the _____ _____ and _____.

1.2.2 The first computer to use integrated circuit technology was the _____.

1.2.3 How does a minicomputer differ from a mainframe computer?

1.2.4 What is the difference between a microcomputer and a microprocessor?

1.2.5 Why are microcontrollers called "hidden computers"?

1.2.6 What is a parallel processor?

1.2.7 Why are RISC processors more efficient than CISC processors?

1.2.8 How does a DSP differ from a conventional microprocessor?

1.3 COMPUTER CODES

Introduction

One of the complications that we human beings have when working with a computer is that we cannot simply tell the computer what we want it to do. For example, suppose that I wish to add two numbers. As a human being, I could ask you for the two numbers, add

---

[8]A modem is a device that converts the 1's and 0's of a digital signal into audio tones that can be transmitted over conventional telephone lines. Modems are discussed in detail in Chapter 10.

them in my head, and announce the result. Compare these steps with those required to make a computer do the same thing:

1. Read the first number input from the keyboard.
2. Store this number in the memory unit.
3. Read the second number from the keyboard and store it in the accumulator.
4. Retrieve the first number from the memory unit and add it to the number in the accumulator, leaving the result in the accumulator.
5. Output the contents of the accumulator to the CRT screen.

There are so many operations required, that it makes you wonder about the usefulness of the computer in the first place! Of course, the computer can do each operation rather quickly—usually in just a few microseconds. Once the program to add two numbers has been written the computer will perform the operations at lightning speed and never make a mistake. Of course, this is the advantage the computer has over us—once programmed to perform a task, it will flawlessly perform that task at rates approaching millions of operations per second!

The problem becomes one of programming the computer—that is, telling it what we want it to do. Unfortunately, the computer does not speak our language and seems unwilling to learn. (People are working on that problem, though!) Therefore, the burden is on us to learn the instructions that will program the computer to perform a particular task.

In this section, we:

- Explain how to convert decimal numbers to binary and hexadecimal and vice versa.
- Show how the ASCII code is used to represent letters of the alphabet, numbers, punctuation symbols, and control codes.

Bits and Bytes

When one is typing at the keyboard of a microcomputer or time-shared terminal, it is easy to forget that computers are simply *on*-and-*off* machines. The logic circuits controlling the computer's operations typically produce +5 V or 0 V, and the binary number system is invoked to describe these digital signals. Assuming a positive logic convention, the +5-V level becomes a logic 1 and the 0-V level a logic 0.

A single digital line can therefore carry only two pieces of information—the line is a 1 or it is a 0. We solve this apparent lack of information-handling capability by combining many digital lines together. Such collections of lines are referred to as a *bus*.

Figure 1.9 shows eight lines representing the data bus of a microprocessor. When written in binary, the data on the bus is

$$11001011$$

where the D7 output is on the left and the D0 output on the right. Each digit in this binary number is referred to as a *bit* (*binary digit*). It has become common practice to refer to 8 bits as a *byte*; 4 bits are often called a *nibble*.

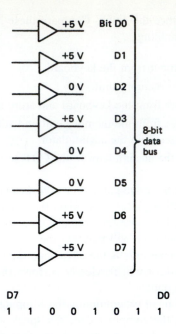

D7							D0
1	1	0	0	1	0	1	1

Figure 1.9 Eight digital lines make up the data bus of a microcomputer. The binary number system is used to describe the data on this bus. In this case, the data word is 11001011.

The important result to note is that by combining eight lines, the information-handling capability of the bus has increased not by a factor of 8, but by a factor of 2^8. This is seen by writing down all possible combinations of the 8 bits, starting with 00000000, 00000001, 00000010, . . . , 11111110, and, finally, 11111111. In doing this exercise, you will discover (or take my word for it) that there are 256 different combinations of 8 bits. The general result is that for *n* bits, there are 2^n unique combinations.

This result is the key to the success of the modern digital computer. If enough bits are used in the data words, we can express even the largest of numbers. Furthermore, we can develop *codes* to represent the letters and punctuation marks of the alphabet. In this way, the computer can process all types of written information.

Binary, Decimal, and Hexadecimal Numbers

At first glance, a binary number is imposing to most of us used to dealing with base-10 numbers. Is 11001011 a large number or a small one? How can we tell?

Any binary number can be converted to its decimal equivalent by adding the powers of 2 represented by the bit positions of the digits of the number. In binary, this is particularly easy because each bit is either a 1 or a 0. As with any number system, the weight of a digit is found as the base (2 in this case) raised to the power corresponding to the digit's position. Numbering the digit positions starting from the right and beginning with 0 results in

$$2^n . . . 2^3 \; 2^2 \; 2^1 \; 2^0$$

The decimal value of the binary number in Fig. 1.9 is therefore found to be

$$
\begin{array}{cccccccc}
1 & 1 & 0 & 0 & 1 & 0 & 1 & 1 \\
\end{array}
$$

$$1 \times 2^7 + 1 \times 2^6 + 0 \times 2^5 + 0 \times 2^4 + 1 \times 2^3 + 0 \times 2^2 + 1 \times 2^1 + 1 \times 2^0 =$$

$$
\begin{array}{ccccccccc}
128 & +64 & +0 & +0 & +8 & +0 & +2 & +1 & = 203
\end{array}
$$

Experienced users of binary simply count 1, 2, 4, 8, 16, 32, and so on, adding up the appropriate powers of 2.

Example 1.1

Convert the following binary words to their decimal equivalents: (a) 101, (b) 11111111, (c) 1100001011.

Solution
(a) $101 = 4 + 1 = 5$
(b) $11111111 = 128 + 64 + 32 + 16 + 8 + 4 + 2 + 1 = 255$
(c) $1100001011 = 512 + 256 + 8 + 2 + 1 = 779$

Computers may "like" binary numbers, but we human beings surely do not. It is very difficult to remember (or even recognize) that 11001011 is actually decimal 203. Because of this, the *hexadecimal* number system is often used. Table 1.3 lists the binary and hexadecimal equivalents of the decimal numbers 0 through 15. The hexadecimal (or simply, hex) number system defines a unique symbol for each of the 16 possible combinations of 4 bits. Note that this requires a little imagination after the symbol 9 has been used.

At first, it might appear that we have only made matters worse. After all, what is the meaning of a number like E3D? The real utility of the hex number system is the ease with which binary numbers can be represented. Grouping the binary digits four at a time, we may convert a binary number to hex by inspection.

For example, our binary number 11001011 becomes CB in hex. Its decimal value is still unrecognizable perhaps, but it is a number that is more easily "carried around."

Example 1.2

Convert the binary numbers in Example 1.1 to hex.

TABLE 1.3 Binary and Hexadecimal Equivalents of the Decimal Numbers 0 through 15

Decimal	Binary	Hexadecimal
0	0000	0
1	0001	1
2	0010	2
3	0011	3
4	0100	4
5	0101	5
6	0110	6
7	0111	7
8	1000	8
9	1001	9
10	1010	A
11	1011	B
12	1100	C
13	1101	D
14	1110	E
15	1111	F

Solution

(a) 101 = 5

(b) 11111111 = FF

(c) 1100001011 = 30B

When we begin our discussion of programming the microprocessor in Chapter 2, the value of hex will become even more apparent. To be fully conversant in hex and binary, you must be able to convert back and forth between the two and their decimal equivalents with ease. The next three examples review the techniques.

Example 1.3

Convert the following hex numbers to decimal and binary:
(a) 3C, (b) 2A92, (c) FFFF.

Solution. The conversion to binary can be made directly by writing the four binary digits that represent each hex digit.

(a) 3C = 0011 1100

(b) 2A92 = 0010 1010 1001 0010

(c) FFFF = 1111 1111 1111 1111

We could now count the binary weights to find the decimal equivalents, but there is a quicker way—convert the hex numbers directly to decimal.

(a) $3C = 3 \times 16^1 + 12 \times 16^0 = 60$

(b) $2A92 = 2 \times 16^3 + 10 \times 16^2 + 9 \times 16^1 + 2 \times 16^0 = 10,898$

(c) $FFFF = 15 \times 16^3 + 15 \times 16^2 + 15 \times 16^1 + 15 \times 16^0 = 65,535$

Example 1.4

Convert the following decimal numbers to binary: (a) 43, (b) 106, (c) 862.

Solution. This can be done by reversing the process used in Ex. 1.1.

(a) $43 = 32 + 8 + 2 + 1 = 2^5 + 2^3 + 2^1 + 2^0 = 101011$

(b) $106 = 64 + 32 + 8 + 2 = 2^6 + 2^5 + 2^3 + 2^1 = 1101010$

(c) $862 = 512 + 256 + 64 + 16 + 8 + 4 + 2 = 2^9 + 2^8 + 2^6 + 2^4 + 2^3 + 2^2 + 2^1 =$ 1101011110

Decimal numbers can also be converted to binary by using the repeated-division-by-2 technique. However, this is a rather laborious process. The next example shows a faster method.

Example 1.5

Convert the following decimal numbers to hexadecimal and then to binary: (a) 94, (b) 299, (c) 48,000.

Solution. The numbers can be converted in a straightforward manner by accumulating the highest power of 16, similar to what was done in Example 1.4. The following technique makes use of a pocket calculator and is suitable for even the largest decimal numbers.

(a) 94/16 = 5.875   Write down the 5.   5

　　.875 × 16 = 14   Write down the 14 (D).   D

The result is $94_{10} = 5D_{16} = 1011101_2$.

(b) 299/256 = 1.16796875   Write down the 1.   1

　　.16796875 × 256 = 43

$$43/16 = 2.6875 \qquad \text{Write down the 2.} \qquad 2$$
$$.6875 \times 16 = 11 \qquad \text{Write down the 11 (B).} \qquad B$$

The result is $299_{10} = 12B_{16} = 100101011_2$.

(c) $48,000/4096 = 11.71875 \qquad \text{Write down the 11 (B).} \qquad B$

$$.71875 \times 4096 = 2944$$
$$2944/256 = 11.5 \qquad \text{Write down the 11 (B).} \qquad B$$
$$.5 \times 256 = 128$$
$$128/16 = 8.0 \qquad \text{Write down the 8.} \qquad 8$$
$$0 \times 16 = 0 \qquad \text{Write down the 0.} \qquad 0$$

The result is $48,000_{10} = BB80_{16} = 1011101110000000_2$.

Note: Once the conversion to hexadecimal has been made, the binary conversion is obtained almost "for free."

Codes

In Fig. 1.1, the program counter of our simple computer is "pointing at" memory cell 7. In that cell is the data word 76. Based on the preceding section, we now know that this data word would actually be stored in binary form as 01001100. But what does this number represent? Should we interpret it literally as decimal 76, or does it represent the *code* for some computer operation?

The answer to this question is that only the computer knows for sure. If the computer is looking for an operation code, it will interpret this byte as an operation code (even if we meant it to be a data byte). If the computer is looking for a data byte, the byte in cell 7 will be interpreted as data. It is up to the programmer to make sure that the proper codes are presented to the computer. This is what computer programming is all about.

The important point we need to make is that a byte may have many interpretations besides its decimal value. For example, the byte 01001100 (decimal 76, hexadecimal 4C) is interpreted as the operation code MOV C,H (copy the contents of the H register into the C register) by an 8080 microprocessor, the operation code JMP by the 6502 microprocessor, and the operation code INCA (increment accumulator A) by the 6800 microprocessor.

And there is still another interpretation for the byte. In 1968 the American National Standards Institute (ANSI) established a 7-bit code for all of the letters of the alphabet, the numerals 0–9, the common punctuation symbols found on most typewriters, and several special-purpose control codes. ANSI called its code the American Standard Code for Information Interchange, or *ASCII* for short (pronounced "ask-E"). A copy of this code is given in Table 1.4.

Although ASCII is a 7-bit code, it is often written in byte (8-bit) form, with bit 8 ignored (assumed to be 0) or used for parity. Examining the table, we see that the byte 01001100 (4C hex) is the code for the capital letter L. Nearly all text information today is encoded in ASCII format, making it possible to transfer data between two different computer systems. Each time you type a key on a computer terminal, the ASCII code for that key is generated and sent to the computer for processing.

Actually, there are many codes in addition to ASCII. The binary-coded decimal (*BCD*) code is useful for decimal arithmetic. The *Gray* code, in which only one bit changes between successive entries in the code is useful for testing digital circuits. The *2's-complement* code, shown in Table 1.5, uses the most significant bit of each word to rep-

TABLE 1.4 American Standard Code for Information Interchange (ASCII)[a]

Least significant bits	Most significant bits							
	0 0000	1 0001	2 0010	3 0011	4 0100	5 0101	6 0110	7 0111
0 0000	NUL	DLE	SP	0	@	P	'	p
1 0001	SOH	DC1	!	1	A	Q	a	q
2 0010	STX	DC2	"	2	B	R	b	r
3 0011	ETX	DC3	#	3	C	S	c	s
4 0100	EOT	DC4	$	4	D	T	d	t
5 0101	ENQ	NAK	%	5	E	U	e	u
6 0110	ACK	SYN	&	6	F	V	f	v
7 0111	BEL	ETB	'	7	G	W	g	w
8 1000	BS	CAN	(	8	H	X	h	x
9 1001	HT	EM	)	9	I	Y	i	y
A 1010	LF	SUB	*	:	J	Z	j	z
B 1011	VT	ESC	+	;	K	[	k	{
C 1100	FF	FS	,	<	L	\	l	|
D 1101	CR	GS	–	=	M	]	m	}
E 1110	SO	RS	.	>	N	^	n	~
F 1111	SI	US	/	?	O	—	o	DEL

[a]Bit 7 of the code is assumed to be 0.

resent the sign (positive or negative) of the word. The *Baudot,* or five-level, code was used on early teletype machines and is now obsolete. The *Extended Binary-Coded Decimal Interchange Code* (EBCDIC) was developed by IBM for its line of Selectric typewriters. And there are yet more codes.

So you can see that there is much more to a group of binary digits than its decimal value; it is up to the user to select and use the appropriate code for the application at hand.

SELF-REVIEW 1.3

1.3.1 How many different binary numbers can be written using 8 bits?

1.3.2 Convert 11010110 to hexadecimal and to binary.

1.3.3 Convert 462 to binary and to hexadecimal.

1.3.4 When encoded in ASCII, the letter "P" has the binary code _____.

1.4 COMPUTER LANGUAGES

Introduction

As mentioned previously, programming the computer requires learning a new language. But which one? There is machine language, assembly language, and a host of high-level languages.

TABLE 1.5 Two's-Complement
Signed Binary Numbers[a]

Decimal	Binary	Hexadecimal
−128	10000000	80
−127	10000001	81
−126	10000010	82
−125	10000011	83
−124	10000100	84
.	.	.
.	.	.
.	.	.
−3	11111101	FD
−2	11111110	FE
−1	11111111	FF
0	00000000	0
+1	00000001	1
+2	00000010	2
.	.	.
.	.	.
.	.	.
+125	01111101	7D
+126	01111110	7E
+127	01111111	7F

[a]Positive numbers are formed without change.
Negative numbers are formed by complementing all bits and adding 1. Thus, −6 becomes 00000110 → 11111001 + 1 =
11111010.

In this section, we:

- Compare machine language programming with assembly language programming.
- Explain what is meant by a high-level computer language.

Machine and Assembly Language Programming

Fundamentally, all computers must be programmed in binary. However, this can be very awkward for human beings. Consider an 8080 microprocessor program that adds two numbers input from a keyboard:

```
11011011
00000000
01000111
11011011
00000000
10000000
11010011
00000000
01110110
```

Not too clear, is it? Of course, it is crystal clear to an 8080 microprocessor. This type of program is referred to as *object code* and is the only code a computer can execute. However, it is nearly impossible for a human being to work with.

Now consider the same program encoded in hexadecimal:

DB
00
47
DB
00
80
D3
00
76

Certainly this is more readable, but the function of the program is still not clear. So let's add the *mnemonics* (abbreviations for the instruction operation codes) corresponding to these hex codes:

Binary	Hex	Mnemonic	Comment
11011011	DB	IN	;INPUT THE FIRST NUMBER
00000000	00	0	;FROM PORT 0 AND SAVE IN REGISTER A.
01000111	47	MOV B,A	;PUT A COPY OF REGISTER A IN REGISTER B.
11011011	DB	IN	;INPUT THE SECOND NUMBER
00000000	00	0	;FROM PORT 0 AND SAVE IN REGISTER A.
10000000	80	ADD B	;ADD REGISTERS A AND B, AND LEAVE THE SUM ;IN REGISTER A.
11010011	D3	OUT	;OUTPUT REGISTER A
00000000	00	0	;TO PORT 0.
01110110	76	HLT	;HALT.

The function of the program now becomes clear. The two numbers to be added are first input from port 0 (to which the keyboard is assumed to be connected). The first number is temporarily saved in register B so that the second input operation will not overwrite it. (*Note:* A register is a storage location within the CPU that is capable of storing data, just as a memory cell can. The 8080 microprocessor has several registers, labeled B, C, D, E, H, and L.) The ADD B instruction adds the contents of registers A and B, leaving the result in Register A (the accumulator). This value is then output to port 0 (to which the CRT is assumed to be connected). Finally, the computer is instructed to halt.

Notice how the operation codes may be represented in binary, in hex, or as a mnemonic. The comments on the far right help make the function of the program clear. Programming the computer by entering only the hexadecimal operation codes is referred to as *machine language* programming. Some computers allow the mnemonics to be entered directly. This is called *assembly language* programming.

Although it is obvious that assembly language is the easiest of the two forms to use, it is well to remember that the computer itself can accept only binary data (object code). What, then, is the usefulness of assembly language?

A special program called an *assembler* is required. Placed in the computer's memory, this program will allow the operator to input the code program in mnemonic form. The assembler program usually comes with some form of *editor* that allows for easy creation of the assembly language file (called the *source code*). When the source code version of the program is completed, the assembler is called on to "look up" the binary codes for the mnemonics and create a new file called the *object code*. This file contains the binary code, which can be loaded into memory and executed.

If you are using a microprocessor trainer to learn microcomputer programming, you will probably be writing your programs in mnemonic form. You will then be required to look up the hex codes for each mnemonic in an assembly language reference chart supplied with the documentation for your microprocessor. This process is called (strangely enough) *hand assembly*.

Now, you might be wondering to yourself how your trainer can accept hex codes when the microprocessor can digest only binary codes. Figure 1.10 should help explain. It shows a diagram of a 16-line-to-4-line encoder. This circuit accepts 16 different inputs (corresponding to the 16 keys, 0 through F, on your trainer's keyboard) and provides a 4-bit binary output, 0000 through 1111. In this way, you are allowed to input data in hex, even though the computer itself will see the data as binary.

High-Level Languages

The BASIC computer language is very popular and is supplied with most personal computer systems. A BASIC program to add two numbers is

```
10 INPUT N1,N2
20 PRINT "SUM = ";N1+N2
30 END
```

A comparison with the original binary program is striking. Of course, the intent of all high-level languages is to let the programmer communicate in a language as similar as possible to his or her own.

Programming in BASIC requires a BASIC *interpreter* or *compiler.* When one uses interpreted BASIC, the application program may be entered into memory without an editor. The command RUN is then given, causing the interpreter to examine each BASIC statement and then execute a sequence of machine code to perform the function.

The use of an interpreter may result in very slow program execution. Worse, if the computer is in a loop, the interpreter will continue to interpret the instructions in the loop over and over. Of course, the computer is so fast that we often do not notice this delay.

For example, the BASIC program given previously to add two numbers might require 10 ms to calculate the sum and print the result. The machine language version could do it in 23 μs (using an 8080 microprocessor with a 2-MHz clock). However, you would have to be pretty quick to notice the difference between 10 ms and 23 μs!

This time delay can become noticeable when large amounts of computing must be done, however. For example, say that we had to perform the addition problem 1 million times. This would require $1,000,000 \times 10$ ms $= 10,000$ s, or 2.8 hours, with the BASIC program. By contrast, the machine language version would require $1,000,000 \times 23$ μs $= 23$ s!

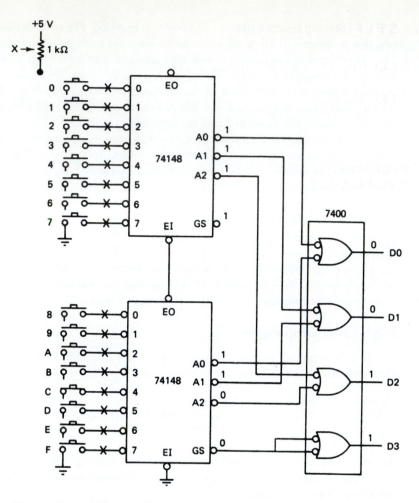

Figure 1.10 A 16-line-to-4-line encoder circuit allows hexadecimal input to a microprocessor trainer. In this example, key C is closed and the binary output is 1100.

A *compiler* is used to convert a high-level language program to object code. Using a compiler is similar to using an assembler, because an editor must be used for creating the application program file.

When the compiler is called on, it compiles the high-level language program into a file containing binary machine code. This has several advantages over the interpreter. For one, the code does not have to be reinterpreted over and over when loops are encountered. In addition, the resulting object code file will run all by itself without the need for the compiler to be resident in memory. This saves memory space and allows for larger programs to be run.

The main disadvantage to using a compiler is that errors will require reinvoking the editor, correcting the errors, and recompiling the program. This can be frustrating when simple syntax errors—missing commas, for example—appear.

SELF-REVIEW 1.4

1.4.1 What is the name of a computer program that inputs mnemonics for instructions and outputs binary object code?

1.4.2 A(n) _____ is a digital circuit that can be used to convert the closing of a switch into a binary number.

1.5 IMPLEMENTING THE THREE-BUS ARCHITECTURE IN HARDWARE

Introduction

Typical 8-bit microprocessors have an 8-bit data bus, a 16-bit address bus, and a four-line control bus. A detailed understanding of these three buses is essential for anyone interested in microprocessor design and engineering.

In this section, we:

- Compare signal levels for TTL and CMOS digital systems.
- Draw a memory map for a processor with 64 KB of memory space.

Digital Signals

Figure 1.11 illustrates the *three-bus architecture* of a typical microprocessor. The 16 lines of the address bus are labeled A0 (least significant bit) through A15 (most significant bit). Similarly, the 8 lines of the data bus are labeled D0 through D7. The 4 lines of the control bus are defined to be consistent with the four types of machine cycles introduced in Section 1.1 (I/O read and write and memory read and write).

Recall that a bus is defined as a collection of lines, each carrying a discrete voltage level. When this voltage level varies with time, we refer to the information on the line as a digital signal.

Most microprocessors and digital circuits provide signals that are *transistor–transistor-logic* (TTL) compatible. In this system, any voltage level less than or equal to 0.4 V is considered a logic 0. A logic 1 is defined as a voltage level greater than or equal to 2.4 V. Typical values are 0.2 V and 3.4 V. Note that a TTL receiver is designed to accept voltages as high as 0.8 V for a logic 0 and as low as 2.0 V for a logic 1. (See Section 4.3 for a discussion of noise immunity.)

Another popular logic family is *complementary metal-oxide semiconductor* (CMOS), devices that produce typical logic levels of 0 V and 5 V. In most cases, TTL devices can drive a nearly unlimited number of CMOS devices (provided that pull-up resistors are used to bring TTL's logic 1 level closer to 5.0 V), but CMOS is limited to one standard TTL load. More detail on TTL-to-CMOS and CMOS-to-TTL interfacing is provided in Chapter 4 and in most digital electronics textbooks.

It is important to remember that digital signals are nearly always switching in time. As an example, Fig. 1.12 shows an oscilloscope photograph of the two low-order (A0 and A1) address lines of a Z-80 microprocessor. We expect these lines to be switching quite

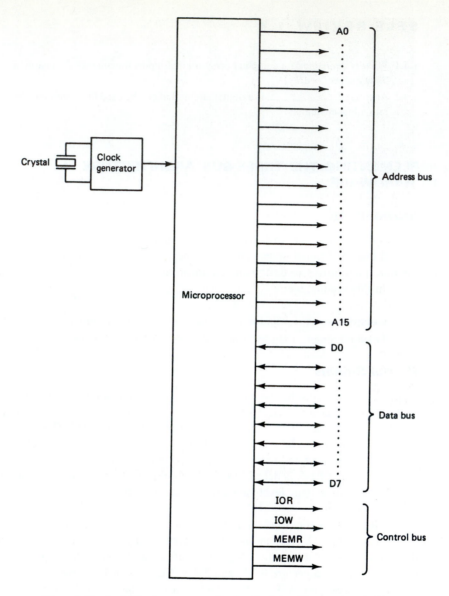

Figure 1.11   An 8-bit microprocessor showing the data, address, and control buses.

frequently, because they must change each time the microprocessor fetches a new instruction from memory. Also, note that the idealized square waves usually drawn (with 0-ns rise and fall times and perfectly square edges) are not realized in practice.

With 16 address lines, 8 data bus lines, and 4 control lines, the conventional dual-trace oscilloscope may not be the ideal tool for troubleshooting microcomputer systems. Instead, what is required is a multichannel instrument with memory that can store the

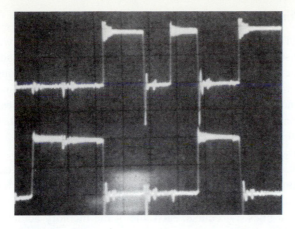

Figure 1.12 Oscilloscope photograph of address lines A0 and A1 on a Z-80 microprocessor. The vertical sensitivity is 2 V/div, and the horizontal time base is 2 μs/div.

contents of the buses over a period of time (several hundred cycles) and present the data in binary, hex, ASCII, or mnemonic form. Such an instrument is called a *logic analyzer* or a *data analyzer* and is an indispensable tool for locating hardware problems in microprocessors.

Figure 1.13 shows the Hewlett-Packard model 1611A logic-state analyzer. This instrument has 32 channels and will store 64 cycles of the input data. The screen display can be in binary, hex, or ASCII, or, with the appropriate personality module, the hex codes can be disassembled and the corresponding mnemonics displayed. Using the logic analyzer as a troubleshooting tool is discussed in detail in Chapter 11.

Figure 1.13 The Hewlett-Packard model 1611A logic-state analyzer. This device has 32 input channels and is ideal for monitoring the buses of a microprocessor system. When the 1611A is used with the optional personality module, the contents of the data bus can be disassembled and displayed in mnemonic form. (Courtesy of Hewlett-Packard.)

Defining the Three Buses

The address bus in Fig. 1.11 carries the address of the memory cell the CPU wishes to read from or write to. With 16 address lines, there are 2^{16}, or 65,536, unique addresses that the CPU can output. These range from 0000 hex to FFFF hex. Strangely enough, this number of addresses is referred to as *64K* of memory space. The apparent misnomer is due to the fact that there is no even power of 2 that comes out to 1000. The closest is 2^{10}, or 1024; therefore, 1K in binary is 1024, and a 1K-bit memory actually has 1024 memory cells. Similarly, a 2K-bit memory has 2048 memory cells, and so on.

Figure 1.14 shows two pictorial representations of the 16-bit address. In Fig. 1.14(a), the high-order 8 bits are shown defining 1 of 256 pages in a book. (Remember that there are 256 unique combinations of 8 bits.) On each page, there are 256 lines, defined by the 8 low-order bits. The total capacity of the book is thus 256 pages with 256 lines per page, or 65,536 total lines. Of course, each line of the memory actually stores one byte (8 bits), and a 64K memory system thus represents 64K $\times$ 8, or 512K, total bits.

In Fig. 1.14(b), the memory space is shown as a *map* with 16 blocks. Each block corresponds to 4K of memory space. This division into 4K blocks is arbitrary, but it is a convenient choice because the most significant hex digit increments by 1 for each 4K block.

Memory maps are useful for showing how much of the memory space of the microprocessor is actually implemented and whether any I/O devices are mapped into that area. (This is called *memory-mapped I/O* and is discussed in Chapter 6). We will return to the memory-map concept throughout the book.

Although the memory lines are all outputs from the microprocessor, the data bus lines must be capable of both inputting and outputting data. Such a bus is referred to as *bidirectional.* A microprocessor with an 8-bit data bus is referred to as an 8-bit machine. All of the microprocessors studied in this book are 8-bit machines, but of course, there are 4-, 8-, 16-, and 32-bit microprocessors—how long will it be until the first 64-bit micro appears?

Last, we come to the control bus. This bus is necessary to control the direction of data flow on the bidirectional data bus and to differentiate between a memory address and an I/O address. For example, when the I/O write (IOW) line is active, the address on the address bus should be interpreted as an I/O address, and not that of a memory cell. Because this occurs during a write cycle, the I/O device should be prepared to receive data from the microprocessor.

You should be able to see that the four lines of the control bus electrically define the type of instruction cycle the microprocessor is performing, as listed in Table 1.1.

SELF-REVIEW 1.5

1.5.1 What are typical high- and low-level output voltages for a standard TTL gate?

1.5.2 Which microprocessor bus is used to indicate whether the current instruction requires data to enter the CPU or leave the CPU?

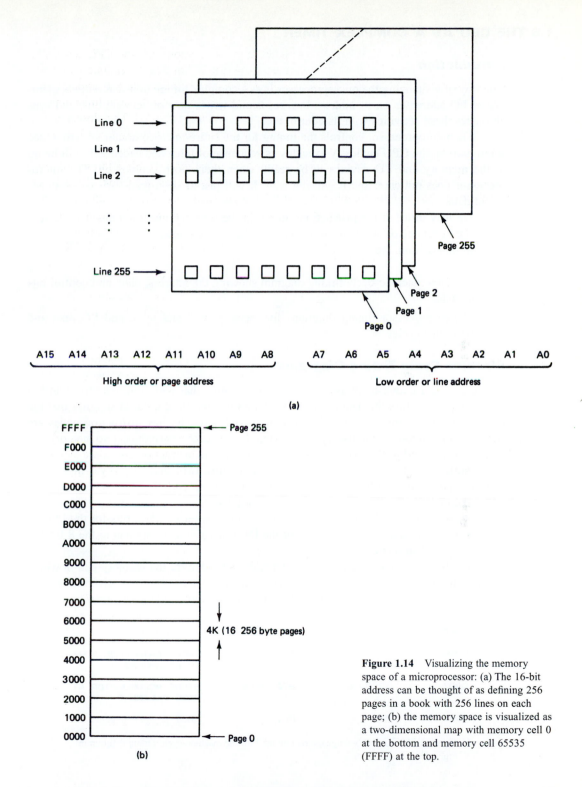

Line 0 →

Line 1 →

Line 2 →

Line 255 →

Page 255

Page 2

Page 1

Page 0

| A15 | A14 | A13 | A12 | A11 | A10 | A9 | A8 |

High order or page address

| A7 | A6 | A5 | A4 | A3 | A2 | A1 | A0 |

Low order or line address

(a)

FFFF ← Page 255
F000
E000
D000
C000
B000
A000
9000
8000
7000
6000
5000   4K (16 256 byte pages)
4000
3000
2000
1000
0000 ← Page 0

(b)

Figure 1.14 Visualizing the memory space of a microprocessor: (a) The 16-bit address can be thought of as defining 256 pages in a book with 256 lines on each page; (b) the memory space is visualized as a two-dimensional map with memory cell 0 at the bottom and memory cell 65535 (FFFF) at the top.

1.6 THE CPU AS A COMPLEX TIMER

Introduction

One way of visualizing the microprocessor is as a complex timing unit that outputs memory or I/O addresses on its address bus, reads and writes data on its data bus, and synchronizes these activities with its control bus.

The microprocessor controls the timing for the entire microcomputer system. Once set in motion, the CPU endlessly executes its sequence of fetch and execute. It will be up to the memory and I/O devices to be ready when their "turn" comes up. The microprocessor does not care, and it will not wait. It will just as soon read garbage as meaningful data.

We may think of the instructions stored in the memory unit as codes that cause a particular sequence of events to occur on the CPU's three buses.

In this section, we:

- Sketch a machine-cycle timing diagram showing the address, data, and control bus signals.
- Sketch processor timing diagrams for memory read and write and I/O read and write bus cycles.

Machine-Cycle Timing Diagrams

Figure 1.15 is a listing of an assembly language routine that will input data from an I/O device at port 3, store the data at memory address 0700H (the capital H signifies that the address should be interpreted in hexadecimal), and halt. The hex instruction codes are shown in the middle of the listing on the same line as each mnemonic. The memory addresses correspond to the locations in memory where the instruction codes are stored.

Notice that the IN and STA instructions require two- and three-byte instruction codes, respectively. The first byte always represents the *op code* for the instruction; thus, DB is the op code for IN and 32 the op code for STA.

We will see that the processors studied in this book use only 8 bits for the I/O address. For this reason, the second byte of the IN instruction corresponds to the 8-bit I/O address—port 3 in this case.

The STA instruction requires a 16-bit address to identify the memory cell in which to store the data. Notice that the processor requires that these bytes be given in reverse order, with the low-order address first (00) and the high-order address last (07).

ADDRESS	OP-CODES	MNEMONICS	COMMENTS
0000	DB 03	IN 3	INPUT DATA FROM PORT 3 TO ACCUMULATOR
0002	32 00 07	STA 0700	STORE ACCUMULATOR AT PAGE 7 LINE 0
0005	76	HLT	HALT

Figure 1.15 Assembly language routine used for the machine-cycle timing diagram in Fig. 1.16.

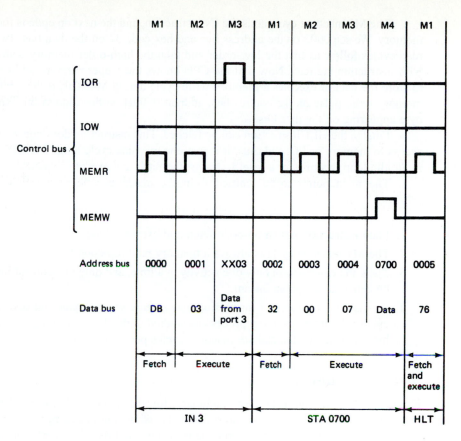

Figure 1.16 Machine-cycle timing diagram. Each instruction produces a unique pattern on the three buses of the microprocessor. This diagram is for the program of Fig. 1.15.

Figure 1.16 is a machine-cycle timing diagram corresponding to the program of Fig. 1.15. The presence of a control signal is shown by a pulse to the logic 1 level. The contents of the address and data buses are given in hex for better readability. The diagram is divided into three major time periods, corresponding to the three separate instructions.

Each instruction begins with an op-code fetch (memory read machine cycle). This cycle is numbered M1 in the figure. Tracing the IN 3 instruction, we see that the second machine cycle (M2) is also a memory read cycle. This is because, during the M1 cycle, only the op code was read. The code instructed the CPU to input data from a port. The M2 memory read cycle identifies the port address. Notice that the address bus increments to 0001 for the M2 cycle.

Once the op code and port address are known, the CPU can execute the instruction by inputting the data from port 3. The M3 cycle shows this execution phase. The I/O read (IOR) control line is pulsed, the address bus outputs 03 (the port address) on A0 through A7, and the bidirectional data bus is configured for data input. It is now up to the I/O device to place its data on the bus.

The M3 machine cycle ends the IN instruction, and the next op code is fetched from memory. We see 0002 on the address bus and hex code 32 on the data bus. Two memory read cycles follow as first the low-order and then the high-order memory address for the STA instruction are read. Now that the CPU knows the proper memory address at which to store the data, it executes a memory write cycle during M4. This is "observed" by the memory write pulse on the control bus, address 0700H on the address bus, and the data byte appearing on the data bus.

Finally, the HLT instruction can be fetched. This instruction does not require further access to memory or I/O, and thus, it is just one machine cycle long. The CPU now halts in an idle loop, waiting for a reset to restart the fetch-and-execute sequence.

The main points to be learned from the machine-cycle timing diagram are as follows:

1. Each instruction has an op-code fetch-and-execute phase.
2. The M1 machine cycle is always a memory read (op-code fetch).
3. The CPU can perform only one activity at a time, and only one control line can thus be active at any given instant.
4. A single microprocessor instruction may require several bytes and several machine cycles; the Intel and Zilog processors studied in this book have a maximum of four bytes per instruction and six machine cycles per instruction.

Instruction Timing

Figure 1.17 is an instruction set summary for the Intel 8080 microprocessor. The mnemonics are listed in alphabetical order, followed by a brief description of the instruction. The binary equivalent of the op code is also given. From this chart, you can see that the IN instruction has the op code 11011011, or DBH (again, H indicates hex).

The chart also includes the number of clock cycles—sometimes called *T states*—required for each instruction. The IN instruction requires 10 clock cycles, the STA instruction requires 13, and the HLT instruction 7. From this information, we can conclude that the program given in Fig. 1.15 will require 30 clock cycles. If the microcomputer system clock is 2.0 MHz, the time required to execute the program is

$$30 \text{ clock cycles} \times \frac{1}{2 \text{ MHz}} = 15 \text{ }\mu\text{s}.$$

The chart in Fig. 1.17 does not indicate how these clock cycles are distributed over the various machine cycles involved. This information can be found in the user's manual for the microprocessor. The important point to remember is that *not all machine cycles are of equal length,* even though Fig. 1.16 gives that impression.

Processor Timing

Figure 1.18 illustrates basic processor timing for memory read and write machine cycles. Each T state is identified as one pulse from the system clock. In this instance both machine cycles are shown as three T states long, but that may not always be true.

INSTRUCTION SET

Summary of Processor Instructions
By Alphabetical Order

Mnemonic	Description	D_7	D_6	D_5	D_4	D_3	D_2	D_1	D_0	Clock [2] Cycles
ACI	Add immediate to A with carry	1	1	0	0	1	1	1	0	7
ADC M	Add memory to A with carry	1	0	0	0	1	1	1	0	7
ADC r	Add register to A with carry	1	0	0	0	1	S	S	S	4
ADD M	Add memory to A	1	0	0	0	0	1	1	0	7
ADD r	Add register to A	1	0	0	0	0	S	S	S	4
ADI	Add immediate to A	1	1	0	0	0	1	1	0	7
ANA M	And memory with A	1	0	1	0	0	1	1	0	7
ANA r	And register with A	1	0	1	0	0	S	S	S	4
ANI	And immediate with A	1	1	1	0	0	1	1	0	7
CALL	Call unconditional	1	1	0	0	1	1	0	1	17
CC	Call on carry	1	1	0	1	1	1	0	0	11/17
CM	Call on minus	1	1	1	1	1	1	0	0	11/17
CMA	Compliment A	0	0	1	0	1	1	1	1	4
CMC	Compliment carry	0	0	1	1	1	1	1	1	4
CMP M	Compare memory with A	1	0	1	1	1	1	1	0	7
CMP r	Compare register with A	1	0	1	1	1	S	S	S	4
CNC	Call on no carry	1	1	0	1	0	1	0	0	11/17
CNZ	Call on no zero	1	1	0	0	0	1	0	0	11/17
CP	Call on positive	1	1	1	1	0	1	0	0	11/17
CPE	Call on parity even	1	1	1	0	1	1	0	0	11/17
CPI	Compare immediate with A	1	1	1	1	1	1	1	0	7
CPO	Call on parity odd	1	1	1	0	0	1	0	0	11/17
CZ	Call on zero	1	1	0	0	1	1	0	0	11/17
DAA	Decimal adjust A	0	0	1	0	0	1	1	1	4
DAD B	Add B & C to H & L	0	0	0	0	1	0	0	1	10
DAD D	Add D & E to H & L	0	0	0	1	1	0	0	1	10
DAD H	Add H & L to H & L	0	0	1	0	1	0	0	1	10
DAD SP	Add stack pointer to H & L	0	0	1	1	1	0	0	1	10
DCR M	Decrement memory	0	0	1	1	0	1	0	1	10
DCR r	Decrement register	0	0	D	D	D	1	0	1	5
DCX B	Decrement B & C	0	0	0	0	1	0	1	1	5
DCX D	Decrement D & E	0	0	0	1	1	0	1	1	5
DCX H	Decrement H & L	0	0	1	0	1	0	1	1	5
DCX SP	Decrement stack pointer	0	0	1	1	1	0	1	1	5
DI	Disable Interrupt	1	1	1	1	0	0	1	1	4
EI	Enable Interrupts	1	1	1	1	1	0	1	1	4
HLT	Halt	0	1	1	1	0	1	1	0	7
IN	Input	1	1	0	1	1	0	1	1	10
INR M	Increment memory	0	0	1	1	0	1	0	0	10
INR r	Increment register	0	0	D	D	D	1	0	0	5
INX B	Increment B & C registers	0	0	0	0	0	0	1	1	5
INX D	Increment D & E registers	0	0	0	1	0	0	1	1	5
INX H	Increment H & L registers	0	0	1	0	0	0	1	1	5
INX SP	Increment stack pointer	0	0	1	1	0	0	1	1	5
JC	Jump on carry	1	1	0	1	1	0	1	0	10
JM	Jump on minus	1	1	1	1	1	0	1	0	10
JMP	Jump unconditional	1	1	0	0	0	0	1	1	10
JNC	Jump on no carry	1	1	0	1	0	0	1	0	10
JNZ	Jump on no zero	1	1	0	0	0	0	1	0	10
JP	Jump on positive	1	1	1	1	0	0	1	0	10
JPE	Jump on parity even	1	1	1	0	1	0	1	0	10
JPO	Jump on parity odd	1	1	1	0	0	0	1	0	10
JZ	Jump on zero	1	1	0	0	1	0	1	0	10
LDA	Load A direct	0	0	1	1	1	0	1	0	13
LDAX B	Load A indirect	0	0	0	0	1	0	1	0	7
LDAX D	Load A indirect	0	0	0	1	1	0	1	0	7
LHLD	Load H & L direct	0	0	1	0	1	0	1	0	16
LXI B	Load immediate register Pair B & C	0	0	0	0	0	0	0	1	10
LXI D	Load immediate register Pair D & E	0	0	0	1	0	0	0	1	10
LXI H	Load immediate register Pair H & L	0	0	1	0	0	0	0	1	10
LXI SP	Load immediate stack pointer	0	0	1	1	0	0	0	1	10

Mnemonic	Description	D_7	D_6	D_5	D_4	D_3	D_2	D_1	D_0	Clock [2] Cycles
MVI M	Move immediate memory	0	0	1	1	0	1	1	0	10
MVI r	Move immediate register	0	0	D	D	D	1	1	0	7
MOV M, r	Move register to memory	0	1	1	1	0	S	S	S	7
MOV r, M	Move memory to register	0	1	D	D	D	1	1	0	7
MOV r1,r2	Move register to register	0	1	D	D	D	S	S	S	5
NOP	No-operation	0	0	0	0	0	0	0	0	4
ORA M	Or memory with A	1	0	1	1	0	1	1	0	7
ORA r	Or register with A	1	0	1	1	0	S	S	S	4
ORI	Or immediate with A	1	1	1	1	0	1	1	0	7
OUT	Output	1	1	0	1	0	0	1	1	10
PCHL	H & L to program counter	1	1	1	0	1	0	0	1	5
POP B	Pop register pair B & C off stack	1	1	0	0	0	0	0	1	10
POP D	Pop register pair D & E off stack	1	1	0	1	0	0	0	1	10
POP H	Pop register pair H & L off stack	1	1	1	0	0	0	0	1	10
POP PSW	Pop A and Flags off stack	1	1	1	1	0	0	0	1	10
PUSH B	Push register Pair B & C on stack	1	1	0	0	0	1	0	1	11
PUSH D	Push register Pair D & E on stack	1	1	0	1	0	1	0	1	11
PUSH H	Push register Pair H & L on stack	1	1	1	0	0	1	0	1	11
PUSH PSW	Push A and Flags on stack	1	1	1	1	0	1	0	1	11
RAL	Rotate A left through carry	0	0	0	1	0	1	1	1	4
RAR	Rotate A right through carry	0	0	0	1	1	1	1	1	4
RC	Return on carry	1	1	0	1	1	0	0	0	5/11
RET	Return	1	1	0	0	1	0	0	1	10
RLC	Rotate A left	0	0	0	0	0	1	1	1	4
RM	Return on minus	1	1	1	1	1	0	0	0	5/11
RNC	Return on no carry	1	1	0	1	0	0	0	0	5/11
RNZ	Return on no zero	1	1	0	0	0	0	0	0	5/11
RP	Return on positive	1	1	1	1	0	0	0	0	5/11
RPE	Return on parity even	1	1	1	0	1	0	0	0	5/11
RPO	Return on parity odd	1	1	1	0	0	0	0	0	5/11
RRC	Rotate A right	0	0	0	0	1	1	1	1	4
RST	Restart	1	1	A	A	A	1	1	1	11
RZ	Return on zero	1	1	0	0	1	0	0	0	5/11
SBB M	Subtract memory from A with borrow	1	0	0	1	1	1	1	0	7
SBB r	Subtract register from A with borrow	1	0	0	1	1	S	S	S	4
SBI	Subtract immediate from A with borrow	1	1	0	1	1	1	1	0	7
SHLD	Store H & L direct	0	0	1	0	0	0	1	0	16
SPHL	H & L to stack pointer	1	1	1	1	1	0	0	1	5
STA	Store A direct	0	0	1	1	0	0	1	0	13
STAX B	Store A indirect	0	0	0	0	0	0	1	0	7
STAX D	Store A indirect	0	0	0	1	0	0	1	0	7
STC	Set carry	0	0	1	1	0	1	1	1	4
SUB M	Subtract memory from A	1	0	0	1	0	1	1	0	7
SUB r	Subtract register from A	1	0	0	1	0	S	S	S	4
SUI	Subtract immediate from A	1	1	0	1	0	1	1	0	7
XCHG	Exchange D & E, H & L Registers	1	1	1	0	1	0	1	1	4
XRA M	Exclusive Or memory with A	1	0	1	0	1	1	1	0	7
XRA r	Exclusive Or register with A	1	0	1	0	1	S	S	S	4
XRI	Exclusive Or immediate with A	1	1	1	0	1	1	1	0	7
XTHL	Exchange top of stack, H & L	1	1	1	0	0	0	1	1	18

NOTES: 1. DDD or SSS – 000 B – 001 C – 010 D – 011 E – 100 H – 101 L – 110 Memory – 111 A.

2. Two possible cycle times, (5/11) indicate instruction cycles dependent on condition flags.

Figure 1.17   Instruction set of the 8080 microprocessor. (Courtesy of Intel Corporation.)

Sec. 1.6   The CPU as a Complex Timer

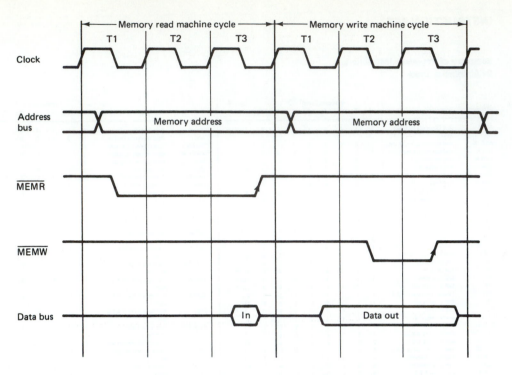

Figure 1.18   Processor timing for memory read and write machine cycles.

Rather than try to show 16 separate lines for the address bus, it is shown as two parallel lines, indicating that some of the lines are a logic 1 level and some a logic 0 level. When these lines cross, a new address is output by the CPU. Similarly, the 8 lines of the data bus are defined only when valid data are present; the lines are left unknown elsewhere.

Examining the memory read machine cycle in the figure, we see that the contents of the address bus become valid during the T1 clock cycle. Near the end of this machine cycle, the memory read ($\overline{\text{MEMR}}$) line becomes active. (The bar drawn above "MEMR" signifies that this line goes low when active.) The memory unit now has available the time until the falling edge of the clock during the T3 cycle to find the data requested by the CPU and place the data on the data bus. This time is referred to as the *access time* of the memory.

Notice that the data bus is expected to receive valid data from the memory when the falling edge of T3 occurs, and at no other time during this machine cycle is data valid on the bus.

The memory write cycle is similar to the memory read cycle, except that the processor now outputs the data instead of the memory unit. To give the memory plenty of time to latch the data, the data bus contains valid data early in the machine cycle. When the memory write ($\overline{\text{MEMW}}$) line goes high, the memory unit will store the byte on the data bus at the address specified by the A0 through A15 address lines.

Figure 1.19 illustrates processor timing for I/O read and write operations. You should be able to see that these are identical to memory read and write cycles, except that the $\overline{\text{IOR}}$ and $\overline{\text{IOW}}$ lines will be active instead of $\overline{\text{MEMR}}$ and $\overline{\text{MEMW}}$.

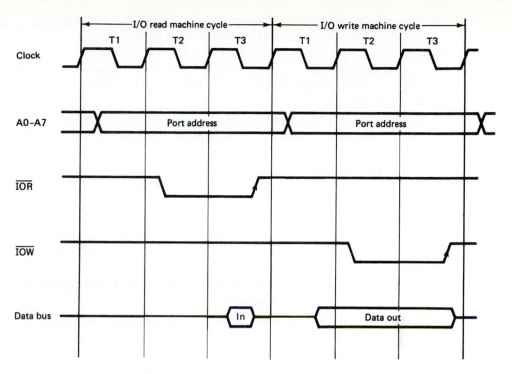

Figure 1.19 Processor timing for I/O read and write machine cycles.

SELF-REVIEW 1.6

1.6.1 The CPU continually follows the sequence _____ and _____.

1.6.2 Each computer instruction is made up of one or more _____ cycles, and each of these requires several clock cycles, or _____ states.

QUESTIONS AND ANSWERS

Q: *What are the three main units of a digital computer?*

A: The central-processing unit (CPU), the memory unit, and the input–output devices.

Q: *What sequence does the CPU continually follow?*

A: Fetch an instruction code from memory, increment the program counter, and execute the instruction.

Q: *How does the microprocessor communicate with the other components in a microcomputer system?*

A: Via the data, address, and control buses.

Q: *What types of activities can occur on the buses of a microprocessor?*

A: A memory read or write operation or an I/O read or write operation.

Q: *What company built the first microprocessor chip? What was its data bus width?*

A: The first microprocessor was the 4-bit 4004, designed and built by Intel.

Q: *What is the difference between a microcontroller and a microprocessor?*

A: A microcontroller is an entire computer on a chip. That is, it contains the CPU, memory, and I/O ports. A microprocessor requires external memory and I/O to build a working computer.

Q: *What is an RISC processor?*

A: A RISC processor is a microprocessor that has been designed to execute instructions very efficiently. It does this by limiting the instruction set to a small number of simple instructions that each execute in one clock cycle.

Q: *What is a digital circuit?*

A: A circuit designed to switch between an ON and an OFF state. TTL and CMOS are the most common digital technologies.

Q: *What is hexadecimal?*

A: A base-16 number system that uses the digits 0–9 and the letters A–F. Hexadecimal provides a way of expressing binary numbers in a more compact and easily remembered form.

Q: *What type of data is stored in the memory of a microcomputer?*

A: Computer instructions, ASCII characters, BCD numbers, and other coded data.

Q: *What is machine language programming?*

A: Programming a computer by writing the instructions in binary or hexadecimal.

Q: *What is a mnemonic instruction?*

A: An abbreviation for a computer instruction. Typically, an assembler is used to convert mnemonics into their binary equivalents. Writing a program using mnemonics is called assembly language programming.

Q: *How much memory can a typical 8-bit microprocessor access?*

A: Assuming a 16-bit address bus, 65,536 locations, or 64 KB (2^{16}).

Q: *What is a machine cycle?*

A: The time during which the computer does one specific operation (a memory read or write or an I/O read or write). Computer instructions are made up of several machine cycles. The first cycle is always a memory read.

Q: *How can you determine the length of time required to execute a computer program?*

A: Each instruction requires a specific number of clock cycles, or T states. Add these up and multiply by the time for one T state to get the length of time required to execute a computer program.

LAB PROJECTS

1.1. BASIC has two functions—CHR$(*n*) and ASC("*X*")—that can be used to print the ASCII equivalent of the number *n* or the ASCII code for the character "*X*". Use these functions to write the following BASIC programs.

    (a) Input a decimal number and output its ASCII character equivalent.

    (b) Input an ASCII character and output its ASCII numeric code.

    (c) Print the entire ASCII character set corresponding to all combinations of 8 binary bits.

1.2. The following four-line BASIC program can be used to convert a decimal number to its 8-bit binary equivalent [stored in the array B(J)]:

```
10 INPUT N
20 FOR J = 7 to 0 STEP −1
30 IF N −2^J < 0 THEN B(J) = 0 ELSE B(J) = 1: N = N − 2^J
40 NEXT J
```

Modify this program so that it will accept decimal numbers as large as 65,535, convert them to 16-bit binary numbers, and print the results.

1.3. The BASIC statement A$ = HEX$($n$) stores the hexadecimal equivalent of the number n in string variable A$. Using this function, modify the program of Lab 1.2 to also print the hexadecimal equivalent of the input number.

1.4. Test the keyboard encoder circuit shown in Fig. 1.10. If a 16-key keypad is unavailable, two 8-switch DIP switches can be substituted.
  (a) Test the output with two or more keys down.
  (b) Test the output with no keys down.
  (c) Modify the circuit to include a KEYDOWN signal that will be active only when one or more of the 16 keys are pressed.
  (d) Add a seven-segment decoder and display to the output so that each key code can be viewed directly.

QUESTIONS AND PROBLEMS

Section 1.1

  1.1. Explain the purpose of the address, data, and control buses. Which are bidirectional?
  1.2. Indicate the source and destination of data for each of the following types of machine cycle:
   (a) memory read
   (b) memory write
   (c) I/O read
   (d) I/O write
  1.3. Referring to Fig. 1.1, describe the contents of the address, data, and control buses when the CPU is writing the data word 26 to memory cell 16.
  1.4. One problem with all stored-program computers is that when they are first turned on, the memory unit contains random data. (The flip-flops that make up the memory cells will power on in a random fashion.) Because these random data cannot be executed with predictable results, the computer is not usable. Can you suggest a different type of memory that could be used to boot up the computer when power is first applied, thereby solving this problem?

Section 1.2

  1.5. Number the following events in order of time (1 = oldest).
     _____ **(a)** The first minicomputer (the PDP-8) is announced.
     _____ **(b)** Intel introduces one of the first 32-bit microprocessors, the 80386.
     _____ **(c)** The transistor is invented at Bell Laboratories.
     _____ **(d)** IBM begins selling a personal computer based on the 8088 microprocessor.

_____ **(e)** IBM announces the first IC-based computer, the model 360.

_____ **(f)** The integrated circuit is invented independently at Texas Instruments and Fairchild Semiconductor.

_____ **(g)** IBM announces its first electronic computer, the vacuum-tube–based model 701.

_____ **(h)** The first processor on a chip, the 4004, is announced by Intel.

_____ **(i)** Cray Research announces its first supercomputer, the Cray-1.

_____ **(j)** Apple, IBM, and Motorola announce the PowerPC RISC.

_____ **(k)** ENIAC is designed and built at the University of Pennsylvania.

1.6. The first microprocessor chip was the _____. It had a _____-bit data bus.

1.7. A _____ is a microprocessor that contains the CPU, memory, and I/O all on a single chip.

Section 1.3

1.8. How many different memory locations can a microprocessor with a 32-bit address bus access?

1.9. Most 8-bit microprocessors have 16 address lines and can therefore access 64K bytes of memory. What happens to this memory capacity when one additional memory line is added? State the general result for adding n additional memory lines.

1.10. Convert the following hex numbers to binary and to decimal.

   (a) FEH

   (b) 2 A9H

   (c) CC00H

   (d) FE027CH

1.11. Convert the following decimal numbers to binary and to hex.

   (a) 19

   (b) 99

   (c) 3784

   (d) 57,629

1.12. Perform the following hexadecimal arithmetic problems. Express your answer in hex and in decimal.

   (a) 2AH + 13H

   (b) CA + 2F

   (c) 6BH − 3CH

   (d) E2 − D7

1.13. One way of expressing a negative number in binary is to use the 2's complement. This is found by complementing all bits and adding 1. Positive numbers are left unchanged. Express the following decimal numbers in 8-bit 2's complement form.

   (a) −23

   (b) −102

   (c) −128

   (d) +47

1.14. With the use of the two's complement, a positive number is indicated when the most significant bit (MSB) of a signed number is a 0. If the MSB is a 1, a negative number is indicated (see Table 1.5), and its magnitude can be found by forming the two's complement and converting to decimal. Following these rules, convert the following 8-bit signed numbers to decimal.

(a) 11010110

(b) 10001111

(c) C3H

(d) 66H

1.15. When the hexadecimal numbers 3C and 92 are added together, the result is CE. Show that in *unsigned* binary this problem corresponds to the decimal addition of 60 + 146 = 206. Now show that using *signed* binary, the same problem corresponds to 60 − 110 = −50.

1.16. Determine the ASCII equivalent of the following hexadecimal numbers.

(a) 26H

(b) 66H

(c) 07H

(d) 1BH

Section 1.4

1.17. What does it mean to "hand assemble" a machine language computer program?

1.18. When you buy an expensive software program, the manufacturer will always supply the object code but seldom the source code. What is the reasoning behind this practice?

1.19. Consider a program written in assembly language, in interpreted BASIC, and in compiled BASIC. Which version will have the shortest execution time? Which one do you think is the easiest to write? Explain why.

1.20. Refer to the keyboard encoder circuit shown in Fig. 1.10. If keys 1 and 7 are both held down, what is the binary output code that will be produced?

*1.21. Refer to Fig. 1.10. Suppose that the connection between EO and E1 of the two encoders breaks open. What would the *symptom* of this problem be? (*Hint:* TTL circuits interpret open pins as logic 1's.)

*1.22. Suppose that key "8" is stuck closed. What would the *symptom* of this problem be?

Section 1.5

1.23. How many decimal memory words are there in a 32K-byte memory unit? How many address lines would be required to access all locations in this memory?

1.24. Refer to Fig. 1.14(a). What is the hexadecimal address corresponding to decimal page 48, line 203?

1.25. A certain microcomputer has a 1K-byte memory beginning at address 1000H. What is the hex address of the *last* byte in this memory?

1.26. Redraw the memory map shown in Fig. 1.14(b) using eight 8K-byte blocks. Indicate the starting address of each block.

Section 1.6

1.27. A single-step circuit will "freeze" all data on the buses of a microcomputer system. Assume that such a circuit is used to test a microprocessor and that the data bus lines are measured with a voltmeter. The results are as follows:

$$\text{bit } D0 = 3.8 \text{ V,} \qquad \text{bit } D1 = 3.5 \text{ V,}$$
$$\text{bit } D2 = 0.1 \text{ V,} \qquad \text{bit } D3 = 0.1 \text{ V,}$$

---

*Throughout the text, problems marked with a * are troubleshooting problems.

ADDRESS	OP CODES	MNEMONICS		COMMENTS
0000	3E 32	MVI	A,32H	LOAD ACCUMULATOR WITH 32H
0002	D3 05	OUT	5	OUTPUT THE CONTENTS OF THE ACCUMULATOR TO I/O PORT 5
0004	32 FF 06	STA	06FFH	STORE THE ACCUMULATOR AT MEMORY LOCATION 06FFH
0007	76	HLT .		HALT

Figure 1.20 8080 microprocessor assembly language routine used for Problems 1.31 through 1.35.

$$\text{bit D4} = 3.5 \text{ V}, \quad \text{bit D5} = 3.4 \text{ V},$$
$$\text{bit D6} = 0.2 \text{ V}, \quad \text{bit D7} = 0.1 \text{ V}.$$

What is the data byte on the bus, interpreted in hexadecimal? What character does the data byte represent as an ASCII code? What operation code does it represent as an 8080 microprocessor instruction?

1.28. The first machine cycle of every instruction is always:
   (a) memory read
   (b) memory write
   (c) I/O read
   (d) I/O write

1.29. The 8080/8085 instruction IN 3 requires three machine cycles. What are they?

1.30. True or false? One machine cycle requires one T state or clock cycle.

1.31. Refer to Fig. 1.20. How many total bytes does the program require?

1.32. In Fig. 1.20, memory location 0005 holds the data byte FF. How will the CPU interpret this byte when the program is run?

1.33. If it is desired to output 26H to I/O port 5, what change should be made to the program in Fig. 1.20?

1.34. Draw a machine-cycle timing diagram for the program in Fig. 1.20. Follow the format shown in Fig. 1.16.

1.35. Calculate the total time required to execute the program in Fig. 1.20 if the system clock frequency is 2 MHz. Figure 1.17 provides T-state information for each 8080 microprocessor instruction.

1.36. The access time of a memory chip is defined as the time from receipt of the memory address until valid data is output by the chip. Referring to Fig. 1.18, estimate the access time required of the memory, assuming a 4-MHz clock signal.

SELF-REVIEW ANSWERS

1.1.1. CPU, memory, I/O.

1.1.2. Address, data, control.

1.1.3. Memory read and write, I/O read and write.

1.2.1. Vacuum tube, transistor.

1.2.2. IBM 360.

1.2.3. A minicomputer is a scaled-down mainframe. It is typically much less costly than a mainframe.

1.2.4. A microcomputer is a computer system built using a microprocessor as the processor.

1.2.5. They are embedded within a product and therefore are not visible as a computer.

1.2.6. Multiple CPUs wired in parallel, each processing a portion of the program simultaneously.

1.2.7. A RISC processor has a simpler control unit because all instructions are of the same length and execute in a single clock cycle. The simplified control logic can operate faster than that of a CISC processor and requires less space on the chip.

1.2.8. A DSP has separate memories for data and instructions, onboard hardware multipliers and adders optimized for execution rates of one clock cycle, arithmetic pipelines to perform simultaneous math operations, hardware optimized for repetitive operations such as DO loops, and multiple serial I/O ports for communicating with a host processor.

1.3.1. 256.

1.3.2. D6, 214.

1.3.3. 1CE, 111001110.

1.3.4. 1010000.

1.4.1. Assembler.

1.4.2. Encoder.

1.5.1. 3.4 V and 0.2 V.

1.5.2. Control bus.

1.6.1. Fetch, execute.

1.6.2. Machine, T.

2

INTRODUCING THE 8080, 8085, AND Z-80 MICROPROCESSORS

OUTLINE

OBJECTIVES

After completing this chapter, you should be able to:

- Identify the support chips required to construct 8080, 8085, and Z-80 CPU modules.
- Associate the function of each 8080, 8085, and Z-80 processor pin with the control bus, address bus, or data bus.
- Explain the functions of the CPU general-purpose, flag, stack, and program counter registers.
- Sketch programming models for the 8080, 8085, and Z-80 processors, showing the internal CPU registers and flags.

- Identify and interpret 8080, 8085, and Z-80 instructions in mnemonic form.
- List the major 8080, 8085, and Z-80 instruction groups, including the data transfer, arithmetic, logical, branch, stack, I/O, machine control, exchange, block transfer, search, and bit manipulation groups.
- List the four addressing modes of the 8080/8085 processors and the six addressing modes of the Z-80 processor.
- Identify the components of an assembly language program, including the address, object codes, label, op-code, operand, and comment fields.
- Hand assemble a simple 8080/85 and Z-80 assembly language program.

OVERVIEW

In Chapter 1 we studied the basic elements of the stored-program computer. We now apply these concepts to hardware, in the form of the Intel 8080 and 8085 and the Zilog Z-80 microprocessors.

We begin the task by forming the basic *CPU module* for each chip. This module will be consistent with the definition of the CPU presented in Chapter 1. Next we carefully "peel the covers off" each processor and develop *programming models* for each chip. Think of the CPU module as the hardware designer's view of the microprocessor, whereas the programming model presents the software designer's view.

The chapter concludes with an introduction to the instruction sets of the three processors, a discussion of addressing modes, and a sample program written in assembly language with hexadecimal instruction codes.

2.1 CPU MODULES FOR THE 8080, 8085, AND Z-80 MICROPROCESSORS

Introduction

As we learned in Chapter 1, to build a microcomputer system we must add a memory interface and input–output devices to the microprocessor. The first step in accomplishing these goals is to construct a *CPU module*—a circuit that generates the system clock signal and provides access to the data, address, and control buses of the processor.

In this section, we:

- Identify the support chips required to construct 8080, 8085, and Z-80 CPU modules.
- Associate the function of each 8080, 8085, and Z-80 processor pin with the control bus, address bus, or data bus.

The 8080 CPU Module

In its day, Intel's 8080 microprocessor was one of the most popular microprocessors in the industry. Indeed, this chip and Motorola's 6800 singlehandedly begat the microprocessor revolution, still ongoing today.

The first samples of the 8080 became available in December 1971, so it is not a new device. However, it is a tribute to the original designers (and the circuit's popularity) that all of the processors studied in this book remain software compatible.

Figure 2.1 provides a pinout for the 8080 and describes the function of each pin. The 8080 shows its age by requiring three power supplies ($+5$ V, -5 V, and $+12$ V) and a two-phase nonoverlapping, non-TTL-compatible clock signal, shown in Fig. 2.2.

The 8080 does not directly furnish the control bus signals we are familiar with from Chapter 1. Instead, it provides a *SYNC* signal that pulses high during the first T cycle of each M1 machine cycle (that is, the first clock pulse of each instruction fetch). When SYNC is high, the data bus carries *status* information that may be latched and decoded to provide a control bus.

Figure 2.3 illustrates basic 8080 instruction cycle timing. Note that when ϕ_1 is high and SYNC is high, the data bus carries a special *status word*. Table 2.1 is a chart listing the 10 unique status words that can be output by the 8080. The status word indicates the type of machine cycle the processor is about to perform. For example, M1 indicates an instruction fetch cycle, M2 a memory read cycle. Using the chart, we can design a decoder to generate the four control bus signals necessary for I/O and memory read and write operations.

Example 2.1

Design a decoder circuit to generate the control bus signals $\overline{\text{MEMR}}$, $\overline{\text{MEMW}}$, $\overline{\text{IOR}}$, and $\overline{\text{IOW}}$ for an 8080 microprocessor.

Solution. Note from Fig. 2.3 that the *DBIN* signal (data bus in) indicates a CPU read operation and the $\overline{\text{WR}}$ signal a CPU write operation. From the status word chart in Table 2.1, only when data bus bit D6 is high is the current machine cycle an I/O read. Thus, D6 can be latched and combined with DBIN to generate the $\overline{\text{IOR}}$ control bus signal. This is shown in Fig. 2.4. Only when DBIN is high and the latched data bus bit D6 is high will $\overline{\text{IOR}}$ be active (that is, low). The other three control signals are developed in a similar manner.

(*Note:* Be sure that you understand the need to combine the status bit and DBIN or $\overline{\text{WR}}$. The status word tells us what is about to happen (that is, the type of machine cycle), but DBIN and $\overline{\text{WR}}$ tell us that the microprocessor is now ready to make it happen. Because the status bits disappear after the T2 state, they must be latched until needed.)

There is more information in the 8080 status word than is absolutely necessary for developing the control bus signals. For example, it is possible to distinguish between three types of memory reads—an *instruction fetch,* a *memory read,* and a *stack read*—by decoding status words 1, 2, and 4, respectively. Usually, this is not done, and only the decoding shown in Fig. 2.4 is provided.

If you are beginning to picture the 8080 as a rather complex chip to interface, you are correct. To make the job simpler, Intel has provided two support devices for the 8080: the *8228 system controller* and the *8224 system clock generator.* With these two chips, we can finally draw the CPU module for an 8080-based microcomputer.

Figure 2.5 illustrates the circuit. The 8224 develops the two-phase clock signal from an external crystal, divides the crystal frequency by 9, forms the two clock phases, and level-shifts the waveforms to the MOS levels required by the 8080. The 8224 also provides a TTL-level clock signal that may be used by other circuits in the system. Because

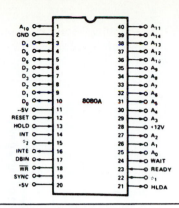

Symbol	Type	Name and Function
A_{15}-A_0	O	**Address Bus:** The address bus provides the address to memory (up to 64K 8-bit words) or denotes the I/O device number for up to 256 input and 256 output devices. A_0 is the least significant address bit.
D_7-D_0	I/O	**Data Bus:** The data bus provides bi-directional communication betweeen the CPU, memory, and I/O devices for instructions and data transfers. Also, during the first clock cycle of each machine cycle, the 8080A outputs a status word on the data bus that describes the current machine cycle. D_0 is the least significant bit.
SYNC	O	**Synchronizing Signal:** The SYNC pin provides a signal to indicate the beginning of each machine cycle.
DBIN	O	**Data Bus In:** The DBIN signal indicates to external circuits that the data bus is in the input mode. This signal should be used to enable the gating of data onto the 8080A data bus from memory or I/O.
READY	I	**Ready:** The READY signal indicates to the 8080A that valid memory or input data is available on the 8080A data bus. This signal is used to synchronize the CPU with slower memory or I/O devices. If after sending an address out the 8080A does not receive a READY input, the 8080A will enter a WAIT state for as long as the READY line is low. READY can also be used to single step the CPU.
WAIT	O	**Wait:** The WAIT signal acknowledges that the CPU is in a WAIT state.
$\overline{WR}$	O	**Write:** The $\overline{WR}$ signal is used for memory WRITE or I/O output control. The data on the data bus is stable while the $\overline{WR}$ signal is active low ($\overline{WR}$ = 0).
HOLD	I	**Hold:** The HOLD signal requests the CPU to enter the HOLD state. The HOLD state allows an external device to gain control of the 8080A address and data bus as soon as the 8080A has completed its use of these busses for the current machine cycle. It is recognized under the following conditions: • the CPU is in the HALT state. • the CPU is in the T2 or TW state and the READY signal is active. As a result of entering the HOLD state the CPU ADDRESS BUS (A_{15}-A_0) and DATA BUS (D_7-D_0) will be in their high impedance state. The CPU acknowledges its state with the HOLD ACKNOWLEDGE (HLDA) pin.
HLDA	O	**Hold Acknowledge:** The HLDA signal appears in response to the HOLD signal and indicates that the data and address bus will go to the high impedance state. The HLDA signal begins at: • T3 for READ memory or input. • The Clock Period following T3 for WRITE memory or OUTPUT operation. In either case, the HLDA signal appears after the rising edge of ϕ_2.
INTE	O	**Interrupt Enable:** Indicates the content of the internal interrupt enable flip/flop. This flip/flop may be set or reset by the Enable and Disable Interrupt instructions and inhibits interrupts from being accepted by the CPU when it is reset. It is automatically reset (disabling further interrupts) at time T1 of the instruction fetch cycle (M1) when an interrupt is accepted and is also reset by the RESET signal.
INT	I	**Interrupt Request:** The CPU recognizes an interrupt request on this line at the end of the current instruction or while halted. If the CPU is in the HOLD state or if the Interrupt Enable flip/flop is reset it will not honor the request.
RESET[1]	I	**Reset:** While the RESET signal is activated, the content of the program counter is cleared. After RESET, the program will start at location 0 in memory. The INTE and HLDA flip/flops are also reset. Note that the flags, accumulator, stack pointer, and registers are not cleared.
V_{SS}		**Ground:** Reference.
V_{DD}		**Power:** +12 ±5% Volts.
V_{CC}		**Power:** +5 ±5% Volts.
V_{BB}		**Power:** -5 ±5% Volts.
ϕ_1, ϕ_2		**Clock Phases:** 2 externally supplied clock phases. (non TTL compatible)

Figure 2.1   8080 microprocessor pinout and descriptions of each pin. (Courtesy of Intel Corporation.)

SILICON GATE MOS 8080A

A.C. CHARACTERISTICS

$T_A = 0°C$ to $70°C$, $V_{DD} = +12V \pm 5\%$, $V_{CC} = +5V \pm 5\%$, $V_{BB} = -5V \pm 5\%$, $V_{SS} = 0V$, Unless Otherwise Noted

Symbol	Parameter	Min.	Max.	Unit	Test Condition
t_{CY}[3]	Clock Period	0.48	2.0	μsec	
t_r, t_f	Clock Rise and Fall Time	0	50	nsec	
$t_{\phi1}$	ϕ_1 Pulse Width	60		nsec	
$t_{\phi2}$	ϕ_2 Pulse Width	220		nsec	
t_{D1}	Delay ϕ_1 to ϕ_2	0		nsec	
t_{D2}	Delay ϕ_2 to ϕ_1	70		nsec	
t_{D3}	Delay ϕ_1 to ϕ_2 Leading Edges	80		nsec	

TIMING WAVEFORMS [14]

(Note: Timing measurements are made at the following reference voltages: CLOCK "1" = 8.0V "0" = 1.0V; INPUTS "1" = 3.3V, "0" = 0.8V; OUTPUTS "1" = 2.0V, "0" = 0.8V.)

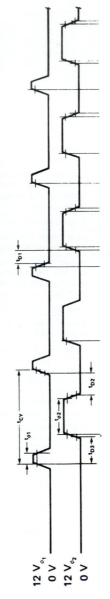

Figure 2.2 The 8080 requires a two-phase nonoverlapping clock signal. The clock levels are not TTL compatible. (Courtesy of Intel Corporation.)

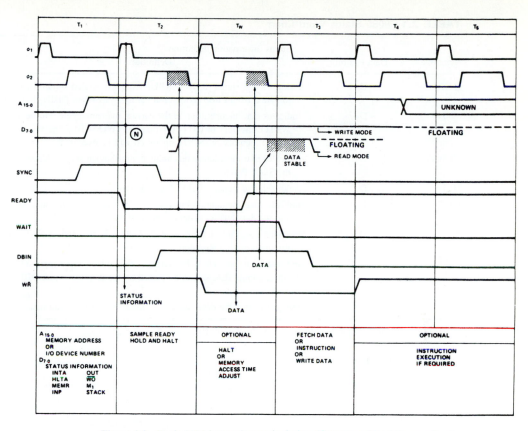

Figure 2.3 Basic 8080 instruction cycle timing. (Courtesy of Intel Corporation.)

of the divide-by-9 feature, a typical 8080A crystal is 18 MHz, resulting in a 2-MHz system clock.

The third chip in the CPU module is the 8228. This circuit takes the place of the 8212 latch and decoder circuitry shown in Fig. 2.4. In addition, it buffers (amplifies) the data bus lines so that they will not be loaded down by the many chips connected to this bus.

In sum, the 8080 is actually a three-chip CPU module requiring the 8224 clock generator and the 8228 system controller. An external crystal determines the system clock frequency. A few lines remain to be explained in Fig. 2.5, and these are covered in Chapters 4 and 6.

The 8085 CPU Module

As the state of the art in semiconductor technology advanced, it became possible for Intel to redesign the 8080 and include the 8224 and 8228 in a single package. The result was the 8085 microprocessor. Although there are several differences between the 8085 and the older 8080, the most important similarity is that the 8085 is *object code compatible* with the 8080. This means that all software written for the 8080 will also run on the 8085, without any changes.

TABLE 2.1 8080 Status Word Chart

Symbols	Data bus bit	Status information definition — Definition
INTA*	D_0	Acknowledge signal for INTERRUPT request. Signal should be used to gate a restart instruction onto the data bus when DBIN is active.
$\overline{WO}$	D_1	Indicates that the operation in the current machine cycle will be a WRITE memory or OUTPUT function ($\overline{WO}$ = 0). Otherwise, a READ memory or INPUT operation will be executed.
STACK	D_2	Indicates that the address bus holds the pushdown stack address from the Stack Pointer.
HLTA	D_3	Acknowledge signal for HALT instruction.
OUT	D_4	Indicates that the address bus contains the address of an output device and the data bus will contain the output data when $\overline{WR}$ is active.
M_1	D_5	Provides a signal to indicate that the CPU is in the fetch cycle for the first byte of an instruction.
INP*	D_6	Indicates that the address bus contains the address of an input device and the input data should be placed on the data bus when DBIN is active.
MEMR*	D_7	Designates that the data bus will be used for memory read data.

*These three status bits can be used to control the flow of data onto the 8080 data bus.

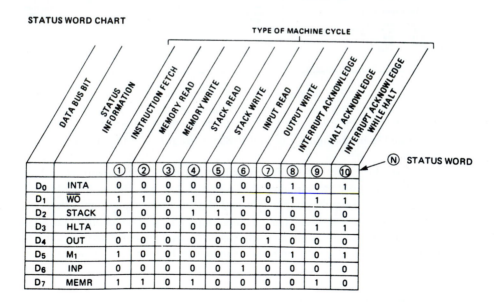

STATUS WORD CHART

Data bus bit	Status information	① Instruction fetch	② Memory read	③ Memory write	④ Stack read	⑤ Stack write	⑥ Input read	⑦ Output write	⑧ Interrupt acknowledge	⑨ Halt acknowledge	⑩ Interrupt acknowledge while halt
D_0	INTA	0	0	0	0	0	0	0	1	0	1
D_1	$\overline{WO}$	1	1	0	1	0	1	0	1	1	1
D_2	STACK	0	0	0	1	1	0	0	0	0	0
D_3	HLTA	0	0	0	0	0	0	0	0	1	1
D_4	OUT	0	0	0	0	0	0	1	0	0	0
D_5	M_1	1	0	0	0	0	0	0	1	0	1
D_6	INP	0	0	0	0	0	1	0	0	0	0
D_7	MEMR	1	1	0	1	0	0	0	0	1	0

Ⓝ STATUS WORD

Source: Courtesy of Intel Corporation.

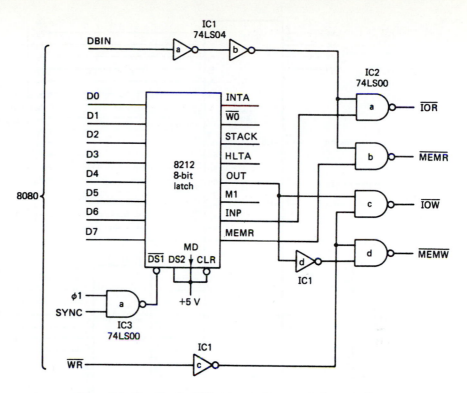

Figure 2.4 Decoding the 8080 status word to generate the control bus.

One of the problems that the 8085 designers (and indeed, all microprocessor designers) had to face was the limited number of pins available in the standard dual-in-line package (DIP). Most manufacturers have settled on the 40-pin package as a component that can be readily handled without breakage and still provide many lines of access to the chip itself.

Another solution to this problem is to share the package pins for several functions. This is what the designers of the 8085 chose to do. They maintained the standard 40-pin package, but combined the low-order address lines (A0 through A7) with the data bus lines (D0 through D7). The resulting lines are labeled *AD0* through *AD7*.

For this scheme to work, a new signal is required to identify when AD0–AD7 represent data and when they represent the low-order address. Intel calls this line *ALE,* for *address latch enable.* When ALE is high, AD0–AD7 carry the low-order address; when ALE switches low, AD0–AD7 represent the bidirectional data bus.

Figure 2.6 provides a pinout and pin description for the 8085. The most significant differences between the 8085 and the 8080 can be summarized as follows:

1. Only one power source is required, +5 V.
2. The clock signal is generated internally from an external crystal or *RC* network connected to X1 and X2. The internal clock runs at one-half the oscillation frequency of this circuit.

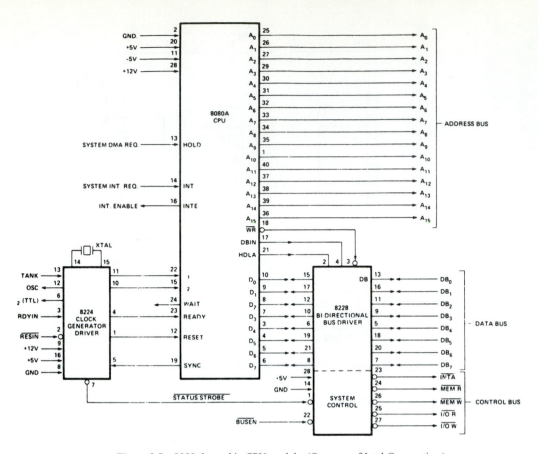

Figure 2.5 8080 three-chip CPU module. (Courtesy of Intel Corporation.)

3. The low-order address lines (A0 through A7) and the data bus lines (D0 through D7) are *multiplexed* onto the same set of eight pins, labeled AD0–AD7. The signal ALE is used to distinguish between the two.

4. The control bus is generated internally, providing the three signals $\overline{RD}$, $\overline{WR}$, and IO/$\overline{M}$.

Figure 2.7 illustrates basic 8085 system timing. Notice that ALE pulses high during the T1 clock pulse of each machine cycle. This provides a means of *demultiplexing* the bus into separate buses A0 through A7 and D0 through D7.

Figure 2.8 illustrates the technique in an 8085 CPU module for standard memory and I/O devices. The 8212 latch is used to demultiplex AD0–AD7. It is enabled by the ALE signal latching A0 through A7 on the falling edge of this signal. The gating array is used to form a control bus consistent with the 8080 CPU module.

Intel has developed special memory and I/O devices that support the multiplexed bus and control signals of the 8085. (See Chapter 7.) When these devices are used, the 8085 becomes a single-chip CPU module. But if standard memory and I/O devices are selected, the CPU module in Fig. 2.8 must be used.

Symbol	Type	Name and Function
A_8-A_{15}	O	**Address Bus:** The most significant 8 bits of the memory address or the 8 bits of the I/O address, 3-stated during Hold and Halt modes and during RESET.
AD_0-7	I/O	**Multiplexed Address/Data Bus:** Lower 8 bits of the memory address (or I/O address) appear on the bus during the first clock cycle (T state) of a machine cycle. It then becomes the data bus during the second and third clock cycles.
ALE	O	**Address Latch Enable:** It occurs during the first clock state of a machine cycle and enables the address to get latched into the on-chip latch of peripherals. The falling edge of ALE is set to guarantee setup and hold times for the address information. The falling edge of ALE can also be used to strobe the status information. ALE is never 3-stated.
$S_0, S_1,$ and IO/$\overline{M}$	O	**Machine Cycle Status:**
$\overline{RD}$	O	**Read Control:** A low level on $\overline{RD}$ indicates the selected memory or I/O device is to be read and that the Data Bus is available for the data transfer, 3-stated during Hold and Halt modes and during RESET.
$\overline{WR}$	O	**Write Control:** A low level on $\overline{WR}$ indicates the data on the Data Bus is to be written into the selected memory or I/O location. Data is set up at the trailing edge of $\overline{WR}$. 3-stated during Hold and Halt modes and during RESET.

Machine Cycle Status table (within $S_0, S_1,$ and IO/$\overline{M}$ row):

IO/$\overline{M}$	S_1	S_0	Status
0	0	1	Memory write
0	1	0	Memory read
1	0	1	I/O write
1	1	0	I/O read
0	1	1	Opcode fetch
1	1	1	Opcode fetch
1	1	1	Interrupt Acknowledge
*	0	0	Halt
*	X	X	Hold
*	X	X	Reset

* = 3-state (high impedance)
X = unspecified

S_1 can be used as an advanced R/$\overline{W}$ status. IO/$\overline{M}$, S_0 and S_1 become valid at the beginning of a machine cycle and remain stable throughout the cycle. The falling edge of ALE may be used to latch the state of these lines.

Figure 2.6 8085 microprocessor pin numbers and definitions. (Courtesy of Intel Corporation.)

Symbol	Type	Name and Function
READY	I	**Ready:** If READY is high during a read or write cycle, it indicates that the memory or peripheral is ready to send or receive data. If READY is low, the cpu will wait an integral number of clock cycles for READY to go high before completing the read or write cycle. READY must conform to specified setup and hold times.
HOLD	I	**Hold:** Indicates that another master is requesting the use of the address and data buses. The cpu, upon receiving the hold request, will relinquish the use of the bus as soon as the completion of the current bus transfer. Internal processing can continue. The processor can regain the bus only after the HOLD is removed. When the HOLD is acknowledged, the Address, Data $\overline{RD}$, $\overline{WR}$, and IO/$\overline{M}$ lines are 3-stated.
HLDA	O	**Hold Acknowledge:** Indicates that the cpu has received the HOLD request and that it will relinquish the bus in the next clock cycle. HLDA goes low after the Hold request is removed. The cpu takes the bus one half clock cycle after HLDA goes low.
INTR	I	**Interrupt Request:** Is used as a general purpose interrupt. It is sampled only during the next to the last clock cycle of an instruction and during Hold and Halt states. If it is active, the Program Counter (PC) will be inhibited from incrementing and an $\overline{INTA}$ will be issued. During this cycle a RESTART or CALL instruction can be inserted to jump to the interrupt service routine. The INTR is enabled and disabled by software. It is disabled by Reset and immediately after an interrupt is accepted.
$\overline{INTA}$	O	**Interrupt Acknowledge:** Is used instead of (and has the same timing as) $\overline{RD}$ during the Instruction cycle after an INTR is accepted. It can be used to activate an 8259A Interrupt chip or some other interrupt port.
RST 5.5 RST 6.5 RST 7.5	I	**Restart Interrupts:** These three inputs have the same timing as INTR except they cause an internal RESTART to be automatically inserted. The priority of these interrupts is ordered as shown in Table 2. These interrupts have a higher priority than INTR. In addition, they may be individually masked out using the SIM instruction.

Symbol	Type	Name and Function
RESET OUT	O	**Reset Out:** Reset Out indicates cpu is being reset. Can be used as a system reset. The signal is synchronized to the processor clock and lasts an integral number of clock periods.
X_1, X_2	I	**X_1 and X_2:** Are connected to a crystal, LC, or RC network to drive the internal clock generator. X_1 can also be an external clock input from a logic gate. The input frequency is divided by 2 to give the processor's internal operating frequency.
CLK	O	**Clock:** Clock output for use as a system clock. The period of CLK is twice the X_1, X_2 input period.
SID	I	**Serial Input Data Line:** The data on this line is loaded into accumulator bit 7 whenever a RIM instruction is executed.
SOD	O	**Serial Output Data Line:** The output SOD is set or reset as specified by the SIM instruction.
V_{CC}		**Power:** +5 volt supply.
V_{SS}		**Ground:** Reference.

Symbol	Type	Name and Function
TRAP	I	**Trap:** Trap interrupt is a non-maskable RESTART interrupt. It is recognized at the same time as INTR or RST 5.5-7.5. It is unaffected by any mask or Interrupt Enable. It has the highest priority of any interrupt. (See Table 2.)
$\overline{RESET\ IN}$	I	**Reset In:** Sets the Program Counter to zero and resets the Interrupt Enable and HLDA flip-flops. The data and address buses and the control lines are 3-stated during RESET and because of the asynchronous nature of RESET, the processor's internal registers and flags may be altered by RESET with unpredictable results. $\overline{RESET\ IN}$ is a Schmitt-triggered input, allowing connection to an R-C network for power-on RESET delay (see Figure 3). Upon power-up, $\overline{RESET\ IN}$ must remain low for at least 10 ms after minimum V_{CC} has been reached. For proper reset operation after the power-up duration, $\overline{RESET\ IN}$ should be kept low a minimum of three clock periods. The CPU is held in the reset condition as long as $\overline{RESET\ IN}$ is applied.

Figure 2.6 (*Continued*)

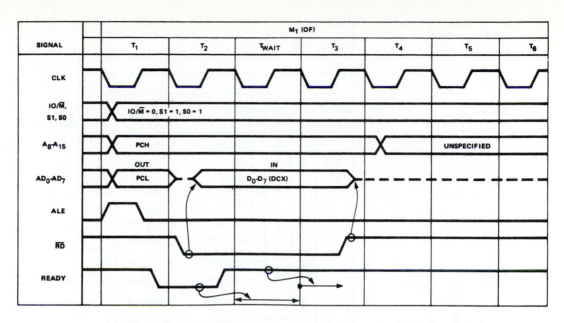

SIGNAL	M₁ (OF)						
	T_1	T_2	T_{WAIT}	T_3	T_4	T_5	T_6
CLK							
IO/M̄, S1, S0	IO/M̄ = 0, S1 = 1, S0 = 1						
A_8-A_{15}	PCH					UNSPECIFIED	
AD_0-AD_7	OUT PCL		IN D_0-D_7 (DCX)				
ALE							
R̄D̄							
READY							

Figure 2.7 Basic 8085 instruction cycle timing. (Courtesy of Intel Corporation.)

What has been gained by this multiplexing scheme? Several new *interrupt* inputs (special inputs to the microprocessor, causing it to suspend its present task temporarily) have been provided, giving the 8085 considerably more flexibility than the 8080 in servicing interrupts. In addition, two new I/O lines—*SID* and *SOD*—are provided and allow rudimentary serial input and output capabilities. (Serial I/O refers to transferring data bit by bit, instead of byte by byte in parallel.) Finally, status information is provided via the two pins *S0* and *S1*. They encode the bus activities as follows:

S1	S0	
0	0	Halt
0	1	Write
1	0	Read
1	1	Fetch

By combining these signals with IO/M̄, it is possible to identify the type of machine cycle in progress. (See Problem 2.9.) Because S0 and S1 are output *early* in the machine cycle, they can be used to generate early read and write control signals. This technique is useful for increasing memory access times allowed by the processor (and allowing slower memory parts to be interfaced).

In sum, the 8085 is software compatible with the 8080, includes an on-chip clock oscillator, requires an external latch for interfacing standard memories, and will require some simple gating to generate 8080-compatible control bus signals.

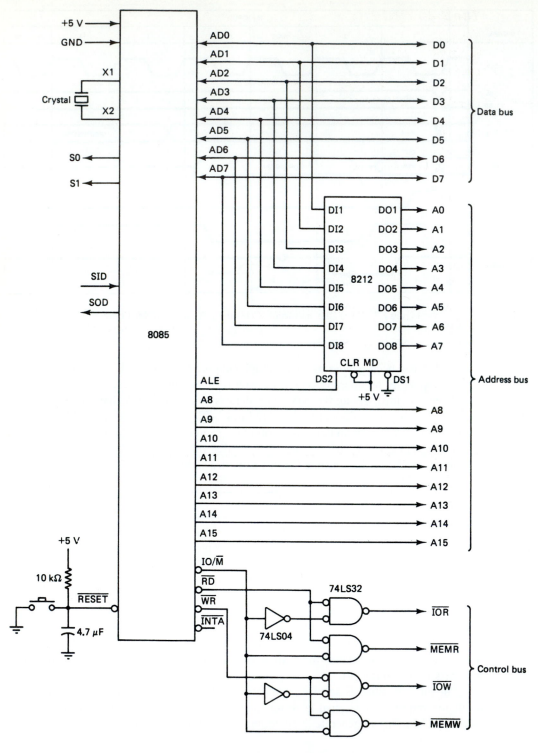

Figure 2.8 8085 CPU module.

The Z-80 CPU Module

The people responsible for the design of the 8080 microprocessor at Intel also designed the Z-80 for Zilog. In fact, Zilog is fond of calling the 8080 a *subset* of the Z-80. Of course, Intel considers the 8085 to be its version of an enhanced 8080.*

Although neither the 8085 nor the Z-80 is pin compatible with the 8080, the Z-80 more closely resembles the 8080 CPU module than does the 8085. The Z-80 also goes a step beyond the 8085 in that it not only is object code compatible, but also has a greatly expanded instruction set compared with that of the 8080. Indeed, some people feel that the instruction set is too complicated. You can judge this for yourself later in the chapter when the instruction sets of the three processors are presented.

Figure 2.9 is a pinout diagram and pin description for the Z-80. Unlike the clock signal of the 8085, that of the Z-80 must be generated external to the chip, but unlike the clock signal of the 8080, that of the Z-80 is a single-phase TTL-compatible signal. A typical clock frequency for the Z-80 is 4 MHz. A single +5-V power source is required.

Also, unlike the address and data buses of the 8085, but similar to those of the 8080, the address and data buses of the Z-80 are not multiplexed. Thus, the Z-80 can be interfaced to standard memory and I/O devices without the need for a low-order address latch.

Basic system timing for an op-code fetch machine cycle is shown in Fig. 2.10. One of the more notable features of the Z-80 is the *refresh address* output on A0 through A7 during T3 and T4 of each M1 machine cycle. This address will increment with each successive M1 cycle and can be used to refresh dynamic memories. (Such use is discussed in more detail in Chapter 5.)

Figure 2.11 illustrates a typical Z-80-based CPU module. The 74LS04 inverters function as a crystal oscillator, supplying the TTL-level clock signal. Zilog recommends pulling the clock output to +5 V through a 330-Ω resistor as shown. Again, a simple gating array is required to produce an 8080-like control bus. Depending on the interface, this combination of gates may not always be needed or may be combined with the address decoding logic. (We study this logic in more detail in Chapter 4 through 8.)

Finally, there are several other control-oriented signals not shown in the CPU module. These are dealt with later, when the subjects of *interrupts* and *DMA* (Chapter 6) and *WAIT* states (Chapter 5) are covered.

In sum, the Z-80 is an enhanced 8080 in a single IC package. Its bus structure is more straightforward than that of either the 8080 or the 8085. It does require an external clock generator, but this can be a simple 74LS04-based crystal oscillator. The Z-80's control bus is very similar to the 8080's and can be made to look exactly like the 8080's with a few simple gates.

---

*While the 8080 and 8085 represent the end of the line for Intel general-purpose 8-bit processors, Zilog has continued to develop the Z-80. CMOS versions are now available with clock speeds as high as 20 MHz. The Z84C90 is essentially a *computer on a chip* based on the Z-80 processor. It incorporates serial and parallel I/O ports, a counter/timer circuit, and a crystal oscillator. Also available is the Z80180. This is a more powerful version of the Z-80 with an expanded instruction set, including 8-bit multiplication. An onboard memory management unit (MMU) allows the more powerful Z-80 to access 1 MB of memory. Like the Z84C90, the Z80180 is highly integrated, incorporating two 16-bit timers, two direct memory access (DMA) channels, and two serial I/O ports. Versions are available with clock speeds as high as 33 MHz.

Z80, Z80A-CPU Pin Description

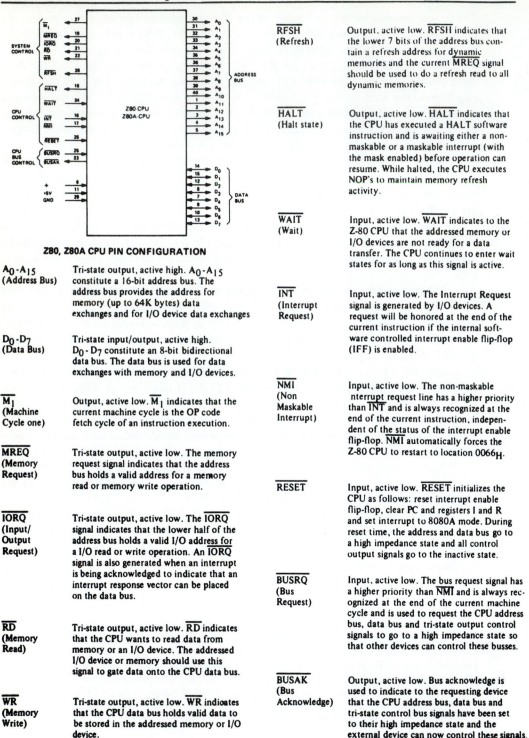

Z80, Z80A CPU PIN CONFIGURATION

A_0-A_{15}
(Address Bus)

Tri-state output, active high. A_0-A_{15} constitute a 16-bit address bus. The address bus provides the address for memory (up to 64K bytes) data exchanges and for I/O device data exchanges

D_0-D_7
(Data Bus)

Tri-state input/output, active high. D_0 - D_7 constitute an 8-bit bidirectional data bus. The data bus is used for data exchanges with memory and I/O devices.

$\overline{M_1}$
(Machine Cycle one)

Output, active low. $\overline{M_1}$ indicates that the current machine cycle is the OP code fetch cycle of an instruction execution.

$\overline{MREQ}$
(Memory Request)

Tri-state output, active low. The memory request signal indicates that the address bus holds a valid address for a memory read or memory write operation.

$\overline{IORQ}$
(Input/ Output Request)

Tri-state output, active low. The $\overline{IORQ}$ signal indicates that the lower half of the address bus holds a valid I/O address for a I/O read or write operation. An $\overline{IORQ}$ signal is also generated when an interrupt is being acknowledged to indicate that an interrupt response vector can be placed on the data bus.

$\overline{RD}$
(Memory Read)

Tri-state output, active low. $\overline{RD}$ indicates that the CPU wants to read data from memory or an I/O device. The addressed I/O device or memory should use this signal to gate data onto the CPU data bus.

$\overline{WR}$
(Memory Write)

Tri-state output, active low. $\overline{WR}$ indicates that the CPU data bus holds valid data to be stored in the addressed memory or I/O device.

$\overline{RFSH}$
(Refresh)

Output, active low. $\overline{RFSH}$ indicates that the lower 7 bits of the address bus contain a refresh address for dynamic memories and the current $\overline{MREQ}$ signal should be used to do a refresh read to all dynamic memories.

$\overline{HALT}$
(Halt state)

Output, active low. $\overline{HALT}$ indicates that the CPU has executed a HALT software instruction and is awaiting either a non-maskable or a maskable interrupt (with the mask enabled) before operation can resume. While halted, the CPU executes NOP's to maintain memory refresh activity.

$\overline{WAIT}$
(Wait)

Input, active low. $\overline{WAIT}$ indicates to the Z-80 CPU that the addressed memory or I/O devices are not ready for a data transfer. The CPU continues to enter wait states for as long as this signal is active.

$\overline{INT}$
(Interrupt Request)

Input, active low. The Interrupt Request signal is generated by I/O devices. A request will be honored at the end of the current instruction if the internal software controlled interrupt enable flip-flop (IFF) is enabled.

$\overline{NMI}$
(Non Maskable Interrupt)

Input, active low. The non-maskable interrupt request line has a higher priority than $\overline{INT}$ and is always recognized at the end of the current instruction, independent of the status of the interrupt enable flip-flop. $\overline{NMI}$ automatically forces the Z-80 CPU to restart to location 0066_H.

$\overline{RESET}$

Input, active low. $\overline{RESET}$ initializes the CPU as follows: reset interrupt enable flip-flop, clear PC and registers I and R and set interrupt to 8080A mode. During reset time, the address and data bus go to a high impedance state and all control output signals go to the inactive state.

$\overline{BUSRQ}$
(Bus Request)

Input, active low. The bus request signal has a higher priority than $\overline{NMI}$ and is always recognized at the end of the current machine cycle and is used to request the CPU address bus, data bus and tri-state output control signals to go to a high impedance state so that other devices can control these busses.

$\overline{BUSAK}$
(Bus Acknowledge)

Output, active low. Bus acknowledge is used to indicate to the requesting device that the CPU address bus, data bus and tri-state control bus signals have been set to their high impedance state and the external device can now control these signals.

Figure 2.9 Z-80 microprocessor pin numbers and definitions. (Courtesy of Zilog, Inc.)

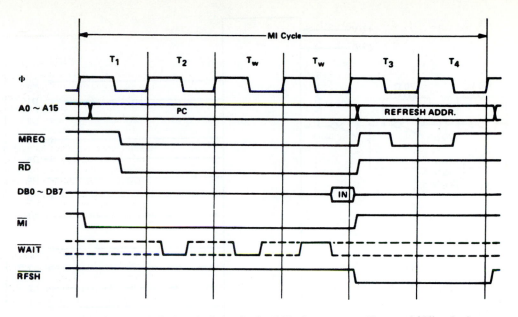

Figure 2.10 Op-code fetch cycle timing for the Z-80 microprocessor. (Courtesy of Zilog, Inc.)

SELF-REVIEW 2.1

2.1.1 The 8080 CPU module requires two support chips: the _____ clock generator and the _____ system controller.

2.1.2 The 8085 CPU module requires an 8-bit latch to demultiplex the _____ and _____ lines.

2.1.3 The Z-80 CPU module requires only an external TTL-compatible _____ generator.

2.2 PROGRAMMING MODELS FOR THE 8080, 8085, AND Z-80 MICROPROCESSORS

Introduction

An understanding of the *CPU module* is essential when your goal is to design and construct a particular microcomputer system. However, when the goal is to develop *software* for a particular processor (that is, control and applications programs), a knowledge of the CPU module is less important.

For example, to write an 8080 assembly language program, we do not need to know how the clock signal is generated or that status information is output at the beginning of each machine cycle. What we do need is a knowledge of the inner workings of the 8080 microprocessor itself. This information is usually presented in the form of a *programming model*.

The programming model is a diagram of the internal registers and flags within the CPU. Recall that we have already seen one special register in Chapter 1: the *accumulator*.

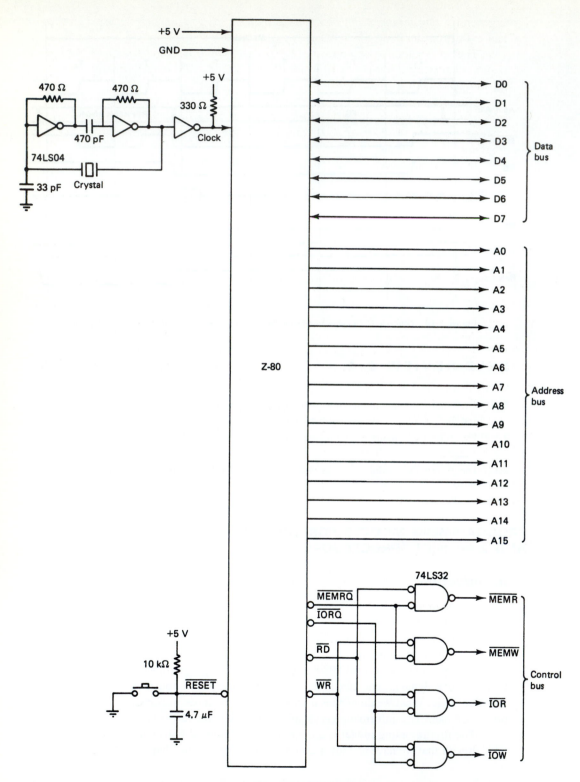

Figure 2.11 Z-80 CPU module.

In general, a register is a storage location in the CPU. The accumulator is special because data in this register can be manipulated mathematically or logically.

The nonaccumulator registers are called *general-purpose registers* and can be used to store temporary information. (Recall how the B register was used for temporary storage in the addition problem in Section 1.4).

Our goal in the current section is to develop programming models for the three processors we are discussing. Once these models are understood, we will be able to make efficient use of the instruction sets of the processors and begin to write assembly language programs.

In this section, we:

- Explain the functions of the CPU general-purpose, flag, stack, and program counter registers.
- Sketch programming models for the 8080, 8085, and Z-80 processors, showing the internal CPU registers and flags.

A Programming Model for the 8080

Figure 2.12 is a programming model for the 8080 microprocessor. The 8080 has six 8-bit general-purpose registers called the *B, C, D, E, H,* and *L* registers. The A register is the accumulator and register F is a special flag register.

There are also two 16-bit registers labeled register *SP* and register *PC.* Register PC is the *program counter,* and its 16-bit length is consistent with the 16-bit address bus of the 8080. As mentioned in Chapter 1, the program counter holds the address of the next instruction the CPU will be fetching from memory.

Register SP is called the *stack pointer register.* It also holds a 16-bit address, but this address is interpreted as pointing to a special section of memory called the *stack.* The stack area of memory can be used to supply a nearly unlimited number of general-purpose registers *external* to the microprocessor. The stack is also used to save the return

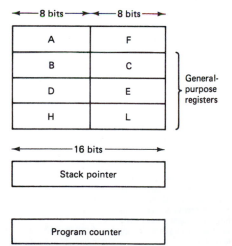

Figure 2.12   Programming model for the 8080 microprocessor.

address when a subroutine call instruction is given. (We will learn more about the stack later in this chapter.)

Recall that all data for the 8080 is 8 bits in length. Therefore, when the CPU fetches an instruction from memory, it will issue a 16-bit address, but it will retrieve only 8 bits, or one byte, of data. The general-purpose registers are intended for storing data bytes, but the stack pointer and program counter registers are used to specify memory locations or addresses.

Some of the 8080 instructions allow the general-purpose registers to be grouped as *register pairs*. Thus, we have the "BC pair," the "DE pair," and the "HL pair." Note that only these pairings are allowed. When used in this manner, the register pair can represent 16-bit numbers.

In some special cases, the number in the register pair can be used as an address. For example, the 8080 instruction MOV M,B is interpreted to mean "Move the data in the B register to the contents of memory whose address is in the HL pair." This is referred to as *register-indirect* addressing. (We will study the different addressing modes of the processors later in the chapter.)

The 8080 Flag Register

Figure 2.13 illustrates the five condition flags of the 8080 and provides a definition of each. These flags are actually 1-bit flip-flops that can be set to a logic 1 or reset to a logic 0. In general, each 8080 instruction will affect all, some, or none of the flags.

You can best understand the flags by studying several examples.

Example 2.2

If register B = 03H and register A = 03H, what is the state of the flags after the command SUB B is given?

S	Z	0	AC	0	P	1	CY

<u>Zero:</u> If the result of an instruction has the value 0, this flag is set; otherwise it is reset.

<u>Sign:</u> If the most significant bit of the result of the operation has the value 1, this flag is set; otherwise it is reset.

<u>Parity:</u> If the modulo 2 sum of the bits of the result of the operation is 0, (i.e., if the result has even parity), this flag is set; otherwise it is reset (i.e., if the result has odd parity).

<u>Carry:</u> If the instruction resulted in a carry (from addition), or a borrow (from subtraction or a comparison) out of the high-order bit, this flag is set; otherwise it is reset.

<u>Auxiliary carry:</u> If the instruction caused a carry out of bit 3 and into bit 4 of the resulting value, the auxiliary carry is set; otherwise it is reset. This flag is affected by single precision additions, subtractions, increments, decrements, comparisons, and logical operations, but is principally used with additions and increments preceding a DAA (Decimal Adjust Accumulator) instruction.

Figure 2.13   8080 flag word and descriptions.

Solution. The description of SUB B is "Subtract the contents of register B from register A, leaving the result in register A." It is obvious that, for this example, register A must contain 0. Because the result is 0, the Z flag will be set. The sign flag will be reset, the P flag will be set, and the AC and CY flags will both be reset.

Ignoring the last four flags for the moment, the point you should note is that the Z flag is set when the result of an arithmetic (or logical) operation is 0.

Example 2.3

If register B = 80H and register A = 03H, what is the state of the flags after the command ADD B is given?

Solution. The description of ADD B is "Add the contents of register B to register A, leaving the result in register A." Thus, register A must contain 83H (10000011). In this case the Z flag will be reset, because the result is not zero. Since no carries were generated, the AC and CY flags will also be reset. The parity flag is reset because the number of 1's in 83H is three (odd parity). The sign flag will be set because the most significant bit of the result is a 1.

Note: With the use of two's-complement arithmetic, the number in the B register actually corresponds to -128 decimal. The 03H in register A represents $+3$ decimal. When the ADD B instruction is given, a *subtraction* operation is actually indicated $(-128 + 3)$, and the result of 83H is equivalent to -125 decimal. The steps in realizing this result are as follows:

1. 80H = 10000000, and because bit 7 is a 1, a negative number is indicated.
2. To determine the decimal value of 80H, find the two's complement by inverting all bits and adding 1:

$$\begin{array}{r} 01111111 \\ + \quad\quad 1 \\ \hline 10000000 \quad\quad \text{or } -128_{10} \end{array}$$

3. Obviously, $-128 + 3 = -125$, and this can be verified by finding the two's complement of the result, 83H:

$$\begin{array}{ll} 10000011 = 83\text{H} & \\ 01111100 & \text{invert all bits} \\ + \quad\quad 1 & \text{add 1 to form two's complement} \\ \hline 01111101 = 7\text{DH or } 125_{10}, & \text{as expected} \end{array}$$

Example 2.4

If register B = 01H and register A = FFH, what is the state of the flags after the command ADD B is given?

Solution. Register A will contain FF + 01 = 00. The S flag will be reset because bit 7 is 0. The Z flag will be set because the result is 0. The AC flag will be set because a carry occurred from bit 3 to bit 4. The P flag will be set because the parity is even, and the CY flag will be set because of the carry out of bit 7.

The point to note here is that an *overflow* during an addition operation will set the CY flag. You will also find that the CY flag acts as a borrow flag for subtraction. For example, if A = 02H and B = 03H, the command SUB B will leave FF in the accumulator and set the CY flag.

The real utility of the flags is that they can be tested by various branch or jump instructions, allowing decision blocks in your program. For example, Fig. 2.14 is a brief 8080 machine language program that will loop through the last two instructions 255 (decimal) times. This can be useful for generating time delays.

The MVI B,FF instruction loads register B with 255 decimal. In the second line, the contents of register B are decremented by 1. The JNZ 0002 instruction (jump if not zero to location 0002) tests the Z flag. If the flag is not set—that is, if the result is not zero—the DCR B instruction is repeated. After 255 cycles the result will be zero, and control will pass to the program segment following the JNZ instruction.

A Programming Model for the 8085

From a programmer's standpoint, the 8085 is nearly identical to the 8080. The programming model shown in Fig. 2.12 still applies, and the flag register shown in Fig. 2.13 is also the same. In fact, the only difference between the two microprocessors is the inclusion in the 8085 of two new instructions with mnemonics *RIM* (read interrupt masks) and *SIM* (set interrupt masks). These commands allow the 8085 to service interrupting devices using its expanded interrupt capabilities. They also allow the input and output of serial data through register A and the SID and SOD pins. (An example that uses the RIM and SIM instructions and the SID and SOD pins is given in Chapter 3.)

A Programming Model for the Z-80

A programming model for the Z-80 microprocessor is shown in Fig. 2.15. As can be seen, the Z-80 is almost like two 8080s in one package. All of the 8080 general-purpose registers, including the A and F registers, have been duplicated. These are called the *alternate register* set and are identified with the prime (') symbol.

In addition to the duplicate set of 8080 registers, the Z-80 contains two new 16-bit registers labeled *IX* and *IY*. These registers are referred to as the X and Y index registers and provide a new addressing mode called *indexed addressing*. For example, the Z-80 mnemonic LD A,(IX+5) is interpreted as "Load register A with the data in the memory location whose address is in index register X, offset by 5." The offset is variable and is summed with the contents of register IX using two's-complement arithmetic.

In addition to registers IX and IY, there are two new 8-bit registers labeled *I* and *R*. The I register is used for mode-2 interrupts and is discussed in Chapter 6. The R register is used for refreshing dynamic memories. The low 7 bits of this register are placed on the low-order address lines (A0 through A6) during T3 and T4 of each M1 machine cycle. The R register is incremented automatically after each M1 machine cycle.

ADDRESS	OP-CODES	MNEMONICS	COMMENTS
0000	06 FF	MVI B,FF	PUT FF INTO REGISTER B
0002	05	DCR B	SUBTRACT 1 FROM B
0003	C2 02 00	JNZ 0002	IF THE RESULT IS NOT ZERO JUMP TO LOCATION 0002

Figure 2.14 8080 machine language program demonstrating a technique for testing the Z flag.

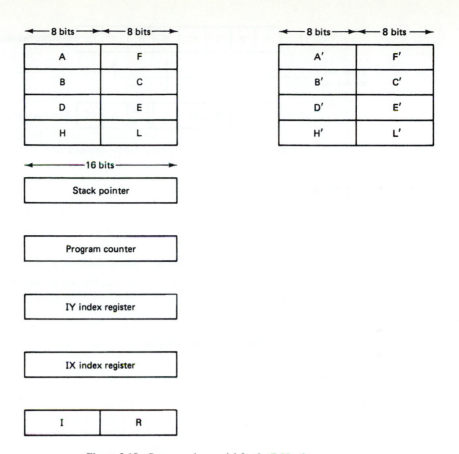

Figure 2.15 Programming model for the Z-80 microprocessor.

Note that, although the Z-80's general-purpose register set is impressive, *only one set is accessible at a time.* The instruction *EXX* will exchange the contents of BC, DE, and HL with BC', DE', and HL', respectively. The instruction EX AF,AF' performs a similar function with the accumulator and flag registers.

The Z-80 Flag Register

Figure 2.16 compares the 8080/85 flag register with the Z-80 flag register. The Z-80 has the same flags as the 8080, but includes two new flags labeled *P/V* and *N.* The P/V flag is set on the basis of the operation being performed. It represents an overflow condition for signed binary arithmetic and, when set, indicates an erroneous result due to data too large to fit into the data space allowed (greater than +127 or less than −128).

For input and logical operations, the P/V flag is set according to the parity of the result—even parity sets the flag, odd parity resets it.

The N flag is used for internal operations and is not testable by the programmer. It is set to a 1 for all subtract operations and a 0 for all additions. Note that in Zilog literature the AC flag is called the H (for half carry) flag.

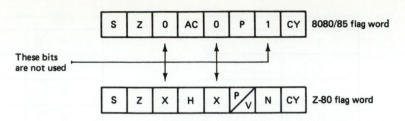

Figure 2.16 8080 and Z-80 flag words compared.

SELF-REVIEW 2.2

2.2.1 A diagram showing the internal CPU registers and flags of a computer is called the

_____ _____.

2.2.2 Which CPU register stores the address of the next instruction to be fetched and executed?

2.2.3 After each instruction is executed, the _____ bits are updated to reflect the result of that instruction.

2.3 INTRODUCING THE INSTRUCTION SETS

Introduction

The instruction set of a microprocessor represents the unique codes that the CPU can interpret, decode, and execute. Recalling the CPU model from Chapter 1, we see that these codes are fetched from the memory unit during the M1 machine cycle, stored in the instruction register, decoded by the CPU, and finally, executed.

The instruction codes cause data to be moved between the general-purpose registers, memory, and I/O devices. They also permit mathematical and logical operations to be performed. The complete set of all operation codes is referred to as the *instruction set*. The 8080 microprocessor recognizes 244 unique operation codes.

In programming a microprocessor, it is absolutely necessary that the programmer understand the programming model for that processor. In addition, he or she must be aware of all *types* of instructions in the processor's instruction set.

Take the time now to browse through the appendices. Included in them are word descriptions of the 8080/85 and Z-80 instruction sets, hexadecimal operation codes, information on T states and machine cycles for each instruction, and details of how each instruction affects the condition flags.

The task before us is to become familiar with this information so that we can begin to write simple (and some not so simple) machine and assembly language programs. But how shall we do this? One approach would be to provide a "blow-by-blow" description of each instruction. But considering that the 8080 and 8085 have over 200 instructions and the Z-80 has over 600 instructions, this would be extremely tedious.

Instead, let us study the instructions in logical *groups*. In particular, we will choose seven types of instructions and study an example of each. This will be a "fast tour" designed to give you an overview of the types of instructions available.

In Chapter 3, a number of programming examples are presented that collectively illustrate the use of most of the processor's instructions in real-world applications. Studying these examples will allow you to compare and contrast the different processors.

In this section, we:

- Identify and interpret 8080, 8085, and Z-80 instructions in mnemonic form.
- List the major 8080, 8085, and Z-80 instruction groups, including the data transfer, arithmetic, logical, branch, stack, I/O, machine control, exchange, block transfer, search, and bit manipulation groups.

Types of Instructions

Let us examine the following seven groups of instructions for the 8080/85 and Z-80 microprocessors:

1. Data transfer group
2. Arithmetic group
3. Logical and rotate group
4. Branch group
5. Stack, I/O, and machine control group
6. Exchange, block transfer, and search group
7. Bit manipulation group

The data transfer group.   Instructions in this group move data from register to register, from memory to a register, or from a register to memory. The data transferred can be 8 or 16 bits (one or two bytes) in length.

Figure 2.17 gives three examples. In the first, data are moved from register B to register A. There are many different versions of this register-to-register transfer, corresponding to all of the 8-bit register combinations.

Hex Op-code	Mnemonic		Symbolic Operation	Description
	8080/85	Z-80		
78	MOV A,B	LD A,B	A ← B	Place a copy of register B in register A.
21 00 07	LXI H,0700	LD HL,0700	HL ← 0700	Load the HL register pair with 0700
DD 2A 00 07	none	LD IX,(0700)	IX ← (0700)	Load the X index register with the contents of memory location 0700 (LSB)* and 0701 (MSB)*.

*Least Significant Byte.
*Most Significant Byte.

Figure 2.17   Examples of a register-to-register data transfer and two 16-bit load operations.

Although the 8080 (and 8085) have a different mnemonic for this instruction from that of the Z-80, the binary (and hex) op code is the same for both. Of course, all of the 8080/85 codes have been duplicated by the Z-80, as mentioned previously.

The second example in Fig. 2.17 illustrates a 16-bit load operation. In this case, the HL register pair is being loaded with the 16-bit word 0700H. (The H indicates a hex number.) Notice that this is a three-byte instruction and that, when it is coded, the order of the data is *backward* (low-order byte first, high-order byte last).

The last example in Fig. 2.17 is unique to the Z-80. Here, the X index register is being loaded with the two data bytes at memory locations 0700H and 0701H. Notice how the parentheses are used to indicate the *contents* of a memory location. The instruction LD IX,0700H (without parentheses) would load 16-bit register X with 0700H.

It is interesting to note that the LD IX,(nnnn) instruction has a two-byte op code (DD 2A). This is the technique the designers of the Z-80 used to obtain more than 600 instructions with an 8-bit word size. The DD op code was not implemented in the 8080/85.

The arithmetic group.   This group includes all of the mathematical commands, such as add, subtract, increment, and decrement. Again, 8- and 16-bit operations are possible.

Figure 2.18 illustrates the basic add operation. The mathematical instructions always occur in the accumulator. Thus, the command ADD B,C does not exist.

The second example in Fig. 2.18 shows a 16-bit addition with the BC and HL register pairs. Sixteen-bit additions are restricted to using the HL pair with one of the other register pairs.

The logical and rotate group.   This group includes the logical operators AND, OR, and EXCLUSIVE-OR. The first example in Fig. 2.19 illustrates the AND operation. Note that each operation is performed *bit by bit.* For example, if register $A = 7FH$ and register $B = 9AH$, the result of the 8080 instruction ANA B is as follows:

$$A = 7F = 01111111$$
$$B = 9A = \underline{10011010}$$
$$A \cdot B = 1A = 00011010$$

Figure 2.19 also shows a compare instruction. In this case, the accumulator is compared against a memory location whose address is held in the HL register pair, an operation known as *register indirect* addressing. Note that the contents of the accumulator are unchanged by this operation. However, the Z flag is set if the two bytes are identical; the CY flag is set if the contents of register A are greater than the contents of HL.

Hex Op-code	Mnemonic		Symbolic Operation	Description
	8080/85	Z-80		
80	ADD B	ADD A,B	$A \leftarrow A+B$	Register B is added to register A. The result is left in register A.
09	DAD B	ADD HL,BC	$HL \leftarrow HL+BC$	Register pair BC is added to register pair HL. The result is left in HL.

Figure 2.18   Examples from the arithmetic group of instructions.

Hex Op-code	Mnemonic 8080/85	Mnemonic Z-80	Symbolic Operation	Description
A0	ANA B	AND B	$A \leftarrow A \cdot B$	Register A is ANDed bit-by-bit with register B. The result is left in register A.
BE	CMP M	CP (HL)	$A - (HL)$	The contents of the memory location whose address is contained in HL is subtracted from the accumulator. The accumulator is unchanged but the condition flags are set.

Figure 2.19 Examples from the logical group of instructions.

Table 2.2 illustrates all of the rotate and shift instructions. The 8080/85 supports only the first four. Notice how the carry flag is used to extend the accumulator to 9 bits for these operations. The 8080/85 restrict the rotates to register A. The Z-80 can rotate the contents of any of the general-purpose registers or memory locations.

The branch group.   Branch instructions are also referred to as jump commands. These commands cause control of the program to be transferred to a new address, breaking the normal sequential flow of a program. The jump instruction can be *conditional* or *unconditional*. In Fig. 2.14 we saw the 8080/85 mnemonic JNZ (jump if not zero). This is a conditional jump.

There are several conditional jump instructions allowing each of the processor condition flags to be tested for a true-or-false condition. For example, two of these are jump if the carry flag is set (JC) and jump if the carry flag is not set (JNC).

The first example in Fig. 2.20 is an *unconditional* jump. Note how this is implemented: The second and third bytes of the instruction are placed in the program counter so that the next instruction fetch cycle automatically occurs from the desired address. Again, the order of these two bytes is "backward."

The Z-80 supports a second type of branch command called the *relative jump,* the second example in Fig. 2.20. In this two-byte instruction, the first byte specifies the op code for the condition to be tested (JR C, JR NC, JR Z, etc.) The second byte specifies a two's-complement offset to be added to the current value of the program counter to determine the new address. This type of relative branching allows a jump forward of 127 bytes or backward of 128 bytes.

The third example in Fig. 2.20 is the subroutine call. The CALL instruction differs from the jump instruction in that control will be transferred to the instruction that follows the CALL when a special RETurn instruction is encountered. This technique allows the subroutine to be used many times from different places in the same program.

The symbolic description of the CALL is rather complex. With reference to Fig. 2.20, the following sequence occurs:

1. The memory location pointed to by register SP − 1 (the stack pointer less 1) is loaded with the high-order byte of the program counter.
2. The memory location pointed at by register SP − 2 is loaded with the low-order byte of the program counter. In other words, the program counter is saved on the stack.

TABLE 2.2 Rotate and Shift Instructions for the 8080/85 and Z-80 Microprocessors

Mnemonic		Symbolic operation
8080/85	Z-80	
RLC	RLCA	
RAL	RLA	
RRC	RRCA	
RAR	RRA	
None	RLC r	
None	RLC (HL)	
None	RLC (IX + d)	
None	RLC (IY + d)	
None	RL m	
None	RRC m	
None	RR m	
None	SLA m	
None	SRA m	
None	SRL m	
None	RLD	
None	RRD	

Courtesy of Zilog, Inc.

Hex	Mnemonic		Symbolic	Description
Op-code	8080/85	Z-80	Operation	
C3 00 01	JMP 0100	JP 0100H	PC ← 0100H	Control is transferred to the address given in bytes 2 and 3 of the instruction.
30 (offset)	none	JR NC, 0100H	PC ← PC+offset	Control is transferred to the address in the PC + offset.
CD 00 01	CALL 0100	CALL 0100H	(SP−1) ← PCH (SP−2) ← PCL PC ← 0100 SP ← SP−2	Control is transferred to the subroutine at 0100H. The return address is stored on the stack. The stack pointer is decremented by 2.
C9	RET	RET	PCL ← (SP) PCH ← (SP+1) SP ← SP+2	Control is transferred to the address on the stack top. The stack pointer is incremented by 2.

Figure 2.20 The branch group includes both conditional and unconditional jumps. Sub-routine calls are also included in this group.

3. The program counter is loaded with the address of the subroutine, in this case 0100H.

4. Register SP is decremented by 2. This protects the stack from being overwritten by another subroutine call and allows *nested* subroutines.

The program now resumes, but at the new address (0100H in this example). When an RET instruction is encountered (see the last example in Fig. 2.20), register SP is incremented by 2 back to its "old" value, and the data on the stack (the return address) are "popped" into the program counter.

Fortunately for the programmer, all of this processing is *transparent,* and you need only remember to balance each subroutine call with a RET instruction. (Subroutines are covered in more detail in Chapter 3.)

The stack, I/O, and machine control group.   We have already seen how the CALL and RET instructions affect the stack. Two other instructions, the *PUSH* and *POP* commands, also utilize this area of memory. Figure 2.21 illustrates the PUSH B and POP

Hex	Mnemonic		Symbolic	Description
Op-code	8080/85	Z-80	Operation	
C5	PUSH B	PUSH BC	(SP−1) ← B (SP−2) ← C SP ← SP−2	The BC register pair is pushed onto the stack top. The stack pointer is decremented by 2.
C1	POP B	POP BC	C ← (SP) B ← (SP+1) SP ← SP+2	The top of the stack is popped into the BC pair. The stack pointer is incremented by 2.

Figure 2.21 The PUSH instruction can be used to store the contents of any of the register pairs in the stack area of memory. The POP command pops data off the stack and into the selected register pair.

B instructions. The PUSH instructions are useful for saving any of the general-purpose registers, the flag register, or the accumulator. Using the 8080/85 mnemonics, there are four versions: PUSH B, PUSH D, PUSH H, and PUSH PSW. PSW is the processor status word and is made up of register A and the flag register. The Z-80 mnemonic is PUSH AF.

Once their contents are pushed onto the stack, these registers are free to be used for some other purpose. The POP command reverses the process, popping the top of the stack into the selected register pair. This is shown as the second example in Fig. 2.21. Great care must be taken in using the stack, as it is a "last-in, first-out" type of memory. This means that registers' contents should be popped off the stack in the *reverse* order in which they were pushed on.

Example 2.5

Explain the operation of the following 8080/85 program:

```
LXI SP,07FFH
PUSH B
PUSH H
POP B
POP H
HLT
```

Solution. The program begins by loading register SP with 07FFH. Now the contents of the register pairs BC and HL are pushed onto the stack. Figure 2.22 shows the stack at this point. Next, the top of the stack (containing the contents of the HL pair) is popped into the BC register pair, the stack pointer is incremented by 2, and the (new) stack top (containing the contents of the BC pair) is popped into the HL register pair. The effect is to exchange the contents of register pairs BC and HL.

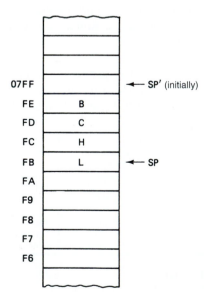

Figure 2.22 After pushing the contents of the BC and HL pairs onto the stack, the stack pointer contains 07FBH. The contents of the HL pair now rest on the top of the stack.

(*Note:* This is the "wrong" way of using the stack when the intent is to save these registers temporarily. In this example, it is an effective way of swapping two register pairs.)

This group also includes the input–output instructions for the three processors, summarized in Table 2.3. The 8080 and 8085 have only two such instructions: IN n (input the data from port n to the accumulator) and OUT n (output the data in the accumulator to port n). Note that for either instruction, the data must pass through the accumulator. (This is not so for the Z-80. The Z-80 commands IN r,(C) and OUT (C),r allow I/O through any of the general-purpose registers except register C, which is used to identify the 8-bit port address.)

In addition, data can be input or output from the memory location specified by the HL pair. In this case, register B is used as a counter, being decremented with each execution of the instruction. The INI and OUTI commands cause the address in HL to increment with each execution, while the IND and OUTD commands cause the HL address pointer to be decremented.

The INIR, INDR, OTIR, and OTDR instructions automatically repeat until the B register contains 0. All of these commands are useful for moving tables of data into or out of memory. One must be careful not to exceed the speed capabilities of the I/O device, however. (See Chapter 6 for a discussion about synchronizing the microprocessor to the I/O device.)

The exchange, block transfer, and search group. These instructions are unique to the Z-80 microprocessor. Figure 2.23 illustrates the EXX command, which swaps all of the Z-80 general-purpose registers with the alternative set of registers.

Another example is the LDDR command. This instruction moves data from the memory location pointed to by register pair HL to the memory location pointed to by register pair DE. LDDR automatically decrements the HL and DE register pair pointers. It is assumed that register pair BC is loaded with the number of bytes to be transferred. After each transfer, the BC byte counter is decremented, and if it is not zero, execution of the instruction continues until all bytes in the block have been moved. Notice that this instruction has a two-byte op code. There are four versions, labeled LDI (increment HL and DE), LDD (decrement HL and DE), LDIR (increment and repeat), and LDDR (decrement and repeat).

Also shown in Fig. 2.23 is the CPI instruction. This is similar to the compare shown in Fig. 2.19, but it uses the BC pair as a counter, automatically decrementing the pair with each execution. If the comparison is true, the Z flag is set.

There are four versions of this instruction, labeled CPI, CPD, CPIR, and CPDR. The I implies that HL is to be incremented and the D that HL is to be decremented. Instructions with the R suffix automatically repeat until BC = 0 or a comparison comes out true.

The bit manipulation group. Included in this group are instructions that allow individual bits of a register or a memory location to be set, reset, or tested. The first example in Fig. 2.24 shows how bit 4 of register C can be tested. If bit 4 is zero, the Z flag will be set; if bit 4 is not zero, the Z flag will be reset.

TABLE 2.3 Input and Output Instructions for the 8080/85 and Z-80 Microprocessors

Mnemonic		Symbolic operation
8080/85	Z-80	
In n	IN A, (n)	A ← (n)
None	IN r, (C)	r ← (C) If r = 110, only the flags will be affected
None	INI	(HL) ← (C) B ← B − 1 HL ← HL + 1
None	INIR	(HL) ← (C) B ← B − 1 HL ← HL + 1 Repeat until B = 0
None	IND	(HC) ← (C) B ← B − 1 HL ← HL − 1
None	INDR	(HL) ← (C) B ← B − 1 HL ← HL − 1 Repeat until B = 0
Out n	OUT (n), A	(n) ← A
None	OUT (C), r	(C) ← r
None	OUTI	(C) ← (HL) B ← B − 1 HL ← HL + 1
None	OTIR	(C) ← (HL) B ← B − 1 HL ← HL + 1 Repeat until B = 0
None	OUTD	(C) ← (HL) B ← B − 1 HL ← HL − 1
None	OTDR	(C) ← (HL) B ← B − 1 HL ← HL − 1 Repeat until B = 0

Source: Courtesy of Zilog, Inc.

Hex Op-code	Mnemonic 8080/85	Mnemonic Z-80	Symbolic Operation	Description
D9	none	EXX	BC ⇔ B'C' DE ⇔ D'E' HL ⇔ H'L'	The primary and alternate register pairs are exchanged.
ED B8	none	LDDR	(DE) ← (HL) DE ← DE−1 HL ← HL−1 BC ← BC−1	Load location (DE) with location (HL), decrement DE, HL and BC; repeat until BC = 0.
ED A1	none	CPI	A − (HL) HL ← HL + 1 BC ← BC − 1	Compare location (HL) with the accumulator, increment HL and decrement BC. The accumulator is unchanged but the condition flags are set.

Figure 2.23 The Z-80 has several block-oriented commands. EXX allows switching between the primary and alternative set of registers. LDDR transfers a block of data from one location in memory to another. CPI is used to compare the contents of the accumulator with all data bytes in a block of memory.

In the second and third examples, bit 6 of register H is set to 1 or reset to 0. Although the 8080 and 8085 have no such instructions, the logical AND and OR instructions can be used to achieve the same result. (See Problems 2.29 and 2.30.)

SELF-REVIEW 2.3

2.3.1 Although the Z-80 uses mnemonics different from those of the 8080/85, the _____ codes for similar instructions are identical.

2.3.2 The data transfer group of instructions allows three different combinations for the source and destination of data. What are they?

2.3.3 Via a certain group of instructions, the sequential flow of a computer program can be altered. What is the group?

2.3.4 Which CPU register identifies the memory location corresponding to the current top of the stack?

Hex Op-code	Mnemonic 8080/85	Mnemonic Z-80	Symbolic Operation	Description
CB 61	none	BIT 4,C	$Z \leftarrow \overline{C}_4$	Test bit 4 of register C and set the Z flag accordingly.
CB 74	none	SET 6,H	$H_6 \leftarrow 1$	Set bit 6 of register H.
CB 97	none	RES 6,H	$H_6 \leftarrow 0$	Reset bit 6 of register H.

Figure 2.24 Bit setting, resetting, and testing is easily accomplished with the Z-80 bit-manipulation instructions.

2.4 ADDRESSING MODES

Introduction

The instruction set of a microprocessor lists the various instructions available to the processor to operate on data. For example, to add the contents of register B to register A, the instruction ADD B (Z-80 mnemonic, ADD A,B) can be used. Another form of the same instruction is ADD M (Z-80 mnemonic, ADD A,(HL)). In this case, the contents of the memory location whose address is stored in the HL register pair are added to the contents of register A.

Comparing these two instructions, we see that the *operation* is the same for both— ADD. However, the *operands* are different. In the first case the source operand is a CPU register, whereas in the second case it is a memory location.

Microprocessors typically have several different ways of specifying the source and destination operands. The various ways are called *addressing modes*.

In this section, we:

- List the four addressing modes of the 8080 processor and the six addressing modes of the Z-80 processor.

The direct addressing mode.   In the *direct* addressing mode, the full 16-bit address is specified as part of the instruction. The 8080/85 mnemonic LDA 1000H means "Load register A with the contents of memory location 1000H." The hex op code for this instruction is 3A 00 10.

The register addressing mode.   The direct addressing mode is a straightforward way of accessing memory, but has the drawback of requiring three memory fetches per instruction—one for the op code and two for the 16-bit address. Programs requiring a large number of memory accesses will execute slowly with this addressing mode, due to the relatively high number of T states required. To solve this problem, microprocessor designers usually include a number of general-purpose registers that can be addressed with a single byte. For example, the 8080/85 instruction MOV A,B copies the data byte stored in register B to register A. This mode is called *register* addressing.

The immediate addressing mode.   Some means of loading the general-purpose registers must, of course, be provided. The *immediate* addressing mode is intended for this purpose. The 8080/85 instruction MVI A,00 has the hex op code 3E 00 and means "Load register A with the data byte immediately following this op code." In this case, the accumulator is loaded with the data byte 00. The Z-80 mnemonic is LD A,00. The immediate mode can also be used to load a register pair with 16 bits of data.

The register indirect addressing mode.   Even with the general-purpose registers, it is still necessary to use memory to store large tables of data or messages that are to be printed when a certain condition occurs. Indeed, *word processors* may need to store tens of thousands of data bytes. To access this large amount of data without having to specify the full 16-bit address for each access, the *register indirect* addressing mode has been developed.

In this mode, the HL register pair is preloaded with a memory address. Now any of a number of special register indirect instructions may be given. For example, the 8080/85 mnemonic MOV A,M means "Move to register A the data stored in the memory location pointed to by the HL register pair." The Z-80 mnemonic is more concise: LD A,(HL), where the parentheses indicate the memory location addressed by HL. The hex op code is the single byte 7E.

Table 2.4 summarizes the four addressing modes of the 8080/85 microprocessors. The mnemonics shown are for the 8080/85, but all four modes are also supported by the Z-80.

The Z-80 relative addressing mode.   When the Z-80 was designed, two new addressing modes were included in its set of instructions. The first is called *relative* addressing, and affects only the Z-80 branch instructions. Normally, a branch instruction requires three bytes—one for the op code and two for the address. This is the *direct* addressing mode supported by the 8080/85. In addition to supporting this direct jump command, the Z-80 has a two-byte jump relative command. (See Section 2.3.) For example, the instruction JR addr will unconditionally transfer control up to 127 locations forward or 128 locations backward relative to the present value of the program counter.

Besides saving one byte, the relative jump has the advantage that the resulting code is *position independent*. This means that programs written with relative jumps can be loaded anywhere in memory, and they will execute properly. We investigate the Z-80's relative addressing mode in more detail in the next chapter.

The Z-80 indexed addressing mode.   The sixth addressing mode for the Z-80 is called *indexed* addressing. This mode utilizes the two 16-bit index registers IX and IY. These registers are used as pointers similar to the HL pair, but with one difference: The instruction specifies an *offset* to be added to the pointer value.

As an example, consider the Z-80 mnemonic LD A,(IX + 20H), which is interpreted as "Load register A with the contents of memory pointed to by index register IX plus 20H." The hex op code is DD 7E 20. The offset is added to register IX or IY using *two's-complement* arithmetic. This means that the offset can range from +127 (7FH) to −128 (80H).

Table 2.5 summarizes the six addressing modes of the Z-80.

TABLE 2.4   8080/85 Addressing Modes[a]

Addressing mode	Sample mnemonic	Symbolic operation	Hex op code
1. Direct	LDA 1000H	A ← (1000H)	3A 00 10
2. Register	MOV A,B	A ← B	78
3. Register indirect	MOV A,M	A ← (HL)	7E
4. Immediate	MVI A,00	A ← 00	3E 00

[a]All four modes are also supported by the Z-80.

TABLE 2.5 Addressing Modes of the Z-80

Addressing mode[a]	Sample mnemonic	Symbolic operation	Hex op code
1. Direct	LD A,(1000H)	A ← (1000H)	3A 00 10
2. Register	LD A,B	A ← B	78
3. Register indirect	LD A,(HL)	A ← (HL)	7E
4. Immediate	LD A,00	A ← 00	3E 00
5. Relative branching	JR PC + 20H	PC ← PC + 20H	18 20
6. Indexed	LD A,(IX + 20H)	A ← (IX + 20H)	DD 7E 20

[a]Modes 1 to 4 are also supported by the 8080/85.

SELF-REVIEW 2.4

2.4.1 Each processor instruction has a source of, and destination for, data. The _____ _____ specify the way these data locations are accessed.

2.4.2 The _____ _____ addressing mode uses a register pair to specify the address of a memory location.

2.5 PUTTING IT ALL TOGETHER: A PROGRAMMING EXAMPLE

Introduction

Let us use our newfound knowledge of the instruction sets to write a microcomputer program that adds two numbers; this is not exactly Space Invaders, but it is a beginning! In Chapter 3, we will progress toward more elaborate and useful programs.

In this section, we:

- Identify the components of an assembly language program, including the address, object codes, label, op code, operand, and comment fields.
- Hand assemble a simple 8080/85 and Z-80 assembly language program.

A simple assembly language program.   Consider the following programming example.

Example 2.6

Write a program to add the contents of memory locations 0700H and 0701H and leave the sum in memory location 0702H. Write the program beginning at location 0600H, and show both the 8080/85 and Z-80 mnemonics.

Solution.   Figure 2.25 is the 8080/85 solution. Note how this program has been laid out. A special form identifies the author, name, and date of the program and includes six *fields* for the program itself: the *address field,* the *object code field,* the *label field,* the *op-code field,* the *operand field,* and the *comment field.* You are encouraged to follow this format as you develop your own programs.

For now, we will concern ourselves only with the assembly language portion of the program and ignore the address and object code fields. The first instruction, LDA 0700H, is

Address	Object codes				Label	Op-code	Operand	Comments
0600	3A	00	07		SUM:	LDA	0700H	; GET FIRST BYTE
0603	47					MOV	B,A	; SAVE IN B
0604	3A	01	07			LDA	0701H	; GET SECOND BYTE
0607	80					ADD	B	;COMPUTE SUM
06C8	32	02	07			STA	0702H	; SAVE SUM
060B	76					HLT		; STOP

Program Name _____

Author _____   Date _____

Figure 2.25 8080/85 programming solution for Example 2.6.

made up of the *op code* LDA and the *operand* 0700H. As the comment field indicates, this instruction is used to fetch the first number to be added (the number stored in 0700H).

The label SUM: is optional and is used here simply to give the addition routine a name. In the next chapter, we will see more useful applications for the label field.

Because additions must occur in the accumulator, the second instruction moves the data byte to register B for temporary storage. Now the LDA 0701H instruction brings in the second number, and we are prepared for the addition: ADD B (add the contents of registers A and B). The sum, which is left in register A, is then stored in memory location 0702H with the direct addressing mode instruction: STA 0702H. HLT ends the program.

Assembling the program.   At this point, the assembly language version of the program is complete. But of course, the 8080/85 cannot execute mnemonics! What we have generated is called the *source code,* but what the microprocessor wants is called the *object code.* We now have two choices: If an 8080/85 assembler is available, the source code can be typed into the computer and the assembler told to assemble the program; if no assembler is available, you will have to "hand assemble" the program.

Hand assembly is a good way to learn machine language programming, but is tedious for lengthy programs. To hand assemble the program of Fig. 2.25, refer to the 8080/85 instruction set index (Appendix A.2), which provides a listing of all 8080 and 8085 instructions. Look up the LDA instruction. You will see 3A LDA Adr. This means that the op code for the instruction is 3A, which is then followed by two bytes representing the 16-bit address (0700H). Recalling that 16-bit numbers are always entered "backwards," we enter 3A 00 07 to the left of the LDA op code under the field labeled "Object Codes."

We continue in this manner, looking up the hex codes for each instruction. Finally, we can complete the address field, which must begin at address 0600H. Notice how the low-

Address	Object codes			Label	Op-code	Operand	Comments
0600	3A	00	07	SUM:	LD	A,(0700H)	;GET FIRST BYTE
0603	47				LD	B,A	;SAVE IN B
0604	3A	01	07		LD	A,(0701H)	;GET SECOND BYTE
0607	80				ADD	A,B	;COMPUTE SUM
0608	32	02	07		LD	(0702H),A	;SAVE SUM
060B	76				HALT		;STOP

Program Name_____

Author_____   Date_____

Figure 2.26   Z-80 programming solution for Example 2.6.

order address increases from instruction to instruction. Don't forget that you are counting in hex, so after address 0609 comes address 060A (not 0610!).

The program is now ready for testing. If you are using a microprocessor trainer. you may use your monitor program to enter the hex codes into memory, starting at address 0600H. Before executing the program, put two numbers in locations 0700H and 0701H. After you run the program, the correct sum should be stored in location 0702H.

The Z-80 version of the program is shown in Fig. 2.26. This program is identical to the 8080/85 version except for the mnemonics. Note in particular that the object code is *exactly* the same. Appendix B.1 can be used to hand assemble the Z-80 version of this program.

SELF-REVIEW 2.5

2.5.1 In general, the mnemonic for each microprocessor instruction has two parts, called the _____ and _____.

2.5.2 List the two ways of generating object code from source code.

QUESTIONS AND ANSWERS

Q: *What are the main parts of a microcomputer CPU module?*
A: The microprocessor, a clock signal generator, and logic to generate the control signals.
Q: *What chips are required to build an 8080 CPU module?*
A: The 8080 processor, the 8224 clock generator, and the 8228 system controller.

Q: *Can the 8085 microprocessor function as a single-chip CPU module?*

A: Yes, when it is interfaced to 8085-family memory and I/O chips. When it is interfaced to standard memory and I/O, a low-order address latch and control logic are required.

Q: *What chips are required to build a Z-80 CPU module?*

A: A TTL-level clock oscillator circuit. If an 8080-like control bus is required, simple logic gates will be needed to generate the signals.

Q: *What are the typical elements found in a microprocessor programming model?*

A: The programming model shows the internal architecture of the processor. Typical elements are the accumulator, general-purpose registers, flag register, stack pointer register, program counter register, and index registers.

Q: *What are condition flags?*

A: The condition flags are flip-flops that can be set or reset, depending on the result of an instruction. The 8080/85 and Z-80 processors have carry, zero, parity, half-carry, sign, overflow, and subtract flags.

Q: *Why are the condition flags important?*

A: The condition flags are important because they can be tested and program flow altered on the basis of their value.

Q: *What is meant by the instruction set of a microprocessor?*

A: A microprocessor's instruction set consists of a list of all of the software commands that the processor can decode and execute.

Q: *What types of instructions can the 8080/85 and Z-80 microprocessors execute?*

A: Instructions for the 8080/85 and Z-80 may transfer data, perform arithmetic, logical, and rotate operations, cause the program to branch to a new location, access the stack or I/O devices, control the processor, exchange and search blocks of data in memory, and manipulate individual bits of a CPU register or memory location.

Q: *What is meant by an addressing mode?*

A: Addressing modes describe the ways a processor can access instruction operands. The 8080/85 has four different addressing modes, and the Z-80 has six.

Q: *What items should be included in an assembly language program?*

A: The following fields are recommended: address, object code, label, op code, operand, and comments.

Q: *What is the difference between hand assembly and machine assembly?*

A: Hand assembly requires you to manually locate the operation codes for each program instruction in a table. An assembler is a computer program that accomplishes this task for you.

LAB PROJECTS

2.1. Obtain a schematic diagram of the microcomputer you are using to support this text or course. Locate the following items on your schematic:
  (a) microprocessor chip
  (b) clock generator/crystal oscillator
  (c) 8 data bus lines
  (d) 16 address bus lines
  (e) I/O and memory control bus lines.

2.2. Sketch a *block diagram* of your computer, showing all of the items from Lab 2.1. Save the diagram so that the memory and I/O can be added at a later time.

2.3. A good way to learn the instruction set of a microprocessor is to execute a single instruction and then return to the system monitor program to examine the effect of the instruction on the CPU registers. For example, a typical sequence might be the following:

(a) Preload register A with 27H.

(b) Load the instruction ADI 3CH (8080/85) or ADD 3CH (Z-80). The hex codes are C6H and 3CH, respectively.

(c) On paper, predict the result:

$$\begin{array}{r} 27\text{H} \\ +\ 3\text{CH} \\ \hline 63\text{H} \end{array}$$

(d) Run the "program."

(e) Examine the A register to confirm or disconfirm your prediction.

With this technique, all of the instructions can be "tested." You should also be able to examine the flags to see how they are affected by each instruction.

2.4. Do Question 2.42 or Question 2.44 in the next section. Now take the hand-assembled listing and load this program into the memory of your computer. Run the program and verify the contents of register A and the flags.

2.5. Make the following changes to the program described in Lab 2.4, and predict the new results in register A and the flags:

(a) Change the data loaded into register B.

(b) Replace one of the rotates with a NOP.

(c) Change the rotates to RRC's (8080/85) or RRCA's (Z-80).

(d) Change the immediate data in the AND instruction.

(e) Change the AND instruction to an OR.

QUESTIONS AND PROBLEMS

Section 2.1 (8080 microprocessor)

2.1. Fill in the blanks: When the SYNC signal is _____, the 8080 outputs status information indicating one of _____ different machine cycles the processor is about to perform.

2.2. True or false? The M1 machine cycle is always an instruction fetch cycle.

2.3. What is the purpose of the 8080 SYNC signal? The 8085 and Z-80 do not need this signal. Why not?

2.4. While SYNC is high, the data bus of an 8080 microcomputer contains the data byte 42H. What type of machine cycle is indicated?

2.5. Refer to Table 2.1. Some types of 8080 machine cycles can be identified by testing only a single bit. List all such types.

2.6. Some 8080-based microcomputers include a front panel with LED indicators to display the different types of machine cycles. Using an 8212 latch, several LEDs, and a few logic gates, design a circuit to display the following types of cycles: instruction fetch, memory read, stack read, stack write, memory write, input read, and output write.

2.7. In an 8080 system with an 8228 controller, how many times will the $\overline{\text{MEMR}}$ control line pulse low during execution of the following program?

```
MVI    A,10H
MVI    B,C9H
ADD    B
STA    0100H
HLT
```

Section 2.1 (8085 microprocessor)

2.8. True or false? ALE pulses high only during the T1 state of an op-code fetch (M1) machine cycle.

2.9. Complete the following table indicating the logic level on each control or status pin for the various machine cycles shown:

Machine cycle	$\overline{\text{RD}}$	$\overline{\text{WR}}$	$\text{IO}/\overline{\text{M}}$	S0	S1
memory read					
memory write					
I/O read					
I/O write					
op-code fetch					

2.10. Using the results of Problem 2.9, design a logic circuit that will produce one active-high pulse for every 8085 M1 (op-code fetch) machine cycle.

2.11. Assume that the program in Problem 2.7 is run on an 8085. Give the name of each required machine cycle and the values of the S0 and S1 status signals for each cycle.

2.12. True or false? Any program written for the 8080 will run without changes on the 8085.

Section 2.1 (Z-80 microprocessor)

2.13. How does the Z-80 indicate that the current machine cycle is an op-code fetch (M1)?

2.14. Complete the following table, indicating the logic level on each Z-80 control or status pin for the machine cycles shown:

Machine cycle	$\overline{\text{RD}}$	$\overline{\text{WR}}$	$\overline{\text{MREQ}}$	$\overline{\text{IORQ}}$	$\overline{\text{M1}}$
memory read					
memory write					
I/O read					
I/O write					
op-code fetch					

2.15. True or false? Any program written for the 8080 will run without changes on the Z-80.

2.16. True or false? Any program written for the Z-80 will run without changes on the 8085.

2.17. Design a logic circuit to detect and store the refresh address output on the Z-80 address bus. (*Hint:* Refer to Fig. 2.10 for refresh timing.)

Section 2.2 (8080/85 microprocessors)

2.18. If register B = C3H and register A = 3EH, determine the contents of register A and the value of the flags after the command ADD B is given.

2.19. Repeat Problem 2.18 if the command is changed to SUB B.

2.20. Determine the value of the flags and register A after the program in Problem 2.7 has been run.

2.21. If the addition in Problem 2.7 is interpreted using two's-complement signed binary numbers, the actual operation is a subtraction. Explain this by showing the decimal equivalent of the data in registers A and B and the result.

2.22. Suppose the program in Fig. 2.14 is run on an 8080 microprocessor with a 2-MHz system clock. How long will it take to execute? Use Fig. 1.17 to look up the number of T states required by each instruction. (*Hint:* The last two instructions are executed 255 times.)

Section 2.2 (Z-80 microprocessor)

2.23. In what ways is the Z-80 programming model the same as the 8080/85? In what ways is it different?

2.24. Repeat Problem 2.18, assuming that a Z-80 processor and the command ADD A,B are given.

2.25. Repeat Problem 2.18, assuming that a Z-80 processor and the command SUB B are given.

2.26. If register A = 60H and register B = 60H and the command ADD A,B is given, a two's-complement overflow results. Explain. How does the Z-80 indicate this condition?

Section 2.3 (8080/85 microprocessors)

2.27. Determine the contents of the accumulator after the following programs have run:

(a)		(b)		(c)	
MVI	A,3CH	MVI	A,27H	MVI	C,7FH
ANI	07H	MOV	B,A	MVI	B,3EH
HLT		INR	A	MOV	A,B
		ANA	B	RLC	
		DCR	A	RLC	
		HLT		ANI	7FH
				HLT	

2.28. Determine the value of the flags after each of the programs in Problem 2.27 has run.

2.29. The instruction ANI 40H can be used to test bit 6 of register A. Explain.

2.30. An OR instruction can be used to force selected bits of a specified register to become high. What is the mnemonic of an instruction that will set bit 5 of register A without changing any of the other bits in this register?

2.31. What is the value of the stack pointer after the following program is run?

```
MOV    SP,07FFH
PUSH   B
CALL   Subroutine
POP    B
ADD    B
PUSH   B
HALT
```

Section 2.3 (Z-80 microprocessor)

2.32. Determine the contents of the accumulator after the following programs have run:

(a) LD	A,3CH	(b) LD	A,27H	(c) LD	C,7FH
AND	07H	LD	B,A	LD	B,3EH
HALT		INC	A	LD	A,B
		AND	B	RLCA	
		DEC	A	RLCA	
		HALT		AND	7FH
				HALT	

2.33. Refer to Appendix B.1 and determine the value of the flags after each of the programs in Problem 2.32 has run.

2.34. The instruction AND 40H can be used to test bit 6 of register A. Explain.

2.35. An OR instruction can be used to force selected bits of a specified register to become high. What is the mnemonic of an instruction that will set bit 5 of register A without changing any of the other bits in this register?

2.36. Explain the difference between the instruction LD BC,(0600H) and the instruction LD BC,0600H.

2.37. What is the value of the stack pointer after the following program is run?

```
LD      SP,07FFH
PUSH    BC
CALL    Subroutine
POP     BC
ADD     A,B
PUSH    BC
HALT
```

Section 2.4 (8080/85 microprocessors)

2.38. Identify the addressing mode for each instruction in the following program:

```
MVI     H,07H
MVI     L,01H
MOV     C,B
INR     C
INR     M
LDA     0600H
```

2.39. In Problem 2.38, the instruction INR M increments the contents of a memory location. What is the address of this memory location?

Section 2.4 (Z-80 microprocessor)

2.40. Identify the addressing mode for each instruction in the following program:

```
LD      IX,0701H
LD      B,(IX + 10H)
AND     B
INC     (HL)
LD      A,(0700H)
```

2.41. In Problem 2.40 the instruction LD B,(IX + 10H) loads register A with the contents of a memory location. What is the address of this memory location?

Section 2.5 (8080/85 microprocessors)

2.42. Using a form similar to Fig. 2.25, hand assemble the program in Problem 2.27(c), starting at address 0600H.

2.43. The codes that follow form an 8080/85 machine language program. Use Appendix A.2 to "decode" this program into the corresponding 8080/85 mnemonics. (*Caution:* Some of the codes represent data, not instructions, depending on the context.)

Address	Code
0600	06
0601	3C
0602	DB
0603	03
0604	17
0605	D2
0606	02
0607	06
0608	A0
0609	D3
060A	05
060B	76

Section 2.5 (Z-80 microprocessor)

2.44. Using a form similar to Fig. 2.26, hand assemble the program in Problem 2.32(c), starting at address 0600H.

2.45. In Fig. 2.26, the instruction LD A,(0700H) has the object code 3A 00 07. If the instruction is changed to LD A,(3C2AH), what is the new object code?

SELF-REVIEW ANSWERS

2.1.1. 8224, 8228

2.1.2. A0–A7 address, D0–D7 data

2.1.3. clock

2.2.1. programming model

2.2.2. program counter

2.2.3. flag

2.3.1. object

2.3.2. memory to register, register to memory, register to register

2.3.3. the conditional-jump or -branch instructions

2.3.4. stack pointer (SP)

2.4.1. addressing modes

2.4.2. register indirect

2.5.1. op code, operand

2.5.2. hand assembly, assembler program

3

PROGRAMMING THE MICROPROCESSOR

OUTLINE

OBJECTIVES

After completing this chapter, you should be able to:

- Show how the register indirect addressing mode can be used to simplify the task of accessing instruction operands.
- Show how the Z-80's indexed addressing mode can be used to access memory elements within a 256-byte memory page.
- Explain how to set up a program loop to perform 32-bit binary addition using the 8080/85 processor.
- Explain how to set up a program loop to perform 32-bit decimal addition using the Z-80 processor.
- Write a Z-80 program that uses the method of repeated addition to multiply two 8-bit numbers.
- Show how the rotate instruction can be used repeatedly to divide a number by two, thereby converting the number to binary.
- Write a program that sets up a memory pointer and a byte counter in order to fill a block of memory.
- Calculate the number of clock cycles required to execute a group of instructions, and thereby create a specific software time delay.
- Write a program that exchanges data with a serial port by synchronizing itself to the data rate of that port via the transmitter and receiver ready flags.
- Write a program that displays on a video terminal the contents of memory in ASCII form.
- Write a program that uses the 8085's SID and SOD I/O pins to read a switch and turn an LED on or off.
- Design the hardware and write the software to allow a Z-80 based computer to function as a frequency counter.
- Write a simple assembly language game program designed to interact with a video terminal.
- Develop a Z-80 program that retrieves note codes from memory and uses them to play music through a loudspeaker.

OVERVIEW

To be truly competent in the microcomputer field, you must be able not only to design microprocessor hardware, but also to program that hardware. If you have just designed and constructed an 8-bit *digital-to-analog converter* for a Z-80 microprocessor, how will you be able to tell if it works? A program is required that exercises the hardware and thoroughly tests its functions. Only then can you be sure that it has met all the design goals.

Like it or not, all of us hardware "types" are going to have to learn some software. We have already laid the groundwork for this task by covering programming models and instruction set groups in Chapter 2. The current chapter presents 14 programming examples for you to study. Each example identifies the processor the program is intended for and any special hardware requirements you will need, and provides a brief description of the new instructions introduced.

The first few examples are easy, but they become more complex as you move further into the chapter. The examples are chosen to illustrate instruction set groups, addressing modes, and programming techniques. Although you may be interested only in one of the processors studied in this book, you are encouraged to study the examples illustrating the other processors as well. For example, in several cases the Z-80 and 8080 solutions to a problem are both provided. And in some of these cases the Z-80 cannot do the job any better than the older 8080. But in other cases the Z-80's greatly expanded instruction set can be taken advantage of to solve the problem more simply.

Finally, you will notice an introduction of *assembly directives,* or *pseudo-ops.* These are not microprocessor instructions, but commands recognizable by an assembler program. Even if you do not have access to an assembler, you will find it convenient to use at least some of these directives in your machine language programs.

Unfortunately, you cannot become a computer programmer by reading a book. You cannot really remember that the low-order address must come first and then the high-order address until you have spent a half hour (or maybe an hour) tracking down the bug caused by using the opposite order. So if you can, run some of the programs yourself. At the end of the chapter, you will find several programming problems. Use them to test your knowledge.

Think of learning to program as learning a new language. You can look up the meaning of each new word (instruction) in a dictionary (instruction set), but you won't truly understand that word until you use it in context. The examples in this chapter will give you that "real-life" context.

3.1 MICROPROCESSOR PROGRAMMING EXAMPLES

Introduction

Each of the examples in this section is in the same format, with the following information given:

1. *Program name and number.*
2. *Processor:* the microprocessor for which the program is intended.
3. *Objective.*
4. *Hardware:* the special (if any) hardware needed to test the program. This generally means a parallel output port or standard video terminal.
5. *Problem statement:* a description of the problem to be solved.
6. *Sample output:* a sample of the output the program should produce.
7. *Discussion:* a brief explanation of the programming technique and flowcharting of the problem.
8. *New instructions:* a description of each new instruction that the example introduces. Included are assembly directives.

9. *Problem solution:* a standard assembly language listing, including the hexadecimal object code.

10. *Summary:* a summary of the key points to be learned.

11. Self-review question(s).

PROGRAM 1: 8080/85 8-Bit Addition

Processor—8080/85

Objective.   Show how the register indirect addressing mode can be used to simplify the task of accessing instruction operands.

Hardware.   Required is a machine language monitor capable of examining memory, depositing data into memory, and running a program.

Problem Statement.   Add the contents of memory locations 0700H and 0701H. Place the sum in memory location 0702H.

Sample Output

$$(0700) = 23H$$
$$(0701) = 6AH$$

Then

$$(0702) = 8DH$$

Discussion.   This problem was first solved at the end of Chapter 2 using the *direct* addressing mode. In this example, we will use *register indirect* addressing. This technique uses the HL register pair as a pointer to a memory location. The INR L command can be used to change the position of the pointer.

New Instructions

ORG   The ORG command is an assembly language *directive.* It instructs the assembler to begin assembling the mnemonics that follow at the address specified in the operand field (in this program, address 0600H). There can be any number of ORG commands within a particular program.

LXI H,Addr   Byte 3 of the instruction is moved into register H. Byte 2 of the instruction is moved into register L. This is a 16-bit register pair load operation using the immediate addressing mode. Other forms are LXI B, LXI D, and LXI SP.

INR L   The contents of register L are incremented by 1. Any of the general-purpose registers may be specified. Similarly, **DCR r** decrements a register.

MOV A,M   The contents of the memory location whose address is in registers H and L are moved to register A. This is a one-byte instruction using the register indirect addressing mode. It saves two bytes and six clock cycles compared with the direct addressing

```
                                  ;8080/85 8-BIT ADDITION
                                  ;
                                  ;THIS PROGRAM WILL ADD THE CONTENTS
                                  ;OF MEMORY LOCATIONS 0700H AND
                                  ;0701H AND STORE THE SUM IN 0702H.
                                  ;
    0600                          ORG      0600H     ;START AT LOCATION 0600H
    0600 210007                   LXI      H,0700H   ;HL POINTS AT FIRST BYTE
    0603 7E                       MOV      A,M       ;SAVE FIRST BYTE IN A
    0604 2C                       INR      L         ;NOW POINT AT SECOND BYTE
    0605 86                       ADD      M         ;ADD IT TO A
    0606 2C                       INR      L         ;ADVANCE POINTER
    0607 77                       MOV      M,A       ;SAVE SUM HERE
    0608 76                       HLT                ;STOP
    0609                          END
```

Figure 3.1   Program 1: 8080/85 8-bit addition.

mode technique (LDA Addr). It may be used with any of the general-purpose registers (MOV B,M, MOV C,M, etc.).

MOV M,A   The contents of register A are moved to the memory location whose address is in registers H and L. This instruction also uses the register indirect addressing mode. It can be used with any of the general-purpose registers (MOV M,B, MOV M,C, etc.).

ADD M   The contents of the memory location whose address is contained in the H and L registers are added to the contents of the accumulator. The result is placed in the accumulator. This instruction uses register indirect addressing.

HLT   The processor is stopped. The registers and flags are unaffected. You may want to replace this instruction with a RET or JMP back to your monitor. If not, only a reset will restart the computer.

END   END is another (optional) assembly directive and must be the last statement in an assembly language program. All statements following END will be ignored by the assembler.

Program Solution.   Figure 3.1 provides a solution to this problem. The program begins by loading the HL pair with the address of the first byte. Now the MOV A,M command brings this byte into the accumulator. Incrementing L results in HL pointing to the second byte, which ADD M then adds this to the contents of the accumulator. A second INR L causes HL to point to the location at which the sum will be stored, and MOV M,A accomplishes this. Statements beginning with a semicolon are comments and are ignored by the assembler.

Summary.   This program solves the addition problem first presented in Chapter 2, with seven instructions versus six for that solution. However, the total number of bytes has been reduced from 12 to 9, due to use of the register indirect addressing mode.

SELF-REVIEW

3.1.1 Rather than specify the address as part of each instruction, the register indirect addressing mode uses the _____ register pair to point to the desired memory location.

PROGRAM 2: Z-80 8-Bit Addition

Processor—Z-80

Objective.   Show how the Z-80's indexed addressing mode can be used to access memory elements within a 256-byte memory page.

Hardware.   Required is a machine language monitor capable of examining memory, depositing data into memory, and running a program.

Problem Statement.   Add the contents of memory locations 0700H and 0701H. Place the sum in memory location 0702H.

Sample Output

$$(0700) = 23H$$
$$(0701) = 6AH$$

Then

$$(0702) = 8DH$$

Discussion.   This is another solution to the addition problem presented in Program 1. The Z-80 *indexed* addressing mode is used. This technique allows reference to a memory location pointed to by the X or Y index registers, but with a two's-complement offset. The technique is convenient when you need to pull values from a table or list with a known offset. Note, however, that the offset cannot be computed at run time.

New Instructions

ORG   The ORG command is an assembly language directive. It instructs the assembler to begin assembling the mnemonics that follow at the address specified in the operand field (in this program, address 0600H). There can be any number of ORG commands within a particular program.

LD IX,nnnn   This command is used to initialize the X index register with a 16-bit value. It uses the immediate addressing mode and requires four bytes. Any of the register pairs IY, SP, BC, DE, and HL can be loaded in this manner (LD rp,nnnn).

LD A,(IX+0)   The accumulator is loaded with the contents of memory pointed to by the X index register, offset by 0. Recall the Z-80 convention of using parentheses to indicate the contents of a memory location. Any of the general-purpose registers can be loaded in this manner. The offset can vary from -128_{10} to $+127_{10}$.

ADD A,(IX+1)   The indexed addressing mode is not restricted to the load instructions. This command adds the contents of memory pointed to by register IX+1 to the accumulator. It thus becomes unnecessary to use a general-purpose register for temporary storage. Only register A can be specified for this instruction.

HALT   The processor is stopped. The registers and flags are unaffected. You may want to replace this instruction with a RET or JMP back to your monitor. If not, only a reset will restart the computer.

END END is another (optional) assembly directive and must be the last statement in an assembly language program. All statements following END will be ignored by the assembler.

Problem Solution. Figure 3.2(a) is a listing of the solution to this problem. The program begins by loading the X index register with the address of the first byte. Now the LD A,(IX+0) command brings this byte into the accumulator. ADD A,(IX+1) adds the two numbers without the need of incrementing a pointer. Similarly, LD (IX+2),A stores the sum. Figure 3.2(b) shows how the X index register is used in the problem.

Lifeboat Assoc.   Z80 Assembler Page 0001

ADDR	CODE	STMT	SOURCE STATEMENT		
		0001	; Z-80 8-BIT ADDITION		
		0002	;		
		0003	; THIS PROGRAM WILL ADD THE CONTENTS		
		0004	; OF MEMORY LOCATIONS 0700H AND		
		0005	;0701H AND STORE THE SUM IN 0702H.		
		0006	;		
>0600		0007	ORG	0600H	;START AT LOCATION 0600H
'0600	DD210007	0008	LD	IX,0700H	;IX POINTS TO FIRST BYTE
'0604	DD7E00	0009	LD	A, (IX+0)	; SAVE IT IN A
'0607	DD8601	0010	ADD	A, (IX+1)	; ADD THE SECOND BYTE
'060A	DD7702	0011	LD	(IX+2), A	; SAVE THE SUM
'060D	76	0012	HALT		; STOP
		0013	END		

ERRORS = 0000

(a)

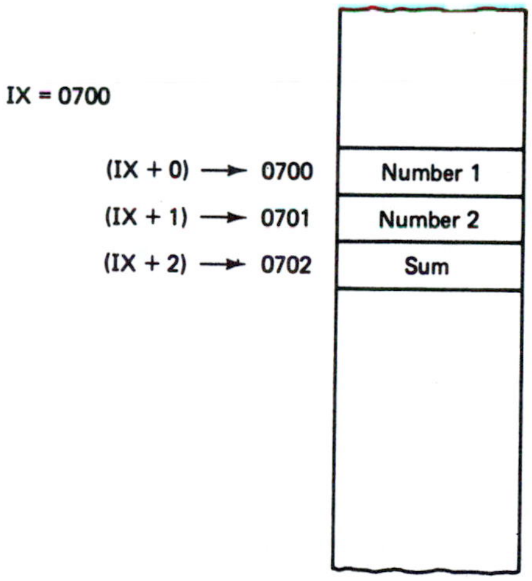

IX = 0700

(IX + 0) ⟶ 0700   Number 1

(IX + 1) ⟶ 0701   Number 2

(IX + 2) ⟶ 0702   Sum

(b)

Figure 3.2 (a) Program 2: Z-80 8-bit addition; (b) the X index register is used to access all three memory locations.

Summary. The 8-bit addition problem has now been solved three ways. Of the three, the Z-80 solution requires the fewest number of instructions—just five. This is due to the *indexed* addressing mode. However, it requires just as many bytes as the 8080 *direct* addressing mode solution in Chapter 2 and three more bytes than the 8080 *register indirect* solution in Program 1. This is because the Z-80 indexed instructions all require two-byte op codes plus an offset.

In general, the indexed addressing mode is most useful when the memory locations are not sequential. The register indirect mode is best for sequential data, because the one-byte command INC HL can be used to advance the memory pointer through the table without the need to specify absolute addresses or an offset.

SELF-REVIEW

3.1.2 Via a two's-complement offset, the _____ addressing mode allows access to 256 consecutive memory locations without the need to increment a memory pointer.

PROGRAM 3: 32-Bit Binary Addition

Processor—8080/85

Objective. Explain how to set up a program loop to perform 32-bit binary addition using the 8080/85 processor.

Hardware. Required is a machine language monitor capable of examining memory, depositing data into memory, and running a program.

Problem Statement. Add the four-byte binary number in 0700H (LSD—least significant digit) through 0703H (MSD—most significant digit) to the four-byte binary number in 0704H (LSD) through 0707H (MSD). Store the sum as a four-byte binary number in 0708H (LSD) through 070BH (MSD).

Sample Output

$$(0703-0700) = 05\ 62\ 21\ 4F$$
$$(0707-0704) = 58\ F3\ CD\ 09$$

Then

$$(070B-0708) = 5E\ 55\ EE\ 58$$

Discussion. Figure 3.3 shows how the 12 bytes of memory are used. In each case, the least significant digit is stored first and the most significant digit last.

The program sets up four trials and proceeds to add the LSDs of the two numbers. The sum is placed in the LSD position of the sum. The process is repeated until all four bytes have been added.

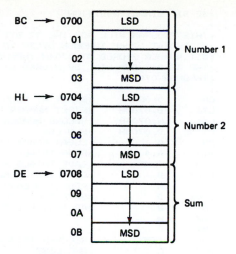

BC → 0700 | LSD
01
02 } Number 1
03 | MSD
HL → 0704 | LSD
05
06 } Number 2
07 | MSD
DE → 0708 | LSD
09
0A } Sum
0B | MSD

Figure 3.3 Memory organization for the 32-bit binary addition problem.

New Instructions:

DS   Define storage. This is an assembly language directive and is used to tell the assembler to set aside a certain number of bytes at the current program position. For example,

TEMP   DS   1

reserves 1 byte of storage with the label (or name) TEMP.

ANA A   The logical AND instructions perform a bit-by-bit AND operation with the contents of the accumulator. Any of the general-purpose registers or (HL) may be specified. In this case, A is being ANDed with itself. This seems illogical, since A will not change. However, the carry flag will be reset. In effect, this is a *reset carry* instruction. Other forms of the instruction are ORA r (OR the contents of the accumulator with those of register r) and XRA r (exclusive-OR the contents of the accumulator with those of register r).

MVI A,nn   All of the general-purpose registers can be loaded in the immediate mode. This two-byte instruction moves the second byte to the selected register.

STA addr   Store the contents of the accumulator at the address in the second and third bytes of the instruction. This is the direct addressing mode, and only the contents of the accumulator can be stored in this manner.

LDAX B   This instruction is identical to MOV A,M, except that register pair B is used as the memory pointer. The other form is LDAX D. Note that LDAX H is not a valid mnemonic—use MOV A,M.

ADC M   Add the contents of memory pointed to by the HL pair, including the carry flag, to the accumulator. Any of the general-purpose registers may be specified (ADC B, ADC C, etc.). It is also possible to add without the carry. In this case, the mnemonic is ADD M (also, ADD B, ADD C, etc.).

INX B   Increment register pair BC. Other forms are INX H, INX D, and INX SP. Note that no flags are affected. (*This is very important!*)

```
                              ;32 BIT BINARY ADDITION
                              ;
                              ;THIS PROGRAM WILL ADD THE 32 BIT NUMBER
                              ;STORED AT 0700H THROUGH 0703H TO THE 32
                              ;BIT NUMBER STORED AT 0704H THROUGH 0707H.
                              ;THE 32 BIT SUM WILL BE STORED AT 0708H
                              ;THROUGH 070BH.
                              ;
0600                  ORG     0600H           ;START AT LOCATION 0600H
0600 010007           LXI     B,0700H         ;FIRST NUMBER LSD
0603 210407           LXI     H,0704H         ;SECOND NUMBER LSD
0606 110807           LXI     D,0708H         ;SUM LSD
0609 A7               ANA     A               ;CLEAR CARRY FLAG
060A 3E04             MVI     A,4             ;FOUR TRIALS
060C 321D06    NEXT   STA     TEMP            ;SAVE TRIALS HERE
060F 0A               LDAX    B               ;GET FIRST NUMBER
0610 8E               ADC     M               ;ADD WITH CARRY TO SECOND
0611 12               STAX    D               ;SAVE THE RESULT
0612 03               INX     B               ;ADVANCE POINTERS
0613 23               INX     H
0614 13               INX     D
0615 3A1D06           LDA     TEMP            ;RECOVER TRIALS
0618 3D               DCR     A               ;ONE LESS
0619 C20C06           JNZ     NEXT            ;CONTINUE TILL DONE
061C 76               HLT
061D           TEMP   DS      1               ;ONE BYTE OF STORAGE
061E                  END
```

Figure 3.4 Program 3: 32-bit binary addition.

JNZ addr   Jump if not zero to addr. This instruction tests the zero flag, allowing control to transfer to an instruction out of the sequential program path.

Program Solution.   Figure 3.4 is the assembly language listing. All three register pairs are used as pointers, leaving the accumulator to hold the number of trials. However, the accumulator must also be used to accumulate the sums. For this reason, a temporary storage location called TEMP is created. LDAX fetches the first number and ADC M adds the second to it. STAX D stores the sum. The process is repeated four times by decrementing TEMP and testing for zero with JNZ NEXT. Note how the label NEXT is used to specify the location to jump to. The whole point of using labels is to avoid the use of specific addresses or variables in the program listing; let the assembler worry about this.

Summary.   Multibyte addition is just an extension of 8-bit addition. One must make sure, however, that the carry propagates along with each addition (but is zero to start with).

SELF-REVIEW

3.1.3 When it is necessary to repeat a group of instructions several times, the _____ and _____ instructions can be used to decrement a loop counter and test for zero.

PROGRAM 4: 32-Bit Decimal Addition

Processor—Z-80

Objective.   Explain how to set up a program loop to perform 32-bit decimal addition using the Z-80 processor.

Hardware.   Required is a machine language monitor capable of examining memory, depositing data into memory, and running a program.

Problem Statement.   Add the four-byte BCD number stored in locations 0700H (LSD) through 0703H (MSD) to the four-byte BCD number in locations 0704H (LSD) through 0707H (MSD). Store the four-byte BCD sum in locations 0708H (LSD) through 070BH (MSD).

Sample Output

$$(0703-0700) = 05\ 62\ 21\ 56$$
$$(0707-0704) = 58\ 53\ 38\ 09$$

Then

$$(070B-0708) = 64\ 15\ 59\ 65$$

Discussion.   Figure 3.3 shows how the 12 bytes of memory are used. In each case, the least significant digit (LSD) is stored first and the most significant digit (MSD) last. The program sets up four trials and proceeds to add the LSDs of the two numbers. After each addition, a *decimal adjust* must be made. This causes a half carry or full carry whenever the sum exceeds 9 (1001). The result is placed in the LSD position of the sum. The process is repeated until all four bytes have been added.

New Instructions

EQU   The EQU assembly directive allows an 8- or 16-bit value to be assigned to a label. This label can then be used throughout the program, making it more readable. In addition, if it is necessary to define a new value, only the EQU statement need be changed and the program reassembled. For example,

```
NUMB1    EQU    0700H
```

assigns the value 0700H to the name NUMB1.

AND A   The logical AND instructions perform a bit-by-bit AND operation with the contents of the accumulator. Any of the general-purpose registers or (HL) may be specified. In this case, A is being ANDed with itself. This seems illogical at first, because A will not change. However, the carry flag will always be reset. In effect, this is a *reset carry* instruction. Other forms of the instruction are OR r (OR the contents of the accumulator with those of register r) and XOR r (exclusive-OR the contents of the accumulator with those of register r).

EX AF,AF′   The Z-80 has an alternative set of general-purpose registers, two accumulators, and two sets of flags. Only one set of registers is active at a particular time, and the exchange command flips back and forth between the two; it is up to you to know which set is active! EX AF,AF′ exchanges the contents of the accumulator and flags. EXX exchanges the contents of the general-purpose registers (B, C, D, E, H, and L). You can also exchange the contents of the HL and DE registers within a particular set with the command EX HL,DE.

LD A,nn   This is an 8-bit load operation using the immediate addressing mode. The second byte of the instruction is moved to register A. Any of the general-purpose registers or the accumulator may be specified.

LD A,(BC)   This instruction uses register indirect addressing to load the accumulator with the contents of memory pointed to by register pair BC. Any of the register pairs may be used when A is the destination. If a general-purpose register is the destination, only the HL pair is allowed to be the pointer.

ADC A,(HL)   Add the contents of memory pointed to by the HL pair, including the carry flag, to the contents of the accumulator. Any of the general-purpose registers may be specified (ADC A,B, ADC A,C, etc.). It is also possible to add without the carry. In this case, the mnemonic is ADD A,(HL) (also, ADD A,B, ADD A,C, etc.).

DAA   This instruction is used after an addition or subtraction operation to adjust the accumulator to a valid BCD number. The adjustment is necessary because of the six invalid BCD codes 1010 through 1111. For example, if the accumulator contains 59H and the command INC A is given, the result is 5AH. Now, if a DAA is executed, the result is 60H.

INC BC   Increment register pair BC. Other forms are INC HL, INC SP, INC IX, and INC IY. Note that no flags are affected. (*This is very important!*) The DEC rp command similarly does not affect any of the flags.

DEC A   Decrement register A. Any of the general-purpose registers may be specified. Similarly, INC r increments a general-purpose register. All flags are affected by these instructions.

JR cc   Jump relative if the specified condition is true; otherwise, continue. This is a two-byte command, with the second byte a two's-complement offset, indicating a jump forward or backward. A significant advantage to using relative jumps in your programs is that *no absolute addresses need be specified.* This means that the resulting code is position independent.

Program Solution.   Figure 3.5 is the assembly language listing of the program. All three register pairs are used as pointers, leaving the accumulator to hold the number of trials. Because the accumulator must also be used to accumulate the sums, the EXX AF,AF′ command is useful for swapping accumulators (and carry flags) and for providing temporary storage for the trials counter. LD A,(BC) fetches the first number, and ADC A,(HL) adds the second to it. After adjusting for decimal, LD (DE),A saves the sum in memory. The process is repeated four times by decrementing the trials counter in A. Notice how the label NEXT is used to specify the location to jump to. The whole point of

```
ADDR    CODE        STMT  SOURCE STATEMENT

                    0001          ;32-BIT DECIMAL ADDITION
                    0002          ;
                    0003          ;THIS PROGRAM WILL ADD THE 32 BIT BCD
                    0004          ;NUMBER STORED AT 0700H THROUGH 0703H TO
                    0005          ;THE 32 BIT BCD NUMBER STORED AT 0704H
                    0006          ;THROUGH 0707H.   THE 32 BIT BCD SUM WILL
                    0007          ;BE STORED AT 0708H THROUGH 070BH.
                    0008          ;
>0700               0009  NUMB1   EQU      0700H
>0704               0010  NUMB2   EQU      0704H
>0708               0011  SUM     EQU      0708H
                    0012          ;
>0600               0013          ORG      0600H           ;PROGRAM STARTS AT 0600H
'0600   010007      0014          LD       BC,NUMB1        ;POINT AT NUMB1
'0603   210407      0015          LD       HL,NUMB2        ;POINT AT NUMB2
'0606   110807      0016          LD       DE,SUM          ;POINT AT SUM
'0609   A7          0017          AND      A               ;CLEAR CARRY
'060A   08          0018          EX       AF,AF'          ;SAVE CARRY STATUS
'060B   3E04        0019          LD       A,4             ;FOUR TRIALS
'060D   08          0020  NEXT    EX       AF,AF'          ;RECOVER CARRY
'060E   0A          0021          LD       A,(BC)          ;GET FIRST NUMBER
'060F   8E          0022          ADC      A,(HL)          ;ADD TO SECOND WITH CARRY
'0610   27          0023          DAA                      ;ADJUST FOR BCD
'0611   12          0024          LD       (DE),A          ;SAVE SUM
'0612   03          0025          INC      BC              ;ADVANCE POINTERS
'0613   23          0026          INC      HL
'0614   13          0027          INC      DE
'0615   08          0028          EX       AF,AF'          ;RECOVER TRIALS
'0616   3D          0029          DEC      A               ;ONE LESS
'0617   20F4        0030          JR       NZ,NEXT         ;CONTINUE FOR FOUR BYTES
'0619   76          0031          HALT                     ;STOP
                    0032          END

ERRORS=0000
```

Figure 3.5   Program 4: 32-bit decimal addition.

using labels is to avoid the use of specific addresses in the program listing—let the assembler worry about this.

Note: If you do not have an assembler, you will have to figure out the argument for each relative jump yourself. There are two techniques. First you must realize that the program counter will be pointing to the instruction *following* JR. In Fig. 3.5, this means that PC = 0619. We want to branch back to location 060D. This is a total of 12 bytes (page 6, line 25 − page 6, line 13). Accordingly, we find the two's complement of 12:

$$00001100 \rightarrow 11110011 + 1 = 11110100 = F4$$

Another technique is useful when the distance to branch is not too far. Starting at location 0618 (the last byte of the JR), we count *backwards* from FF until the desired location is reached. Try it. It really works!

Summary.   Multibyte decimal addition is just an extension of 8-bit decimal addition. One must make sure, however, that the carry propagates along with each addition (but is zero to start with) and that the accumulator is properly adjusted for decimal.

SELF-REVIEW

3.1.4 When it is necessary to repeat a group of instructions several times, the _____ and _____ instructions can be used to decrement a loop counter and test for zero.

3.1.5 Following the addition of two BCD numbers, the _____ instruction should be used to ensure that the result is a valid BCD number.

PROGRAM 5: 8-Bit Multiplication

Processor—Z-80

Objective. Write a Z-80 program that uses the method of repeated addition to multiply two 8-bit numbers.

Hardware. Required is a machine language monitor capable of examining memory, depositing data into memory, and running a program.

Problem Statement. Multiply the byte in 0700H (the multiplier) by the byte in 0701H (the multiplicand), and store the 16-bit product in 0702H (LSB) and 0703H (MSB).

Sample Output

$$(0700) = A3H = 163_{10}$$
$$(0701) = 3AH = 58_{10}$$

Then

$$(0702) = EEH$$
$$(0703) = 24H \ (24EEH = 9454_{10})$$

Discussion. Figure 3.6(a) illustrates the conventional method for forming the product of two 8-bit numbers. Note the following points:

1. The partial product grows in size with each addition. It is 9 bits long after the second bit is considered and 10 bits long after the third bit is considered. Eventually, it becomes the product and can be 16 bits long.

2. Although it appears that we can simply rotate the multiplicand left with each addition for which the multiplier bit is a 1, this will require a 16-bit register for the multiplicand and another for the partial products.

3. There are no Z-80 instructions for rotating a 16-bit register. However, the command ADD HL,HL will double the contents of the HL pair (effectively, a shift left).

4. Consider the technique shown in Fig. 3.6(b). This multiplication is done by starting with the leftmost bit of the multiplier and shifting right. The result is the same, however.

5. Assume that the HL pair is used to hold the partial products and a general-purpose register is used to hold the multiplicand. Figure 3.7 shows the addition corresponding

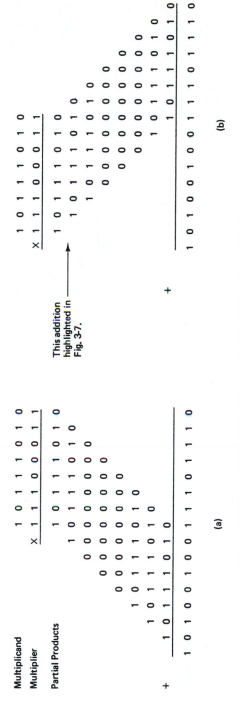

Figure 3.6 Binary multiplication: (a) conventional technique; (b) multiplication begins with the leftmost bit of the multiplier. The method in (b) is easiest to implement with the Z-80.

105

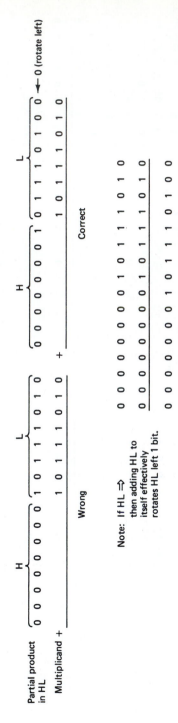

Figure 3.7 The partial-product addition in line three of Fig. 3.6(b). If the partial product in the HL pair is first rotated left, the addition will be correct.

to line 3 of Fig. 3.6(b). If the HL pair is rotated left one bit position, the addition will be correct.

The programming algorithm is now clear. We add HL to itself to perform a rotate left and then test the leftmost bit of the multiplier. If this bit set, the multiplicand is added to the partial product. If the bit is reset, no action need be taken. (There is no point in adding zero.) When all 8 bits have been tested, HL contains the answer.

New Instructions

ADD HL,HL   This was discussed earlier. The Z-80 allows 16-bit addition, but the result must always be in the HL pair. The contents of any of the register pairs may be added to HL (ADD HL,BC, ADD HL,DE, and ADD HL,SP). The zero flag is not affected, but the carry flag will be set if a carry out of bit 15 occurs.

RLCA   Rotate the contents of the accumulator left circular. Bit 7 is rotated into the carry and into bit 0. The Z-80 features many different rotate and shift instructions (see Table 2.2), including the ability to rotate (HL).

DJNZ   Decrement the B register and jump relative if not zero. This is a handy instruction that utilizes the B register as a counter. There are no other forms of the instruction.

LD (addr),HL   Save the HL pair at address addr (L) and addr+1 (H). Any of the register pairs may be specified, including the IX and IY index registers.

LD L,D   The contents of any general-purpose register may be copied into any other general-purpose register. In this case, a copy of D is placed in L. D remains unchanged.

Program Solution.   Figure 3.8 is the assembly language listing of the program. The B register is used as the bit counter—thinking ahead to the DJNZ instruction. The multiplier is loaded into the accumulator, and register E holds the multiplicand. Register D is set to zero in preparation for the ADD HL,DE, which forms the partial product. The program now proceeds as described in the foregoing discussion. RLCA is used to test the multiplier bit, and the 16-bit sum is finally stored with the use of the LD (PRDCT),HL command.

Summary.   Most 8-bit microprocessors do not have multiplication (or division) instructions, and (rather complex) routines must be written to accomplish this function. The problem is further compounded by a lack of 16-bit rotate instructions. The ADD HL,HL instruction can be used to advantage in this instance.

SELF-REVIEW

3.1.6 Two 8-bit numbers can be multiplied together by repeatedly totaling the partial product left by adding the multiplicand for each 1 bit of the _____.

3.1.7 To rotate the contents of the HL register pair left one bit, the instruction _____ should be used.

```
ADDR    CODE        STMT  SOURCE STATEMENT

                    0001        ;Z-80  8-BIT MULTIPLICATION
                    0002        ;
                    0003        ;THIS PROGRAM WILL MULTIPLY THE 8-BIT
                    0004        ;NUMBER IN 0700H TIMES THE 8-BIT NUMBER
                    0005        ;IN 0701H.   THE 16-BIT PRODUCT WILL BE
                    0006        ;STORED IN 0702H (LSB) AND 0703H (MSB).
                    0007        ;
>0700               0008  DATA  EQU     0700H               ;ADDRESS OF FIRST BYTE
>0702               0009  PRDCT EQU     0702H               ;ADDRESS OF PRODUCT
                    0010        ;
>0600               0011        ORG     0600H               ;PROGRAM STARTS AT 0600H
'0600   0608        0012        LD      B,8                 ;BIT COUNTER
'0602   210007      0013        LD      HL,DATA             ;POINT AT MULTIPLIER
'0605   7E          0014        LD      A,(HL)              ;GET IT
'0606   23          0015        INC     HL                  ;ADVANCE POINTER
'0607   5E          0016        LD      E,(HL)              ;E HOLDS MULTIPLICAND
'0608   1600        0017        LD      D,0                 ;PREPARE FOR 16-BIT ADD
'060A   6A          0018        LD      L,D                 ;HL MUST START WITH 0
'060B   62          0019        LD      H,D                 ;
'060C   29          0020  MTPY  ADD     HL,HL               ;ROTATE PART PROD LEFT
'060D   07          0021        RLCA                        ;TEST MULTIPLIER
'060E   3001        0022        JR      NC,SKIP             ;NO ADD IF 0
'0610   19          0023        ADD     HL,DE               ;ADD MULTIPLICAND
'0611   10F9        0024  SKIP  DJNZ    MTPY                ;DO 8 TIMES
'0613   220207      0025        LD      (PRDCT),HL          ;SAVE THE PRODUCT
'0616   76          0026        HALT                        ;STOP
                    0027        END
```

ERRORS=0000

Figure 3.8   Program 5: Z-80 8-bit multiplication.

PROGRAM 6: BCD-to-Binary Conversion

Processor—Z-80

Objective.   Show how the rotate instruction can be used to repeatedly divide a number by two, thereby converting it to binary.

Hardware.   Required is a machine language monitor capable of examining memory, depositing data into memory, and running a program.

Problem Statement.   Convert the eight-digit BCD number stored in 0700H through 0703H to a 24-bit binary number, and store the result in 0704H through 0706H.

Sample Output.   Figure 3.9 illustrates the memory usage and shows the BCD number 13,964,829 stored in 0700H through 0703H. The 24-bit binary result is D5161DH and is stored in 0704H through 0706H.

Discussion.   This problem can be solved by using the *repeated-division-by-2* technique for converting decimal numbers to binary. In this method, the decimal number is repeatedly divided by 2, and the remainder (which must be 0 or 1), recorded. The first remainder becomes the least significant bit (LSB), and the remainder from the last division is the most significant bit (MSB).

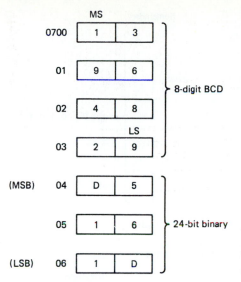

Figure 3.9 Memory usage for the BCD-to-binary conversion program. Four bytes are required for the eight-digit BCD number, and the result is stored as a 24-bit binary number.

Figure 3.10(a) illustrates the method (for 8 bits) in decimal, and Fig. 3.10(b) shows the same problem done in binary. Note that in binary, division by 2 is simply a rotate-right operation. We must make sure that the result is always a valid BCD number, however. Whenever a rotate operation results in bit 7 or 3 being set, 3 must be subtracted from the corresponding nibble to achieve the correct result.

The solution to this problem requires that we rotate the 4-byte, eight-digit BCD number right one bit, test bits 3 and 7 of each byte, and then use the carry flag to accumulate the binary result. A flowchart is presented in Fig. 3.11.

New Instructions

PUSH AF and **POP AF**   The accumulator and flag registers are pushed onto the top of the stack area of memory. The stack pointer register is decremented by 2. This is a convenient and quick way of saving a register pair when it must temporarily be used for something else. In this example the carry status needs to be saved, but the status of bits 3 and 7 of the accumulator must also be tested and corrected. PUSH AF is used to save the carry value and POP AF recovers it. In general, PUSH rp loads the top of the stack with a register pair, and POP rp pops the top of the stack into the selected register pair. Because PUSH and POP access only the top of the stack, great care must be taken to ensure that you know what is currently on the top. If you do not, erroneous data may be popped into your register pair.

BIT 7,A   AND the contents of register A with 10000000, and set the zero flag accordingly. This instruction can be used to test any bit of any register, indexed memory location, or (HL). Similar instructions exist to set any bit (SET b,r) or reset any bit (RES b,r).

SUB nn   Subtract the immediate data byte nn from the accumulator. Other forms of this instruction allow the contents of a general-purpose register or memory location to be subtracted from the contents of the accumulator [SUB r, SUB (HL), etc.]. Similar forms exist for the add instruction [ADD nn, ADD r, ADD (HL), etc.].

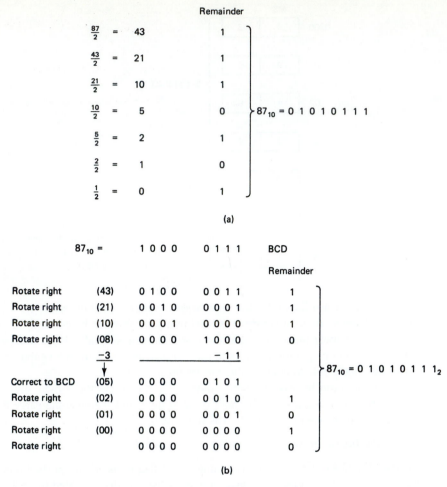

Figure 3.10 The repeated-division-by-2 algorithm applied to (a) a decimal number and (b) its BCD equivalent.

Program Solution.   Figure 3.12 is the assembly language listing of the program. It follows the flowchart very closely.

Summary.   Converting a BCD number to binary is a straightforward process once the repeated-division-by-2 algorithm is understood. In this process, the rotate commands are useful for dividing or multiplying by 2 and extracting the remainder.

SELF-REVIEW

3.1.8 To divide a register by 2, rotate the contents of that register _____ one bit. The remainder, if any, will be stored in the _____ flag.

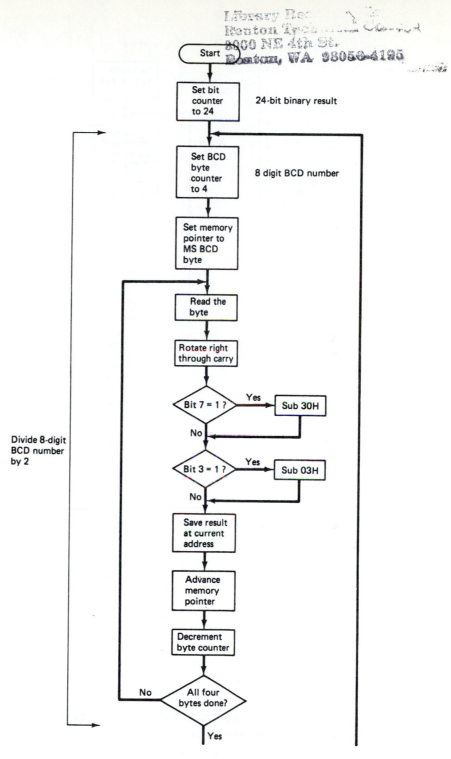

Figure 3.11 Flowchart for the BCD-to-binary conversion routine.

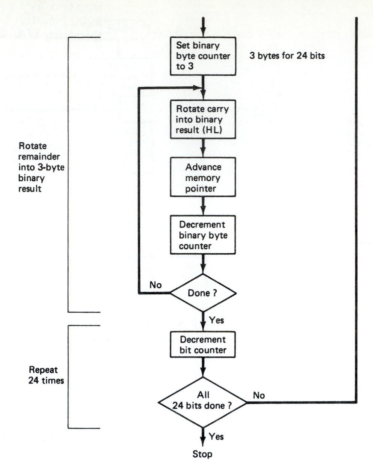

Figure 3.11 *(Continued)*

3.1.9 After the instruction BIT 7,A, the zero flag will be _____ if bit 7 of register A is a 1.

PROGRAM 7: Filling a Block of Memory

Processor—8080/85 (version 1) and Z-80 (version 2)

Objective. Write a program that sets up a memory pointer and a byte counter in order to fill a block of memory.

```
ADDR    CODE        STMT  SOURCE STATEMENT

                    0001        ;Z-80 BCD TO BINARY CONVERSION ROUTINE
                    0002        ;
                    0003        ;THIS PROGRAM WILL CONVERT THE 8 DIGIT BCD
                    0004        ;NUMBER STORED IN 0700H (MSB) THROUGH 0703H
                    0005        ;TO A 24-BIT BINARY NUMBER AND STORE THE
                    0006        ;RESULT IN 0704H (MSB) THROUGH 0706H.
                    0007        ;
 >0700              0008 START  EQU   0700H          ;MSB OF BCD NUMBER
 >0018              0009 BITS   EQU   24             ;BITS IN BINARY RESULT
 >0004              0010 BYTES  EQU   4              ;BCD BYTES
 >0003              0011 BIN    EQU   3              ;BINARY BYTES IN RESULT
                    0012        ;
 >0600              0013        ORG   0600H          ;PROGRAM STARTS AT 0600H
'0600   0E18        0014        LD    C,BITS         ;LOAD BIT COUNTER
                    0015        ;
                    0016        ;DIVIDE EACH BCD DIGIT BY TWO
                    0017        ;
'0602   0604        0018 LOOP   LD    B,BYTES        ;LOAD BCD BYTE COUNTER
'0604   210007      0019        LD    HL,START       ;MEMORY POINTER
'0607   A7          0020        AND   A              ;CLEAR CARRY
'0608   7E          0021 DIV    LD    A,(HL)         ;FETCH BYTE
'0609   1F          0022        RRA                  ;DIVIDE BY 2
'060A   F5          0023        PUSH  AF             ;SAVE CARRY STATUS
'060B   CB7F        0024        BIT   7,A            ;ERROR IF SET
'060D   2802        0025        JR    Z,TEST3        ;CHECK BIT 3 IF NOT
'060F   D630        0026        SUB   30H            ;CORRECT HIGH ORDER NIBBLE
'0611   CB5F        0027 TEST3  BIT   3,A            ;ERROR IF SET
'0613   2802        0028        JR    Z,SAVE         ;SAVE IT IF NOT
'0615   D603        0029        SUB   03H            ;CORRECT LOW ORDER NIBBLE
                    0030        ;
                    0031        ;SAVE THIS RESULT
                    0032        ;
'0617   77          0033 SAVE   LD    (HL),A         ;SAVE THE CORRECTED RESULT
'0618   23          0034        INC   HL             ;PREPARE FOR NEXT BYTE
'0619   F1          0035        POP   AF             ;RECOVER CARRY
'061A   10EC        0036        DJNZ  DIV            ;TEST FOR LAST BYTE
                    0037        ;
                    0038        ;CARRY FLAG HOLDS THE REMAINDER OF THE DIVISION
                    0039        ;SO ROTATE THIS INTO THE BINARY RESULT.
                    0040        ;
'061C   0603        0041        LD    B,BIN          ;BYTE COUNTER
'061E   CB1E        0042 ANSWR  RR    (HL)           ;(HL) ACCUMULATES RESULT
'0620   23          0043        INC   HL             ;NEXT BYTE
'0621   10FB        0044        DJNZ  ANSWR          ;TEST FOR DONE
                    0045        ;
                    0046        ;THIS MUST BE DONE 24 TIMES FOR A 24-BIT RESULT
                    0047        ;
'0623   0D          0048        DEC   C              ;BUMP BIT COUNTER
'0624   20DC        0049        JR    NZ,LOOP        ;AND CONTINUE
'0626   76          0050        HALT                 ;UNTIL ALL BITS TESTED
                    0051        END
```

Figure 3.12 Program 6: Z-80 eight-digit BCD-to-24-bit binary conversion program.

Hardware. Required is a machine language monitor capable of examining memory, depositing data into memory, and running a program.

Problem Statement. Fill the block of memory whose beginning address is stored at BEGIN with the total number of bytes stored at BYTES. Fill the block with the character FILL. Provide 8080/85 and Z-80 solutions.

Sample Output.   If

$$BEGIN = 0700H$$
$$BYTES = 1000H$$
$$FILL = 2BH$$

then all memory from 0700H through 16FFH will contain 2BH.

Discussion.   The 8080/85 solution to the problem uses the HL pair as a memory pointer and the MOV M,A instruction to fill the memory location. A second register pair is used as a byte counter. Because the DCX rp instruction does not affect any flags, first the contents of the low-order register of rp are moved to the accumulator, and then the contents of the high-order register of rp are ORed with the accumulator. A zero result means that the register pair contains zero.

The Z-80 does not have to go through these contortions. Its powerful LDI command decrements the byte counter and moves data pointed to by HL to the address pointed to by DE. By holding the HL address constant (at FILL), the block is filled automatically.

New Instructions

DW or **DEFW**   The define word assembly directive allows you to define the contents of two consecutive memory locations. Usually, the pseud-op is used with a label, as in the code

```
START     DW      0700H
```

START then becomes an address whose contents are 07H (START + 1) and 00 (START). Make sure that you see the difference between DW and EQU. The EQU directive assigns a value to a label; DW assigns an address (two consecutive bytes) to a label and allows you to specify the contents of that address.

DB or **DEFB**   The define byte assembly directive is the same as DW except that only one byte is defined.

The following are new 8080 instructions:

EQU   The EQU assembly directive allows an 8- or 16-bit value to be assigned to a label. This label can then be used throughout the program, making it more readable. In addition, if it is necessary to define a new value, only the EQU statement need be changed and the program reassembled. For example,

```
NUMB1     EQU     0700H
```

assigns the value 0700H to the name NUMB1.

LDA addr   Load the accumulator with the contents of memory specified in bytes two and three of the instruction. Only register A may be loaded in this manner.

LHLD   Load register L with the contents of memory whose address is specified in bytes two and three of the instruction. Load register H with the contents of the next memory location. Only the HL pair may be loaded in this manner. A similar instruction is SHLD, which stores the HL pair at the address specified in the instruction.

XCHG   Exchange the HL pair with the DE pair. LHLD followed by XCHG is a convenient way of loading the DE register pair from memory.

PUSH PSW and **POP PSW**   The accumulator and flag registers are pushed onto the top of the stack area of memory. The stack pointer register is decremented by 2. This is a convenient and quick way of saving a register pair or the flags when they must temporarily be used for something else. In general, PUSH rp loads the top of the stack with a register pair, and POP rp pops the top of the stack into the selected register pair. Because PUSH and POP access only the top of the stack, great care must be taken to ensure that you know what is currently on the top. If you do not, erroneous data may be popped into your register pair.

DCX rp   Decrement the indicated register pair. *No flags are affected!*

MOV r,r   Copy data from one register pair to another. The contents of the source register are not changed.

JZ addr   Jump if zero to addr. This instruction tests the ZERO flag, which has been set or reset in a previous instruction. All of the 8080/85 condition flags can be tested in this manner. The jump instructions are what allow the processor to break out of its normal sequential flow and provide decision points in the program.

The following are new Z-80 instructions:

LDI   Transfer the data byte pointed to by HL to the memory location pointed to by DE. Decrement the BC register pair (acting as a byte counter), and increment HL and DE.

```
                        ;8080/85 BLOCK FILL PROGRAM
                        ;
                        ;BLOCK BEGINS AT ADDRESS (START)
                        ; (BYTES) IS TOTAL BYTES IN THE BLOCK
                        ; (FILL) IS THE CHARACTER TO WRITE TO THE BLOCK
                        ;
    0600                ORG     0600H   ;PROGRAM STARTS AT 0600H
    0600 3A1D06         LDA     FILL    ;GET FILL CHARACTER
    0603 2A1B06         LHLD    BYTES   ;GET NUMBER OF BYTES
    0606 EB             XCHG            ;DE NOW BYTE COUNTER
    0607 2A1906         LHLD    START   ;HL HOLDS START ADDRESS
    060A 77      LOOP   MOV     M,A     ;WRITE A BYTE
    060B F5             PUSH    PSW     ;SAVE A
    060C 23             INX     H       ;ADVANCE MEMORY POINTER
    060D 1B             DCX     D       ;BUMP BYTE COUNTER
    060E 7A             MOV     A,D     ;PREPARE TO TEST IF
    060F B3             ORA     E       ;D=E=0
    0610 CA1706         JZ      DONE    ;IF SO THEN DONE
    0613 F1             POP     PSW     ;ELSE RECOVER A
    0614 C30A06         JMP     LOOP    ;AND WRITE ANOTHER BYTE
    0617 F1      DONE   POP     PSW     ;RESTORE STACK POINTER
    0618 76             HLT             ;STOP
                        ;FILL THESE LOCATIONS WITH THE DESIRED
                        ;BLOCK DATA
    0619 0007    START  DW      0700H   ;BLOCK STARTING ADDRESS
    061B 0010    BYTES  DW      1000H   ;NUMBER OF BYTES
    061D 2B      FILL   DB      2BH     ;FILL CHARACTER
```

Figure 3.13   Program 7: 8080/85 version of the block fill program.

```
ADDR    CODE         STMT SOURCE STATEMENT
                     0001        ;Z-80  BLOCK FILL PROGRAM
                     0002        ;
                     0003        ;BLOCK BEGINS AT ADDRESS (START).
                     0004        ;(BYTES) IS TOTAL BYTES IN THE BLOCK.
                     0005        ;(FILL) IS THE CHARACTER TO WRITE TO THE BLOCK.
                     0006        ;
 >0600               0007        ORG      0600H         ;PROGRAM STARTS AT 0600H
'0600   ED5B1206'    0008        LD       DE,(START)    ;DE HOLDS FILL ADDRESS
'0604   ED4B1406'    0009        LD       BC,(BYTES)    ;BC IS BYTE COUNTER
'0608   211606'      0010        LD       HL,FILL       ;HL POINTS AT BYTE TO XFER
'060B   EDA0         0011 LOOP   LDI                    ;FILL THE LOCATION
'060D   2B           0012        DEC      HL            ;POINT AT SAME BYTE
'060E   EA0B06'      0013        JP       PE,LOOP       ;CONTINUE UNTIL BC=0
'0611   76           0014        HALT                   ;STOP
                     0015        ;
                     0016        ;FILL THESE LOCATIONS WITH THE
                     0017        ;DESIRED BLOCK DATA
'0612   0007         0018 START  DEFW     0700H         ;BLOCK STARTING ADDRESS
'0614   0010         0019 BYTES  DEFW     1000H         ;NUMBER OF BYTES
'0616   2B           0020 FILL   DEFB     2BH           ;FILL CHARACTER
                     0021        END

ERRORS=0000
```

Figure 3.14   Program 7: Z-80 version of the block fill program.

There are several forms of this instruction, including LDD, LDDR, and LDIR. The LDD versions decrement HL and DE, and the LDI versions increment HL and DE. The two commands ending with R repeat until BC = 0.

JP PE,Loop   Jump if parity even to LOOP. The P/V flag is set if BC ≠ 0 after the LDI instruction. Thus, JP PE,Loop causes the program to loop until BC = 0 (and the P/V flag is reset).

Program Solutions.   Figure 3.13 is the 8080/85 solution and Fig. 3.14 is the Z-80 solution.

Summary.   Filling a block of memory requires two register pairs, one to act as a memory pointer and a second to act as a byte counter. With the 8080/85, loading and testing these register pairs requires several instructions. With the Z-80, the LDI instruction makes the job much simpler. The final result is as follows:

8080/85:   15 instructions and 25 bytes
Z-80:   7 instructions and 18 bytes

SELF-REVIEW

3.1.10 When decrementing or incrementing one of the 16-bit register pairs, _____ of the flags are affected.

3.1.11 The ORA E will set the zero flag only if registers A and E are _____.

3.1.12 The Z-80 instruction LDI transfers the byte in memory pointed to by register _____ to the location pointed to by register_____.

PROGRAM 8: Square-Wave Generator

Processor—8080

Objective.   Calculate the number of clock cycles required to execute a group of instructions and thereby create a specific software time delay.

Hardware.   Required are a machine language monitor and a latched output port.

Problem Statement.   Create a variable-rate square-wave generator using bit 0 of an available output port.

Sample Output.   With the program running and a logic probe or oscilloscope connected to bit 0 of the chosen output port, a pulse condition should be observed.

Discussion.   Generating a square wave with a microprocessor is much easier than it might at first seem. By simply incrementing the accumulator and giving the OUT command, bit 0 of the output port will toggle back and forth between a 1 and a 0—hence a square wave. Controlling the frequency of this oscillation is not so easy. In this example a subroutine will be called, causing the microprocessor to count down to zero from some large number. By calculating the number of clock cycles required and knowing the system clock frequency, the period for one-half cycle can be calculated.

New Instructions

OUT nn   The contents of the accumulator are output to the port whose address is specified in byte two of the instruction. The corresponding input instruction is IN nn. Note that for both instructions, the data must go through the accumulator; no general-purpose registers may be specified.

CALL addr   Jump to the subroutine at the address specified in bytes two and three of this instruction. Save the return address on top of the stack. Subroutines are very useful because they represent sections of a program that can be shared by other parts of the program. This, in turn, saves memory space that would otherwise be filled duplicating the subroutine function. What makes the CALL different from a JMP is the RET instruction.

RET   Return to the address stored on top of the stack. Unlike JMP, a subroutine can return to the main program when it is complete. It should be obvious that great care must be taken to balance each CALL with a RET. Similarly, PUSHes and POPs must be balanced, or you may return from a subroutine using a PUSHed (but not POPped) register pair as the address!

Program Solution.   Figure 3.15 provides a solution to this problem. The number of clock cycles for each instruction is indicated at the far right of the listing. This information can be obtained from the instruction set summary in Table A.1 of Appendix A. By changing the DELAY equate, the frequency of the square wave can be controlled. The PUSH D and PUSH PSW instructions make the subroutine "transparent"—the contents of the registers and flags are not changed. As discussed in Program 7, the DCX instruction does not affect the flags, and therefore, the MOV A,D and ORA E instructions are used to determine when DE has been counted down to zero.

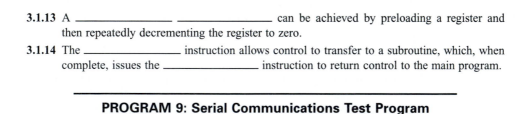

```
                          ;8080 SQUARE WAVE GENERATOR
                          ;
                          ;CHANGE THE OPORT EQU TO MATCH YOUR HARDWARE
                          ;
                          ;TOTAL CLOCK CYCLES ARE:
                          ;(24 X DE) + 62(SUB) + 42(MAIN ROUTINE)
                          ;THE 24 CYCLES OF THE LOOP ARE HIGHLIGHTED.
                          ;IF DE = 20829 = 515DH THEN THE TOTAL CLOCK
                          ;CYCLES WILL BE 500,000.  FOR A 1MHZ COMPUTER
                          ;THIS RESULTS IN A 1HZ SQUARE WAVE AT BIT 0.
                          ;
0001 =        OPORT   EQU     1           ;OUTPUT PORT 1
515D =        DELAY   EQU     515DH       ;1HZ SQUARE WAVE
                          ;
0600                  ORG     0600H       ;START AT 0600H
0600 D301     AGAIN   OUT     OPORT       ;OUTPUT A LEVEL           (10)
0602 CD0906           CALL    WAIT        ;NOW WAIT                 (17)
0605 3C               INR     A           ;TOGGLE THE OUTPUT BIT    (5)
0606 C30006           JMP     AGAIN       ;MAKE A SQUARE WAVE       (10)
                          ;
                          ;THIS IS THE WAIT SUBROUTINE
0609 D5       WAIT    PUSH    D           ;SAVE DE                  (11)
060A F5               PUSH    PSW         ;AND PSW                  (11)
060B 115D51           LXI     D,DELAY     ;16 BIT COUNT             (10)
060E 1B       LOOP    DCX     D           ;BUMP COUNTER            .(5)
060F 7A               MOV     A,D         ;PREPARE TO TEST         .(5)
0610 B3               ORA     E           ;FOR DE = 0              .(4)
0611 C20E06           JNZ     LOOP        ;IF NOT - CONTINUE       .(10)
0614 F1               POP     PSW         ;DONE SO RECOVER PSW      (10)
0615 D1               POP     D           ;AND DE - NOTE THE ORDER  (10)
0616 C9               RET                 ;TIMES UP                 (10)
0617                  END
```

Figure 3.15   Program 8: 8080 square-wave generator.

Summary.   Time delay routines are good choices for subroutines. With the use of a 16-bit counter, a wide range of delay values can be achieved. However, care must be used when testing for 0, because the 16-bit decrement instructions do not affect any flags.

SELF-REVIEW

3.1.13 A _____ _____ can be achieved by preloading a register and then repeatedly decrementing the register to zero.

3.1.14 The _____ instruction allows control to transfer to a subroutine, which, when complete, issues the _____ instruction to return control to the main program.

PROGRAM 9: Serial Communications Test Program

Processor—Z-80

Objective.   Write a program that exchanges data with a serial port by synchronizing itself to the data rate of that port via the transmitter and receiver ready flags.

Hardware. Required are a machine language monitor and serial terminal with bit-testable receiver and transmitter ready flags. The terminal must be set to the *full-duplex* mode.

Problem Statement. Monitoring the receiver and transmitter ready flags, "echo" each keystroke from the terminal's keyboard back to the terminal for display. This will verify the communications link between computer and terminal.

Sample Output. With the test program running, the terminal will appear to be a typewriter displaying each character exactly as it is typed on the keyboard. Stopping the program will cease all output.

Discussion. Computer terminals (or video terminals) are most often interfaced to a computer via a serial data link. Because the computer can input or output data to the terminal much faster than the terminal can accept the data, *ready flags* are required. The receiver ready flag says, "I am ready to give you a byte of data." Similarly, the transmitter ready flag says, "I am ready to transmit another byte of data." With the use of these ready flags, the computer is *synchronized* to the slower data rate of the terminal. (More detail on interfacing a terminal to a microcomputer is presented in Chapter 9.)

New Instructions

IN A,(nn) and **OUT (nn),A**   These are the basic input and output commands compatible with the 8080 and 8085. The port address is restricted to 8 bits, and all data must flow through the accumulator.

IN r,(C) and **OUT (C),r**   The Z-80 can also input or output data with any of the general-purpose registers. In these instructions, register C holds the port address. A third group of I/O instructions uses (HL) as the source or destination of data. These instructions are listed in Table 2.3.

Problem Solution. Figure 3.16 is the assembly language listing of the program. If you wish to test this program, change the equates to match your hardware. RMSK and TMSK are logical *masks*. When their contents are ANDed with those of the accumulator, the result is zero if the test bit is zero and not zero if the test bit is set. The program begins by waiting for the receiver ready flag to be set, indicating that a character has been typed. The IN B,(C) command works nicely here, saving the character in B while the program continues by testing the transmitter ready flag. When the latter is set, the contents of register B—the character that is received—are echoed back to the terminal.

Summary. An "echo back" program is an effective and simple way to test a serial communications line. Care must be taken to synchronize the computer to the data rate of the terminal. This can be accomplished by monitoring the receiver and transmitter ready flags.

SELF-REVIEW

3.1.15 A _____ is a binary pattern that allows specific bits to be tested via an AND instruction.

```
ADDR    CODE        STMT  SOURCE STATEMENT
                    0001        ;SERIAL COMMUNICATIONS TEST PROGRAM
                    0002        ;
                    0003        ;THIS PROGRAM WILL ECHO EACH KEYSTROKE
                    0004        ;BACK TO THE TERMINAL FOR DISPLAY.
                    0005        ;
                    0006        ;CHANGE THE EQUATES BELOW TO MATCH YOUR
                    0007        ;SYSTEM HARDWARE.
                    0008        ;
                    0009        ;SPORT IS THE STATUS PORT AND DPORT IS
                    0010        ;THE DATA PORT.  TMSK AND RMSK ARE THE
                    0011        ;MASKS REQUIRED TO TEST THE TERMINAL
                    0012        ;READY FLAGS.
                    0013        ;
  >0003             0014  SPORT EQU   3             ;STATUS PORT
  >0002             0015  DPORT EQU   2             ;DATA PORT
  >0001             0016  TMSK  EQU   1             ;BIT 0 IS XMTR READY
  >0002             0017  RMSK  EQU   2             ;BIT 1 IS RECEIVER READY
                    0018        ;
  >0600             0019        ORG   0600H         ;PROGRAM BEGINS AT 0600H
                    0020        ;
  '0600   0E02      0021        LD    C,DPORT       ;C IS THE DATA PORT ADDR
  '0602   DB03      0022  CIN   IN    A,(SPORT)     ;GET READY STATUS
  '0604   E602      0023        AND   RMSK          ;TEST RECEIVER
  '0606   28FA      0024        JR    Z,CIN         ;WAIT FOR A KEYSTROKE
  '0608   ED40      0025        IN    B,(C)         ;READ IT
                    0026        ;
                    0027        ;REGISTER B HOLDS THE CHARACTER.  NOW ECHO
                    0028        ;IT BACK TO TERMINAL.
                    0029        ;
  '060A   DB03      0030  COUT  IN    A,(SPORT)     ;GET READY STATUS
  '060C   E601      0031        AND   TMSK          ;TEST TRANSMITTER
  '060E   28FA      0032        JR    Z,COUT        ;WAIT UNTIL READY
  '0610   ED41      0033        OUT   (C),B         ;NOW TRANSMIT IT
  '0612   18EE      0034        JR    CIN           ;LOOP FOREVER

ERRORS=0000
```

Figure 3.16   Program 9: serial communications test program.

PROGRAM 10: Hex Dump

Processor—8080/85

Objective.   Write a program that displays on a video terminal the contents of memory in ASCII form.

Hardware.   Required are a machine language monitor and serial terminal with bit-testable receiver and transmitter ready flags.

Problem Statement.   Using a standard video terminal with 24 lines and 80 characters per line, output the contents of memory, beginning with the address stored in (START). (BYTES) holds the total number of bytes to be dumped.

Sample Output.   Figure 3.17 shows the output of the program with (START) = 0700H and (BYTES) = 0040H. (The data shown represent random data at these locations in memory.)

```
0700  A3 67 E6 2F 55 9F E6 22 21 5B C6 99 1C 9A AF 48
0710  4A 6B 7E 88 38 17 29 8C CE D4 B3 5A 22 71 2B 9E
0720  BC 4E 6A 73 88 19 26 37 3D EE 6A BE A5 62 77 21
0730  CC 42 75 49 A0 E2 8C 3B 11 AA 72 9B 1E 8A 90 EC
```

Figure 3.17 Sample output from the 8080/85 hex dump program.

Discussion.   The main difficulty in solving this problem is converting the hexadecimal data stored in memory to ASCII format so that it will be readable on the terminal. The hex numbers 0 through 9 must be translated to 30H through 39H—simply add 30H. The hex letters A through F must be translated to 41H through 46H—add 37H. (For example, 0AH + 37H = 41H = ASCII A.)

Another feature of the program will require that the terminal's transmitter ready status be monitored before each character is output. (Recall the discussion of Program 9.)

Finally, the output should be formatted on the screen, with the address shown on the left, spaces between bytes of data, and line feeds between successive lines.

New Instructions

CPI nn   Compare the contents of the accumulator with the immediate data byte that follows. The accumulator is not changed by this instruction, but the condition flags are affected. The Z flag is set if the comparison is true. If the contents of the accumulator are *less than* the data byte, the carry flag is set. The instruction CPI 0AH will set the carry flag if the contents of the accumulator are less than 0A. (This condition can be used to identify the hex numbers 0 through 9). Other forms of the instruction are CMP r (compare the contents of the accumulator with those of a general-purpose register) and CMP M (compare the contents of the accumulator with the contents of memory pointed to by HL).

RZ   Return if the zero flag is set. Any of the condition flags can be tested in this manner. Be careful, however: If the condition never occurs, you will never return to your intended location!

Problem Solution.   Figure 3.18 is a flowchart of the problem. Two subroutines have been incorporated into the program. COUT waits for the terminal to be reset and then outputs the character in the B register. HXAS converts the two-digit hex number in register A to two separate ASCII numbers and passes them on to COUT, at which point they are printed. The assembly language solution to the problem is presented in Fig. 3.19.

Note: Studying a program as complex as the one in Fig. 3.19 lets you appreciate the power of an assembler program. Much more than generating the machine code, the assembler lets you *document* your program so that it can be easily modified at a later date. Figure 3.20 is a copy of the hex dump program, but without any of the comments. Try figuring out what it does!

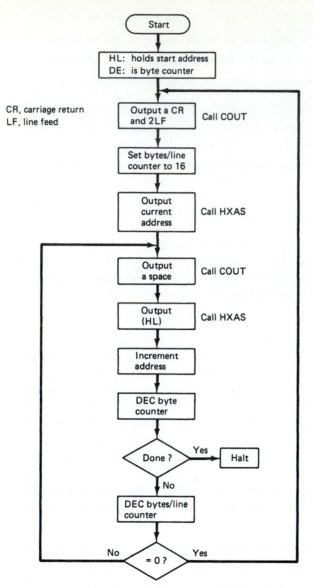

CR, carriage return
LF, line feed

Figure 3.18 Flowchart of the 8080/85 hex dump program.

Summary. A hex dump routine is a useful utility as part of a monitor program. The main problems to be overcome in its development are the conversion to ASCII of the hex data and the necessary screen formatting.

SELF-REVIEW

3.1.16 By adding 30H to the hex numbers 0–9 or 37H to the hex numbers A–F, a hexadecimal number is converted to its _____ equivalent.

Processor—8085

Objective. Write a program that uses the 8085's SID and SOD I/O pins to read a switch and turn an LED on or off.

Hardware. Required are a machine language monitor, a 7404 inverter, a light-emitting diode (LED), two resistors, and one switch, as shown in Fig. 3.21.

Problem Statement. Use the SID and SOD lines of the 8085 microprocessor, and construct a 1-bit I/O port.

Sample Output. With the program running, opening the switch should light the LED; closing the switch should turn off the LED.

Discussion. The serial input data (*SID*) line of the 8085 can be tested with the *RIM* instruction, which will set bit 7 of the accumulator according to the SID status. In a similar manner, the *SIM* instruction will cause bit 7 of the accumulator to be output to the serial output data (*SOD*) line of the 8085. This output will remain unchanged until another SIM is executed.

New Instructions

SIM Set interrupt masks. This instruction allows any of the 8085 RST 5.5, 6.5, or 7.5 interrupt inputs to be "masked." When masked, interrupts on that pin are ignored by the processor. In addition, the RST 7.5 interrupt flag can be reset with a SIM instruction. (Interrupts are discussed in detail in Chapter 6.) If bit 6 of the accumulator is set when the SIM instruction is executed, bit 7 of the accumulator is output to the SOD line as discussed earlier.

RIM Read interrupt masks. Executing this instruction causes the accumulator to be loaded with the current interrupt mask status (as set by the SIM instruction), the interrupt enable status, and the status of any hardware interrupts that are pending. RIM also reads the value of the SID input line and stores this value in accumulator bit 7.

Problem Solution. Figure 3.22 is the assembly language listing of the program. The RIM instruction is used to test the status of the SID line. The SIM instruction is then used to turn the LED ON or OFF, depending on the position of the switch.

Summary. The 8085 SID and SOD lines can be used to pass status information about an I/O device, to turn on valves, relays, or LEDs, to detect switch closings, or to read and write serial data. The RIM instruction is used to test the SID input, and the SIM instruction is used to control the SOD output.

SELF-REVIEW

3.1.17 To read the status of the 8085's SID input, use the _____ instruction. To control the status of the 8085's SOD output, use the _____ instruction.

```
                                  ;8080/85 HEX DUMP ROUTINE
                                  ;
                                  ;THIS PROGRAM WILL DUMP THE CONTENTS OF
                                  ;MEMORY WITH BEGINNING ADDRESS STORED IN
                                  ;(START) AND WITH TOTAL NUMBER OF BYTES
                                  ;STORED IN (BYTES).
                                  ;
                                  ;THE FOLLOWING HARDWARE EQUATES CAN BE
                                  ;CHANGED TO MATCH YOUR HARDWARE.  AN
                                  ;80 CHARCATER BY 24 LINE CRT TERMINAL IS
                                  ;ASSUMED.
                                  ;
0003 =            SPORT  EQU      3        ;TERMINAL STATUS PORT
0001 =            TMSK   EQU      1        ;TRANSMITTER READY FLAG MASK
0002 =            DPORT  EQU      2        ;TRANSMITTER DATA PORT
                                  ;
                                  ;THE FOLLOWING EQUATES WILL MAKE THE PROGRAM
                                  ;MORE READABLE.
000D =            CR     EQU      0DH      ;CARRIAGE RETURN IN ASCII
000A =            LF     EQU      0AH      ;LINE FEED
0020 =            SPACE  EQU      20H      ;SPACE
0010 =            BLINE  EQU      16       ;BYTES/LINE IN THE DUMP
                                  ;
0600                     ORG      600H     ;START AT 600H
                                  ;BEGIN BY LOADING HL WITH START ADDRESS AND
                                  ;DE WITH THE NUMBER OF BYTES TO OUTPUT
                                  ;
0600 2A3B06             LHLD     BYTES    ;GET NUMBER OF BYTES
0603 EB                 XCHG              ;DE IS BYTE COUNTER
0604 2A3906             LHLD     START    ;HL IS MEMORY POINTER
                                  ;
                  NEWL    ;BEGIN EACH NEW LINE WITH A CR AND 2 LF
                                  ;
0607 060D               MVI      B,CR     ;CARRIAGE RETURN
0609 CD5906             CALL     COUT     ;PRINT IT
060C 060A               MVI      B,LF     ;LINE FEED
060E CD5906             CALL     COUT     ;PRINT IT
0611 CD5906             CALL     COUT     ;ONE MORE
                                  ;
                                  ;LOAD THE BYTES/LINE COUNTER AND SAVE
                                  ;
0614 0610               MVI      B,BLINE  ;BYTES/LINE
0616 C5                 PUSH     B        ;COUT ALSO USES B
                                  ;
                                  ;PRINT THE STARTING ADDRESS FOR THIS LINE
                                  ;
0617 7C                 MOV      A,H      ;GET THE HIGH ORDER ADR
0618 CD3D06             CALL     HXAS     ;CONVERT TO ASCII AND PRINT
061B 7D                 MOV      A,L      ;GET THE LOW ORDER ADR
061C CD3D06             CALL     HXAS     ;CONVERT TO ASCII AND PRINT
                                  ;
                  NEWC    ;NOW PRINT THE HEX EQUIVALENT OF THE MEMORY
                          ;BYTE POINTED AT BY HL
                                  ;
061F 0620               MVI      B,SPACE  ;FIRST A SPACE
0621 CD5906             CALL     COUT     ;PRINT IT
0624 7E                 MOV      A,M      ;GET THE BYTE
0625 CD3D06             CALL     HXAS     ;CONVERT TO ASCII AND PRINT
                                  ;
                                  ;ADVANCE THE MEMORY POINTER AND
                                  ;TEST FOR DONE
                                  ;
0628 23                 INX      H        ;ADVANCE POINTER
```

Figure 3.19 Program 10: 8080/85 hex dump program.

```
0629 1B              DCX     D         ;BUMP BYTE COUNTER
062A 7A              MOV     A,D       ;PREPARE TO TEST
062B B3              ORA     E         ;IF DE=0
062C CA3806          JZ      DONE      ;IF SO WE'RE DONE
                     ;
                     ;IF NOT DONE THEN TEST FOR END OF LINE
                     ;
062F C1              POP     B         ;RECOVER BYTES/LINE
0630 05              DCR     B         ;END OF LINE?
0631 CA0706          JZ      NEWL      ;GO TO NEWLINE
0634 C5              PUSH    B         ;ELSE SAVE BYTES/LINE
0635 C31F06          JMP     NEWC      ;AND GO TO NEW CHARACTER
                     ;
              DONE   ;THIS IS PROGRAM END.  IF YOU ARE USING
                     ;THIS ROUTINE AS PART OF A MONITOR YOU
                     ;CAN MAKE THIS A RET.
0638 76              HLT               ;STOP
                     ;
                     ;DEFINE SOME SPACE FOR THE STARTING
                     ;ADDRESS AND BYTES TO DUMP
                     ;
0639 0007     START  DW      0700H     ;0700 IS AN EXAMPLE
063B 4000     BYTES  DW      0040H     ;4 LINES FOR EXAMPLE
                     ;
                     ;

              HXAS   ;********************************
                     ;*          HXAS                 *
                     ;*   SUBROUTINE TO CONVERT THE HEX  *
                     ;*   CHARACTER IN A TO ASCII AND CALL *
                     ;*   COUT.  REGISTERS A,B AND C ARE  *
                     ;*   SCRAMBLED UPON RETURN         *
                     ;********************************
                     ;
063D 0E02            MVI     C,2       ;2 ASCII DIGITS PER BYTE
063F F5              PUSH    PSW       ;SAVE THE CHARACTER
0640 OF              RRC               ;EXCHANGE MSD WITH LSD
0641 OF              RRC
0642 OF              RRC
0643 OF              RRC
0644 E60F     CONV   ANI     0FH       ;MASK THE HIGH 4 BITS
0646 FE0A            CPI     0AH       ;CHECK FOR 0-9 HEX
0648 DA4D06          JC      NUMB      ;AND GO TO NUMB
064B C607            ADI     07H       ;LETTERS HAVE A 37H OFFSET
064D C630     NUMB   ADI     30H       ;NUMBERS HAVE A 30H OFFSET
                     ;
                     ;REGISTER A NOW HOLDS THE ASCII BYTE.
                     ;PRINT IT AND THEN CHECK IF BOTH DIGITS
                     ;HAVE BEEN CONVERTED
                     ;
064F 47              MOV     B,A       ;COUT WANTS CHARAC IN B
0650 CD5906          CALL    COUT      ;PRINT IT
0653 0D              DCR     C         ;TEST DIGIT COUNTER
0654 C8              RZ                ;IF ZERO WE'RE DONE
0655 F1              POP     PSW       ;RECOVER THE CHARACTER
0656 C34406          JMP     CONV      ;ELSE DO ONE MORE
                     ;
                     ;


                     ;
              COUT   ;****************************************
                     ;*               COUT                   *
                     ;*   THIS SUBROUTINE WILL WAIT FOR THE    *
                     ;*   TRANSMITTER READY FLAG AND THEN      *
                     ;*   OUTPUT THE CONTENTS OF THE B         *
                     ;*   REGISTER TO THE SERIAL DATA PORT     *
                     ;****************************************
                     ;
0659 DB03            IN      SPORT     ;GET TRANSMITTER STATUS
065B E601            ANI     TMSK      ;MASK READY FLAG
065D CA5906          JZ      COUT      ;WAIT UNTIL READY
0660 78              MOV     A,B       ;GET THE CHARACTER
0661 D302            OUT     DPORT     ;SHOW IT
0663 C9              RET               ;DONE
0664                 END
```

Figure 3.19   *(Continued)*

```
0600    LHLD  063B
0603    XCHG
0604    LHLD  0639
0607    MVI   B,0D
0609    CALL  0659
060C    MVI   B,0A
060E    CALL  0659
0611    CALL  0659
0614    MVI   B,10
0616    PUSH  B
0617    MOV   A,H
0618    CALL  063D
061B    MOV   A,L
061C    CALL  063D
061F    MVI   B,20
0621    CALL  0659
0624    MOV   A,M
0625    CALL  063D
0628    INX   H
0629    DCX   D
062A    MOV   A,D
062B    ORA   E
062C    JZ    0638
062F    POP   B
0630    DCR   B
0631    JZ    0607
0634    PUSH  B
0635    JMP   061F
0638    HLT
0639    NOP
063A    NOP
063B    NOP
063C    NOP
063D    MVI   C,02
063F    PUSH  PSW
0640    RRC
0641    RRC
0642    RRC
0643    RRC
0644    ANI   0F
0646    CPI   0A
0648    JC    064D
064B    ADI   07
064D    ADI   30
064F    MOV   B,A
0650    CALL  0659
0653    DCR   C
0654    RZ
0655    POP   PSW
0656    JMP   0644
0659    IN    03
065B    ANI   01
065D    JZ    0659
0660    MOV   A,B
0661    OUT   02
0663    RET
0664
```

Figure 3.20 Program 10 without the comments or assembly directives.

PROGRAM 12: Frequency Counter

Processor—Z-80

Objective. Design the hardware and write the software to allow a Z-80-based computer to function as a frequency counter.

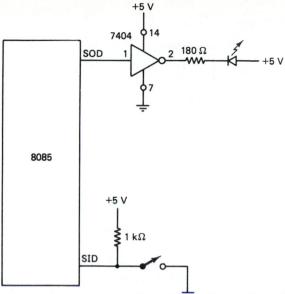

Figure 3.21 One-bit input and output port for the 8085.

Hardware. Required are a machine language monitor, a 5-Hz, 50% duty cycle square wave, two decoded seven-segment displays, one 8-bit output port, and one square-wave generator to supply the unknown frequency to be measured. (See Fig. 3.23 for details.)

Problem Statement. Measure the frequency of the input square wave by counting pulses during one-half period of the 5-Hz square wave. Show the frequency with a resolution of 10 Hz on the two seven-segment displays.

```
          ;8085 1-BIT I/O PORT
          ;
          ;THIS PROGRAM MONITORS A SWITCH CONNECTED
          ;TO SID AND CONTROLS AN LED CONNECTED TO SOD.
          ;WHEN THE SWITCH IS CLOSED THE LED IS OFF.
          ;WHEN THE SWITCH IS OPENED THE LED LIGHTS.
          ;
0600      ORG       0600H           ;PROGRAM STARTS AT 0600H
          ;
          ;TEST THE SID LINE AND BRANCH ACCORDINGLY
          ;
0600 20   CHECK RIM                  ;GET SID STATUS
0601 17         RAL                  ;TO CARRY
0602 D20B06     JNC       OFF        ;IF 0 TURN OFF LED
          ;
          ;ITS HIGH SO TURN ON LED
          ;
0605 3EC0       MVI       A,0C0H     ;PROGRAM SOD HIGH
0607 30         SIM                  ;TURN ON LED
0608 C30006     JMP       CHECK      ;CONTINUE MONITORING
          ;
060B 3E40  OFF  MVI       A,40H      ;PROGRAM SOD TO A 0
060D 30         SIM                  ;TURN OFF LED
060E C30006     JMP       CHECK      ;CONTINUE MONITORING
```

Figure 3.22 Program 11: 8085 1-bit I/O port.

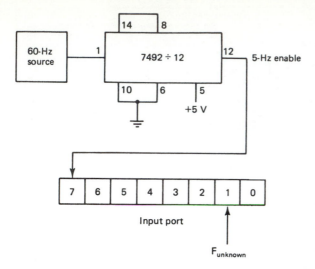

Figure 3.23 Hardware for the frequency counter program. The 7492 is connected as a divide-by-12 counter that produces a 5-Hz, 50% duty cycle enable signal from a TTL-compatible 60-Hz square-wave input.

Sample Output. If the input square wave has a frequency of 654 Hz, the seven-segment displays should show 65. If the input frequency is 60 Hz, the displays should show 06.

Discussion. Figure 3.23 shows the hardware required for this problem. If one uses a microprocessor trainer, the two seven-segment displays could be replaced by the displays on the trainer. A video terminal can also be used with a hex-to-ASCII conversion routine.

The 5-Hz, 50% duty cycle enable signal can easily be generated from a 60-Hz source (based on the line frequency) and divide-by-12 counter as shown.

Figure 3.24 illustrates the waveforms for the counter. The low period of the enable signal has arbitrarily been selected as the *count time.* If three pulses are counted during this 0.1-s interval, the frequency is 30 pulses per second, or 30 Hz. Figure 3.25 is a detailed flowchart of the program.

New Instructions. There are no new instructions.

Problem Solution. Figure 3.26 is the assembly language listing of the program. Two methods of bit testing are used in this program. When the status bit to be tested is bit 0 or bit 7, a rotate instruction followed by a test of the carry flag requires the fewest bytes. The Z-80 BIT n,r command can also be used, but requires 2 bytes. The DAA in-

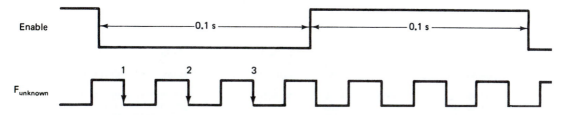

Figure 3.24 Typical waveforms for the frequency counter circuit. The computer will count three falling edges during the 0.1-s enable period and display 03 or 30 Hz.

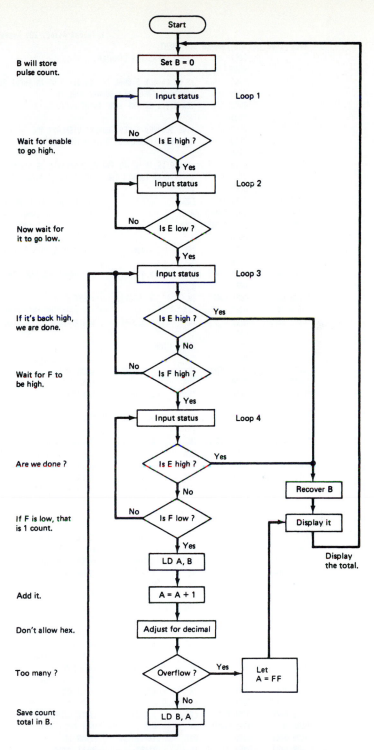

Figure 3.25 Flowchart for the Z-80 frequency counter.

```
ADDR  CODE      STMT SOURCE STATEMENT
                0001          ;Z-80 FREQUENCY COUNTER
                0002          ;
                0003          ;5 HZ ENABLE SIGNAL (E) ON BIT 7 OF AN INPUT PORT.
                0004          ;UNKNOWN FREQUENCY SQUARE WAVE (F)
                0005          ;ON BIT 1 OF THE SAME INPUT PORT.
                0006          ;
                0007          ;TWO DECODED SEVEN SEGMENT DISPLAYS ARE
                0008          ;ASSUMED CONNECTED TO AN OUTPUT PORT.
                0009          ;
                0010          ;RANGE IS 10 HZ TO 990 HZ DISPLAYED AS 01-99.
                0011          ;OVERRANGE CAUSES THE DISPLAY TO GO DARK.
                0012          ;
>00FF           0013 DARK  EQU     0FFH          ;CODE FOR DARK DISPLAY
>0001           0014 SPORT EQU     1             ;THIS IS THE INPUT PORT
>0001           0015 DPORT EQU     1             ;THIS IS THE OUTPUT PORT
                0016          ;
>0600           0017        ORG     0600H         ;PROGRAM STARTS AT 0600H
                0018          ;
'0600 0600      0019 START LD      B,0           ;B COUNTS FALLING EDGES
                0020          ;
'0602 DB01      0021 LOOP1 IN      A,(SPORT)     ;TEST E
'0604 17        0022        RLA                   ;BY ROTATING INTO CARRY
'0605 30FB      0023        JR      NC,LOOP1      ;WAIT FOR E TO BE HIGH
                0024          ;
                0025          ;E IS HIGH
                0026          ;
'0607 DB01      0027 LOOP2 IN      A,(SPORT)     ;NOW WAIT
'0609 17        0028        RLA                   ;FOR E TO
'060A 38FB      0029        JR      C,LOOP2       ;GO LOW
                0030          ;
                0031          ;E IS LOW SO BEGIN COUNTING
                0032          ;
'060C DB01      0033 LOOP3 IN      A,(SPORT)     ;CHECK E AGAIN
'060E 17        0034        RLA                   ;IF IT IS HIGH
'060F 3817      0035        JR      C,DONE        ;STOP COUNTING
'0611 CB4F      0036        BIT     1,A           ;CHECK F
'0613 28F7      0037        JR      Z,LOOP3       ;WAIT FOR F HIGH
                0038          ;
                0039          ;F IS HIGH
                0040          ;
'0615 DB01      0041 LOOP4 IN      A,(SPORT)     ;CHECK E AGAIN
'0617 17        0042        RLA                   ;IF IT IS HIGH
'0618 380E      0043        JR      C,DONE        ;STOP COUNTING
'061A CB4F      0044        BIT     1,A           ;CHECK F
'061C 20F7      0045        JR      NZ,LOOP4      ;WAIT FOR F LOW
                0046          ;
                0047          ;FOUND 1 FALLING EDGE
                0048
'061E 78        0049        LD      A,B           ;RECOVER THE COUNT
'061F 3C        0050        INC     A             ;ADD 1
'0620 27        0051        DAA                   ;KEEP IT DECIMAL
'0621 3803      0052        JR      C,OVFL        ;TOO MANY?
'0623 47        0053        LD      B,A           ;SAVE THE COUNT
'0624 18E6      0054        JR      LOOP3         ;CONTINUE
                0055          ;
'0626 06FF      0056 OVFL  LD      B,DARK        ;DARK DISPLAY
'0628 78        0057 DONE  LD      A,B           ;GET THE COUNT
'0629 D301      0058        OUT     (DPORT),A     ;SHOW IT
'062B 18D3      0059        JR      START         ;NEXT CYCLE
                0060        END
ERRORS=0000
```

130   **Figure 3.26** Program 12: Z-80 frequency counter.

struction is used to prevent frequencies such as 6A from being displayed. (Instead, 70 is shown.)

Summary. This program presents an effective way to detect rising or falling edges of a pulse. With the technique it employs, a frequency counter is easily implemented. Other applications include detecting patterns on a serial pulse train, implementing software UARTs (parallel-to-serial and serial-to-parallel converters), and attaining real-time motor speed control.

SELF-REVIEW

3.1.18 Falling edges of an input pulse can be counted in software by waiting for the input bit to be _____ and then to be _____.

3.1.19 One way of testing the value of a bit is to give an AND instruction and then test the zero flag. Another way is to use a rotate instruction and test the _____ flag.

PROGRAM 13: The Game of NIM

Processor—8080/85

Objective. Write a simple assembly language game program designed to interact with a video terminal.

Hardware. Required are a machine language monitor and serial terminal.

Problem Statement. The game of NIM is played with 15 sticks. When it is your turn, you may pick 1, 2, or 3 sticks. The player to pick up the last stick wins. In this case, the 8080/85 is to be programmed as the opponent.

Sample Output

First move:	You pick 1—14 sticks remain.
	Computer picks 2—12 sticks remain.
Second move:	You pick 2—10 sticks remain.
	Computer picks 2—8 sticks remain.
Third move:	You pick 3—5 sticks remain.
	Computer picks 1—4 sticks remain.
Fourth move:	You pick 1 (sadly!)—3 sticks remain.
	Computer picks 3—It wins!

Discussion. The strategy behind this game is to have a table of choices for the computer to pick from, depending on the number of sticks remaining. If each possible move is studied carefully, the computer can (almost always) be assured of winning.

The remainder of the problem is mainly one of formatting messages on the terminal's screen so that the user knows what the current state of the game is.

New Instructions

LXI SP, addr   Load the stack pointer register with the 16-bit address that follows. This is an important instruction that is easily forgotten. If you use a development system or microprocessor trainer, the stack is defined by the operating system as soon as power is applied. But if you are writing the operating system or developing a piece of stand-alone software, the stack pointer must be initialized.

XTHL   Exchange the top of the stack with the HL pair. This instruction can be useful when it is desired to examine the top of the stack. It can also be used to cause a jump to the address stored on the stack. In that case the instruction PCHL—load the program counter with the address in HL—should be used. In this program, XTHL is used because it takes a very large number of clock cycles—18 for the 8080 and 16 for the 8085. Putting a pair of XTHL commands in a program loop does not change any CPU registers, but can generate a long time delay when that is desired.

Problem Solution.   Figure 3.27 is a flowchart for NIM, and the assembly language listing of the program is presented in Fig. 3.28. NIM uses five subroutines, whose functions are summarized in Fig. 3.29. Pay particular attention to the PRMSG—print message—subroutine. This routine greatly simplifies the task of outputting messages to the terminal. The HL pair is simply pointed to one of the eight messages (located at the end of the assembly listing), and PRMSG is called. Note how the assembler allows the input of ASCII data between apostrophes (') but converts it to hex in the object code column.

Summary.   Game programs can be fun to develop, and they provide an interesting way of improving your assembly language skills. In such programs, an extensive use of subroutines simplifies program development.

SELF-REVIEW

3.1.20 To locate selected data in a table, point the _____ register pair at the base of the table, and then add the offset of the desired byte.

3.1.21 To store an ASCII message in memory, enclose the message between _____, and use the _____ operator to name that message.

PROGRAM 14: Computer Music

Processor—Z-80

Objective.   Develop a Z-80 program that retrieves note codes from memory and uses them to play music through a loudspeaker.

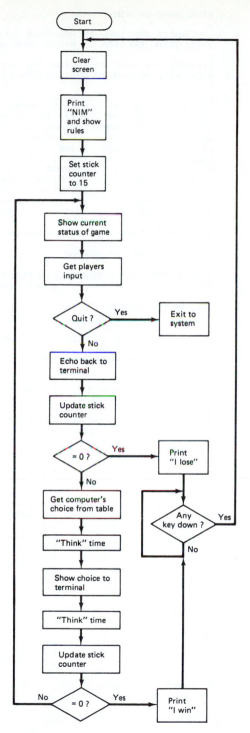

Figure 3.27 Flowchart for the game of NIM.

```
                                        ;THE GAME OF NIM
                                        ;
                                        ;AN ASCII TERMINAL IS REQUIRED - CHANGE THE
                                        ;FOLLOWING EQUATES TO MATCH YOUR HARDWARE
                                        ;
                                        ;ESCAPE THE GAME BY TYPING THE QUIT CHARACTER
                                        ;YOU WILL RETURN TO SYSTEM (SEE EQUATES)
                                        ;
                                        ;
0000 =                                  SYSTEM     EQU   0       ;SYSTEM REBOOTS AT 0
0051 =                                  QUIT       EQU   'Q'     ;EXIT BY TYPING Q
001B =                                  ESC        EQU   1BH     ;ESCAPE SEQUENCE
000D =                                  CR         EQU   0DH     ;CARRIAGE RETURN
000A =                                  LF         EQU   0AH     ;LINE FEED
007A =                                  CSCREEN    EQU   7AH     ;ESC Z CLEARS SCREEN
0000 =                                  DELAY      EQU   0       ;ADJUST FOR 3-5S THINK TIME
0002 =                                  DPORT      EQU   2       ;TERMINAL DATA PORT
0003 =                                  SPORT      EQU   3       ;TERMINAL STATUS PORT
0002 =                                  RMSK       EQU   2       ;BIT 2 IS DATA READY
0001 =                                  TMSK       EQU   1       ;BIT 1 IS TRANSMITTER READY
                                        ;
                                        ;SET UP A STACK AND BEGIN PROGRAM AT 0100H
0100                                               ORG   100H
0100 312E03                                        LXI   SP,STKTOP
                                        ;
                                        ;AN IN DPORT WILL RESET DATA READY FLAG
0103 DB02                               START      IN    DPORT    ;MAKE SURE FLAG RESET
                                        ;
                                        ;CLEAR THE SCREEN
0105 061B                                          MVI   B,ESC    ;ESCAPE SEQUENCE
0107 CD8201                                        CALL  COUT
010A 067A                                          MVI   B,CSCREEN ;CLEAR SCREEN
010C CD8201                                        CALL  COUT
010F CDA101                                        CALL  WAIT     ;TIME TO CLEAR SCREEN
                                        ;
                                        ;SHOW NIM
0112 21D701                                        LXI   H,NIM    ;POINT AT NIM MESSAGE
0115 CD8F01                                        CALL  PRMSG    ;PRINT MESSAGE
                                        ;
                                        ;PRINT THE INSTR AND SET STICK COUNTER TO 15
0118 210E02                                        LXI   H,INSTR  ;POINT AT INSTR
011B CD8F01                                        CALL  PRMSG
011E 160F                                          MVI   D,0FH    ;D IS THE STICK COUNTER
                                        ;
0120 CDB301                             TURN       CALL  UPDATE   ;SHOW STICKS REMAINING
                                        ;
                                        ;GET USERS CHOICE
0123 218802                                        LXI   H,UCHCE  ;DISPLAY USERS CHOICE
0126 CD8F01                                        CALL  PRMSG    ;MESSAGE
0129 CD7B01                                        CALL  CRDY     ;WAIT FOR KEY DOWN
012C DB02                                          IN    DPORT    ;AND READ THE KEY
012E FE51                                          CPI   QUIT     ;TEST FOR QUIT
0130 CA0000                                        JZ    SYSTEM   ;AND EXIT TO SYSTEM
0133 F5                                            PUSH  PSW      ;ELSE SAVE IT ON STACK
0134 47                                            MOV   B,A      ;COUT WANTS IT IN B
0135 CD8201                                        CALL  COUT     ;ECHO TO TERMINAL
                                        ;
                                        ;UPDATE THE STICK COUNTER
0138 F1                                            POP   PSW      ;RECOVER THE NUMBER
0139 E603                                          ANI   3        ;STRIP OFF ASCII
013B 47                                            MOV   B,A      ;SAVE IT
013C 7A                                            MOV   A,D      ;GET STICK COUNTER
013D 90                                            SUB   B        ;UPDATE IT
```

Figure 3.28   Program 13: The game of NIM.

```
013E  CA6601              JZ    UWIN;       ;IF 0 YOU WIN
0141  57                  MOV   D,A         ;ELSE SAVE IT
0142  CDB301              CALL  UPDATE      ;AND SHOW IT
                          ;
                          ;LOOK UP COMPUTERS CHOICE
0145  21D002              LXI   H,MCHCE     ;POINT AT MY CHOICE
0148  CD8F01              CALL  PRMSG       ;PRINT IT
0148  CDA101              CALL  WAIT        ;TIME TO "THINK"
014E  21DF02              LXI   H,TBL       ;POINT AT SELECTIONS
0151  85                  ADD   L           ;FORM OFFSET
0152  6F                  MOV   L,A         ;HL POINTS AT CHOICE
0153  7E                  MOV   A,M         ;SHOW IT BY
0154  C630                AD1   30H         ;FORMING ASCII VALUE
0156  47                  MOV   B,A         ;PUTTING IN B
0157  CD8201              CAL   COUT        ;AND CALLING COUT
                          ;
                          ;UPDATE THE STICK COUNTER AND SEE IF I WON
015A  CDA101              CALL  WAIT        ;MORE "THINK" TIME
015D  7A                  MOV   A,D         ;GET THE STICK COUNTER
015E  96                  SUB   M           ;UPDATE COUNTER
015F  CA6C01              JZ    IWIN        ;IF 0 I WIN
0162  57                  MOV   D,A         ;ELSE SAVE COUNTER
0163  C32001              JMP   TURN        ;NEXT TURN
                          ;
                          ;WINNERS COME HERE
0166  219602       UWIN   LXI   H,LOST      ;POINT AT I LOOSE
0169  C36F01              JMP   SKIP        ;SKIP NEXT
016C  21A102       IWIN   LXI   H,WON       ;POINT AT I WIN
016F  CD8F01       SKIP   CALL  PRMSG       ;PRINT MESSAGE
0172  CD7801              CALL  CRDY        ;ANY KEY RESTARTS GAME
0175  C30301              JMP   START
                          ;
                          ;THE FOLLOWING ARE THE SUBROUTINES
                          ;
                          ;CRDY: RETURN WHEN ANY KEY IS DOWN
0178  F5           CRDY   PUSH  PSW         ;MAKE TRANSPARENT
0179  DB03         CRDY1  IN    SPORT       ;GET STATUS
017B  E602                ANI   RMSK        ;MASK DATA READY
017D  CA7901              JZ    CRDY1       ;LOOP UNTIL READY
0180  F1                  POP   PSW
0181  C9                  RET
                          ;
                          ;COUT: OUTPUT THE CHARACTER IN B
0182  F5           COUT   PUSH  PSW         ;MAKE TRANSPARENT
0183  DB03         COUT1  IN    SPORT       ;GET STATUS
0185  E601                ANI   TMSK        ;MASK TRANSMITTER READY
0187  CA8301              JZ    COUT1       ;LOOP UNTIL READY
018A  78                  MOV   A,B         ;GET THE CHARACTER
018B  D302                OUT   DPORT       ;OUTPUT IT
018D  F1                  POP   PSW         ;RECOVER STATUS
018E  C9                  RET
                          ;
                          ;PRMSG: PRINT THE MESSAGE POINTED AT BY HL
                          ;AND TERMINATED BY 0
018F  F5           PRMSG  PUSH  PSW         ;MAKE TRANSPARENT
0190  C5                  PUSH  B
0191  7E           PRMSG1 MOV   A,M         ;GET A BYTE
0192  B7                  ORA   A           ;SET THE FLAGS
0193  CA9E01              JZ    MOVR        ;AND RETURN IF DONE
0196  47                  MOV   B,A         ;COUT WANTS IT IN B
0197  CD8201              CAL   COUT        ;PRINT IT
019A  23                  INX   H           ;NEXT BYTE
0198  C39101              JMP   PRMSG1      ;LOOP UNTIL DONE
```

Figure 3.28 (*Continued*)

```
019E  C1               MOVR      POP    B
019F  F1                         POP    PSW
01A0  C9                         RET
                        ;
                        ;WAIT: WAIT A FEW SECONDS
01A1  F5               WAIT      PUSH   PSW        ;MAKE TRANSPARENT
01A2  C5                         PUSH   B
01A3  010000                     LXI    B,DELAY    ;16 BIT COUNTER
01A6  E3               LOOP      XTHL              ;18 CLOCK CYCLES
01A7  E3                         XTHL              ;MUST USE IN PAIRS
01A8  E3                         XTHL
01A9  E3                         XTHL
01AA  0B                         DCX    B          ;BUMP COUNTER
01AB  78                         MOV    A,B        ;TEST BC FOR 0
01AC  B1                         ORA    C          ;BY ORING THEM
01AD  C2A601                     JNZ    LOOP       ;LOOP UNTIL DONE
01B0  C1                         POP    B
01B1  F1                         POP    PSW
01B2  C9                         RET
                        ;
                        ;UPDATE: PRINT THE UPDATE MESSAGE
01B3  F5               UPDATE    PUSH   PSW        ;MAKE TRANSPARENT
01B4  C5                         PUSH   B
01B5  21AA02                     LXI    H,UP1      ;POINT AT THERE ARE NOW
01B8  CD8F01                     CALL   PRMSG      ;AND PRINT IT
01BB  7A                         MOV    A,D        ;GET STICK COUNTER
01BC  FE0A                       CPI    0AH        ;IS IT LESS THAN 10?
01BE  DAC801                     JC     UNITS      ;YES
01C1  0631                       MVI    B,31H      ;FIRST DIGIT IS ASCII 1
01C3  CD8201                     CALL   COUT       ;PRINT IT
01C6  D60A                       SUI    0AH        ;OFFSET FOR SECOND DIGIT
01C8  C630             UNITS     ADI    30H        ;FORM ASCII OFFSET
01CA  47                         MOV    B,A        ;COUT WANTS IT IN B
01CB  CD8201                     CALL   COUT       ;PRINT IT
01CE  21BC02                     LXI    H,MEND     ;POINT TO MESSAGE END
01D1  CD8F01                     CALL   PRMSG      ;PRINT IT
01D4  C1                         POP    B
01D5  F1                         POP    PSW
01D6  C9                         RET
                        ;
                        ;THESE ARE THE MESSAGES CALLED BY PRMSG
                        ;
01D7  2020202020       NIM       DB     '                           '
01F5  4E494D202D                 DB     'NIM - A GAME OF SKILL'
020A  0D0A0A00                   DB     CR,LF,LF,0
                        ;
020E  4920484156       INSTR     DB     'I HAVE 15 STICKS.   YOU MAY PICK '
022E  312C32204F                 DB     '1,2 OR 3 STICKS.   THEN I WILL '
024C  5049434B2E                 DB     'PICK.'
0251  0D0A                       DB     CR,LF
0253  594F552057                 DB     'YOU WIN IF YOU PICK UP THE LAST '
0273  312C203220                 DB     '1, 2 OR 3 STICKS.'
0284  0D0A0A00                   DB     CR,LF,LF,0
0288  594F555245       UCHCE     DB     'YOURE CHOICE:'
0295  00                         DB     0
                        ;
0296  0D0A             LOST      DB     CR,LF
0298  594F552057                 DB     'YOU WIN!'
02A0  00                         DB     0
                        ;
02A1  0D0A             WON       DB     CR,LF
02A3  492057494E                 DB     'I WIN!'
02A9  00                         DB     0
```

Figure 3.28   (*Continued*)

```
02AA 0D0A0A         ;
                    UP1       DB    CR,LF,LF
02AD 5448455245               DB    'THERE ARE NOW '
02BB 00                       DB    0
                    ;
02BC 2053544943     MEND      DB    ' STICKS REMAINING'
02CD 0D0A00                   DB    CR,LF,0
                    ;
02D0 4D59204348     MCHCE     DB    'MY CHOICE IS: '
02DE 00                       DB    0
                    ;
                    ;THIS IS THE TABLE OF SELECTIONS FOR THE COMPUTER
02DF 0001020301     TBL       DB    0,1,2,3,1
02E4 0102030101               DB    1,2,3,1,1
02E9 0101010102               DB    1,1,1,1,2
                    ;
                    ;SET UP THE STACK AREA HERE
02EE                STACK     DS    64          ;STORAGE FOR STACK
032E =              STKTOP    EQU   $           ;TOP OF STACK
032E                END
```

Figure 3.28 *(Continued)*

Hardware. Required are a machine language monitor, latched output port, loud-speaker, and transistor driver. (See Fig. 3.30.)

Problem Statement. When the transistor in Fig. 3.30 is switched between *saturation* and *cutoff* at an audio-frequency rate, a tone will be heard from the speaker. Set up a song table in memory such that when the notes are pulled from the table, a simple song is played through the speaker.

Sample Output. When the program is running, the song stored in memory is heard from the speaker. The note codes supplied with this program will play "Daisy."

Discussion. The theory behind single-note computer music is quite simple. By substituting square waves for sine waves, time delays can be generated corresponding to the periods of the various musical notes. Figure 3.31 illustrates the general case. The

Subroutine Name	Function	Registers Changed
CRDY	Return when any key is pressed.	none
COUT	Print the character in register B.	none
PRMSG	Print the ASCII string pointed at by HL and terminated by 0.	HL is incremented to end of string.
WAIT	3–6 second time delay set by DELAY equate.	none
UPDATE	Print the message: "There are now xx sticks remaining."	HL is incremented to end of message.

Figure 3.29 Five subroutines used in the 8080/85 version of NIM.

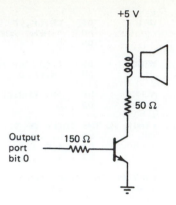

Figure 3.30 Driving a loudspeaker with 1 bit of an output port.

square wave shown has a one-half period of Δt. Consider the following time delay routine (T states are shown in brackets):

```
       CYCLE   LD    E,N          ;N is a number
[4]    LOOP    DEC   E
[4]            NOP
[4]            NOP
[4]            NOP
[4]            NOP
[12]           JR    NZ,LOOP
               CPL                ;COMPLEMENT ACCUMULATOR
               OUT   (nn),A
               JR    CYCLE
```

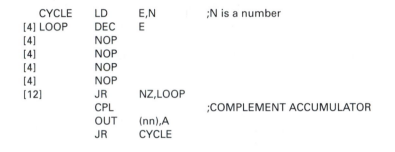

1. All notes will play for 0.25 s minimum.

2. Δt is determined by delay parameter in the E register.

3. N is found as 0.25 s/Δt.

4. Example: For middle C, f = 256 Hz

$$\Delta t = \frac{1}{2} \times \frac{1}{f} = 32 \times E \times \frac{1}{4\,\text{MHz}}$$

$$E = \frac{4\,\text{MHz}}{64f} = 244 = \text{F4H}$$

and N = 0.25s $\times$ 2 $\times$ f = 128 = 80H

Figure 3.31 Calculating E and N for the computer music program. The Δt time-delay loop has $32 \times E$ clock cycles, where E denotes the contents of the E register.

This routine has a loop with $32 \times E$ clock cycles. As explained in Fig. 3.31, a 4-MHz Z-80 would require $E = 244$ to generate the proper period for middle C.

A not-so-obvious point is that higher frequency notes will require less total time for the same number of cycles than is required by lower frequency notes. If a fixed time period (say, 0.25 s) is chosen for each note's duration, a second parameter can be calculated. Call this the number of cycles (N). Figure 3.31 shows how to make this calculation. N is 128 for middle C. This means that 128 "half periods" of middle C will last for 0.25 s.

Now a two-byte-per-entry table can be created that holds the values of E (the time delay for the frequency generator) and N (the number of cycles) for each note it is desired to be able to play. (See Fig. 3.32.) This data table becomes a permanent part of the music program. A second table called the *note table* is also required. This table holds the codes for the notes in the song to be played. A new song is created by changing the codes in this table.

A final problem remains to be solved. In music there are eighth notes, quarter notes, half notes, and full notes. Thus, each note to be played should have two attributes: a note code and a duration code. With some sacrifice in the total number of notes possible, this information can be encoded into 1 byte. Figure 3.33 illustrates one technique.

Address	Data	Note	Note code
0	80	Middle C	0
1	F4		
2	88	C#	1
3	E6		
4	90	D	2
5	DA		
6	98	D#	3
7	CD		
8	A2	E	4
9	C2		
A	AB	F	5
B	B7		
C	B5	F#	6
D	AD		
E	C0	G	7
F	A3		
10	CC	G#	8
11	99		
12	DB	A	9
13	91		
14	E4	A#	A
15	89		
16	F2	B	B
17	81		
18	00	High C	C
19	7A		

N

Δt

Figure 3.32 Data table for Program 14. Each note has two entries. The first number is N, the number of cycles required for a duration of 0.25 s. The second number is E, the value required in the time-delay loop for that note's frequency.

Sec. 3.1   Microprocessor Programming Examples   **139**

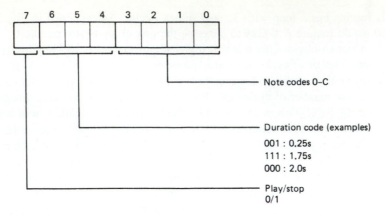

Figure 3.33 Each note in the song table is 1 byte long. The low 4 bits define 1 of 13 notes according to the code in Fig. 3.32. Bits 4 through 6 select one of eight note lengths from 0.25 s to 2.0 s. Bit 7 is used to detect the last note in the song table. If this bit is a 1, the program will stop.

New Instructions

RET NZ   Return from a subroutine call if the zero flag is not set. Any of the condition flags can be tested in this manner. Be careful, however: If the condition never occurs, you will never return to your intended location!

CPL   Complement accumulator. This instruction is useful to produce the toggling effect required in this program.

RLD   This instruction is difficult to explain in words, but is clear when diagrammed as in Fig. 3.34. It amounts to a 12-bit rotate with the accumulator making up the top 4 bits and HL the bottom byte. The RRD instruction is similar, but rotates the contents of HL right. In this program, RLD is useful for examining the two separate nibbles of the note code.

Program Solution.   Figure 3.35 is a flowchart of the program. The tables are those mentioned previously. Each note is assigned a code between 0 and 12. Middle C is note 0 and high C is note 12 (0CH). If it is desired to play high C for 0.5 s, the hex code is 2C (2×0.25 s and note 12 or 0CH). If bit 7 is set in the note code, the program terminates.

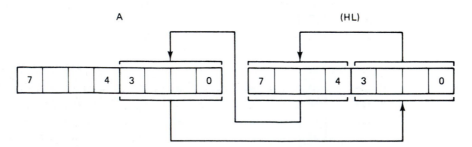

Figure 3.34 The Z-80 RLD instruction is actually a 12-bit rotate command in which bits 4 through 7 of the accumulator are unchanged.

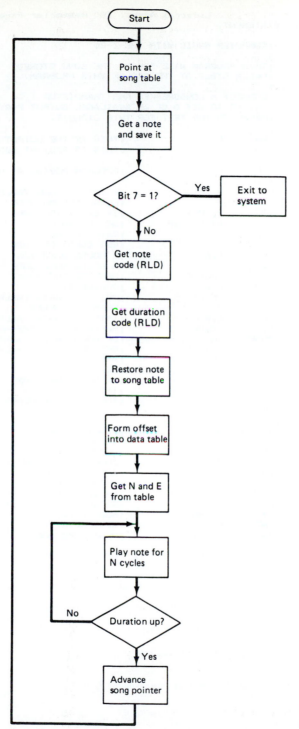

Figure 3.35 Flowchart for the Z-80 computer music program.

```
ADDR      CODE        STMT  SOURCE STATEMENT

                      0001        ;COMPUTER MUSIC WITH THE Z-80
                      0002        ;
                      0003        ;THIS PROGRAM WILL "PLAY" THE SONG STORED
                      0004        ;UNDER STBLE AT THE END OF THIS PROGRAM.
                      0005        ;
                      0006        ;CONNECT A LOUDSPEAKER AND TRANSISTOR
                      0007        ;DRIVER TO BIT 0 OF AN AVAILABEL OUTPUT PORT.
                      0008        ;REFER TO THE TEXT FOR THIS CIRCUIT.
                      0009        ;
  >0000               0010 PORT   EQU     0              ;THIS IS THE OUTPUT PORT
  >0000               0011 SYSTEM EQU     0000           ;THIS IS RESTART ADDRESS
                      0012        ;
  >0600               0013        ORG     0600H          ;PROGRAM BEGINS AT 0600H
                      0014        ;
 '0600  214A06'       0015        LD      HL,STBLE       ;POINT AT SONG TABLE
 '0603  97            0016 NUNOTE SUB     A              ;CLEAR ACCUMULATOR
 '0604  CB7E          0017        BIT     7,(HL)         ;IF BIT 7 IS HIGH
 '0606  C20000        0018        JP      NZ,SYSTEM      ;GO TO SYSTEM
 '0609  4E            0019        LD      C,(HL)         ;SAVE THE NOTE
 '060A  ED6F          0020        RLD                    ;GET DURATION CODE
 '060C  47            0021        LD      B,A            ;B HOLDS DURATION
 '060D  ED6F          0022        RLD                    ;A HOLDS NOTE CODE
 '060F  71            0023        LD      (HL),C         ;RESTORE THE NOTE
 '0610  87            0024        ADD     A,A            ;DOUBLE IT
 '0611  113006'       0025        LD      DE,DTBLE       ;POINT AT DATA TABLE
 '0614  83            0026        ADD     A,E            ;FORM AN OFFSET
 '0615  5F            0027        LD      E,A            ;INTO THE DATA TABLE
 '0616  EB            0028        EX      DE,HL          ;HL POINTS AT THE NOTE
 '0617  D5            0029        PUSH    DE             ;DE HOLDS ADDR IN STBLE
 '0618  56            0030 NOTE   LD      D,(HL)         ;GET NUMBER OF CYCLES
 '0619  23            0031        INC     HL             ;AND
 '061A  5E            0032 CYCLES LD      E,(HL)         ;DELTA T
 '061B  1D            0033 LOOP   DEC     E              ;THIS IS THE LOOP
 '061C  00            0034        NOP                    ;THAT DETERMINES
 '061D  00            0035        NOP                    ;THE NOTE FREQUENCY
 '061E  00            0036        NOP                    ;
 '061F  00            0037        NOP                    ;
 '0620  20F9          0038        JR      NZ,LOOP        ;COUNT E DOWN
 '0622  2F            0039        CPL                    ;TOGGLE THE
 '0623  D300          0040        OUT     (PORT),A       ;OUTPUT PORT
 '0625  15            0041        DEC     D              ;BUMP CYCLE COUNTER
 '0626  20F2          0042        JR      NZ,CYCLES      ;AND CONTINUE
 '0628  2B            0043        DEC     HL             ;CORRECT POINTER
 '0629  10ED          0044        DJNZ    NOTE           ;UNTIL DURATION IS UP
 '062B  D1            0045        POP     DE             ;RECOVER ADDR IN STBLE
 '062C  EB            0046        EX      DE,HL          ;NOW IN HL
 '062D  23            0047        INC     HL             ;NEXT NOTE
 '062E  18D3          0048        JR      NUNOTE         ;PLAY SOME MORE
                      0049        ;
                      0050        ;THIS IS THE DATA TABLE FOR THE 13 NOTES
                      0051        ;FROM MIDDLE C TO HIGH C.
                      0052        ;
 '0630  80F488E6      0053 DTBLE  DEFB    80H,0F4H,88H,0E6H,90H,0DAH,98H,0CDH
        90DA98CD
 '0638  A2C2ABB7      0054        DEFB    0A2H,0C2H,0ABH,0B7H,0B5H,0ADH,0C0H
        B5ADC0
 '063F  A3CC99D8      0055        DEFB    0A3H,0CCH,99H,0D8H,91H,0E4H,89H
        91E489
 '0646  F281007A      0056        DEFB    0F2H,81H,0,7AH
                      0057        ;
```

Figure 3.36 Program 14: computer music with the Z-80.

```
                              0058              ;THESE NOTES CORRESPOND TO "DAISY"
                              0059              ;
'064A    3C393530   0060  STBLE    DEFB    3CH,39H,35H,30H,12H,14H,15H,22H,15H,40H
         12141522
         1540
'0654    373C3935   0061           DEFB    37H,3CH,39H,35H,12H,14H,15H,27H,19H,47H
         12141527
         1947
'065E    191A1917   0062           DEFB    19H,1AH,19H,17H,3CH,19H,17H,45H,17H,29H
         3C191745
         1729
'0668    15221512   0063           DEFB    15H,22H,15H,12H,60H,10H,25H,19H,27H,10H
         60102519
         2710
'0672    25192719   0064           DEFB    25H,19H,27H,19H,1AH,1CH,19H,15H,27H,10H
         1A1C1915
         2710
'067C    7580       0065           DEFB    75H,80H

ERRORS=0000
```

Figure 3.36   (*Continued*)

The values for N and E are stored in the data table and are selected by doubling the note code and adding to a pointer set to point to the top of the table. High C is found as the 25th and 26th entries in the table. Middle C corresponds to the first and second entries.

Figure 3.36 is the assembly language listing of the program.

Summary.   The principle behind single-note computer music is simple, but implementing a useful program can be complicated. To minimize the amount of memory required for each note, the note code and duration can be encoded into a single byte. The Z-80 RLD instruction is useful for such nibble-organized data.

SELF-REVIEW

3.1.22 To generate an audio tone, use the _____ instruction in a loop to complement 1 bit of an output port at an audio rate.

QUESTIONS AND ANSWERS

Q: *What is the advantage of the indirect and indexed addressing modes, compared with that of the direct addressing mode?*

A: The indirect and indexed addressing modes require fewer bytes to code and, accordingly, execute faster. This is because the address of the memory location to be accessed need not be coded as part of the instruction. (The HL pair holds this address.)

Q: *When should the indexed addressing mode be used?*

A: The indexed addressing mode allows an offset to be added to the memory pointer. Therefore, this mode is useful for extracting nonsequential data from a table.

Q: *What caution should be observed in doing multibyte addition?*

A: After adding the first digits with the ADD instruction, one should use the ADC instruction for subsequent digits. This procedure ensures that low-order carries are accounted for.

Q: *What caution should be observed in doing decimal addition?*

A: After giving the ADD instruction the DAA instruction should be executed. This will ensure that the result is a valid BCD number.

Q: *How can a binary number easily be multiplied or divided by 2?*

A: Use the rotate-left (multiplication) or rotate-right (division) instructions.

Q: *How do you create a software time delay?*

A: Load a register with a large number, and then use the DCR–JNZ instructions to create a loop. The time delay will equal the value loaded into the register, times the number of clock cycles required to execute the DCR and JNZ instructions.

Q: *What does it mean to synchronize a peripheral to a microprocessor?*

A: Typically, a peripheral supplies a ready flag that indicates when the device is ready to receive data. A masking technique can be used to test this bit, ensuring that the microprocessor sends data to the peripheral only when it is ready. In this way, the microprocessor and peripheral are synchronized.

Q: *What is the purpose of the 8085's SID and SOD I/O lines?*

A: The SID and SOD I/O lines are 1-bit (serial) input and output lines. The 8085 can send and receive data through these lines using the SIM and RIM instructions, respectively.

Q: *How can a computer be programmed to play a musical note?*

A: One way is to repeatedly toggle an output port bit that is connected to a loudspeaker. With the use of a software time delay, the frequency of these oscillations can be set to the audio range.

LAB PROJECTS

3.1. Modify the 8-bit addition in Program 1 (8080/85) or Program 2 (Z-80) so that the result of (0700)—(0701) is stored in 0702.

3.2. Write a Z-80 or 8080/85 program to move a block of data in memory beginning at address SOURCE to address DEST. Assume that the number of bytes in the block is stored in two sequential memory locations named NUMB. SOURCE and DEST are defined with EQU statements.

3.3. Write a Z-80 or 8080/85 program to search the source block of memory identified in Lab 3.2 for the smallest element. Store the result in memory location SMALL.

3.4. Write a Z-80 or 8080/85 program to search the source block of memory identified in Laboratory Project 3.2 for the byte stored in memory location OLD. Replace all occurrences with the byte stored in memory location NEW.

3.5. Write a Z-80 or 8080/85 program to convert the two hex digits stored in location 0700H to two ASCII digits and store the results in locations 0701H (LSD) and 0702H (MSD). For example, if (0700H) = A4H, then (0701H) = 34H and (0702H) = 41H.

3.6. Modify the communications test routine in Program 9 to send to the terminal an ASCII message stored in memory beginning at location MSG and terminated with the "$" symbol.

3.7. Connect a DIP switch and LEDs to an available input and output port as shown in Fig. 3.37. Write a Z-80 or 8080/85 program to "read" the value of the switches and turn on the corresponding LEDs (i.e., when switch 0 is closed, LED 0 should come on, etc.). Several other

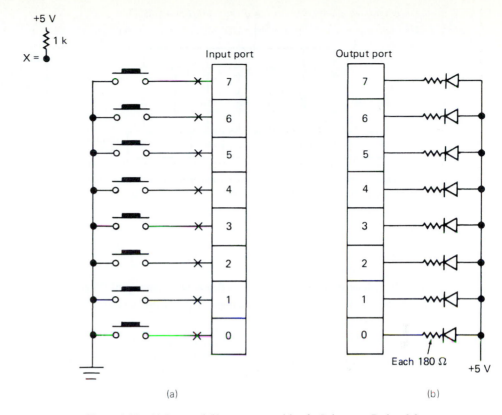

Figure 3.37 (a) Input and (b) output port wiring for Laboratory Project 3.8.

programs are possible. (*Example:* Turn all LEDs on only when switches 0 *and* 1 are closed *and* switches 3 *or* 4 are open, etc.).

3.8. Wire the 8085 circuit shown in Fig. 3.21. Now write a program that monitors the SID input line. When this line switches from high to low, turn on the LED connected to SOD. Turn off the LED on the next high-to-low transition of SID. Continue in this manner, toggling the LED with each high-to-low SID transition.

3.9. Connect the seven segments of a common anode LED display to the output port of your computer as shown in Fig. 3.38. Connect an eight-switch DIP switch to an input port as shown in Fig. 3.37(a). Now write a Z-80 or 8080/85 program that reads switches 0–3 and displays the corresponding hex number on the display. (*Hint:* Use a data table for the seven-segment codes.)

3.10. With a seven-segment display connected as described in Laboratory Project 3.10, write a Z-80 or 8080/85 program that causes a slow count from 0 through F to appear in the display.

QUESTIONS AND PROBLEMS

8080/85-Specific Questions

3.1. List the changes required in Program 1 if the two numbers to be added are stored in locations C000H and C001H.

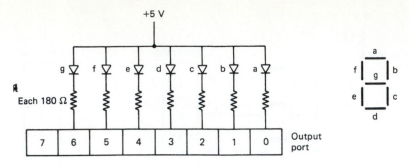

Figure 3.38 Seven bits of a computer output port can be used to drive a seven-segment display. There is no need for a conventional seven-segment decoder.

3.2. Compare the times required for the 8-bit addition in Program 1 using a 2-MHz 8080 and a 2-MHz 8085.

3.3. Why is it necessary to clear the carry flag at the beginning of Program 3?

3.4. Assume that Program 3 is run with memory preloaded as follows:

0700	3C
0701	27
0702	FF
0703	80
0704	DE
0705	F9
0706	1A
0707	69

Determine the contents of memory locations 0708–070B after the program has run.

3.5. What is the address of the last byte in the memory block filled by the program in Fig. 3.13 (Program 7)? What character is written to the block?

*3.6. The following instructions are intended to form a time delay loop:

```
        LHLD    FFFFH
AGAIN   DCX     H
        JNZ     AGAIN
```

Debugging reveals that the loop is executed only once. What is wrong?

3.7. Assuming a 2-MHz 8080, what are the maximum and minimum square-wave frequencies produced by Program 8?

3.8. What is the frequency of the square wave at bit D7 of the output port in Program 8? What change is required to make all 8 bits of the output port operate at the same frequency?

3.9. Calculate the value of DELAY required for the WAIT subroutine in Program 8 to produce a 1-Hz square wave using a 3-MHz 8085AH.

3.10. In Program 10, the HXAS subroutine begins by exchanging the MSD and LSD. Explain why.

3.11. What change is necessary in Program 10 to cause the output to appear as follows?

```
0700    A3
0701    67
0702    E6
etc.
```

3.12. In Program 11 what change is required to make the LED light when the switch *closes*?

3.13. Analyze Program 13, and determine the number of sticks the computer will pick if 11 sticks remain and you pick 2.

3.14. Explain how the PRMSG subroutine in Program 13 detects the end of the string to be printed.

Z-80-Specific Questions

3.15. Describe the changes required in Program 2 if the two numbers to be added are stored in locations D780H and D781H. Assume that the sum is to be stored in location D782H.

3.16. Calculate the time required to execute the 8-bit addition of Program 2 using a 4-MHz Z-80 processor.

3.17. In Program 4, the instruction JR NZ,NEXT has the op code 20 F4. Show that F4 is actually the two's complement of the displacement to memory location NEXT.

3.18. Refer to the sample output of Program 4. Determine the output produced by this program if the DAA instruction is omitted.

3.19. Determine the contents of the HL pair after the following instructions have been executed:

```
LD      HL,679A
ADD     HL,HL
```

Verify that the result is the same as rotating the HL pair left one bit.

3.20. Calculate the execution time for the 8-bit multiplication routine in Program 5, assuming a 4-MHz Z-80 processor.

3.21. What is the largest BCD number that Program 6 will convert correctly?

3.22. In Program 6, if the BCD number to be converted is 8,693,721, determine the contents of memory locations 0700–0706 after the first pass of the program (i.e., the first time the JR NZ,LOOP instruction in location 0624 is run). Assume that locations 0704–0706 all initially store zeros.

3.23. What does the following program accomplish?

```
LD      DE,0100H
LD      BC,0100H
LD      HL,A000H
LDIR
HALT
```

3.24. How would the operation of Program 7 in Fig. 3.14 be changed if the DEC HL instruction in location 060D were deleted?

3.25. If the receiver ready flag in Program 9 were active in the low state instead of the high state, what changes would be required to make this program run correctly?

3.26. The terminal test routine in Program 9 can be stopped only with a processor reset. Modify the program so that typing control-R causes an exit back to memory location MONITOR.

***3.27.** Find all errors in the following routine written to count rising edges of the signal applied to bit 0 of input port C3H.

```
TEST1    IN     A,C3H
         RLA
         JR     C,TEST1
TEST2    IN     A,C3H
         RRA
         JR     Z,TEST2
         INC    B           ;B is the edge counter
```

3.28. How could the frequency-divider hardware of Program 9 be modified to allow 1-Hz resolution without changing the program? What would the maximum count frequency be with this modification?

3.29. Refer to Program 14 and Fig. 3.32, and verify the calculations for E and N for note F (342 Hz).

3.30. Refer to Program 14 in Fig. 3.36. What is the first note of the song "Daisy"? How long is it played?

3.31. Determine the contents of register A and (HL) after execution of the following instructions:

```
LD     A,D7H
LD     (HL),A
RLD
```

SELF-REVIEW ANSWERS

3.1.1. HL

3.1.2. indexed

3.1.3. DCR, JNZ or JZ

3.1.4. DEC, JR NZ

3.1.5. DAA

3.1.6. multiplier

3.1.7. ADD HL,HL

3.1.8. right, carry

3.1.9. reset

3.1.10. none

3.1.11. 0000 0000

3.1.12. HL, DE

3.1.13. time delay

3.1.14. CALL, RET

3.1.15. mask

3.1.16. ASCII

3.1.17. RIM, SIM

3.1.18. high, low

3.1.19. carry

3.1.20. HL

3.1.21. apostrophes, DB

3.1.22. CPL

4

BUILDING THE MICROCOMPUTER, PART 1: THE BUSES

OUTLINE

OBJECTIVES

After completing this chapter, you should be able to:

- Compare asynchronous and synchronous logic designs.
- Describe the 8080, 8085, and Z-80 clock signals and show how these signals can be generated.
- Show how to construct a reset circuit for the 8080, 8085, and Z-80 microprocessors.
- Compute the high- and low-level noise immunity for TTL and CMOS logic circuits.

- Calculate the maximum number of loads that can be driven by a logic circuit without exceeding its output drive capabilities.
- Compare open-collector and tristate bus buffers.
- Show how to construct a bidirectional bus buffer.
- Identify the function of each component in typical 8080, 8085, and Z-80 CPU modules.
- Show how to troubleshoot the buses of a microprocessor using a single-stepping circuit.
- Explain the operation of single-stepping circuits for the 8080, 8085, and Z-80 processors.
- Explain the operation of a Z-80 jump-on-reset circuit.

OVERVIEW

The design of a microcomputer system must begin with the *CPU module*. This module will establish the basic system timing, provide an orderly means of starting up the processor, and afford access to the system buses. If the microcomputer is to be expandable, buffering and loading considerations must be taken into account in designing these buses.

It is also wise to think ahead to the testing phase of the design. Perhaps a *single-stepping* circuit should be designed into the module. This kind of circuit should allow the microprocessor to be stepped one machine cycle at a time—freezing all data, addresses, and control signals on the buses.

When reset, the 8080, 8085, and Z-80 all force their program counters to location 0000. This requires a start-up program (usually in a read-only memory chip) permanently mapped to page 0 of the processor's memory space. However, low memory is often used by application programs; therefore, another useful addition to the CPU module is a *jump-on-reset circuit*. This circuit intercepts the reset signal and directs the processor to a new location in memory.

Basic CPU modules for the 8080, 8085, and Z-80 microprocessors were presented in Chapter 2. In the current chapter, we expand on those designs and pay particular attention to the electrical characteristics of digital signals on a bus.

4.1 GENERATING THE SYSTEM CLOCK

Introduction

All microprocessors require a synchronizing clock signal. The frequency of this signal determines the speed of the processor. Clock generator circuits employ crystal oscillators to ensure a stable operating frequency.

In this section, we:

- Compare asynchronous and synchronous logic designs.
- Describe the 8080, 8085, and Z-80 clock signals and show how these signals can be generated.

Synchronous vs. Asynchronous Logic

The design of a digital system may be *synchronous* or *asynchronous*. In an asynchronous digital network, the outputs of the circuit change whenever the inputs change. That is, the outputs are not synchronized to any timing signal. Most combinational logic networks are examples of asynchronous logic.

Figure 4.1 illustrates a simple combinational logic circuit in which the inverter is assumed to have a propagation delay time twice that of the AND gate. As designed, the circuit is "looking for" the condition SELECT1 = 1 AND SELECT2 = 0. Although this condition never occurs, a false output is produced due to the propagation delay time of the inverter.

Figure 4.2 shows how the same circuit is modified to become a synchronous logic circuit. The SENABLE (synchronized ENABLE) output is synchronized to the clock signal and can change only on the rising edge of the clock. By choosing the clock period long enough for all propagation delays to expire, false outputs are prevented.*

The maximum clock frequency of a microprocessor is determined by the propagation delays of its internal gates. These, in turn, are set by the type of technology used to manufacture the chip. For example, bipolar processors (which use npn transistors) are faster than NMOS processors (which use n-channel metal-oxide semiconductor transistors).

In choosing the clock frequency of a microcomputer, consideration must be given to the overall effect on the system. A 6-MHz 8085 processor may be desirable to mini-

---

*The sum of the flip-flop setup and hold times should exceed the pulse width of the false output.

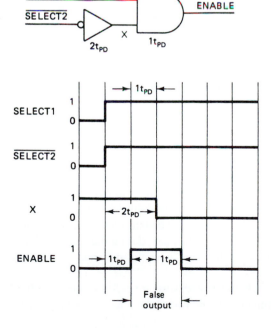

Figure 4.1 In an asynchronous logic network, the outputs change when the inputs change. This may lead to temporary false outputs, due to the unequal propagation delay paths from input to output.

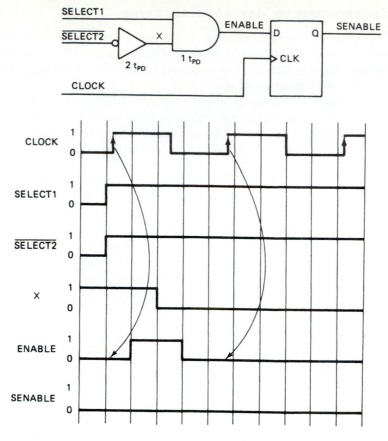

Figure 4.2 In a synchronous logic network, the output can change only in synchronism with a clock signal. By choosing the clock period to exceed the worst-case propagation delay path, no false outputs occur.

mize instruction execution times, but it will also require memory devices that can operate at this higher speed.

The 8080 Clock

The 8080 and 8085 microprocessors both use *two-phase non-overlapping* clock signals. (See Fig. 2.2 for the case of the 8080.) The advantage of this type of clock signal is that two different timing periods and four clock edges are available to synchronize different activities of the processor. For example, the 8080 and 8085 break each instruction into several machine cycles, each of which is further divided into several clock periods, or T states.

Figure 4.3 shows the activities that take place during the four (or five) T states of an 8080 instruction fetch machine cycle. Note how the different timing intervals of the nonoverlapping clocks are used.

Generating the 8080 clock signal with discrete components is difficult because of the non-TTL levels and asymmetry of the two clock phases. As discussed in Chapter 2,

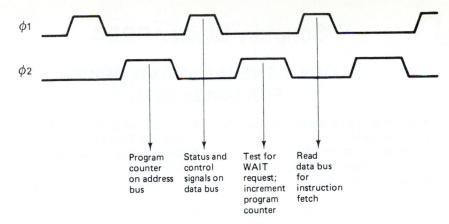

ϕ1

ϕ2

Program	Status and	Test for	Read
counter	control	WAIT	data bus
on address	signals on	request;	for
bus	data bus	increment	instruction
		program	fetch
		counter	

Figure 4.3   The 8080 and 8085 microprocessors use a two-phase nonoverlapping clock signal. The processor activities shown are for an 8080.

Intel produces an integrated clock generator circuit for the 8080 called the 8224. This circuit is shown in Fig. 4.4. Interfacing the 8224 to the 8080 is extremely simple, as shown in Fig. 4.5. The clock frequency is determined by a crystal connected between pins 14 and 15. The crystal frequency should be nine times greater than the desired system frequency.

There are actually three different versions of the 8080 microprocessor, and these are listed in Table 4.1. The maximum operating frequency is 3 MHz for the 8080A-1. The power dissipation is obtained from the data sheets in Table C.1 of Appendix C. Remember that the 8080 requires +5-V, +12-V, and −5-V power sources.

In sum, the 8224 clock generator is the logical choice for developing clock signals in 8080-based microprocessor systems. This chip is specifically designed to interface with the 8080 CPU and 8228 system controller.

The 8085 Clock

Internally, the 8085 requires the same nonoverlapping clock signal as the 8080. However, in redesigning the 8080, the 8085 designers incorporated the 8224 clock generator (or its equivalent) on board. As a result, generating the 8085 clock signal is very simple. Figure 4.6(a) shows the connections. Unlike the 8080 crystal, the 8085 crystal should be twice the desired system operating frequency. Also, an external clock driver, an *LC* tuned circuit, or an *RC* circuit can each be used to generate the clock signal.

Table 4.2 provides data on the maximum operating frequency and power dissipation for the five versions of the 8085. This information is obtained from the data sheets in Table C.2.

The Z-80 Clock

The Z-80 requires a single-phase 0-V to 5-V clock signal. This signal can be generated with the 74LS04 oscillator circuit shown in Fig. 4.7. Because the typical high-level output voltage of a TTL gate is only 3.3 V, and the minimum high level required at the Z-80 clock input is 4.4 V, a 330-Ω pull-up resistor is required.

Schottky Bipolar **8224**

CLOCK GENERATOR AND DRIVER
FOR 8080A CPU

- **Single Chip Clock Generator/Driver for 8080A CPU**
- **Power-Up Reset for CPU**
- **Ready Synchronizing Flip-Flop**
- **Advanced Status Strobe**
- **Oscillator Output for External System Timing**
- **Crystal Controlled for Stable System Operation**
- **Reduces System Package Count**

The 8224 is a single chip clock generator/driver for the 8080A CPU. It is controlled by a crystal, selected by the designer, to meet a variety of system speed requirements.

Also included are circuits to provide power-up reset, advance status strobe and synchronization of ready.

The 8224 provides the designer with a significant reduction of packages used to generate clocks and timing for 8080A.

PIN CONFIGURATION

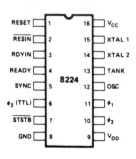

BLOCK DIAGRAM

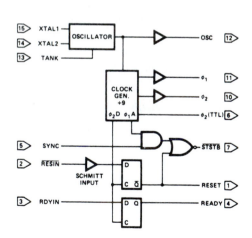

PIN NAMES

RESIN	RESET INPUT		XTAL 1	CONNECTIONS
RESET	RESET OUTPUT		XTAL 2	FOR CRYSTAL
RDYIN	READY INPUT		TANK	USED WITH OVERTONE XTAL
READY	READY OUTPUT		OSC	OSCILLATOR OUTPUT
SYNC	SYNC INPUT		ϕ_2 (TTL)	ϕ_2 CLK (TTL LEVEL)
STSTB	STATUS STB (ACTIVE LOW)		V_{CC}	+5V
ϕ_1	8080		V_{DD}	+12V
ϕ_2	CLOCKS		GND	0V

Figure 4.4 8224 clock generator. 8080 designers are strongly advised to use this circuit to generate the 8080 clock signals. (Courtesy of Intel Corporation.)

154

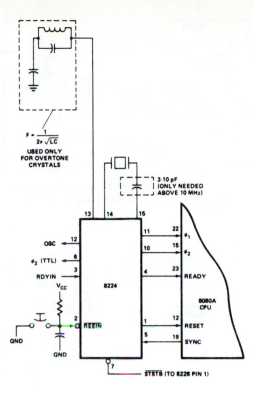

$$F = \frac{1}{2\pi \sqrt{LC}}$$

USED ONLY
FOR OVERTONE
CRYSTALS

3-10 pF
(ONLY NEEDED
ABOVE 10 MHz)

OSC

ϕ_2 (TTL)

RDYIN

V_{CC}

8224

RESIN

GND

GND

ϕ_1

ϕ_2

READY

8080A
CPU

RESET

SYNC

STSTB (TO 8228 PIN 1)

Figure 4.5 The 8224 connects directly to the 8080, requiring only an external crystal at nine times the system frequency. (Courtesy of Intel Corporation.)

It is unfortunate that the Z-80 designers did not incorporate this clock circuit on board, as in the 8085, but two package pins are saved with the technique (compared with the 8085).*

The Z-80 processor is manufactured using two different technologies: *n*-channel MOS (NMOS) and (complementary MOS (CMOS). Parts in the NMOS series are numbered Z840004, Z840006, and Z840008 and correspond to clock rates of 4 MHz, 6.17 MHz, and 8 MHz, respectively. Parts in the CMOS series are numbered Z84C0006, Z84C0008, Z84C0010, and Z84C0020 and correspond to clock rates of 6.17 MHz, 8 MHz, 10 MHz, and 20 MHz, respectively. Because of the low power consumption, most new designs use the CMOS parts. Table 4.3 provides data on clock frequency and power dissipation for these parts.

*The Z84090 KIO chip, a Z-80 support chip, does include an onboard crystal oscillator. (See Chapter 8.)

TABLE 4.1 Speed and Power Specifications for Three Versions of the 8080 Microprocessor

	8080A	8080A-1	8080A-2
f_{max} (MHz)	2	3	2.5
P_D (mW)	1245	1245	1245

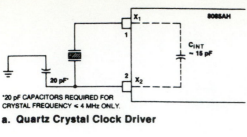

a. Quartz Crystal Clock Driver

*20 pF CAPACITORS REQUIRED FOR
CRYSTAL FREQUENCY ≤ 4 MHz ONLY.

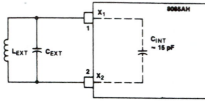

b. LC Tuned Circuit Clock Driver

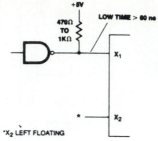

*X₂ LEFT FLOATING

**d. 1-6 MHz Input Frequency External Clock
Driver Circuit**

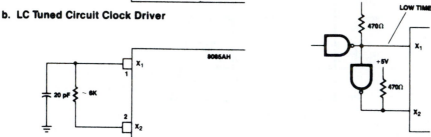

c. RC Circuit Clock Driver

**e. 1-12 MHz Input Frequency External Clock
Driver Circuit**

Figure 4.6 Different techniques for generating the 8085 clock signal: (a) quartz crystal clock driver; (b) *LC* tuned circuit clock driver; (c) *RC* circuit clock driver; (d) 1–6-MHz input frequency external clock driver circuit; (e) 1–12-MHz input frequency external clock driver circuit. (Courtesy of Intel Corporation.)

SELF-REVIEW 4.1

4.1.1 The higher a microprocessor's clock frequency, the _____ the computer will operate.

4.1.2 Comparing the 8080, 8085, and Z-80, we see that only the _____ microprocessor has a "built-in" clock generator.

TABLE 4.2 Speed and Power Specifications for Several Versions of the 8085 Microprocessor

	8085A	8085A-2	8085AH	8085AH-1	8085AH-2
f_{max} (MHz)	3	5	3	6	5
P_D (mW)	850	850	675	1000	675

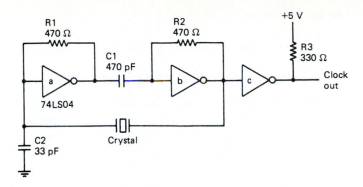

Figure 4.7 A TTL oscillator can be used to generate the Z-80 system clock signal.

TABLE 4.3 Speed and Power Specifications for Several Versions of the Z-80 Microprocessor

	Z84C0006	Z84C0008	Z84C0010	Z84C0020
f_{max} (MHz)	6	8	10	20
P_D (mW)	150	200	250	500

4.2 RESETTING THE MICROPROCESSOR

Introduction

In Chapter 1, we conveniently sidestepped one significant problem of the stored-program computer: How do we put the "very first" program in memory? Certainly, once it is there, we can use the keyboard to enter new programs or give commands to load other programs from a magnetic tape or disk. But how does that first program get in?

What is needed is a permanent program stored in memory that can never be lost or written over, even when power is removed. I imagine that you are already ahead of me and realize that this is exactly the purpose of a read-only memory, or *ROM*. A ROM chip is *nonvolatile,* which means that its contents are not lost when power is removed.

Usually, a ROM is used to hold a "bootstrap" loader. This is a special program that is called upon only once to "boot up" the operating system. Once the operating system is loaded, the keyboard becomes active and new programs can be written or loaded from the disk.

But one problem remains. When power is first applied to the microprocessor, all of its registers, including the program counter, contain random data. Accordingly, some means must be found to point the program counter to the bootstrap ROM. This is the purpose of the *reset* switch.

As mentioned earlier in this chapter, resetting the 8080, 8085, or Z-80 causes the program counter to be loaded with 0000. Therefore, this is the logical address for the bootstrap ROM chip. (In Section 4.7, we show how to force a reset to *any* location in memory.)

In this section, we:

• Show how to construct a reset circuit for the 8080, 8085, and Z-80 microprocessors.

Reset Circuits for the 8080, 8085, and Z-80

Circuits for resetting the 8080, 8085, and Z-80 are shown in Fig. 4.8. The purpose of the switch should be clear, but the *RC* network requires some explanation.

When power is first applied to the system, it would be convenient to have the microprocessor reset itself without the need to push the reset button. In this way, simply turning on the computer could cause the bootstrap program to load the operating system—this is sometimes called a *turnkey* system.

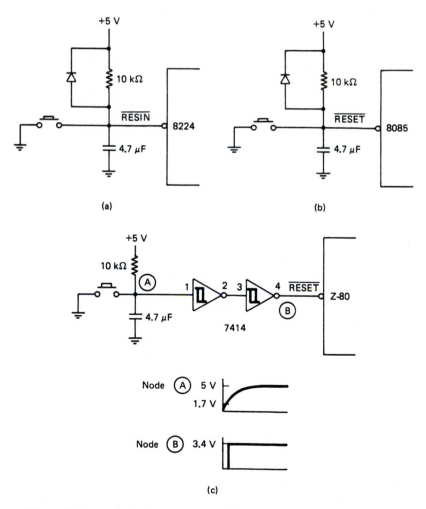

Figure 4.8   Reset circuits for the (a) 8080, (b) 8085, and (c) Z-80 microprocessors.

With the *RC* network connected to the reset input as shown in Fig. 4.8, the capacitor will hold the reset pin low for several time constants when power is first applied. The result is called a *power-on-reset* circuit.

Because the reset signal obtained across the capacitor is a rising exponential and not a sharp square wave, a Schmitt trigger is used to square up the waveshape. The 7414 shown in Fig. 4.8(c) will switch to a low-level output when its input exceeds 1.7 V. The input will then have to go below 0.9 V before the output will switch back high. That is, the logic 1 and logic 0 switching points are not the same.

A circuit with two different switching thresholds is said to have *hysteresis*. This property is characteristic of all *Schmitt* triggers and is useful for cleaning up waveshapes with excessive ringing or for signals that pass relatively slowly through the TTL switching threshold.

The 8224 and 8085 both incorporate Schmitt triggers at their reset inputs, but the Z-80 does not. Note that this is another good reason for selecting the 8224 as a support component to the 8080.

SELF-REVIEW 4.2

4.2.1 When reset, the 8080, 8085, and Z-80 all load their program counter with the address _____.

4.2.2 Via a _____ circuit, the CPU's RESET input will be held low for several time constants, ensuring an orderly start-up of the computer.

4.3 ELECTRICAL CHARACTERISTICS OF A BUS

Introduction

A bus can be defined as a set of lines used to transport data between a transmitter and a receiver. Usually, we lump together common signal lines and refer to them collectively as a bus. Thus, we have the *address bus,* the *data bus,* and the *control bus.* In many microcomputer systems, these signals and others are all wired to a common *backplane,* or *motherboard,* and are referred to as the system bus.

A properly designed system bus must consider such problems as noise immunity, ac and dc loading, reflection problems due to high-speed logic pulses, and cross talk between parallel conductors.

In this section, we:

- Compute the high- and low-level noise immunity for TTL and CMOS logic circuits.
- Calculate the maximum number of loads that can be driven by a logic circuit without exceeding its output drive capabilities.

Noise Immunity

In a microcomputer system there are typically three types of buses, and these are described in Table 4.4. In all cases, the transmitter places a logic 1 (called V_{OH} for "V_{out}

TABLE 4.4 Microcomputer Buses

Type	Description	Example
1	One transmitter, many receivers	Address bus
2	One receiver, many transmitters	CPU control lines (WAIT, INT, etc.)
3	Many transmitters and receivers (bidirectional)	Data bus

high") or a logic 0 (called V_{OL} for "V_{out} low") on the bus. This signal propagates down the bus line and is received as a V_{IL} (input voltage low) or V_{IH} (input voltage high).

The values for V_{OL}, V_{OH}, V_{IL}, and V_{IH} are dependent on the logic family used. Table 4.5 indicates values for TTL, CMOS, and low-power Schottky TLL (LSTTL). A minimum requirement for any bus system to work is that

$$V_{OH} > V_{IH} \qquad \text{and} \qquad V_{OL} < V_{IL}.$$

The amount by which these requirements are exceeded is called the *noise immunity*.

Example 4.1

Assume that a 7400 TTL gate is driving a bus line with a 74LS04 receiver. Calculate the worst-case noise immunity for the bus.

Solution. The minimum-output high level for the 7400 gate is 2.4 V. The 74LS00 will accept a logic 1 input as low as 2.0 V. Therefore, the logic-1-level noise immunity is 2.4 V − 2.0 V = 0.4 V.

The maximum logic-0-level output voltage for the 7400 gate is 0.4 V. The 74LS00 will accept a logic-0-level input as high as 0.8 V, so the logic-0-level noise immunity is 0.8 V − 0.4 V = 0.4 V.

The 0.4 V of noise immunity calculated in the preceding example means that the bus can tolerate a noise impulse that pulls the V_{OH} level down by 0.4 V or the V_{OL} level up by 0.4 V. Noise immunity levels for a CMOS transmitter driving a CMOS receiver are greater than 1 V.

TABLE 4.5 Logic-Level Specifications for the TTL, LSTTL, and CMOS Logic Families

	Description	TTL	LSTTL	CMOS[a]
V_{OH}	Minimum logic 1 output voltage	2.4 V	2.7 V	4.6 V
V_{OL}	Maximum logic 0 output voltage	0.4 V	0.5 V	0.4 V
V_{IL}	Maximum acceptable logic 0 input voltage	0.8 V	0.8 V	1.5 V
V_{IH}	Minimum acceptable logic 1 input voltage	2.0 V	2.0 V	3.5 V
I_{IL}	Maximum logic-0-level input source current	−1.6 mA	−0.4 mA	−1 μA
I_{IH}	Maximum logic-1-level input sink current	40 μA	20 μA	1 μA
I_{OH}	Maximum logic-1-level output source current	−400 μA	−400 μA	−360 μA
I_{OL}	Maximum logic-0-level output sink current	16 mA	8 mA	0.36 mA

[a]Data given for the CD4001BC.

Bus Loading

Noise immunity is a characteristic of the logic family used and cannot be changed. However, a problem that can be designed out is the loading of the transmitter by the receiver or receivers on the bus. In general, each receiver added to the bus will require an additional amount of *source* current from the transmitter in the high state and an additional amount of *sink* current into the transmitter in the low state. The situation is diagrammed in Fig. 4.9.

All of the output voltage specifications in Table 4.5 are for worst-case loading conditions, indicated as I_{OL} and I_{OH} in the bottom two lines of the table. Using these data, we can expect a 7400 output to be no lower than 2.4 V when the transmitter is sourcing a 400-μA load and no greater than 0.4 V when sinking a 16-mA load. The amount of loading to be

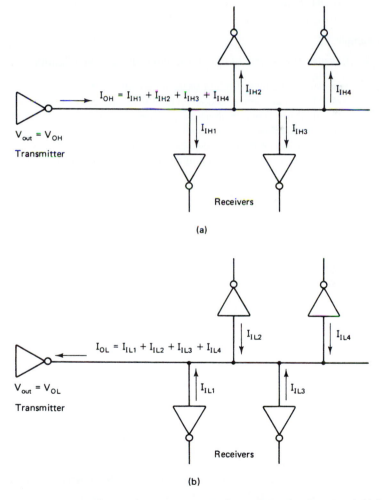

Figure 4.9 A transmitter sends source current to the receivers when its output is high (a) and receives sink current from the receivers when its output is low (b).

expected for a given logic family is shown in Table 4.5 as I_{IL} and I_{IH}. Negative currents mean that the direction of the current is out of the device. (That is, a source current.)

Example 4.2

Calculate the number of 74LS04 receivers that a 7400 transmitter can safely drive without exceeding its drive capabilities.

Solution. In the logic 1 state, a 74LS04 presents one 20-μA load per input. The 7400 transmitter can supply 400 μA of drive current in the 1 state and thus can safely drive 400 μA/20 μA = 20 74LS04 receivers.

In the logic 0 state, the 74LS04 receiver presents a 0.4-mA load per input. The 7400 transmitter can supply 16 mA of drive current in the 0 state and thus can safely drive 16 mA/0.4 mA = 40 74LS04 receivers.

The logic 1 state is therefore the worst case, and the bus should be limited to 20 74LS04 receivers.

Example 4.3

Calculate the number of CD4001 receivers that a 7400 transmitter can safely drive.

Solution. The input loading factor for a CMOS gate is almost negligible (1 μA), and one would think that there would be no limit to the number of CMOS receivers a TTL transmitter could drive. However, there are two problems. The first is that the V_{OH} level for TTL does not meet the minimum V_{IH} requirement for CMOS. This means that the logic 1 output of a TTL gate may not be interpreted as a logic 1 input by the CMOS gate. This problem can be solved fairly simply by the use of a pull-up resistor as shown in Fig. 4.10.

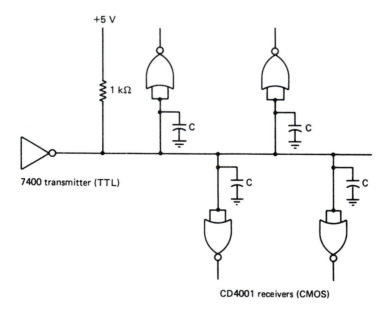

Figure 4.10   When a TTL transmitter is used to drive a bus line with CMOS receivers, a resistor is required to pull up the TTL V_{OH} level to near 5 V.

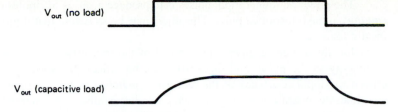

Figure 4.11 When a transmitter drives a capacitive load, the output of a logic gate will be delayed and become distorted as shown.

The second problem is caused by the capacitive nature of the CMOS input. A TTL gate typically has 1.5 pF of capacitance per input, but a CMOS gate can be as high as 7.5 pF per input.

Consider a TTL transmitter driving 10 CMOS receivers. The total capacitive load (ignoring wiring capacitance) could be as high as 75 pF (compared with only 15 pF for 10 TTL loads). This large capacitive load will distort the output signal from the TTL gate, as shown in Fig. 4.11. The effect will be to lower the bandwidth of the bus—that is, restrict the bus to low frequencies.

The 7400 data sheet indicates a maximum capacitive load of 15 pF. Checking the CD4001 data sheet shows 5 pF per input. The 7400 transmitter can thus drive just three CD4001 loads.

Reflections

The physical nature of a bus is usually a number of parallel traces on a printed circuit (PC) board or a bundle of wire-wrap wire. A pulse placed on this bus is affected in a manner similar to the way radio-frequency signals on a high-frequency transmission line are affected.

Figure 4.12 illustrates the effect of placing a long and a short pulse on an open-circuited bus line. This model is a reasonable one for a microcomputer bus because of the high input resistance of a TTL or CMOS logic gate acting as a receiver. The pulse propagates down the line at approximately 2 ns/ft. Because of the open circuit, the current reaching the end of the line is forced to turn around and head back to the transmitter, a process called *reflection*.

If the input pulse is very short, the effect is a series of reflected pulses. Depending on the amplitude and duration of these pulses, clocked devices such as flip-flops and latches may produce erroneous results.

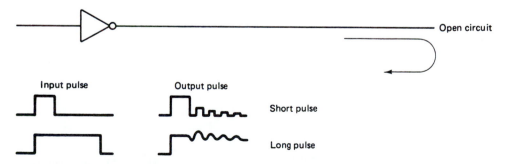

Figure 4.12 Effect of reflections on long and short pulses placed on an open-circuited bus line.

The effect on longer input pulses is to produce a series of ripples (sometimes called *ringing*) in the transmitted pulse. This effect may be so severe that it produces momentary invalid logic levels.

Ideally, a receiver placed on the end of the transmission line would absorb all of the energy in the pulse, and there would be no reflection. However, this action occurs only if the input resistance of the receiver is *matched* to the resistance of the transmission line. PC board traces and wire-wrap bundles exhibit a characteristic impedance (resistance plus reactance) of 100 to 200 Ω. Therefore, one means of minimizing reflections is to terminate each bus line with a 100- to 200-Ω resistor to ground. This arrangement is referred to as *passive termination*. Unfortunately, this has the undesirable effect of producing a dc load on the transmitter. The V_{OH} level will be pulled down and the V_{OL} level pulled up. A better solution is to use a voltage-divider configuration that biases the bus line in the middle of the TTL-level threshold and simultaneously matches the characteristic impedance of the line. Such a circuit is called an *active terminator* and is shown in Fig. 4.13.

Because of the receiver input resistance and the resistance of the line, voltage division ensures that the amplitude of the reflected pulse will always be less than the amplitude of the incident pulse. Eventually, the reflections will die out. For this reason, short bus lines (less than 3 ft) are not seriously affected by reflections. Of course, the closer the receiver is matched to the characteristic impedance of the bus line, the greater is the attenuation factor for the reflected waves. There is no reflection with a matched load.

In some cases, coaxial cable is used as a transmission line between receiver and transmitter. The center conductor in this cable is surrounded by a grounded shield, or braid. This shielding prevents capacitive coupling between adjacent conductors called cross talk.

An alternative to coaxial cable is the twisted pair. The signal wire and a ground conductor are twisted together to form an inexpensive transmission line. The ground wire again forms a protective shield.

With either type of transmission line, the cable length should be restricted to 15 to 30 ft when driven by TTL. Greater cable lengths introduce unacceptably large capacitive loads. Special line drivers and receivers are available for these long lines.

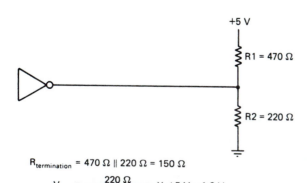

$R_{termination} = 470\ \Omega \parallel 220\ \Omega = 150\ \Omega$

$V_{bus} = \dfrac{220\ \Omega}{220\ \Omega + 470\ \Omega} \times +5\ V = 1.6\ V$

Figure 4.13 Active termination of a bus line minimizes reflections without producing a significant dc load on the transmitter.

SELF-REVIEW 4.3

4.3.1 The difference between a transmitter's worst-case high- or low-level output voltage and a receiver's worst-case high- or low-level input threshold voltage is called _____ _____ _____.

4.3.2 As the number of receivers connected to a bus line increases, the transmitter's high-level output voltage will _____, and its low-level output voltage will _____.

4.4 BUS BUFFERING TECHNIQUES

Introduction

Bus buffering refers to the various methods required to ensure that valid logic levels are carried on the bus. In Section 4.3, we learned that a microprocessor has three types of buses. (See Table 4.4.) Each one of these requires a different buffering technique.

In this section, we:

- Compare open-collector and tristate bus buffers.
- Show how to construct a bidirectional bus buffer.

Type 1 Bus

The type 1 bus is characterized by a single transmitter and several receivers. The address bus is an example of a type 1 bus. The need for buffering can best be seen with an example.

Example 4.4

Suppose that a Z-80 microprocessor is interfaced to a 32K-byte memory consisting of 16 HM6116 2K × 8 RAM chips. In addition to driving the RAM chips, assume that each address line must also drive three TTL loads used for address decoding. Is a buffer required?

Solution. Figure 4.14 illustrates the interface for the A0 address line. (In general, the arrangement is duplicated for all 16 address lines.) Because the HM6116s are MOS devices, they require only a small drive current—10 μA in this case. The three TTL loads will require 1.6 mA each in the low state and 40 μA each in the high state. The total loading on the Z-80 A0 address line is thus

$$
\begin{array}{r}
16 \times 10\ \mu A = 160\ \mu A \\
+ \quad 3 \times 40\ \mu A = 120\ \mu A \\
\hline
280\ \mu A \text{ in the logic 1 state}
\end{array}
$$

and

$$
\begin{array}{r}
16 \times 10\ \mu A = 160\ \mu A \\
+ \quad 3 \times 1.6\ mA = 4.8\ mA \\
\hline
4.96\ mA \text{ in the logic 0 state.}
\end{array}
$$

The data sheet for the Z-80 in Appendix C.3 indicates an I_{OH} of 250 μA and an I_{OL} of 1.8 mA. The 32K memory interface will exceed both of these specifications, and therefore, a special buffer will be required.

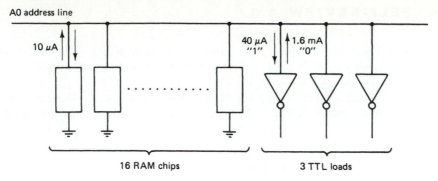

Figure 4.14   Loading considerations for the A0 address line in Example 4.4.

The result obtained in Example 4.4 should come as no surprise: Microprocessors are MOS devices and, as such, have very limited drive capabilities. As a general rule, a bus buffer should be used whenever the bus loading exceeds the drive capabilities of the microprocessor or when it is necessary to drive receivers off the main CPU card. The latter requirement is due to the capacitive loading associated with the edge connectors and backplane wiring in a multicard system.

Special buffers are available for this application, and Fig. 4.15 shows several common varieties. The 74LS241 and 74LS244 are particularly attractive because they contain eight buffers in one package. A data sheet for these devices is shown in Fig. 4.16.

Example 4.5

Assume that a type 1 bus similar to that of Fig. 4.9 is to be buffered with a 74LS244 transmitter. Calculate the number of standard TTL loads that can be driven by this transmitter. How many loads can be driven if each input is also buffered by a 74LS244?

Solution.   From the data sheet in Fig. 4.16, the high-level output drive capability of the 74LS244 is 3 mA at V_{OH} = 2.4 V. This means that 3 mA/40 μA = 75 standard TTL loads can be driven in the high state.

In the low state the 74LS244 can sink 12 mA, and thus, 12 mA/1.6 mA = 7.5 standard TTL loads can be driven.

When the loads are also buffered with 74LS244s, the high-level drive current required drops to 20 μA/input, and 3 mA/20 μA = 150 loads can be driven.

In the low state the buffered load requires only 0.2 mA, and the calculation is 12 mA/0.2 mA = 60 loads.

To summarize, for a type 1 bus with 74LS244 transmitters, seven standard TTL loads or 60 74LS244-buffered loads can be driven.

The lesson from the foregoing example should be clear: Not only is it advantageous to use a buffer for the transmitter, but also, buffering each receiver input greatly increases the number of receivers that can be safely driven.

Tristate Buffers with Hysteresis

Another advantage to the 74LS240 series of buffers is that each gate has a built-in *Schmitt* trigger. As mentioned previously, this is a circuit with a dual switching threshold—a

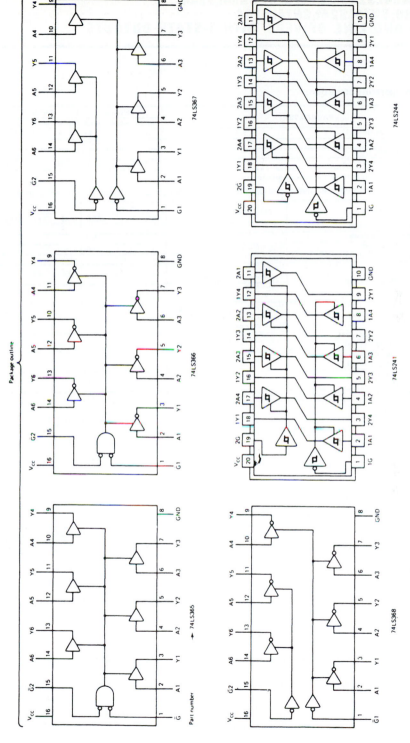

Figure 4.15 Common bus buffers for use with microprocessors. (From J. Uffenbeck, *Hardware Interfacing with the Apple II Plus*, Prentice-Hall, Inc., Englewood Cliffs, N.J., 1983, and Texas Instruments.)

recommended operating conditions

PARAMETER	SN54LS'			SN74LS'			UNIT
	MIN	NOM	MAX	MIN	NOM	MAX	
Supply voltage, V_{CC} (see Note 1)	4.5	5	5.5	4.75	5	5.25	V
High-level output current, I_{OH}			−12			−15	mA
Low-level output current, I_{OL}			12			24	mA
Operating free-air temperature, T_A	−55		125	0		70	°C

NOTE 1: Voltage values are with respect to network ground terminal.

electrical characteristics over recommended operating free-air temperature range (unless otherwise noted)

PARAMETER		TEST CONDITIONS[†]		SN54LS'			SN74LS'			UNIT
				MIN	TYP[‡]	MAX	MIN	TYP[‡]	MAX	
V_{IH}	High-level input voltage			2			2			V
V_{IL}	Low-level input voltage					0.7			0.8	V
V_{IK}	Input clamp voltage	V_{CC} = MIN,	I_I = −18 mA			−1.5			−1.5	V
	Hysteresis ($V_{T+} - V_{T-}$)	V_{CC} = MIN		0.2	0.4		0.2	0.4		V
V_{OH}	High-level output voltage	V_{CC} = MIN, V_{IH} = 2 V, V_{IL} = V_{IL} max, I_{OH} = −3 mA		2.4	3.4		2.4	3.4		V
		V_{CC} = MIN, V_{IH} = 2 V, V_{IL} = 0.5 V, I_{OH} = MAX		2			2			
V_{OL}	Low-level output voltage	V_{CC} = MIN, V_{IH} = 2 V, V_{IL} = V_{IL} max	I_{OL} = 12 mA			0.4			0.4	V
			I_{OL} = 24 mA						0.5	
I_{OZH}	Off-state output current, high-level voltage applied	V_{CC} = MAX, V_{IH} = 2 V, V_{IL} = V_{IL} max	V_O = 2.7 V			20			20	μA
I_{OZL}	Off-state output current, low-level voltage applied		V_O = 0.4 V			−20			−20	
I_I	Input current at maximum input voltage	V_{CC} = MAX,	V_I = 7 V			0.1			0.1	mA
I_{IH}	High-level input current, any input	V_{CC} = MAX,	V_I = 2.7 V			20			20	μA
I_{IL}	Low-level input current	V_{CC} = MAX,	V_{IL} = 0.4 V			−0.2			−0.2	mA
I_{OS}	Short-circuit output current[♦]	V_{CC} = MAX		−40		−225	−40		−225	mA
I_{CC}	Supply current	Outputs high	V_{CC} = MAX	All	17	27		17	27	mA
		Outputs low		'LS240	26	44		26	44	
			Outputs open	'LS241, 'LS244	27	46		27	46	
		All outputs disabled		'LS240	29	50		29	50	
				'LS241, 'LS244	32	54		32	54	

[†] For conditions shown as MIN or MAX, use the appropriate value specified under recommended operating conditions.

[‡] All typical values are at V_{CC} = 5 V, T_A = 25°C.

[♦] Not more than one output should be shorted at a time, and duration of the short-circuit should not exceed one second.

switching characteristics, V_{CC} = 5 V, T_A = 25°C

PARAMETER		TEST CONDITIONS	'LS240			'LS241, 'LS244			UNIT
			MIN	TYP	MAX	MIN	TYP	MAX	
t_{PLH}	Propagation delay time, low-to-high-level output	C_L = 45 pF, R_L = 667 Ω, See Note 2		9	14		12	18	ns
t_{PHL}	Propagation delay time, high-to-low-level output			12	18		12	18	ns
t_{PZL}	Output enable time to low level			20	30		20	30	ns
t_{PZH}	Output enable time to high level			15	23		15	23	ns
t_{PLZ}	Output disable time from low level	C_L = 5 pF, R_L = 667 Ω, See Note 2		15	25		15	25	ns
t_{PHZ}	Output disable time from high level			10	18		10	18	ns

NOTE 2: Load circuit and voltage waveforms are shown on page 3-11.

Figure 4.16 Electrical specifications for the 74LS240, 74LS241, and 74LS244. (Courtesy of Texas Instruments.)

property also called *hysteresis*. Figure 4.17 shows the effect that a Schmitt trigger can have on a waveform with excessive ringing due to reflections.

All of the buffers in Fig. 4.15 also have *tristate* capability. This means that in addition to the two logic states, a third output state called the tristate can be realized. This state is actually a high-impedance, or open, circuit. A model of a tristate gate is shown in Fig. 4.18.

Tristate buffers allow several transmitters to control the same bus line. By placing all but one transmitter in the tristate mode (OFF), no interference occurs. This property will be taken advantage of in the type 3 bus.

Type 2 Bus

The type 2 bus has many transmitters, but only one receiver. This type of bus cannot be realized with standard TTL gates. Figure 4.19 shows why. Everything is fine as long as both transmitters "want" the same level on the bus. But as is shown in the figure, when one output is high and the other is low, the bus line can become indeterminate. What is worse, an excessive current may flow from the logic 1 output to the logic 0 output, possibly damaging both devices. This is called *bus contention*.

One solution to this problem is to use tristate gates for the transmitters. By enabling only one transmitter at a time, bus contention is eliminated. The problem with this technique is that extra logic will be required to ensure that only a single transmitter is enabled at a particular time.

Another solution is to use an *open collector* (or open drain) bus, as shown in Fig. 4.20. In this scheme, the transmitters have open-collector output stages. This means that they can pull the bus down to a logic 0—by saturating their output transistor—but they require an external pull-up resistor to force a logic 1 onto the bus.

We can write the following logic equation for the WAIT signal in Fig. 4.20:

$$\overline{\text{WAIT}} = \overline{\text{T1}} + \overline{\text{T2}}.$$

This connection is referred to as a "wired OR." An open-collector bus normally sits in the high state and is activated by any one transmitter pulling the bus line low. For this reason, the receiver is normally a control function activated by a low logic level—that

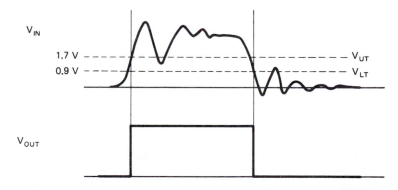

Figure 4.17 Effect of hysteresis on a waveform with excessive ringing. All 74LS240 series buffers have hysteresis.

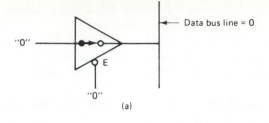

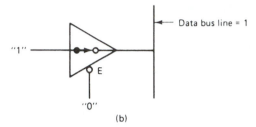

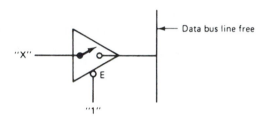

Figure 4.18 Tristate gates are commonly used to shunt data onto a data bus. In (a) and (b), the tristate gate is enabled and the data bus line is connected to the input logic level. In (c), the tristate gate is disabled and its output appears as an open circuit. The data bus line is now free to be controlled by another transmitter on the line. (From J. Uffenbeck, *Hardware Interfacing with the Apple II Plus,* Prentice-Hall, Inc., Englewood Cliffs, N.J., 1983.)

is, an active-low input. Examples are the Z-80 $\overline{\text{HALT}}$, $\overline{\text{WAIT}}$, $\overline{\text{INT}}$, $\overline{\text{NMI}}$, and $\overline{\text{BUSRQ}}$ inputs.

A disadvantage of this type of bus is that it is not possible to tell which transmitter pulled the bus line low. To do so may require the processor to read a status port—a technique called *polling*—to determine the activating device.

In many cases, the CPU "does not care" what pulled the bus line low. For example, when the $\overline{\text{WAIT}}$ line is low, the microprocessor enters a wait, or idling, state. Such a state

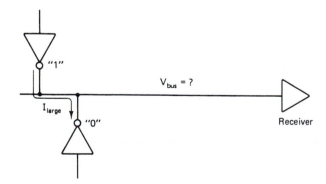

Figure 4.19 A type 2 bus has several transmitters and one receiver. If standard TTL gates are used, problems occur when one transmitter tries to drive the bus high and another tries to drive it low.

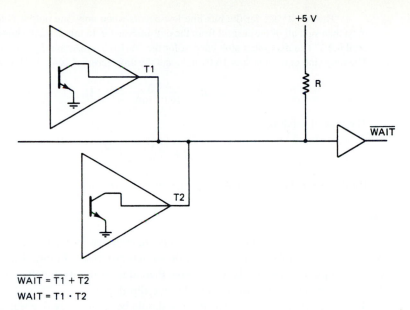

$$\overline{\text{WAIT}} = \overline{\text{T1}} + \overline{\text{T2}}$$
$$\text{WAIT} = \text{T1} \cdot \text{T2}$$

Figure 4.20 Type 2 bus realized with open-collector gates. This connection is called a "wired OR."

is usually requested by a slow memory circuit that cannot respond quickly enough with data for the processor. In that case, the processor waits until the memory is ready (when the $\overline{\text{WAIT}}$ line is released back high) and then continues. The specific memory device requesting the WAIT is unimportant.

The value of the pull-up resistor used with an open-collector bus is not arbitrary. This is because loading of the transmitters must be considered.

Example 4.6

Suppose that the open-collector bus in Fig. 4.20 has five transmitters, each using a 7401 open-collector NAND gate. Suppose further that the receiver is the $\overline{\text{WAIT}}$ input of a Z-80 microprocessor. Calculate the value of the pull-up resistor.

Solution. When all transmitters are OFF, the pull-up resistor must supply a leakage current to each collector and the Z-80 input. According to the data sheet on Z-80 dc characteristics in Appendix C.3, the leakage current is 10 μA for the $\overline{\text{WAIT}}$ input. The 7401 data sheet indicates 250 μA maximum leakage per collector. The total current is thus 5×250 μA + 10 μA = 1.26 mA.

The high level presented to the $\overline{\text{WAIT}}$ input must not be less than 2.4 V. Therefore, for the pull-up resistor, we must have

$$R \leq \frac{2.6 \text{ V}}{1.26 \text{ mA}} = 2 \text{ k}\Omega.$$

The general result is

$$R \leq \frac{5 \text{ V} - 2.4 \text{ V}}{(n \times I_{\text{LKG}}) + I_{\text{IH}}}.$$

The worst case for the bus line low occurs when only one output is low, as the driver must then sink all of the current from the pull-up resistor. In this case, the bus line must not exceed 0.4 V. The maximum sink current for the 7401 is 16 mA, and I_{IL} for the Z-80 is 10 μA. The total sink current is thus 16.01 mA, and the drop across R is 4.6 V. Hence, we must have

$$R \geq \frac{4.6 \text{ V}}{16.01 \text{ mA}} = 287 \ \Omega.$$

The general result is

$$R \geq \frac{5 \text{ V} - 0.4 \text{ V}}{I_{OL} + I_{IL}}.$$

For this particular bus, R must be greater than 287 Ω, but less than 2 kΩ.

Type 3 Bus

The type 3 bus is a *bidirectional* bus that has many transmitters and many receivers. The most common example is the data bus of a microprocessor. Figure 4.21 illustrates data flow from an input device to the CPU. Note that all transmitters are shown as tristate gates and all receivers are shown as latches (D-type flip-flops).

The necessity for tristate transmitters should be clear: Only one transmitter can control the bus at a particular time. The need for receiver latches may not be so clear. What we must remember is that data is placed on the bus for a very brief time. For example, when an input instruction is performed, the data bus holds the op code for the IN instruction during the M1 machine cycle. During the next machine cycle, it holds the port address. Finally, during the third machine cycle, the input device is enabled and places the actual data onto the bus. Because each machine cycle is only four or five clock periods long, each receiver must quickly latch the data when its turn comes up.

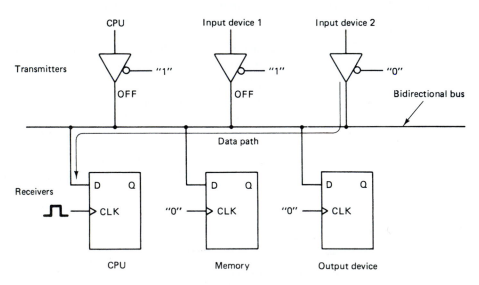

Figure 4.21 Data flow on a bidirectional bus line.

And that is the main problem with the type 3 bus: How does a receiver (or transmitter) know when its turn has come? The answer to this question involves address bus and control bus *decoding* techniques, which are covered in detail in the next two chapters. But the concept is simple enough. If the control bus I/O read line is active, and if the address bus holds "our" port address, it is time to put the data on the bus (time to enable the tristate transmitter).

On the other hand, if the I/O write line is active and the address bus holds "our" address, it is time to clock the flip-flop and store the present contents of the data bus. For this reason, all three buses (control, address, and data) are involved in the transfer of data between a receiver and a transmitter on the data bus.

The drive capabilities of the CPU data bus lines are no better than those of the address lines. In addition, the routing of the data bus lines to other cards and peripherals causes capacitive and reflective problems. Buffers will again be required.

The technique for buffering a data bus line is slightly more complex, due to the bidirectional nature of the bus. Figure 4.22 shows the method. Two tristate gates are required for each bus line with separate READ and WRITE enables. These enable signals must be derived from the control bus of the microprocessor.

Special bus transceivers are available for this application, and Fig. 4.23 shows several common types. The 74LS245 is particularly well suited to such an application, as it contains eight tristate pairs and has separate *enable* and *direction* controls.

A special circuit is available for the 8080 that combines the functions of a bidirectional bus buffer and a status word decoder. This circuit is the 8228 system controller shown in Fig. 4.24. It is designed to interface directly with the 8080 and uses the $\overline{\text{STSTB}}$ signal generated by the 8224 to latch the 8080 status word. (See Section 2.1 for a discussion of the 8080 status word.) Note that all of the common control bus signals are generated directly by the 8228.

The 8228 is an important support device for 8080-based microprocessor designs. It provides full data bus buffering, generates all control bus signals, and supports the 8080's vectored interrupt technique by allowing multiple-byte restart instructions or automatic insertion of an RST 7 instruction. (See Chapter 6.)

The 8228 has an I_{OH} of 1 mA and an I_{OL} of 10 mA, compared with the 74LS245's 3 mA and 12 mA, respectively. Additional buffering of the 8228 data bus may therefore be required.

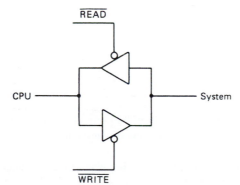

Figure 4.22 Bidirectional bus buffer. Only one gate is enabled at a particular time.

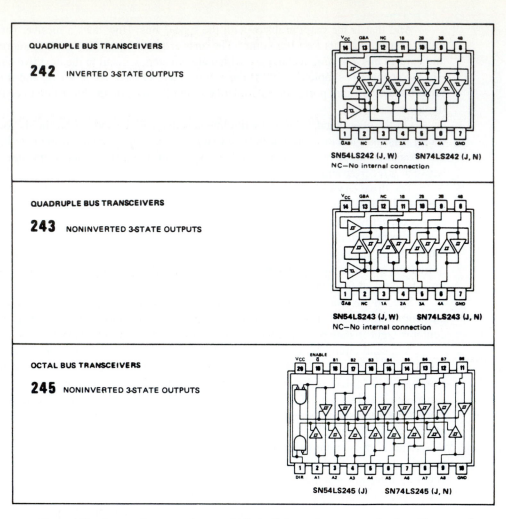

Figure 4.23 Common bus transceivers useful for buffering a microprocessor data bus. (Courtesy of Texas Instruments.)

SELF-REVIEW 4.4

4.4.1 Why is it desirable to buffer *receiver inputs* as well as transmitter outputs?

4.4.2 An _____ bus is useful when several transmitters share a common bus-request line.

4.4.3 The output of a tristate bus buffer may be high, low, or an _____ _____.

Schottky Bipolar **8228**

SYSTEM CONTROLLER AND BUS DRIVER
FOR 8080A CPU

- **Single Chip System Control for MCS™-80 Systems**
- **Built-in Bi-Directional Bus Driver for Data Bus Isolation**
- **Allows the use of Multiple Byte Instructions (e.g. CALL) for Interrupt Acknowledge**

- **User Selected Single Level Interrupt Vector (RST 7)**
- **28 Pin Dual In-Line Package**
- **Reduces System Package Count**

The 8228 is a single chip system controller and bus driver for MCS-80. It generates all signals required to directly interface MCS-80 family RAM, ROM, and I/O components.

A bi-directional bus driver is included to provide high system TTL fan-out. It also provides isolation of the 8080 data bus from memory and I/O. This allows for the optimization of control signals, enabling the systems deisgner to use slower memory and I/O. The isolation of the bus driver also provides for enhanced system noise immunity.

A user selected single level interrupt vector (RST 7) is provided to simplify real time, interrupt driven, small system requirements. The 8228 also generates the correct control signals to allow the use of multiple byte instructions (e.g., CALL) in response to an INTERRUPT ACKNOWLEDGE by the 8080A. This feature permits large, interrupt driven systems to have an unlimited number of interrupt levels.

The 8228 is designed to support a wide variety of system bus structures and also reduce system package count for cost effective, reliable, design of the MCS-80 systems.

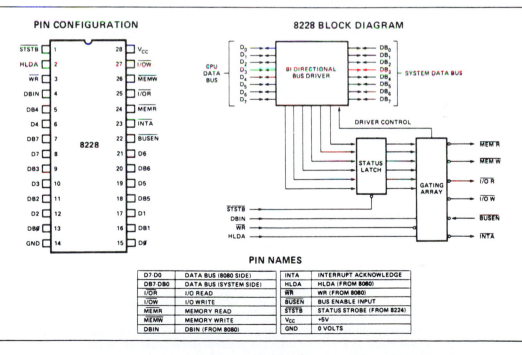

Figure 4.24 The 8228 system controller. This chip includes a bidirectional bus buffer and decoding logic to generate the 8080 control bus signals. (Courtesy of Intel Corporation.)

TOWARD MORE READABLE LOGIC DIAGRAMS

Have you ever noticed that most digital electronics textbooks seem to favor logic 1s over logic 0s? For example, a two-input AND gate is drawn as

and has the word interpretation: *"Output C will be high whenever inputs A AND B are high."* But couldn't we also say: *"Output C will be low whenever inputs A OR B are low"*? This gate would have the symbol

In effect, this "new" gate is an OR gate that works on logic 0s instead of logic 1s. Sometimes this type of gate is called a *negative logic* OR gate. Unfortunately, the term "negative logic" scares a lot of folks. No one but the military would use negative logic!

But let's backtrack a moment. What's wrong with an OR gate that operates on 0s? I can think of many cases where the digital signal is asserted (applied or turned on) with a logic 0. The enable input on most buffers requires a 0. The asynchronous set and reset inputs of flip-flops are always active low (activated by a logic 0). Indeed, all of the control bus signals output by the microprocessor are active low.

So maybe there is some merit to this negative logic OR gate. Let's consider an example. As we have seen, the Z-80 control bus signals are similar but not identical to the 8080 control bus signals. If we wish to generate the 8080 $\overline{IOR}$ signal, we must note that the Z-80 indicates an I/O operation by asserting $\overline{IORQ}$. A read operation is indicated by $\overline{RD}$ = 0.

Using conventional logic we would conclude that $\overline{IOR}$ can be generated by inverting $\overline{IORQ}$ and $\overline{RD}$, ANDing the two terms, and inverting the result.

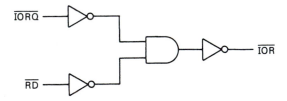

But why not let the word statement of the problem define the circuit? *"Whenever $\overline{IORQ}$ is low AND $\overline{RD}$ is low, generate a signal $\overline{IOR}$ that is low."* The circuit is

You may not recognize this gate at first, but it is just an OR gate. Now we could have made up a truth table for this problem and recognized the OR function, but letting the problem speak for itself is much simpler.

In either case, recognizing the OR function, why not draw the OR symbol? This is an important point. If we were to use the OR gate symbol, the word interpretation would become: "*Whenever $\overline{IORQ}$ is high OR $\overline{RD}$ is high, output $\overline{IOR}$ should be high.*" Although this is correct, it does not convey the designer's intent.

The key is to remember that there are really only two logic functions: AND and OR. If you need to AND two signals that are active low, draw the AND symbol with inversion circles on each input. If the output of this gate should also be active low, draw a circle on the output. If the output should be active high, omit the circle.

Forget about NAND and NOR gates. Let the problem define the logic symbol. Later you can go back and (using De Morgan's theorem if necessary) determine the part number of the symbol.

For example, the negative input positive output AND gate

is actually a NOR gate. This can be seen by applying De Morgan's theorem:

$$C = \overline{A} \cdot \overline{B} = \overline{A + B}$$

A convenient "trick" that makes this conversion easy to remember is to visualize the opposite gate type (ANDs become ORs and ORs become ANDs) with all inputs and outputs inverted.

Throughout this book you will find a "mixed logic" symbology. Positive and negative logic are intermixed—and not because I am trying to make the diagrams more confusing; just the opposite. Learn to "read" the word description of each logic function. Your logic diagrams will become clearer and fewer gates will be required.

4.5 CPU MODULES FOR THE 8080, 8085, AND Z-80

Introduction

Basic CPU modules for the 8080, 8085, and Z-80 microprocessors were presented in Chapter 2. These modules were conceptual circuits that did not take into account real-world problems such as bus loading.

In this section, we:

- Identify the function of each component in typical 8080, 8085, and Z-80 CPU modules.

The 8080 CPU Module

As discussed in Chapter 2, the 8080 is really a three-chip microprocessor. This can be seen in Fig. 4.25. The 8224 clock generator is used to generate the two-phase clock signals and also to synchronize the WAIT and system reset requests. It also generates the status strobe signal required by the 8228.

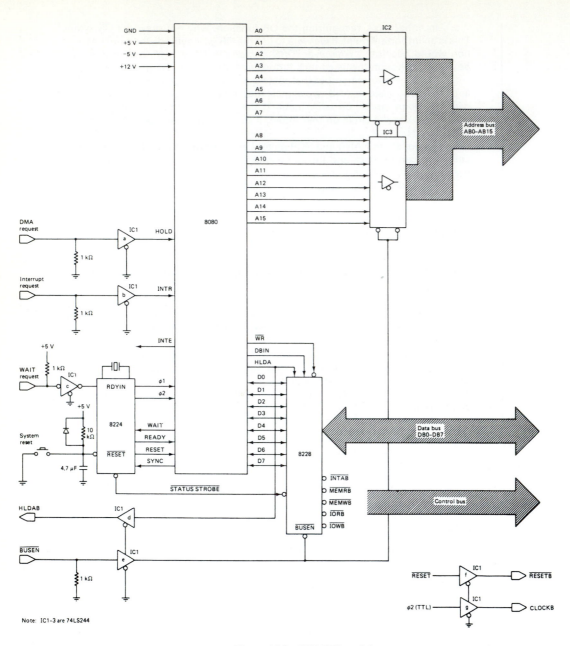

Figure 4.25 8080 CPU module.

The 8228 is used to buffer the system data bus and to generate the five control bus signals. A new control signal, interrupt acknowledge (INTA), has been included in the control bus. This signal is important for interrupt-driven I/O and is discussed in Chapter 6.

The address bus is buffered by two 74LS244s. Note that the names of the signals have a "B" appended to them, to indicate their buffered status. This is important: The signals A0 and AB0 are usually the same—but not always. (For example, with direct memory access, A0 is tristated but AB0 is output by the direct memory access controller.) Throughout this book, a signal whose name has the letter B appended represents a *buffered* version of that signal.

Note that all three buses can be tristated by driving the BUSEN input high. This allows another master to control the system buses.

The remaining signals—DMA request, interrupt request, INTE, and HLDAB—are explained in Chapter 6.

The 8085 CPU Module

Unlike the 8080, the 8085 requires no special support devices. However, examining the CPU module diagram in Fig. 4.26 reveals a considerable number of TTL devices. There are two reasons for this. First, because of the multiplexed address and data bus lines (AD0–AD7), a latch is required to separate the two buses. This is the function of IC6, a 74LS373 8-bit latch that contains eight D flip-flops with a common active-high enable input (G).

AD0–AD7 carry the low-order address when the address latch enable (ALE) signal is high. When ALE switches low, the 74LS373 stores this address.

The second reason for the complexity of the CPU module is the need to decode the control bus signals. This is done by IC8 and inverter IC5b. In Chapter 7 we will see that Intel supplies special memory and I/O devices that interface directly with the 8085's multiplexed address/data bus and are compatible with its control bus. If these devices are used, the CPU module can be simplified considerably.

Again, 74LS244s are used to buffer the control and address buses. A 74LS245 is used to buffer the data bus. Note that the direction control of this device is derived from the RD control signal. Because IC8 and IC7 are 74LS parts, no buffering is required on the RD signal.

A BUSEN input is again provided to allow the three buses to be placed in a tristate condition. Notice that the 74LS373 latch has the unique capability of tristating its outputs when OE is high. In addition, the output drive capability is identical to a 74LS244 in the low state and 2.6 mA (versus 3 mA for the 74LS244) in the high state. Thus, the 74LS373 is ideally suited to this application, latching the low-order address, allowing its outputs to be tristated for direct memory access, and providing full buffering for AB0 through AB7. (*Note:* The 8212 latch shown in Fig. 2.8 can also be used for this purpose, but it has only 1 mA of high-level drive capability.)

Five active-high input interrupt requests are provided, labeled INTR, TRAP, and RST 5.5–7.5. The jumper connections allow these inputs to be grounded when not used. DMA request and HLDAB are discussed in Chapter 6.

The Z-80 CPU Module

The Z-80 CPU module is presented in Fig. 4.27. Again, no special support devices are needed, although separate ICs are required to generate the clock signal and interface the system reset signal.

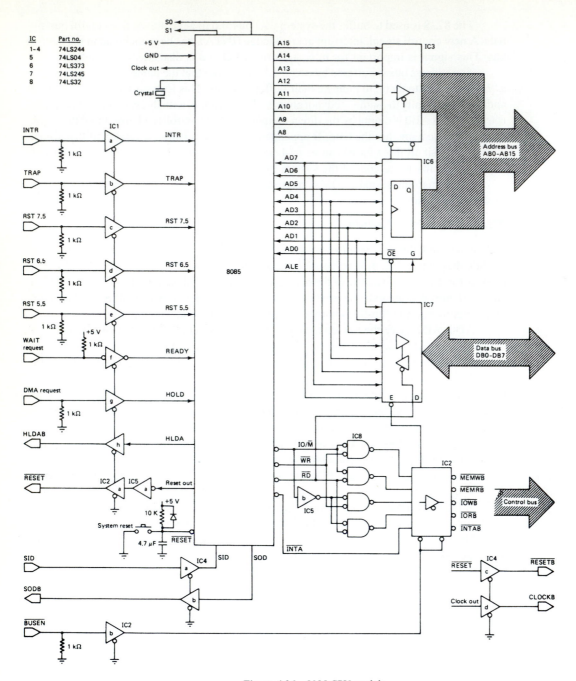

Figure 4.26 8085 CPU module.

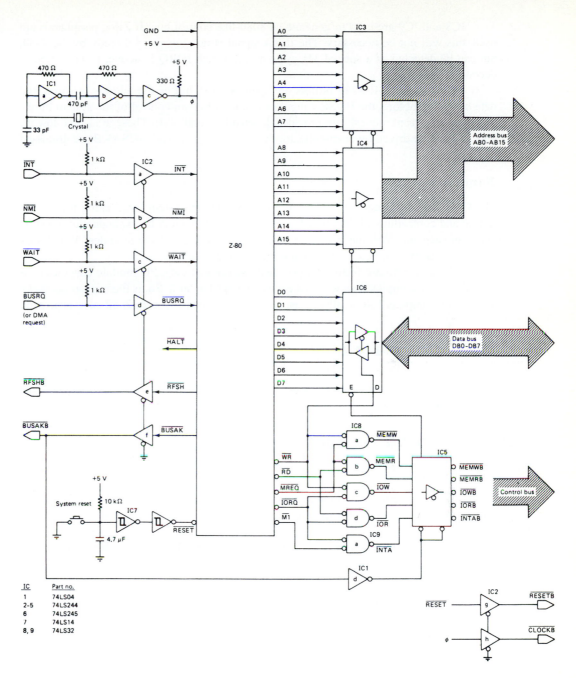

Figure 4.27 Z-80 CPU module.

IC8 and IC9 are used to generate an 8080-like control bus. If Zilog peripherals are used, this will not be necessary. The $\overline{INTA}$ signal is not generated directly by the Z-80, but can be detected as a special M1 cycle during which $\overline{IORQ}$ is active. IC9a is used to decode this signal.

74LS244 and 74LS245 buffers are again used to buffer the address, control, and data buses. As before, the $\overline{BUSEN}$ input can be used to gain control of the system buses.

Two interrupt requests are provided, labeled $\overline{INT}$ and $\overline{NMI}$. These are active-low inputs and can be driven by open-collector gates. Both signals and $\overline{BUSAKB}$ are discussed in Chapter 6.

Summary

The CPU module forms the "brain" of a microcomputer system, originating the system timing and controlling all data transfers. In designing this module, expandability must be taken into account. Will the system be able to drive all of the RAM modules? Will it support direct memory access and interrupt-driven I/O?

Taking all of these factors into account, we see that the CPU module becomes considerably more complex than was first envisioned in Chapter 2. So, is the microprocessor a single-chip computer? Not really—least not the 8080, the 8085, or the Z-80 microprocessor.

SELF-REVIEW 4.5

4.5.1 Explain why several chips are required to build CPU modules for the 8080, 8085, and Z-80 processors.

4.6 SINGLE-STEPPING THE MICROPROCESSOR

Introduction

When testing and troubleshooting a microcomputer interface, the first task is to isolate the problem to hardware or software. One way of doing this is to step the processor one instruction—or even one machine cycle—at a time. The advantage, of course, is to be able to examine the contents of the various CPU registers and flags after each instruction has executed. When stepping machine cycles, the signals on the buses can be monitored to allow troubleshooting of the external hardware.

In this section, we:

- Show how to troubleshoot the buses of a microprocessor using a single-stepping circuit.
- Explain the operation of single-stepping circuits for the 8080, 8085, and Z-80 processors.

Troubleshooting

Suppose that we have interfaced a digital-to-analog converter (DAC) to a Z-80 microcomputer, but find that it does not work. The circuit might look something like Fig. 4.28.

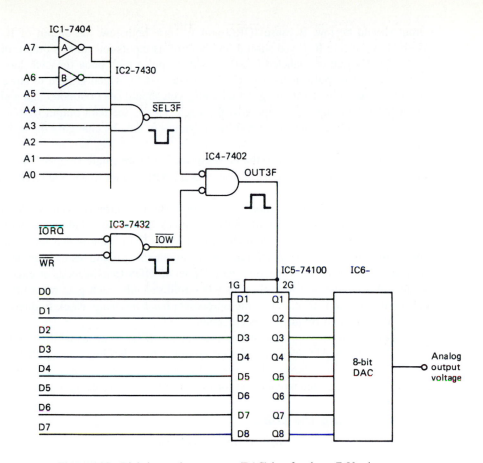

Figure 4.28 Digital-to-analog converter (DAC) interfaced to a Z-80 microprocessor.

Let's assume that a hardware single-stepper is available and attempt to debug the circuit. First we will need a simple test program. (Be sure to use a *simple* test program; we want to debug hardware, not software.)

A suitable program might be the following:

```
LOOP    LD      A,0      ;PUT A TEST PATTERN IN REGISTER A
        OUT     (3F),A   ;OUTPUT TO PORT 3F
        JP      LOOP     ;LOOP
```

Start the program running and then press the single-step switch. The program will stop in a *WAIT* state with all three buses holding valid data. Pushing the STEP key should cause the computer to execute one machine cycle. Now using a logic probe, we can examine each of the buses. What we are looking for is the M3 cycle of the OUT instruction. You can quickly find this cycle by monitoring the $\overline{IORQ}$ or $\overline{WR}$ control bus signal. When either of these lines goes low, you have found the M3 cycle. (Do you know why?)

Now checking the low-order address bus, we should observe the binary code 00111111. This is the port address (3FH). All inputs to IC2 should be high, and its output should be low. Because $\overline{IORQ}$ and $\overline{WR}$ are both low, the output of IC3 should also be low. Testing IC4, you should find both of its inputs low and its output high.

The IC4 output—labeled OUT3F—should pulse high once for each loop through the program. This pulse is used to clock the latch (IC5), which is used to store the contents of the data bus. Examining the data bus, you should see 00000000 and a similar result at the Q1 through Q8 outputs of the latch. This is the data output by the OUT instruction. You can test the latch for different values of data by changing the test pattern in the LD instruction.

I think you can appreciate the power of the hardware single-stepper. By freezing the data on the microprocessor buses, it becomes a simple matter to test the hardware and locate any faults.

You might think that a good way to single-step a microprocessor would be to slow down the clock signal or manually pulse the clock input. Then, individual clock periods could be monitored. Unfortunately, this won't work. The reason is that internally the microprocessor uses *dynamic* logic, a design technique that minimizes the number of circuit components by using the capacitive gate inputs of MOS transistors as storage elements. Because this charge will leak away in a few milliseconds, each gate must be repeatedly recharged. For that reason, every microprocessor has a *minimum* clock frequency in addition to its maximum frequency specification.

Most single-step circuits utilize the built-in *WAIT* state capability of the microprocessor. In the WAIT state the microprocessor "idles," holding valid addresses, control signals, and data on its buses. (This is true for most microprocessor chips, but not all—to be sure, check the technical manuals for the chip that you are using.)

Single-Stepping the 8080

Figure 2.3 illustrates basic 8080 instruction-cycle timing. After the T1 state, in which the processor has output a valid memory or I/O address and set up its control signals, the READY input line is sampled. If this input is found low, a WAIT state is entered and is identified by the WAIT output going high. The 8080 remains in the WAIT state, sampling the READY input during each successive clock cycle. When READY is again found high, the instruction cycle continues with the T3 state.

The READY input is intended for interfacing slow memory devices to the 8080. Normally, the processor gives the memory three clock periods (until state T3) to place its data on the bus. This situation is shown in Fig. 2.3. If three clock periods are not enough time, a WAIT-state generator can be built to force a number of WAIT states to occur before state T3. It is important to note that the processor does not "automatically" insert these WAIT states—a circuit must be designed to request them.

An 8080 single-step circuit based on the WAIT-state principle is shown in Fig. 4.29. The operation of this circuit is as follows:

1. With switch S1 in the RUN position, the output of IC1C will be high. As shown in Fig. 4.4, the RDYIN input of the 8224 is synchronized to the $\phi2$ clock and applied to the 8080 READY input. Because RDYIN is high, the processor is in the RUN mode.

2. In the RUN mode the WAIT output is low, and this asynchronously sets the D flip-flop IC2.

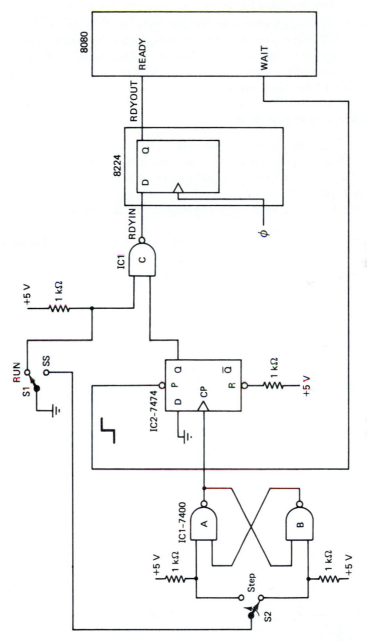

Figure 4.29 8080 single-step circuit.

3. When S1 is switched to the single-step position, the output of IC1C goes low, forcing the READY input of the 8080 low on the next rising edge of the ϕ2 clock. The 8080 will enter the WAIT mode during the next T2 clock cycle, and the three buses will become available for testing.

4. To advance the program one machine cycle, the step switch can be pushed. This clocks IC2, forcing its Q output low relinquishing the WAIT request. The processor again begins running—forcing WAIT low and setting IC2. Of course, this pulls the RDYIN line of the 8224 low, and the 8080 will again enter the WAIT mode when the next T2 machine cycle occurs.

Single-Stepping the 8085

WAIT-state timing for the 8085 is the same as for the 8080 and can be seen in Fig. 2.7. The main difference between the two processors is that no WAIT signal is available from the 8085. This turns out to not be a problem, as the address latch enable (*ALE*) signal can be used in its place.

Figure 4.30 is the 8085 single-stepping circuit. Its operation is as follows:

1. With switch S1 in the run mode, the READY line of the 8085 is held high and the processor runs normally.

2. Because each machine cycle begins with an ALE pulse, the Q output of IC2 will be high.

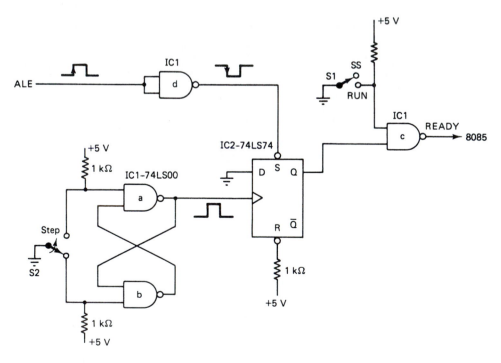

Figure 4.30 8085 single-step circuit.

3. Moving S1 to the single-step position causes the IC1C output to go low, and the 8085 will enter the WAIT mode after T2 of the next machine cycle.

4. Single-stepping by one machine cycle is accomplished by pushing S2. This action clocks IC2, forcing its Q output low relinquishing the WAIT request. The 8085 now runs until the next ALE pulse—one machine cycle later—and then reenters the WAIT mode.

Single-Stepping the Z-80

WAIT-state timing for the Z-80 is similar to that for the 8080 and 8085 and is shown in Fig. 2.10 for an op-code fetch machine cycle. Zilog prefers to call the READY input $\overline{WAIT}$, and this line is sampled with the falling edge of ϕ during the T2 clock period of each machine cycle. If $\overline{WAIT}$ is found low, the processor enters a WAIT state with valid addresses, control signals, and data on its buses. This WAIT state will persist indefinitely until the $\overline{WAIT}$ input is found high on the falling edge of ϕ. At this time, program execution continues normally with the T3 state of the current machine cycle.

A single-step circuit for the Z-80 is shown in Fig. 4.31. The operation of this circuit is as follows:

1. When power is first applied or when the reset switch (not shown) is pushed, IC2A is reset and IC2B is set.

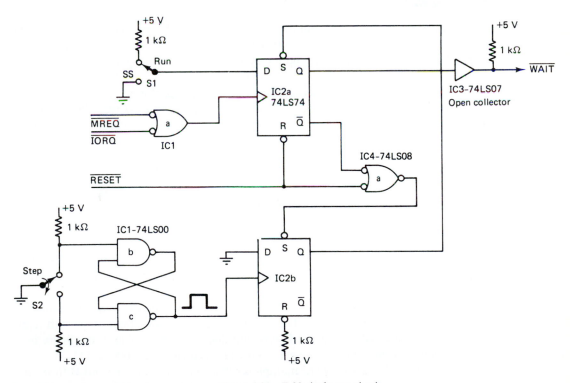

Figure 4.31   Z-80 single-step circuit.

2. With switch S1 in the RUN position, any I/O or memory request will set flip-flop IC2A and cause the $\overline{\text{WAIT}}$ line to go high. The processor will run normally.

3. When S1 is switched to the single-step position, any I/O or memory request will reset IC2A and cause $\overline{\text{WAIT}}$ to go low. This will in turn cause the Z-80 to enter a WAIT state as soon as T2 of the next machine cycle occurs.

4. Pushing the STEP switch now resets IC2B, sets IC2A, and forces $\overline{\text{WAIT}}$ high. The Q output of IC2A also sets IC2B, and this allows the next I/O or memory request to again clock the $\overline{\text{WAIT}}$ line low. The effect is to execute one machine cycle each time the STEP switch is pushed.

SELF-REVIEW 4.6

4.6.1 When troubleshooting microprocessor hardware, which is more desirable, a circuit that single-steps instructions or one that single-steps machine cycles?

4.6.2 Machine-cycle single-step circuits work by forcing the CPU into a _____ state in which valid data is held on all three buses.

4.7 A POWER-ON-JUMP CIRCUIT FOR THE Z-80

Introduction

As discussed in Section 4.2, resetting the 8080, 8085, or Z-80 microprocessor causes the program counter to be loaded with 0000. This generally means that a ROM chip must be mapped to page 0 in order to boot up the system. However, having a ROM in this location may be incompatible with some operating systems.

For example, the operating system often uses page 0 for storing system variables, all three processors use locations on page 0 for storing *interrupt vectors* (see Chapter 6 for a discussion of interrupts), and commercial software is often written to begin in location 0.

What is needed is a *jump-on-reset* circuit that forces the processor to some location other than 0 when a reset occurs.

In this section, we:

• Explain the operation of a Z-80 jump-on-reset circuit.

Circuit Description

Figure 4.32 shows how a jump-on-reset circuit for the Z-80 can be constructed. This type of circuit "tricks" the processor into reading the op code for a jump instruction whenever the reset line is pulled low.

Because a jump instruction is three bytes long, three separate data bytes will have to be gated onto the Z-80 data bus. The circuit in Fig. 4.32 uses a three-stage shift register made up of three edge-triggered D-type flip-flops. The truth table in the figure indicates the action taken as the shift register moves sequentially from 000 to 111.

The 74LS257 is a 4-bit word multiplexer that routes word A or word B to its output, depending on the select (S) input. The outputs of the 74LS257 are tri-stated and

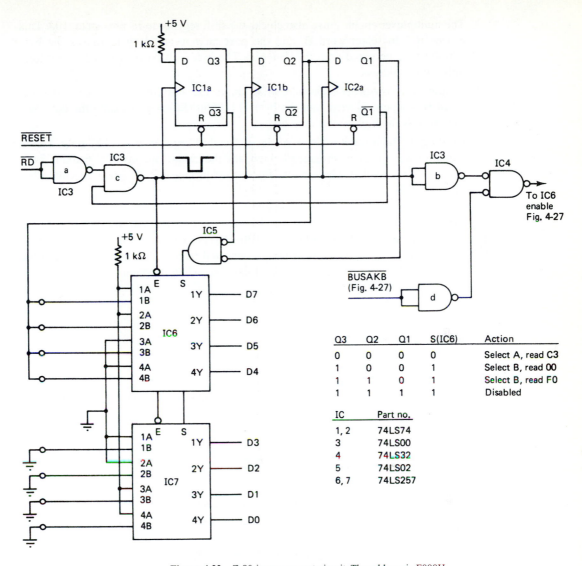

Figure 4.32 Z-80 jump-on-reset circuit. The address is F000H.

become active only when the enable ($\overline{\text{E}}$) input is low. This is necessary in order to drive the bus without conflicts.

The operation of the circuit is as follows:

1. When the $\overline{\text{RESET}}$ line is driven low, the shift register is reset to 000, causing the 74LS257 select input to be low (select word A).

2. When $\overline{\text{RESET}}$ returns high, the Z-80 begins an instruction fetch cycle and $\overline{\text{RD}}$ goes low. This enables the tristate outputs of the 74LS257 through IC3C. The A inputs of the two multiplexers are hardwired to 11000011 or C3H (the op code for a JP instruction).

3. The multiplexer enable pulse also clocks the shift register to its next state, 100. This causes IC5 to select word B, and the next memory read cycle causes the byte 00000000 to be gated onto the data bus. The byte will be interpreted as the low-order jump address.

4. Reading the low-order address also advances the shift register to the 110 state. Word B is again selected, and the byte 11110000 (F0) is gated onto the data bus. This byte is the high-order jump address.

5. Reading the high-order address advances the shift register to the 111 state. The Q output of IC2A is now permanently high, and the tristate outputs of IC6 and IC7 are permanently disabled. The circuit effectively "disappears." Program execution begins at F000H.

The circuit in Fig. 4.32 is designed to interface directly with the Z-80 data bus. These lines are labeled D0 through D7 (not DB0–DB7) in Fig. 4.27. The enable input (pin 19) of the 74LS245 transceivers must be disconnected from IC1D and connected to the output of IC4. This will turn off the external data bus when the jump-on-reset circuit is active.

SELF-REVIEW 4.7

4.7.1 Why is a power-on-jump circuit necessary?

4.7.2 The op code for a jump instruction is C3H. How does the circuit in Fig. 4.32 generate this op code?

QUESTIONS AND ANSWERS

Q: *How is the clock signal for the 8080 microprocessor generated?*

A: The best approach is to use the 8224 clock driver and a crystal whose frequency is nine times the system operating frequency.

Q: *How is the clock signal for the 8085 microprocessor generated?*

A: The 8085 incorporates an on-chip clock oscillator circuit requiring only an external crystal whose frequency is twice the system operating frequency.

Q: *How is the clock signal for the Z-80 microprocessor generated?*

A: The Z-80 requires an external crystal oscillator circuit. This circuit can be built with three 74LS04 inverters. The system operates at the frequency of the oscillator.

Q: *What is the purpose of the processor's reset input?*

A: The reset input allows the processor's program counter to be forced to location 0000, where a start-up program is stored.

Q: *What kinds of buses are found in a microcomputer system?*

A: There are three different types: (1) buses with one transmitter and several receivers (the address bus); (2) buses with one receiver and many transmitters (the READY or WAIT input); and (3) buses with many transmitters and receivers (the data bus).

Q: *What is meant by the noise immunity of a logic circuit?*

A: The noise immunity is the amount a signal can pulse high or low and still be properly interpreted by the receiver. Typical values are 0.4 V for TTL and 1.0 V for CMOS.

Q: *When are bus buffers required?*

A: Bus buffers are required whenever the receiver loading exceeds the drive capabilities of the transmitter or when bus lines are driven off-card through connectors.

Q: *When are open-collector logic gates used?*

A: Open-collector gates are used for processor control functions. In these applications, the bus line is held high via a pull-up resistor. The line is then pulled low to request service.

Q: *How is it possible for several transmitters and receivers to share the same bus?*

A: The transmitters are connected to the bus via tristate gates, and only one such gate is enabled at a time. When disabled, the tristate gate appears to be an open circuit.

Q: *What is the function of a hardware single-step circuit?*

A: This is a circuit that steps through computer instructions one machine cycle at a time. Such a circuit is useful for troubleshooting purposes because valid data is held on the buses after each cycle is completed.

Q: *What is a jump-on-reset circuit?*

A: This is a circuit that allows the processor to jump to any location in memory upon reset. With such a circuit, applications programs can use page 0 for processors that normally reset to location 0.

LAB PROJECTS

4.1. Study the schematic diagram of the microcomputer you are using to support this text and the course in which it is being used. Locate and redraw the following on a separate sheet of paper:
   (a) clock generator (note the crystal frequency)
   (b) reset circuit (look for a power-on-reset circuit)
   (c) address buffers (look for an enable signal)
   (d) bidirectional data bus buffers (look for enable and direction control signals)
   (e) control bus buffers (look for an enable signal)
   (f) single-step circuit

4.2. Use an oscilloscope to observe and measure the system clock signal. Compare the measured value with your predictions from Lab 4.1.

4.3. Set up an open-collector bus circuit like that shown in Fig. 4.33. Calculate a value for the pull-up resistor.
   (a) What is the normal (inactive) state of the bus?
   (b) Make up a truth table in terms of SW1–SW3 and OUT.
   (c) What equivalent logic function does the circuit perform?

4.4. Set up a bidirectional data bus circuit like that shown in Fig. 4.21. Use one 74LS244 for the transmitter and two 74LS74s for the receivers.
   (a) With all transmitters disabled, what is the logic level on the bus?
   (b) Enable one of the transmitters. Note that its data input now controls the bus.
   (c) Send data from one transmitter to one receiver. (Set the data, enable the transmitter, and then clock the flip-flop of the receiver.)
   (d) Why don't the other receivers also store this data?

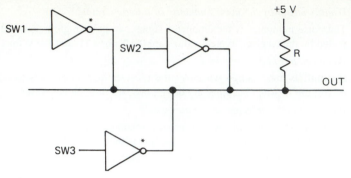

* Open collector outputs (7405, 7406, 7416, 7417, etc.)

Figure 4.33 Circuit for Lab 4.3.

(e) What happens if two transmitters simultaneously try to control the bus? (Don't try it!) What prevents this from happening in a practical computer system?

4.5. If your computer does not have a single-step circuit, try building and interfacing one of those presented in this chapter. You may want to make the circuit a permanent addition to your computer.

4.6. Try running the single-step test program presented in Section 4.6. The 8080/85 mnemonics are as follows:

```
LOOP    MVI   A,0      ;test pattern
        OUT   3FH      ;any port will do
        JMP   LOOP     ;cycle forever
```

With the program running,
(a) observe the $\overline{\text{IOW}}$, IO/$\overline{\text{M}}$, or $\overline{\text{IORQ}}$ line with a logic probe. The line should be pulsing.
(b) switch to single-step mode. Repeatedly press the STEP switch until the I/O write machine cycle has been found.
(c) measure the contents of the data bus. You should see 00.
(d) measure the I/O address on address lines A7–A0. You should see 3FH.
(e) repeat (c) and (d) using a different test pattern and port address.

QUESTIONS AND PROBLEMS

Section 1.1

4.1. If the inverter and AND gate in Fig. 4.1 have equal propagation delays, will the false output still occur?

4.2. If $t_{PD} = 0.5$ μs, what is the maximum clock frequency for the synchronous circuit in Fig. 4.2?

4.3. Refer to Appendices A and B, and determine the minimum number of T states for any one 8080, 8085, or Z-80 instruction. Refer to Fig. 4.3 and describe the CPU activity for each state.

4.4. Suppose you are designing CPU modules for the 8080, 8085, and Z-80. If the clock speed is to be 3 MHz, what crystal frequency should you select for each processor? Of the three CPU chips, which do you expect will require the most supply current?

Section 4.2

4.5. Why does a computer require a RESET input?

*4.6. Suppose the capacitor in Fig. 4.8 becomes open. What would the *symptom* of this problem be?

4.7. What is the purpose of the Schmitt trigger buffers in the Z-80 reset circuit in Fig. 4.8?

Section 4.3

4.8. The 74LS00 can source 400 μA in the high state and sink 8 mA in the low state. Based on this information, how many standard TTL loads (I_{IH} = 40 μA and I_{OL} = 1.6 mA) can this chip drive?

4.9. Calculate the worst-case noise immunity for the interface described in Problem 4.8.

4.10. Refer to Table 4.5, and calculate the maximum number of LSTTL loads a CMOS CD4001 can safely drive without exceeding its drive capabilities.

4.11. Calculate the worst-case noise immunity for the interface described in Problem 4.10.

4.12. What special considerations must be made when one interfaces a TTL transmitter with several CMOS receivers?

4.13. What causes "ringing" on a bus line? How can its effect be minimized?

Section 4.4

4.14. If one unit load (1 UL) equals 40 μA of source current in the high state and 1.6 mA of sink current in the low state, what is the output drive capability of the 74LS244, expressed in unit loads? (Assume that V_{OH} = 2.4 V and V_{OL} = 0.5 V.)

4.15. The circuit in Fig. 4.34 uses tristate transmitters connected to a common bus line. Under what conditions will the bus line be low? Write the logic equation for $\overline{OUT}$ in terms of inputs A, B, and C.

4.16. Standard TTL provides 0.4 V of noise immunity in the high and low states. This value can be improved by using a Schmitt trigger buffer with hysteresis, such as the 74LS244. Assuming a high-level switching threshold of 1.7 V and a low-level threshold of 0.9 V, calculate the noise immunity for a standard TTL gate driving a 74LS244.

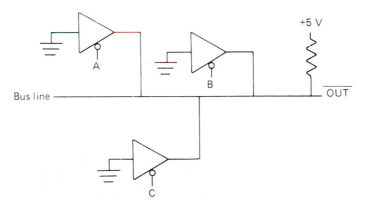

Figure 4.34   Circuit for Problem 4.13.

4.17. Suppose that the noisy ringing signal shown in Fig. 4.35 is applied to the 74LS244 buffer described in Problem 4.16. Sketch the output waveform produced by this gate.

*4.18. What, if anything, is wrong with the microprocessor bus interface shown in Fig. 4.36?

4.19. Redesign the bus interface in Fig. 4.36 using 7405 open-collector gates. Calculate the value of the pull-up resistor required.

4.20. Why do receivers on the data bus, but not on the address bus, need to be *latches*?

4.21. Study the 74LS245 logic diagram in Fig. 4.23, and then complete the following function table:

DIR	ENABLE (G)	Description
0	0	B = input, A = output
0	1	
1	0	
1	1	

Section 4.5

4.22. Refer to the 8080 CPU module in Fig. 4.25. Which of the following is not a function of the 8228?
(a) Bidirectional data bus buffer
(b) Clock generator
(c) Control bus decoder/buffer

4.23. Refer to the 8085 CPU module in Fig. 4.26. (a) Which chip decodes the multiplexed address/data bus? (b) What is the function of IC7? (c) Under what conditions will the MEMWB output be low?

4.24. Refer to the Z-80 CPU module in Fig. 4.27. (a) What is the purpose of IC1a–c? (b) What type of logic gate is IC8? (c) Under what conditions will output $\overline{\text{IORB}}$ be low?

Section 4.6

*4.25. If the output of IC2 in Fig. 4.28 is shorted to a logic 0, the circuit will still appear to work. What change to the test program will be required to detect this fault? How would you locate the bad IC?

*4.26. If $\overline{\text{WR}}$ in Fig. 4.28 is replaced by $\overline{\text{RD}}$, the circuit will not work. Describe the troubleshooting procedure you would use to locate this problem.

4.27. True or false? The single-step circuits in Figs. 4.29–31 cause the microprocessor to operate in "slow motion," one clock cycle at a time.

4.28. In the 8080 single-step circuit in Fig. 4.29, pushing the STEP switch in the SS mode forces RDYIN _____, causing the CPU to execute one machine cycle and the WAIT output to momentarily go _____.

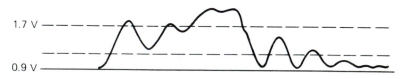

1.7 V

0.9 V

Figure 4.35 Waveform for Problem 4.15.

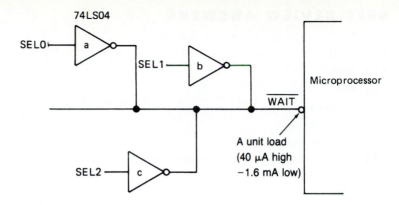

Figure 4.36 Circuit for Problems 4.18–19.

4.29. In the 8085 single-step circuit in Fig. 4.30, the Q output of the flip-flop is continually _____ by the rising edge of ALE. With the mode switch in the SS position, the READY input will be forced _____ at the beginning of each machine cycle.

4.30. In the Z-80 single-step circuit in Fig. 4.31, when S1 is in the SS position, the Q output of IC2a is continually _____ at the beginning of each memory or I/O machine cycle. Pushing the STEP switch momentarily _____ IC2a, allowing the CPU to run one machine cycle.

4.31. Describe the function of the circuit in Fig. 4.37. (*Hint:* Consider the charging and discharging time constant paths.)

4.32. Modify the Z-80 single-step circuit so that it single-steps *instructions* instead of machine cycles.

*4.33. Suppose that the Q output of IC2 in the 8085 single-step circuit in Fig. 4.30 is stuck low. What would the symptom of this problem be? How would you troubleshoot the problem?

*4.34. Suppose that the Q output of IC2b in the Z-80 single-step circuit in Fig. 4.31 is stuck high. What would the symptom of this problem be? How would you troubleshoot the problem?

Section 4.7

4.35. In Fig. 4.32, what is the purpose of IC4?

4.36. Add a switch to the Z-80 jump-on-reset circuit in Fig. 4.32 so that in one position a normal reset to location 0000 occurs and in the other a jump to the hardwired address occurs.

4.37. Modify the jump-on-reset circuit in Fig. 4.32 so that a jump to location D800H is performed upon reset.

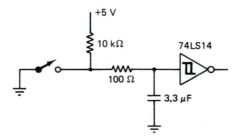

Figure 4.37 Circuit for Problem 4.31.

SELF-REVIEW ANSWERS

4.1.1. faster

4.1.2. 8085

4.2.1. 0000

4.2.2. power-on-reset

4.3.1. noise immunity

4.3.2. decrease, increase

4.4.1. Buffered outputs have greater output current capabilities. Buffered inputs require minimal current from the driver.

4.4.2. open-collector

4.4.3. open circuit

4.5.1. A clock generator and reset circuit are required, as well as address, data, and control bus buffers.

4.6.1. A machine-cycle single-stepper is most useful, as it allows the data on the buses to be traced.

4.6.2. WAIT

4.7.1. A power-on-jump circuit is required to force the CPU to begin program execution at an address other than 0000 (perhaps because this address is used to store program data).

4.7.2. The instruction is hardwired onto the A inputs of IC6 and IC7.

5

BUILDING
THE MICROCOMPUTER, PART 2:
ADDING MEMORY

OUTLINE

OBJECTIVES

After completing this chapter, you should be able to:

- Show that computer memory can be classified on the basis of its application, speed, and capacity.
- Provide examples of main, secondary, and archival computer memory.
- Define the important timing parameters for 8080, 8085, and Z-80 memory read and write cycles.
- Illustrate 8080, 8085, and Z-80 WAIT-state generator circuits that are useful for interfacing slow memory devices.
- Describe typical applications for ROM and RAM memory.

- Show how to draw a memory map for a microcomputer system.
- Compare programmable, one-time programmable, UV-light erasable, and electrically erasable read-only memory technologies.
- Compare static and dynamic RAM technologies on the basis of their bit density, access time, and power consumption.
- Design and verify the timing for RAM and ROM memory interfaces.
- Compare several different address-decoding techniques, including those making use of full, partial, block, ROM, and PAL decoders.
- Describe common DRAM control signals and access time parameters.
- Compare conventional DRAMs with page-mode, extended-data-out, and synchronous DRAM technologies.

OVERVIEW

The concept of a memory unit is essential to the stored-program computer. It is from this unit that the CPU fetches instructions directing it in some task. But within a particular computer system, there may be several types of memories, each with its own ranking, or *hierarchy*.

Most important is the *main* or *prime* memory, which interfaces directly with the CPU over the system three-bus architecture. But there is also *secondary* memory, for mass storage of application programs and data files. And a third type of memory, called *archival storage,* may be present in some systems for backup purposes.

The type memory used in a particular microcomputer system depends on the intended application for that system. Microcontrollers often store all of their program instructions in main memory and require no secondary storage. On the other hand, a microcomputer intended for business applications requires an extensive library of software stored on secondary storage devices such as a floppy disk drive or hard drive. In this chapter we are concerned only with main memory, leaving the topic of secondary storage to Chapter 10.

But even narrowing the discussion to main memory presents us with a myriad of technologies. There are, of course, *RAM* and *ROM*—random access and read-only memory—but there also are *PROM, EPROM, E^2PROM,* and flash memory, to name a few others. And even RAM comes in two "flavors": *static* and *dynamic.* So nothing is simple anymore!

We will begin by letting the performance characteristics of memory define a hierarchy of memory systems. Then we will turn to the microprocessor, to see that it defines the timing for all main memory. And we cannot change that timing, so our next task becomes one of choosing memory devices that will be compatible with the system needs and timing.

Our end goal is the design of a main memory module compatible with the CPU modules designed in Chapter 4. This is accomplished in Sections 5.5 and 5.6.

5.1 MEMORY HIERARCHIES

Introduction

In a computer system, the term *memory* refers to a device or circuit that stores digital information. In most cases, this information represents a computer program—hence the term *stored-program computer.* It is desirable to store other kinds of information as well.

A word processor, for example, creates text files. Storing this information as a computer file allows it to be edited at a later date. If the media used for storage is portable, information can be shared with other users.

In this section, we:

- Show that computer memory can be classified on the basis of its application, speed, and capacity.
- Provide examples of main, secondary, and archival computer memory.

Main Memory

The fetch-and-execute principle mandates a type of memory that interfaces with the microprocessor using the data, address, and control buses. The two qualifications for this *main memory* are as follows:

1. It must be able to communicate with the processor at the system frequency. This means that a 6-MHz processor will require faster memory devices than will a 1-MHz processor.
2. Each cell in the memory must be randomly accessible via its own unique address.

Main memory is *executable* memory. It must be capable of keeping up with the microprocessor. This means that main memory must supply data "instantly" when its address appears on the bus and must allow random storage of variables when needed.

Today, main memory is built almost exclusively with semiconductor technology. In fact, one can measure the state of the art in semiconductor processing by observing the storage capacities of currently available memory parts. Table 5.1 highlights the developments to date.

Secondary Storage

But most computer systems will require more than main memory. Let's see why. A typical microcomputer used for data processing will require several high-level languages and application programs. Examples might be a 16K BASIC interpreter or compiler, a 35K word processor, a 24K database management program, a 6K editor, and numerous application programs and data files from 1K to 40K bytes in length. It soon becomes apparent that all of these programs and languages cannot fit in main memory at once.*

In fact, it is not uncommon for large programs to exceed 64K bytes in length. These programs can be used only by loading smaller portions at a time into memory. For these reasons, there is a need for a secondary storage medium with the following attributes:

1. It must provide relatively fast access; an application program should load in 1 to 30 s.
2. Access can be random or sequential.
3. The storage medium must be portable, so that programs and data files can be transported between machines or stored for safekeeping.
4. It must be nonvolatile.

---

*Assuming an 8-bit processor with a 64K memory.

TABLE 5.1 Important Dates in Semiconductor Memory Technology

Date	Part no.	Organization	Description
1968	1101	256 × 1	Static RAM
1970	1103	1K × 1	Dynamic RAM
1972	2102	1K × 1	Static RAM
1973	4027	4K × 1	Dynamic RAM
1976	4116	16K × 1	Dynamic RAM
1977	2114	1K × 4	Static RAM
1981	4164	64K × 1	Dynamic RAM
1984	41256	256K × 1	Dynamic RAM
1987	511000	1M × 1	Dynamic RAM
1990	514000	4M × 1	Dynamic RAM
1992	TMS417400	4M × 4	Dynamic RAM
1994	ATT7C1024	128K × 8	Static RAM
1995	TMS464800	8M × 8	Dynamic RAM
1996	TMS626802	1M × 8 × 2 banks	Synchronous Dynamic RAM
1998	MT48LC32M4A2TG	32M × 4	Synchronous Dynamic RAM
1999	Micron	64M × 4	Synchronous Dynamic RAM

A typical secondary storage device is the *floppy disk drive*. Data is transferred to main memory from a floppy disk at rates as high as 500,000 bits per second. This means that a 24K applications program could load in less than 1 s.

The data on a floppy disk is stored in sectors, with 512 bytes per sector. Data from a floppy disk is read by locating the appropriate sectors. Data bytes within a given sector must be searched sequentially, meaning that the access is not truly random.

Floppy disks are made from a Mylar base and coated with a magnetic compound. Logic 1's and 0's are stored on the disk as flux transitions when current through the disk drive's read/write head is reversed. This makes floppy disks *nonvolatile* (the contents are not lost when the disk is removed from the disk drive) and easily transportable.

The main disadvantage of the floppy disk is the limited amount of storage available on one diskette. This amount can range from 360K bytes to 2.88 MB in some double-sided drives. Although it sounds like a lot of storage capacity, computer programmers have been known to "eat" that much memory for breakfast!*

For truly large amounts of storage, *hard-disk* technology must be employed. Hard disks are available with capacities varying from several hundred to several thousand megabytes. Once considered a luxury, hard drives come installed on nearly all microcomputers today.

Archival Storage

Just like floppy disks, hard disks are used for secondary storage, but they are less portable. This necessitates a third type of memory in the hierarchy, called *archival storage*. The important properties of archival storage are as follows:

1. It must be nonvolatile.
2. It is accessed infrequently.

_____

*Zip drives provide 100MB of storage using removeable magnetic cartridges similar to floppy disks.

TABLE 5.2 Microcomputer Memory Hierarchies

Type of memory	Speed (access time/byte)	Capacity (bytes)	Example
Main	< 0.1 μs	1K to 256 M	Semiconductor RAM
Secondary	< 1 μs	100K to 20G	Hard drive
Archival	< 100 μs	1 M to 100 G	Magnetic tape

3. High speed and random access are not essential.
4. It must be portable.

Magnetic tape is the most common medium used for archival storage. Low-cost (analog) devices can store 500 MB to 2 GB of information using 1/4″ tape cartridges. Data rates are typically under 1 MB/minute. More expensive (digital audiotape, or DAT) devices can store tens of gigabytes (1000 MB) and provide speeds in excess of 600 MB/minute.

Archival storage is used for making backup copies of important data files that are infrequently used. It provides protection against loss of data due to operator error or system "crashes."

Table 5.2 summarizes the three major memory hierarchies. The remainder of the chapter deals with main memory. Chapter 10 considers secondary storage techniques in more detail.

SELF-REVIEW 5.1

5.1.1 Memory that interfaces directly to the address, control, and data buses of the microprocessor is called _____ memory.

5.1.2 List two examples of common secondary storage devices.

5.1.3 A tape drive is an example of a(n) _____ storage device.

5.2 THE MICROPROCESSOR DEFINES THE MEMORY TIMING

Introduction

At first glance, interfacing main memory to a microprocessor can seem quite complex. There are read cycle times, chip-select access times, output enable access times, write cycle times, and numerous setup and hold times.

Naturally, these timing specifications should be carefully studied. However, if we view the microprocessor as the source of the timing signals, there is little we can do other than to verify that a certain memory chip will or will not meet the timing specifications for a particular processor.

Certainly, we cannot change the sequence of events that occur on the three buses during a memory read or write cycle. At best, we can slow the processor down by adding wait states.

In this section, we:

- Define the important timing parameters for 8080, 8085, and Z-80 memory read and write cycles.
- Illustrate 8080, 8085, and Z-80 WAIT-state generator circuits that are useful for interfacing slow memory devices.

Memory-Read-Cycle Timing

Figure 5.1 is a sort of *generic* memory-read-cycle timing diagram. It shows the sequence of events on a microprocessor's address, data, and control buses when a memory read machine cycle is performed.

For clarity, the address bus is shown as two parallel lines. This should be interpreted as meaning that some of the address lines are high and others are low. When the lines cross, a new address is output by the processor. The actual address is not important for this discussion.

A similar drafting convention is used for the data bus. Because the data on the bus may not always be valid, hash lines are used to indicate unknown or invalid data.

The memory cycle begins with the output of a memory address on A0 through A15. This is followed by the $\overline{\text{MEMR}}$ line going low, indicating a memory read machine cycle. The microprocessor now turns its internal data bus around so that it is ready to receive data.

At this point, it is up to the memory to place valid data on the data bus before the rising edge of $\overline{\text{MEMR}}$. When $\overline{\text{MEMR}}$ does go high, the contents of the data bus will be gated into the microprocessor, and the memory read cycle will have ended.

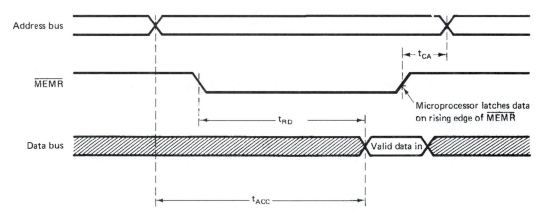

Figure 5.1 Typical memory read cycle for a microprocessor. The memory must respond with valid data t_{ACC} seconds after the memory address is placed on the bus by the processor.

There are three major time periods of importance in this read cycle:

t_{RD}: $\overline{MEMR}$ to valid data. This is the maximum amount of time after $\overline{MEMR}$ goes low that valid data can be placed on the bus by the memory. If t_{RD} is exceeded, the microprocessor may not be able to latch the data byte before $\overline{MEMR}$ goes high at the end of the cycle.

t_{ACC}: address access time. This is the maximum amount of time the memory has to decode the address and place the selected data byte on the data bus. If the memory requires more time than t_{ACC}, WAIT states will be required.

t_{CA}: $\overline{MEMR}$ to new address. This is the minimum amount of time after $\overline{MEMR}$ goes high before a new address will appear on the bus. t_{CA} does not have to be met by the memory, but ensures that $\overline{MEMR}$ will be high when a new address is output by the processor. If this were not done, it would be possible for one memory device to be putting new data onto the bus while the previous memory device was still outputting its data. This could result in bus contention (two transmitters driving the same bus line).

Table 5.3 indicates values for these three times for the 8080A, the 8085AH, and the Z840004 (4 MHz Z-80) microprocessors. These data are obtained from the data sheets in Appendix C. The terms in the equations represent terminology used in the data sheets.

Note that the Z-80 timing specifications shown in the table are for an op-code fetch machine cycle. When the Z-80 performs a general memory read (not an op-code fetch), an additional half clock period is allotted.

Memory-Write-Cycle Timing

Figure 5.2 illustrates the sequence of events during a memory write cycle. The same nomenclature is used as in the memory-read-cycle diagram.

The cycle begins with the output of an address on A0 through A15 by the microprocessor. In order to give the memory a *data write setup time,* valid data is output on D0 through D7 early in the machine cycle. The $\overline{MEMW}$ line then goes low, identifying the memory write cycle.

The memory now has until the rising edge of $\overline{MEMW}$ to latch the data. After this time, the contents of the data bus will become undefined. There are two major periods during this memory write cycle:

t_{DW}: data valid to end of write. This is the minimum amount of time that valid data will be held on the bus before $\overline{MEMW}$ goes high. t_{DW} can be thought of as a *setup time* for the memory. If the memory requires more than that amount of time, valid data may not be properly written.

t_{AW}: address valid to end of write. This is the minimum amount of time that a valid address will be held on the bus before $\overline{MEMW}$ goes high. t_{AW} corresponds to the amount of time that the memory chip has to decode the address and write the data byte into the selected cell.

Table 5.4 lists times for these specifications for the 8080A, 8085AH, and Z840004 microprocessors. The data is obtained from the data sheet in Appendix C. Again, the terms used in the equations refer to specifications mentioned on the particular data sheets.

TABLE 5.3 Memory Read Timing Specifications for the 8080A, 8085AH, and Z840004 Microprocessors

Microprocessor	t_{RD} (max)	Equation used	t_{ACC} (max)	Equation used	t_{CA} (min)	Equation used
8080A* (2 MHz)	464 ns	$2\,t_{CY} - t_{DSS} - t_{DC} - t_{DS2}$	650 ns	$2\,t_{CY} - t_{DA} - t_{DS2}$	330 ns	$t_{CY} - t_{DF} - t_{RR} + t_{DA}$
8085 AH (3 MHz)	300 ns	t_{RD}	575 ns	t_{AD}	120 ns	t_{CA}
Z840004 (4 MHz)	195 ns	$t_3 + t_1 - t_{13} - t_{15}$	325 ns	$2\,t_{CY} - t_5 - t_{15} - t_6$	25 ns	$t_6 - t_{14}$

*Numbers obtained from the 8080A, 8224, and 8228 data sheets.

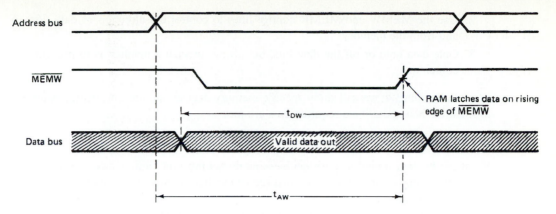

Figure 5.2 Typical memory write cycle for a microprocessor. The memory must latch the data word within t_{AW} seconds after its address is output by the microprocessor.

(*Note:* The data in Tables 5.3 and 5.4 do not include time delays lost in buffers and decoders. This could easily account for another 100 to 150 ns and should be taken into account when comparing the specifications with a particular memory device. (See Section 5.5.)

Comparing t_{AW} in Table 5.4 with t_{ACC} in Table 5.3 reveals that the memory read timing is the most critical. For this reason, memory devices are usually characterized by their t_{ACC} specification—the address access time.

Memory Interfacing Requirements

The task of connecting a particular memory device to a microprocessor is called *memory interfacing.* From the timing diagrams presented in Figs. 5.1 and 5.2, we can define three general requirements:

1. Build a circuit that examines the address bus and outputs a pulse when the address is intended for the particular memory device. This circuit is called an *address decoder.*

TABLE 5.4 Memory Write Timing Specifications for the 8080A, 8085AH, and Z-80A Microprocessors

Microprocessor	t_{DW} (min)	Equation used	t_{AW} (min)	Equation used
8080A* (2 MHz)	656 ns	$2t_{CY} - t_{D3} - t_{DD} + t_{DC} + t_{WR}$	1176 ns	$3\,t_{CY} - t_{D3} - t_{DA} + t_{DC} + t_{WR}$
8085AH (3 MHz)	420 ns	t_{DW}	670 ns	$t_{AC} + t_{CC}$
Z-80A (4 MHz)	265 ns	$2\,t_{CY} - t_{53} - t_{12}$	500 ns	$t_2 + t_4 + 2\,t_{CY} + t_{32} - t_6$

*Numbers obtained from the 8080A, 8224, and 8228 data sheets.

2. Use the $\overline{\text{MEMW}}$ and $\overline{\text{MEMR}}$ control lines to control the direction of data flow to and from the memory.

3. Gate data onto or off the data bus, but always in such a manner as to prevent bus contention.

In Section 5.4, we will study specific memory devices and present several examples to illustrate how these three requirements are met.

Interfacing Slow Memory

What can be done about memory devices that do not meet the timing specifications listed in the preceding section? First, we must recognize that the memory cannot be "too fast" for the microprocessor—only too slow.

Usually, the speed of a memory is measured by considering its address access time (or simply, access time). Thus, a Z-80A microprocessor will give a memory device 325 ns of access time (ignoring buffer propagation delays). A memory device with a 500-ns access time will be too slow, meaning that it will not have enough time to decode the memory address and gate the proper data byte onto the data bus.

Nothing can be done to speed up the memory device—except to buy faster parts—but the microprocessor can be slowed down. Two methods are possible. In the first, the system clock can be set to a lower frequency. However, this penalizes the entire system because of one slow memory device.

A better solution is to have the slow memory device request a *WAIT* state (or states). This can be done by activating the processor's $\overline{\text{WAIT}}$ or READY input line. Recalling the single-step circuits in Chapter 4, we see that the 8080, 8085, and Z-80 all examine this input during T2 of each machine cycle. If the input is found low, the processor enters an idle state, but holds valid data on its address, data, and control buses. This idle state will persist until the READY or $\overline{\text{WAIT}}$ input is found high one or more clock periods later. In that way, an integral number of clock periods can be added to the access time provided the memory by the microprocessor.

Figure 5.3 is a simple *brute-force* WAIT-state generator for the 8080. It adds one WAIT state to all machine cycles (memory read or write and I/O read or write), regardless of the memory device selected. A similar circuit for the 8085 is shown in Fig. 5.4.

A WAIT-state generator for the Z-80 is shown in Fig. 5.5. The signal VALID ADR is presumed to go low whenever the slow memory device is accessed. As we will see, this

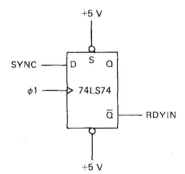

Figure 5.3 8080 WAIT-state generator. One clock period is added to all machine cycles.

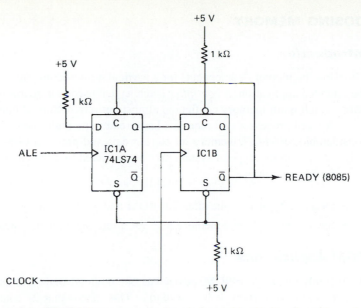

Figure 5.4 8085 WAIT-state generator. One clock period is added to all machine cycles.

signal can be derived from an address decoder. In this way, WAIT states are requested only when the slow memory device is selected. (See Problem 5.11 for an analysis of the timing of such a circuit.)

SELF-REVIEW 5.2

5.2.1 The length of time required by a memory chip to decode a memory address and output valid data is called the _____ _____ time.

5.2.2 To accommodate slow memory parts, the microprocessor can be slowed down by adding _____ states.

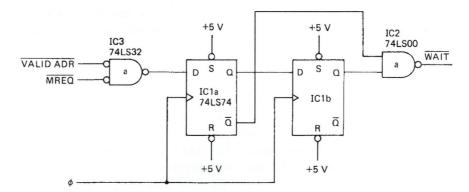

Figure 5.5 Z-80 WAIT-state generator. WAIT states will be generated only for the slow memory device.

5.3 CHOOSING MEMORY

Introduction

Choosing the memory components for a particular microcomputer system will depend on the intended application. A *controller* (such as that used in a microwave oven) will require only a small main memory configured almost entirely with read-only memory devices.

A word processor will require a large read/write main memory for storing text and considerable secondary memory for storing data and program files. The amount of read-only memory in this type of system may be restricted to a bootstrap loader.

In this section, we:

- Describe typical applications for ROM and RAM memory.
- Show how to draw a memory map for a microcomputer system.

ROM Applications

A read-only memory, or ROM, device has one main attribute that makes it very useful in a microcomputer system: It is *nonvolatile*. This means that its contents will not be lost when power is removed from the device.

ROMs are used in microcomputers to store bootstrap loader programs (see Section 4.2), software for dedicated controllers (e.g., in the microwave oven), and application programs in turnkey systems (a BASIC interpreter or a word processor program can be stored in one or two ROMs, for example).

The advantage of using ROM memory is that it is instantly available when power is applied. This immediate availability allows the operator to simply *turn the key* and begin using the application program. Thus, ROM-based microcomputers can appear to be appliances rather than computers.

The disadvantage of a ROM is that it occupies memory space that cannot be written into. This may not be a problem in the dedicated controller, but can take away valuable main memory from a word processor or other data-processing system.

Another disadvantage is that ROMs are not easily programmed. Although custom devices can be programmed at the factory, doing so is practical only with large volumes (many thousands of units). Field-programmable devices must be programmed one at a time and must be individually removed from the circuit board—a slow and costly process.*

RAM Applications

Read/write memories are commonly referred to as random-access memories, or RAMs. Of course, ROMs are also random-access memories, so the acronym is not really correct. Nevertheless, it has become common practice to refer to read/write memory as RAM—I suppose it would be difficult to pronounce RWM!

The most important property of a RAM is that it is *programmable*. Application programs can be quickly loaded into RAM from a disk or tape and then executed by the mi-

---

*E^2PROM and flash memory devices can be programmed onboard. Special software is required, however. These devices are covered in the next section.

croprocessor. RAM is also used for storing temporary data such as BASIC program variables, the system stack, and disk drive directories.

The amount of RAM a particular microcomputer system has available dictates the maximum size of an application program. Most microcomputer owners are familiar with the *OM* error—out of memory!

The single most important limitation of RAM is that it is *volatile:* Turn the power off and all information is lost. It is this property of RAM that necessitates some form of secondary storage in most microcomputer systems.

The Memory Map

Usually, a microcomputer system will have a mix of ROM and RAM. For example, there might be 16K of ROM, and 12K of RAM, and the rest of the memory space may be left unimplemented or open. In developing software for such a system, it is convenient (and perhaps mandatory) to know exactly where in the memory space of the processor these RAM and ROM chips are located. This is the purpose of the *memory map*.

Example 5.1

A certain microcomputer has the following memory specifications:

1. 2716 2K ROM at address 0
2. 2732 4K ROM at address F000H
3. Eight HM6116 2K RAMs immediately following the 2716 in memory space

Draw a memory map for this computer.

Solution. In Chapter 1 we divided the 16-bit memory address into a *high-order,* or page, address and a *low-order,* or line, address. (See Fig. 1.14.) Keeping this analogy in mind, we can think of the high-order byte as a page counter. For a 2K memory, there are eight 256-byte pages.

The 2716 ROM in this example will extend from location 0000 to location 07FFH. This is eight full pages, with the ninth page beginning at address 0800H. In a similar manner, the HM6116 RAM addresses can be found. These are shown in Fig. 5.6.

The 2732 is a 4K-byte ROM and thus occupies sixteen 256-byte pages. This corresponds to the range 0000 to 0FFFH (page 0 through page 15), with address 1000H marking the beginning of the second 4K block. Figure 1.14(b) shows a memory map marked in 4K-block segments. In the current example, the 2732 will occupy 16 pages of memory, from F000H to FFFFH.

Note that most of the memory space is still left open.

SELF-REVIEW 5.3

5.3.1 List several applications for read-only memory.

5.3.2 Explain the terms *volatile memory* and *nonvolatile memory.*

5.3.3 An 8KB RAM chip is interfaced to a computer beginning at address 1000H. What is the address of the last byte in this memory chip?

5.3.4 A drawing showing the specific range of memory addresses associated with each of the memory devices in a computer is called a _____ _____.

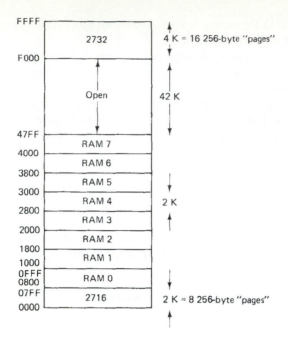

FFFF	
	2732
F000	
	Open
47FF	
4000	RAM 7
3800	RAM 6
3000	RAM 5
2800	RAM 4
2000	RAM 3
1800	RAM 2
1000	RAM 1
0FFF	
0800	RAM 0
07FF	
0000	2716

4 K = 16 256-byte "pages"

42 K

2 K

2 K = 8 256-byte "pages"

Figure 5.6 Memory map for Example 5.1.

5.4 RAM AND ROM TECHNOLOGIES

Introduction

If you could build the ideal memory chip, what characteristics would it have? The *access time*—the time required to read or write data to the chip—would be very short (near 0 ns). The data, once written, would never be lost, even if power were interrupted (i.e., the part would be *nonvolatile*). The chip itself would be very *dense,* requiring only a small amount of printed circuit board space. And finally, *power consumption* would be minuscule to minimize the current drain on the system power supply or battery.

In this section, we examine several different main memory technologies. Each meets some of the preceding criteria, but falls short in others. ROMs, for example, are nonvolatile, but cannot be easily written to. Static RAMs (SRAMs) can be read from or written to and have very short access times, but lose their data when power is turned off. Dynamic RAMs (DRAMs) provide very high bit densities, but are relatively slow and also volatile. Flash memory comes the closest to our ideal, as it is nonvolatile, has relatively high bit densities, and has (memory read) access times comparable to that of DRAMs. However, single bytes cannot be written; instead, the entire chip (or a subset of it) must first be erased and then the new data block written.

In this section, we:

- Compare programmable, one-time programmable, UV-light erasable, and electrically erasable read-only memory technologies.
- Compare static and dynamic RAM technologies on the basis of their bit density, access time, and power consumption.

Mask-Programmable ROMs

It is possible to view a ROM as a device with n inputs and m outputs. For each of the 2^n input combinations, there is one output word of m bits. This relationship is shown in Fig. 5.7.

A ROM is made up of an address decoder, a programmable memory array, and a set of output buffers. In Fig. 5.7, $n = 4$ and $m = 5$. When a 4-bit address is applied to the ROM, one of the 16 row lines will go low. A diode connected between a row line and a column line will program that output bit low (via the conducting diode). The absence of a diode will program a logic 1 (via the column pull-up resistors).

In essence, a ROM is nothing more than a *truth table generator,* providing one *m*-bit output word for each possible input combination. Because of this feature, ROMs can be used to replace combinational logic networks.

A mask-programmable ROM is a ROM in which the diode connections are programmed at the factory according to a truth table supplied by the user. In this way, the manufacturer can sell the same ROM chip to many different customers, altering only the mask that defines the diode connections.

The economics of integrated-circuit manufacture are such that it would be impractical to make only one ROM chip. The integrated-circuit dies are grouped together on a wafer containing several hundred potential ROM chips. Because there is no guarantee that a particular wafer will be found to be good when tested, several wafers must be manufactured. For this reason, mask-programmable ROMs are limited to production runs of several thousand parts. Needless to say, it is imperative that the truth table supplied to the manufacturer be accurate!

Field-Programmable ROMs

There are several types of ROMs that can be programmed by the original equipment manufacturer (OEM) or end user. These devices are referred to as *programmable read-only memories,* or PROMs.

One type of PROM uses a low-current fusible link in series with each diode in the array. (See Fig. 5.8.) By applying a current pulse to the desired location, the fuse can be melted and a logic 1 permanently programmed. Of course, once a fuse has been "blown," it cannot be altered. Fusible-link PROMs are therefore referred to as *one-time programmables* or OTPs.

UV-light erasable PROMs (EPROMs).   A more versatile—but more expensive—type of PROM is the UV-EPROM. This device can be programmed, erased, and reprogrammed many times over by the user. EPROMs use a floating-gate avalanche-injection MOS (FAMOS) transistor cell to store charge. (See Fig. 5.9(a).) Applying a special programming voltage V_{pp} to the chip causes a high electric field to be developed in the channel region of the transistor. This in turn causes electrons to jump the silicon dioxide barrier between the channel region and the floating gate.

During programming, the select gate is given a positive bias, which helps attract these electrons to the floating-gate electrode. Because the floating gate is surrounded by silicon dioxide (an excellent insulator), the injected charge is effectively trapped. The storage period is projected to exceed 20 years.

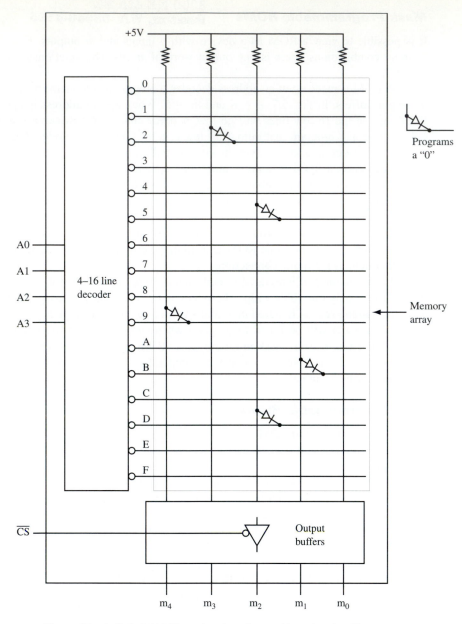

Figure 5.7 A diode ROM illustrating the n-input address decoder, $2^n \times m$ memory array, and m output buffers. (From J. Uffenbeck, *Microcomputers and Microprocessors: The 8080, 8085, and Z-80*. Prentice Hall, Englewood Cliffs, N.J., 1991.)

Cells with trapped charge cause the transistor to be biased on, whereas those cells without trapped charge are biased off. Blank EPROMs have no trapped charge, and each cell stores a logic 1. The EPROM can be erased by subjecting each gate to ultraviolet (UV) light with a wavelength of 2537 angstroms. The electrons on the floating gate ab-

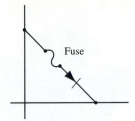

Figure 5.8 OTP ROMs use titanium tungsten (TiW) fuses that can be selectively "blown" using a special programmer.

sorb photons from the UV-light source and acquire enough energy to reverse the programming process and return to the substrate.

EPROMs are placed in special ceramic packages with quartz windows to allow erasure. Commercial erasers are available that will erase several EPROMs at once in 15 to 20 minutes. In practice, the EPROM window should be covered with an opaque label, because normal room fluorescent lighting could erase the device. (Intel reports that approximately three years of exposure to fluorescent lighting or one week of direct sunlight would be required.)

UV EPROMs are programmed by wiring their V_{pp} programming pin to $+13$ V. The data to be written is then applied to the data-out lines, the desired address is applied to the address

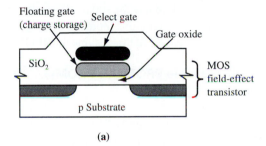

(a)

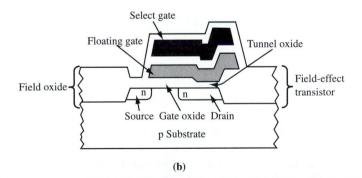

(b)

Figure 5.9 (a) Basic UV EPROM cell structure. A logic 0 is stored by trapping charge on the floating-gate electrode. (b) The E^2PROM has a thin tunnel oxide covering the drain diffusion of the MOS transistor. Electrons are able to "tunnel" through this thin oxide to or from the floating gate. In this way, programming and erasure are both done electrically. (Courtesy of Intel Corporation.)

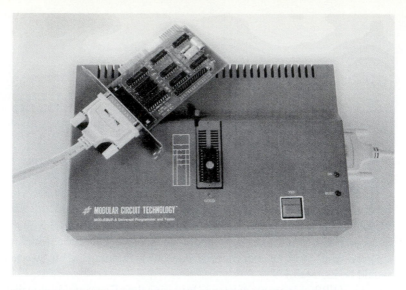

Figure 5.10 EPROM programmer consisting of a PC interface card and programming module.

lines, and the pin is pulsed low for 100 μs. Typically, all this is accomplished using a PC, an interface card, and a programming module. (See Fig. 5.10.) Proprietary software is then used to program the selected EPROM. A typical EPROM can be programmed in 2–5 s.

Electrically erasable PROMs (E^2PROMs). The UV EPROM has a number of disadvantages:

1. The device must be removed from the circuit board in order to be erased.
2. Byte erasure is not possible—all cells are erased when they are exposed to UV light.
3. The quartz window package is expensive.

Because of these problems, much research has been devoted to developing an electrically erasable nonvolatile memory device. Two different technologies have emerged: electrically erasable PROMs (or E^2PROMs) and flash memory. Both devices can be programmed and erased without removing the chip from its socket. In addition, byte and bulk erasure modes are possible.

Figure 5.9(b) shows the difference between the FAMOS cell and the E^2PROM cell. As with the FAMOS cell, a floating gate and select gate are used in the E^2PROM cell. However, a very thin tunnel oxide is provided over the drain diffusion of the MOS transistor. With a positive voltage applied to the select gate, electrons are attracted to the floating gate. Applying a positive voltage to the drain terminal discharges (erases) the cell.

Because the gate oxide over the drain is so thin, the process is controlled by a tunneling phenomenon instead of avalanche injection. Tunneling has the advantage that a large amount of charge can be injected during the write cycle but only a small amount of charge is lost during a read cycle. Data retention is said to be greater than 10 years.

Unfortunately, each read and write cycle causes a small amount of charge to be trapped in the gate oxide. Eventually, the E^2PROM will not be able to be reprogrammed. Still, its lifetime is between 10,000 and 1,000,000 read/write cycles.

E^2PROM read access times are comparable to those of present EPROM chips, but write times are slow (typically, 25 ms) compared with those of conventional RAM devices. For this reason, WAIT states are required for all write cycles.

Flash memory. In recent years, E^2PROMs, with their complex cell structures, have fallen out of favor and been replaced by *flash memory*. As with E^2PROMs, flash memory parts can be electrically erased and reprogrammed without removing the chip from the circuit board. Unlike the situation with E^2PROMs, however, the entire chip (or a sub-block) must be erased at one time; individual byte erasure is not possible.

Despite this limitation, flash memory offers several advantages over E^2PROM. First, the flash memory cell is much simpler to manufacture, thus lowering costs and improving reliability. In addition, very *dense* memory parts can be manufactured. Intel's 28F020, for example, provides 2 million bits of storage organized as 256K bytes. As shown in Fig. 5.11, flash memory devices are available in credit-card-sized Personal Computer Memory Card International Standard (PCMCIA) units that store more than 40 MB of nonvolatile read/write memory. These cards effectively function as *silicon hard disks*.

Figure 5.11 PCMCIA modem and Ethernet adapter.

Figure 5.12 provides a description of the 28F020 256K $\times$ 8 CMOS flash memory. Note the following about this chip:

1. Its typical erase time is 2 s.
2. A single byte can be written in 10 s. Four seconds are required to write to all 256K locations.
3. 100,000 erase/program cycles are allowed.
4. The chip's read access time is 70 ns (comparable to that of high-speed dynamic RAMs, or DRAMs), but slower than that of static RAM).
5. Two power supplies are required: V_{CC} = 5 V and V_{PP} = 12 V. (The latter is required for programming only.)
6. The chip's current consumption is typically 10 mA. (Similar-sized DRAMs typically require 65–90 mA.)
7. Only bulk (entire-chip) erasure is possible.

Flash memory components differ from conventional memory parts in that access is controlled via an onboard command register. Typically, V_{PP} is raised to 12 V, and one, two, or three commands are written to the chip. Table 5.5 provides the details. For example, to read from the memory array, a 00 data byte is written first; subsequent reads then occur from the memory array. Similarly, to erase the chip, two write cycles with the data byte 20H are required.

A recent development in flash memory technology is the introduction of the *boot block* memory device. Figure 5.13 lists key features of the 28F400B. This chip provides 4 million bits of storage, organized as 256K 16-bit words or 512K 8-bit bytes. The memory is further divided into seven memory blocks as follows:

1	Boot block	16 KB
2	8-KB parameter blocks	16 KB
1	Main block	96 KB
3	128-KB main blocks	384 KB
		512 KB

These blocks are located sequentially in memory, but the boot block can be placed at the top or bottom of the memory space. In addition, each block can be individually erased. The boot block can also be locked via a special input pin. When this pin is low, no program or erase cycles are possible within the block.

There are numerous applications for flash memory, each taking advantage of the nonvolatile nature of the part, along with the capability to (occasionally) reprogram some or all memory locations:

1. In Chapter 3, we learned that DOS stores boot-up code and BIOS routines in ROM. With conventional ROM technology, BIOS updates require that the user locate and replace the ROM BIOS chips, a task unsuited to most users. With flash memory, however, BIOS upgrades are accomplished by running a software program that erases the flash ROM and reprograms it with the new code. This is a relatively routine task. In fact, it could even be accomplished remotely by a technician with a modem connection to the target computer.

intel®

28F020
2048K (256K x 8) CMOS FLASH MEMORY

- **Flash Electrical Chip-Erase**
  - **— 2 Second Typical Chip-Erase**

- **Quick-Pulse Programming Algorithm**
  - **— 10 μs Typical Byte-Program**
  - **— 4 Second Chip-Program**

- **100,000 Erase/Program Cycles**

- **12.0V ±5% V$_{PP}$**

- **High-Performance Read**
  - **— 70 ns Maximum Access Time**

- **CMOS Low Power Consumption**
  - **— 10 mA Typical Active Current**
  - **— 50 μA Typical Standby Current**
  - **— 0 Watts Data Retention Power**

- **Integrated Program/Erase Stop Timer**

- **Command Register Architecture for Microprocessor/Microcontroller Compatible Write Interface**

- **Noise Immunity Features**
  - **— ±10% V$_{CC}$ Tolerance**
  - **— Maximum Latch-Up Immunity through EPI Processing**

- **ETOX Nonvolatile Flash Technology**
  - **— EPROM-Compatible Process Base**
  - **— High-Volume Manufacturing Experience**

- **JEDEC-Standard Pinouts**
  - **— 32-Pin Plastic Dip**
  - **— 32-Lead PLCC**
  - **— 32-Lead TSOP**
  - (See Packaging Spec., Order #231369)

- **Extended Temperature Options**

Intel's 28F020 CMOS flash memory offers the most cost-effective and reliable alternative for read/write random access nonvolatile memory. The 28F020 adds electrical chip-erasure and reprogramming to familiar EPROM technology. Memory contents can be rewritten: in a test socket; in a PROM-programmer socket; on-board during subassembly test; in-system during final test; and in-system after-sale. The 28F020 increases memory flexibility, while contributing to time-and cost-savings.

The 28F020 is a 2048-kilobit nonvolatile memory organized as 262,144 bytes of 8 bits. Intel's 28F020 is offered in 32-pin plastic DIP, 32-lead PLCC, and 32-lead TSOP packages. Pin assignments conform to JEDEC standards for byte-wide EPROMs.

Extended erase and program cycling capability is designed into Intel's ETOX (EPROM Tunnel Oxide) process technology. Advanced oxide processing, an optimized tunneling structure, and lower electric field combine to extend reliable cycling beyond that of traditional EEPROMs. With the 12.0V V$_{PP}$ supply, the 28F020 performs 100,000 erase and program cycles well within the time limits of the Quick-Pulse Programming and Quick-Erase algorithms.

Intel's 28F020 employs advanced CMOS circuitry for systems requiring high-performance access speeds, low power consumption, and immunity to noise. Its 70 nanosecond access time provides no-WAIT-state perform-ance for a wide range of microprocessors and microcontrollers. Maximum standby current of 100 μA trans-lates into power savings when the device is deselected. Finally, the highest degree of latch-up protection is achieved through Intel's unique EPI processing. Prevention of latch-up is provided for stresses up to 100 mA on address and data pins, from −1V to V$_{CC}$ + 1V.

With Intel's ETOX process base, the 28F020 levers years of EPROM experience to yield the highest levels of quality, reliability, and cost-effectiveness.

Figure 5.12 Description of the 28F020 256K × 8 flash memory part. (Courtesy of Intel Corporation.)

TABLE 5.5 Flash Memory Command Definitions (Courtesy of Texas Instruments)

Command	Bus cycles required	First bus cycle			Second bus cycle		
		Operation	Address[1]	Data[2]	Operation	Address[1]	Data[2]
Read Memory	1	Write	X	00H			
Read Intelligent Identifier Codes[3]	3	Write	X	90H	Read	[3]	[3]
Set Up Erase/Erase	2	Write	X	20H	Write	X	20H
Erase Verify	2	Write	EA	A0H	Read	X	EVD
Set Up Program/Program	2	Write	X	40H	Write	PA	PD
Program Verify	2	Write	X	C0H	Read	X	PVD
Reset[4]	2	Write	X	FFH	Write	X	FFH

[1]IA = Identifier address: 00H for manufacturer code, 01H for device code.
EA = Address of memory location to be read during erase verify.
PA = Address of memory location to be programmed.
Addresses are latched on the falling edge of the write-enable pulse.

[2]ID = Data read from location IA during device identification (Mfr = 89H, Device = BDH).
EVD = Data read from location EA during erase verify.
PD = Data to be programmed at location PA. Data is latched on the rising edge of write-enable.
PVD = Data read from location PA during program verify. PA is latched on the Program command.

[3]Following the Read Intelligent ID command, two read operations access manufacturer and device codes.

[4]The second bus cycle must be followed by the desired command register write.

2. Networks have become increasingly popular in recent years, and many PCs today are equipped with Ethernet network interface cards. These cards must be configured with I/O addresses and interrupt numbers. Although this can be accomplished with "jumpers," most cards today use flash memory to allow these settings to be specified via software and then stored by the card.

3. Laser printers typically require cards to support various fonts. With flash memory, users can select the fonts they want and download them to the printer. If a different set of fonts is desired, the old one can be erased and a new set programmed.

4. In the automotive industry, flash ROMs can be used to store "trouble codes" that provide diagnostic information to the mechanic. The nonvolatile nature of the flash memory part allows these codes to be stored for several weeks or months after the actual fault occurs. The codes can then be studied by the technician at the next service interval.

Static RAM

Static RAM, or SRAM, is a type of RAM that uses a flip-flop as its basic storage element. Figure 5.14 shows a typical SRAM memory cell. In this cell, Q1 and Q2 form a cross-coupled flip-flop, with Q3 and Q4 acting as pull-up resistors. Transistors Q5 and Q6 provide access to the cell. To write data into the flip-flop, the row-select line is made active, turning on transistors Q5 and Q6. Now to store a logic 1, the COLUMN line is driven high and COLUMN low. Via Q5, the high level on the COLUMN line is applied to the gate of Q2, turning this transistor on and forcing its drain lead low.

intel®

28F400BX-T/B, 28F004BX-T/B
4 MBIT (256K x16, 512K x8) BOOT BLOCK FLASH
MEMORY FAMILY

- ■ x8/x16 Input/Output Architecture
  - 28F400BX-T, 28F400BX-B
  - For High Performance and High Integration 16-bit and 32-bit CPUs

- ■ x8-only Input/Output Architecture
  - 28F004BX-T, 28F004BX-B
  - For Space Constrained 8-bit Applications

- ■ Optimized High Density Blocked Architecture
  - One 16-KB Protected Boot Block
  - Two 8-KB Parameter Blocks
  - One 96-KB Main Block
  - Three 128-KB Main Blocks
  - Top or Bottom Boot Locations

- ■ Extended Cycling Capability
  - 100,000 Block Erase Cycles

- ■ Automated Word/Byte Write and Block Erase
  - Command User Interface
  - Status Registers
  - Erase Suspend Capability

- ■ SRAM-Compatible Write Interface

- ■ Automatic Power Savings Feature
  - 1 mA Typical I_{CC} Active Current in Static Operation

- ■ Very High-Performance Read
  - 60/80 ns Maximum Access Time
  - 30/40 ns Maximum Output Enable Time

- ■ Low Power Consumption
  - 20 mA Typical x8 Active Read Current
  - 25 mA Typical x16 Active Read Current

- ■ Reset/Deep Power-Down Input
  - 0.2 μA I_{CC} Typical
  - Acts as Reset for Boot Operations

- ■ Extended Temperature Operation
  - −40°C to +85°C

- ■ Write Protection for Boot Block

- ■ Hardware Data Protection Feature
  - Erase/Write Lockout During Power Transitions

- ■ Industry Standard Surface Mount Packaging
  - 28F400BX: JEDEC ROM Compatible
    44-Lead PSOP
    56-Lead TSOP
  - 28F004BX: 40-Lead TSOP

- ■ 12V Word/Byte Write and Block Erase
  - V_{PP} = 12V ±5% Standard
  - V_{PP} = 12V ±10% Option

- ■ ETOX III Flash Technology
  - 5V Read

Figure 5.13 The 28F004B is a boot block flash memory part. Unlike conventional flash memory parts, individual blocks can be erased and reprogrammed. (Courtesy of Intel Corporation.)

Similarly, the low level on $\overline{\text{COLUMN}}$ forces Q1 off, and its drain lead pulls high, reinforcing the high level applied to the gate of Q2. In effect, the cell latches itself into the applied state. Row-select transistors Q5 and Q6 can now be turned off, and the information is retained. To store a logic 0, the process is repeated, but this time the COLUMN input is driven low and $\overline{\text{COLUMN}}$ high.

To read the data stored by the SRAM cell, the row-select line is again made active, but this time the voltage *difference* between the column lines is sensed. A positive

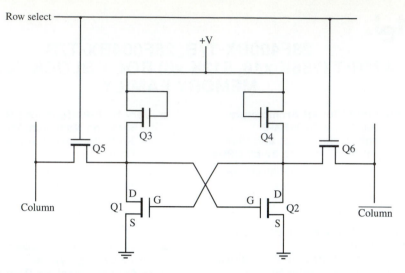

Row select

+V

Q3 Q4

Q5 Q6

Column

D G Q1 G D Q2

S S

Column

Figure 5.14 Basic six-transistor static memory cell. (From J. Uffenbeck, *Microcomputers and Microprocessors: The 8080, 8085, and Z-80*. Prentice Hall, Englewood Cliffs, N.J., 1991.)

voltage indicates that a logic 1 is stored. A negative voltage between these same lines indicates that a logic 0 is stored.

Because of the SRAM's internal latching mechanism, data are retained without the need for any refresh signals. For this reason, the cell is referred to as *static*. However, if power is removed from the cell, the data is lost. Furthermore, when power is reapplied, the state of each flip-flop will be unpredictable.

SRAM applications. To avoid inserting WAIT states, most high-speed microcomputer systems require a *cache* memory subsystem.* These systems are normally designed using SRAMs, because they provide the fastest access times of any of the current memory technologies. The 7C1024-15 SRAM, for example, provides 128K bytes of storage and has an access time of just 15 ns. Four of these chips would allow a 32-bit-wide, 512K-byte cache to be constructed. Most microcomputer system boards have sockets designed to accommodate several different sizes of SRAM chips. In this way, the user can adjust the size of the cache as needed, based on the amount of installed DRAM and cost.

Dynamic RAM

If we assume that one of the goals of main memory technology is to produce a high-bit-density component, a part that requires six transistors per cell may not be the best choice. It is this drawback of static RAM that has led designers to *dynamic* RAM (DRAM) technology.

Figure 5.15 shows the internal structure of a DRAM. The memory cell has been shrunk to a single bit-select transistor and storage capacitor. Each cell in the array is identified by its

---

*Cache memory, a special kind of memory interfaced between the microprocessor and its main memory, is designed to hold information that the processor is likely to require in the near future.

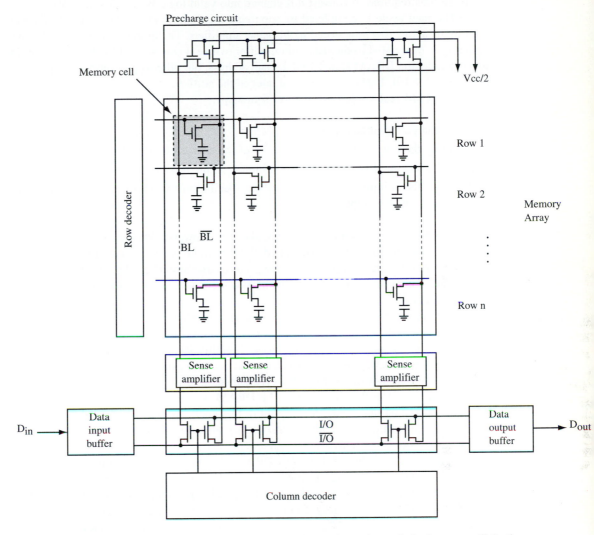

Column 1   Column 2   . . . .   Column n

Precharge circuit

Memory cell

$V_{CC}/2$

Row 1

Row 2

Memory
Array

Row n

Row decoder

$\overline{BL}$

BL

Sense
amplifier

Sense
amplifier

Sense
amplifier

D_{in}

Data
input
buffer

I/O
$\overline{I/O}$

Data
output
buffer

D_{out}

Column decoder

Figure 5.15   Dynamic RAMs use an MOS transistor and capacitor as the basic storage cell. Particular cells are selected via a row and column address.

unique row and column address. A 1-Mb chip for example, might be organized as 1024 rows by 1024 columns.

Data is read from the DRAM by sensing the voltage on the bit cell capacitor. The row address decoder turns on all of the transistors in a given row. The charge on the selected capacitors is then placed on the bit-sense lines (BL and $\overline{BL}$). However, because these capacitors are very tiny, the charge stored is also very tiny. The precharge circuit is used to precharge the bit-sense lines to $V_{CC}/2$ volts. When the row transistors are turned on, this level is either increased (if the capacitor is charged) or decreased (if the capacitor is empty). The amount of change is very small however, typically only 100 mV. Differential amplifiers (sense amplifiers) are thus required to convert this change into valid logic levels (0 V or 5 V).

The read cycle is completed by supplying a column address that is used to select 1 bit in the active row now stored in the sense amplifiers. The output of the selected sense amplifier is then gated to the data output buffer, where it can be read by the processor. In this example, the DRAM stores 1 bit at each address, but other organizations are possible ($\times$ 4, $\times$ 8, $\times$ 16). These are discussed later in the section.

A DRAM read cycle thus requires four steps:

1. Precharge the bit-sense lines.
2. Apply the row address and turn on all of the transistors in that row.
3. Sense and amplify the potential difference on the bit-sense lines.
4. Apply the column address to select the specific bit (or bits) in the selected row to be gated to the output.

DRAM write cycles are similar to read cycles. However, after the bit-sense lines are precharged and the row address is applied, the data to be written is gated through one of the sense amplifiers and allowed to change the charge stored on the selected capacitor. That is, if a 1 is to be written, the charge level is increased, and if a 0 is to be written, the charge level is decreased.

You may be familiar with the DRAM's greatest shortcoming: The storage node is not perfect and will become discharged over a period of time. This necessitates a *refresh* operation—that is, we must sense the charge, amplify it, and then rewrite the data. Depending on the DRAM, a refresh must be carried out once every 1–16 ms per memory cell.

Refresh may not be as difficult to implement as it may at first seem. Referring to Fig. 5.15, note that each time a row in the DRAM is accessed, the precharge circuit restores the charge on that capacitor—and all of the other capacitors in that row. Thus, simply reading (or writing) the contents of memory also refreshes the memory. In Section 5.6, we discuss different DRAM refresh strategies.

Because of their high bit density, DRAMs form the "core" memory for most microcomputer systems. For example, it is not uncommon for a microcomputer to have 16 MB of DRAM main memory, 2 MB of DRAM video memory, and another 2–4 MB of hard-disk DRAM cache memory. To minimize the amount of circuit board space required to support all of these DRAMs, the chips are commonly soldered onto thin circuit boards called *single in-line memory modules,* or SIMMs. (See Fig. 5.16.) Single-byte (30-pin) and 4-byte (72-pin) SIMMs are available. Figure 5.17 shows the pin-outs for an 8M $\times$ 32 (32 MB) 72-pin SIMM. The equivalent schematic is shown in Fig. 5.18.

Many system boards are now designed to accept *dual in-line memory modules* (DIMMs) instead of SIMMs. With a total of 168 pins, DIMMs are 8 bytes wide—twice the width of 72-pin SIMMs.

Memory Organization

The organization of a memory chip refers to the way in which the storage cells are arranged to provide access to external data. For example, a particular chip may have a total of 16 MB of storage that may be accessed externally in several different ways:

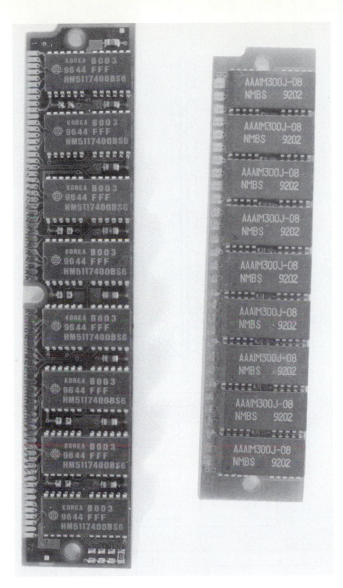

Figure 5.16 High bit density memory arrays are constructed by soldering DRAM chips to small circuit boards. The resulting component is referred to as a SIMM—*single in-line memory module*, 30- and 72-pin SIMMs are popular.

- 16M $\times$ 1 (i.e., 16 M bits)
- 4M $\times$ 4 (i.e., 4 M nibbles)
- 2M $\times$ 8 (i.e., 2 M bytes)
- 1M $\times$ 16 (i.e., 16 M words)

SRAMs and ROMs are typically arranged $\times$ 8, referred to as *byte-wide*. The organization of a memory chip is important because it determines how many chips will be required in a memory interface.

Sec. 5.4   RAM and ROM Technologies

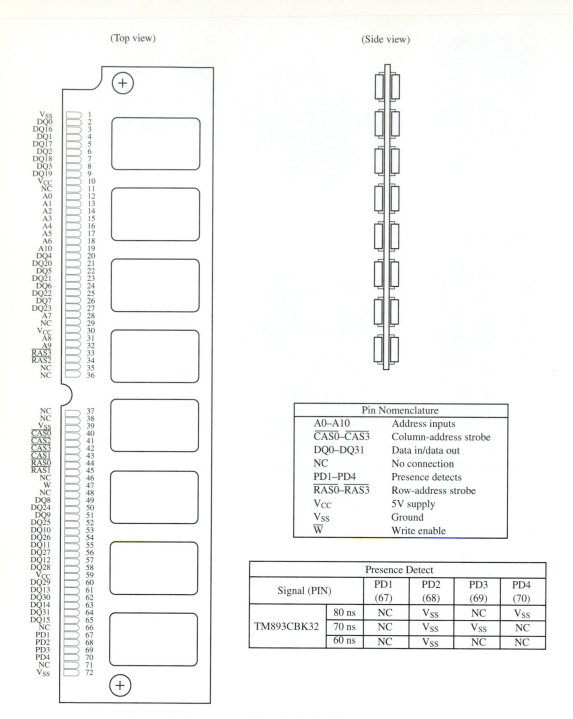

Figure 5.17 Pinouts for an 8M × 32 (32 MB) SIMM. (Courtesy of Texas Instruments.)

Functional block diagram (side 1)

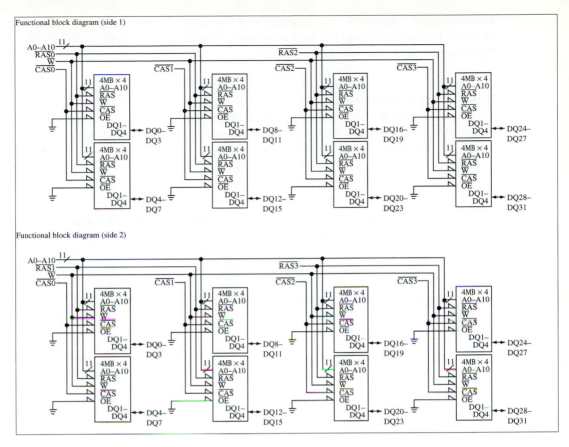

Functional block diagram (side 2)

Figure 5.18 Equivalent circuit for the 32 MB SIMM shown in Figure 7.11. (Courtesy of Texas Instruments.)

Example 5.2

It is desired to design a 32-KB memory board. Calculate the total number of memory chips required if the board is built using the following SRAM parts:

(a) 2114 1K $\times$ 4
(b) 2147 4K $\times$ 1
(c) 6116 2K $\times$ 8
(d) 62256 32K $\times$ 8

Solution

(a) With $\times$ 4 organization, two 2114s will be required per byte and 64 total chips will thus be needed.
(b) With $\times$ 1 organization, eight 2147s will be required per 4K bytes, and thus, 64 chips will again be needed.
(c) One chip supplies 2K bytes, and thus, a total of 16 chips will be needed.
(d) This single chip supplies the full 32K bytes.

Memory part numbers. Interpreting the part number of a memory chip is tricky, because no particular standard has been established. Nevertheless, one can usually identify four components of the part number, namely,

$$\text{WWW XX YYYYY–ZZ.}$$

WWW is the *manufacturer code,* XX identifies the *type* of memory (EPROM, SRAM, DRAM, etc.), YYYYY represents the total *bit storage* of the chip, and ZZ represents the *access time* in nanoseconds. As an example, suppose a certain memory chip has the number MC27256-10. We interpret this number as follows:

- WWW = MC, the code for a Motorola semiconductor
- XX = 27, the code used to identify EPROMs*

---

*The XX code for DRAMs is typically 41 or 51, flash memories use 28, and SRAMs are often indicated by 62 or 7C. Use caution, however; there are many inconsistencies.

TABLE 5.6 Specifications for Common Memory Chips

Part number	Manufacturer	Technology	Total bits	Organization	Access time
TMS4164-100	Texas Instruments	DRAM	64K	64K × 1	100 ns
TMS4464-80	Texas Instruments	DRAM	256K	64K × 4	80 ns
UPD411000-60	NEC	DRAM	1M	1M × 1	60 ns
HY514256P-60	Siemens	DRAM	1M	256K × 4	60 ns
TMS44100-70	Texas Instruments	DRAM	4M	4M × 1	70 ns
TMS417400-60	Texas Instruments	DRAM	16M	4M × 4	60 ns
TMS464800-60	Texas Instruments	DRAM	64M	8M × 8	60 ns
TMM2016-150	Toshiba	SRAM	16K	2K × 8	150 ns
HM6264LP-10	Hitachi	SRAM	64K	8K × 8	100 ns
HM62256LP-12	Hitachi	SRAM	256K	32K × 8	120 ns
HM62832-12	Hitachi	SRAM	256K	32K × 8	12 ns
ATT7C1024-15	AT&T	SRAM	1M	128K × 8	15 ns
TMS27C128-15	Texas Instruments	EPROM	128K	16K × 8	150 ns
TMS27C256-12	Texas Instruments	EPROM	256K	32K × 8	120 ns
TMS27C512-80	Texas Instruments	EPROM	512K	64K × 8	80 ns
27C101-70	Microchip Technology	EPROM	1M	128K × 8	70 ns
TMS27C210A-120	Texas Instruments	EPROM	1M	64K × 16	120 ns
27C201-100	Microchip Technology	EPROM	2M	256K × 8	100 ns
27C401-80	Microchip Technology	EPROM	4M	512K × 8	80 ns
TMS27C240-80	Texas Instruments	EPROM	4M	256K × 16	80 ns
28F256-120	Intel	Flash	256K	32K × 8	120 ns
TMS29F256-170	Texas Instruments	Flash	256K	32K × 8	170 ns
28F010-65	Intel	Flash	1M	128K × 8	65 ns
28F020-70	Intel	Flash	2M	256K × 8	70 ns
29LV040-25PC	Atmel	Flash	4M	512K × 8	250 ns

- YYYY = 256, the total storage capacity of the chip (256K bits)
- ZZ = 10, i.e., the access time is 100 ns

Notice that the part number does not give a hint as to how the chip's 256K bits are organized. However, EPROMs are almost always bytewide, and thus, we surmise that this particular chip provides 32K bytes (32K × 8 = 256K).

One might think that the −10 in the part number indicates 10 ns of access time. However, most manufacturers use only two digits to represent access time; users therefore have to make an *educated guess* as to the actual access time. Because EPROMs are relatively slow, with access times generally 100 ns or more, we conclude that for this chip the correct access time is 100 ns. Table 5.6 gives examples of part numbers for several other common memory chips.

The Universal Site

A number of semiconductor manufacturers have chosen to adopt a standard pin configuration for bytewide memories. This configuration is called the *byte-wide universal memory site*. Figure 5.19 gives details.

The universal memory site can accommodate EPROMs, E^2PROMs, static RAMs, and quasi-static RAMs. Figure 5.20 shows some examples. Note that although the standard is based on a 28-pin package, 24-pin devices such as the 2716 EPROM can be used by plugging the device into the bottom 24 pins.

One of the advantages of this scheme is that developmental software can be debugged in static RAM, where changes are easily made. Once tested, an EPROM can be programmed and plugged into the same socket, but with full confidence that the software has been debugged.

Example 5.3

Show how the universal memory site can be designed to accommodate the 2K 2716 EPROM or the 16K 27128 EPROM.

Solution.   Figure 5.21 is the circuit. The jumpers are shown in the 27128 position. The decoder is necessary to determine the value of the high-order address bits that will enable the EPROM. Notice that the 2716 plugs into the low 24 pins of the socket.

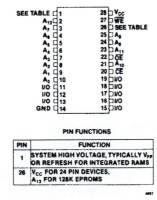

Figure 5.19 Pin configuration for the bytewide universal memory site. (Courtesy of Intel Corporation.)

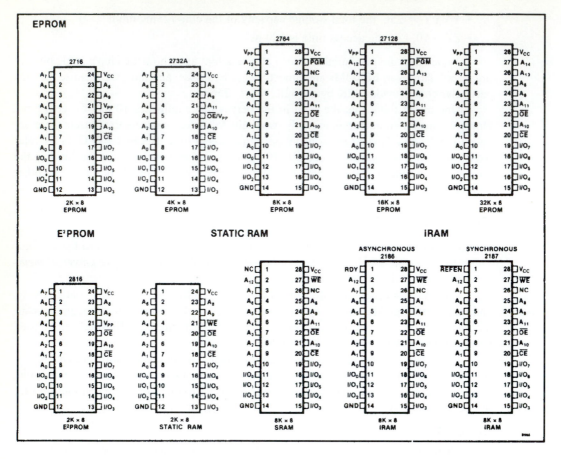

Figure 5.20 Bytewide universal memory site. (Courtesy of Intel Corporation.)

SELF-REVIEW 5.4

5.4.1 The diode ROM in Fig. 5.7 can store _____ words, where each word is _____ bits wide.

5.4.2 Fusible-link PROMs are said to be _____ _____ _____.

5.4.3 Which of the following PROMs can be erased without requiring the chip to be removed from its socket?
 (a) UV-EPROM
 (b) E^{2}PROM
 (c) OTP ROM
 (d) Mask-programmable ROM

5.4.4 _____ memory offers bit densities comparable to that of DRAMs, but is limited to _____ erase/program cycles.

5.4.5 _____ provides the fastest memory access times.

5.4.6 The storage cell for a DRAM is actually a _____.

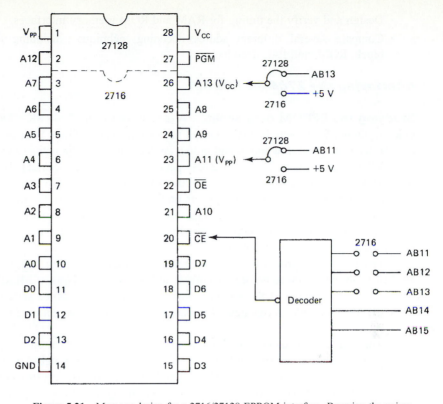

Figure 5.21 Memory design for a 2716/27128 EPROM interface. By using the universal memory site, 2716 designs can be upgraded to the larger 27128 without redesigning the circuit board.

5.4.7 Seventy-two-pin SIMMs are _____ bytes wide.

5.4.8 A certain SRAM stores 1 Mb of data. If this chip is organized × 8, it stores _____ bytes.

5.4.9 A memory chip with part number 4164-10 probably uses _____ technology, stores _____ bits, and has an access time of _____ ns.

5.5 INTERFACING STATIC RAM AND ROM TO THE MICROPROCESSOR

Introduction

Connecting a memory device to the three-bus architecture of a microprocessor is called *memory interfacing.* This process requires a careful consideration of the control signals required by the memory component in order to ensure compatibility with the host microprocessor. In addition, because the timing of the microprocessor cannot be changed (except to add WAIT states), the worst-case time delays of the interface circuitry and the memory device should be summed and verified to be within the specifications of the processor.

In this section, we:

- Design and verify the timing for RAM and ROM memory interfaces.
- Compare several different address-decoding techniques including full, partial, block, ROM, and PAL decoders.

Interfacing the 2764 8K EPROM

Studying the EPROM data sheet. A data sheet for the 2764 8K EPROM is provided in Figure 5.22. Note that two control lines are provided. These lines are called *chip enable* ($\overline{CE}$), an active-low input, and *output enable* ($\overline{OE}$), also an active-low input.

When the $\overline{CE}$ input is high, the 2764 operates in *standby* mode, and power consumption is reduced from 500 mW maximum to 200 mW maximum. The $\overline{CE}$ input should be driven low only when a valid address appears on the address bus from the microprocessor.

The second control input is $\overline{OE}$, and this line enables the internal tristate buffers to place the data word on the output lines. Intel recommends that $\overline{OE}$ be driven by the processor $\overline{MEMR}$ control signal.

From the microprocessor memory read timing diagram in Fig. 5.1, it is clear that $\overline{MEMR}$ is always removed before the current address changes. Thus, if $\overline{MEMR}$ is used to control $\overline{OE}$, the outputs of the memory will be in a high-impedance state (the tristate) when the memory address changes. This feature is a safety precaution used to prevent bus contention.

The task of interfacing the 2764 to any of the three CPU modules presented in Chapter 4 should now be straightforward. Address lines AB0 through AB12 connect directly to the chip, as do data lines DB0 through DB7. The $\overline{MEMR}$ control signal can connect to the $\overline{OE}$ input. These connections are shown in Fig. 5.23(a).

Three address lines, AB13 through AB15, are unused in this scheme. These lines should be *decoded* and used to control the $\overline{CE}$ input. For example, if the decoder requires that AB13 AND AB14 AND AB15 all be high to produce a low output, the EPROM will occupy the memory space from E000H through FFFFH, as shown in Fig. 5.23(b).

Because there are eight combinations of the three address lines AB13 through AB15, there are eight possible slots in the 64K memory space that this chip can occupy. These slots are listed in Fig. 5.23(b).

So what is in the box labeled "Decoder"? It must be a circuit that recognizes one of the eight patterns shown in Fig. 5.23(b) and causes a low-level output when that input appears. For the case AB13 = AB14 = AB15 = 1, the circuit is simply a three-input *NAND* gate, shown in Fig. 5.24(a). By adding inverters, any of the eight patterns can be decoded. Note that a three-input OR gate can also be used as a decoder, as shown in Fig. 5.24(c).

Verifying the timing. Now that we have determined the proper connections for the 2764 interface, we should verify that the timing specifications are compatible with the microprocessor.

Consider first the *address access time,* as defined in Fig. 5.1. This is the amount of time the processor will allow the memory to place valid data on the bus after it has output a memory address. For the 2764, a maximum of 250 ns is required.

Because we are deriving the $\overline{CE}$ signal from the address bus, the time t_{CE} must also be considered. Referring to the data sheet in Appendix D.1, we see that this is also 250 ns maximum.

2764
64K (8K x 8) UV ERASABLE PROM

- ■ **200 ns (2764-2) Maximum Access Time ... HMOS*-E Technology**
- ■ **Compatible with High-Speed 8mHz iAPX 186...Zero WAIT State**
- ■ **Two Line Control**
- ■ **Pin Compatible to 27128 EPROM**

- ■ **int_eligent Programming™ Algorithm**
- ■ **Industry Standard Pinout ... JEDEC Approved**
- ■ **Low Active Current...100mA Max.**
- ■ **±10% V_{CC} Tolerance Available**

The Intel 2764 is a 5V only, 65,536-bit ultraviolet erasable and electrically programmable read-only memory (EPROM). The standard 2764 access time is 250 ns with speed selection available at 200 ns. The access time is compatible with high-performance microprocessors such as Intel's 8 mHz iAPX 186. In these systems, the 2764 allows the microprocessor to operate without the addition of WAIT states. The 2764 is also compatible with the 12 MHz 8051 family.

An important 2764 feature is the separate output control, Output Enable ($\overline{OE}$) from the Chip Enable control ($\overline{CE}$). The $\overline{OE}$ control eliminates bus contention in microprocessor systems. Intel's Application Note AP-72 describes the microprocessor system implementation of the $\overline{OE}$ and $\overline{CE}$ controls on Intel's EPROMs. AP-72 is available from Intel's Literature Department.

The 2764 has a standby mode which reduces power consumption without increasing access time. The maximum active current is 100 mA, while the maximum standby current is only 40 mA. The standby mode is selected by applying a TTL-high signal to the $\overline{CE}$ input.

±10% V_{CC} tolerance is available as an alternative to the standard ±5% V_{CC} tolerance for the 2764. This can allow the system designer more leeway with regard to his power supply requirements and other system parameters.

The 2764 is fabricated with HMOS*-E technology, Intel's high-speed N-channel MOS Silicon Gate Technology.

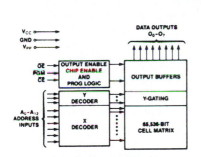

Figure 1. Block Diagram

NOTE: INTEL 'UNIVERSAL SITE'-COMPATIBLE EPROM PIN CONFIGURATIONS ARE SHOWN IN THE BLOCKS ADJACENT TO THE 2764 PINS

Figure 2. Pin Configurations

MODE SELECTION

MODE \ PINS	$\overline{CE}$ (20)	$\overline{OE}$ (22)	$\overline{PGM}$ (27)	A_9 (24)	V_{PP} (1)	V_{CC} (28)	Outputs (11–13, 15–19)
Read	V_{IL}	V_{IL}	V_{IH}	X	V_{CC}	V_{CC}	D_{OUT}
Output Disable	V_{IL}	V_{IH}	V_{IH}	X	V_{CC}	V_{CC}	High Z
Standby	V_{IH}	X	X	X	V_{CC}	V_{CC}	High Z
Program	V_{IL}	V_{IH}	V_{IL}	X	V_{PP}	V_{CC}	D_{IN}
Verify	V_{IL}	V_{IL}	V_{IH}	X	V_{PP}	V_{CC}	D_{OUT}
Program Inhibit	V_{IL}	X	X	X	V_{PP}	V_{CC}	High Z
int_eligent Identifier	V_{IL}	V_{IL}	V_{IH}	V_H	V_{CC}	V_{CC}	Code
int_eligent Programming	V_{IL}	V_{IH}	V_{IL}	X	V_{PP}	V_{CC}	D_{IN}

1. X can be V_{IH} or V_{IL}
2. V_H = 12.0V ± 0.5V

PIN NAMES

A_0-A_{12}	ADDRESSES
$\overline{CE}$	CHIP ENABLE
$\overline{OE}$	OUTPUT ENABLE
O_0-O_7	OUTPUTS
$\overline{PGM}$	PROGRAM
N.C.	NO CONNECT

*HMOS is a patented process of Intel Corporation

Figure 5.22 Specifications for the Intel 2764 8K-byte UV EPROM. (Courtesy of Intel Corporation.)

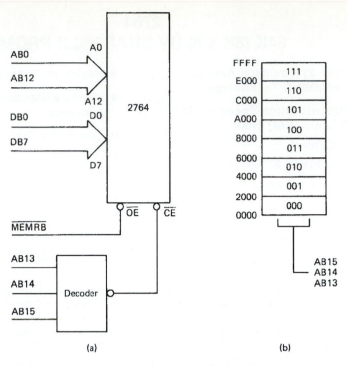

(a)   (b)

Figure 5.23 (a) 2764 EPROM interface to any of the CPU modules presented in Chapter 4; (b) address lines AB13 through AB15 are decoded to select one of eight possible 8K slots in the processor's memory space.

Finally, the time t_{RD} in Fig. 5.1 (memory read to valid data) is considered. This corresponds to the time t_{OE} in the 2764 ac waveforms and is specified as 100 ns maximum in Appendix D.1.

Table 5.7 compares these times with those calculated in Section 5.2 for the 8080A, the 8085AH, and the Z-80A. Be sure that you interpret the numbers correctly. In all cases,

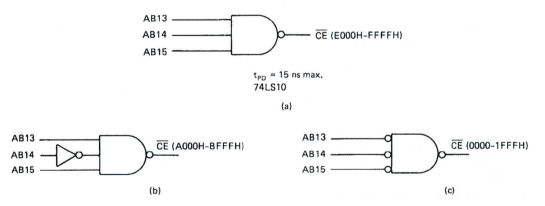

Figure 5.24 A three-input NAND gate (a) and (b) or a three-input OR gate (c) can be used to decode the three address lines in Fig. 5.23(a).

TABLE 5.7 Timing Parameters for the 2764 EPROM Interface in Fig. 5.20

Processor	t_{ACC} (ns)[a]		t_{CE} (ns)[b]		t_{RD} (ns)[c]	
	μP	Memory	μP	Memory	μP	Memory
8080A (2 MHz)	590	250	555	250	404	100
8085AH (3 MHz)	515	250	480	250	218	100
Z-80A (4 MHz)	265	250	230	250	113	100

[a]Microprocessor times have been reduced by 60 ns from those given in Table 5.3. This accounts for the buffer delays, as explained in Fig. 5.25.

[b]See note a. An additional 35 ns has been subtracted from the microprocessor times to account for the delay through the address decoder logic. (See Fig. 5.25.)

[c]See note a. An additional 22 ns has been subtracted from the 8085 and Z-80 times to account for the $\overline{MEMR}$ logic on the CPU module.

the microprocessor provides a *timing window* in which the event must occur. For example, the 8080A provides a 590-ns access-time window during which the memory must decode the address and come up with valid data. In this particular case 250 ns is required by the memory, which is well within the specification. Notice, however, that the 2764 is too slow for the faster Z-80 processor, and one WAIT state will be required. (Or select the 2764-2 part.)

Observe that the numbers used in Table 5.7 are smaller than those given in Table 5.3. Figure 5.25 helps explain why. When the microprocessor issues an address, it is buffered and placed on the system address bus. This introduces one time delay. Another buffer at the memory module site introduces a second delay.

The memory access time now occurs as the data byte is retrieved from the memory array. The data byte is then buffered and placed on the system data bus, introducing a third buffer time delay. Finally, the CPU module buffers the data off the bus, introducing a fourth buffer delay.

The propagation delay path for t_{CE} is further increased by the decoder logic (assume a NAND gate and an inverter), and this adds another 35 ns of time delay to this parameter.

Finally, the memory read control bus logic (one 74LS32 OR gate) on the 8085 and Z-80 CPU modules (see Figs. 4.26 and 4.27, respectively) contributes another 22 ns to their t_{RD} specifications.

The accumulation of all these buffer delays (each assumed to be the worst-case delay) deletes as much as 60 ns from the t_{AC} timing window, 95 ns from the t_{CE} timing window, and 82 ns from the t_{RD} timing window.

The timing considerations for the 8085 are more complex still, due to the need for a low-order address latch. Assuming that a 74LS373 octal buffer/latch is used, as shown in Fig. 4.26, the worst-case time delays introduced by this buffer will be the same as if a standard buffer were used. Therefore, the same derating numbers can be applied to the 8085 processor.

Alternative decoding schemes. The decoding techniques shown in Fig. 5.24 provide *full decoding*: All address lines are tested by the decoder. Sometimes, however, a *partial* decoding scheme is used in which some of the address lines are not tested.

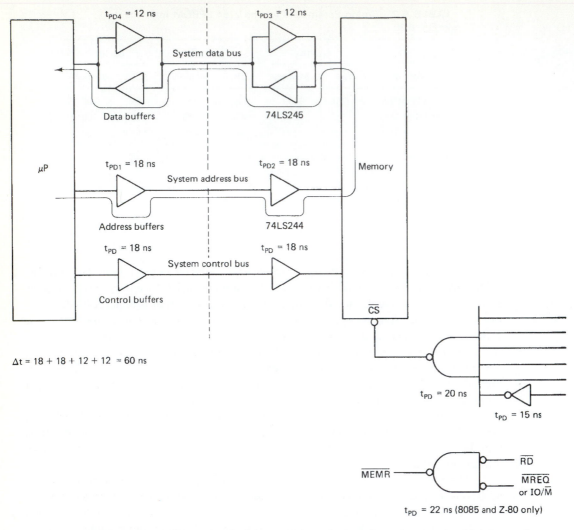

Figure 5.25 Buffers onto and off the system buses increase the total propagation delay times and have the effect of shortening the timing windows provided by the microprocessor.

Figure 5.26(a) illustrates a 2764 interface that places the EPROM in the first 8K slot of the processor's memory space. This is done by using only address line AB15 to generate the $\overline{CE}$ signal. When AB15 is low, the memory will be enabled and respond to addresses in the range 0000 to 1FFFH.

There is an undesirable side effect to this decoding scheme, however: The 8K memory "wraps around," or folds back on itself, and also resides in the 8K slot from 2000H to 3FFFH, the slot from 4000H to 5FFFH, and the slot from 6000H to 7FFFH. This configuration is shown in Fig. 5.26(b). These "extra" slots correspond to the unused combinations of address lines AB13 and AB14.

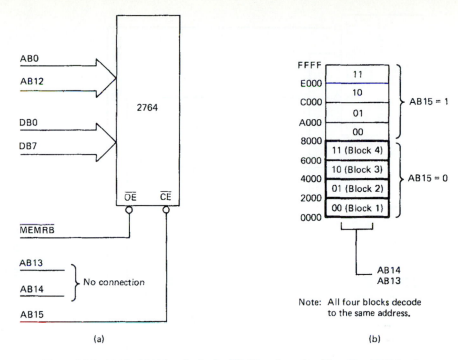

Figure 5.26 (a) The 2764 decoder is simplified by using only address line AB15 for the CE input; (b) the result is four 8K slots, all decoding to the same chip.

Because of the partial decoding, the 2764 cannot tell the difference between address 0000 and address 2000H. The reason is that the only difference is address line AB13, and this line is not tested.

So why should we use partial decoding? In some microcomputer systems, the amount of memory required is minimal and it is known that the system will not be expanded at a later date; these conditions might be met by a dedicated hardware controller such as that found in a microwave oven, for example. In this case, partial decoding simplifies the decoder logic by eliminating the NAND gate, which can save circuit-board space and help reduce costs.

Figure 5.27 shows another decoding scheme. In this circuit, a 74LS138 three-line-to-eight-line decoder (also made by Intel as the 8205) is used to generate eight separate EPROM select signals corresponding to the eight memory slots shown in Figs. 5.23(b) and 5.26(b). By using these eight signals as CE inputs to eight separate EPROMS, a 64K-byte EPROM interface can be constructed.

Note that all address and data lines are connected in parallel in this interface. What allows the scheme to work is that only one EPROM can be enabled at a time, depending on the value of address lines AB13 through AB15. The output lines of the disabled devices will be in a high-impedance state and therefore will not interfere with the selected EPROM.

The decoding technique shown in Fig. 5.27 is called *block decoding,* as it divides the memory space into eight separate memory blocks.

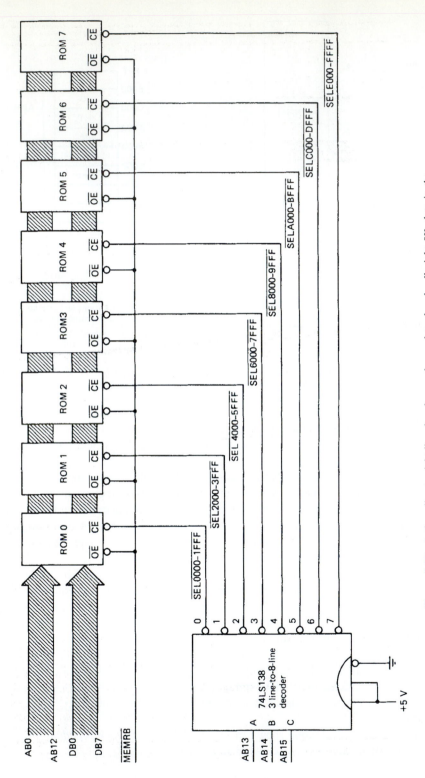

Figure 5.27 A three-line-to-eight-line decoder can be used to decode all eight 8K slots in the processor's memory space. In this case, a 64K-byte EPROM interface is built.

In sum, many different decoding schemes are possible, but the objective is always to prevent bus contention by enabling only one memory device at a time.

Interfacing the 2167 16K Static RAM

Chip architecture. Appendix D.2 is a data sheet for the NEC μPD2167 16K × 1 static RAM. This is a high-speed MOS RAM chip having a maximum access time of only 70 ns. It also has *separate* data-in and data-out lines. This means that data to be written should be applied to the data-in pin, but data to be read should be read from the data-out pin. This feature will require special attention when interfacing to the system's bidirectional data bus.

Unlike the 2764, the 2167 has only one memory control line, called *chip select* ($\overline{CS}$). When $\overline{CS}$ is low, the memory is activated, and data are placed on the data-out pin if the write enable ($\overline{WE}$) input is high. If $\overline{WE}$ is low, data placed on the data-in pin will be stored. $\overline{CS}$ should normally be kept high, as the data-out pin is then in a tristate, and power consumption is reduced from 850 mW to 150 mW.

The 2167 competes with bytewide devices like the HM6116 2K × 8 SRAM, but offers the advantage of a narrow-profile package. This means that more DIPs can be accommodated on one circuit board, allowing large memory arrays to be constructed.

The 2167's principal disadvantage is that it is not pin compatible with any of the "universal memory components" discussed in Section 5.4. A board built with 2167s must be dedicated to an SRAM function of a particular size.

Verifying the timing. The 2167 is a fast device, as is soon discovered when one studies the timing parameters in Table 5.8. The memory access time is five to nine times faster than the window opening provided by any of the microprocessors. Note that the data sheet indicates two memory read cycles. Read cycle 1 occurs when the $\overline{CS}$ input is permanently enabled. Read cycle 2 is the more common case and occurs when the $\overline{CS}$ input is driven by an address decoder.

The microprocessor access times in Table 5.8 do not include time delays through the buffers and decoder logic, but it is clear that the 2167 is much faster than required.

A write cycle occurs when $\overline{CS}$ is brought low, output data are placed on the data-in pin, and the $\overline{WE}$ input is taken low. The $\overline{CS}$ input should be driven by an address decoder and the $\overline{WE}$ input by the processor $\overline{MEMWB}$ control line. With this convention, the write parameters agree exactly with the definitions of t_{DW} and t_{AW} in Fig. 5.2. From Table 5.8, it is clear that the 2167 easily meets these requirements.

TABLE 5.8 Timing Parameters for the 2167 Static RAM Interface in Fig. 5.28

Processor	t_{ACC} (ns)		t_{DW} (ns)		t_{AW} (ns)	
	μP	2167-2	μP	2167-2	μP	2167-2
8080A	650	70	656	30	1176	55
8085AH	575	70	420	30	670	55
Z-80A	325	70	265	30	500	55

A 32K RAM module.   Figure 5.28 is a diagram of a 32K RAM module based on the 2167 SRAM. Note the following observations:

1. Because the 2167 is 1 bit wide, eight chips are required to store a byte. For example, RAMs 0 and 8 store data bit 0, RAMs 1 and 9 store bit 1, and so on.
2. Two banks of 16K are required for the 32K module. BANK0 consists of RAMs 0 through 7; BANK1 consists of RAMs 8 through 15.
3. Address lines AB0 through AB13 are wired in parallel to each of the memory chips. However, only one bank of chips will be enabled at a particular time.

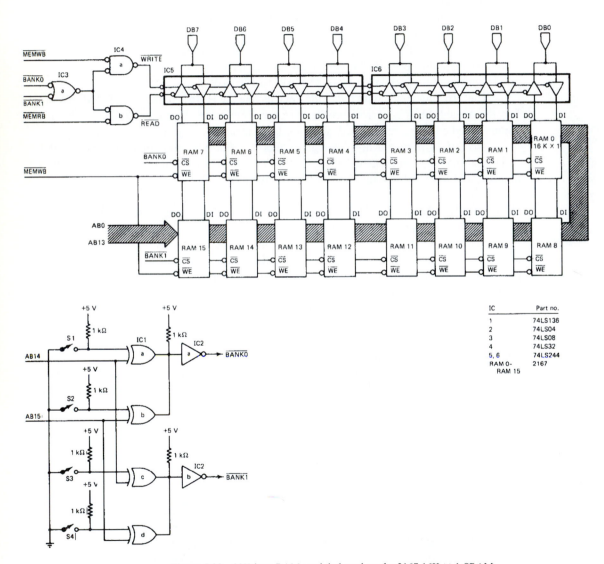

Figure 5.28   32K-byte RAM module based on the 2167 16K × 1 SRAM.

4. Address lines AB14 and AB15 are decoded to provide two bank-select signals, BANK0 and BANK1. These signals are obtained from the wired-OR outputs of the open-collector *exclusive-OR* gates IC1a–d. For example, if switches S1 and S2 are open, then BANK0 will be selected only if AB14 AND AB15 are both low. If either of these address lines is high, BANK0 will be held high and RAMs 0 through 7 disabled.

5. The purpose of switches S1 through S4 is to allow each 16K bank to be moved to one of four possible 16K slots in the processor's memory space. In this way, other memory modules can be accommodated that might otherwise conflict with a fixed address module. Figure 5.29 explains how the switches are to be set for a particular 16K slot.

6. The bidirectional data bus must be broken into separate data-in and data-out lines to accommodate the 2167. This is the purpose of tristate buffers IC5 and IC6.

During a memory read, the processor outputs a 16-bit address on AB0 through AB15. The bank decoder examines AB14 and AB15 and, depending on the settings of switches S1 through S4, causes one of the bank select lines to go low. This, in turn, selects one row of RAM chips.

Each RAM chip in the selected row now decodes address lines AB0 through AB13 and places the selected bit on its data-out (DO) pin.

The buffer control logic is enabled by either bank-select signal, and because this is a memory read operation, the READ output goes low. This signal is used to enable the buffers connected to each data-out line, and the data byte is thereby gated onto the microprocessor system data bus.

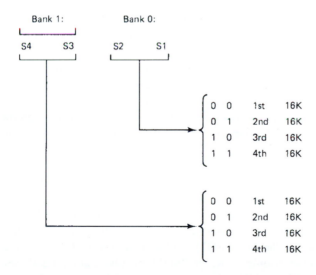

Example: S4 S3 S2 S1 = 1 1 0 1   (closed-closed-open-closed)

         Bank 0 = 4000–7FFF

         Bank 1 = C000–FFFF

Figure 5.29 Switches S1 through S4 select one of four 16K slots for each memory bank in Fig. 5.25.

The sequence of events for a memory write is similar, except that the $\overline{\text{MEMWB}}$ signal causes each RAM chip in the selected row to prepare to receive data on its data-in pin.

The buffer control logic causes $\overline{\text{WRITE}}$ to go low and enables the buffers connected to the data-in pin of each RAM. The microprocessor places the data byte to be written onto the system data bus, allowing each RAM chip to latch its particular data bit. When $\overline{\text{MEMWB}}$ goes high, the cycle has ended.

Although not shown in Fig. 5.28, address lines AB0 through AB15 and the $\overline{\text{MEMRB}}$ and $\overline{\text{MEMWB}}$ control signals are all assumed to be buffered before connecting to the system address and control bus. The resulting RAM module can then be connected to any of the CPU modules designed in Chapter 4.

Interfacing a RAM/ROM Module

A practical microcomputer system will require a certain amount of ROM memory for its operating system and a certain amount of RAM memory for read/write applications. In this section, we study a RAM/ROM module that provides 12K of ROM and 16K of RAM.

Designing the hardware. Combining ROM and RAM memory components in a single memory module is no more difficult than designing an all-ROM or all-RAM module. In this case, we will use the 2167 16K-bit SRAM, the 2764 8K-byte EPROM, and the 2732 4K-byte EPROM. The main complication in such an interface is the address decoding required for the three different block sizes.

Figure 5.30 is a schematic diagram of the module. The memory array consists of the eight 2167 SRAMs and the 2764 and 2732 EPROMs. The address bus is wired in parallel to each chip, and the chip-select inputs are driven with the signals $\overline{\text{RAM}}$, $\overline{\text{ROM1}}$, and $\overline{\text{ROM2}}$.

The system data bus must be broken into separate data-in and data-out lines to accommodate the 2167 SRAMs. Note that the EPROM data lines are wired in parallel with the data-out pins of the RAMs. This configuration will not cause a conflict if the address decoding ensures that only one type of memory is enabled at a particular time. (Recall that the data lines of the memory devices go to a high-impedance state when their chip-select inputs are high.)

Buffer control logic is again used to control the direction of data flow through the tristate buffers IC2 and IC3. IC5 ensures that the buffers are disabled for addresses outside the range of this module.

ROM address decoder. Perhaps the most interesting feature of the RAM/ROM module in Fig. 5.30 is the address decoder. Rather than use standard combinational logic, a 74S287 256×4 *fusible-link PROM* has been chosen. This has the advantage of allowing the memory map of the module to be *programmed,* instead of hardwired, into the chip.

The desired memory map for the RAM/ROM module is shown in Fig. 5.31. Because the smallest block size in the module is 4K, the PROM must have at least a 4K resolution. This means that address lines AB12 through AB15 must be examined by the PROM. The 16 combinations of AB12 through AB15 correspond to the 16 4K blocks of memory in the processor's 64K memory space. Similarly, address lines AB11 through AB15 would be required if a 2K resolution were desired.

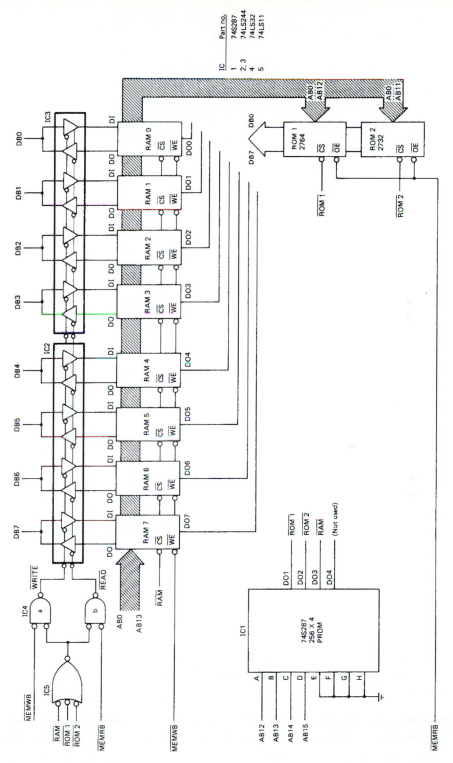

Figure 5.30 12 K-ROM, 32K-RAM memory module using a fusible-link PROM decoder.

241

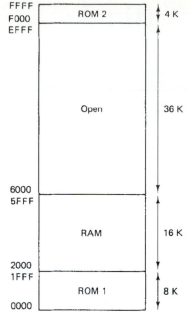

FFFF		
F000	ROM 2	4 K
EFFF		
	Open	36 K
6000		
5FFF		
	RAM	16 K
2000		
1FFF		
	ROM 1	8 K
0000		

Figure 5.31 Memory map for the RAM/ROM module in Fig. 5.30.

The 74S287 has eight (address) inputs, labeled A through H. We will require only lines A through D and connect these inputs to address lines AB12 through AB15. By grounding PROM inputs E through H, only the first 16 words in the 256-word PROM will be used.

What data should be stored in these 16 locations? To answer this question, we must develop a *truth table* and assign functions to each PROM output pin. This is done in Fig. 5.32.

Although there are four output pins (corresponding to the 4-bit word size), only three outputs are required. These are arbitrarily chosen as shown in Figs. 5.30 and 5.32.

Once the output definitions are determined, the truth table can be completed. Studying the addresses in the memory map in Fig. 5.31, we see that the ROM1 output should be low when AB15 through AB12 = 0000 or 0001. All other combinations should produce ROM1 high.

Similarly, the RAM output should be low when AB15 through AB12 = 0010, 0011, 0100, or 0101. Finally, the 4K EPROM (ROM2) is enabled when AB15 through AB12 = 1111.

Table 5.9 is a data table for the 74S287 PROM and lists, in hex format, the 4-bit data words to be stored in the PROM. Because an *unprogrammed* data bit stores a 1, the unused DO4 data bit is assumed to be 1 in this table.

Figure 5.33 lists the step-by-step programming procedure recommended by Texas Instruments for the 74S287.

PAL address decoder. Many designers today use *programmable array logic* devices, or PALs, instead of ROMs for replacing combinational logic. A PAL consists of

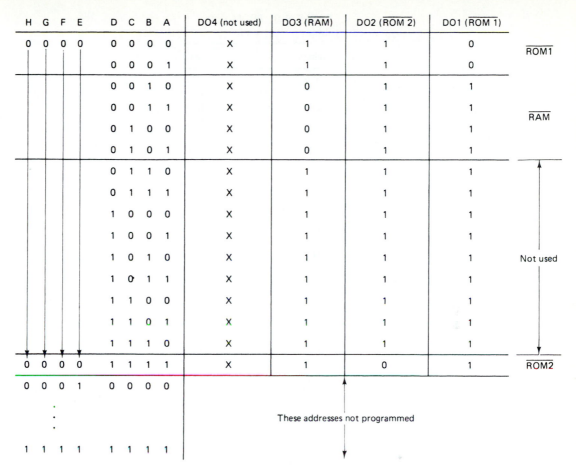

H G F E	D C B A	DO4 (not used)	DO3 ($\overline{\text{RAM}}$)	DO2 ($\overline{\text{ROM 2}}$)	DO1 ($\overline{\text{ROM 1}}$)	
0 0 0 0	0 0 0 0	X	1	1	0	$\overline{\text{ROM1}}$
	0 0 0 1	X	1	1	0	
	0 0 1 0	X	0	1	1	
	0 0 1 1	X	0	1	1	$\overline{\text{RAM}}$
	0 1 0 0	X	0	1	1	
	0 1 0 1	X	0	1	1	
	0 1 1 0	X	1	1	1	
	0 1 1 1	X	1	1	1	
	1 0 0 0	X	1	1	1	
	1 0 0 1	X	1	1	1	
	1 0 1 0	X	1	1	1	Not used
	1 0 1 1	X	1	1	1	
	1 1 0 0	X	1	1	1	
	1 1 0 1	X	1	1	1	
	1 1 1 0	X	1	1	1	
0 0 0 0	1 1 1 1	X	1	0	1	$\overline{\text{ROM2}}$
0 0 0 1	0 0 0 0			↑		
. . .				These addresses not programmed		
1 1 1 1	1 1 1 1			↓		

Figure 5.32 Truth table for the PROM decoder in Fig. 5.30. The table corresponds to the memory map in Fig. 5.31.

a programmable array of AND and OR gates. Figure 5.34 shows the PAL10L8. This chip has 10 input pins and 8 output pins. Note that each output is obtained from a two-input NOR gate, and each of these inputs is driven by AND gates. Inverters on each input pin allow the complement of that input to be easily obtained.

In Fig. 5.34, the intersection of a vertical and a horizontal line represents a possible AND input. To program the chip, first place an "X" at each desired intersection to form a "map" of the intended circuit. For example, an X at row 0, column 5, and row 0, column 8, programs the product term

$$\overline{\text{INPUT3}} \cdot \text{INPUT4}$$

Two such product terms can be formed for each OR gate. In the ROM address decoder example, we saw that the signal ROM1 should be active whenever AB15, AB14, and AB13 are low. This could be programmed via a PAL as

$$O_{19} = \overline{\text{INPUT1}} \cdot \overline{\text{INPUT2}} \cdot \overline{\text{INPUT3}}$$

TABLE 5.9 PROM Data Table

Address	Data
0	E
1	E
2	B
3	B
4	B
5	B
6	F
7	F
8	F
9	F
A	F
B	F
C	F
D	F
E	F
F	D
10	F
.	F
.	F
.	F
FF	F

The data in the truth table in Fig. 5.32 are converted to a PROM address and hex data word in preparation for programming.

where pins 1, 2, and 3 are connected to AB13–15. Pin 19 then becomes the ROM1 output signal.

PALs are more easily programmed than ROMs because each output maps to a single programming combination. With a ROM, several hundred locations may have to be programmed for each output. PALs are programmed using a fusible-link technique similar to that of a bipolar PROM.

SELF-REVIEW 5.5

5.5.1 The _____ _____ determines the range of addresses occupied by a memory chip.

5.5.2 What is the effect of address and data bus buffers on memory timing?

5.5.3 When _____ decoding is used, the same memory module occupies more than one address.

5.5.4 By using a _____ or _____ chip, the logic of an address decoder can be made programmable.

step-by-step programming procedure

1. Apply steady-state supply voltage (V_{CC} = 5 V) and address the word to be programmed.

2. Verify that the bit location needs to be programmed. If not, proceed to the next bit.

3. If the bit requires programming, disable the outputs by applying a high-logic-level voltage to the chip-select input(s).

4. Only one bit location is programmed at a time. Connect each output not being programmed to 5 V through 3.9 kΩ and apply the voltage specified in the table to the output to be programmed. Maximum current out of the programming output supply during programming is 150 mA.

5. Step V_{CC} to 10.5 V nominal. Maximum supply current required during programming is 750 mA.

6. Apply a low-logic-level voltage to the chip-select input(s). This should occur between 10 μs and 1 ms after V_{CC} has reached its 10.5-V level. See programming sequence of Figure 3.

7. After the X pulse time (1 ms) is reached, a high logic level is applied to the chip-select inputs to disable the outputs.

8. Within 10 μs to 1 ms after the chip-select input(s) reach a high logic level, V_{CC} should be stepped down to 5 V at which level verification can be accomplished.

9. The chip-select input(s) may be taken to a low logic level (to permit program verification) 10 μs or more after V_{CC} reaches its steady-state value of 5 V.

10. At a Y pulse duty cycle of 35% or less, repeat steps 1 through 8 for each output where it is desired to program a bit.

NOTES: A) V_{CC} should be removed between program pulses to reduce dissipation and chip temperatures. See Figure 3.
B) When verification indicates that a bit did not program, repeat steps 3 through 9. If the bit did not program after the second application of a 1-ms X pulse, repeat steps 3 through 9 using an X pulse time of 10 to 20 ms. Regardless of the X duration, the total average pulse time of Y should be no more than 35% of the programming cycle.

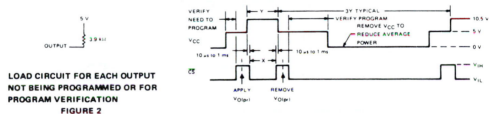

LOAD CIRCUIT FOR EACH OUTPUT
NOT BEING PROGRAMMED OR FOR
PROGRAM VERIFICATION
FIGURE 2

FIGURE 3—VOLTAGE WAVEFORMS FOR PROGRAMMING

Figure 5.33 Programming procedure for the 74S287 fusible-link PROM. (Courtesy of Texas Instruments.)

5.6 INTERFACING DYNAMIC RAM TO THE MICROPROCESSOR

Introduction

Because of their dynamic nature, DRAMs are more complex to interface than SRAMs. The memory address must be supplied in row and column format, and because of the capacitive nature of the storage cell, the entire chip must be refreshed on a periodic basis. The timing required to accomplish these operations is critical; if it is not observed, data will be lost.

In this section, we:

- Describe common DRAM control signals and access-time parameters.
- Compare conventional DRAMs with page-mode, extended data-out, and synchronous DRAM technologies.

10L8

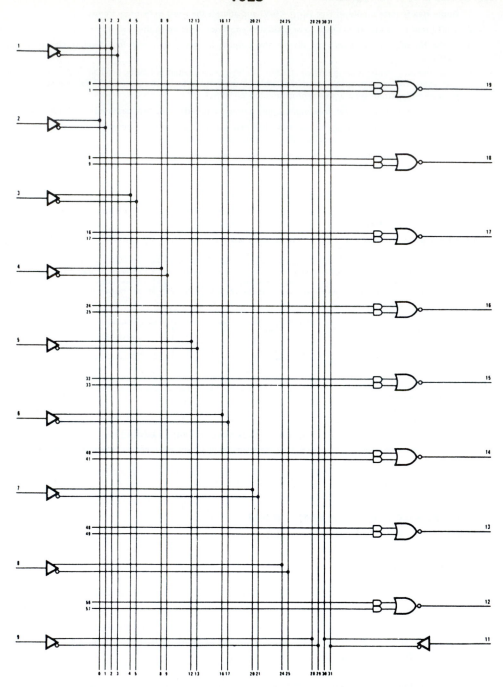

Figure 5.34 The PAL10L8 has 10 inputs and 8 outputs. (Courtesy of Monolithic Memories, Inc. PAL is a registered trademark of Monolithic Memories, Inc. PLF is a trademark of Monolithic Memories, Inc.)

Timing Diagrams for Dynamic RAM

Appendix D.2 contains a data sheet for the Intel 2164A 64K $\times$ 1 dynamic RAM. From the logic symbol for this device, it is clear that only eight address lines are provided. Normally, one would expect a 64K device to require 16 address lines. Because that many pins would require a large package, the designers have chosen to time-multiplex the address bus into a *row address* (A0 through A7) and a *column address* (A8 through A15).

Figure 5.35 illustrates the basic timing for memory read and write cycles. Two clock signals are required: the row address strobe ($\overline{RAS}$), and the column address strobe ($\overline{CAS}$).

A read or write cycle begins with the falling edge of the $\overline{RAS}$ clock signal (1). This operation will latch the address currently applied to the chip, which should correspond to the low-order, or row, address. During the timing window t_{RCD}, the row address must be held stable to meet the t_{RAH} row address hold specification and then changed to the high-order, or column, address. The falling edge of $\overline{CAS}$ will latch this address (2).

If a memory read cycle is in progress, the falling edge of $\overline{CAS}$ will also gate data onto the data-out pin of the RAM. The access time is measured from the falling edge of $\overline{RAS}$ to valid data at the data-out pin (t_{RAC}; 3).

The memory read cycle must include the cycle *precharge* time t_{RP}. This is the time required to charge the bit sense line (see Fig. 5.15) in preparation for the next memory cycle. The memory read cycle time is the sum of t_{RAC} and t_{RP}. The 2164A-15 has a 150-ns access time (t_{RAC}), but a 260-ns cycle time.

From the microprocessor's standpoint, the access time is the important parameter; the precharge time is a unique requirement of the dynamic RAM only. The effect of the precharge is to cause the cycle time to be greater than the access time. Fortunately, this does not affect the microprocessor. Why? A minimum of four clock periods is required for any one microprocessor machine cycle. This requirement prevents the processor from requesting consecutive memory cycles with periods shorter than 4T, or 1µs, at 4 MHz. This time is much longer than the memory cycle time.*

Page mode. Modern PCs routinely operate with clock frequencies greater than 100 MHz and require only two clock cycles per memory cycle (<20 ns/cycle). To these machines, the DRAM access times are very slow—even using today's 60-ns DRAMs. For this reason, most PCs are designed with high-speed SRAM *cache memories*. In these systems, DRAM accesses occur infrequently—only when a cache miss occurs. When the DRAMs are accessed, one cache line's worth of data will be read or written. Notice that this implies read or write cycles to *consecutive* memory locations.

Accordingly, most DRAMs support a fast *page mode* that can be taken advantage of in this situation. After the $\overline{RAS}$ clock falls low, all of the memory cells in the selected row pass their data on to the sense amplifiers. In the case of the 2164A, the column address is 8 bits wide, and each row therefore stores 256 bits (one page).

With one page of data stored in the sense amplifiers, the $\overline{CAS}$ clock can now be used to select random (or consecutive) memory locations on this page. The advantage, of

---

*Of course, with a faster processor, the cycle time becomes more important.

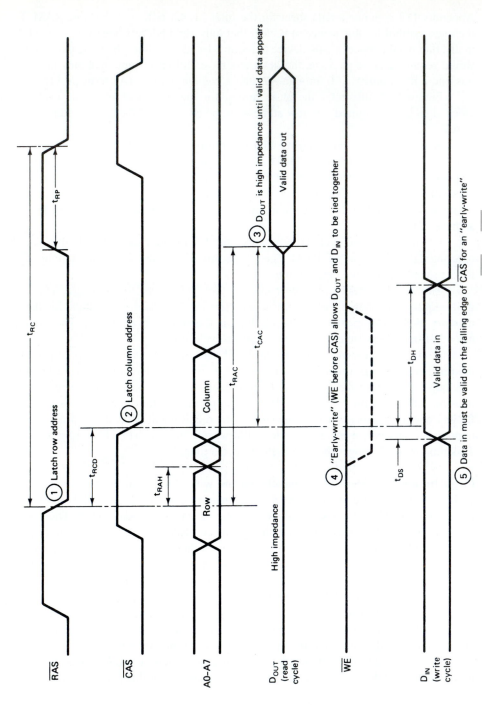

Figure 5.35 Dynamic RAM timing diagrams. Two clock signals ($\overline{RAS}$ and $\overline{CAS}$) are required to latch the multiplexed row and column addresses.

248

course, is that the column access time t_{CAC} is faster than the row access time t_{RAC}. (For the 2164A, t_{RAC} is 150 ns, while t_{CAC} is 125 ns.)*

Extended data out (EDO). Conventional DRAMs have the drawback that during the time $\overline{CAS}$ is high—the $\overline{CAS}$ precharge time—the output data is turned off. In order to maintain a reasonable valid data-out window, the width of the $\overline{CAS}$ low pulse must be extended. The effect is to increase the cycle time of the memory (and decrease the overall system performance).

EDO DRAMs offer one new feature: During the $\overline{CAS}$ precharge time, valid data remains on the output pins. That is, $\overline{CAS}$ no longer turns the output data off. This simple change has far-reaching effects: Because the time when valid data is available has been extended to the end of the memory cycle, the cycle time can be reduced while a reasonable data-out window is still maintained. In practice, most systems using EDO DRAMs achieve a 20–30% reduction in memory cycle times.

Synchronous DRAM (SDRAM). The drawback to conventional DRAM (and SRAM) technology has always been the *asynchronous* nature of the part. DRAMs in particular require a complex sequencing of row and column address clocks before data can be accessed. As processor clock speeds move well past 100 MHz, it becomes increasingly difficult to work with parts that deliver their data only after some (unsynchronized) time delays occur.

With synchronous DRAMs, the control signals ($\overline{RAS}$ and $\overline{CAS}$) are latched on the rising edge of the system clock. The data output is then available on a subsequent rising edge of the clock. Notice that with this type of memory, the access time is synchronized to the system clock: As the clock frequency speeds up, the memory speeds up. WAIT states thus become a thing of the past.

Of course the "trick" is to manufacture SDRAMs that can keep up with clock frequencies of 100 MHz or more. Accordingly, most SDRAMs have a *burst mode* of operation. In this mode, the processor programs the SDRAM for 1-, 2-, 4-, or 8-byte bursts. Then, when a memory access occurs, the SDRAM returns as many as 8 bytes in one burst (1 byte per clock pulse) without the need for a new memory address. With a 100-MHz clock, a new byte is supplied every 10 ns.

Refresh

As mentioned in Section 5.4, the storage cell for a dynamic RAM is a capacitor. And because this capacitor is not perfect, the charge in each memory cell must be rewritten at least once every 2 ms, or data will be lost. In the case of the 2164, the memory array consists of four quadrants arranged as 128 rows by 128 columns. Because the row lines of all four quadrants are the same, the refresh operation can be accomplished by sequencing through all 128 row addresses. This means that the refresh address is 7 bits wide.

Although a refresh operation will occur whenever a read or write cycle occurs, we usually cannot guarantee that every row of the DRAM will be accessed at least once every 2 ms. (An exception to this might be "screen" memory used in a memory-mapped video display interface.)

---

*With modern DRAMs, the improvement is even better. For example, the 417400-60 4M × 4 DRAM has a 60-ns row access time, but just 15 ns for the column access time.

The technique most commonly used in DRAM controllers is called $\overline{RAS}$-only refresh and is illustrated in Fig. 5.36. In this scheme, only a row address is output to the DRAM, and no data is read or written during the cycle. Sequencing through all 128 row addresses will refresh the memory. Of course, during this time, the processor will be unable to access the memory.

A third method of refreshing a DRAM is called *hidden refresh*. The timing is illustrated in Fig. 5.37. After completing a normal memory cycle, the $\overline{CAS}$ clock is left low. This will maintain data on the data-out pin. Now any number of $\overline{RAS}$ clocks can be applied as the row address is incremented. Hidden refresh is essentially a $\overline{RAS}$-only refresh, but with the $\overline{CAS}$ clock held low. The technique can be used to "hide" refresh cycles among processor cycles which require that data be held on the bus, but do not require a new memory or I/O access.

There are three methods of distributing the necessary refresh cycles over the 2-ms refresh period:

1. *Burst refresh:* In this technique, the processor is forced into a WAIT state and all 128 rows are refreshed in one "burst." Normal processing is then resumed until the next refresh period is required. Because one 2164A refresh cycle can take 260 ns or longer, the time to refresh all 128 rows will exceed 30 μs. During this time, the memory cannot be accessed.

2. *Distributed refresh:* Rather than refreshing the entire memory at once, the refresh cycles can be distributed over the entire 2-ms period. This will require a refresh cycle every 2 ms/128 cycles = 15.6 μs. Most DRAM controllers use a distributed refresh technique.

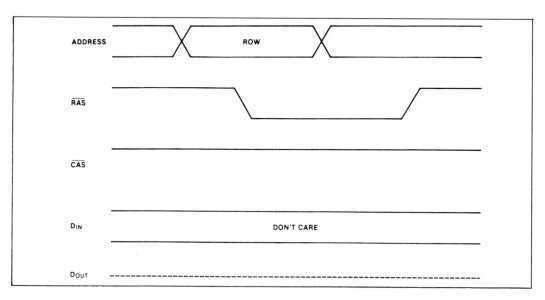

Figure 5.36 $\overline{RAS}$-only refresh cycle. The microprocessor cannot access the memory during this refresh time. (Courtesy of Intel Corporation.)

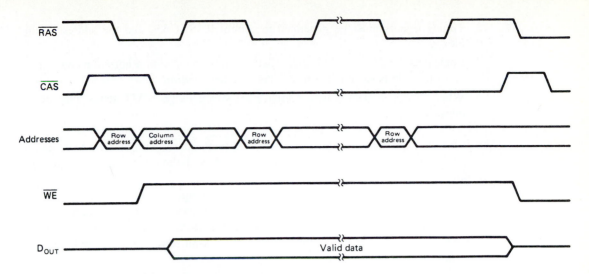

Figure 5.37 Hidden refresh cycle. D_{OUT} is maintained valid throughout the cycle.

3. *Transparent refresh:* Ideally, we would like to "sneak" the refresh cycles into the microprocessor timing at points when access to the memory is not required. In this way, the refresh operations would be "transparent" and never slow the processor down. The usual technique is to identify the *M1* or op-code fetch machine cycle. After this cycle, several clock periods are often consumed while instructions are executed. For example, the 8080 instruction INR r requires five T states. After state T3, the contents of the buses are no longer important. During states T4 and T5, the selected register is accessed and then incremented. One refresh cycle could easily be performed during this time.

Using transparent refresh, the microprocessor must never cease fetching op codes, or data will be lost. This puts a restriction on certain types of processor activities, such as DMA transfers. Transparent refresh is also not suitable for the newer generation of high-speed microprocessors, because the execution phase of an instruction may not be sufficiently long at the faster clock speeds. Another problem occurs with processors such as the Intel 8086 16-bit microprocessor. This processor *prefetches* instructions while previous instructions are being executed. Thus, the "dead time" on the bus used for refresh is effectively eliminated.

The 8203 DRAM Controller

Several problems are associated with interfacing a dynamic RAM memory:

1. During normal processor read and write cycles the DRAM must receive a memory address from the processor, but during refresh operations it must receive a special "refresh address." This is called *address multiplexing*.
2. Each row in the DRAM memory must be refreshed at least once every 2 ms.

3. Timing signals must be generated to control $\overline{RAS}$, $\overline{CAS}$, and the address multiplexer.

4. Logic must be designed to decide whether a refresh cycle or a normal memory read or write cycle is to be performed. This is called *arbitration*.

5. When refresh interferes with normal processor activity, WAIT states must be requested.

This is a formidable list of problems to be solved (particularly with discrete logic gates). Fortunately, all of the problems have, in fact, been solved in the form of the *dynamic RAM controller*.

Figure 5.38 presents a block diagram and pin configuration for the Intel 8203 dynamic RAM controller. The 8203 accepts a 16-bit address from the microprocessor at AH0–AH7 (the high-order, or column, address) and AL0–AL7 (the low-order, or row, address). These two bytes are then multiplexed with an 8-bit refresh counter and are available at outputs $\overline{OUT0}$ through $\overline{OUT7}$.

The refresh counter cycles through 256 states at least once every 4 ms. In this way, the 8203 is compatible with 128-row or 256-row refresh RAMs. The refresh rate and all other system timing are controlled by a crystal connected to X0 and X1. Any frequency between 18.432 and 25 MHz can be used for this crystal.

Note that the 8203 directly generates the $\overline{CAS}$, $\overline{RAS}$, and $\overline{WE}$ signals required by the DRAM array. When used for controlling 16K devices, the $\overline{RAS0}$ through $\overline{RAS3}$ outputs allow four 16K banks. In this case, the address is broken into two 7-bit groups: A0 through A6 and A7 through A13. A14 and A15 are then connected to B0 and B1 and determine which of the four banks is to be selected.

Figure 5.39 illustrates a 128K dynamic RAM interface using two banks of 2164 64K DRAMs. In this circuit, the 8203 is used in the 64K mode by grounding pin 35 ($16K/\overline{64K}$). In the 64K mode, four of the pins change function. The number of banks is reduced to two, as the $\overline{RAS2}$ and $\overline{RAS3}$ outputs are now used for address output 7 and bank-select input B0. The former bank-select inputs, B0 and B1, are now used for the additional address inputs AL7 (A7) and AH7 (A15).

Refreshing of the two banks occurs automatically by the 8203 at least once every 2 ms. During the refresh time, $\overline{RAS0}$ and $\overline{RAS1}$ are both enabled, and therefore, both 64K banks are refreshed simultaneously using the "RAS-only" technique.

Of course, the processors we have studied cannot directly access 128K of memory and do not have an address line AB16 (connected to B0 in Fig. 5.39). However, an output port (basically a flip-flop) could be used to control the 8203 B0 input. In this way, an output instruction could be used to flip from one 64K bank to another.

The 8203 uses a *distributed refresh* technique, and an internal refresh timer and an arbitrator determines when to perform a refresh cycle so that RAM data are never lost. However, an external refresh can also be performed using the REFRQ input. This input would be used to implement "transparent refresh," for example.

Because the 8203 will perform a refresh cycle *asynchronously* with respect to the CPU, it is likely that the microprocessor will request a memory cycle during a refresh operation. If this should occur, the arbitration logic will finish the refresh cycle and then honor the memory request. Similarly, a memory cycle will be allowed to be completed

8203
64K DYNAMIC RAM CONTROLLER

- **Provides All Signals Necessary to Control 64K (2164) and 16K (2117, 2118) Dynamic Memories**

- **Directly Addresses and Drives Up to 64 Devices Without External Drivers**

- **Provides Address Multiplexing and Strobes**

- **Provides a Refresh Timer and a Refresh Counter**

- **Provides Refresh/Access Arbitration**

- **Internal Clock Capability with the 8203-1 and the 8203-3**

- **Fully Compatible with Intel® 8080A, 8085A, iAPX 88, and iAPX 86 Family Microprocessors**

- **Provides System Acknowledge and Transfer Acknowledge Signals**

- **Refresh Cycles May be Internally or Externally Requested (For Transparent Refresh)**

- **Internal Series Damping Resistors on RAS, CAS and WE Outputs**

- **Available in EXPRESS**
  —Standard Temperature Range

The Intel® 8203 is a Dynamic Ram System Controller designed to provide all signals necessary to use 2164, 2118 or 2117 Dynamic RAMs in microcomputer systems. The 8203 provides multiplexed addresses and address strobes, refresh logic, refresh/access arbitration. Refresh cycles can be started internally or externally. The 8203-1 and the 8203-3 support Advanced-Read mode and an internal crystal oscillator. The 8203-3 is a ±5% V_{CC} part.

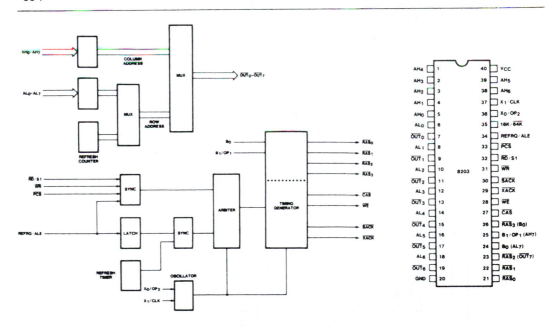

Figure 5.38 Intel 8203 dynamic RAM controller. (Courtesy of Intel Corporation.)

Sec. 5.6   Interfacing Dynamic RAM to the Microprocessor   **253**

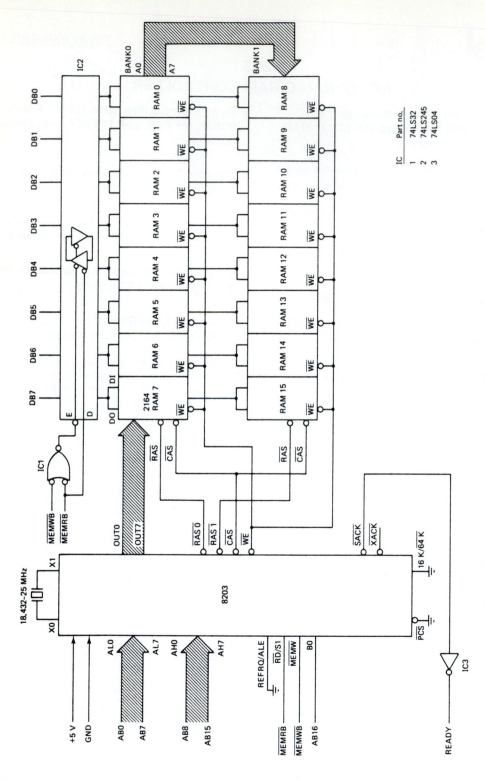

Figure 5.39 128K dynamic RAM module. For the 8080, 8085, or Z-80, A16 can be simulated with 1 bit of an output port.

before a pending refresh cycle is executed. The arbitrator gives a memory cycle the priority, but also ensures that a refresh cycle will be delayed by at most one memory cycle.

For this scheme to work, the 8203 provides a control signal called system acknowledge (SACR), which should be connected to the processor's READY or $\overline{WAIT}$ input. This signal goes low early in a memory cycle and acknowledges the CPU's request for memory access. If the $\overline{SACK}$ signal is not received by the microprocessor, a refresh cycle is in progress and the microprocessor is forced to enter a WAIT state.

Some microprocessors provide an early indication of the type of machine cycle, which can be used by the 8203 to decrease memory access time. This is the purpose of the ALE and $\overline{RD}$/S1 inputs. These pins are directly compatible with the same signal names on the 8085, 8088, and 8086 microprocessors. The feature is called the *advanced read* mode.

The Z-80 as a Refresh Controller

Recall from Chapter 2 that the Z-80 outputs a 7-bit refresh address during T3 and T4 of every M1 machine cycle. The timing was shown in Fig. 2.10. Using this feature of the Z-80, one can build a *transparent refresh controller*.

Unfortunately, the RAS and CAS timing signals and the address multiplexing must still be built with discrete logic. And because the refresh address is limited to 7 bits, 256-row RAMs cannot be used. Multiple banks of 64K will also require additional bank-select logic.

SELF-REVIEW 5.6

5.6.1 DRAM chips use a time-multiplexed address bus. What does this mean?

5.6.2 Typically, DRAMs are characterized by their row access time. This is the time from the falling edge of _____ to valid data out.

5.6.3 When operated in page mode, the _____ clock is used to retrieve data from a DRAM.

5.6.4 EDO DRAMs allow faster memory _____ _____ by extending the time valid data available through the $\overline{CAS}$ precharge time.

5.6.5 When operated in _____ mode, SDRAMs can supply as many as 8 bytes in one cycle—1 byte per clock pulse.

5.6.6 Most DRAMs use a _____ - _____ refresh in which each row address is output in sequence once during the refresh period.

QUESTIONS AND ANSWERS

Q: *What are the three common memory hierarchies?*

A: Main memory, secondary storage, and archival storage.

Q: *What is meant by the access time of a memory chip?*

A: The access time is the time from receipt of the memory address by the chip until valid data appears on the output pins of that chip.

Q: *What can be done about a memory part whose access time is too slow for the microprocessor?*

A: The memory interface must cause one or more WAIT states to be inserted. This will in turn cause an integral number of system clock states to be added to the access time provided to the memory by the processor.

Q: *What are typical applications for ROM memory parts?*

A: Because they are nonvolatile, ROMs are used to store bootstrap loader programs and control-software for products with embedded microcontrollers.

Q: *What are typical applications for RAM memory parts?*

A: Because it can be read from and written to, RAM memory is used for temporary storage of user programs and data.

Q: *List several different ROM memory technologies.*

A: Mask programmable, fusible link, UV-light erasable, and electrically erasable.

Q: *What is flash memory?*

A: Flash memory is a type of nonvolatile read/write memory available with very high bit densities and with memory read access times comparable to that of DRAMs. FLASH memory parts are divided into blocks, with each block individually erasable.

Q: *What are two main RAM technologies?*

A: Static RAM (SRAM) and dynamic RAM (DRAM). SRAMs use four to six transistors per cell, do not require refresh, and provide the fastest access times of any memory technology. DRAMs use a capacitor as the storage cell and thus require periodic refreshing. DRAMs provide the highest bit density of any memory technology.

Q: *What determines the specific range of addresses to which a memory chip is mapped?*

A: The address decoder.

Q: *How is an address decoder built?*

A: The simplest decoder is a NAND (or AND) gate. Programmable decoders can be built using a PROM or PAL chip.

Q: *What is the purpose of a DRAM's $\overline{RAS}$ and $\overline{CAS}$ clocks?*

A: DRAMs receive a memory address in the form of a row address followed by a column address. The $\overline{RAS}$ and $\overline{CAS}$ clock signals strobe these addresses into the DRAM one after the other.

Q: *How does a synchronous DRAM (SDRAM) compare with a conventional DRAM?*

A: Conventional DRAMS are asynchronous. After the row and column addresses have been supplied, a time delay occurs, and the data appears on the output pins. With a synchronous DRAM, the system clock strobes the row and column addresses into the chip. The next system clock pulse strobes the data onto the output pins.

Q: *What are three different ways of performing a DRAM memory refresh?*

A: Burst, transparent, and distributed.

LAB PROJECTS

5.1. Study the schematic diagram of the microcomputer you are using to support this text or course. Now answer the following questions:

(a) How much RAM does your system have?

(b) How much ROM?

(c) What types of memory chips are used? What is the organization of these chips (2K × 8, 16K × 1, etc.)?

(d) Does your system buffer the address, data, and control buses?

5.2. On separate sheets of paper, draw schematic diagrams of the RAM and ROM interfaces. Be sure to include the address decoding logic.

5.3. Sketch a *memory map* for your computer showing the address range occupied by each RAM and ROM chip. Can the memory of your computer be expanded? If so, include this information in your map.

5.4. Build a 16-word-by-4-bit diode ROM similar to Fig. 5.7. On one side of a piece of perf board, horizontally mount 16 bare copper wires—one for each byte. On the other side, mount eight vertical bit lines and 1K pull-up resistors. Connect the word lines to the output of a 74LS154, and connect the bit lines to the input of a 74LS244. For fun, program the ROM with the seven-segment codes for your name. Do this by soldering diodes between the appropriate row and column wires. Connect a binary counter to the address inputs and a seven-segment display to the data outputs.

5.5. The circuit in Fig. 5.40 can be used to test the operation of a 2K × 8 RAM. As the diagram shows, only 16 of the 2048 memory locations can be accessed, because there are just four data switches. Write data to the RAM by selecting an address, holding the $\overline{WE}$ switch low, and then setting the data to be written on the DIP switch. When $\overline{WE}$ goes high, the data will be written. To read the data back, hold the $\overline{OE}$ switch low. (*Note:* Connect the memory data bus to an 8-bit input port of your computer. Now write a program to read the port and display its contents. This will make monitoring the memory's data bus very easy.)

5.6. If you have access to a PROM programmer and eraser, program a PROM to implement the following truth table:

I2	I1	I0	O0	O1	O2	O3
0	0	0	0	0	1	1
0	0	1	0	1	1	0
0	1	0	0	1	1	0
0	1	1	0	1	1	0
1	0	0	0	1	1	0
1	0	1	0	1	1	0
1	1	0	0	1	1	0
1	1	1	1	1	0	0

(*Note:* The four outputs correspond to the AND, OR, NAND, and NOR of the inputs I2, I1, and I0.)

5.7. Write a program to test the memory of your computer. The program returns the location of any error. Several different types of tests are possible:

(a) *Checkerboard test:* Write AAH to the even bytes and 55H to the odd bytes. Read and verify all locations. Then repeat, reversing the even and odd bytes. (*Note:* This test is good for locating adjacent shorted data or address lines.)

(b) *Complement test:* Read a byte, complement and save it, and write it to memory. Compare the contents of memory with the saved byte. Complement memory and move on to the next byte. (*Note:* This test does not alter the contents of memory.)

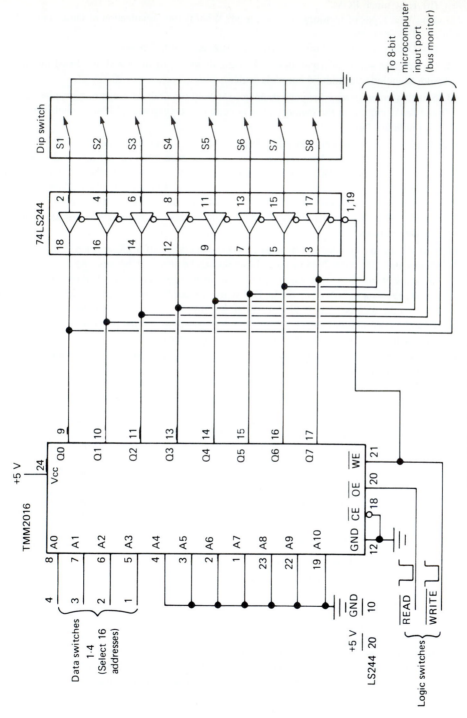

Figure 5.40 $2K \times 8$ RAM test circuit for Lab Project 5.5.

258

(c) *Walking-bit test:* (1) Write the following test pattern to memory:

```
0000    0000
0000    0001
0000    0010
 .       .
 .       .
 .       .
1000    0000
1111    1110
1111    1101
 .       .
 .       .
0111    1111
```

(2) Read the pattern back and verify it. (3) Shift the test pattern by one bit position and go to step 1. (4) Repeat the test until all memory locations have stored all 17 data patterns. (*Note:* This test is very thorough, and identifying the faulty RAM chip in the event of a failure is quite easy—see Problem 5.45.)

QUESTIONS AND PROBLEMS

Section 5.1

5.1. Classify each of the following as main memory, secondary storage, or archival storage:
   (a) 1.44M-byte floppy disk drive
   (b) 800M-byte hard drive
   (c) 32K bytes of RAM interfaced to a Z-80 microprocessor as addresses 0000 to 7FFFH
   (d) 32K bytes of ROM interfaced to an 8085 microprocessor as addresses 0000 to 7FFFH
   (e) 2G-byte cartridge tape drive

5.2. A certain floppy disk drive can store 1.44 MB of information. How can such a drive be used with a microcomputer that has only 64K bytes of memory space?

5.3. True or false? Each byte of main memory has its own unique address.

Section 5.2

5.4. A certain memory chip is advertised as having an *access time* of 100 ns. What does this mean?

5.5. Typically, a memory chip stores data on the _____ edge of the _____ _____ signal.

5.6. The 3-MHz 8085AH microprocessor "expects" to receive valid data from memory _____ ns after the MEMR signal becomes active.

5.7. A 4-MHz Z-80A microprocessor provides _____ ns of data-setup time before clocking the memory with the trailing edge of MEMW.

5.8. Refer to Appendix C.2, and add another entry to Tables 5.3 and 5.4 for the 6-MHz 8085AH-1. (*Hint:* Use the equations given in the tables.)

5.9. Refer to Appendix C.3, and add another entry to Tables 5.3 and 5.4 for the 6-MHz Z-80B. (*Hint:* Use the equations given in the tables.)

5.10. Draw a timing diagram for the 8085 WAIT-state generator in Fig. 5.4. Be sure to include the clock, ALE, Q1A, Q1B, and READY signals.

5.11. Draw a timing diagram for the Z-80 WAIT state generator in Fig. 5.5. Be sure to include the clock, $\overline{MREQ}$, Q1A, Q1B, and $\overline{WAIT}$ signals.

5.12. Modify the 8085 WAIT-state generator circuit in Fig. 5.4 so that it requests WAIT states only for memory read or write machine cycles—not I/O cycles.

*5.13. Suppose that a solder splash shorts to ground the SET inputs of IC1A and IC1B in the 8085 WAIT-state generator circuit in Fig. 5.4. How would this fault affect the operation of the circuit?

*5.14. Refer to the Z-80 WAIT-state generator circuit shown in Fig. 5.5. Which of the following could account for the $\overline{WAIT}$ output to be permanently high?
   (a) The S input of IC1a is shorted to ground.
   (b) The S input of IC1b is shorted to ground.
   (c) The connection between $\overline{MREQ}$ and IC3 is open.
   (d) The clock signal is too slow.

Section 5.3

5.15. Can a practical microcomputer be built with ROM memory only (i.e., no RAM)? Explain.

5.16. True or false? In a typical microcomputer system, ROM is used to store a bootstrap loader program, which in turn causes the applications software to be loaded into RAM.

5.17. An 8K-byte memory is interfaced to a microcomputer system beginning at address A000H. What is the hex address of the *last* byte in this memory?

5.18. A microcomputer system has RAM from address 0000 to 7FFFH and ROM from B000H to FFFFH. How many total bytes of RAM does this system have? How many bytes of ROM? How much of the memory space is unused?

5.19. Draw the memory map corresponding to Problem 5.18.

5.20. Draw a memory map showing the starting and ending address of each memory chip in the following system:
   (a) 2 8K-byte RAM chips beginning at address 0000.
   (b) 1 1K-byte RAM chip beginning at address B000H
   (c) 4 2K-byte ROM chips beginning at address E000H

Section 5.4

5.21. What is the "word" stored at address 1101 in the diode ROM in Fig. 5.7?

5.22. Which of the following types of ROM are user programmable?
   (a) fusible-link PROM
   (b) UV-EPROM
   (c) mask-programmable ROM
   (d) E^2PROM

5.23. Which of the types of ROM listed in Problem 5.22 are erasable?

5.24. Match each of the listed phrases with one of the following memory technologies: mask-programmable ROM, OTP ROM, UV-E^2PROM, flash memory, SRAM, DRAM. Some phrases may have more than one answer.
   (a) Volatile
   (b) Capacitor storage cell
   (c) Fastest access times
   (d) Nonvolatile and byte erasable
   (e) Nonvolatile with access times comparable to that of DRAMs

(f) Fusible links

(g) SIMMs

(h) Quartz glass window

5.25. A 64K-byte memory is to be constructed using 64K × 1 DRAM chips or 8K × 8 SRAM chips. How many chips are required for each design? What are the advantages and disadvantages of each choice?

5.26. True or false? To refresh a 64K-byte DRAM, all 65,536 cell addresses must be accessed once every 2 ms.

5.27. Show how a 24-pin socket should be wired to accommodate a 2K × 8 2716 EPROM or a 2K × 8 6116 SRAM. Use jumper wires to select the ROM or RAM device.

Section 5.5

5.28. Refer to Fig. 5.41 for the following questions:

(a) Is this a ROM or RAM memory interface?

(b) What is the total memory capacity of the interface?

(c) For what *range* of memory addresses is 2732B enabled?

(d) How can the data buses of the two 2732s be wired in parallel without causing bus contention?

5.29. Redesign the memory interface in Fig. 5.41 to cover the address range 4000–5FFFH.

5.30. Suppose the output of ICIC in Fig. 5.41 fails in such a way that it is "stuck" high. How would this affect the operation of the circuit?

5.31. If address line AB15 is removed from IC1A in Fig. 5.41 and that input is grounded, the memory interface becomes *partially decoded*. To what range of addresses will each memory chip now respond?

5.32. The circuit in Fig. 5.42 is suitable as a ROM block decoder. For what *type* of bus cycles and *range* of memory addresses will output "9" be active? What size of ROM chips should be used?

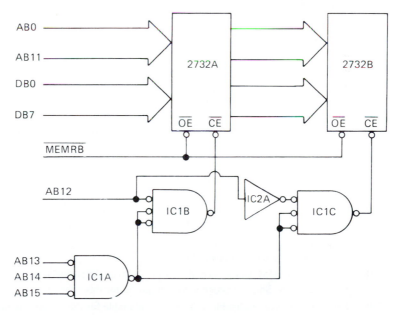

Figure 5.41   Memory interface for Probs. 28–31.

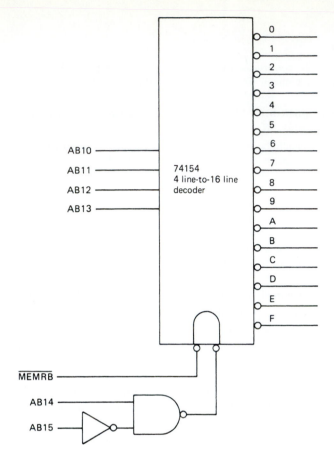

Figure 5.42 Circuit for Problem 5.32.

5.33. A certain memory interface uses buffers onto and off of the system address, data, and control buses. If the memory chips have a 150-ns access time, the address buffers a 25-ns propagation delay time, and the data bus buffers a 30-ns propagation delay time, calculate the minimum access time necessary to avoid WAIT states.

5.34. For each circuit in Fig. 5.43, determine the range of addresses for which the output is active, the active sense of the output (active high or low), and the total number of bytes in the address range.

5.35. Design a 2716-based 16K EPROM memory interface that begins at address 8000H. (*Hint:* Use a 74LS138 three-to-eight-line block decoder.)

5.36. Refer to the 32K-byte RAM module in Fig. 5.28. What switch settings are required to map BANK0 to the range 0000–3FFFH and BANK1 to the range 4000–7FFFH?

5.37. Design a 2167-based 16K-byte memory interface that begins at address C000H. Be sure to include bidirectional data bus buffers.

5.38. The 74S287 PROM address decoder in Fig. 5.30 could be replaced by a 74LS154 4-line-to-16-line decoder. Show the connections required for this change.

5.39. Determine the new truth table and PROM data table for the memory interface in Fig. 5.30 if the memory map is changed to agree with Fig. 5.44.

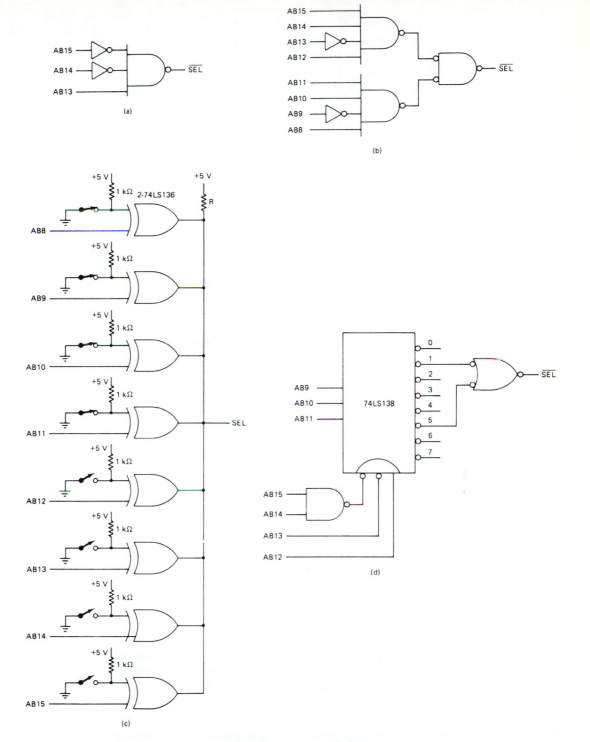

Figure 5.43 Circuit for Problem 5.34.

Chap. 5   Questions and Problems   **263**

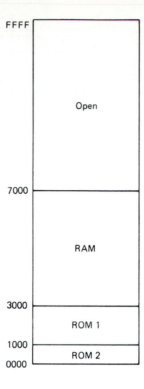

FFFF	
	Open
7000	
	RAM
3000	
	ROM 1
1000	
0000	ROM 2

Figure 5.44 New memory map for the RAM/ROM module in Fig. 5.30.

5.40. Replace all of the combinational logic (except the buffers) in the memory interface in Fig. 5.30 with a single fusible-link PROM. Specify the PROM required, the input and output assignments, the truth table, and the data table required.

5.41. Suppose a PAL10L8 is to be programmed to replace the 74S287 PROM address decoder in Fig. 5.30. Write the logic equations for $\overline{ROM1}$, $\overline{ROM2}$, and $\overline{RAM}$ in terms of A15–A12. (*Hint:* Refer to the truth table in Fig. 5.32.)

*5.42. A memory test is run on the 32K-byte memory shown in Fig. 5.28 with BANK0 mapped to cover addresses 0000–3FFFH and BANK1 mapped to cover addresses 4000–7FFFH. The test reports an error at address 57E3H, bit 4. Which RAM chip is indicated?

*5.43. A memory test is run on the 32K-byte memory in Fig. 5.28 and reports errors at *all* memory locations. Further testing shows that each location appears to be storing random data despite attempts to write particular data patterns. What do you think is wrong with this interface? What would you check?

*5.44. The "walking 1's" memory test writes a 1 to each possible bit position. Which bit (0–7) do you think is in error in the walking 1's test report that follows?

```
Error at 2300H    wrote: 00000000    read: 00000001
Error at 2300H    wrote: 00000010    read: 00000011
Error at 2300H    wrote: 00000100    read: 00000101
Error at 2300H    wrote: 00001000    read: 00001001
              .                .                .
              .                .                .
              .                .                .
Error at 2300H    wrote: 10000000    read: 10000001
```

Section 5.6

5.45. The *access time* of a DRAM chip is measured from the falling edge of _____ to _____ _____ .

5.46. A certain DRAM has address pins numbered A0–A8 and is organized × 16. What is the total storage capacity of this chip in bits?

5.47. Number the following DRAM timing parameters in order (1 = shortest, 3 = longest)
  a. _____ row access time
  b. _____ memory cycle time (nonpage mode)
  c. _____ column access time

5.48. A certain DRAM requires a 7-bit refresh address and has a 300-ns cycle time. How long would a *burst refresh* cycle take for this memory chip? Express your answer as a percentage of the 2-ms refresh period.

5.49. In Fig. 5.39, which control signal selects the active 64K memory bank? Can both banks ever be active simultaneously?

5.50. Which of the following DRAM refresh controller components are "built in" to the Z-80 microprocessor?
  a. address multiplexer
  b. $\overline{RAS}$ and $\overline{CAS}$ clock generator
  c. refresh address generator

SELF-REVIEW ANSWERS

5.1.1. main

5.1.2. floppy and hard-disk drives

5.1.3. archival

5.2.1. address access

5.2.2. WAIT

5.3.1. Nonvolatile storage of a bootstrap loader, microcontroller software, applications software (BASIC in ROM)

5.3.2. Volatile: Contents of memory are lost when power is removed. Nonvolatile: Contents of memory are retained, even when power is removed.

5.3.3. 1000H + 1FFFH = 2FFFH

5.3.4. memory map

5.4.1. 16,5

5.4.2. one-time programmable

5.4.3. (b)

5.4.4. Flash, 100,000

5.4.5. SRAM

5.4.6. capacitor

5.4.7. 4

5.4.8. 128K

5.4.9. DRAM, 64K, 100

5.5.1. address decoder

5.5.2. They decrease the access time alloted the memory by the CPU.

5.5.3. partial

5.5.4. ROM, PAL

5.6.1. The address is split into a row and column address and is clocked in separately on the same set of pins via the $\overline{\text{RAS}}$ and $\overline{\text{CAS}}$ clock signals.

5.6.2. $\overline{\text{RAS}}$

5.6.3. $\overline{\text{CAS}}$

5.6.4. cycle times

5.6.5. burst

5.6.6. $\overline{\text{RAS}}$-only

6

BUILDING THE MICROCOMPUTER, PART 3: INPUT/OUTPUT

OUTLINE

OBJECTIVES

After completing this chapter, you should be able to:

- Explain the role of the address, data, and control buses in 8080, 8085, and Z-80 I/O machine cycles.
- Design an 8-bit input and an 8-bit output port compatible with the 8080, 8085, and Z-80 microprocessors.
- Compare port-mapped I/O with memory-mapped I/O.
- Explain the hardware and software required to interface a matrix keypad to a microprocessor using memory-mapped I/O.

- Explain the relationship between a peripheral's BUSY/READY, STROBE, and AC-KNOWLEDGE signals.
- Explain what is meant by the term *handshaking logic*.
- Describe the handshaking signals commonly available with a parallel printer.
- Write a parallel-printer control program using programmed I/O and calculate its maximum data transfer rate.
- Compare the interrupt capabilities of the 8080, 8085, and Z-80 microprocessors.
- Write a parallel-printer control program using interrupt-driven I/O and calculate its maximum data transfer rate.
- Explain how a peripheral can be interfaced using direct memory access (DMA).
- Compare the byte, burst, and block modes of DMA operation.

OVERVIEW

The last block to be discussed in the building of our microcomputer is the input–output, or I/O, block. We might call this the *user interface*. Try to imagine a microcomputer without any input or output devices. Internally, the CPU might be executing a "magnificent" program. But without a means to communicate with this program, the CPU might as well execute NOPs.

There are basically two hardware techniques for getting data into and out of a computer. The first is the *parallel* interface and is the most natural for the microprocessor. Data is read and written from the I/O devices in 8-bit bytes, much as from read/write memory. All data bits are transferred in parallel.

The second technique is the *serial* interface. This method does not come as naturally to the microprocessor, but it does have its advantages. A parallel-to-serial converter is used to transmit the 8 data bits serially—that is, one after the other in time. Similarly, a serial-to-parallel converter is used to re-form the parallel data bytes. The advantage of this technique is that only three wires are required to implement the interface: serial data in, serial data out, and ground. The main disadvantage is a speed penalty: It takes at least eight times as long to transmit the byte 1 bit at a time as it will to transmit all 8 bits at once.

Nevertheless, serial data communication is quite popular today. Perhaps one reason is that many computer peripherals cannot handle data as fast as a parallel interface would output it anyway. Another reason is that three conductor cables are considerably cheaper than eight or nine.

Finally, the 1's and 0's output by a serial computer interface can be converted into audio tones and transmitted over the telephone network by a *modem*. This technique allows communication over thousands of miles by using the existing wiring of the various telephone companies.

Because serial communication is so popular, Chapter 9 is devoted entirely to this subject. In the current chapter, we concentrate on parallel I/O techniques. This would be a fairly simple topic if all computer peripherals were as fast as the microprocessor. But, of course, they are not: Data come off a terminal as fast as the operator can type and can be output to a printer only as fast as the printer can print. Often, the microprocessor must sit and wait—sometimes for a relatively long time—until the peripheral is ready to receive or transmit more data.

A few peripherals are actually faster than the microprocessor. Magnetic disk interfaces, particularly hard-disk drives, can transfer data at rates as high as 5 million bits per second. For these peripherals, special data transfer processors (called *DMA controllers*) are required.

So once again we begin a chapter by saying, "Nothing is simple anymore!"

6.1 PARALLEL I/O: INTERFACING TO A TYPE 3 BUS

In this section, we:

- Explain the role of the address, data, and control buses in 8080, 8085, and Z-80 I/O machine cycles.
- Design an 8-bit input and an 8-bit output port compatible with the 8080, 8085, and Z-80 microprocessors.

Introduction

The design of a microcomputer input or output port involves all three system buses. Figure 4.21 illustrated the data path from an input device to the microprocessor. Data are input to the CPU by tristate transmitters and received by clocked latches. The bidirectional data bus is required for all data transfers. We defined this bus to be a *type 3* bus in Chapter 4.

Before we actually design an input or output port, let us review the timing for the two I/O operations, keeping in mind the type 3 bus model in Fig. 4.21.

I/O Machine Cycles and Timing

Table 6.1 lists typical input and output instructions for the 8080, 8085, and Z-80 microprocessors. Notice that the 8080 and 8085 are restricted to using the accumulator for all I/O operations. The Z-80 can use register C to hold the port address and then input or output data with any of the other general-purpose registers. The Z-80 can also use HL as a source or destination of data.

Each I/O instruction leaves its own unique set of "footprints" on the three system buses. Understanding this information, we can readily design microcomputer input and output ports.

Figure 6.1 summarizes the information in Table 6.1 in the form of a "generic" timing diagram for an I/O read and I/O write machine cycle. The I/O read cycle [Figure 6.1 (a)] is identical to a memory read cycle with the following changes:

1. The port address is 8 bits long instead of 16. The 8080 and 8085 duplicate this address on A0 through A7 and A8 through A15. The Z-80 outputs the port address on A0 through A7 only.
2. The $\overline{\text{IOR}}$ control signal, instead of $\overline{\text{MEMR}}$, is active. Remember that $\overline{\text{IOR}}$ is active when IO/$\overline{\text{M}}$ = 1 and $\overline{\text{RD}}$ = 0 for the 8085 and when $\overline{\text{IORQ}}$ = 0 and $\overline{\text{RD}}$ = 0 for the Z-80.
3. For the Z-80 only, one WAIT state is added.

TABLE 6.1 I/O Instructions for the 8080, 8085, and Z-80 Microprocessors

Microprocessor	Instruction	Data bus	Control bus	Address bus
8080	IN nn	Data	$\overline{\text{IOR}} = 0$	A0–A7 and A8–A15 = nn
	OUT nn	Accumulator	$\overline{\text{IOW}} = 0$	A0–A7 and A8–A15 = nn
8085	IN nn	Data	$\text{IO}/\overline{\text{M}} = 1$ $\overline{\text{RD}} = 0$	AD0–AD7 and A8–A15 = nn
	OUT nn	Accumulator	$\text{IO}/\overline{\text{M}} = 1$ $\overline{\text{WR}} = 0$	AD0–AD7 and A8–A15 = nn
Z-80	IN A,(nn)	Data	$\overline{\text{IORQ}} = 0$ $\overline{\text{RD}} = 0$	A0–A7 = nn A8–A15 = accumulator
	OUT (nn),A	Accumulator	$\overline{\text{IORQ}} = 0$ $\overline{\text{WR}} = 0$	A0–A7 = nn A8–A15 = accumulator
	IN r,(C)	Data	$\overline{\text{IORQ}} = 0$ $\overline{\text{RD}} = 0$	A0–A7 = C A8–A15 = accumulator
	OUT(C),r	r	$\overline{\text{IORQ}} = 0$ $\overline{\text{WR}} = 0$	A0–A7 = C A8–A15 = accumulator

The critical timing parameters for an I/O read cycle are t_{RD} and t_{RH}. t_{RD} is the time the microprocessor gives the input port-select logic to gate its data onto the data bus. This amounts to the time required to enable the tristate transmitter in Fig. 4.21.

t_{RH} is the amount of time the microprocessor requires that data be held stable after IOR returns high. This parameter is 0 ns for all three processors, which means that data

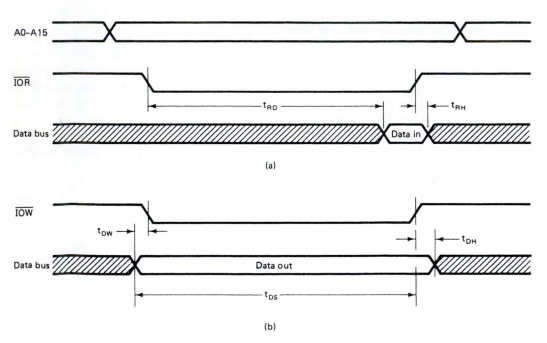

Figure 6.1 Timing relationships for (a) I/O read and (b) I/O write machine cycles.

TABLE 6.2 I/O Timing Specifications for the 8080, 8085, and Z-80 Microprocessors

	I/O read		I/O write		
Microprocessor	t_{RD} (max.)	t_{RH} (min.)	t_{DW} (min.)	t_{DS} (min.)	t_{DH} (min.)
8080A (2 MHz)	464 ns	0	156 ns	656 ns	119 ns
8085AH (3 MHz)	300 ns	0	−40 ns	420 ns	100 ns
Z-80A (4 MHz)	475 ns	0	−10 ns	600 ns	60 ns

can be removed as soon as $\overline{\text{IOR}}$ disappears. Specifications for t_{RD} and t_{RH} are given for the 8080A, 8085AH, and Z-80A in Table 6.2.

Figure 6.1(b) illustrates an I/O write machine cycle. This cycle is identical to a memory write cycle with the following exceptions:

1. The port address is again 8 bits instead of 16.
2. $\overline{\text{IOW}}$, instead of $\overline{\text{MEMW}}$, is active.
3. For the Z-80 only, one WAIT state is added.

The memory write cycle begins with the output of the port address on A0 through A15. Next, the data to be written is placed on D0 through D7, and the $\overline{\text{IOW}}$ line is brought low. Table 6.2 provides specifications for the three timing parameters shown in Fig. 6.1(b).

The first parameter is t_{DS}, the amount of time that data is on the bus before $\overline{\text{IOW}}$ is removed (goes high). Normally, data should be latched by the output port on the rising edge of $\overline{\text{IOW}}$; thus, t_{DS} corresponds to a setup time for the output port data latch.

The second important timing parameter is t_{DH}, the amount of time that data remain stable after $\overline{\text{IOW}}$ has gone high. This time is provided by the microprocessor to satisfy the hold-time requirements of many latches.

The last timing parameter is t_{DW}, the amount of time that data are stable before the falling edge of $\overline{\text{IOW}}$. From Table 6.2, t_{DW} is actually *negative* for the 8085 and Z-80 microprocessors, meaning that $\overline{\text{IOW}}$ goes low *before* the data are stable. This is an important point, because, if the falling edge of $\overline{\text{IOW}}$ is used to clock the output port latch, erroneous information may be stored.

Designing an 8-Bit Input Port

On the basis of the preceding discussion, we can conclude that the hardware for a microcomputer input port must do all of the following:

1. Examine the address bus for a specific port address.
2. When the port address is present AND $\overline{\text{IOR}}$ = 0, generate a *device-select pulse* (DSP).
3. Gate data onto the data bus through eight tristate transmitters enabled by the DSP.

Sec. 6.1   Parallel I/O: Interfacing to a Type 3 Bus

Example 6.1

Design a microcomputer interface to read the value that is set on an eight-position DIP switch. Use input port address 3FH. Calculate t_{RD}, and verify that this specification is met for all processors listed in Table 6.2.

Solution. The circuit diagram is given in Fig. 6.2. Two inverters and an eight-input NAND gate are used to decode the port address output on address lines AB0 through AB7. The output of IC2 will go low each time the low-order address bus contains 3FH. Notice that this could occur many times in the execution of a typical program, because there are 256 separate pages that have a low-order address of 3FH.

When, and only when, the instruction IN 3FH [Z-80 mnemonic IN A,(3FH)] is executed, the low-order address will be 3FH *and* the $\overline{\text{IOR}}$ line will be low. This will cause the output of IC3 to go low, generating a device-select pulse (labeled $\overline{\text{IN3F}}$ in Fig. 6.2). The $\overline{\text{IN3F}}$ DSP is used to enable the 74LS244, causing the settings of the eight switches to be placed onto the data bus. The microprocessor latches this data byte and stores it in the accumulator on the rising edge of $\overline{\text{IOR}}$.

The time delays associated with each component in this interface are shown as Δt in the figure. Also shown are the propagation delays associated with the address buffers, the 8085 and Z-80 $\overline{\text{IOR}}$ logic (actually on the CPU module), and the bidirectional bus buffers (also part of the CPU module).

First note that we do not need to consider the delays through the address decoder. This is because the port address is output well ahead of the $\overline{\text{IOR}}$ signal (180 ns for the Z-80A), and the $\overline{\text{SEL3F}}$ output thus arrives at IC3 well before $\overline{\text{IORB}}$. When $\overline{\text{IORB}}$ does arrive—delayed through buffers on the CPU module and I/O module—the $\overline{\text{IN3F}}$ DSP is generated. The total time delay to this point is

$$t_{DSP} = 2 \times t_{BUF} + t_{IC3}$$
$$= 36 \text{ ns} \quad + 22 \text{ ns}$$
$$= 58 \text{ ns}$$

This time should be increased by 37 ns for the 8085 and 22 ns for the Z-80, due to the $\overline{\text{IOR}}$ control logic shown in the upper left corner of Fig. 6.2.

Once the DSP is generated, the 74LS244 buffer responds (after a 30-ns delay), and the data appear on the system data bus. The data bus buffers on the CPU module add an additional 12 ns of delay, resulting in a total read time of

$$t_{RD} = t_{DSP} \quad + t_{BUF244} + t_{BUF245}$$
$$= 58 \text{ ns} \quad + 30 \text{ ns} \quad + 12 \text{ ns}$$
$$= 100 \text{ ns}$$

The results for the 8085 and Z-80 are 137 ns and 122 ns, respectively. This additional delay is due to the $\overline{\text{IOR}}$ logic, as mentioned before. Comparing these numbers with the specifications in Table 6.2, we see that the input port in Fig. 6.2 is considerably faster than required.

It is interesting to note that the t_{RD} specification for the 6-MHz version of the 8085 drops from 300 ns to only 75 ns, but is still 300 ns for the 6-MHz Z-80B. The Z-80 adds an extra WAIT state to its I/O instructions, purposely giving the select logic more time to output its data.

Note also that the time delays indicated in Fig. 6.2 are *worst-case* numbers; typical devices will have delays only 50 to 60% of these times. However, designing to typical

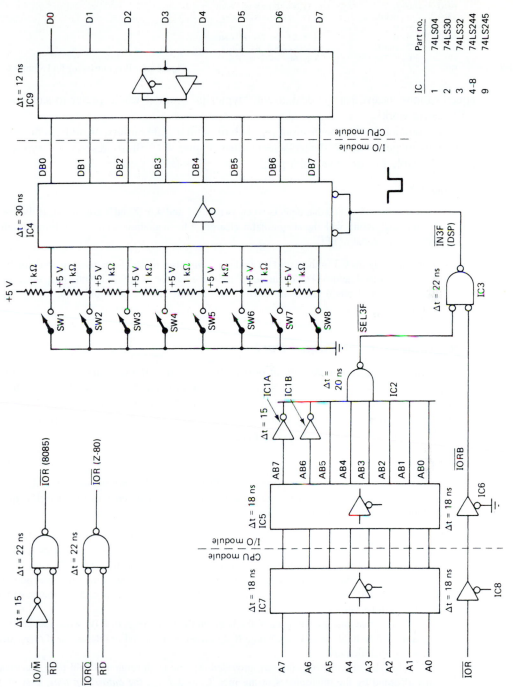

Figure 6.2 Hardware for the input port in Example 6.1.

IC	Part no.
1	74LS04
2	74LS30
3	74LS32
4–8	74LS244
9	74LS245

273

```
EX6-2     IN    A,(3FH)     ;READ INPUT PORT
          LD    B,A         ;SAVE A COPY
          AND   09H         ;TEST BITS 0 AND 3
          JR    Z,DONE      ;IF ZERO RETURN
          LD    A,B         ;RETRIEVE COPY
          AND   42H         ;TEST BITS 6 AND 1
          JR    Z,DONE      ;IF ZERO RETURN
          LD    A,FFH       ;ELSE ACC = FF
DONE      RET
```

Figure 6.3   Program listing for Example 6.2.

specifications means that the design will "typically" work! I would prefer to say that it will *always* work!

In sum, a microcomputer input port is built with tristate buffers, an address decoder, and logic to generate the device-select pulse. Figure 4.15 illustrates several types of buffers suitable for use in an input port.

Example 6.2

Write a Z-80 subroutine that detects when switches 1 and 4 or 2 and 7 are closed. If the condition is met, return with the accumulator cleared; if the condition is not met, return with the accumulator equal to FFH.

Solution.   Figure 6.3 is the program listing. A *masking* technique is used to monitor bits 0 and 3 or bits 1 and 6. For example, if the accumulator is ANDed with 09H, the result will be 0 only if bits 0 and 3 are also 0. In this way, any bit or combination of bits can be tested.

Designing an 8-Bit Output Port

The design of a microcomputer output port requires the use of a latch to "catch" data that is output on the system data bus. This operation was illustrated in Fig. 4.21, in which all receivers of data are shown as flip-flops. Again, a *DSP* must be generated, this time by combining the address-select signal and the $\overline{\text{IOW}}$ control signal. The DSP is then used to clock the latch connected to the system data bus.

Example 6.3

Design an 8-bit output port using partial decoding such that the port maps to any address between 80H and FFH. Calculate t_{DS} and t_{DH} for the circuit, and verify that the specifications in Table 6.2 are met for all processors.

Solution.   The circuit diagram is provided in Fig. 6.4. Because of the partial decoding requirement, there is no need for a separate address-decoder circuit: Port addresses between 80H and FFH can easily be identified whenever address line A7 is high. The DSP signal used to clock the latch should combine A7 and $\overline{\text{IOW}}$. In this way, whenever the low-order address bus holds an address between 80H and FFH *and* the $\overline{\text{IOW}}$ line is active, the contents of the data bus will be latched.

Notice that data are strobed into the latch on the rising edge of $\overline{\text{IOW}}$ when the data bus is guaranteed to hold valid data. Change IC2 to a NOR gate, and problems could occur due to the t_{DW} specification.

This circuit will work correctly, provided that the latch setup and hold-time specifications afforded by the microprocessor are met. Consider t_{DS}, the *data setup time*, first. Any data that is output by the microprocessor must propagate through the CPU module buffers (after a 40-ns delay) and then the I/O module buffers (after an 18-ns delay). The 74LS374

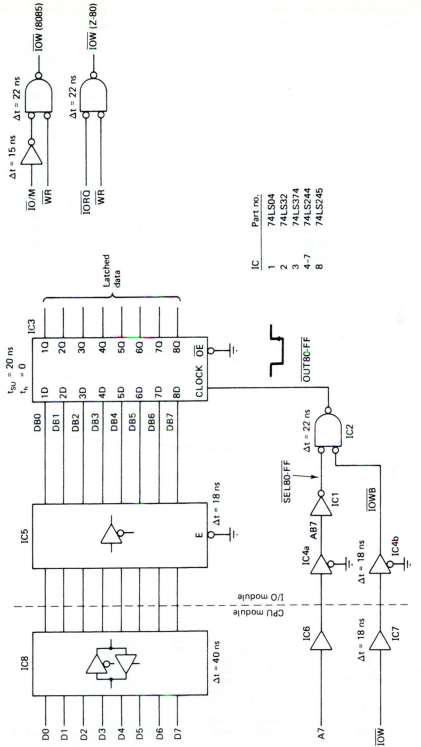

Figure 6.4 Hardware for the output port in Example 6.3. The buffers on either side of the dashed lines are part of the CPU module and I/O modules as recommended in Chapter 4.

275

latch requires that data be stable on its inputs for at least 20 ns prior to the strobe signal. Thus, the setup time required by the output port interface in Fig. 6.4 is

$$t_{DS} = t_{BUFCPU} + t_{BUFI/O} + t_{SUlatch}$$
$$= 40 \text{ ns} + 18 \text{ ns} + 20 \text{ ns}$$
$$= 78 \text{ ns}$$

Referring to Table 6.2, we see that 78 ns is well within the specifications for all of the processors.

Last we must consider the *hold-time* requirement. Some latches require that data be held for a brief period after the clock edge occurs. This requirement ensures that data will be internally latched by the device. The 74LS374 latch used in Fig. 6.4 has a 0-ns hold-time requirement. This means that data need be held stable only until the clock edge occurs.

The 74LS374 clock signal (the $\overline{\text{OUT80-FF DSP}}$) is derived from the address-decoding logic and $\overline{\text{IOW}}$ signal. In this case, we are concerned with the trailing edge of $\overline{\text{IOW}}$—that is, the point in time when $\overline{\text{IOW}}$ returns high. To meet the hold-time specification of the 74LS374, data must be stable until the clock input goes high. Due to the CPU module and I/O module buffers (IC7 and IC4b) and IC2, the rising edge of $\overline{\text{IOW}}$ will be delayed. During this time, the data must be held stable. Thus, the hold time for the circuit in Fig. 6.4 is

$$t_{DH} = t_{BUFCPU} + t_{BUFI/O} + t_{IC2}$$
$$= 18 \text{ ns} + 18 \text{ ns} + 22 \text{ ns}$$
$$= 58 \text{ ns}$$

This time must be increased to 95 ns for the 8085 and 80 ns for the Z-80, due to the extra $\overline{\text{IOW}}$ logic required for these processors. Checking with Table 6.2, we find that the 8080 and 8085 are within specifications (barely), but the Z-80 is 20 ns out of specifications. One way of rationalizing this is to note that if the Z-80 does remove data 20 ns too soon, the 74LS374 will not "realize" it until after the propagation delays of the two data bus buffers. Assuming typical delays for these gates, 39 ns would be required, and the hold time would be met with 19 ns to spare.

In sum, the design of a microcomputer output port requires decoding the port address and combining this signal with $\overline{\text{IOW}}$ to generate a DSP that is then used to clock a latch and store the contents of the data bus. Table 6.3 lists several commonly available latches suitable for microcomputer output ports.

Example 6.4

Write a Z-80 program that turns output bits 2 and 4 on (high) in Fig. 6.4 if switches 1 and 4 or 2 and 7 of the input port in Fig. 6.2 are closed. If these switches are open, then turn on output bits 0 and 5.

Solution. The program listing is provided in Fig. 6.5. After turning all outputs off, the program checks the input port by calling the subroutine in Fig. 6.3. Depending on the status of

```
EX6-4     SUB    A             ;CLEAR ACCUMULATOR
          OUT    (80H),A       ;TURN ALL BITS OFF
LOOP      CALL   EX6-2         ;TEST BITS
          OR     A             ;SET FLAGS
          JR     NZ,NMET       ;CONDITION NOT MET
          LD     A,14H         ;BITS 2 AND 4 ON
          JR     CMET          ;CONDITION MET
NMET      LD     A,21H         ;BITS 0 AND 5 ON
CMET      OUT    (80H),A       ;PROGRAM THE PORT
          JR     LOOP          ;CYCLE AGAIN
```

Figure 6.5 Program listing for Example 6.4.

TABLE 6.3 Latches Suitable for Use in Microcomputer Output Ports

MSI/LSI functions

Functional index/selection guide

Latches

Description	No. of bits	Clear	Outputs	Typical delay time	TYP total power dissipation	Device type and package			
						−55°C to 125°C		0°C to 70°C	
Multimode Buffered	8	Low	Q	11 ns	410 mW	SN54S412	J	SN74S412	J, N
Addressable	8	Low	Q	12 ns	300 mW	SN54259	J, W	SN74259	J, N
		Low	Q	17 ns	110 mW	SN54LS259	J, W	SN74LS259	J, N
Transparent	8	None	Q	19 ns	120 mW	SN54LS373	J	SN74LS373	J, N
		None	Q	7 ns	525 mW	SN54S373	J	SN74S373	J, N
Dual 4-Bit with Independent Enable	8	Low	Q	11 ns	250 mW	SN54116	J, W	SN74116	J, N
		None	Q	15 ns	320 mW	SN54100	J, W	SN74100	J, N
Dual 2-Bit with Independent Enable	4	None	$Q, \overline{Q}$	15 ns	160 mW	SN5475	J, W	SN7475	J, N
		None	$Q, \overline{Q}$	30 ns	80 mW	SN54L75	J	SN74L75	J, N
		None	$Q, \overline{Q}$	11 ns	32 mW	SN54LS75	J, W	SN74LS75	J, N
		None	Q	15 ns	160 mW	SN5477	W		
		None	Q	30 ns	80 mW	SN54L77	T		
		None	$\overline{Q}, Q$	10 ns	35 mW	SN54LS77	W		
		None	$Q, \overline{Q}$	12 ns	32 mW	SN54LS375	J, W	SN74LS375	J, N
QUAD $\overline{S}$-$\overline{R}$ (SSI)	4	None	Q	12 ns	90 mW	SN54279	J, W	SN74279	J, N
		None	Q	12 ns	19 mW	SN54LS279	J, W	SN74LS279	J, N

Source: Courtesy of Texas Instruments, Inc.

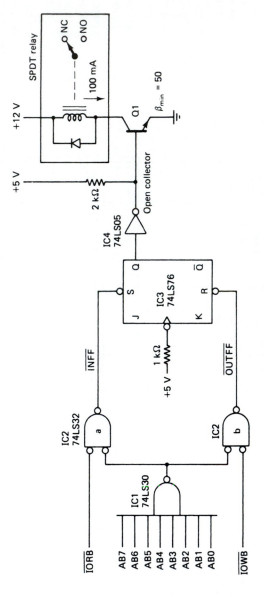

Figure 6.6 Using device-select pulses (DSPs) to control a relay. An OUT FF instruction will turn on the relay and an IN FF instruction will turn it off.

the accumulator, the appropriate bit pattern is output to port 80H to turn on the proper output pins. The program loops continuously, responding immediately to a change at the input port.

Applications for the Device-Select Pulse

In some control applications, the device-select pulse (DSP) alone is sufficient for the interface. An example of such a circuit is shown in Fig. 6.6. The OUTFF DSP is used to reset the flip-flop and the $\overline{\text{INFF}}$ DSP to set it. The Q output of the flip-flop is used to control a relay through the 74LS05 open-collector buffer and transistor Q1.

The 8080/85 command OUT FF will reset the flip-flop and turn on the relay. The transistor is required because the relay coil requires 100 mA of current when it is energized—well beyond the sink capabilities of the flip-flop Q output. Chapter 11 provides more details on interfacing to non-TTL-compatible peripherals.

What data should be in the accumulator when the OUT FF command is given? Because no connection is made to the data bus, it does not matter. Only the DSP is used. Similarly, no data are input when the IN FF instruction is executed. (Due to the nature of a TTL gate—open inputs "look like" logic 1's—the accumulator will probably store FFH.)

SELF-REVIEW 6.1

6.1.1 The 8080, 8085, and Z-80 output a(n) _____ -bit I/O address, allowing access to _____ different I/O ports.

6.1.2 Which of the three processors—the 8080, 8085, or Z-80—adds a WAIT state to all I/O cycles?

6.1.3 The signal used to activate an I/O port is called the _____ _____ pulse.

6.2 MEMORY-MAPPED I/O

Introduction

We began Section 6.1 by noting the similarities between a memory read or write cycle and an I/O read or write cycle. Thinking about this similarity some more, we might note that a read/write memory is made up of (8-bit) latches for storing data and tristate buffers for reading the data back out—the same hardware as that required for an I/O port. What if we designed a 1-byte memory interface? For all intents and purposes, this would, in fact, be an I/O port and not really a memory location.

This is the essence of *memory-mapped* I/O: All microprocessors are capable of memory-mapped I/O if they are capable of interfacing to memory. In fact, for many microprocessors—the 6800 and 6502 microprocessors, for example—only memory-mapped I/O is possible. These processors have no IN or OUT instructions; all I/O operations are performed using normal memory-reference commands.

But this is precisely the advantage of memory-mapped I/O: The 8080 has only two I/O instructions, but it has numerous memory-reference instructions. The instruction MOV M,B becomes an I/O instruction: Copy the contents of register B into the output port whose address is stored in the HL pair.

In this section, we:

- Compare port-mapped I/O with memory-mapped I/O.
- Explain the hardware and software required to interface a matrix keypad to a microprocessor using memory-mapped I/O.

Designing an 8-Bit Memory-Mapped Input Port

Figure 6.7 is the schematic diagram of an 8-bit memory-mapped input port. This diagram should be compared with Fig. 6.2, which is the corresponding I/O-mapped input port. (*Note: I/O mapped* is the term used for conventional I/O, which employs the IN and OUT instructions.) The only difference between the two circuits is in the selection logic. Because a memory address is 16 bits long, the address decoder must decode more bits. In Fig. 6.7, two 74LS30s are required, and the port address is arbitrarily chosen to be FF3FH.

Any memory reference to address FF3FH will be decoded and cause $\overline{\text{SEL FF3F}}$ to go low. By combining this signal with $\overline{\text{MEMRE}}$, any memory read from address FF3FH will cause the $\overline{\text{IN FF3F DSP}}$ signal to become active and enable the tristate buffer.

Example 6.5

List several instructions that can be used to read the contents of the switch in the memory-mapped interface in Fig. 6.7.

Solution. Many instructions can be used:

Mnemonic		
8080/85	Z-80	Comment
LDA FF3FH	LD A,FF3FH	;LOAD THE ACCUMULATOR DIRECT
LDAX B	LD A,(BC)	;BC = FF3FH
MOV C,M	LD C,(HL)	;HL = FF3FH
	LD D,(IX + d)	;IX = FF3FH AND d = 0

One of the disadvantages of memory-mapped I/O is the requirement to decode 16 bits, versus 8 with the conventional I/O-mapped interface. Because of this requirement, *partial decoding* is often used. For example, if the portion of the decoder enclosed in dashed lines in Fig. 6.7 is removed—that is, A0 through A7 are no longer decoded—the resulting circuit is no more complex than Fig. 6.2. The price for this simplification is that the port now occupies memory from FF00H through FFFFH.

The preceding discussion points out the main drawback to memory-mapped I/O: It "steals" memory space from the processor. Consider a memory implemented with 16K RAM chips and one memory-mapped input port at FFFFH. Because the memory and I/O cannot be allowed to have the same address, the maximum memory capacity may be re-

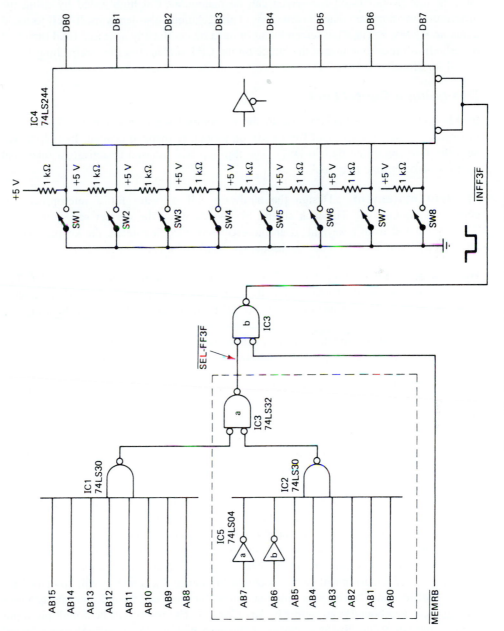

Figure 6.7 Memory-mapped input port at address FF3FH.

stricted to 48K. This problem can be overcome by detecting address FFFFH and disabling the RAM, but you can see the problem.

Memory mapping is a popular technique for interfacing a *video display generator*. Objects and characters on the screen can be manipulated at high speed by using the processor's memory reference instructions. This technique also lends itself well to using dynamic RAMs, because the screen memory must be continually accessed (and therefore refreshed) in order to maintain the image on the CRT screen. In effect, refreshing is obtained for "free."

Designing a Digital Lock

In this section, we consider the use of the microprocessor as a controller. The microprocessor will receive its input from a 10-digit memory-mapped keypad. Its output will be a flip-flop controlled by two DSPs. The flip-flop will be used to activate a relay that controls an electronic door lock.

Problem statement. Design the hardware and software for a microprocessor-controlled digital lock. The lock should be opened when the correct sequence of six digits is entered from a keypad. If an incorrect sequence is entered, the keypad should be disabled for at least 1 minute to discourage "trial and error."

Hardware. The electronic lock will use the relay control circuit shown in Fig. 6.6. The relay contacts are assumed connected to the lock in such a way that an OUT FF command will turn on the relay and open the lock. An IN FF command will turn off the relay and close the lock.

Figure 6.8 shows the memory-mapped keypad interface. The 10 keys are assumed to be normally open push-button switches arranged in two columns as shown.

Reading the keypad. In interfacing any keyboard to a microcomputer, three problems must be solved:

1. Detect that a key is down.
2. "Debounce" the key closure.
3. Encode the key.

In Fig. 6.8, a key closure is detected by doing a memory read from address FF03H. This will enable the tristate buffers and cause the two column inverters, IC1A and IC1B, to put 0 V on the column lines. If no key is down, the row lines will be pulled high by the resistors, and the data will be inverted and read as 00000000. However, if any key is down, the result will be nonzero—00010000 if key 4 is down, for example.

Whenever a mechanical switch is closed or opened, the contacts will "bounce" for several milliseconds. During this time, the microprocessor will be led into falsely interpreting these key bounces as legitimate key closures. The result will be a multiple input of the same key value. Switches can be *debounced* with hardware (using cross-coupled gates—or see Problem 4.31 for another technique) or with software.

Figure 6.9 is a flowchart illustrating how the keypad can be debounced in software. Because the microprocessor can execute the entire program before you can even take your

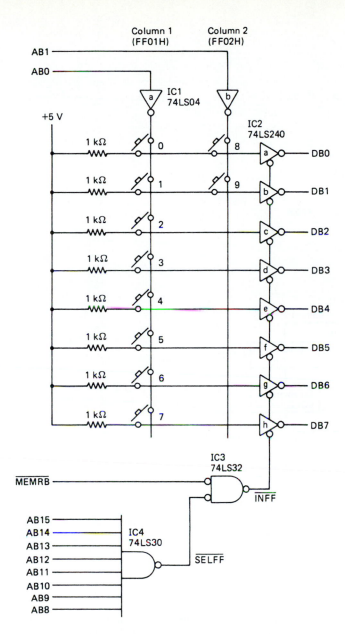

Figure 6.8 Memory-mapped keypad interface for the digital lock design problem.

finger off one key, the program begins by waiting until the keyboard is clear. Once this condition is detected, a 20-ms wait is inserted to allow the key to bounce upon being released.

Next, the program waits for a key to be pressed. When this condition is detected, another 20-ms wait is inserted to allow the key to stop bouncing. Now the encoding process can begin. First, the column with the key closed must be determined. This is done by reading from address FF01 (column 1) and testing for a nonzero result. A zero result indicates that the key which is down must be in column 2 and address FF02 should be read.

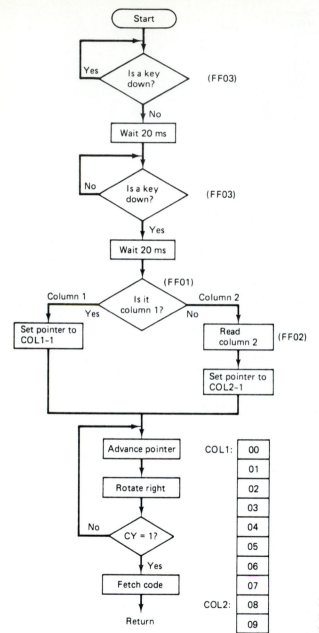

Figure 6.9 Flowchart to detect a key closure, debounce the key, and encode it using the hardware in Fig. 6.8.

Now that the proper column is known, a pointer into a data table is initialized. In this table are stored the values we wish to assign each key—in this case, the numerals 0 through 9.

All that remains is to locate the actual key that is down. This is done by rotating the data word right and testing the carry flag. For example, after five rotate rights, the carry

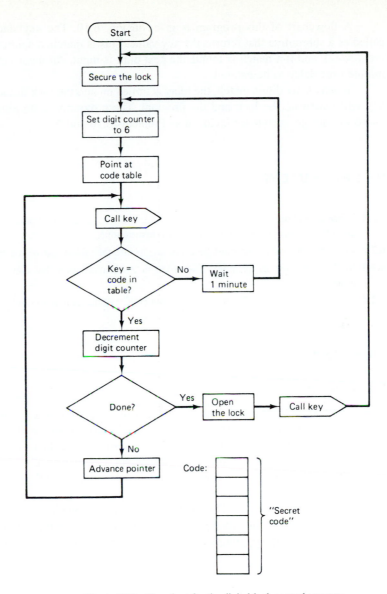

Figure 6.10 Flowchart for the digital lock control program.

flag will be set if key 4 was held down. By advancing the memory pointer with each rotate, it will end up pointing at 04. This character can be moved to a register and the routine ended.

Developing the control software. The keyboard encoding routine flow-charted in Fig. 6.9 is only part of the control program. The main program determines the number of digits in the sequence, checks each input as it is typed against the "secret code," and, finally, unlocks the door.

A flowchart of this program is given in Fig. 6.10. The keyboard read routine is called as a subroutine that returns the key value. This is matched against a table (the *"secret code"*), and if a match is found, the next digit is input. An incorrect digit causes a 1-minute time delay to be entered.

When all six digits match, the relay is turned on and the lock unlocked. Pushing any key will reactivate the lock and the program. The programs to go along with the flowcharts are not given, but are included as Problems 6.16 and 6.17.

SELF-REVIEW 6.2

6.2.1 When an I/O port is _____ _____, that port can be accessed using any of the processor's memory-reference instructions.

6.2.2 List three problems that must be overcome to interface a keypad with a microprocessor.

6.2.3 In Fig. 6.8, give an example of an 8080 or Z-80 instruction that can be used to read column 1.

6.2.4 In Fig. 6.8, if just key 2 is held down, what code will the instruction in Question 6.2.3 return?

6.3 HANDSHAKING LOGIC

Introduction

Why was the block "Is a key down?" required in the digital lock problem? What would have happened if the microprocessor simply read the keyboard without waiting for this block? I think you know the answers to these questions. The data input from the keypad is *asynchronous* with respect to the microprocessor. Unless we wait for a key to be down, the program will try to process nonexistent data, or it might read the same key many times over.

This is a critical point. The microprocessor must somehow *synchronize* itself with the peripheral. That is, the processor must be able to adjust to the data rate of the I/O device, whether the operator enters data at the rate of 5 characters per second or 1 character per hour.

In most cases, the microprocessor is much faster than the peripheral. Consider a line printer capable of printing 100 characters per second (cps). This corresponds to one character every 10 ms. If the Z-80 instruction *OTIR* is used to output data to the printer, the Z-80A will output 190,476 characters per second! Unless some means of synchronizing the printer and microprocessor is found, data will be lost.

Most slow peripherals, such as printers and plotters, are mechanical devices and limited in their maximum speed. To interface to these devices, the microprocessor must be slowed down—certainly, the peripheral cannot be speeded up.

For some peripherals, the microprocessor is too slow. A high-density $3\frac{1}{2}''$ floppy disk transfers data at a rate of 500,000 bits per second. Hard disks can transfer millions of data bits per second. Interfacing to these devices is particularly interesting because they cannot be slowed down and the microprocessor cannot be speeded up!

In this section, we:

- Explain the relationship between a peripheral's BUSY/READY, STROBE, and ACKNOWLEDGE signals.
- Explain what is meant by the term *handshaking logic*.

BUSY, $\overline{READY}$, and ACKNOWLEDGE Flags

It has become common practice, regardless of the interfacing technique used, to utilize a set of *handshaking* signals between the microprocessor and its peripherals. Figure 6.11 illustrates the technique. In addition to the data lines, the peripheral now supplies a *BUSY/READY* flag. When this line is high, the peripheral is busy and cannot accept new data. When the line is low, the peripheral is ready for new data.

The handshaking sequence begins with the processor checking the BUSY/$\overline{READY}$ flag of the peripheral. Finding it low (not busy), the processor outputs a strobe pulse (or DSP). This tells the I/O device that data are on the bus and should be latched. The peripheral now sets its BUSY/$\overline{READY}$ flag while the character is being received and processed (printed in the case of a printer).

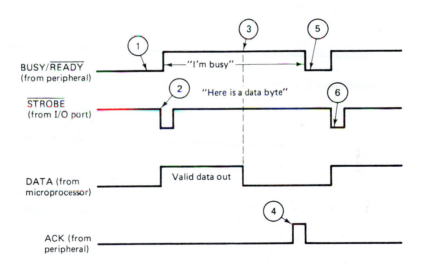

Microcomputer	Peripheral
1. Read BUSY/$\overline{READY}$	BUSY/$\overline{READY}$ = 0
2. Strobe data to peripheral	BUSY/$\overline{READY}$ = 1
3. Read BUSY/$\overline{READY}$	BUSY/$\overline{READY}$ = 1 (still busy)
4. —	ACK = 1 (data byte accepted)
5. Read BUSY/$\overline{READY}$	BUSY/$\overline{READY}$ = 0
6. Strobe data to peripheral	BUSY/$\overline{READY}$ = 1

Figure 6.11 Handshaking signals allow the microprocessor and peripheral to be synchronized for data transfers.

Eventually, an *acknowledge* signal is output by the peripheral. This signal acknowledges receipt of the data and indicates that new data can be placed on the bus. The term "handshake" comes from the CPU "extending its hand" with the strobe signal and the peripheral "extending its hand" back with the acknowledge (ACK) signal.

Three techniques are commonly used to interface a peripheral that utilizes handshaking logic:

1. Programmed I/O
2. Interrupt-driven I/O
3. Direct memory access

SELF-REVIEW 6.3

6.3.1 Handshaking logic is required to _____ a microprocessor with a slow I/O device.

6.3.2 When a peripheral's BUSY/READY flag is _____, the device is ready to receive data.

6.4 PROGRAMMED I/O

Introduction

Programmed I/O is so called because a special I/O program is in full control of all data transfers. With the use of a software technique called *polling,* the microprocessor is synchronized to the speed of the peripheral.

In this section, we:

• Describe the handshaking signals commonly available with a parallel printer.
• Write a parallel-printer control program using programmed I/O and calculate its maximum data transfer rate.

Polling

The classic example of programmed I/O is the parallel-printer interface, sometimes called a "Centronics parallel printer interface" after the name of the printer manufacturer. Figure 6.12 illustrates the hardware.

A 74LS373 level-triggered (not edge-triggered) latch is used to store the data byte. This latch is referred to as *transparent,* because the data input is gated to the output pins whenever the latch's enable input is high. Data is latched when the enable input goes low. Notice that the requirement of latching the data with the rising edge of $\overline{IOW}$ is still met.

The address decoder is designed to decode port 0. Its output, $\overline{SEL\ 0}$, is shared with a 1-bit input port for the BUSY/READY flag and the output port latch.

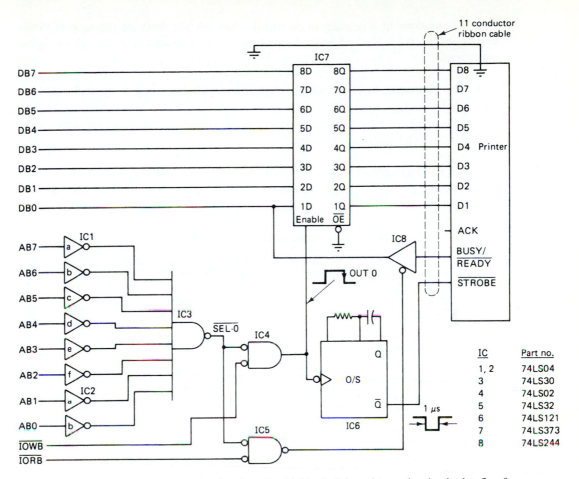

Figure 6.12 Parallel-printer interface. Handshaking logic is used to synchronize the data flow from microprocessor to printer.

The $\overline{\text{STROBE}}$ signal requires some explanation. $\overline{\text{STROBE}}$ is the signal generated by the I/O port which tells the printer that valid data is on the bus and should be latched and printed. At first glance, it would appear that the OUT0 DSP could be inverted and used for this purpose. However, most parallel printers have a *minimum* $\overline{\text{STROBE}}$ pulse width of 0.5 μs or longer. Assuming a 3-MHz 8085, the OUT0 signal has only a 400-ns pulse width. With a Z-80A, the pulse width is somewhat longer (~470 ns) due to the extra WAIT state inserted in Z-80 I/O cycles, but is still a bit too fast for the printer. As a result, the OUT0 DSP is used to trigger IC6, a 74LS121 one-shot. The pulse width is set for approximately 1 μs.

Finally, note that the interface will require an 11-conductor cable between the computer and printer. Because all signals are TTL levels, the cable length should be limited to 10 to 20 ft. This is one of the disadvantages of parallel I/O; an RS-232 serial port can do the same job using only three wires and drive a cable several thousand feet long. We discuss this in detail in Chapter 9.

Let us develop a program to control the flow of data from the output port to the printer in Fig. 6.12. We will write the program as a subroutine with the following assumptions:

1. The characters to be printed are stored in a table beginning at symbolic address DATA.
2. The number of bytes to be printed will be stored in a memory location called NUMB. (NUMB) must be a number less than 256.

An 8080/85 subroutine to accomplish the task is listed in Fig. 6.13. After pointing the HL pair at the head of the data table and loading register B with the number of bytes

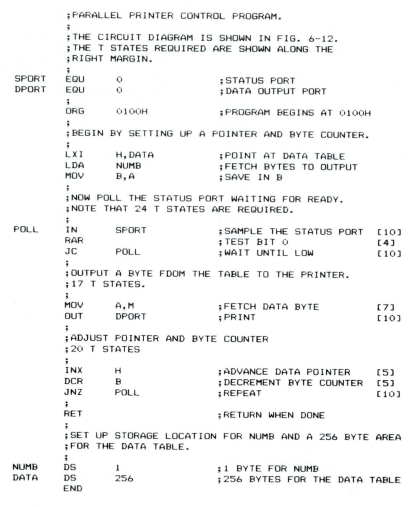

```
        ;PARALLEL PRINTER CONTROL PROGRAM.
        ;
        ;THE CIRCUIT DIAGRAM IS SHOWN IN FIG. 6-12.
        ;THE T STATES REQUIRED ARE SHOWN ALONG THE
        ;RIGHT MARGIN.
        ;
SPORT   EQU     0               ;STATUS PORT
DPORT   EQU     0               ;DATA OUTPUT PORT
        ;
        ORG     0100H           ;PROGRAM BEGINS AT 0100H
        ;
        ;BEGIN BY SETTING UP A POINTER AND BYTE COUNTER.
        ;
        LXI     H,DATA          ;POINT AT DATA TABLE
        LDA     NUMB            ;FETCH BYTES TO OUTPUT
        MOV     B,A             ;SAVE IN B
        ;
        ;NOW POLL THE STATUS PORT WAITING FOR READY.
        ;NOTE THAT 24 T STATES ARE REQUIRED.
        ;
POLL    IN      SPORT           ;SAMPLE THE STATUS PORT  [10]
        RAR                     ;TEST BIT 0              [4]
        JC      POLL            ;WAIT UNTIL LOW          [10]
        ;
        ;OUTPUT A BYTE FDOM THE TABLE TO THE PRINTER.
        ;17 T STATES.
        ;
        MOV     A,M             ;FETCH DATA BYTE         [7]
        OUT     DPORT           ;PRINT                   [10]
        ;
        ;ADJUST POINTER AND BYTE COUNTER
        ;20 T STATES
        ;
        INX     H               ;ADVANCE DATA POINTER    [5]
        DCR     B               ;DECREMENT BYTE COUNTER  [5]
        JNZ     POLL            ;REPEAT                  [10]
        ;
        RET                     ;RETURN WHEN DONE
        ;
        ;SET UP STORAGE LOCATION FOR NUMB AND A 256 BYTE AREA
        ;FOR THE DATA TABLE.
        ;
NUMB    DS      1               ;1 BYTE FOR NUMB
DATA    DS      256             ;256 BYTES FOR THE DATA TABLE
        END
```

Figure 6.13 Control program for the parallel-printer interface in Fig. 6.12. A polling technique is used.

to be output, the program falls into a loop called POLL. In this loop, the status of bit 0 of input port 0 is continually tested. In essence, the program is waiting for the printer to be READY.

When the $\overline{\text{BUSY/READY}}$ flag finally goes low, the character to be printed is output—generating the OUT0 DSP and the 1-μs $\overline{\text{STROBE}}$ signal—the data pointer advanced, and the byte counter decremented. If more data remain to be output, control is transferred back to POLL; if not, the RET is executed.

The key point to note about this routine is the POLL loop. The technique of continually checking the peripheral's $\overline{\text{BUSY/READY}}$ flag is called *polling*, and in fact, programmed I/O is often referred to as polling. The technique has its advantages: The control program is always in control of the peripheral and the hardware required is not too complex.

Polling also has its disadvantages. The polling loop in Fig. 6.13 requires 24 T states using an 8080 or 12 μs with a 2-MHz clock. If the printer can accept characters at a 100-cps rate, 10 ms, or 10,000 μs, must elapse between outputting each character. This means that the subroutine in Fig. 6.13 will figuratively ask the question *"Are you ready?"* and receive the reply *"NO!"* 833 times before getting a *"YES!"*—a rather *inefficient* use of the microprocessor.

But what about this inefficiency? Does it really matter? Will the CPU wear itself out continually testing the $\overline{\text{BUSY/READY}}$ flag? The answer is "not likely." The inefficiency is important only in a *multitasking* environment.

Multitasking means using the processor to do several tasks at once. This used to be a skill reserved for large mainframe computers and minicomputers, but no longer: It is becoming common practice to use a microcomputer to edit a file on a word processor while the same program is printing another file. And why not? Certainly, it is a better use of your time than waiting for the (perhaps lengthy) file to be printed.

However, to perform multitasking efficiently, special hardware is usually required. (See Sections 6.5 and 6.6.) This can add additional cost and complexity to the microcomputer system.

Data Transfer Rate

An important characteristic of any I/O interface is the *maximum data transfer rate*. Let us calculate this number assuming an 8080 processor for the subroutine in Fig. 6.13. What we are interested in is the rate at which characters can be output by the program.

When the processor runs at its fastest rate, the polling routine will need to be executed only once for each output. This will require 24 T states, as mentioned previously. Once ready, data is fetched from the table and output, and the pointer and byte counter are adjusted and tested. This requires an additional 37 T states. The total time for one cycle through the program is therefore 61 T states, or 30.5 μs, with a 2-MHz 8080 processor. This time corresponds to 32,787 bytes per second.

We can put this number into perspective by considering that a high-density floppy disk transfers data at 62,500 bytes per second. Thus, polling could be used to interface with that peripheral. Note, however, that the transfer rate for a typical hard drive is greater than 1 million bytes per second!

Example 6.6

Rewrite the polling routine in Fig. 6.13, assuming a Z-80 microprocessor. Calculate the maximum transfer rate with a 4-MHz clock.

Solution. The program is given in Fig. 6.14. The polling loop actually requires one additional T state compared with the loop in the 8080 program, but the data output loop is reduced from 37 T states to 26 T states because of the special Z-80 output instruction *OUTI*. The cycle time of the program is 51 × 250 ns = 12.75 μs. The data transfer rate is 78,431 bytes per second.

Priorities

The polling concept can be extended to more than one peripheral. In that case, a special status input port is dedicated to the BUSY/READY flags. This port is shown in Fig. 6.15. One 8-bit input port can supply the status of eight peripherals.

```
                 ;PARALLEL PRINTER CONTROL PROGRAM (Z-80 VERSION)
                 ;
                 ;THE CIRCUIT DIAGRAM IS SHOWN IN FIG. 6-12.
                 ;THE T STATES REQUIRED ARE SHOWN ALONG THE
                 ;RIGHT MARGIN.
                 ;
SPORT    EQU     0                    ;STATUS PORT
DPORT    EQU     0                    ;DATA OUTPUT PORT
         ;
         ORG     0100H                ;PROGRAM BEGINS AT 0100H
         ;
         ;BEGIN BY SETTING UP A POINTER AND BYTE COUNTER
         ;
         LD      HL,DATA              ;POINT AT DATA TABLE
         LD      A,(NUMB)             ;FETCH BYTES TO OUTPUT
         LD      B,A                  ;SAVE IN B
         ;
         ;WE WILL USE OUTI SO PUT DPORT IN C
         ;
         LD      C,DPORT              ;C HOLDS DPORT ADDRESS
         ;
         ;NOW POLL THE STATUS PORT WAITING FOR READY.
         ;NOTE THAT 25 T STATES ARE REQUIRED.
         ;
POLL     IN      A,(SPORT)            ;SAMPLE THE STATUS PORT    [11]
         RRA                          ;TEST BIT 0                [4]
         JP      C,POLL               ;WAIT UNTIL LOW            [10]
         ;
         ;OUTPUT A BYTE FROM THE TABLE TO THE PRINTER.
         ;NOTE THAT OUTI "AUTOMATICALLY" ADJUSTS HL AND B.
         ;26 T STATES
         ;
         OUTI                         ;OUTPUT BYTE; INCREMENT HL [16]
         JP      NZ,POLL              ;REPEAT UNTIL 0            [10]
         ;
         RET                          ;RETURN WHEN DONE
         ;
         ;SET UP STORAGE LOCATION FOR NUMB AND A 256-BYTE AREA
         ;FOR THE DATA TABLE.
         ;
NUMB     DEFS    1                    ;1 BYTE FOR NUMB
DATA     DEFS    256                  ;256 BYTES FOR THE DATA TABLE
         END
```

Figure 6.14 Z-80 polling routine for the printer interface in Fig. 6.12.

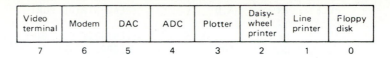

Video terminal	Modem	DAC	ADC	Plotter	Daisy-wheel printer	Line printer	Floppy disk
7	6	5	4	3	2	1	0

Figure 6.15 One 8-bit input port can be used to monitor the BUSY/$\overline{\text{READY}}$ status of eight separate peripherals.

A routine can now be written to poll each device (test bit 0, then bit 1, etc.) and branch to the appropriate peripheral service routine when the device is ready. What happens if two devices are ready at the same time? Obviously, the first one to be polled will be serviced first. In fact, this suggests that the polling routine can be written in such a way that *priorities* are assigned to each peripheral.

For example, suppose that we start polling with bit 0 and proceed to bit 7. Each time a flag is found indicating that a certain peripheral is ready, that peripheral is serviced and the polling restarts at bit 0. Using the device assignments shown in Fig. 6.15, this scheme assigns the highest priority to the floppy-disk drive and the lowest priority to the video terminal.

When several peripherals are controlled in a programmed I/O environment, the *response time* of the polling routine (in addition to the transfer rate) must be considered. For example, consider the polling program listed in Fig. 6.16. This program inputs the status from port 0 and then proceeds to test each bit in order. Because so many devices have to be polled, the response time—the time from BUSY/$\overline{\text{READY}}$ = READY to the start of the service routine—can be quite long.

Example 6.7

Calculate the worst-case response time for the video terminal, using the polling routine in Fig. 6.16. Assume that the service routine for each peripheral requires 50 T states and the system clock is 2 MHz.

Solution. In a bad case, the terminal's BUSY/$\overline{\text{READY}}$ flag will be ready just after servicing a previous character from the terminal. The terminal will have to wait for the JMP POLL instruction to execute and then all of the other peripherals to be polled. In a worse case, each of these devices will require service, and the video terminal's service routine will not be entered until a total response time of

$$T = [10 + 11 + (14 + 50) \times 7] \times 500 \text{ ns} = 234.5 \text{ μs}$$

The preceding example points out a major disadvantage of polling: Although the individual transfer rate can be quite high, the response time can be quite slow when many peripherals are involved. The scheme can become totally unacceptable when the response time is so long as to lose data.

But now consider the video terminal. Even when operated at a relatively fast 19,200 bits/s, it cannot accept data faster than one character every 469 μs, and you certainly cannot type that fast. For this peripheral, a 234.5-μs wait is no problem.

Note: The "worst case" in Example 6.7 is not really the worst case. If we assume that each service routine branches back to address POLL in Fig. 6.16 (as it should), the floppy disk could require service continually, and none of the other peripherals would

```
POLL    IN      A,0             ;READ STATUS PORT          [11]
        ;
        RAR                     ;TEST BIT 0                [4]
        JC      FD              ;FLOPPY DISK               [10]
        ;
        RAR                     ;TEST BIT 1                [4]
        JC      LP              ;LINE PRINTER              [10]
        ;
        RAR                     ;TEST BIT 2                [4]
        JC      LAS             ;LASER PRINTER             [10]
        ;
        RAR                     ;TEST BIT 3                [4]
        JC      PL              ;PLOTTER                   [10]
        ;
        RAR                     ;TEST BIT 4                [4]
        JC      ADC             ;ANALOG-DIGITAL CONV.      [10]
        ;
        RAR                     ;TEST BIT 5                [4]
        JC      DAC             ;DIGITAL-ANALOG CONV.      [10]
        ;
        RAR                     ;TEST BIT 6                [4]
        JC      MOD             ;MODEM                     [10]
        ;
        RAR                     ;TEST BIT 7                [4]
        JC      TERM            ;TERMINAL                  [10]
        ;
        JMP     POLL            ;REPEAT                    [10]
```

Figure 6.16 Polling can be extended to several peripherals. This routine tests the BUSY/READY status of all eight peripherals in Fig. 6.15. T states are listed along the right margin for an 8080.

ever be serviced. This is another disadvantage of polling; when several peripherals are involved, the highest priority devices may cause the low-priority devices to become "starved" for service.

SELF-REVIEW 6.4

6.4.1 Programmed I/O requires that a software program _____ the I/O device to determine if it is ready to exchange data.

6.4.2 When is programmed I/O inefficient?

6.4.3 How are priorities determined when several peripherals are controlled via programmed I/O?

6.5 INTERRUPT-DRIVEN I/O

Introduction

One alternative to programmed I/O is to use the microprocessor's built-in interrupt capabilities. Most microprocessors have at least one interrupt input pin. The input on this pin is sampled by the processor during the last clock cycle of the last machine cycle of every instruction. (The 8085 tests on the second-to-last clock cycle.) If the interrupt input is found active, control is transferred to a special *interrupt service routine* (ISR).

In this section, we:

- Compare the interrupt capabilities of the 8080, 8085, and Z-80 microprocessors.
- Write a parallel-printer control program using interrupt-driven I/O and calculate its maximum data transfer rate.

The Interrupt Cycle

Figure 6.17 flowcharts a typical interrupt cycle. At time 1, normal processing is occurring—perhaps the editing of a word-processing file. At time 2, an interrupt occurs. The processor finishes its current instruction and then saves the program counter on the stack at time 3. Control is then transferred to the ISR at time 4, and this routine is executed during time 5. The ISR ends with a RET instruction at time 6, causing the program counter to be popped from the stack. Having recovered its "old address," the processor continues normal processing at time 7.

Now suppose that the interrupt was generated by the BUSY/READY flag of a printer. In this case, the ISR would be a routine to feed the printer another character. This might require 20 to 100 µs of processing time. But remember, the printer requires 10,000 µs to print the character (at 100 cps). This leaves 9900 µs for the processor to continue its editing (or some other) task.*

Interrupt-driven I/O has the advantage that the processor responds to the peripheral only when the peripheral is ready. And with the use of the processor's special interrupt input, there is no need to poll for this condition. Thus, the microprocessor is used more efficiently.

---

*Most printers today have buffers that can be filled at high speed. Once the buffer is full, a relatively long delay occurs while the buffer is emptied and the data are printed. During this time, the printer cannot accept data.

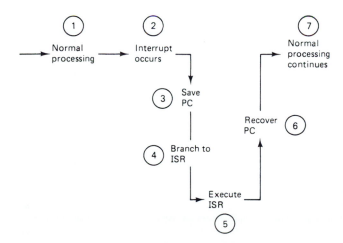

Figure 6.17 When an interrupt occurs, normal processing is suspended while a special interrupt service routine (ISR) is executed. Normal processing resumes when this routine is completed.

In order to implement interrupt-driven I/O, several problems must be solved, including the following:

1. Hardware must be added to generate the interrupt.
2. The address of the ISR must be determined at interrupt time.
3. Some processor activities—for example, disk operations—cannot be allowed to be interrupted, or loss of data may result.
4. If several peripherals are to be interfaced, each must be recognized, but must have its own ISR.
5. What happens if two devices request interrupts simultaneously?

There is also a danger in using interrupts that are not present in programmed I/O. That is, hardware now controls the program flow instead of software. And because the source of the interrupt is *asynchronous* with respect to the processor, any program can be interrupted at any time. Too many interrupts can cause the microprocessor to become asynchronous—the programmer actually loses control of his or her own machine!

Generating an Interrupt

Throughout this book, I have stressed the similarities between the various processors studied. Indeed, once the CPU modules have been designed, nearly all of the memory and I/O interfaces presented can be used with any 8-bit processor.

Not so with interrupts: Every processor seems to have its own unique way of handling interrupt requests. In this section, we discuss interrupt-driven I/O in general and provide specific details for the 8080, 8085, and Z-80 microprocessors.

For most microprocessors (including the Z-80, but not the 8080 or 8085), the interrupt request input is interfaced using a type 2 bus. This is an open-collector bus line characterized by one receiver and many transmitters. That way, any number of interrupting devices may be interfaced. (Determining which device generated the interrupt is another matter, however.) The type 2 interrupt bus is shown in Fig. 6.18(a).

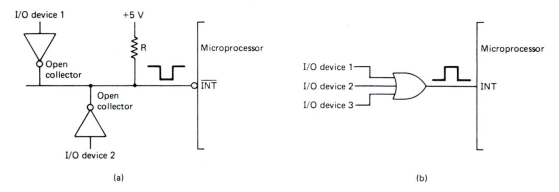

(a)   (b)

Figure 6.18 The interrupt request pin at the microprocessor may require (a) an active-low signal or (b) an active-high signal.

Some processors, including the 8080 and 8085, require that the interrupt input be driven high. For these processors, an OR gate must be used to provide the processor with a single interrupt request. This technique is shown in Fig. 6.18(b).

It is not uncommon for a microprocessor to have more than one interrupt input pin, and with such a processor, it may be possible for each peripheral to have its own dedicated interrupt input. Table 6.4 lists several important interrupt features of the 8080, 8085, and Z-80 microprocessors. Note in particular that the 8080 has only one interrupt input, the Z-80 has two, and the 8085 has five. The Z-80's $\overline{\text{INT}}$ input has three separate modes of operation controlled by software.

Remembering that the processor will not service an interrupt request until the end of the current instruction, we must take care that the processor has indeed received the interrupt request. In most cases, the processor will generate a special *interrupt acknowledge* signal called $\overline{\text{INTA}}$. This signal can be used to remove the interrupt request once it has been acknowledged, as shown in Fig. 6.19.

The 8085 *RST 7.5* and Z-80 *NMI* inputs are edge triggered. An internal flip-flop is set when the appropriate edge occurs, thus ensuring that the processor will "remember" that an interrupt is pending. The circuit in Fig. 6.19 is not required to have these inputs.

The 8085's *RST 6.5* and *5.5* inputs are neither acknowledged nor edge triggered. In driving these input pins, care must be taken to ensure that the interrupt is long enough not to be missed by the processor, but not so long as to be counted twice.

The 8085 *TRAP* input is both level triggered and edge triggered. On the rising edge of the TRAP signal, an internal latch is set, but the request will be acknowledged only if the TRAP input remains high. After the internal acknowledgment has occurred, the interrupt request can be removed. The TRAP input will not be recognized again until it has returned low and then high. This feature prevents false triggering due to noise or logic glitches. For that reason, TRAP has a minimum pulse width, but not a maximum.

Maskable and Nonmaskable Interrupts

The interrupt inputs of a microprocessor can be classified as *maskable* or *nonmaskable*. A maskable interrupt is an interrupt that can be turned off or disabled by the CPU. For example, all three processors include the instruction *DI*—disable interrupts. When this command is given, maskable interrupts cannot be serviced. Interrupts are automatically disabled whenever a $\overline{\text{RESET}}$ occurs or immediately after the receipt of an interrupt request.

The 8080 provides a special output signal called *interrupts enabled* (*INTE*). When this signal is high, it indicates that interrupt requests will be honored by the processor. The signal turns out not to be too important, and neither the 8085 nor the Z-80 provides a similar output.

A nonmaskable interrupt cannot be ignored by the CPU and must be serviced. Obviously, this type of interrupt should be used with great caution. Classically, it is reserved for a power-fail indication. If the computer system should lose power, the filter capacitors in the power supply will be able to hold up the supply voltages for several milliseconds. During this time, important data in RAM can be quickly written to disk or E^2PROM for safekeeping by the nonmaskable ISR.

TABLE 6.4 Important Interrupt Features of the 8080, 8085, and Z-80 Microprocessors

		Interrupt request			Interrupt response					
Micro-processor	Input	Type	Trigger	Priority	Type	Address	Acknowledge signal	PC saved?	Software maskable?	Type of return
8080	INTR	Maskable	High level until sampled	—	Vectored	RST p[a]	$\overline{\text{INTA}} = 0$	No[b]	No[c]	RET
8085	TRAP	Nonmaskable	↑ Edge and level[d] ⌐ Latched	1	Direct	0024H	None	Yes	No	RET
	RST 7.5	Maskable	↑ Latched	2	Direct	003CH	None	Yes	Yes	RET
	RST 6.5	Maskable	High level until sampled	3	Direct	0034H	None	Yes	Yes	RET
	RST 5.5	Maskable	High level until sampled	4	Direct	002CH	None	Yes	Yes	RET
	INTR	Maskable	High level until sampled	5	Vectored	RST p[a]	$\overline{\text{INTA}} = 0$	No[b]	No[c]	RET
Z-80	$\overline{\text{NMI}}$	Nonmaskable	⌐ Latched	1	Direct	0066H	None	Yes	No	RETN[e]
	$\overline{\text{INT}}$ mode 0	Maskable	Low level until sampled	2	Vectored	RST p[a]	$\overline{\text{IORQ}} = 0$ $\overline{\text{M1}} = 0$	No[b]	No[c]	RET
	$\overline{\text{INT}}$ mode 1	Maskable	Low level until sampled	2	Direct	0038H	$\overline{\text{IORQ}} = 0$ $\overline{\text{M1}} = 0$	Yes	No[c]	RET
	$\overline{\text{INT}}$ mode 2	Maskable	Low level until sampled	2	Indirect	I register + 7-bit vector points to vector table	$\overline{\text{IORQ}} = 0$ $\overline{\text{M1}} = 0$	Yes	No[c]	RETI[f]

[a] A call instruction (or any other) may also be used.

[b] Using an RST instruction saves the PC.

[c] The DI instruction disables all maskable interrupts.

[d] Triggered on the rising edge, but must be held high until internally sampled.

[e] Restores premaskable interrupt status.

[f] Used by Zilog peripherals to reset IEO flag.

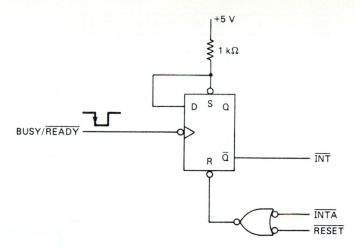

Figure 6.19 The microprocessor's interrupt acknowledge signal (INTA) can be used to remove the interrupt request after it has been received by the microprocessor.

The Z-80 $\overline{\text{NMI}}$ input and the 8085 TRAP input are examples of nonmaskable interrupts. The 8080 does not have a nonmaskable interrupt.

With the Z-80 NMI input, a special *return from nonmaskable interrupt (RETN)*, should be used. This instruction restores the pre-NMI status of the internal interrupt-enable flip-flop. Such restoration is necessary because an $\overline{\text{NMI}}$ request will reset the flip-flop, inhibiting further maskable interrupts.

In addition to the DI instruction, the 8085 has the command *set interrupt mask (SIM)*. This instruction can be used to mask any combination of the RST 5.5 through 7.5 inputs. Figure 6.20(a) shows the bit assignments for the interrupt masks.

Example 6.8

Write an 8085 program that enables the RST 7.5 and RST 5.5 inputs.

Solution. The SIM instruction will copy the contents of the accumulator into the interrupt masks according to Fig. 6.20(a) if bit 3 is a 1. Thus, the correct byte to load into the accumulator is X0X01010. (X implies a "don't care" condition.) The program is

```
MVI A,0AH      ;MASK PATTERN
SIM            ;WRITE IT
EI             ;ENABLE INTERRUPTS
```

Note that DI overrides the SIM command.

The SIM instruction can also be used to reset the internal RST 7.5 flip-flop. However, this will be done automatically when the RST 7.5 interrupt request is serviced.

The 8085 *read interrupt mask (RIM)* command can be used to determine the current status of the interrupt masks. The bit assignments are shown in Fig. 6.20(b). A RIM should be performed immediately after a TRAP occurs so that the pre-TRAP interrupt status can be restored with a SIM. RIM and SIM are thus analogous to the Z-80's RETN instruction.

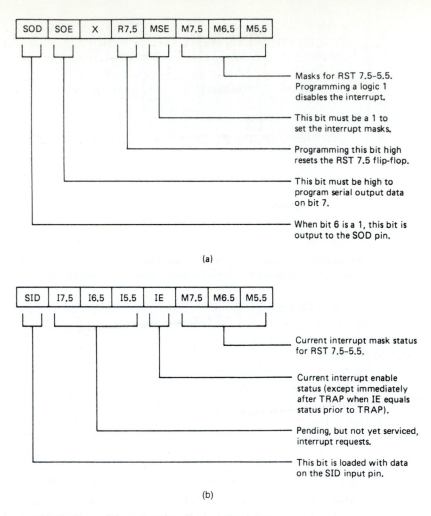

Figure 6.20 (a) The RST 5.5–7.5 inputs of the 8085 microprocessor can be masked using the SIM instruction; (b) the status of these interrupts can be read using the RIM instruction.

Branching to the Interrupt Service Routine

Once an interrupt occurs, control must be transferred to the address of the ISR. There are three techniques for doing this:

1. Vectored interrupts
2. Direct interrupts
3. Indirect interrupts

Vectored interrupts. With *vectored* interrupts, the interrupting device supplies a vector indicating the address of the ISR. All three processors support this type of interrupt—the 8080 and 8085 on the INTR pin and the Z-80 on its $\overline{\text{INT}}$ pin. As indicated in Table 6.4, the Z-80 uses the $\overline{\text{INT}}$ pin for all three of its interrupt modes. The instructions IM 0, IM 1, and IM 2 are used to specify the desired technique: vectored, direct, and indirect, respectively.

During vectored interrupts, a special interrupt-acknowledge machine cycle is executed by the processor. This cycle is similar to an instruction fetch cycle, except that the control bus signal $\overline{\text{INTA}}$ is active instead of $\overline{\text{MEMR}}$. The Z-80 does not generate the $\overline{\text{INTA}}$ signal directly, but during an interrupt-acknowledge cycle it causes M1 and $\overline{\text{IORQ}}$ to be active simultaneously. These two signals can be combined to generate the $\overline{\text{INTA}}$ signal. (See the diagram of the Z-80 CPU module in Fig. 4.27.)

The $\overline{\text{INTA}}$ signal can be used to reset the interrupt request as shown in Fig. 6.19. It is also used to gate an interrupt vector onto the system data bus. (See Fig. 6.21.) During the interrupt-acknowledge cycle, the CPU reads the data off the bus just as it would in a normal memory read cycle.

Although any instruction can be gated into the microprocessor during the interrupt-acknowledge cycle, the most logical instruction to use is one of the eight restart instructions, RST 0 through RST 7 (8080/85 mnemonics). These instructions are 1-byte calls to locations on page 0 of the processor's memory space. For example, an RST 4 (Z-80 mnemonic RST 20) will cause a subroutine call to address 0020H. The op code of RST 4 in binary is 11100111.

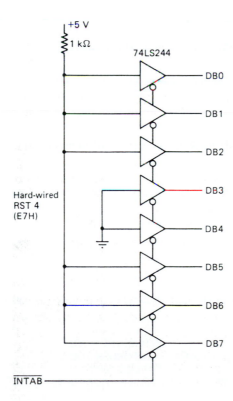

Figure 6.21 The $\overline{\text{INTA}}$ signal is used to gate a restart vector onto the microprocessor data bus.

TABLE 6.5 Restart Instructions Used with
Vectored Interrupts

Op Code	Mnemonic		Restart address
	8080/85	Z-80	
C7	RST 0	RST 0	0000H
CF	RST 1	RST 08	0008H
D7	RST 2	RST 10	0010H
DF	RST 3	RST 18	0018H
E7	RST 4	RST 20H	0020H
EF	RST 5	RST 28H	0028H
F7	RST 6	RST 30H	0030H
FF	RST 7	RST 38H	0038H

Table 6.5 lists the eight restart instructions and indicates the vector address of each. Note that only 8 bytes of memory separate each address. Studying Fig. 6.21, you can see that when $\overline{INTA}$ goes low, an RST 4 (op code = E7H) will be gated onto the system data bus. The processor will execute this instruction by saving the program counter on the stack and branching to location 0020H. The ISR in this location should terminate with a RET instruction, and normal processing can then continue.

Direct interrupts. *Direct interrupts* are supported by the 8085 with the use of the TRAP and RST 5.5 through 7.5 inputs. The Z-80 $\overline{INT}$ input is put in the direct interrupt mode by executing an IM 1 instruction. The Z-80 $\overline{NMI}$ input is also a direct interrupt.

Generating an interrupt on one of these pins causes a direct branch to a specific location in memory without the need for an interrupt vector. For example, activating the 8085's RST 5.5 input will cause a branch to location 002CH. In all cases, the program counter is automatically saved on the stack before the branch occurs.

Note that the 8085 TRAP input and the Z-80 $\overline{NMI}$ input are nonmaskable. All of the other inputs are maskable.

Indirect interrupts. Only the Z-80 supports this mode. It is specified by executing an IM 2 instruction. The mode is similar to the vectored interrupt technique, except that the vector gated onto the bus is combined with the Z-80's I register to form a 16-bit pointer into a vector table. The two consecutive bytes stored in this table are used as the address for the ISR.

Example 6.9

Using the interface shown in Fig. 6.21, determine the ISR address defined by the following Z-80 program:

```
IM 2          ;INTERRUPT MODE 2
LD A,0FFH     ;HIGH-ORDER ADDRESS
LD I,A        ;IN REGISTER I
EI            ;ENABLE INTERRUPTS
```

Solution. The high-order address is specified by the contents of register I. In this case, page FF is defined. When an interrupt occurs, the low-order address will be read from the interrupt-acknowledge circuit, but bit 0 will be ignored. (The entries in the vector table must start at an even address.) In this example, the vector is 11100111, so the full address will be FFE6H. The processor will thus branch to the low-order address stored in FFE6H and high-order address stored in FFE7H.

Indirect interrupts allow the ISR to be located anywhere in the processor's memory space. Hence, they offer the maximum flexibility. Direct interrupts are the easiest of the interrupts to implement, as no external hardware is required. Vectored interrupts offer the advantage that eight separate peripherals can share the same interrupt request line, yet each branch to a separate service routine. However, each routine is limited to 8 bytes on page 0.

Response Time and Transfer Rate

Interrupt-driven I/O is clearly a more efficient interfacing technique than programmed I/O. But how do the two compare with regard to *response time* and *transfer rate*?

Table 6.6 calculates the worst-case response time for each of the interrupt inputs on the 8080, 8085, and Z-80 microprocessors. This is the maximum time required from generation of the interrupt signal by the peripheral to execution of the first instruction in the ISR.

In the worst case, the interrupt request will occur just after the interrupt input is sampled in the last T state of an instruction. This means that the interrupt will not be serviced until the end of the next instruction. The wait could be as long as 18 T states for an 8080 or 8085 and 23 T states for a Z-80 (depending on the instruction).

Unlike the 8080 or 8085, the Z-80 inserts two WAIT states in the interrupt-acknowledge cycle for maskable interrupts. The two states are used to allow arbitration logic time to settle out and to enable the highest priority device. We will discuss this more in the next section.

TABLE 6.6 Interrupt Response Times for the 8080, 8085, and Z-80 Microprocessors

Micro-processor	Interrupt input	Extra T state	One instruction: worst-case T states	WAIT states	RST T states	Total T states	Total time (μs)
8080A (2 MHz)	INTR	1	0–18	0	11	12–30	6–15
8085AH (3 MHz)	INTR TRAP RST 5.5–7.5	1	0–18	0	12	13–31	4.3–10.3
Z-80A (4 MHz)	NMI	1	0–23	0	10	11–34	2.8–8.5
	INT-Mode 0	1	0–23	2	11	14–37	3.5–9.3
	INT-Mode 1	1	0–23	2	10	13–36	3.25–9
	INT-Mode 2	1	0–23	2	17[a]	20–43	5–10.8

[a] 19 T states required to fetch low-order vector, save program counter, and branch to address in the vector table.

After acknowledging the interrupt, the processor either fetches a restart instruction from the data bus (if the 8080/85 INTR or Z-80 INT mode 0 input is active) or automatically inserts the restart instruction (if the 8085 TRAP or RST 5.5–7.5 or Z-80 NMI or INT mode 1 input is active). In either case 10, 11, or 12 T states are required.

When the Z-80 INT input is used in mode 2, 17 T states (plus 2 WAIT states) are required to fetch the low-order address vector, save the program counter on the stack, and get the jump address from the interrupt table in memory.

The total required T states shown in Table 6.6 can be compared with 24 or 25 T states for the response time for the polling routines in Figs. 6.13 and 6.14. Thus, polling is slightly faster than interrupts in the worst case. In the best case, interrupts will be faster.

But what happens as more peripherals are added? Examining the polling routine in Fig. 6.16, the laser printer (LAS) will not be serviced until at least 53 T states have elapsed (11 + 14 + 14 + 14), and probably longer if one of the higher priority devices is being serviced. If interrupts were used, as soon as the printer requested service, the processor would respond. The total response time would still be found using the numbers in the table.

It should be clear that the response time for programmed I/O begins to exceed interrupt-driven I/O as soon as a second peripheral is added to the polling routine.

Another advantage of interrupts is that one service routine can interrupt another. In fact, if the ISR is written so as to be *reentrant,* an interrupt can even interrupt itself. This action prevents the response time from being degraded due to having to wait for a previous service routine to finish, as would occur with polling. Of course, the interrupted service routine will be suspended while the most recent interrupt is serviced, thereby degrading the transfer rate of the first routine.

Let us consider the *transfer rate* of an ISR by developing a routine to service a printer each time its BUSY/READY flag indicates that the printer is ready. We will assume the following:

1. A supervisor program is used to write into memory locations DATA and DATA + 1 the address of a data table for the printer. This program also writes into memory location NUMB—the number of bytes that are to be printed.

2. When it is desired to print the data file, the supervisor enables interrupts and then proceeds with some other activity.

3. When ready, the printer generates an interrupt, and control is temporarily transferred to the printer ISR.

4. The printer ISR must fetch a data byte from the table, output it to the printer, test for the last byte, and reenable interrupts if more data are to be output.

Figure 6.22 is an 8080 listing of the printer ISR. Note that the routine is broken into six sections as follows:

1. *Save the environment.* If interrupts are to work at all, the ISR must not be allowed to change any CPU registers. If they are allowed to do so, the interrupted program may "crash" when the ISR returns control to it.

```
                    ;SAMPLE INTERRUPT SERVICE ROUTINE FOR THE 8080.
                    ;
                    ;NOTE THE SIX ACTIVITIES PERFORMED BY THIS PROGRAM.
                    ;T STATES ARE INDICATED IN THE RIGHT MARGIN.
                    ;
                    ;SUPERVISOR PROGRAM PRESUMED TO HAVE LOADED (DATA) AND (NUMB).
                    ;
        DPORT   EQU     1                ;OUTPUT DATA PORT
                    ;
                ORG     0100H            ;PROGRAM BEGINS AT 0100H
                    ;
                    ;[1]  SAVE THE ENVIRONMENT
                    ;
                PUSH    H                ;                                [11]
                PUSH    PSW              ;                                [11]
                PUSH    B                ;                                [11]
                    ;
                    ;[2]  RESTORE PRINTING ENVIRONMENT
                    ;
                LHLD    DATA             ; (DATA) STORES ADDRESS OF       [16]
                                         ;CURRENT DATA BYTE TO BE OUTPUT
                LDA     NUMB             ; (NUMB) STORES BYTES REMAINING  [13]
                                         ;TO BE OUTPUT
                MOV     B,A              ;SAVE NUMB IN B                  [5]
                    ;
                    ;[3]  PRINT THE DATA BYTE - ADJUST POINTER AND COUNTER
                    ;
                MOV     A,M              ;FETCH THE BYTE                  [7]
                OUT     DPORT            ;PRINT                           [10]
                INX     H                ;ADVANCE POINTER                 [5]
                DCR     B                ;DECREMENT BYTE COUNTER          [5]
                JZ      DONE             ;IF DONE SKIP EI                 [10]
                    ;
                    ;[4]  SAVE PRINTING ENVIRONMENT
                    ;
                SHLD    DATA             ;SAVE POINTER                    [16]
                MOV     A,B              ;FETCH BYTE COUNTER TO A         [5]
                STA     NUMB             ;SAVE IT                         [13]
                EI                       ;REENABLE THE INTERRUPTS         [4]
                    ;
                    ;[5]  RESTORE CPU ENVIRONMENT
                    ;
        DONE    POP     B                ;                                [10]
                POP     PSW              ;                                [10]
                POP     H                ;                                [10]
                    ;
                    ;[6]  RETURN
                    ;
                RET                      ;                                [10]
                    ;                                           TOTAL = [182]
                    ;
                    ;SET UP STORAGE LOCATION FOR DATA AND NUMB.
                    ;
        DATA    DS      2                ;2 BYTES FOR DATA ADDRESS
        NUMB    DS      1                ;1 BYTE FOR THE BYTE COUNTER
                END
```

Figure 6.22 Typical ISR. This routine could be used to output data to a printer. Note that six specific activities are required of the program.

2. *Variables used by the ISR must be recovered.* Certainly, the CPU registers cannot be used to hold these values. It will be difficult to use the stack area because the top of the stack will contain a return address when the ISR is entered.

3. *The peripheral can now be serviced.* In this case, data is output to the printer and a test is made for the last byte.

Sec. 6.5   Interrupt-Driven I/O   **305**

4. *The variables used by the ISR must now be saved and interrupts reenabled.* If EI is not given, the next interrupt (and all succeeding interrupts) will be missed.

5. *Restore the environment.* All registers used by the ISR are restored to their original values.

6. *An RET instruction returns control to the interrupted program.*

In general, all ISRs must include the foregoing six activities.

We can calculate the maximum transfer rate for this program by assuming that the next interrupt occurs just as the RET instruction is executed. In this case, control is immediately transferred back to the printer ISR, and the next byte is output. The time required between bytes equals the response time in Table 6.6 (assuming no extra instruction), plus the time taken to execute the routine in Fig. 6.22—182 T states for an 8080 processor. The total T states are thus $182 + 11 = 193$ T states.

Assuming a 2-MHz 8080, 96.5 μs is required for each transfer. Of course, a 100-cps printer requires 10,000 μs per character, so the interrupt routine should work very nicely with this peripheral. But if the routine were used to read or write data from a floppy disk drive, it would be too slow—recall that a 3½″ floppy disk drive requires data every 16 μs.

It is interesting to note that the polling routine used to accomplish the same function (see Fig. 6.13) required only 61 T states, and data could be transferred every 30.5 μs. Why is the polling scheme faster than the interrupt-driven technique?

What we must remember is that although polling is inefficient, it is relatively fast when servicing a *single peripheral.* Interrupts, on the other hand, require a great deal of software overhead to save the program counter and any CPU registers used by the ISR. The instructions used for the task must be executed every time the ISR is executed. The polling routine may also have to save the contents of these registers, but that need only be done once, when the polling routine is first entered.

In sum, we can say that, compared with interrupt-driven I/O, polling is an inefficient use of the resources of the microprocessor, but this matters only in a multitasking environment. In servicing a single peripheral, polling will usually result in the highest data transfer rate.

Multiple Interrupts: The Priority Problem

We have already mentioned that one ISR can interrupt another. This can occur, however, only in either of two special cases:

1. The first ISR executes an EI instruction early in the routine.
2. The second interrupt is nonmaskable.

Remember that once an interrupt is acknowledged, maskable interrupts are automatically disabled. This is done to protect the ISR from being interrupted before it has had a chance to perform its task. By contrast, a nonmaskable interrupt can never be blocked, even if the DI instruction is executed.

When *nested* interrupts—that is, interrupts within interrupts—are used, care must be taken that the stack area not grow so large as to overwrite the program or any of its data tables.

Example 6.10

Suppose that an 8085 microprocessor has received three interrupt requests in the following order: RST 7.5, RST 6.5, and RST 5.5. If these three interrupts are nested, to what depth does the stack penetrate if all registers within the CPU must be saved? Assume that the stack pointer initially points to location FFFFH.

Solution. Each ISR must begin with the sequence

```
PUSH PSW
PUSH B
PUSH D
PUSH H
EI
```

This means that the stack will grow by 10 bytes (do not forget the program counter!) with each new interrupt request. Figure 6.23 illustrates that, after the third interrupt, the stack will have moved down 30 bytes to address FFE1.

This example again illustrates that caution must be applied when using interrupts. When interrupts are enabled, the hardware is in control. If you forget this, one peripheral may cause hundreds of interrupts per second, quickly overwriting your program. The result is a "fatal" crash, which is especially hard to debug because there is no program left to examine!

It is also possible for the microcomputer to become *interrupt bound*. This occurs with long ISRs or multiple interrupt requests. The processor may never get back to its main task.

When a microcomputer is interrupt bound, "software time" is no longer equal to real time. A software timing loop that is repeatedly interrupted will become inaccurate. Monitoring the edges of a pulse train is another example. If interrupted, the software may miss an edge. In both cases, the software is delayed by the ISR and no longer runs in real time.

Another problem to be considered with multiple interrupts is the possibility of two requests arriving simultaneously. Because the processor does not test for an interrupt request until the end of the current instruction, two interrupt requests do not actually have to arrive at the same instant to appear simultaneous to the microprocessor.

This problem has an easy solution and a hard one. The easy solution is provided by the microprocessor itself. The Z-80 and the 8085 both prioritize their interrupts. (See Table 6.4.) For example, for the 8085, an RST 7.5 will be serviced before an RST 6.5 or RST 5.5.

Of course, a nonmaskable interrupt has the highest priority, but this priority extends only to *pending* interrupts, not working ISRs. For instance, in Example 6.10, an RST 5.5 was used to interrupt an RST 6.5. When this is not desired, it is up to the programmer to be sure not to enable interrupts until the ISR has completed its task. In that way, only a nonmaskable interrupt will be able to interrupt the executing ISR.

Interrupt no.		Stack address	
0		FFFFH	65,535
1	RST 7.5	FFF5H	65,525
2	RST 6.5	FFEBH	65,515
3	RST 5.5	FFE1H	65,505

Figure 6.23 Nested interrupts cause the stack to move downward in memory.

Prioritizing works well with direct interrupts, but another technique must be used when one interrupt line is shared by several peripherals. This is typically the case when the vectored interrupt line is used. In fact, it is the only technique available to the 8080.

As shown in Fig. 6.18, any number of peripheral devices can easily be connected to the interrupt request pin if an open-collector bus or an OR gate connection is used. The problem for the processor is determining which peripheral is requesting the interrupt and resolving any simultaneous requests by two or more devices. Three techniques are commonly used:

1. *Polling.* The interrupt request signal from each device can be used to set 1 bit of a register wired as an input port. When an interrupt occurs, the ISR polls this input port to "see" who requested service. A priority is automatically established by the order of the polling. This technique is very simple, but has the negative effect of degrading response time.

2. *Priority interrupt controller* (*PIC*). Figure 6.24 illustrates a solution to the problem using hardware. The 8-line-to-3-line priority encoder (74148) generates a 3-bit binary code corresponding to the active input. If two or more inputs are present simultaneously, the highest numbered will be encoded. The 3 bits are inverted and combined to form a restart instruction that is enabled onto the data bus by $\overline{\text{INTA}}$. Note that the encoder $\overline{\text{GS}}$ output can be used to generate the interrupt request. The Intel 8259A PIC is covered in Chapter 7. This chip incorporates all of the features of the circuit in Fig. 6.24, but gates call instructions, instead of restart instructions, onto the data bus. The 8259A will accommodate 64 separate interrupts in a cascaded mode.

3. *Daisy chain.* This technique is illustrated in Fig. 6.25. Each peripheral has an interrupt enable input (IEI) and an interrupt enable output (IEO). An interrupt request can be made only if IEI is high. In the figure, peripheral number 2 is requesting an interrupt, causing its IEO to be low. This, in turn, disables devices 3 and 4. Note that device number 1 is still able to request an interrupt because it has a higher priority. The $\overline{\text{INTA}}$ signal can be used to reset the IEO of the interrupting device.

Note: All Zilog peripheral interface chips support the daisy-chain technique, each having an IEI and IEO pin. However, rather than use the $\overline{\text{INTA}}$ signal, a special return instruction can be output by the Z-80 called *return from interrupt* (RETI). The peripheral devices monitor the data bus for the unique RETI 2-byte op code ED 4D ($\overline{\text{M1}}$ is active for both bytes) and, if IEI is high, reset IEO when this op code is detected.

The daisy-chain technique is particularly versatile when the Z-80's mode 2 interrupts are selected. The peripheral devices can be programmed with the interrupt vector, and this byte will automatically be gated onto the data bus during the $\overline{\text{INTA}}$ cycle ($\overline{\text{M1}}$ and $\overline{\text{IORQ}}$). (Chapter 8 provides more detail on this topic.)

Summary: 8080, 8085, and Z-80 interrupt requests

As you have seen, each processor has its own unique methods of handling interrupt requests. The following is a summary of the important points for each.

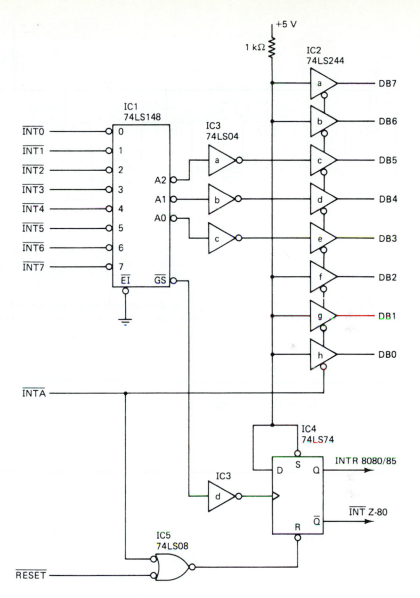

Figure 6.24 Hardware solution to the multiple-interrupts problem. This circuit will accept eight interrupt requests, prioritize them, and generate a separate restart instruction for each.

The 8080:

1. There is one interrupt input, labeled INTR.
2. INTR can be masked with the DI instruction, but is automatically disabled whenever an interrupt request is acknowledged.
3. INTR must be driven high to request an interrupt.

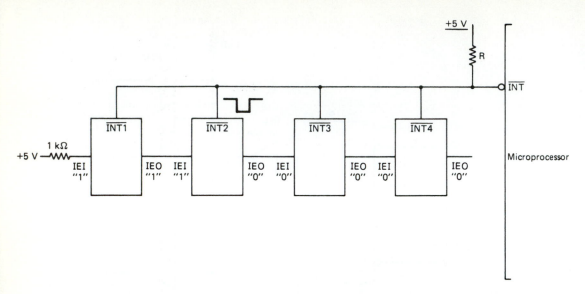

Figure 6.25 Daisy-chain approach to solving the multiple-interrupts problem. IEI is the interrupt enable input and IEO is the interrupt enable output. Only when IEI is high can the peripheral request an interrupt.

4. A vectored interrupt scheme is used. $\overline{\text{INTA}}$ is used to gate a restart instruction onto the data bus.

5. Eight different restart locations are possible.

6. Multiple interrupts are best handled using the 8259 programmable interrupt controller (PIC).

7. After a system reset, INTR is disabled.

The 8085:

1. There are five interrupts, labeled TRAP, RST 7.5, RST 6.5, RST 5.5, and INTR.

2. Only TRAP is nonmaskable.

3. RST 7.5 is rising-edge triggered, TRAP is rising-edge and level triggered. All of the other interrupts are active-high level triggered.

4. INTR is a vectored interrupt identical to INTR on the 8080.

5. TRAP and RST 7.5–5.5 are direct interrupts. See Table 6.4 for the ISR address.

6. The SIM instruction can be used to mask any of the RST interrupts in addition to the DI instruction, which disables all maskable interrupts.

7. After a TRAP, the RIM instruction should be the first instruction in the ISR. This will save the pre-TRAP interrupt status, which can be restored with a SIM instruction when the ISR is completed.

8. Multiple interrupts can be handled by dedicating a separate interrupt to each peripheral. The 8259 PIC can also be used when multiple interrupts are interfaced through INTR.

9. After a system reset, all maskable interrupts are disabled and all three RST mask bits are set.

The Z-80:

1. The Z-80 has two interrupt pins: $\overline{\text{INT}}$ and $\overline{\text{NMI}}$.

2. $\overline{\text{NMI}}$ is a falling-edge-triggered nonmaskable direct interrupt. Its restart address is 0066H.

3. The ISR for an $\overline{\text{NMI}}$ should end with RETN so that the pre-NMI maskable interrupt status will be retained.

4. $\overline{\text{INT}}$ is active-low level-triggered and can be used in three separate modes, labeled modes 0, 1, and 2.

5. When programmed for mode 0 (IM 0), $\overline{\text{INT}}$ behaves as a vectored interrupt identical to INTR on the 8080.

6. When programmed for mode 1 (IM 1), $\overline{\text{INT}}$ behaves as a direct interrupt with a restart address of 0038H.

7. When programmed for mode 2 (IM 2), $\overline{\text{INT}}$ behaves as an indirect interrupt using the address in memory pointed to by the contents of register I (the high-order address) and the 7 most significant bits read from the data bus during an interrupt acknowledge (the low-order address).

8. After a reset, the contents of the I register = 0, the interrupt mode = 0, and maskable interrupts are disabled.

9. $\overline{\text{INTA}}$ must be derived from $\overline{\text{M1}} \cdot \overline{\text{IORQ}}$.

10. Multiple interrupts are best handled with Z-80 peripheral interface chips that support a daisy-chain priority technique. When this technique is utilized, all ISRs should terminate with the RETI instruction, as this instruction is used by the support devices to reset the interrupt-enable output status.

SELF-REVIEW 6.5

6.5.1 Why is interrupt-driven I/O more efficient than programmed I/O?

6.5.2 What is an ISR?

6.5.3 What is a nonmaskable interrupt?

6.5.4 List three ways of transferring control to an ISR.

6.5.5 Why is it important for an ISR to save the CPU registers it is about to use?

6.5.6 List three methods suitable for prioritizing simultaneous interrupt requests.

6.6 DIRECT MEMORY ACCESS

Introduction

We have now seen two different methods of transferring data between a peripheral and a microcomputer. The *polling technique* synchronizes the microprocessor to the peripheral at the expense of processing efficiency. *Interrupt-driven I/O* is more natural: The processor responds only when called upon. This results in more efficient use of the microprocessor at the expense of greater software overhead. The result is a (usually) faster response time than with polling, but a slower data transfer rate.

A third method of transferring data is called *direct memory access,* or DMA. With DMA, the peripheral is synchronized to main memory, not the microprocessor. Because memory access times are very short, the transfer rate can be very high.

In this section, we:

- Explain how a peripheral can be interfaced using direct memory access (DMA).
- Compare the byte, burst, and block modes of DMA operation.

The Processor Bottleneck

To appreciate DMA, you must understand that the real bottleneck in transferring data is the microprocessor itself. When a text file is output to a disk drive, we are concerned with transferring data from memory to that drive. However, to accomplish the transfer we first move the data into the processor and then output the data to the drive's I/O port. The microprocessor acts as a "middleman" in this process, with the result that the data transfer rate is decreased.

The DMA approach is to "turn off" the processor and let the disk drive access the data file in memory itself: a sort of *direct memory access.* If the memory can supply a new byte of data every 200 ns, data can be transferred at a rate of 5 million bytes per second!

The challenge to DMA is building a controller that allows the peripheral to take over the job of the CPU temporarily while it directly accesses the system memory. Figure 6.26 illustrates one type of DMA controller (DMAC) similar to the Intel 8237. As you might imagine, all three system buses are involved in the interface.

A handshaking logic scheme is used between the DMAC and the microprocessor and between the peripheral and the DMAC. A DMA request is initiated by the peripheral by using its BUSY/READY flag to assert DMARQ. The DMAC responds by asserting BUSRQ (Z-80) or HOLD (8080/85). The microprocessor responds by finishing the current machine cycle, asserting BUSAK (Z-80) or HOLDA (8080/85) and then setting its data, address, and control bus signals in a tristate mode. The DMAC alerts the peripheral that it has been selected for DMA by applying DMACK.

The memory and I/O devices now find themselves directly interfaced to the DMAC, just as if it were the microprocessor. Two classes of DMA are now possible. In *sequential DMA,* the DMAC performs a read operation, fetching the data byte from the DMAC. Next, a write operation is performed, transferring the data byte to the I/O port. The opposite sequence is also possible: Read a byte from the I/O port and write the byte to memory. Generally, two to four clock periods are required for each read or write operation (four to eight for the total transfer).

Simultaneous DMA provides the fastest transfers, with read and write operations performed at the same time. This requires MEMR and IOW (or IOR and MEMW) to be active simultaneously. In that way, data does not flow through the DMAC at all, but rather, moves directly from memory to the I/O port (or vice versa). The result is a twofold improvement in speed compared with the sequential approach.

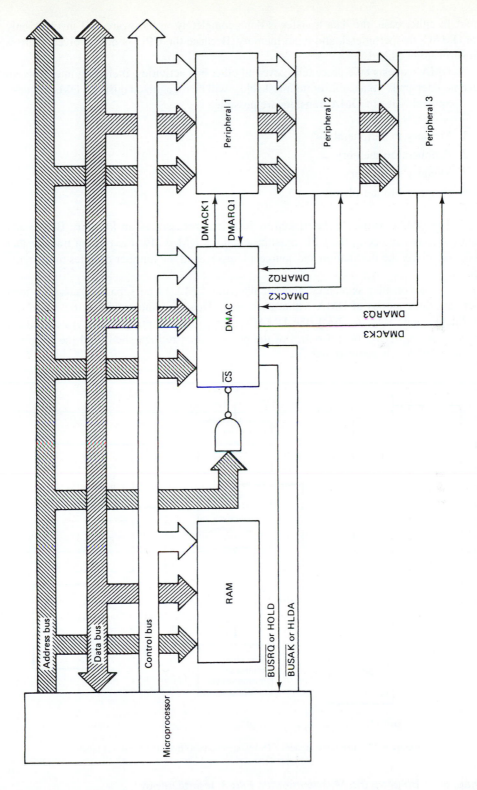

Figure 6.26 A DMA controller allows the peripheral to interface directly with memory without CPU intervention. This direct communication permits the data transfer rate to approach the access time of the memory.

313

In either case, the data transfer is done completely in hardware and involves only the DMAC, the peripheral, and main memory. Because the CPU is not involved, there is no software overhead.

DMA requests take precedence over all other bus activities, including interrupts. In fact, no interrupts—maskable or nonmaskable—will be recognized during a DMA request.

Several types of DMA transfers are possible:

1. Memory to peripheral
2. Peripheral to memory
3. Memory to memory
4. Peripheral to peripheral

The DMAC is usually interfaced to the microprocessor as an I/O port. Before any data transfers can occur, the CPU must program the DMAC for the type of transfer that is to take place, the destination and source addresses, and the number of bytes to be transferred.

If you consider sequential and simultaneous DMA to be separate "classes," then there are three modes of DMA within each class. These are shown in Fig. 6.27. In *byte*, or single, mode [Fig. 6.27(a)], the DMAC, after gaining control of the system buses, transfers a single data byte. Control of the buses is then relinquished until the peripherals' READY flag is again active.

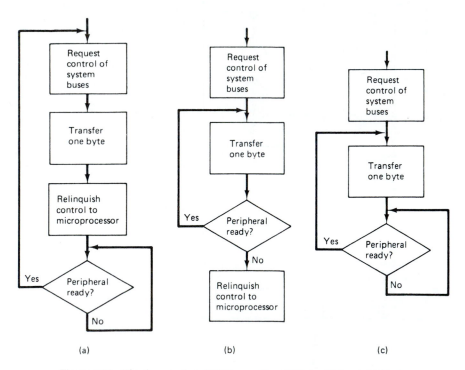

Figure 6.27 The three modes of DMA operation: (a) byte, (b) burst, (c) block.

The *burst,* or demand mode, shown in Fig. 6.27(b), is intended for peripherals that have high-speed data buffers. After the DMAC gains control of the buses, data is transferred until the peripheral's READY flag is no longer active. Control of the buses is then relinquished to the CPU. When READY again becomes active, another burst of DMA occurs. The advantage of this technique is that the buffer can be filled very rapidly by the DMAC and then emptied at the peripheral's leisure.

A third type of DMA is called *block-* or continuous-, mode DMA [Fig. 6.27(c)]. This is similar to burst mode, except that control of the buses is not relinquished until the entire data block has been transferred. The technique is very effective with a high-speed peripheral that can keep up with the DMAC. Slow peripherals will cause long periods of inactivity on the buses as the DMAC waits for the READY flag.

Because the DMA request line is sampled at the end of each machine cycle (not instruction cycle), the response time for DMA will be no longer than one machine cycle plus one T state. This is a worst case of six T states for an 8080 or seven T states for an 8085 or Z-80.

The design of a DMA controller is not a simple task, and this is probably the main disadvantage of the technique. The DMAC is actually a highly specialized *transfer processor* rivaling the microprocessor itself in complexity. Most microprocessors are now supported by special single-chip DMA controllers. Intel offers the 8237 Programmable DMA Controller to support the 8080 and 8085, and Zilog offers the Z-80 DMA to support the Z-80. These devices are discussed in detail in Chapters 7 and 8.

SELF-REVIEW 6.6

6.6.1 When DMA data transfers are used, the peripheral is synchronized to _____, not the microprocessor.

6.6.2 What is meant by simultaneous DMA?

6.6.3 List three different DMA modes for transferring data.

QUESTIONS AND ANSWERS

Q: *What is the key component in a microcomputer output port?*

A: A latch is the key component in a microcomputer output port. It is used to "catch" the data when the processor performs an I/O write cycle.

Q: *What is the key component in a microcomputer input port?*

A: A tristate buffer is the key component in a microcomputer input port. It is used to place the input data onto the data bus when the processor performs an I/O read cycle.

Q: *What is a device-select pulse?*

A: A device-select pulse is a signal that goes active when the processor is writing to or reading from a specified I/O port. Typically, this signal is used to enable a tristate buffer (input port) or a latch (output port).

Q: *What is a memory-mapped I/O port?*

A: A memory-mapped I/O port is a port that is enabled by a memory read or write signal and thus resides in the memory space (not I/O space) of the processor.

Q: *What is meant by handshaking signals?*

A: Handshaking signals are input and output signals exchanged between the processor and an I/O device. They provide a means of synchronizing the processor to the data rate of the peripheral.

Q: *What is meant by programmed I/O?*

A: Programmed I/O is an interfacing technique in which the processor continually asks (polls) the peripheral to see whether it is ready to exchange data. This is an inefficient I/O method because the processor is forced to spend all of its time polling the I/O device.

Q: *What is meant by interrupt-driven I/O?*

A: Interrupt-driven I/O is an interfacing technique in which the peripheral interrupts the processor when it is ready to exchange data. This technique is more efficient than programmed I/O because the processor can do other tasks while waiting for the I/O device to be ready.

Q: *List three common types of interrupts.*

A: Three common types of interrupts, are direct interrupts, indirect interrupts, and vectored interrupts.

Q: *What is meant by a priority structure, as applied to I/O devices?*

A: The order in which the processor responds to multiple I/O requests is referred to as the processor's priority structure. The device with the highest priority gets serviced first.

Q: *Which I/O technique provides the highest data transfer rate?*

A: Direct memory access (DMA) provides the fastest data transfers by synchronizing the peripheral to main memory.

LAB PROJECTS

6.1. Study the schematic diagram of the microcomputer you are using to support this text or course. You should have a user-accessible 8-bit input and output port.*
   (a) What is the part number of the chip used as the output port latch?
   (b) What is the part number of the chip used as the input port buffer?
   (c) To what addresses (or range of addresses) are the two ports mapped?

6.2. Sketch a schematic diagram of the input and output ports you located in Lab Project 6.1. Be sure to include the address-decoding logic.

6.3. Sketch an I/O map of your computer, showing the address ranges occupied by each input and output port. Identify the function of each port (e.g., keyboard, LED display, speaker, user, etc.).

6.4. Design an I/O port address decoder circuit that provides one input and one output device-select pulse (DSP). Test your circuit by writing a program that causes each DSP to pulse at a 1-Hz rate. Use a logic probe to verify that the circuit is operating properly.

6.5. Use the DSP signals from Lab Project 6.4 to add an input and/or output port to your computer. Write a simple program to test your circuit.

6.6. Use the DSP signals from Lab Project 6.4 to build a circuit similar to Fig. 6.6. Connect 1 bit of an input port to a switch, and write a program to monitor the switch and turn a relay on and off. It can be fun to use a photocell in place of the switch.

---

*Some systems use special parallel I/O chips like the 8255 PPI or Z-80 PIO. These are covered in detail in Chapters 7 and 8.

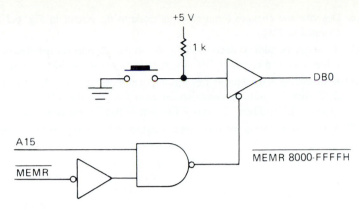

Figure 6.28 One-bit memory-mapped input port for Lab Project 6.7.

6.7. Figure 6.28 is a 1-bit memory-mapped input port. Build this circuit and write a program to read the switch. (*Note:* You may have to adjust the address decoder to avoid conflicts with the memory of your computer. Refer to your system memory map.)

6.8. Using a technique similar to the one used in Chapter 3, Program 12, write a program to count and display the number of falling edges generated by the bouncing switch in Lab Project 6.7.

6.9. Design an interrupt interface such that pushing a switch will cause control to transfer to a vectored interrupt of your choice. Write a simple test program—jump to monitor—to test your hardware.

6.10. Use the interrupt hardware from Lab Project 6.9, and write a "reaction timer" program. Have your program show 00 in its display and then begin a rapid count. When interrupted—by the operator's pushing the switch—the display should "freeze," showing the operator's reaction time.

QUESTIONS AND PROBLEMS

Section 6.1

6.1. Can an input port and an output port share the same address? Explain.

6.2. What data is output by the following Z-80 program? To which port(s) is the data output?

```
LD      C,27H
LD      B,3CH
OUT     (C),B
INC     C
OUT     (C),B
HALT
```

6.3. Write an 8080/85 program that is the equivalent of the Z-80 program in Problem 6.2.

6.4. True or false? For all three processors, valid data will be read by the CPU on the *falling/rising* edge of the $\overline{IOR}$ control signal.

6.5. True or false? When designing an output port care must be taken to latch the data bus on the falling edge of the $\overline{IOW}$ control signal.

6.6. Describe the changes required to be made to the circuit in Fig. 6.2 if the port address is changed to 72H.

6.7. Redesign the address decoder in Fig. 6.2 so that the port address can be set to any one of 256 values via an eight-option DIP switch. (*Hint:* Use two 74LS85 4-bit magnitude comparators.)

*6.8. A technician is troubleshooting the output port of Fig. 6.4. A logic probe connected to DB0–DB7 shows a pulsing condition on each line, but the 1Q–8Q latch outputs are steady. "There's the problem," he says. "The latch is bad." What is wrong with this logic?

*6.9. A technician testing the relay control circuit of Fig. 6.6 uses the following test program:

```
LOOP    IN      FFH
        CALL    DELAY       ;10-s delay
        OUT     FFH
        CALL    DELAY       ;10-s delay
        JMP     LOOP
```

Which of the following could be a cause of the relay's never coming on?
(a) Register A must be loaded with 00 before the OUT instruction is given.
(b) The DELAY subroutine is changing the values of the CPU registers, causing the program to fail.
(c) The 2k resistor is actually a 220k resistor.
(d) The flip-flop Q output is stuck low.

*6.10. In Fig. 6.16, the relay is found to always be on. Which of the following could account for this problem?
(a) The output of IC2a is shorted to ground.
(b) The output of IC2b is shorted to ground.
(c) The collector–emitter of Q1 is shorted.
(d) The relay coil has accidentally been wired to +5 V.

Section 6.2

6.11. Which of the following instructions could be used to output data to a memory-mapped output port?

8080/85 mnemonic		Z-80 mnemonic	
(a) MOV	A,B	LD	A,B
(b) STA	1000H	LD	(1000H),A
(c) STAX	D	LD	(DE),A
(d) MOV	B,M	LD	B,(HL)
(e) MOV	M,C	LD	(HL),C

6.12. Study the circuit shown in Fig. 6.29. Is this circuit an input or output port? Is it I/O mapped or memory mapped? To what address or *range* of addresses will the port respond?

6.13. Write a program to read the contents of the port in Fig. 6.29 and branch to location READY if bit 0 or bit 1 is low.

6.14. Refer to the memory-mapped keypad interface of Fig. 6.8. Suppose the instruction LDA FF03H (8080/85) or LD A, (FF03H) (Z-80) is given and the data byte 41H is read. Which key or keys are being held down?

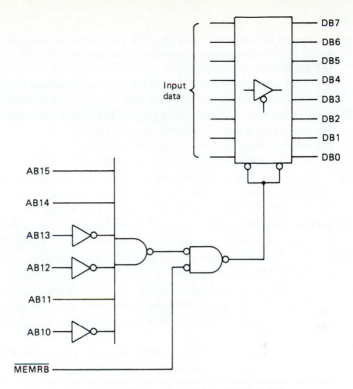

Figure 6.29 I/O port for Problems 6.12 and 6.13.

6.15. If keys 3 and 7 are both held down, what key value will be encoded by the interface in Fig. 6.8 and the software in the flowchart of Fig. 6.9?

6.16. Write the program corresponding to the keyboard encoder in the flowchart of Fig. 6.9.

6.17. Write the program corresponding to the digital lock in the flowchart of Fig. 6.10.

6.18. Can the instruction SHLD 1000H (8080/85) or LD (1000H),HL (Z-80) be used as a 16-bit memory-mapped output instruction? Explain. What is the corresponding input instruction?

Section 6.3

6.19. Explain the handshaking signals exchanged between a computer and a peripheral by completing the following table:

Signal	Output by	Purpose
BUSY/READY		
STROBE		
ACK		

6.20. What is meant by *synchronizing* a microprocessor with a peripheral?

6.21. Answer the following questions about the parallel-printer interface of Fig. 6.12.

   (a) Is this interface memory mapped or I/O mapped?

   (b) What is the data port address?

   (c) What is the size (number of bits) and purpose of the input port?

   (d) Sketch a timing diagram showing $\overline{\text{IOW}}$, the OUT0 DISP, and $\overline{\text{STROBE}}$.

6.22. Refer to the parallel-printer control program in Fig. 6.13 (8080/85) or Fig. 6.14 (Z-80).

   (a) What is the purpose of memory location NUMB?

   (b) Where is the data stored that is to be printed?

   (c) How does the program detect the end of the data?

*6.23. A programmer plans to use the printer control programs in Figs. 6.13 and 6.14 to print a 700-byte document. Her plan is to change the define-storage operator to 1024 and then load NUMB with 700. Unfortunately, this will not work. Why not?

*6.24. Suppose the printer cable in Fig. 6.12 is wired *incorrectly* such that the D2 and D1 printer data lines are exchanged. What would the symptom of this problem be?

6.25. Describe the changes required to be made to the program of Fig. 6.13 or Fig. 6.14 if the output of IC8 is wired to DB7. (See Fig. 6.12.)

6.26. Calculate the maximum transfer rate for the printer control program of Fig. 6.13, assuming a 6-MHz 8085AH-1. Remember to recalculate the T states for an 8085.

6.27. Calculate the maximum transfer rate for the printer control program of Fig. 6.14, assuming a 6-MHz Z-80B.

6.28. Suppose that a floppy disk drive and 100-cps printer are interfaced to a microcomputer. The $\overline{\text{BUSY}}/\text{READY}$ status bit assignments are shown in Fig. 6.30(a). Write a polling routine that monitors these flags and branches to the appropriate service routine as shown in Fig. 6.30(b). Write your program so that the disk drive has the highest priority.

Section 6.5

6.29. List three situations that will cause maskable interrupts to be blocked by the 8080, 8085, and Z-80 microprocessors.

6.30. True or false? Nonmaskable interrupts have a higher priority than maskable interrupts.

6.31. True or false? When interrupts are enabled, a maskable interrupt can interrupt a nonmaskable interrupt service routine.

6.32. The 8085 SIM instruction returns the byte 34H. How is this byte interpreted?

6.33. Write an 8085 program to mask the RST 7.5 and RST 6.5 interrupt inputs. All other interrupt inputs should be enabled.

6.34. Suppose that memory location 0030H stores a jump instruction to a printer interrupt service routine. Sketch a schematic diagram of the circuit required to *vector* to this interrupt.

6.35. The 8080/85 INTR and the Z-80 $\overline{\text{INT}}$ inputs are maskable and level triggered. To guarantee acceptance by the CPU, how long must an interrupt request on one of these inputs be held active? Why is a circuit such as Fig. 6.19 useful with this type of interrupt?

6.36. Why do direct interrupts *not* require the interrupt-acknowledge bus cycle?

6.37. True or false? With regard to the 8080/85 INTR and Z-80 mode 0 INT inputs, using an 8-bit interrupt vector allows _____ different interrupt service routines to be set up.

6.38. A printer is to be interfaced to the Z-80 using mode 2 interrupts. The service routine begins at address 1000H, and the interrupt vector is stored at address FE30H. Sketch a schematic

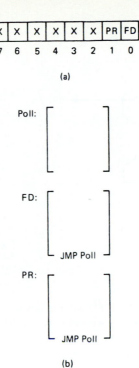

```
        X  X  X  X  X  X  PR FD
        7  6  5  4  3  2  1  0
                (a)


   Poll:  ⌈                    ⌉
          │                    │
          │                    │
          ⌊                    ⌋


   FD:    ⌈                    ⌉
          │                    │
          │                    │
          ⌊ JMP Poll           ⌋


   PR:    ⌈                    ⌉
          │                    │
          │                    │
          ⌊ JMP Poll           ⌋

                (b)
```

Figure 6.30   (a) Status bit assignments and (b) program organization for Problem 6.27.

diagram of the hardware required and write the instruction sequence needed to initialize the Z-80 for this interrupt.

*6.39. A technician is testing a Z-80 computer that uses interrupts. He finds that a mode 1 interrupt on $\overline{\text{INT}}$ is ignored if preceded by an interrupt on $\overline{\text{NMI}}$. However, if the machine is reset and the mode 1 interrupt occurs alone, the $\overline{\text{INT}}$ interrupt is serviced. The code for a system RESET, $\overline{\text{INT}}$ interrupt, and $\overline{\text{NMI}}$ interrupt is as follows:

```
RESET        IM      1
             EI
             JP      MONITOR
INT_ISR      . . . . . .
             . . . . . .
             RET
NMI_ISR      . . . . . .
             . . . . . .
             RET
```

Studying this code, the technician says, "Aha, I see the problem." What has he found?

6.40. The circuit in Fig. 6.31 is intended as an 8085 program "break" key. Pushing the switch should force the CPU to run a *monitor* program. Write the initialization sequence required to enable this circuit. At what address should the monitor program (or a jump to the monitor program) be loaded?

6.41. Suppose the ISR for the 8085 interrupt control circuit in Fig. 6.31 requires 30 μs to execute and then reenables interrupts. Since it is not possible to hold the switch down for that short

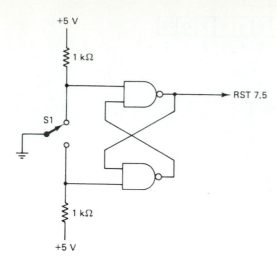

+5 V

1 kΩ

S1

RST 7.5

1 kΩ

+5 V

Figure 6.31 Circuit for Problems 6.40 and 6.41.

a time, it might appear that the CPU will run this interrupt several times. Why doesn't that happen? Is it really necessary to debounce the switch?

6.42. It is a common myth that a CPU's response time is much faster when the CPU uses interrupts versus polling. Under what conditions is this true? When is it false?

*6.43. A programmer has written the ISR shown in Fig. 6.32 to control a printer connected to an 8080/85. What is wrong with her program?

6.44. Figure 6.33 is the schematic for a programmable interrupt controller (PIC) used to interface three peripherals—IREQ1, IREQ2, and IREQ3. Answer the following questions about this circuit:

(a) What is the restart instruction associated with each interrupt?

(b) What is the purpose of the 3-bit memory-mapped input port?

(c) To what *range* of addresses will the memory-mapped port respond?

```
ISR         PUSH    PSW             ;SAVE ENVIRONMENT
            PUSH    B
            ;
            POP     H               ;RECOVER OLD DATA POINTER
            POP     B
            ;
            MOV     A,M             ;PRINT THE CHARACTER
            OUT     1
            ;
            INX     H               ;ADJUST POINTER AND COUNTER
            DCR     B
            JZ      DONE
            ;
            PUSH    B               ;SAVE COUNTER AND POINTER
            PUSH    H
            EI                      ;REENABLE INTERRUPTS
            ;
DONE        POP     B               ;RESTORE CPU ENVIRONMENT
            POP     PSW
            RET
```

Figure 6.32 ISR for Problems 6.43.

Input	Priority	Address
IREQ1	1	0100H
IREQ2	2	0200H
IREQ3	3	0300H

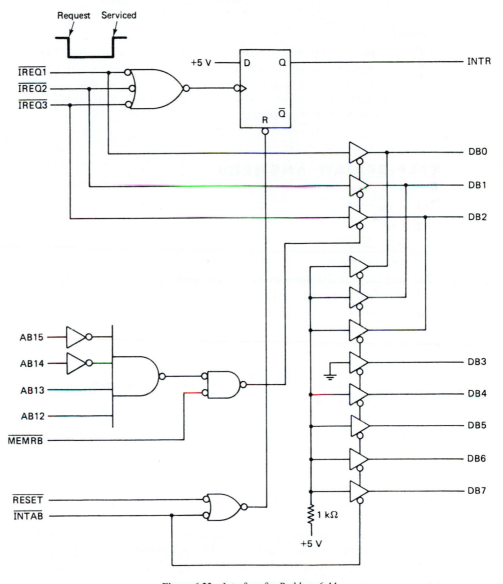

Figure 6.33 Interface for Problem 6.44.

(d) Write an ISR that will cause control to transfer to the addresses shown in the following table when an interrupt occurs:

Input	Priority	Address
IREQ1	1	0100H
IREQ2	2	0200H
IREQ3	3	0300H

Section 6.6

6.45. Is the response time for DMA faster or slower than that for interrupts? Explain.

6.46. Some printers have buffers that allow them to accept several hundreds (or thousands) of characters before they issue the BUSY flag. The characters are then printed from the buffer at the speed of the printer. Which mode of DMA—byte, burst, or block—would be best suited for this type of peripheral?

SELF-REVIEW ANSWERS

6.1.1. 8, 256

6.1.2. Z-80

6.1.3. device-select

6.2.1. memory mapped

6.2.2. detect key pressed, debounce the key, encode the key with a value

6.2.3. LDA FF3FH (LD A,FF3FH)

6.2.4. 04H

6.3.1. synchronize

6.3.2. low

6.4.1. poll

6.4.2. If the I/O device is very slow, the CPU will spend all of its time polling the peripheral to see if it is ready for new data.

6.4.3. The first device polled has the highest priority.

6.5.1. The CPU is able to run another program while it waits for the peripheral to become ready.

6.5.2. The interrupt service routine—the program the CPU executes when an interrupt is received.

6.5.3. An interrupt to which the CPU must respond.

6.5.4. Vectored, direct, indirect

6.5.5. If the registers are altered, the system may "crash" when control is returned to the interrupted program.

6.5.6. Unless they are built into the microprocessor (e.g., the 8085 RST 7.5, 6.5, 5.5 inputs), priorities can be established via polling, a PIC, or a daisy-chain technique.

6.6.1. memory

6.6.2. Data is transferred directly between the peripheral and memory without passing through the DMAC.

6.6.3. burst, byte, block

7

SPECIAL-PURPOSE SUPPORT DEVICES: THE 8080/85 FAMILY

OBJECTIVES

After completing this chapter, you should be able to:

- Determine, from a schematic diagram, the memory and I/O port address ranges for a typical 8755A interface.
- Specify the control word to program the 8755A I/O port bits as inputs or outputs.
- Describe the three operating modes of the 8255A PPI.
- Show how to interface a parallel printer using mode 0 and mode 1 of the 8255A PPI.
- Describe the six operating modes of the 8254 programmable interval timer.
- Write an 8080/8085 frequency counter program using the 8254 as an event counter.

- Describe how to interface the 8259A PIC in single and cascade mode.
- Program the 8259A PIC and specify the initialization and operation control words.
- Describe the sequence of events that must occur for the 8237A DMAC to transfer data with a peripheral.
- Calculate the data transfer rate for the 8237A DMAC.
- Show how to provide bus buffers for a DMA controller.
- Show how to control the direction of a bidirectional bus buffer when a DMA controller is used.

OVERVIEW

One of the unmistakable trends in microprocessor technology today is the integration of the special-purpose I/O interface circuitry into a single programmable device. Such a support device interfaces to the microprocessor over the system data bus and is capable of receiving special initialization codes that program its function.

As an example, consider the Intel 8255A programmable peripheral interface (PPI). This 40-pin device has 24 separate I/O pins organized as three 8-bit ports. By giving the command

OUT (control port)

a control word can be written to the device. If, for example, the accumulator contains 90H, the PPI is programmed for 16 lines of output and 8 lines of input.

In this chapter, we examine several programmable I/O devices made by Intel Corp. to support the 8080 and 8085 microprocessors. Table 7.1 lists some of the devices

TABLE 7.1 I/O Support Devices for the 8080 and 8085 Microprocessors

Part number	Description
8155/56[a]	RAM with I/O and timer
8185[a]	1K $\times$ 8 RAM
8755/8355[a]	EPROM/ROM with I/O
8231	Arithmetic processing unit
8237	Programmable DMA controller
8251	Programmable communications interface
8254	Programmable interval timer
8255	Programmable peripheral interface
8256	Multifunction universal asynchronous receiver/transmitter
8259A	Programmable interrupt controller
8272	Single/double-density floppy-disk controller
8275	Programmable CRT controller
8279	Programmable keyboard display interface
8295	Dot matrix printer controller
82720	Graphics display controller

[a]Compatible with the 8085 multiplexed address and data bus.

currently available, which range from the five chips designed especially for the multiplexed data and address bus of the 8085 to complex DMA processors, CRT controllers, floppy-disk controllers, and programmable keyboard/display interfaces. Although these devices have been designed to interface with the 8080 or 8085, most can also be interfaced to the Z-80 (and most other 8-bit microprocessors). Of course, Zilog also supplies a family of support devices for the Z-80, and these are covered in detail in Chapter 8.

7.1 THE 8755A 16K EPROM WITH I/O

Introduction

Table 7.2 describes the memory and I/O capabilities of the five 8085 support devices available from Intel. The concept of combining memory and I/O functions on one chip was pioneered by Intel and allows a minimal 8085 microcomputer system to be built from three to five chips.

All of the 8085 support devices interface directly to the processor's multiplexed address and data bus without the need for a low-order address latch. In this section we will cover the 8755A, which contains a 2K × 8 EPROM and two bit-programmable 8-bit I/O ports. Note that the 8355 is identical to the 8755A, except that the ROM is mask programmable at the factory. Thus, all comments regarding the 8755A (except for EPROM programming instructions) apply equally to the 8355.

In this section, we:

- Determine, from a schematic diagram, the memory and I/O port address ranges for a typical 8755A interface.
- Specify the control word to program the 8755A I/O port bits as inputs or outputs.

Interfacing the 8755A ROM

Figure 7.1 is a block diagram and pinout of the 8755A. In interfacing to the ROM portion of this device, 11 address lines (A0–A10) are required to select one of the 2048 8-bit

TABLE 7.2 Special Support Devices for the 8085 Microprocessor

Device	Memory	I/O
8355	2K PROM	16-bit programmable I/O lines organized as two 8-bit I/O ports
8755A	2K EPROM	Same as 8355
8185	1K × 8 RAM	None
8155[a]	256 × 8 RAM	Two 8-bit byte programmable I/O ports, one 6-bit control port for handshake, one 14-bit timer
8156[b]	256 × 8 RAM	Same as 8155

[a]Active-low CE input.
[b]Active-high CE input.

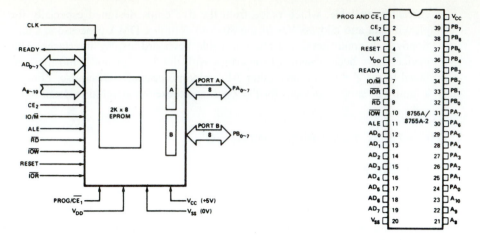

Figure 7.1 Block diagram and pinout for the 8755A 2K × 8 EPROM with I/O. (Courtesy of Intel Corporation.)

words in the memory array. The AD0 through AD7 bus lines from the 8085 connect directly to the 8755A, as does the multiplex control signal ALE.

Because the data on the bus can be directed to the I/O ports or the ROM, the 8085's $IO/\overline{M}$ output control signal is required to distinguish between an I/O address and a memory address. There are two chip-enable inputs, labeled $\overline{CE1}$ and CE2. Data from the ROM is placed onto the data bus by the 8755A when both chip-select inputs are active,—i.e., when $IO/\overline{M} = 0$ and $\overline{RD} = 0$.

Example 7.1

Design a fully decoded 8755A EPROM interface at addresses F800H through FFFFH.

Solution. The circuit diagram is shown in Fig. 7.2. The address/data bus connections and control bus connections are all straightforward ($\overline{IOR}$ and $\overline{IOW}$ will be explained in the next section), connecting to the signals of the same names on the 8085. The system clock signal is required to synchronize WAIT state requests.

Address lines A11 through A15 define 32 different "slots" the 2K PROM can occupy in the 8085's 64K memory space. In this case the topmost slot is desired, and the 74LS30 NAND gate functions as an address decoder for the range F800H through FFFFH. The CE2 input is not used and is therefore permanently enabled.

The 8755A was intended to facilitate the design of minimum-package-count 8085 microcomputer systems. In such systems, it is likely that the full memory space will not be implemented and partial decoding can be used. For example, in Fig. 7.2, connecting A15 to CE2 and grounding $\overline{CE1}$ would place the PROM in the top 32K of memory space from 8000H through FFFFH. No address decoder would be required. Up to five 8755As can be interfaced to the 8085 in this way without the need for an address decoder.

There are two versions of the 8755A, each with a different speed: the 8755A, with an access time of 450 ns, and the 8755A-2, with a 300-ns access time. The first is suitable in 8085 systems up to 3 MHz, while the 8755A-2 should be used in 5-MHz designs.

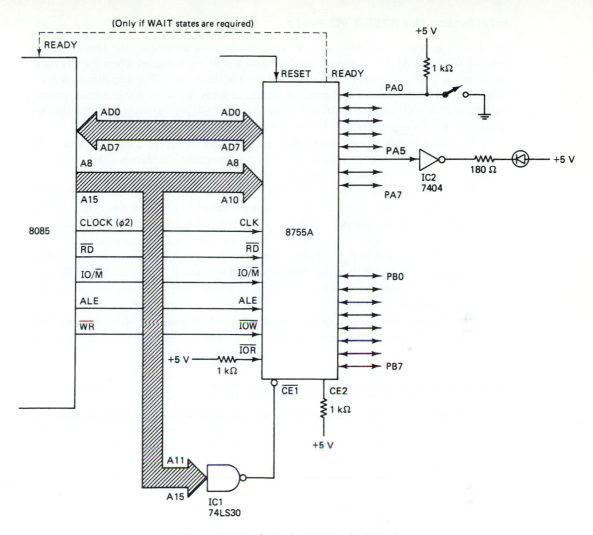

Figure 7.2 Interfacing the 8755A to the 8085 microprocessor.

Automatic WAIT states are inserted by the 8755A if its READY output is connected to the 8085 READY input. Whenever the chip selects are active and ALE = 1, the READY output of the 8755A will go low for one clock period. If WAIT states are not desired, the READY output should be left open.

In larger 8085 systems, the buffer and address decoding logic may cause the chip-enable inputs to become valid after ALE has gone low. In this case, the READY output will never go low and WAIT states cannot be requested. The chip-enable logic will have to be redesigned to ensure a valid CE signal before ALE goes low.

The 8755A is programmed by raising the V_{DD} supply to 25 V and pulsing $\overline{CE1}$ to 5 V for 50 ms. Commercial programmers are available for this purpose. Erasure is accomplished by exposure to an ultraviolet-light source for 15 to 30 minutes.

Sec. 7.1   The 8755A 16K EPROM with I/O

Interfacing the 8755A I/O Ports

The 8755A appears to the 8085 as four separate I/O ports defined by the four combinations of AD0 and AD1. (Address lines A2 through A10 are not used when the I/O ports are accessed.) Table 7.3 lists the definitions of each of these ports. The data direction ports (DDRA and DDRB) control the direction of data at ports A and B. For example, writing F0H to DDRA will program PA0–PA3 as inputs and PA4–PA7 as outputs. Note that resetting the 8755A will clear both DDRs, configuring them as inputs.

It is also possible to read from a port defined as an output (read back the data written) or to write to a port defined as an input. In the latter case, the data will be stored, but not placed on any output pin until that pin is defined as such.

When configured as an output port, each pin can supply 400 μA in the high state and sink 2 mA in the low state. This corresponds to one standard TTL load or five LSTTL loads. When configured as an input port, each pin presents a nearly insignificant 10-μA load.

In interfacing to the I/O ports of the 8755A, the 8085 $\overline{WR}$ output is normally connected to $\overline{IOW}$, as shown in Fig. 7.2. The $\overline{IOR}$ input should not be connected to $\overline{RD}$. This is because the $\overline{IOW}$ and $\overline{IOR}$ inputs override the IO/$\overline{M}$ and $\overline{RD}$ inputs. With $\overline{IOR}$ connected to $\overline{RD}$, a normal memory read cycle could access the PROM and one of the I/O ports simultaneously.

It is recommended that $\overline{IOR}$ be connected to +5 V and $\overline{IOW}$ connected to $\overline{WR}$. Table 7.4 describes the control bus combinations required to read the PROM or access the I/O ports.

Example 7.2

Determine the port addresses for the 8755A interface in Fig. 7.2.

Solution. Recall that the 8085 (and the 8080) duplicates the I/O port address on A0–A7 and A8–A15 in performing an I/O operation. For 8755A I/O operations, it is only necessary for CE1 and CE2 to be active. AD0 and AD1 then select one of four internal I/O ports. In Fig. 7.2, the port addresses can be found by noting the following:

1. A11–A15 (A3–A7): These lines must be high to enable the 8755A via its $\overline{CE1}$ input.
2. A8–A9 (A0–A1): These two lines select one of four internal ports, as shown in Table 7.3.
3. A10 (A2): This line is not examined.

Because A10 is not decoded, two sets of ports, F8H–FBH and FCH–FFH, are defined. Table 7.3 lists the two possible sets of port addresses. Address line A10 can be combined with the IO/$\overline{M}$ signal from the 8085 if partial decoding is not desired. (See Problem 7.2.)

TABLE 7.3 I/O Ports of the 8755A

AD1	AD0	Name	Function	Port address in Fig. 7.2
0	0	I/O port A	I/O on pins PA0–PA7	F8 or FC
0	1	I/O port B	I/O on pins PB0–PB7	F9 or FD
1	0	DDRA	Data direction for the 8 bits of port A*	FA or FE
1	1	DDRB	Data direction for the 8 bits of port B*	FB or FF

*A logic 1 programs an output bit, a logic 0 an input bit.

TABLE 7.4 Control Bus Signal Combination Required to Access the PROM and I/O Ports of the 8755A

$\overline{IOR}$	$\overline{IOW}$	$\overline{RD}$	$IO/\overline{M}$	Function	Active address lines
1	1	0	0	ROM read	AD0–AD10
1	0	1	0	Not allowed	—
1	1	0	1	I/O port read	AD0 and AD1[a]
1	0	1	1	I/O port write	AD0 and AD1[a]

[a]Table 7.3 defines the particular ports selected by the four combinations of the AD0 and AD1 address lines.

Figure 7.3 illustrates a decoding scheme that allows the ROM address and port address to be independent (at the expense of several more TTL gates).

Example 7.3

Write a program to monitor the switch connected to PA0 in Fig. 7.2 and turn on the LED connected to PA5 when the switch is closed.

Solution. The program is as follows:

```
        MVI   A,20H    ;DDRA CONTROL WORD
        OUT   FEH      ;DDRA ACCESS (COULD ALSO USE FAH)
LOOP    IN    FCH      ;SAMPLE PORT A (COULD ALSO USE F8H)
        RAR            ;TEST BIT 0
        JC    OFF      ;CY MEANS SWITCH IS OPEN
        MVI   A,20H    ;MAKE PA5 HIGH (LED ON)
        JMP   LED      ;
OFF     MVI   A,0      ;MAKE PA5 LOW (LED OFF)
LED     OUT   FCH      ;OUTPUT TO PA5
        JMP   LOOP
```

Note that, because only PA0 and PA5 need to be defined, the DDRA control word is XX1XXXX0. Choosing the don't cares to be 0 results in the control word 20H.

Three-Chip 8085 Microcomputer System

Figure 7.4 illustrates a complete 8085 microcomputer system requiring only three chips. The system features 1K of RAM using the 8185 1K × 8 static RAM, 2K of EPROM, and 16 I/O lines using the 8755A. Because the system is so small, no buffering is required and partial decoding can be used.

Is such a system practical? Absolutely. The 16 I/O lines could be used to monitor sensors and activate alarms in a home security system. In an automobile, the I/O lines could be used to monitor engine operating conditions such as flow rates, temperatures, and pressures. A control program in the 8755A can supervise these activities using the 1K of RAM in the 8185 for a stack area and for storage of temporary variables.

The system could also be used as the basis for an 8085 microprocessor trainer. With a memory-mapped keyboard similar to that developed in Chapter 6 and with port A or B of the 8755A to drive two seven-segment hex-decoded displays, one I/O port would remain for experimentation.

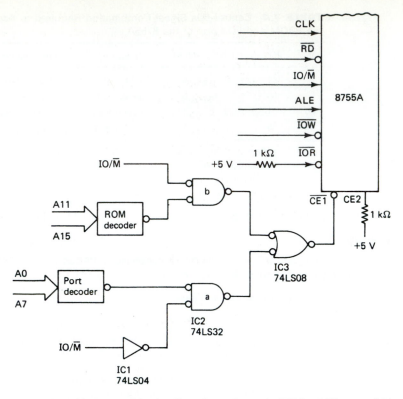

Figure 7.3 With the use of the decoding scheme shown, the ROM and I/O ports of the 8755A may have separate and independent addresses.

SELF-REVIEW 7.1

7.1.1 The 8755A contains _____ bytes of ROM and _____ bit-programmable I/O ports.

7.1.2 To program port A of the 8755A so that pins PA0–PA3 are outputs and pins PA4–PA7 are inputs, we output the byte _____ to DDRA.

7.2 THE 8255A PROGRAMMABLE PERIPHERAL INTERFACE

Introduction

The 8255A is a general-purpose I/O interfacing device that provides 24 I/O lines organized as three 8-bit I/O ports labeled A, B, and C. Pin definitions and a block diagram are provided in Fig. 7.5. Unlike the 8755A, the 8255A is such that individual bits cannot be programmed as inputs or outputs. Instead, all of the bits in port A or port B are programmed as a single byte. The four high- and four low-order bits of port C can be programmed as two separate nibbles, however.

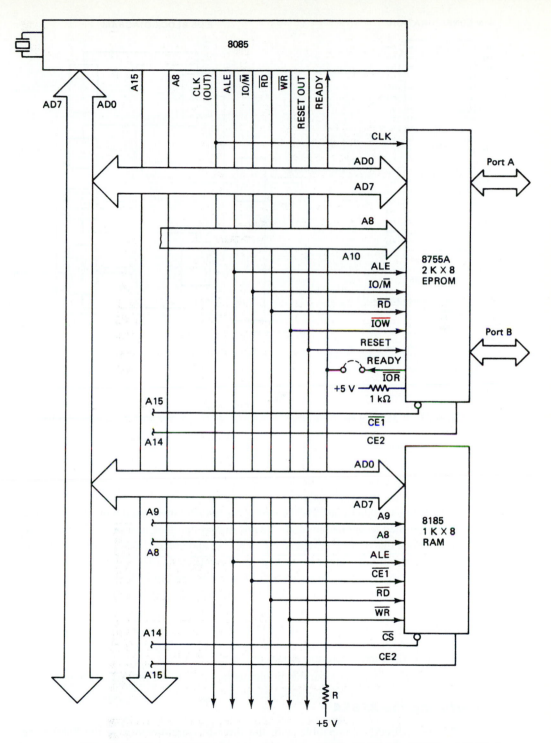

Figure 7.4 Three-chip 8085 microcomputer system with 1K of RAM, 2K of ROM, and 16 I/O pins.

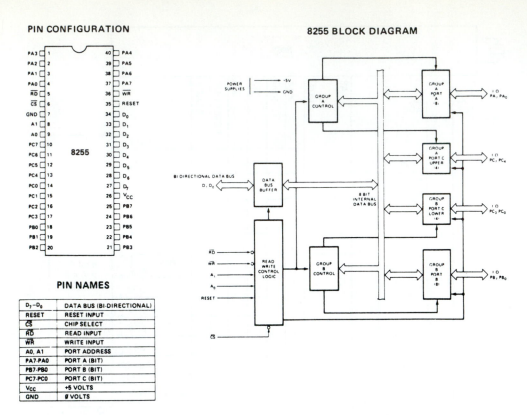

PIN CONFIGURATION

8255 BLOCK DIAGRAM

PIN NAMES

D_7–D_0	DATA BUS (BI-DIRECTIONAL)
RESET	RESET INPUT
CS	CHIP SELECT
RD	READ INPUT
WR	WRITE INPUT
A0, A1	PORT ADDRESS
PA7-PA0	PORT A (BIT)
PB7-PB0	PORT B (BIT)
PC7-PC0	PORT C (BIT)
V_{CC}	+5 VOLTS
GND	0 VOLTS

Figure 7.5 8255A programmable peripheral interface. 24 I/O pins are provided. (Courtesy of Intel Corporation.)

The 8255A is a very versatile device. It can be programmed to look like three simple I/O ports (mode 0), two handshaking I/O ports (mode 1), or a bidirectional I/O port with five handshaking signals (mode 2). The modes can also be intermixed. For example, port A can be programmed to operate in mode 2 while port B operates in mode 0. There is also a bit set/reset mode that allows individual bits of port C to be set or reset for control purposes.

Because the input–output block is a fundamental part of any microcomputer, and because the 8255A is an excellent choice for a universal parallel I/O device, we cover this chip in detail in this section. Several examples will be presented to help you appreciate its capabilities.

In this section, we:

- Describe the three operating modes of the 8255A PPI.
- Show how to interface a parallel printer using mode 0 and mode 1 of the 8255A PPI.

Interfacing the 8255A

The 8255A is directly compatible with the three-bus architecture of the 8080 micro-processor, as is illustrated in Fig. 7.6. Because the CPU modules for the Z-80 and 8085

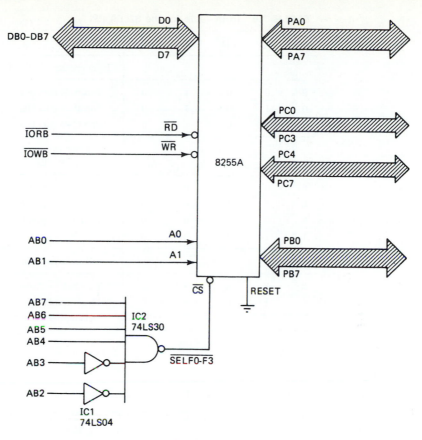

Figure 7.6 The 8255A interfaces directly to the three-bus architecture of the 8080 microprocessor.

examined in Chapter 4 have been made to present 8080-like control buses, these processors will also interface directly to the 8255A.

Notice the bidirectional data bus connection. All communications with the programmable peripheral interface (PPI) occur over these eight lines. In fact, to the microprocessor, the 8255A appears to be four I/O locations corresponding to the four combinations of the A0 and A1 address line inputs. The specific port address is controlled by the chip-select ($\overline{CS}$) input. Only when this pin is low can the PPI be accessed.

Table 7.5 summarizes the possible read and write operations that may be performed with the chip. When $\overline{RD}$ is low, any of the three data ports can be read by applying the appropriate combination to A0 and A1. When A0 and A1 are both high, the control port is accessed. This is a special register in the 8255A that controls the operating mode of the device. Note that the control port can only be written to, not read from.

When the PPI is not accessed ($\overline{CS} = 1$ or $\overline{RD}$ AND $\overline{WR} = 1$), the data bus connections are in a high-impedance state, and the processor is free to communicate with other devices in the microcomputer system.

TABLE 7.5 Truth Table for the 8255A PPI

A_1	A_0	$\overline{RD}$	$\overline{WR}$	$\overline{CS}$	
					Input operation (READ)
0	0	0	1	0	Port A → data bus
0	1	0	1	0	Port B → data bus
1	0	0	1	0	Port C → data bus
					Output operation (WRITE)
0	0	1	0	0	Data bus → port A
0	1	1	0	0	Data bus → port B
1	0	1	0	0	Data bus → port C
1	1	1	0	0	Data bus → control
					Disable function
X	X	X	X	1	Data bus → tristate
1	1	0	1	0	Illegal condition
X	X	1	1	0	Data bus → tristate

Source: Courtesy of Intel Corporation.

Example 7.4

Determine the addresses of ports A, B, and C and the control port in the interface in Fig. 7.6.

Solution. The $\overline{CS}$ input will be driven low whenever the low-order address lines A2 through A7 = 111100. This can occur during memory or I/O machine cycles. However, the $\overline{RD}$ (connected to $\overline{IORB}$) and $\overline{WR}$ (connected to $\overline{IOWB}$) inputs are active only for I/O machine cycles. For example, port A is accessed as input or output port F0H (111100 00). The following table applies to all four ports:

Port	I/O address
A	F0
B	F1
C	F2
Control	F3

Mode 0: Basic I/O

Once the PPI has been interfaced to the CPU module, the operating mode must be selected. As mentioned in the introduction to this section, three modes are possible in addition to a bit set/reset operation. When unconditional, or *nonhandshaking, I/O* is required, mode 0 should be selected. But how is the mode determined?

A single control word written to the control port (port F3H in Fig. 7.6) determines the 8255A operating mode. Figure 7.7 shows the two types of control words possible. When bit 7 of the control word is a 0, the *bit set/reset* mode is selected. If bit 7 is a 1, any

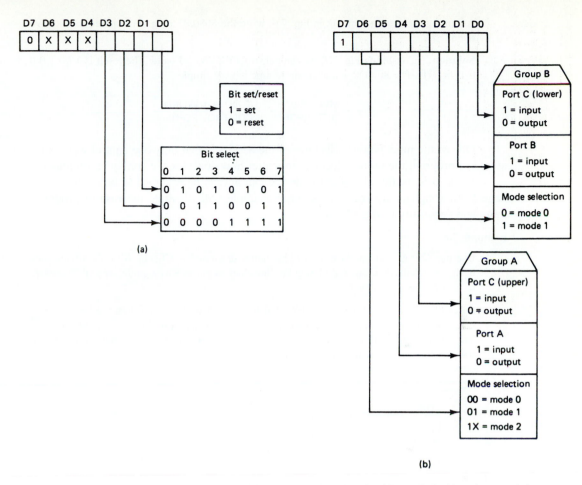

Figure 7.7 There are two types of 8255A control words. When bit 7 = 0, the bit set/reset mode is selected. When bit 7 = 1, any of modes 0–2 can be selected. (a) Bit set/reset format; (b) Mode definition format.

of the three port modes (0 through 2) can be selected. The bit set/reset mode is covered in the next section, so let's turn our attention to the mode set control word.

Examining Fig. 7.7, you can see that the three ports are broken into two groups for mode selection. Port A and the high-order bits of port C can be programmed for any of the modes 0 through 2. Port B and the low-order bits of port C can be programmed to operate in mode 0 or 1 only.

Example 7.5

The following mode 0 port configuration is desired:

>*Port A:* input
>*Port B:* output
>*Port C (upper):* output
>*Port C (lower):* input

Assuming the interface circuit in Fig. 7.6, write the 8080/85 program required to initialize the 8255A.

Solution. Consulting Fig. 7.7, we can construct the control word. The result is 1 00 1 0 0 0 1, or 91H. The 8080/85 initialization routine is very simple:

```
MVI   A,91H      ;CONTROL WORD
OUT   0F3H       ;CONTROL PORT
```

One of the most powerful features of the 8255A is that only one control word is required to program the mode selection, no matter how complex the configuration may be.

Mode 0 is useful when the I/O device can always be assumed to be ready and no handshaking signals are required. Another example will illustrate the ease of programming and versatility of the 8255A.

Example 7.6

Use the 8255A, and interface the 10-key matrix discussed in Chapter 6 for the digital lock design problem. (See Fig. 6.8.) Using the flowchart in Fig. 6.9 as a guide, write the software to encode the 10-key switches.

Solution. The 8255A interface illustrated in Fig. 7.6 will be used with the key switches connected as shown in Fig. 7.8. Unlike the interface in Chapter 6, this circuit is *I/O mapped*. The column lines will be controlled by PC6 and PC7, programmed as outputs. The key matrix can be scanned by reading from port B.

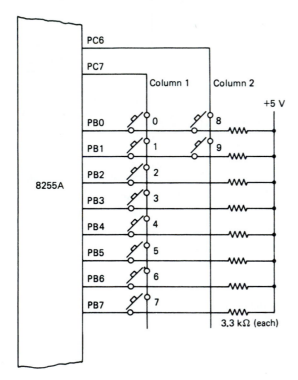

Figure 7.8 Interfacing a 10-key switch matrix to the 8255A. Port B is programmed as an input port and port C (upper) as an output port.

In Chapter 6, the column lines were forced low by reading from the appropriate memory-mapped I/O address. In Fig. 7.8, the column lines are forced low by outputting 0's on PC6 and PC7. Although the row lines are not inverted, this can easily be accomplished with the *CMA* instruction. A program is provided in Fig. 7.9. Notice that because port C (lower) and port B are not used, they can become "don't cares" in determining the 8255A control word. In this case at hand, their control bits were arbitrarily chosen as 0's.

The software required to scan and encode the key switches in Fig. 7.8 is slightly more complex than that required of the similar interface in Chapter 6. There, the memory-mapped interface was able to control the column lines by reading from a specific address. The 8255A interface must use port C for that purpose. This requires a few extra instructions to program PC6 and PC7.

Incidentally, the 8255A can also be interfaced to the microprocessor using memory-mapped I/O. In that case, the four I/O ports occupy four consecutive memory locations. This can have its advantages, especially with the Z-80: The IX or IY index register can be pointed at port A, and then an offset can be used to access the other three ports without the need for specifying the full 16-bit address with each access.

The Bit Set/Reset Mode

When bit 7 of the 8255A control word is a 0, the bit set/reset mode is active. In this mode, any single bit of port C can be set to a logic 1 or reset to a logic 0. Note that only one bit can be set or reset at a time. This feature can be taken advantage of to generate strobe signals.

Example 7.7

Use the 8255A and the bit set/reset feature of port C to interface a parallel printer. Write the control software, assuming that a data table is stored at symbolic address DATA and a byte counter is stored at address NUMB.

Solution. The circuit diagram is shown in Fig. 7.10. Port A has been arbitrarily chosen as the data port, and PC0 is used to monitor the printer's BUSY/READY status. PC7 will be used to generate the strobe pulse. This interface can be compared with that of Fig. 6.12. Again, an 11-conductor cable is required between computer and printer.

Of course, the software is what makes the circuit work. The control program for the printer is shown in Fig. 7.11. The 8255A is programmed for mode 0 with port A an output, port C (lower) an input, and port C (upper) an output. Port B is a "don't care" condition. After the control word is written to port F3 (the control port), the bit set control word 0XXX1111 is used to hold PC7—the printer STROBE input—high.

The program then drops into a polling routine, testing PC0 for a 0. When PC0 is ready, data are output to port A, and the printer's STROBE input is brought low (control word 0XXX1110). This begins the STROBE pulse. The INR A instruction and OUT F3 force the STROBE line back high. STROBE will be low during the execution of these two instructions, which takes 15 T states with an 8080 or 14 T states with an 8085. The result will be a STROBE pulse width of 7.5 μs on a 2-MHz 8080.

The data pointer is then incremented and the byte counter decremented. If more data remain to be printed, control is transferred back to the polling routine. If not, the program returns, via the RET instruction.

```
                ;PROGRAM TO READ THE MATRIX KEYBOARD IN FIG. 7-8
                ;
                ;BEGIN BY INITIALIZING THE 8255
                ;
                MVI     A,82H           ;8255 MODE 0 CONTROL WORD
                OUT     0F3             ;CONTROL PORT
                ;
                ;PREPARE TO TEST BOTH COLUMNS BY MAKING PC6 AND PC7 LOW
                ;
                SUB     A               ;CLEAR ACCUMULATOR
                OUT     0F2             ;PORT C
                ;
                ;LOOP UNTIL ALL KEYS ARE UP
                ;
KDWN            CALL    KREAD           ;CHECK KEYBOARD
                JNZ     KDWN            ;IF NOT ZERO A KEY IS DOWN
                ;
                ;WAIT FOR BOUNCE TIME AND THEN LOOP UNTIL A
                ;KEY IS DOWN
                ;
                CALL    DELAY           ;10-20 MS DELAY
KUP             CALL    KREAD           ;CHECK KEYBOARD
                JZ      KUP             ;IF ZERO NO KEYS ARE DOWN
                ;
                ;A KEY IS DOWN - BUT WHICH COLUMN?  TEST COLUMN 1
                ;
                CALL    DELAY           ;WAIT FOR IT TO STOP BOUNCING
                MVI     A,40H           ;MAKE COLUMN 1 = 0
                OUT     0F2             ;PORT C
                CALL    KREAD           ;CHECK KEYBOARD
                JNZ     COL1            ;IF NOT ZERO ITS COLUMN 1
                ;
                ;IT MUST BE COLUMN 2
                ;
                MVI     A,80H           ;MAKE COLUMN 2 = 0
                OUT     0F2             ;PORT C
                CALL    KREAD           ;CHECK KEYBOARD
                ;
                ;KEY VALUE IS IN ACCUMULATOR - SET COLUMN POINTER
                ;
                LXI     H,COL2          ;POINT AT COLUMN 2
                JMP     LKUP            ;LOOK UP KEY VALUE
                ;
COL1            LXI     H,COL1          ;POINT AT COL1
                ;
                ;LKUP NOW FINDS THE CORRECT KEY VALUE FROM A TABLE
                ;
LKUP            INX     H               ;ADVANCE POINTER
                RAR                     ;TEST BIT
                JNC     LKUP            ;CONTINUE UNTIL CARRY IS SET
                MOV     A,M             ;FETCH THE CODE
                RET                     ;RETURN TO MAIN
                ;
                ;THIS IS THE KREAD SUBROUTINE
                ;
KREAD           IN      0F1             ;READ PORT B
                CMA                     ;COMPLEMENT
                ORA     A               ;SET FLAGS
                RET
                ;
                ;DEFINE BYTES FOR THE KEY VALUES
COL1            DB      0,0,1,2,3,4,5,6 ;FIRST BYTE IS NEVER READ
COL2            DB      7,8,9
```

Figure 7.9 This subroutine scans the key switch matrix in Fig. 7.8 and returns with the key value (0–9) in the accumulator.

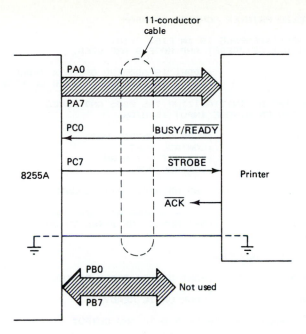

Figure 7.10 Parallel-printer interface using the 8255A in a combined bit set/reset and mode 0 format.

This example also illustrates that the bit set/reset feature does not override the mode selection, but works in addition to the selected mode (0 through 2). However, as we shall see, the main purpose of the bit set/reset feature is for setting *interrupt masks* in mode 1 and mode 2.

Electrical Characteristics of the Ports

All three 8255A ports have an I_{OL} specification of 1.7 mA and an I_{OH} specification of 200 μA. This means that they can drive one standard TTL load or four LSTTL loads. A special feature of ports B and C is that any set of eight lines can source 1 mA at 1.5 V. This feature is useful for driving solid-state relays and transistor drivers. (More details on these techniques are presented in Chapter 11.) Note that the outputs *cannot* sink the typical 10- to 20-mA current required to light an LED, and a TTL buffer should be used, as shown in Fig. 7.2 for the 8755A.

The 8255A comes in two versions, with different speeds: the 8255A and the 8255A-5. The first has a t_{RD} specification of 250 ns, making it compatible with all versions of the 8080 and the 3-MHz version of the 8085. The 8255A-5 has a 200-ns t_{RD} specification. This is not fast enough for the 5- and 6-MHz versions of the 8085, but, interestingly enough, is compatible with the Z-80A and Z-80B processors. The reason is that the Z-80 inserts one WAIT state into its I/O operations.

Mode 1: Strobed I/O

Mode 1 is intended for handshaking and interrupt-driven I/O interfaces. In this mode, ports A and B are programmed as data ports and port C is programmed to carry status signals. One of the unique features of mode 1 is that data transfers can take place without direct CPU intervention.

Sec. 7.2   The 8255A Programmable Peripheral Interface   **341**

```
;8255 PARALLEL PRINTER CONTROL PROGRAM
;
;THE HARDWARE INTERFACE IS IN FIG. 7-10.
;A COMBINED BIT SET/RESET AND MODE 0 ARE USED.
;
DATA    EQU     ADDR1           ;ADDR1 IS ADDRESS OF DATA TABLE
NUMB    EQU     ADDR2           ;ADDR2 IS ADDRESS OF BYTE COUNTER
;
;PROGRAM BEGINS BY INITIALIZING THE 8255 AND MAKES
;SURE THE PRINTER STROBE INPUT IS HIGH.
;
        MVI     A,81H           ;MODE 0 CONTROL WORD
        OUT     0F3H            ;CONTROL PORT
        MVI     A,0FH           ;BIT SET PC7 HIGH
        OUT     0F3H            ;CONTROL PORT
;
;POINT AT THE DATA TABLE AND RETRIEVE BYTE COUNTER
;
        LXI     H,DATA          ;TABLE BEGINS AT LOCATION DATA
        LDA     NUMB            ;GET NUMBER OF BYTES TO OUTPUT
        MOV     B,A             ;SAVE IN B
;
;POLL THE BUSY/READY FLAG
;
POLL    IN      0F2H            ;PORT C BUSY/READY STATUS
        RAR                     ;POLL PC0
        JC      POLL            ;LOOP UNTIL READY
;
;PRINTER IS READY - FETCH DATA BYTE AND OUTPUT IT
;
        MOV     A,M             ;RETRIEVE BYTE FROM TABLE
        OUT     0F0H            ;PORT A
;
;PULSE PC7 TO STROBE THE PRINTER
;
        MVI     A,0EH           ;BIT RESET PC7 LOW
        OUT     0F3H            ;CONTROL PORT
        INR     A               ;BIT SET PC7 HIGH
        OUT     0F3H            ;CONTROL PORT
;
;ADVANCE POINTER AND TEST BYTE COUNTER
;
        INX     H               ;POINT AT NEXT BYTE
        DCR     B               ;BUMP BYTE COUNTER
        JNZ     POLL            ;CONTINUE TILL EMPTY
        RET                     ;AND THEN RETURN
```

Figure 7.11 Control program for the 8255A interface in Fig. 7.10.

The four possible configurations for the 8255A, when operated in mode 1, are shown in Fig. 7.12. These correspond to the four combinations of ports A and B as inputs and outputs. The two separate control words shown in Fig. 7.12(a) and (b) illustrate the fact that port A, port B, or both ports can be programmed for mode 1 operation. This means that it is possible to program port A for mode 1 while using port B in mode 0, for example.

Input port timing.   When port A or port B is programmed as an input port, three control signals—IBF, STB, and INTR—are dedicated to supporting data transfers on the port. Table 7.6 explains the purpose of each of these signals, and Fig. 7.13 illustrates the timing involved.

When the peripheral device has data for the microprocessor, it places the data on the port A or port B input lines and then pulses the 8255A STB input. The PPI replies by

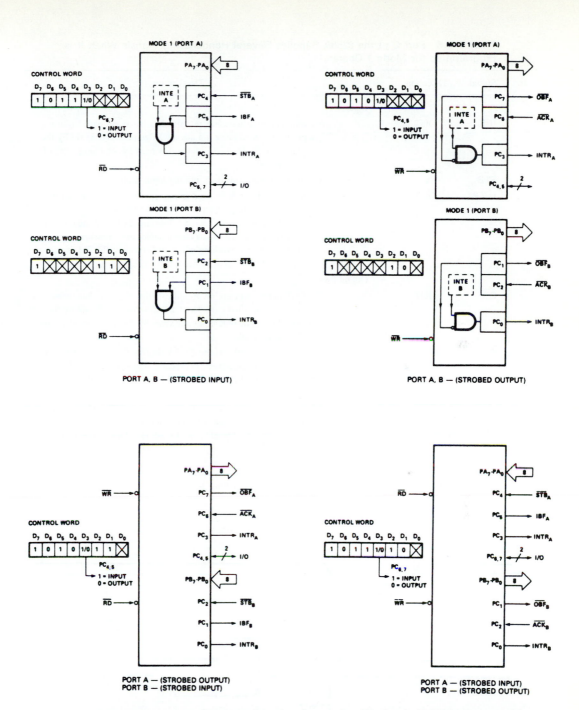

Figure 7.12 Four possible I/O configurations for ports A and B when the 8255A is programmed for mode 1 operation. Port C becomes a status port in this mode. (Courtesy of Intel Corporation and from J. Uffenbeck, *Hardware Interfacing with the Apple II Plus,* Prentice-Hall, Inc., Englewood Cliffs, NJ, 1983.)

TABLE 7.6 Port C of the 8255A Supplies Several Handshaking Signals When it is Programmed for Mode 1 Operation

Signal	Direction	Description
		Input Port
IBF	OUT	A 1 on this output indicates that the data has been loaded into the input latch—in essence, an acknowledgement. IBF is set by the falling edge of the $\overline{STB}$ input and is reset by the rising edge of the $\overline{RD}$ input.
$\overline{STB}$	IN	A 0 on this input loads data into the input latch.
INTR	OUT	A 1 on this output can be used to interrupt the CPU when an input device is requesting service. INTR is set by the rising edge of $\overline{STB}$ if IBF is a 1 and INTE is a 1. It is reset by the falling edge of $\overline{RD}$. This procedure allows an input device to request service from the CPU simply by strobing its data into the port. INTE A is controlled by bit set/reset of PC4 and INTE B by bit set/reset of PC2.
		Output Port
$\overline{OBF}$	OUT	The $\overline{OBF}$ output will go low to indicate that the CPU has written data to the specified port. The $\overline{OBF}$ flip-flop will be set by the rising edge of the $\overline{WR}$ input and reset by the falling edge of the $\overline{ACK}$ input signal.
$\overline{ACK}$	IN	A 0 on this input informs the 8255A that the data from port A or port B has been accepted. In essence, this is a response from the peripheral device indicating that it has received the data output by the CPU.
INTR	OUT	A 1 on this output can be used to interrupt the CPU when an output device has accepted data transmitted by the CPU. INTR is set by the rising edge of $\overline{ACK}$ if $\overline{OBF}$ is a 0 and INTE is a 1. It is reset by the falling edge of $\overline{WR}$. INTE A is controlled by bit set/reset of PC6 and INTE B by bit set/reset of PC2.

Source: J. Uffenbeck, *Hardware Interfacing with the Apple II Plus,* Prentice-Hall, Inc., Englewood Cliffs, NJ, 1983.

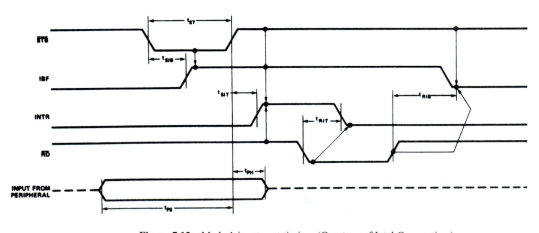

Figure 7.13 Mode 1 input port timing. (Courtesy of Intel Corporation.)

latching the data and raising its input-buffer-full (IBF) line. This is a signal to the peripheral that data have been latched, but not yet read by the microprocessor.

If the interrupts-enabled (INTE) bit of the input port has been set, IBF will also cause the INTR output of that port to go high. The processor now has the choice of polling the IBF line by reading the mode 1 status word (see Fig. 7.14) or letting INTR generate an interrupt, thereby alerting the processor that the input buffer is full.

In either case, the processor should branch to a routine that reads the data port. The falling edge of $\overline{RD}$ causes the 8255A INTR output to be reset, and the rising edge of RD resets IBF. The data transfer is now complete, and the peripheral (monitoring IBF) can strobe in the next byte of data.

Output port timing. When port A or port B is programmed as a mode 1 output port three lines of port C—OBF, ACK, and INTR—are dedicated to supporting this function. Descriptions of the activities of these lines are provided in Table 7.6. Figure 7.15 illustrates output port timing.

Assuming that data has been previously written to one of the data ports, the peripheral monitors output buffer full ($\overline{OBF}$). When this line is low, data is available to be read by the peripheral. Using $\overline{OBF}$ as a $\overline{STROBE}$ input, the peripheral latches the data byte and responds with an acknowledge ($\overline{ACK}$) pulse. The falling edge of this pulse resets $\overline{OBF}$ high, and if INTE is high, the rising edge causes INTR to go high also.

Again, the CPU has the choice of polling $\overline{OBF}$ by reading the mode 1 status word (see Fig. 7.14) or allowing INTR to alert it that $\overline{OBF}$ is high and the peripheral is ready for more data. In either case, the processor should write a new byte of data to the output port. The falling edge of $\overline{WR}$ will reset INTR, and the rising edge of $\overline{WR}$ will force $\overline{OBF}$ low. The peripheral, monitoring $\overline{OBF}$, can latch the new data byte, and the cycle repeats.

Polling versus interrupts. The advantages of polling and interrupts have been discussed previously. Let us make sure that we appreciate what is involved in each technique when we use the 8255A in mode 1.

When polling is used, an input read from port C (an IN F2 instruction for the hardware shown in Fig. 7.6) will load the accumulator with the mode 1 status word shown in Fig. 7.14. Note that if port A is programmed as an input port and port B as an output, the status word will be made up of the GROUP A bits as an input and the GROUP B bits as an output. Standard bit-testing techniques can be used to monitor $\overline{OBF}$ or IBF.

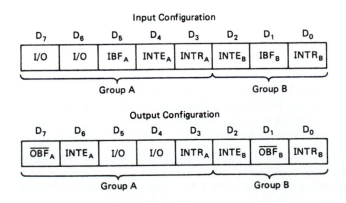

Figure 7.14 Format of mode 1 status word.

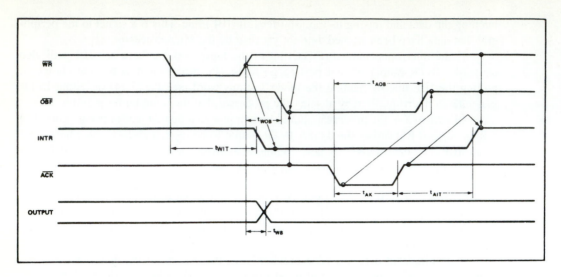

Figure 7.15 Mode 1 output port timing. (Courtesy of Intel Corporation.)

Note also that PC6 and PC7 (port A = input) or PC4 and PC5 (port A = output) are not involved in the handshaking logic and can be programmed as general-purpose input and output lines. This configuration is shown in Fig. 7.12. These ports can also be read as part of the mode 1 status word.

When interrupts are used, the INTR output will be set as $\overline{ACK}$ goes high (the buffer is available for more data) or as $\overline{STB}$ goes high (the input buffer contains data to be read). INTR can be set only if the corresponding INTE bit has been previously set by the processor. This is where the bit set/reset mode comes in.

Referring to Table 7.6, we see that INTE is controlled as follows.

Port	Type	Name	Controlled by bit set/reset of:
A	Input	INTEA	PC4
A	Output	INTEA	PC6
B	Input	INTEB	PC2
B	Output	INTEB	PC2

A few examples should help illustrate how the control word is formed and how interrupts are enabled.

Example 7.8

Determine the 8255A control word to be used in programming port A as a mode 1 input port and port B as a mode 1 output port. INTEA and INTEB should both be enabled, and the two unused port C lines should be defined as outputs. Assuming the hardware shown in Fig. 7.6, write the 8080/85 initialization routine required.

Solution. The desired port configuration is shown in Fig. 7.12(d). With PC6 and PC7 programmed as outputs, the control word is 1011010X. Setting INTEA will require a bit set for PC4, and setting INTEB will require a bit set for PC2. The initialization routine is as follows:

```
MVI   A,0B4H      ;CONTROL WORD
OUT   0F3H        ;CONTROL PORT
MVI   A,09H       ;BIT SET PC4
OUT   0F3H        ;CONTROL PORT
MVI   A,05H       ;BIT SET PC2
OUT   0F3H        ;CONTROL PORT
```

Example 7.9

Repeat Example 7.8 with port B programmed as a mode 0 output port. Program all free pins of port C as inputs.

Solution. Refer to Fig. 7.12(a) to determine the port A portion of the control word, which is 10111XXX. Now refer to Fig. 7.7 for the GROUP B (or port B) portion of the control word. The last 3 bits should be 001. The resulting control word is 10111001. Only INTEA will need to be set, requiring a bit-set operation on PC4. The program is as follows:

```
MVI   A,0B9H      ;CONTROL WORD
OUT   0F3H        ;CONTROL PORT
MVI   A,09H       ;BIT SET PC4
OUT   0F3H        ;CONTROL PORT
```

Note that PC0 through PC2 and PC6 and PC7 are all available as general-purpose inputs.

As a final example, let us again use the 8255A to interface a parallel printer, but this time program the PPI for mode 1. To make the interface more interesting, we will use *interrupts* to control the flow of data. (Refer to the timing diagram in Fig. 7.15 for the discussion that follows.)

The circuit diagram is shown in Fig. 7.16. Port A has been chosen as the data output port, requiring the ACKA signal from the printer to be connected to PC6. The OBFA output from the 8255A will serve as the STROBE input to the printer. Note that BUSY/READY is not used.

Assuming that there is no data presently in the 8255A port A buffer, OBFA will be high, ACKA from the printer will be high, and if INTEA is set, INTRA will be high. Assuming that the processor has enabled its interrupt structure, the interrupt request will be honored. The interrupt service routine will respond to the interrupt request by fetching a data byte from a table and outputting it to port A. This will reset INTRA and force OBFA low, strobing the printer.

A period of time will now elapse as the character is printed. Eventually, ACK will go low as the printer acknowledges receipt and printing of the character. This will reset OBFA and force INTRA high, requesting another interrupt. The cycle then repeats until all of the data has been output.

It is interesting to note that INTRA is "automatically" removed by the 8255A when the processor does the I/O write to port A. Because of this, a synchronizing flip-flop is not required between INTRA and the processor.

Initializing the 8255A will require defining port A as a mode 1 output port and bit setting PC6 to enable INTEA. The 8080/85 code is as follows:

```
MVI   A,0A0H      ;CONTROL WORD = 1010XXXX
OUT   0F3H        ;CONTROL PORT
MVI   A,0DH       ;BIT SET PC6
OUT   0F3H        ;CONTROL PORT
```

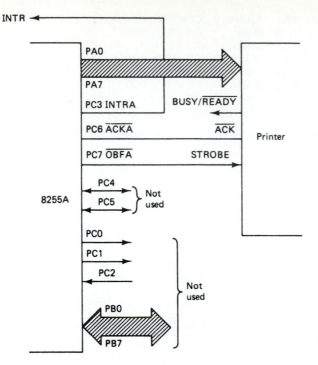

Figure 7.16 Interrupt-driven parallel-printer interface using the 8255A in mode 1.

The interrupt service routine is identical to Fig. 6.22 with one change:

```
DPORT    EQU    0F0H    ;PORT A
```

Mode 2: Strobed Bidirectional I/O

When operated in mode 2, port A of the 8255A becomes a *bidirectional* data port supported by five handshaking signals. (See Fig. 7.17.) The handshaking signals are identical to those provided in mode 1, except that they now refer only to port A. This particular

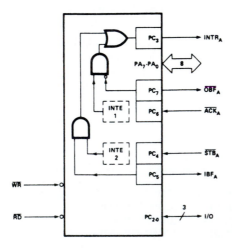

Figure 7.17 Mode 2 for the 8255A. Port A is a bidirectional port in this mode, supported by five handshaking signals from port C. (Courtesy of Intel Corporation.)

mode of operation is useful for transferring data between two computers. (An example is presented later in the section.)

When port A is programmed to operate in mode 2, port B can operate in mode 0 or mode 1. If port B is programmed for mode 0, PC0–PC2 can be programmed as mode 0 inputs or outputs. If port B is programmed for mode 1, then PC0–PC2 become handshake signals for this port.

Considering all of the possible combinations, we see that there are four configurations of the 8255A in mode 2. These are shown in Fig. 7.18. As an example, if we choose to program port A for mode 2, port B as a mode 0 input port, and PC0–PC2 as mode 0 output pins, the control word is 11XXX010.

Input port timing. Figure 7.19 is a timing diagram illustrating the sequence of events as a data byte is transferred first to the 8255A by the peripheral and then from the 8255A back to the peripheral. The numbers in the diagram are keyed to the explanation. We begin with the peripheral outputting a byte to the 8255A:

1. Data is output by the peripheral.
2. The peripheral applies an $\overline{\text{STB}}$ pulse to the 8255A.
3. When the data are latched, IBF goes high.
4. After $\overline{\text{STB}}$ returns high with IBF still set, INTR goes high, requesting an interrupt if this feature is used.
5. Polling or interrupts can now be used to service the peripheral. The 8255A buffer is read when $\overline{\text{RD}}$ goes low.
6. The falling edge of $\overline{\text{RD}}$ resets INTR.
7. The rising edge of $\overline{\text{RD}}$ resets IBF.

Output port timing. The following sequence occurs as the processor outputs a byte of data to the peripheral through the 8255A:

8. Data are output by the processor and latched by the 8255A. (Note that the peripheral bus is in a high-impedance state at this time.)
9. The rising edge of $\overline{\text{WR}}$ causes $\overline{\text{OBF}}$ to switch low. ("The output buffer is full.")
10. The peripheral acknowledges $\overline{\text{OBF}}$ by causing $\overline{\text{ACK}}$ to go low.
11. On the falling edge of $\overline{\text{ACK}}$, the 8255A releases its data onto the bus.
12. $\overline{\text{OBF}}$ returns high. ("The output buffer is empty.")
13. The rising edge of $\overline{\text{ACK}}$ sets INTR, requesting an interrupt if this feature is used.
14. Polling or interrupts can now be used to write the next data byte to the 8255A.

A subtle point that we should not miss concerning mode 2 operation is that only a single INTR output is available. This raises the question of how the processor can determine whether the interrupt requires data to be read or written—that is, who requested the interrupt? Two solutions are possible.

As discussed in Chapter 6, polling can be used when several interrupt requests must share the same input line. The mode 2 status word is shown in Fig. 7.20. With this

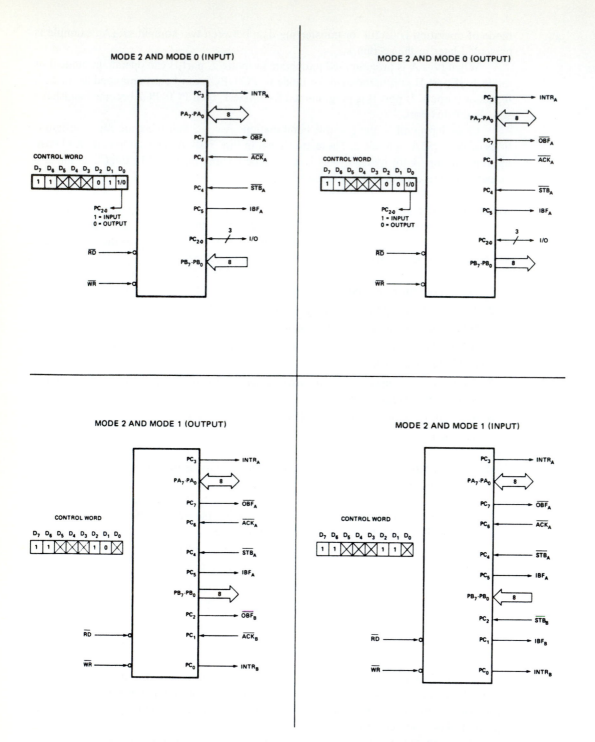

Figure 7.18 Four possible configurations of the 8255A when programmed for mode 2. (Courtesy of Intel Corporation.)

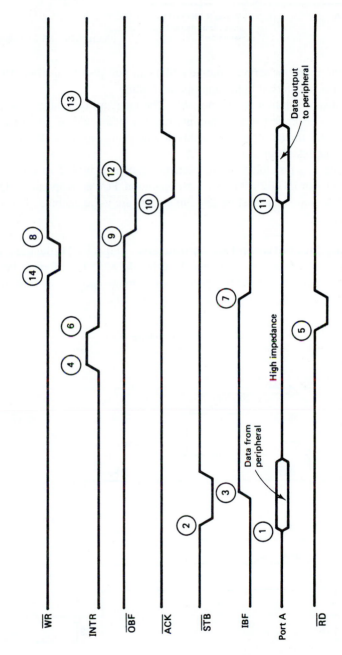

Figure 7.19 Input and output timing relationships for mode 2. The numbers are keyed to the text.

351

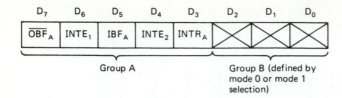

| D₇ | D₆ | D₅ | D₄ | D₃ | D₂ | D₁ | D₀ |

| $\overline{\text{OBF}}_A$ | INTE₁ | IBF_A | INTE₂ | INTR_A | | | |

Group A   Group B (defined by mode 0 or mode 1 selection)

Figure 7.20 Mode 2 status word.

technique, the interrupt service routine (ISR) can poll port C, testing IBFA and $\overline{\text{OBFA}}$. Control is then transferred to the appropriate routine.

A hardware solution is also possible. The interrupt request can be combined with $\overline{\text{OBF}}$ or IBF to generate two separate interrupts, which could be connected to the 8085's RST 5.5 and 6.5 inputs, or a programmable interrupt controller (PIC) could be used to generate unique restart instructions.

Note that it is possible to mask interrupts generated by IBF or $\overline{\text{OBF}}$. This is done by resetting INTE1 or INTE2 with a *bit-reset* operation. PC6 corresponds to INTE1 and PC4 to INTE2. The same bits must be set if interrupts are to be enabled. This can be seen by studying Fig. 7.17.

Exchanging data between two computers.   Figure 7.21 illustrates a technique for exchanging data between two computers by using the 8255A in mode 2. Port A becomes a common data path between the two processors, with the output port control signals of one connected to the input port control signals of the other.

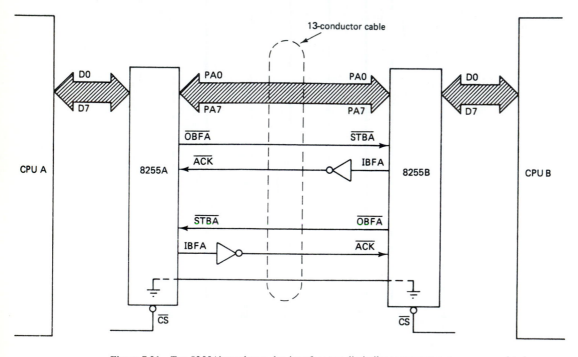

Figure 7.21   Two 8255A's can be used to interface two dissimilar computers over a common data bus.

When CPU A outputs data to its 8255A, the $\overline{\text{OBF}}$ signal strobes 8255B, causing the IBF signal (which is inverted) to come back as an acknowledge pulse. This, in turn, gates data onto the bidirectional data bus. CPU B reads the data, terminating the IBF pulse and forcing $\overline{\text{ACK}}$ of 8255B high. This, in turn, releases $\overline{\text{OBF}}$, and the transfer is complete. The process works in reverse when CPU B wishes to write a byte of data to CPU A.

Each processor in Fig. 7.21 will require four separate routines for the data transfer to work:

1. The 8255A initialization routine
2. An ISR or polling routine to monitor IBF and $\overline{\text{OBF}}$
3. A receiver program to read the data byte when IBF goes high
4. A transmitter program to output a data byte when $\overline{\text{OBF}}$ goes low

One of the interesting features about the interface in Fig. 7.21 is that it will allow the transfer of data files between two dissimilar computers. For example, one processor could be an 8085 and the other a 6800. Of course, 8085 binary object-code files will not run on a 6800, but high-level language ASCII files could be transferred. Another application is transferring data files between two computers with a similar processor, but different floppy-disk formats.

SELF-REVIEW 7.2

7.2.1 When operated in mode 0, the 8255A contains _____ user I/O ports and _____ control port.

7.2.2 Which bit of the 8255A control port selects the mode-set or reset mode?

7.2.3 Determine the 8255A control word to program port A as an output and ports B and C as inputs. Assume mode 0.

7.2.4 Which 8255A operating mode supplies two parallel I/O ports with handshaking signals?

7.2.5 What are the two main uses of the 8255A bit set/reset mode?

7.2.6 When operated in mode 2, the 8255A supplies one _____ I/O port and five handshaking signals.

7.3 THE 8254 PROGRAMMABLE INTERVAL TIMER

Introduction

Many microprocessor interfacing problems require accurate time delays for generating square-wave signals and strobe pulses. In some cases, the microprocessor is called upon to count events and take some action after a prescribed number of pulses. In a real-time clock, for example, a 1-Hz interrupt signal is required to provide the "heartbeat" of the clock.

It is for these kinds of applications that the 8254 has been designed. The 8254 provides three separate 16-bit timing registers, each of which can be programmed as a *timer* or an *event counter*. For example, by loading counter 0 with 868_{10} and specifying mode 3, a divide-by-868 50%-duty-cycle square wave is generated. The clock input can be the system clock or an external signal with an upper limit of 10 MHz (8254-2).

Programming consists of writing a byte to the control port, selecting one of six possible operating modes. These modes allow operation of the machine as an event counter, a one-shot, a square-wave generator, a divide-by-N counter, or a hardware- or software-triggered strobe. Each counter can hold a 16-bit number, which is counted down to zero (called a *terminal count*) at a rate set by that register's clock input. When the terminal count occurs, an interrupt can be requested, a strobe pulse generated, a one-shot pulse terminated, or the logic level of a square wave toggled.

The 8254 is actually a "superset" of the 8253A timer, having the exact same pinout as the latter and being software compatible with it. There are two differences, however: The 8253A has no read-back mode, which means that the status of a particular counter cannot be read back once it has been programmed, and the 8253A is limited to 2 MHz for its maximum clock frequency.

In this section, we:

- Describe the six operating modes of the 8254 programmable interval timer.
- Write an 8080/8085 frequency counter program using the 8254 as an event counter.

Interfacing the 8254

Figure 7.22 provides a block diagram and pinout for the 8254 programmable timer. To the microprocessor, the timer appears to be four separate I/O ports selected by the A0 and A1 input address lines. The $\overline{\text{RD}}$ and $\overline{\text{WR}}$ inputs determine whether data are to be

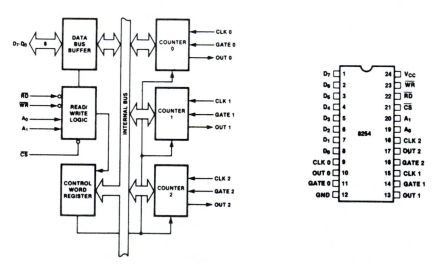

Figure 7.22 Block diagram and pin descriptions for the 8254 programmable interval timer (PIT). Three separate timers/counters are provided. (Courtesy of Intel Corporation.)

TABLE 7.7 Read/Write Operation Summary for the 8254 PIT

$\overline{CS}$	$\overline{RD}$	$\overline{WR}$	A_1	A_0	
0	1	0	0	0	Write into Counter 0
0	1	0	0	1	Write into Counter 1
0	1	0	1	0	Write into Counter 2
0	1	0	1	1	Write Control Word
0	0	1	0	0	Read from Counter 0
0	0	1	0	1	Read from Counter 1
0	0	1	1	0	Read from Counter 2
0	0	1	1	1	No Operation (Tristate)
1	X	X	X	X	No Operation (Tristate)
0	1	1	X	X	No Operation (Tristate)

Source: Courtesy of Intel Corporation.

read or written using the eight lines of the bidirectional data bus. Table 7.7 lists the possible I/O operations. As with the 8255A, no operation is possible unless the chip-select ($\overline{CS}$) input is low. Note that reading from the control register (A0A1 = 11, $\overline{RD}$ = 0) is not possible; the read-back control word should be used.

Figure 7.23 illustrates a typical I/O-mapped interface to the three-bus system architecture.

Example 7.10

Determine the I/O port addresses for the three counters and control port in the 8254 interface of Fig. 7.23.

Solution. Only when the $\overline{CS}$ input is low is the device selected. A low $\overline{CS}$ input occurs when AB7–AB0 = 111100XX. In this case, the Xs are not really "don't cares," but specify the counter to be accessed. The four addresses are as follows:

Address F0: counter 0
Address F1: counter 1
Address F2: counter 2
Address F3: control register

Programming the 8254

The 8254 is programmed by writing a single byte (for each counter) to the control port, followed by 1 or 2 bytes to specify the *initial count*. Three forms of the control word are possible, as shown in Fig. 7.24. The standard control word is used to specify the operating mode and the counter selected. Note that each counter can have a different operating mode and be programmed to operate as a *binary* or *BCD* counter.

Example 7.11

Write a program to specify counter 0 for mode 0 BCD operation with an initial count of 3648_{10}. Program counter 2 for mode 3 operation in binary with an initial count of FFH.

Sec. 7.3   The 8254 Programmable Interval Timer

355

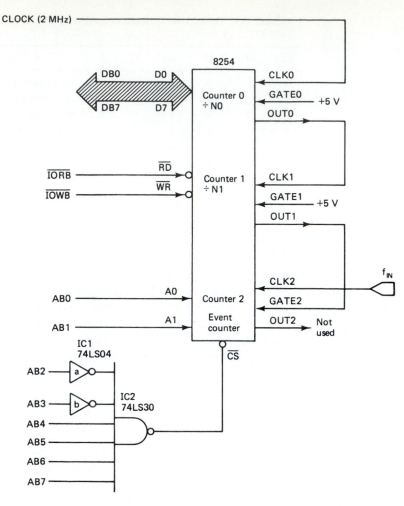

CLOCK (2 MHz)

8254

DB0   D0   CLK0

Counter 0   GATE0   +5 V

DB7   D7   ÷ N0

OUT0

$\overline{RD}$

$\overline{IORB}$ Counter 1   CLK1

$\overline{WR}$ ÷ N1

$\overline{IOWB}$ GATE1   +5 V

OUT1

f_{IN}

CLK2

A0

AB0   Counter 2   GATE2

A1   Event   OUT2   Not

AB1   counter   used

IC1 $\overline{CS}$
74LS04

AB2   a

AB3   b   IC2
74LS30

AB4

AB5

AB6

AB7

Figure 7.23 Interfacing the 8254 to the three-bus system architecture. Four I/O ports are required. The connections shown are for a frequency counter application.

Solution. The control words must first be determined. For counter 0, the control word is 00 11 000 1, which selects counter 0, 2 bytes for the initial count, mode 0, and BCD. For counter 2, the control word is 10 01 X11 0, which selects counter 2, 1 byte for the initial count, mode 3, and binary.

The program is shown in Fig. 7.25. First the control words are written, followed by the 2 bytes for counter 0 and then the single byte for counter 2. Note that the order of programming does not matter, except that the control word must be specified first. If 2 bytes are required for the initial count, both must be written.

When control bits D4 and D5 are 00, the *counter latch* command is specified. This mode latches the current value of the counter specified by bits D7 and D6. Latching is important because reading an unlatched counter may give erroneous results if the count is in the process of changing.

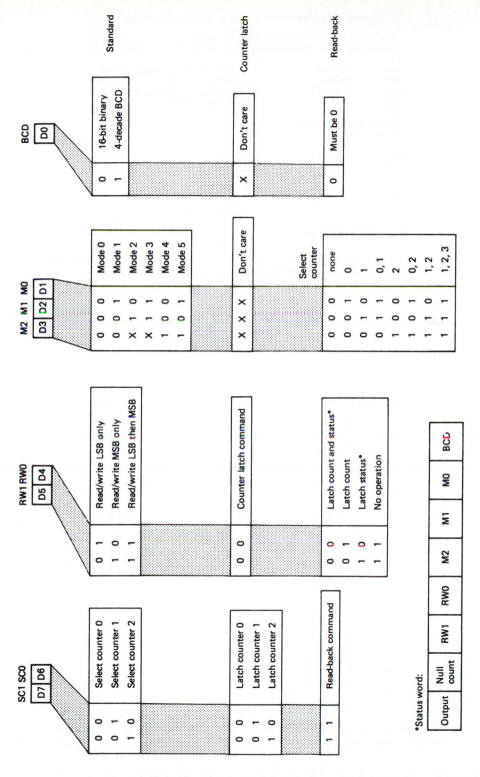

Figure 7.24 8254 control word. The standard form specifies the operating mode. The counter latch and read-back commands are used when the present count or status is to be read.

357

```
;PROGRAM TO DEMONSTRATE 8254 INITIALIZATION
;
;COUNTER 0 IS PROGRAMMED FOR MODE 0, BCD, 16-BITS
;COUNTER 2 IS PROGRAMMED FOR MODE 3, BINARY, 8-BITS
;
MVI     A,31H           ;COUNTER 0 CONTROL WORD
OUT     OF3H            ;CONTROL PORT
MVI     A,96H           ;COUNTER 2 CONTROL WORD
OUT     OF3H            ;CONTROL PORT
;
;LOAD COUNTER 0 WITH 3648H
;LOAD COUNTER 2 WITH FFH
;
MVI     A,48H           ;LSB
OUT     OFOH            ;COUNTER 0
MVI     A,36H           ;MSB
OUT     OFOH            ;COUNTER 0
MVI     A,OFFH          ;LSB
OUT     OF2H            ;COUNTER 2
;
;PROGRAM CONTINUES
```

Figure 7.25   Programming the 8254 consists of a control word followed by 1 or 2 bytes to specify the initial count. In this example, only counters 0 and 2 are programmed.

When the counter latch command is given, the count for that counter will be latched until read; the counter itself will continue to count. Note that 16-bit counters must be read twice to fetch the least significant byte (LSB) and then the most significant byte (MSB). Once a counter is read, the latches revert to following the count, and another latch command must be given if it is desired to read the count again.

The third form of the control word facilitates the *read-back* command. This command allows the count to be latched at any or all counters and/or allows a special status word to be latched. Bits D6 and D7 must both be high for this control word.

When the read-back control word is specified, bits D4 and D5 are used to select the status or count latch mode. Bits D3, D2, and D1 are used to select the particular counter. For example, if D3 D2 D1 = 101 and D5 D4 = 01, counters 0 and 2 will have their counts latched. In this respect, the read-back command takes the place of several counter latch commands.

By making bit D4 low, a special status word will be latched for the specified counter. The form of this byte is shown near the bottom of Fig. 7.24. By examining the byte, you can determine the operating mode of the counter (BCD or binary, any of operating modes 0–5, and 8 or 16 bits) and the logic level on the output pin. When the null count is high, the counter has not yet been loaded with the initial count and should not be read. When the null count is low, the counter is available for reading.

Example 7.12

Write a program that does all of the following:

1. Latches the count for counter 0
2. Latches the status for counter 1
3. Latches the count and status for counter 2

Solution.   The control word for counter 0 is 11 01 001 0. (See Fig. 7.24.) Similarly, the control word for counters 1 and 2 are 11 10 010 0 and 11 00 100 0, respectively. The program is shown in Fig. 7.26. Note that it is possible to program all three counters at once if the same count/status is desired.

The only way that the current mode of a particular counter can be determined is by using the read-back command and specifying the status byte. Once the command has been given, the selected counter can be read to obtain the status byte. If the status byte and count are both specified, the first read will return the status byte, and the second byte (and the third if a 16-bit counter has been programmed) will return the latched count.

In all cases, remember that the control word is written to the control port, but all read operations must be from the selected counter, as specified with the A0 and A1 inputs.

Mode Definitions

As mentioned in the introduction, the 8254 can operate in one of six modes (selected by the standard form of the control word). The following is a brief description of each of these modes:

Mode 0: Event counter. If the GATE input is a 1, the counter will be decremented from its initial count with the falling edge of the second pulse on the CLK input and each succeeding clock pulse thereafter. OUT will go high when the count reaches 0 (the terminal count). OUT can be used as an interrupt input to the processor.

Mode 1: Hardware-triggered one-shot. On the rising edge of GATE, OUT will go low until the initial count has been decremented to 0. OUT will then return high. The active-low pulse width is equal to the initial count times the period of the CLK input.

Mode 2: Divide-by-N counter. If the GATE input is high, OUT will go low for one period of the signal at the CLK input after the initial count has been decremented to 1. The initial count will then automatically be reloaded and the cycle repeated. OUT is initially high.

Mode 3: Square-wave generator. This mode is identical to mode 2, except that the duty cycle of the output will be 50%. If the initial count is an odd number, OUT will be high for one more clock cycle than it is low.

```
;PROGRAM TO DEMONSTRATE THE 8254 READ-BACK COMMAND
;
MVI     A,0D2H           ;LATCH COUNT FOR COUNTER 0
OUT     0F3H             ;CONTROL PORT
;
MVI     A,0E4H           ;LATCH STATUS FOR COUNTER 1
OUT     0F3H             ;CONTROL PORT
;
MVI     A,0C8H           ;LATCH COUNT AND STATUS FOR
                         ;COUNTER 2
OUT     0F3H             ;CONTROL PORT
;
;INPUT INSTRUCTIONS CAN NOW BE USED TO READ THE STATUS
;AND COUNT OF A PARTICULAR COUNTER
```

Figure 7.26 Program for Example 7.12.

Mode 4: Software-triggered strobe. If the GATE input is high, OUT will go low for one period of the CLK input N clock cycles after writing the initial count (N). To produce the strobe a second time, the initial count must be rewritten.

Mode 5: Hardware-triggered strobe. The rising edge of the GATE input will cause the initial count to be decremented to 0. When terminal count occurs, OUT will go low for one period of the CLK input.

A Design Example

In Chapter 3, Program 12 presented the hardware and software to convert the Z-80 into a frequency counter. That circuit provided 10-Hz resolution and a maximum frequency of 990 Hz. In this example, we will use the 8254 to provide a frequency counter with 1-Hz resolution and a maximum frequency of 9999 Hz. With a coarser resolution, frequencies approaching the 10-MHz limit of the (8254-2) clock input can be measured.

Hardware. Figure 7.23 shows the connections required. Counters 0 and 1 are programmed as divide-by-2000 square-wave counters. Assuming a 2-MHz system clock, we see that this results in a frequency at OUT 1 of

$$\frac{2 \times 10^6}{2000 \times 2000} = 0.5 \text{ Hz}$$

A 0.5-Hz square wave has a 2-s period and, by connecting this signal to GATE2, enables counter 2 (programmed as an event counter) for 1 s. During this counting interval, counter 2 will be decremented from its initial count—9999—to some value that depends on the number of clock pulses received at the counter's CLK2 input pin.

Software. The software must initialize the three counters and then monitor OUT1. When the latter is low, the counting period will have ended and the count can be recovered. By subtracting this number from 9999, the total number of clock pulses received during the 1-s counting interval (and thus the frequency) can be calculated.

Example 7.13

Assume that counter 2 contains 3275 just after OUT1 goes low. What is the frequency of the CLK2 input? Assume the hardware in Fig. 7.23.

Solution. The input frequency is found by subtracting 3275 from the initial count of 9999:

$$\begin{array}{r} 9999 \\ -3275 \\ \hline 6724 \text{ Hz} \end{array}$$

It is interesting to notice that programming counter 2 for binary operation allows a maximum frequency of 65,535 Hz. However, a binary-to-decimal conversion routine will be required.

Figure 7.27 provides a solution to the 8254 frequency counter problem. Note the following points:

1. Counters 0 and 1 are programmed to operate in mode 3 binary with an initial count of 2000.

```
;Program to use the 8254 as a frequency counter
;
;The hardware is shown in Fig. 7.23
;
;Program counters 0 and 1 for square wave mode
;
         MVI      A,36H               ;Counter 0, mode 3, binary
         OUT      0F3H                ;Control port
         MVI      A,76H               ;Counter 1, mode 3, binary
         OUT      0F3H                ;Control port
;
;Make each counter a divide-by 2000 (07D0H)
;
         MVI      A,0D0H              ;LSB
         OUT      0F0H                ;Counter 0
         OUT      0F1H                ;Counter 1
         MVI      A,07H               ;MSB
         OUT      0F0H                ;Counter 0
         OUT      0F1H                ;Counter 1
;
;Make counter 2 an event counter
;
CYCLE    MVI      A,0B1H              ;Counter 2, mode 0, BCD
         OUT      0F3H                ;Control port
         MVI      A,99H               ;Initial count is 9999
         OUT      0F2H                ;LSB
         OUT      0F2H                ;MSB
;
;Counter 2 is now counting pulses - done when
;OUT1 goes low
;
;Check to see if the counting period has ended
;
WAIT1    CALL     STAT                ;Counter 1 to carry
         JC       WAIT1               ;Wait until low
;
;Now latch count and status for counter 2 and test
;for overflow
;
         MVI      A,0C8H              ;Read-back counter 2
         OUT      0F3H                ;Control port
         IN       0F2H                ;First read is status
         RAL                          ;Test output
         JC       OVFLW               ;If set then overflow
;
;Read the count and adjust for display
;
         IN       0F2H                ;Get LSB
         CALL     ADJ                 ;Subtract from 99
         INR      A                   ;First clock pulse not counted
         OUT      0                   ;LSB display assumed at port 0
         IN       0F2H                ;Get MSB
         CALL     ADJ                 ;Subtract from 99
         OUT      1                   ;MSB display assumed at port 1
;
;Check to see if the next counting period has begun
;
```

Figure 7.27 Frequency counter program for the 8254 interface in Fig. 7.23.

```
WAIT2   CALL    STAT            ;Counter 1 to carry
        JNC     WAIT2           ;Wait until high
        JMP     CYCLE           ;Start again
        ;
        ;If overflow then come here and show FF in displays
        ;
OVFLW   IN      0F2H            ;Finish the reads
        IN      0F2H            ;
        MVI     A,0FFH          ;Overflow display code
        OUT     0               ;LSB display
        OUT     1               ;MSB display
        JMP     WAIT2           ;Wait for next counting peri
        ;
        ;This routine subtracts the count from 99
ADJ     MOV     B,A             ;Move count to B
        MVI     A,99H           ;Initial count
        SUB     B               ;Adjust
        RET                     ;
        ;
        ;This routine reads the status of Counter 1
        ;and stores in the carry flag
STAT    MVI     A,0E4H          ;Read-back counter 1
        OUT     0F3H            ;Control port
        IN      0F1H            ;Counter 1 status
        RAL                     ;Move OUT1 to carry
        RET                     ;Done
        END
```

Figure 7.27   *(Continued)*

2. Counter 2 is programmed for mode 0 BCD. By letting this counter operate in BCD, the (nontrivial) software required to convert from binary to decimal is avoided. However, the maximum frequency is limited to 9999 Hz.

3. Two decoded seven-segment displays are assumed wired to ports 0 and 1 to display the frequency. If an ASCII terminal is used, a BCD-to-ASCII conversion routine will be required.

4. The status of OUT1 is polled using the read-back command word for counter 1. When OUT1 is low, the event counter is disabled and the latched count (and status) is read and subtracted from 9999.

5. If OUT2 is high, the terminal count has been reached and an overflow condition is detected; FFFF is output to the displays.

6. The cycle repeats after rewriting 9999 to counter 2.

8254 Electrical Characteristics

There are two versions of the 8254, each with a different speed. The 8254 has a 220-ns access time and a maximum clock frequency of 8 MHz. The 8254-2 has a 185-ns access time and an upper frequency limit of 10 MHz.

The GATE and CLK inputs present 10-μA dc loads, and the OUT output can source 400 μA in the high state and sink 2 mA in the low state. This means that one standard TTL load or five LSTTL loads can be driven.

SELF-REVIEW 7.3

7.3.1 The 8254 contains _____ programmable counters/timers in one package.

7.3.2 List the three types of control words that can be output to the 8254.

7.3.3 Which 8254 operating mode should be selected to produce a 50%-duty-cycle square wave?

7.3.4 When operated as a counter, the 8254 can be programmed to count in binary or _____.

7.4 THE 8259A PROGRAMMABLE INTERRUPT CONTROLLER

Introduction

Of the 8080, 8085, and Z-80, the 8080 is the least capable when it comes to servicing interrupts. Only the single INTR line is provided, compared with the 8085's five interrupt inputs and the two interrupt inputs of the Z-80. This disadvantage is more an indication of the 8080's age than it is of a poor design. The solution to the problem is to expand the chip set required for an 8080 microcomputer system so that it includes a *programmable interrupt controller* (PIC).

Indeed, that is one of the rationales behind the 8259A PIC, which is designed to support any of the 8080, 8085, 8086, or 8088 series of microprocessors built by Intel. In that capacity, it probably has more capabilities than are required by a 2-MHz 8080. And although the 8259A PIC is compatible with the 8085's INTR input, it is difficult to imagine a situation in which the 8085's present interrupt capabilities would be inadequate.

The 8259A PIC functions as an overall system interrupt manager designed to enhance the vectored interrupt capabilities of the 8080, 8085, 8086, and 8088 microprocessors. When operated in the 8080/85 mode, the 8259A PIC can do all of the following:

1. Accept eight separate interrupt requests (cascadable to 64).
2. Gate the three bytes for a CALL instruction onto the system data bus in response to INTA.
3. Assign priorities and arbitrate simultaneous interrupts.
4. Program the interrupt inputs for a level or edge trigger.
5. Program the vector address and a 4- or 8-byte address interval.

The 8259A is a very powerful device and, indeed, has capabilities beyond the needs of most (relatively) low-speed 8080 or 8085 microcomputer systems. An 8-bit, 2-MHz 8080 microprocessor with more than a few interrupt inputs will quickly become overtaxed. In such systems, distributed processing techniques or higher speed processors will usually provide better service.

On the other hand, a 16-bit, 10-MHz 8086 microprocessor might be used in a multiuser, multitasking environment requiring several 8259As in cascade. Keep this perspective in mind; the 8259A is a very versatile, but complex, device, and many of its features are best taken advantage of with the 16-bit 8088 or 8086.

In this section, we:

- Describe how to interface the 8259A PIC in single and cascade mode.
- Program the 8259A PIC and specify the initialization and operation control words.

Interfacing the 8259A

Figure 7.28 provides a block diagram of the PIC and gives the pin definitions. To the programmer, the PIC appears to be two I/O ports (or memory locations) specified by the A0 address input. However, as we shall see later in this section, seven separate registers can be written to. The specific address of the PIC is controlled by an address decoder connected to the $\overline{CS}$ input.

Figure 7.29 illustrates a typical interface between the PIC and the three-bus system architecture. In this example, ports F0H and F1H have been selected arbitrarily. The eight interrupt requests are received at IR0 through IR7 and can be programmed to be active high, level sensitive, or rising-edge triggered.

Assuming that the active interrupt is not masked, the 8259A requests an interrupt from the microprocessor by driving the INT output high. The processor, upon completing its current instruction, issues $\overline{INTA}$, which is buffered and received by the 8259A as $\overline{INTAB}$. Three bytes are then gated onto the system data bus. The first is 11001101, the op code for a CALL instruction. When this byte is received by the 8228 (in an 8080 system) or the 8085, two additional $\overline{INTA}$ pulses are output and used to gate in the 16-bit restart address corresponding to the active interrupt.

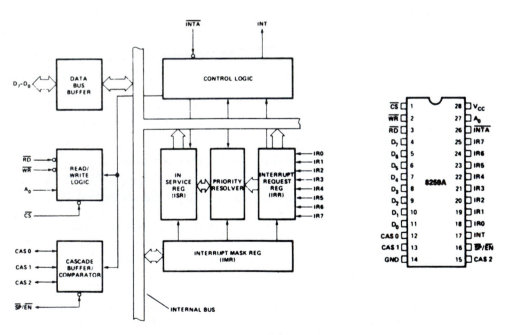

Figure 7.28 Block diagram and pin definitions for the 8259A programmable interrupt controller (PIC). (Courtesy of Intel Corporation.)

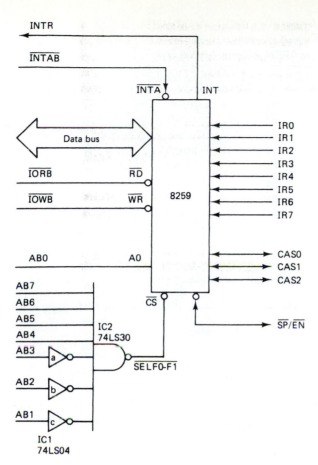

Figure 7.29 Interfacing the 8259A PIC to the three-bus system architecture. Two ports are required and in this case correspond to I/O port addresses F0H and F1H.

Note that the 8259A does not allow each interrupt input to have its own independent address. Instead, a base address can be programmed and a 4- or 8-byte *interval* specified. For example, if the base address is 0100H and the interval is 4, eight restart locations will exist, as shown in Table 7.8. Normally, instructions to jump to the appropriate interrupt service routine would be stored in these locations, and the 32 bytes of memory from 0100 to 011F would be referred to as a "jump table."

In cascading the 8259A, the CAS0 through CAS2 input–output pins are used. This configuration is illustrated in Fig. 7.30. One 8259A is defined to be the master ($\overline{\text{SP/EN}}$ = +5 V), and two other 8259As are defined as slaves ($\overline{\text{SP/EN}}$ = 0 V). CAS0 through CAS2 become outputs from the master and inputs to the slave. These lines are used by the master to identify the active slave device.

Notice that each 8259A in this design has its own I/O address (determined by the address decoder connected to the $\overline{\text{CS}}$ input) and communicates with the CPU over the bidirectional data bus. However, all interrupt requests to the processor must go through the master, and no slave can respond to an $\overline{\text{INTA}}$ unless its CAS0 through CAS2 inputs are active.

TABLE 7.8 Restart Locations
When the 8259A Base Address
is 0100H and the Interval is 4

Interrupt request	Restart address
IR0	0100H
IR1	0104H
IR2	0108H
IR3	010CH
IR4	0110H
IR5	0114H
IR6	0118H
IR7	011CH

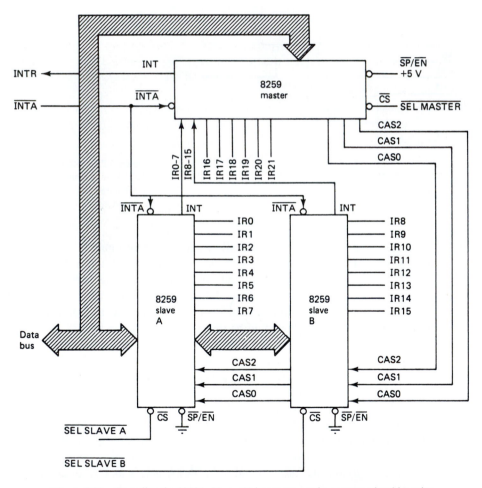

Figure 7.30 Cascading the 8259A. Up to 64 interrupts can be accommodated by using one master and eight slaves.

Arbitration Modes

The 8259A has been designed to handle a large number of interrupt requests. Each of the eight interrupt inputs within one PIC can be assigned a priority for use in the event of a multiple interrupt request—that is, simultaneous interrupts. The following six different operating modes can be programmed:

1. *Fully nested.* This is the default mode and assigns IR0 the highest priority and IR7 the lowest. In the fully nested mode, when one interrupt is being serviced, all others of equal or lower priority are "remembered" (in the interrupt request register—IRR), but not serviced. One bit of the in-service register (ISR) will be set corresponding to the active input.

When the interrupt service routine has finished, a special *nonspecific end-of-interrupt* (EOI) instruction must be given. This instruction will reset the highest in-service bit (which, in the fully nested mode, will correspond to the active input). The EOI instruction is given by writing an *operation control word* (to be described shortly) to the command register. This instruction should be included as part of the interrupt service routine.

By writing a special *initialization control word,* it is also possible to program the 8259A to insert automatically the nonspecific end-of-interrupt command. In this case, the in-service bit will be reset on the trailing edge of the last INTA pulse. Later in this section you will learn how to program the 8259A and write the initialization and operation control words.

2. *Rotating equal priority.* This mode is intended for applications in which all devices have an equal priority. In this scheme, the currently executing interrupt is given the lowest priority after completing its service routine. The technique is shown in Fig. 7.31. Two interrupt requests are received, IR1 and IR6 in Fig. 7.31(a). IR1 has the highest priority and is therefore serviced first. After being serviced, IR1 is assigned the lowest priority. This is shown in Fig. 7.31(b).

IR6 is then serviced and assigned the lowest priority, as shown in Fig. 7.31(c). This technique prevents infrequent interrupt requests from being "starved" for service due to heavy traffic on other interrupt inputs.

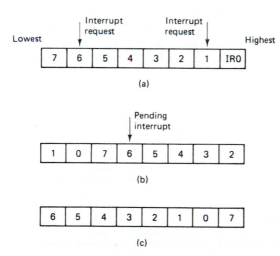

Figure 7.31 Rotating equal priority. In this technique, the current interrupt is assigned the lowest priority after being serviced. In (a), IR1 is serviced. Then, in (b), it is assigned the lowest priority. Next, IR6 is serviced and then is assigned lowest priority in (c).

The priority rotation can be accomplished automatically or with the special non-specific EOI command (given at the end of the interrupt service routine).

3. *Rotating specific priority.* If a specific EOI control word is written to the 8259A, the priority structure after servicing the current interrupt can be fixed in the service routine. This is done by specifying the lowest priority input as part of the EOI control word. Referring to Fig. 7.31(a), we see that a specific EOI control word could assign IR7 the lowest priority, with the result that the priority structure after servicing IR1 would look the same as Fig. 7.31(a), not Fig. 7.31(b).

The advantage is that the service routine can set the priorities on the basis of program execution rather than a fixed rotation scheme. The result is greater flexibility for the programmer.

4. *Basic mask.* This mode allows any of the IR0 through IR7 inputs to be masked by writing a 1 to their corresponding bit position in the interrupt mask register (IMR). This interrupt will then be ignored in all other modes.

5. *Special mask.* Normally, a lower priority interrupt cannot interrupt a higher priority interrupt. However, if the currently executing service routine writes a 1 to the interrupt mask register (IMR) ("masking itself") and the special mask mode is selected, interrupts of a lower (as well as higher) priority level than the masked bit will be accepted.

6. *Polled.* In this mode, the INT output is not used. Instead, the 8259A prioritizes the IR0 through IR7 inputs and provides a status port that can be polled. The status byte has the form shown in Fig. 7.32.

Programming the 8259A

Programming the 8259A requires two to four *initialization control words* (ICWs). These bytes specify the vector address, select a 4- or 8-byte interval between addresses, identify the single or cascaded mode, select the automatic or normal EOI mode, and program the type of trigger. Once the bytes have been written, the PIC is ready to receive interrupt requests.

The default arbitration scheme after initialization is the *fully nested* normal EOI mode in which only higher level interrupt requests can interrupt an in-service request and an EOI command is required at the end of each interrupt service routine. In addition, the interrupt mask register (IMR) is cleared—that is, no masks are applied—IR7 is assigned lowest priority, and the special mask mode is cleared. Changes to any of these operating modes will require writing one to three *operation control words* (OCWs).

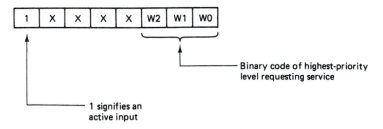

Figure 7.32   In the polled mode, the 8259A acts as a prioritized status port.

Initialization control words. Figure 7.33 describes the bit assignments for ICW1 through ICW4. In all cases, ICW1 and ICW2 must be written. These bytes program the base address that, together with the interval, will be gated onto the data bus during $\overline{INTA}$.

ICW3 should be written only when one or more slave PICs are to be used. ICW4 is required to specify an 8086 or 8088 processor, to enable the auto EOI mode and special fully nested mode (for cascaded PICs), and to select the buffered mode for slave and master. The latter selection is required when data bus buffers are used between the PIC and the system data bus.

The steps required for 8259 initialization are shown in flowchart form in Fig. 7.34.

Example 7.14

The 8259A is to be used to interface eight level-triggered interrupt inputs. The following jump table will be used to service the interrupts:

Address	Op code	Interrupt
E000	JMP ISR 0	IR0
E004	JMP ISR 1	IR1
E008	JMP ISR 2	IR2
E00C	JMP ISR 3	IR3
E010	JMP ISR 4	IR4
E014	JMP ISR 5	IR5
E018	JMP ISR 6	IR6
E01C	JMP ISR 7	IR7

Write the 8080/85 initialization routine, assuming the hardware interface in Fig. 7.29.

Solution. Only ICW1 and ICW2 need be written. Note that ICW1 is accessed when A0 = 0 (thus, port F0 is selected in Fig. 7.29) and ICW1 is accessed when A0 = 1 (thus, port F1 is selected in Fig. 7.29). The code is as follows:

```
MVI   A,1EH      ;000 1 1 1 1 0 (INIT. CODES)
OUT   0F0H       ;ICW1 PORT
MVI   A,0E0H     ;1110 0000 (BASE ADDRESS)
OUT   0F1H       ;ICW2 PORT
```

Note that if ICW3 and ICW4 are required, they are written to the same address as ICW2. The 8259A, by noting bits D0 and D1 of ICW1, will interpret the next two writes as ICW3 and ICW4.

Operation control words. As explained previously, the operation control words (OCWs) are required only when the default conditions (obtained after initialization) must be changed and to give the nonautomatic EOI command at the end of each service routine.

Figure 7.35 details the bit definitions for the three operation control word registers. OCW1 controls the interrupt masks: Logic 1's written to OCW1 will cause the selected interrupts to be masked and ignored by the 8259A.

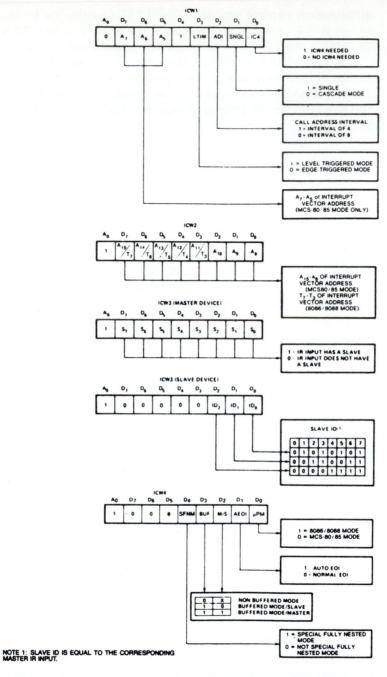

Figure 7.33 8259A initialization control word format. (Courtesy of Intel Corporation.)

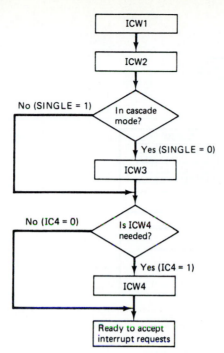

Figure 7.34 8259A initialization sequence. (Courtesy of Intel Corporation.)

The operating modes (see "Arbitration Modes") are selected by writing to OCW2. The following eight commands can be given, usually at the end of the interrupt service routine:

1. *Nonspecific EOI.* Use this command at the end of each service routine during operation in the fully nested mode. The command resets the highest in-service interrupt bit. While this bit is set, interrupts of equal or lower priority are inhibited. The command is automatically inserted by the 8259A if bit D1 of ICW4 is programmed high.

2. *Specific EOI.* Use this command to force a specific in-service bit to be reset. The command should be used only when the fully nested structure is not implemented. Bits 0–2 select the in-service bit.

3. *Rotate on nonspecific EOI.* This command should be given when all peripherals have equal priority. It causes an automatic rotation of the priorities, as illustrated in Figure 7.31.

4. *Rotate in automatic EOI mode (Set).* This command activates the automatic rotate on nonspecific EOI mode. In this mode, the PIC automatically performs a nonspecific EOI command, and the nonspecific EOI command at the end of each interrupt service routine need not be given. (See Example 7.15.)

5. *Rotate in automatic EOI mode (Clear).* This command deactivates the automatic rotate on nonspecific EOI mode.

6. *Rotate on specific EOI.* This command allows the programmer to specify the bottom priority in the rotate mode. For example, if IR4 is programmed as the lowest priority device, then IR5 will have the highest priority.

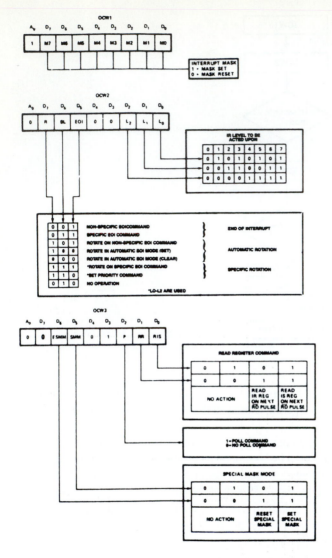

Figure 7.35 8259A operation control word (OCW) format. (Courtesy of Intel Corporation.)

7. *Set priority.* This command alters the priority by specifying the lowest priority device. Note that set priority is not an EOI command, however.

8. *No operation.*

OCW3 is used to enable the *interrupt request register,* IRR (that is, the status of pending interrupts), or the *in-service register,* ISR (that is, the interrupts currently being serviced), for a subsequent read operation. The polling mode is selected with bit D2. Bits D5 and D6 control the special mask mode.

The correct address to use when writing the ICWs and OCWs can be confusing, but Table 7.9 should help explain the matter. ICW1 is written with A0 = 0 and has bits 4,3 = 1X. The PIC recognizes this pattern as ICW1 and expects the initialization sequence, ICW2 through ICW4, to follow.

TABLE 7.9 8259A Initialization and Operation Control Word Summary

Name	$\overline{RD}$	$\overline{WR}$	A0	Special requirements	Comments
Initialization begins.					
ICW1	1	0	0	Bits 4,3 = 1X	This begins initialization sequence.
ICW2	1	0	1	None	First write with A0 = 1 after ICW1 must be ICW2.
ICW3	1	0	1	None	This write must follow ICW2 if specified in ICW1 (bit 1 = 0).
ICW4	1	0	1	None	This write must follow ICW3 if specified in ICW1 (bit 0 = 1).
Initialization is now complete.					
OCW1	1	0	1	None	This write sets the interrupt mask bits.
OCW2	1	0	0	Bits 4, 3 = 00	Bits 4, 3 identify as noninitialization command. Used to select mode.
OCW3	1	0	0	Bits 4, 3 = 01	Bits 4, 3 separate ICW1, OCW2, and OCW3. Bits 0, 1 determine input status registers to be read.
The following read operations may be specified:					
IRR	0	1	0	None	If OCW3 bits 1, 0 = 10, the pending interrupts will be read.
ISR	0	1	0	None	If OCW3 bits 1, 0 = 11, the current in-service interrupts will be read.
IMR	0	1	1	None	Read the interrupt mask bits. This is the read corresponding to OCW1.

The OCWs are more complex. All write operations with A0 = 1 *after initialization is complete* will be directed to OCW1. If A0 = 0, bits 4 and 3 determine whether the byte is to be interpreted as OCW2, OCW3, or ICW1 (begin a new initialization).

Finally, note that three registers can be read. IRR and ISR are controlled by the data written to bits 0 and 1 of OCW3. The interrupt mask register, IMR, is read when A0 = 1 and a read cycle is performed.

Example 7.15

Assume that the initialization codes in Example 7.14 have been written to the 8259A in Fig. 7.29. Now write the proper operation control words for a fully nested priority structure. Mask IR1, IR3, and IR6, and enable the ISR for a read. What code should be used at the end of each interrupt service routine?

Solution. The fully nested structure defaults after initialization; thus, only two control words are required. (See Fig. 7.35.) The program is as follows:

```
MVI   A,4AH    ;INTERRUPT MASK WORD − 01001010
OUT   0F1H     ;OCW1
MVI   A,0BH    ;READ ISR − 00001011
OUT   0F0H     ;BITS 4,3 = 01 => OCW3
```

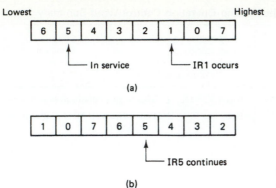

Lowest   Highest

| 6 | 5 | 4 | 3 | 2 | 1 | 0 | 7 |

└── In service   └── IR1 occurs

(a)

| 1 | 0 | 7 | 6 | 5 | 4 | 3 | 2 |

└── IR5 continues

(b)

Figure 7.36 In-service register for Example 7.16.

Each interrupt service routine must end by giving the nonspecific EOI command (resetting the in-service bit). A typical routine would end with the following code:

```
MVI   A,20H      ;NONSPECIFIC EOI − 00100XXX
OUT   0F0H       ;BITS 4,3 = 00 => OCW2
RET
```

(*Note:* If rotate in automatic EOI mode is set, the preceding OCW2 is not required.)

Example 7.16

Assume that Fig. 7.36(a) shows the current interrupt priority and in-service status for the 8259A in Fig. 7.29. What changes are required to the OCWs given in Example 7.15 if the rotate in automatic EOI mode is desired? If IR1 occurs while IR5 is in service, will IR1 be serviced? What will the new priority structure become?

Solution. The only change required to the OCWs in Example 7.15 is the inclusion of a command to rotate in automatic EOI mode:

```
MVI   A,80H      ;ROTATE IN AUTOMATIC EOI − 10000XXX
OUT   0F0H       ;BITS 4,3 = 00 => OCW2
```

Because IR1 is of a higher priority than IR5, the IR5 service routine will be suspended and the IR1 routine executed. Figure 7.36(b) shows the priority structure after the IR1 routine has finished. IR1 has become the lowest priority, and the IR5 service routine can now continue. When the IR5 routine finishes, it will become the lowest priority.

SELF-REVIEW 7.4

7.4.1 A single 8259A can accept as many as ＿＿＿＿＿＿＿＿ different interrupt requests.

7.4.2 When an interrupt occurs, the 8259A automatically gates a 3-byte ＿＿＿＿＿＿＿＿ instruction onto the data bus of the microprocessor.

7.4.3 What is the difference between an initialization control word (ICW) and an operation control word (OCW)?

7.4.4 Which 8259A operating mode should be selected if all interrupting devices have equal priority?

7.4.5 An 8259A PIC receives simultaneous interrupts on IR3 and IR5. If the PIC is operated in the fully nested mode, which input will be serviced?

7.5 THE 8237A PROGRAMMABLE DMA CONTROLLER

Introduction

Direct memory access, or DMA, was introduced in Chapter 6. DMA is an alternative to programmed or interrupt-driven I/O. The main advantage is the high speed at which data transfers can take place. The 8237A DMA controller can transfer data between memory and an I/O port as fast as 1.6 megabytes per second (MB/s). This figure compares with less than 33,000 bytes per second using polling (with a 2-MHz 8080A).

Not all applications of DMA involve high-speed peripherals. Buffered printers can also be interfaced using DMA. Each time the printer's BUSY/READY flag indicates READY, the buffer of the printer can be filled using DMA at high speed, the DMA transfer becomes complete, and the microprocessor resumes normal processing as the printer empties its buffer.

The advantage to using a DMA controller (DMAC) for this printer application is that the controller can be programmed to keep track of the source address and word count without CPU intervention. If interrupts were used, an interrupt service routine would be required, and considerable processing time would be spent recovering and storing program variables.

The disadvantage of DMA is that the processor must idle while the DMA transfer takes place. This is not really a disadvantage when the transfer occurs in "bursts," as in the printer example. On the other hand, if the printer does not have a buffer and the DMAC must insert *WAIT* states to synchronize itself to the printer's data rate, interrupts would provide a better solution. This is because the processor would be allowed to perform some other task while waiting for the printer to be ready.

Another disadvantage of DMA is that no pre- or postprocessing can be done by the DMAC. If this is required, it will have to be done before or after the data have been transferred.

In the past, the biggest limitation to using DMA has been the complexity of designing the DMA controller, or DMAC. This is where the 8237A comes in: It provides all of the features required for DMA transfers in a single 40-pin chip and interfaces in a straightforward manner to the system three-bus architecture. Among the features of the 8237A DMAC are the following:

1. There are four DMA channels.
2. Each channel is capable of transferring up to 64K bytes.
3. Fixed or rotating priorities may be assigned.
4. Hardware or software may request the DMA transfer.
5. Block or single-byte transfers may be specified.
6. Data transfers between I/O and memory or from memory to memory are possible.

In this section, we:

- Describe the sequence of events that must occur for the 8237A DMAC to transfer data with a peripheral.
- Program the 8237A DMAC and specify the transfer mode, source and destination addresses, command byte, and transfer channels.

Interfacing the 8237A

Figure 7.37(a) is a block diagram and pinout definition for the 8237A programmable DMAC. Figure 7.37(b) provides a description of the pin functions. Before we begin a detailed study of this device, it would be wise to review the basic DMA concept.

DMA is an interfacing technique in which a special data transfer processor—the DMAC—takes over and controls the three buses of the microcomputer system. This is done by requesting a special *HOLD* state (called DMA REQUEST in Figs. 4.25 through 4.27) from the processor. The microprocessor acknowledges the request by asserting hold acknowledge (HLDA) and then setting all of its system buses into a tristate condition. These lines are then free to be controlled by the DMAC.

There is a problem in larger systems where all bus lines on the CPU module are buffered. Although the buffers "see" high impedances on their inputs (from the "tristated" microprocessor), they will (usually) convert these impedances to logic 1 levels on their outputs, causing bus contention problems with the DMAC. For this reason, the CPU modules must include a signal (called BUSEN in Figs. 4.25 and 4.26) that will allow the bus buffers to be tristate. As shown in Figs. 4.25 and 4.26, driving BUSEN high disables all three system buses.

Figure 7.38 illustrates how the 8237A DMAC can be interfaced to any of the CPU modules presented in Chapter 4. Note that a high-order address latch is required. During the time when ADSTB is high and a DMA transfer is taking place, D0–D7 hold the high-order address bits. The falling edge of ADSTB latches this byte into the 74LS373 latch. For the remainder of the DMA transfer, D0–D7 function as a bidirectional data bus.

Let us list the steps required for the 8237A in Fig. 7.38 to make a data transfer with a peripheral:

1. Before the transfer can take place, the DMAC must be programmed with the memory address, byte count, and type of transfer to be performed. In the case of the 8237A, the DMAC appears to be 16 consecutive I/O ports selected with A0–A3 and IOR and IOW. Note that the device cannot be memory mapped: MEMR and MEMW are output pins (for the DMAC) only.

2. A DMA transfer can now be requested on one of the four channels by a peripheral asserting DREQ.

3. If the 8237A is enabled and the active channel is not masked, the DMAC asserts HRQ, requesting a HOLD state from the CPU.

4. The CPU responds by completing the current machine cycle, putting its buses in a tristate condition, and then issuing HLDA.

5. The DMAC alerts the peripheral to the HLDA acknowledgment by outputting DACK to the peripheral. This signal is normally used to *chip select* (CS) the peripheral's data port.

6. The 8237A now outputs the high-order memory address on D0–D7 and raises AEN and ADSTB. The address represents the source or destination of the data transfer. AEN enables the tristate outputs of the latch and is also used to disable the system buses via BUSEN.

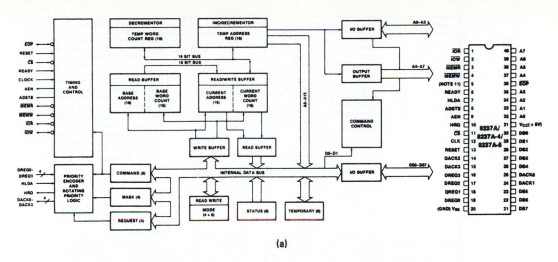

(a)

Symbol	Type	Name and Function
V_{CC}		**Power:** +5 volt supply.
V_{SS}		**Ground:** Ground.
CLK	I	**Clock Input:** Clock Input controls the internal operations of the 8237A and its rate of data transfers. The input may be driven at up to 3 MHz for the standard 8237A and up to 5 MHz for the 8237A-5.
CS	I	**Chip Select:** Chip Select is an active low input used to select the 8237A as an I/O device during the Idle cycle. This allows CPU communication on the data bus.
RESET	I	**Reset:** Reset is an active high input which clears the Command, Status, Request and Temporary registers. It also clears the first/last flip/flop and sets the Mask register. Following a Reset the device is in the Idle cycle.
READY	I	**Ready:** Ready is an input used to extend the memory read and write pulses from the 8237A to accommodate slow memories or I/O peripheral devices. Ready must not make transitions during its specified setup/hold time.
HLDA	I	**Hold Acknowledge:** The active high Hold Acknowledge from the CPU indicates that it has relinquished control of the system busses.
DREQ0–DREQ3	I	**DMA Request:** The DMA Request lines are individual asynchronous channel request inputs used by peripheral circuits to obtain DMA service. In fixed Priority, DREQ0 has the highest priority and DREQ3 has the lowest priority. A request is generated by activating the DREQ line of a channel. DACK will acknowledge the recognition of DREQ signal. Polarity of DREQ is programmable. Reset intializes these lines to active high. DREQ must be maintained until the corresponding DACK goes active

Symbol	Type	Name and Function
DB0–DB7	I/O	**Data Bus:** The Data Bus lines are bidirectional three-state signals connected to the system data bus. The outputs are enabled in the Program condition during the I/O Read to output the contents of an Address register, a Status register, the Temporary register or a Word Count register to the CPU. The outputs are disabled and the inputs are read during an I/O Write cycle when the CPU is programming the 8237A control registers. During DMA cycles the most significant 8 bits of the address are output onto the data bus to be strobed into an external latch by ADSTB. In memory-to-memory operations, data from the memory comes into the 8237A on the data bus during the read-from-memory transfer. In the write-to-memory transfer, the data bus outputs place the data into the new memory location.
IOR	I/O	**I/O Read:** I/O Read is a bidirectional active low three-state line. In the Idle cycle, it is an input control signal used by the CPU to read the control registers. In the Active cycle, it is an output control signal used by the 8237A to access data from a peripheral during a DMA Write transfer.
IOW	I/O	**I/O Write:** I/O Write is a bidirectional active low three-state line. In the Idle cycle, it is an input control signal used by the CPU to load information into the 8237A. In the Active cycle, it is an output control signal used by the 8237A to load data to the peripheral during a DMA Read transfer.
EOP	I/O	**End of Process:** End of Process is an active low bidirectional signal. Information concerning the completion of DMA services is available at the bidirectional EOP pin. The 8237A allows an external signal to terminate an active DMA

(b)

Figure 7.37 (a) Block diagram and pin definitions for the 8237A DMAC; (b) pin descriptions. (Courtesy of Intel Corporation.)

Symbol	Type	Name and Function
		service. This is accomplished by pulling the EOP input low with an external EOP signal. The 8237A also generates a pulse when the terminal count (TC) for any channel is reached. This generates an EOP signal which is output through the EOP Line. The reception of EOP, either internal or external, will cause the 8237A to terminate the service, reset the request, and, if Autoinitialize is enabled, to write the base registers to the current registers of that channel. The mask bit and TC bit in the status word will be set for the currently active channel by EOP unless the channel is programmed for Autoinitialize. In that case, the mask bit remains clear. During memory-to-memory transfers, EOP will be output when the TC for channel 1 occurs. EOP should be tied high with a pull-up resistor if it is not used to prevent erroneous end of process inputs.
A0–A3	I/O	**Address:** The four least significant address lines are bidirectional three-state signals. In the Idle cycle they are inputs and are used by the 8237A to address the control register to be loaded or read. In the Active cycle they are outputs and provide the lower 4 bits of the output address.
A4–A7	O	**Address:** The four most significant address lines are three-state outputs and provide 4 bits of address. These lines are enabled only during the DMA service.

Symbol	Type	Name and Function
HRQ	O	**Hold Request:** This is the Hold Request to the CPU and is used to request control of the system bus. If the corresponding mask bit is clear, the presence of any valid DREQ causes 8237A to issue the HRQ. After HRQ goes active at least one clock cycle (TCY) must occur before HLDA goes active.
DACK0–DACK3	O	**DMA Acknowledge:** DMA Acknowledge is used to notify the individual peripherals when one has been granted a DMA cycle. The sense of these lines is programmable. Reset initializes them to active low.
AEN	O	**Address Enable:** Address Enable enables the 8-bit latch containing the upper 8 address bits onto the system address bus. AEN can also be used to disable other system bus drivers during DMA transfers. AEN is active HIGH.
ADSTB	O	**Address Strobe:** The active high, Address Strobe is used to strobe the upper address byte into an external latch.
MEMR	O	**Memory Read:** The Memory Read signal is an active low three-state output used to access data from the selected memory location during a DMA Read or a memory-to-memory transfer.
MEMW	O	**Memory Write:** The Memory Write is an active low three-state output used to write data to the selected memory location during a DMA Write or a memory-to-memory transfer.

Figure 7.37 *(Continued)*

7. ADSTB then goes low, causing the high-order address to be latched. D0–D7 change to become the data bus and A0–A7 become the low-order address bus.

8. The DMAC is now in control of the buses, and three types of data transfers are possible, as listed in Fig. 7.39. Highlighted in this figure is the transfer of a data byte from memory to an I/O device. Note the unusual condition of the control bus: Two signals—MEMR and IOW—are active simultaneously. Although this can never happen when the CPU is in control, it is the normal case when the DMAC is in control. Data read from RAM is output directly to the I/O device without going through the DMAC.

9. Only one channel of the 8237A is required for the transfer. In the special case of a memory-to-memory transfer, two channels are required, one programmed with the source address (the 8237A requires channel 0) and the other with the destination address (channel 1 is required). In this case, DREQ and DACK are not required.

10. Data is transferred between RAM and the I/O device (in Fig. 7.39) until the byte counter is zero (called the *terminal count*). It is also possible to halt the transfer with an external end-of-process (EOP) input to the DMAC. In either case, HRQ and AEN are removed, relinquishing control of the system buses to the processor.

A timing diagram illustrating these same activities is presented in Fig. 7.40.

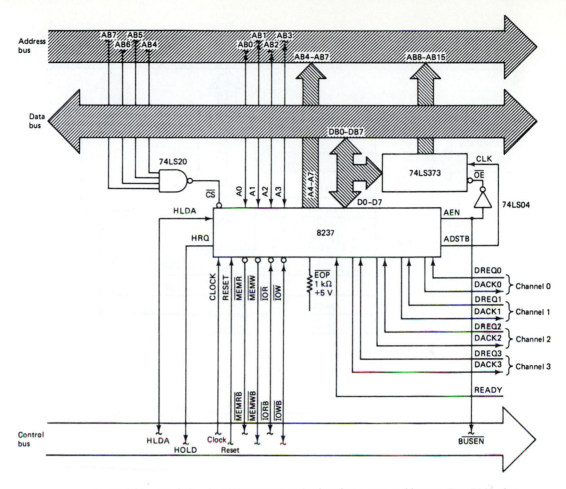

Figure 7.38 Interfacing the 8237A DMAC to the three-bus system architecture. Four DMA channels are provided.

Response Time and Transfer Rate

As mentioned in Chapter 6, the CPU responds within one machine cycle of a HOLD request. This means that a maximum of six T states can elapse between the DMA request and the start of the DMA transfer. (Recall that, with interrupts, the 8080 and 8085 required 12–31 T states to respond to the request.)

When a DMA transfer is to occur, the response time is usually not the main concern. This is because the DMA processor is dedicated to transferring large blocks of data—unlike interrupt-driven or polled I/O, in which the processor must monitor a BUSY/READY flag and then quickly respond with a data byte before the next transaction is to occur.

The 8237A has two basic modes of operation: *idle* and *active*. In the idle state, the device can be programmed by the processor for an upcoming active state during which the DMA transfer will take place. Figure 7.41 illustrates the activities that occur during each of the six possible clock states.

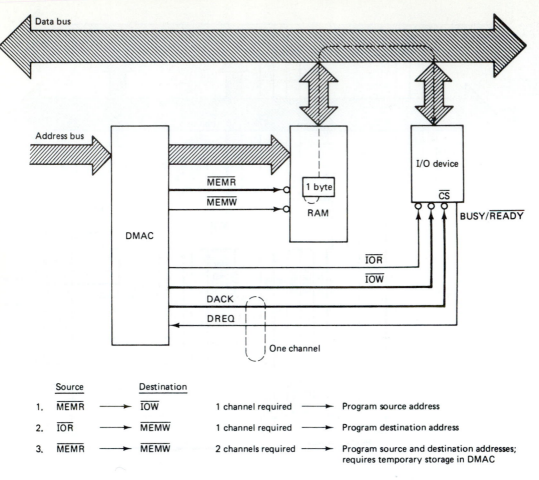

Data bus

Address bus

MEMR
MEMW

1 byte
RAM

DMAC

I/O device

$\overline{CS}$

BUSY/$\overline{READY}$

$\overline{IOR}$

$\overline{IOW}$

DACK

DREQ

One channel

	Source		Destination		
1.	$\overline{MEMR}$	→	$\overline{IOW}$	1 channel required →	Program source address
2.	$\overline{IOR}$	→	$\overline{MEMW}$	1 channel required →	Program destination address
3.	$\overline{MEMR}$	→	$\overline{MEMW}$	2 channels required →	Program source and destination addresses; requires temporary storage in DMAC

Figure 7.39 The 8237A can support three types of data transfers. The case highlighted is a transfer from memory to an I/O device. Note that $\overline{MEMR}$ and $\overline{IOW}$ are simultaneously low for this transfer.

After a DREQ occurs, the DMAC moves from state S1 to S0, waiting for HLDA from the processor. In the S1 state the high-order address is output. Note that this address changes only once every 256 data transfers. For this reason, the 8237A automatically deletes state S1, except when the high-order address must change.

During S2 the low-order address is output, and during S3 the control signals appear. The actual data transfer occurs during state S4. Assuming that the high-order address does not change, three clock states (S2, S3, and S4) will be required for one data transfer. The clock period ranges from 200 ns for the 8237A-5 to 320 ns for the 8237A. The transfer rate (for the 8237A-5) is thus found to be

$$\frac{1}{3 \times 200 \text{ ns}} = \frac{1}{.6 \text{ μs}} = 1.6 \text{ MB/s}$$

In Chapter 6 we calculated the transfer rate for a 2-MHz 8080 using polling to be 32,787 bytes per second. The rate was 78,431 bytes per second with a 4-MHz Z-80. It is

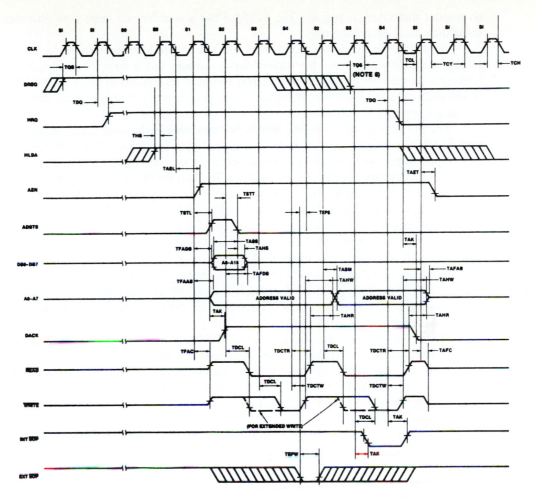

Figure 7.40 8237A DMA transfer timing. (Courtesy of Intel Corporation.)

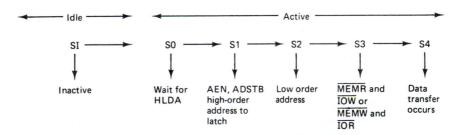

Figure 7.41 The 8237A has an idle and an active mode. In the active mode, data transfers typically require only states S2, S3, and S4.

no wonder that DMA is popular: The 8237A-5 has a transfer rate more than 20 times faster than the Z-80 polling rate!

Of course, the I/O device and memory must be able to keep up with the DMAC to achieve this high transfer rate. For semiconductor memory, this is no problem. A memory read cycle (essentially the same as the address access time) consists of states S2–S4. This is 600 ns for the 8237A-5, but, as we have seen in Chapter 5, memory access times of 600 ns are considered very slow.

The I/O device may be another matter, however. One of the most common applications of DMA is to interface a serial disk drive—a floppy disk or hard disk. A floppy disk will output (or require) a new data byte once every 16 μs—a very fast rate when polling is to be used, but very slow for a DMA transfer. To interface this peripheral, the READY input of the 8237A must be used. This line is pulled low by the floppy disk controller while it retrieves (or writes) a new byte of data. The DMAC's READY input is similar to the microprocessor's READY input and is sampled during state S3. If this input is found low, the three buses "mark time," holding valid data until READY again returns high.

Although the floppy disk interface does not require it, the 8237A is capable of an even faster data rate if *compressed timing* is used. In this mode, state S3 is eliminated; it is used just to extend the pulse width of the $\overline{\text{IOR}}$ and $\overline{\text{IOW}}$ control signals, allowing data transfers only with states S2 and S4. This would require memory devices with access times of less than 400 ns for the 8237A-5.

Memory-to-memory data transfers require twice the time required for memory-to-I/O transfers. This is because one set of S states is required to read the data byte and another to write it; $\overline{\text{MEMR}}$ and $\overline{\text{MEMW}}$ cannot be allowed to be simultaneously low, as they can with the memory and I/O control signals. In addition, a temporary register within the 8237A DMAC is required to save the data byte before the write cycle occurs.

Memory-to-memory transfers are useful when a large block of memory is to be transferred or when a block of memory is to be filled with a certain character.

Programming the 8237A

Each channel of the 8237A has a 16-bit *current address register* and a 16-bit *current word register*. The current address register holds the memory address for the next DMA transfer. The current word register acts as a 16-bit down counter and is programmed with the total number of bytes to be transferred, less 1. The terminal count occurs when this register rolls over from 0000 to FFFF.

Each of these registers is backed up by a *base address register* and *base word register* that contain the initial values when programmed. This allows an autoinitialize sequence to occur (if such a sequence is programmed) that rewrites the current address and current word registers when the terminal count (or EOP) occurs.

Table 7.10 indicates the control signal codes required to access the registers for each channel. Note that the current address and word count registers can only be read, not written. Because the base address and word count are likely to require 16 bits, an internal flip-flop is used to gate these 2 bytes into the DMAC. In this way, the first write to the base and current address register is interpreted as the low-order address and the second write as the high-order address. A similar arrangement is used with the word count register.

TABLE 7.10 Address Register and Word Count Register Control Codes for the 8237A DMAC

Channel	Register	Operation	$\overline{CS}$	$\overline{IOR}$	$\overline{IOW}$	A3	A2	A1	A0	Internal flip-flop	Data buses D80—D87
0	Base and Current Address	Write	0	1	0	0	0	0	0	0	A0–A7
			0	1	0	0	0	0	0	1	A8–A15
	Current Address	Read	0	0	1	0	0	0	0	0	A0–A7
			0	0	1	0	0	0	0	1	A8–A15
	Base and Current Word Count	Write	0	1	0	0	0	0	1	0	W0–W7
			0	1	0	0	0	0	1	1	W8–W15
	Current Word Count	Read	0	0	1	0	0	0	1	0	W0–W7
			0	0	1	0	0	0	1	1	W8–W15
1	Base and Current Address	Write	0	1	0	0	0	1	0	0	A0–A7
			0	1	0	0	0	1	0	1	A8–A15
	Current Address	Read	0	0	1	0	0	1	0	0	A0–A7
			0	0	1	0	0	1	0	1	A8–A15
	Base and Current Word Count	Write	0	1	0	0	0	1	1	0	W0–W7
			0	1	0	0	0	1	1	1	W8–W15
	Current Word Count	Read	0	0	1	0	0	1	1	0	W0–W7
			0	0	1	0	0	1	1	1	W8–W15
2	Base and Current Address	Write	0	1	0	0	1	0	0	0	A0–A7
			0	1	0	0	1	0	0	1	A8–A15
	Current Address	Read	0	0	1	0	1	0	0	0	A0–A7
			0	0	1	0	1	0	0	1	A8–A15
	Base and Current Word Count	Write	0	1	0	0	1	0	1	0	W0–W7
			0	1	0	0	1	0	1	1	W8–W15
	Current Word Count	Read	0	0	1	0	1	0	1	0	W0–W7
			0	0	1	0	1	0	1	1	W8–W15
3	Base and Current Address	Write	0	1	0	0	1	1	0	0	A0–A7
			0	1	0	0	1	1	0	1	A8–A15
	Current Address	Read	0	0	1	0	1	1	0	0	A0–A7
			0	0	1	0	1	1	0	1	A8–A15
	Base and Current Word Count	Write	0	1	0	0	1	1	1	0	W0–W7
			0	1	0	0	1	1	1	1	W8–W15
	Current Word Count	Read	0	0	1	0	1	1	1	0	W0–W7
			0	0	1	0	1	1	1	1	W8–W15

Source: Courtesy of Intel Corporation.

Example 7.17

Suppose that channel 0 (the source) and channel 1 (the destination) of the DMAC interface in Fig. 7.38 are to be used for a memory-to-memory DMA transfer. Determine the port addresses for these two channels and write an 8080/85 initialization routine to load the address and word count registers if 100 bytes are to be transferred. Assume that the source address is 1000H and the destination address is F000H.

Solution. The 74LS20 connected to the $\overline{CS}$ input forces AB4–AB7 to be high to enable the 8237A. Referring to Table 7.10 to select bits AB0–AB3, we find the following port addresses:

Port F0: base and current address for channel 0
Port F1: base and current word count for channel 0
Port F2: base and current address for channel 1
Port F3: base and current word count for channel 1

The initialization program is as follows:

```
MVI   A,00    ;LSB SOURCE AND DESTINATION ADDRESS
OUT   0F0H    ;CHANNEL 0
OUT   0F2H    ;CHANNEL 1
MVI   A,10H   ;MSB SOURCE ADDRESS
OUT   0F0H    ;CHANNEL 0
MVI   A,0F0H  ;MSB DESTINATION ADDRESS
OUT   0F2H    ;CHANNEL 1
MVI   A,63H   ;LSB WORD COUNT LESS 1
OUT   0F3H    ;CHANNEL 1
MVI   A,00    ;MSB WORD COUNT
OUT   0F3H    ;CHANNEL 1
```

Note that you may intermix address and word count writes between the two channels. The first write will be interpreted as the LSB and the second as the MSB. For memory-to-memory transfers, it is necessary only to write the word count to channel 1.

The DMA *transfer mode* of the 8237A must also be programmed. There are four choices (a flowchart of modes 1 through 3 was given in Fig. 6.27):

1. *Single transfer.* A single byte is transferred, the word count is decremented, and the current address register is incremented or decremented as programmed. DREQ must be held active until DACK is received. If DREQ is active throughout the transfer, control will be passed back to the microprocessor for one machine cycle before beginning the next transfer.
2. *Block transfer.* Data is transferred until the terminal count (TC) or EOP occurs. DREQ must be held active until DACK occurs.
3. *Demand transfer.* Data is transferred as long as DREQ is active. When DREQ goes inactive, the current address and word count do not change, allowing the I/O device to resume the transfer where it left off. TC or EOP will terminate the transfer.
4. *Cascade mode.* In this mode, one 8237A serves as a master and the other 8237A's as slaves. The configuration is shown in Fig. 7.42. Each of the slaves is programmed for one of the three transfer modes just listed. Each slave provides the memory address for the transfer, but the master prioritizes the HOLD requests from the slaves.

In addition to the preceding four transfer modes, a *memory-to-memory* transfer mode can be specified, as illustrated in Example 7.17. This mode is limited to block transfers, and channel 0 must be used for the source and channel 1 for the destination.

Four registers are used to program the transfer mode and select various operating features of the 8237A. The bit descriptions of these registers are provided in Fig. 7.43. Each of the registers is a *write-only* register.

1. *Command register.* This register controls the operation of the 8237A. Note that the chip can be disabled by making bit D2 a 1. If rotating priority is selected, the last DREQ honored will be assigned the lowest priority.
2. *Mode register.* The memory access portion of the DMA transfer may be programmed for a read, write, or verify operation. When programmed for verification

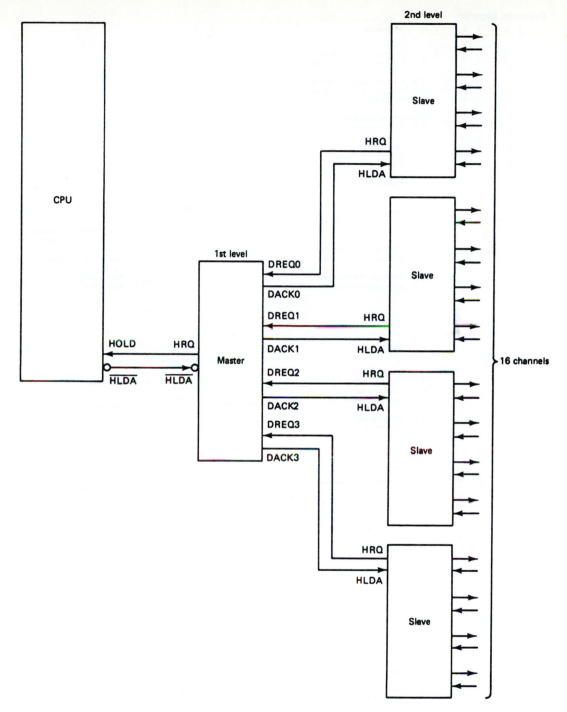

Figure 7.42 The cascade mode. All hold requests must be processed by the master.

Command Register

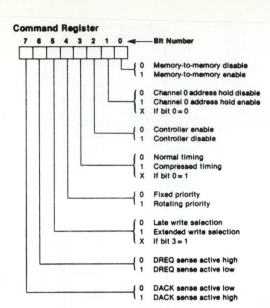

(a)

Mask Register

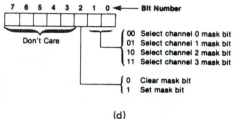

(d)

All four bits of the Mask register may also be written with a single command.

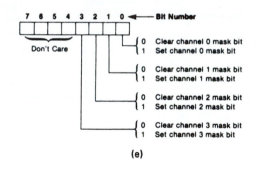

(e)

Mode Register

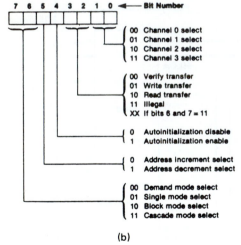

(b)

Request Register

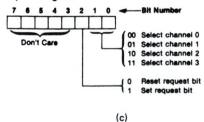

(c)

Figure 7.43 These four registers control the programming mode of the 8237A: (a) command register, (b) mode register, (c) request register, (d) and (e) mask register. (Courtesy of Intel Corporation.)

386

of transfers, the 8237A outputs addresses, but not the control signals. The mode register is also used to program autoinitialization and to increment or decrement addresses.

3. *Request register.* This register allows software, instead of DREQ, to initiate the DMA transfer. When the 8237A is programmed for memory-to-memory transfers, setting the request bit for channel 0 begins the transfer. Software requests are not maskable.

4. *Mask register.* This register is used to mask the DREQ for each channel. Clearing the mask bit enables that channel for DMA requests. Mask bits may be cleared individually or collectively, as shown in Fig. 7.43(d).

Two registers are read-only: the status register shown in Fig. 7.44(a) and the temporary register shown in Fig. 7.44(b). The temporary register contains the last byte transferred during a memory-to-memory transfer.

Three ports of the 8237A are not really ports at all, but use the *device-select pulse* created by an OUT instruction:

1. *Clear first/last flip-flop:* This instruction resets the internal flip-flop for ports 0–7. (See Table 7.10.) The next memory access will therefore be the low-order byte for the memory address or word count.

2. *Master clear.* The 8237A enters an idle state, with the command, status, request, and temporary registers and internal first/last flip-flop all reset and with all mask register bits set.

3. *Clear mask register.* This command enables all four channels to accept DMA requests on their DREQ inputs by clearing all bits in the mask register.

Table 7.11 summarizes the possible read and write functions associated with each of the 16 (base) port addresses of the DMAC. Using the address decoder in Fig. 7.38, the

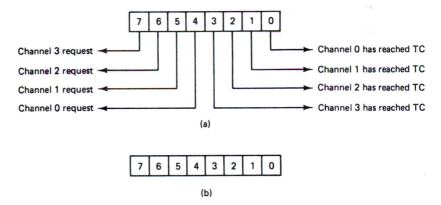

(a)

(b)

Figure 7.44 (a) The status register indicates (with a logic 1) which registers have reached TC and which channels have a pending DMA request. The bits are cleared upon reset and after a status read. (b) The temporary register holds data during a memory-to-memory DMA transfer. Reading this register reveals the last data byte transferred in the previous memory-to-memory transfer.

TABLE 7.11 Port Addresses of the 8237A DMAC

A3–A0	$\overline{\text{IOR}}$	$\overline{\text{IOW}}$	Function	
0	0	1	Read current address	
0	1	0	Write current address	Channel 0
1	0	1	Read current word count	
1	1	0	Write current word count	
2	0	1	Read current address	
2	1	0	Write current address	Channel 1
3	0	1	Read current word count	
3	1	0	Write current word count	
4	0	1	Read current address	
4	1	0	Write current address	Channel 2
5	0	1	Read current word count	
5	1	0	Write current word count	
6	0	1	Read current address	
6	1	0	Write current address	Channel 3
7	0	1	Read current word count	
7	1	0	Write current word count	
8	0	1	Read status register	
8	1	0	Write command register	
9	0	1	Invalid	
9	1	0	Write request register	
A	0	1	Invalid	
A	1	0	Write single mask register bit	
B	0	1	Invalid	
B	1	0	Write mode register	
C	0	1	Invalid	
C	1	0	Clear first/last flip-flop (DSP)	
D	0	1	Read temporary register	
D	1	0	Master clear (DSP)	
E	0	1	Invalid	
E	1	0	Clear mask register (DSP)	
F	0	1	Invalid	
F	1	0	Write all mask register bits	

8237A requires I/O ports F0 through FF. (Ports FC, FD, and FE are controlled by device-select pulses and do not actually transfer data.)

Figure 7.45 is a flowchart of the steps required to initialize the 8237A and illustrates the action taken by the DMAC once it is programmed. Note that it might be wise to disable the DMAC until initialization is complete if a DREQ could be received during this time.

Example 7.18

In Example 7.17, the initialization routine required to program the word count and address registers for a 100-byte memory-to-memory transfer was written. Using this routine as a

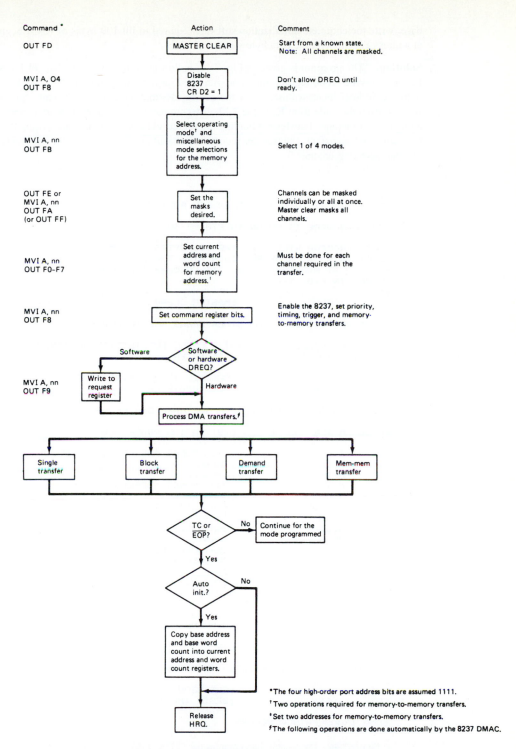

Command *	Action	Comment
OUT FD	MASTER CLEAR	Start from a known state. Note: All channels are masked.
MVI A, O4 OUT F8	Disable 8237 CR D2 = 1	Don't allow DREQ until ready.
MVI A, nn OUT FB	Select operating mode† and miscellaneous mode selections for the memory address.	Select 1 of 4 modes.
OUT FE or MVI A, nn OUT FA (or OUT FF)	Set the masks desired.	Channels can be masked individually or all at once. Master clear masks all channels.
MVI A, nn OUT F0–F7	Set current address and word count for memory address.‡	Must be done for each channel required in the transfer.
MVI A, nn OUT F8	Set command register bits.	Enable the 8237, set priority, timing, trigger, and memory- to-memory transfers.
	Software or hardware DREQ?	
MVI A, nn OUT F9	Software → Write to request register Hardware → Process DMA transfers.ƒ	

Single transfer   Block transfer   Demand transfer   Mem-mem transfer

TC or EOP? — No → Continue for the mode programmed

Auto init? — No

Yes → Copy base address and base word count into current address and word count registers.

Release HRQ.

*The four high-order port address bits are assumed 1111.
†Two operations required for memory-to-memory transfers.
‡Set two addresses for memory-to-memory transfers.
ƒThe following operations are done automatically by the 8237 DMAC.

Figure 7.45   Programmer's flowchart for the 8237A DMAC.

Sec. 7.5   The 8237A Programmable DMA Controller

base, write the complete initialization software required to fill 100 bytes of RAM beginning at address F000H with the data byte stored at 1000H.

Solution. The program is given in Fig. 7.46. Following a master clear, channel 1 is specified as the write mode register and is programmed for autoinitialization and a block transfer with the address incrementing. Next, the source, destination, and word count registers are written using the code from Example 7.17. The command register is then written, specifying a memory-to-memory transfer but holding the source address constant (thus writing the same byte with each transfer). The transfer request is initiated by writing a 1 to bit 2 of the request register, selecting channel 0.

```
;8237 MEMORY-TO-MEMORY TRANSFER ROUTINE
;
;THE HARDWARE IS SHOWN IN FIG. 7-38
;
;THIS PROGRAM WILL FILL THE 100 BYTES OF RAM
;BEGININING AT ADDRESS F00OH WITH THE DATA BYTE
;STORED AT ADDRESS 1000H.  IT FOLLOWS THE FLOW
;CHART IN FIG. 7-45.
;
OUT      OFDH              ;MASTER CLEAR
;
;SKIP THE DISABLE - NO OTHER DREQS ARE INVOLVED.
;
;PROGRAM CHANNEL 1 FOR WRITE MODE, AUTOINITIALIZATION,
;ADDRESS INCREMENT, BLOCK TRANSFER
;
MVI      A,95H             ;CHANNEL 1 OPERATING MODE
OUT      OFBH              ;MODE REGISTER
;
;NO MASKS ARE REQUIRED  (FOR SOFTWARE DMA REQUEST)
;
;PROGRAM THE SOURCE AND DESTINATION ADDRESSES
;
MVI      A,00              ;LSB SOURCE AND DESTINATION ADD
OUT      OFOH              ;CHANNEL O
OUT      OF2H              ;CHANNEL 1
MVI      A,1OH             ;MSB SOURCE ADDRESS
OUT      OFOH              ;CHANNEL O
MVI      A,OFOH            ;MSB DESTINATION ADDRESS
OUT      OF2H              ;CHANNEL 1
MVI      A,63H             ;LSB WORD COUNT LESS 1
OUT      OF3H              ;CHANNEL 1
MVI      A,00              ;MSB WORD COUNT
OUT      OF3H              ;CHANNEL 1
;
;NOW PROGRAM COMMAND REGISTER FOR MEMORY-TO-MEMORY
;TRANSFER WITH ADDRESS HOLD FOR CHANNEL O
;
MVI      A,03              ;CONTROL WORD
OUT      OF8H              ;COMMAND REGISTER
;
;INITIALIZATION IS COMPLETE
;
;WRITE TO REQUEST REGISTER TO BEGIN TRANSFER
;
MVI      A,04              ;SET REQUEST BIT FOR CHANNEL O
OUT      OF9H              ;BEGIN THE TRANSFER
;
;DMA TRANSFER NOW OCCURS
```

Figure 7.46 DMA control program for the 8237A DMAC in Example 7.18.

A Design Example: Interfacing a Floppy Disk Drive

One common application for DMA in a microcomputer system is a floppy disk drive interface. This is because the floppy disk requires large blocks of data to be read or written at relatively high speed—a good match for the DMA controller.

Figure 7.47 is a diagram of an interface between the 8237A DMAC and the Western Digital WD2793 floppy disk controller (FDC).

Similar to the other programmable controllers we have studied in this chapter, the WD2793 appears as four I/O or memory locations selected by A0 and A1 when its chip-select input is low. Data are transferred to or from the FDC when A1 A0 = 11. The other three combinations of A0 and A1 select control functions and allow the status of the controller to be read.

After programming is complete, the FDC is ready to transfer data with the 8237A DMAC. Typically, the control program will request a disk operation by writing to one of the three low port addresses of the FDC. As an example, suppose that we wish to write 1024 bytes of data to the floppy disk. Upon receipt of the write sector command, the FDC loads the head (which contacts the medium), and the ID field is searched for the correct track number, sector number, and side number.

The correct position on the diskette having been found, the FDC asserts a data request (DRQ). This signal indicates that the data register is empty and ready for 1 byte of data. DRQ requests a DMA transfer from channel 0 of the 8237A. (See Fig. 7.47.)

Assuming that the DMAC has been properly programmed, DACK0 acknowledges the request, chip-selects the FDC, and accesses the data port of the WD2793 (A1 A0 = 11). The DMAC now fetches a data byte from its current address and transfers it directly to the FDC on D0–D7. The address is then incremented or decremented and the word counter decremented. If TC does not occur, the DMAC prepares to transfer another byte.

With four states per transfer and 200 ns per state, the entire operation requires 0.8 μs. But the floppy disk is not ready for the next byte for at least 16 μs (assuming $3\frac{1}{2}$-inch high-density drive). For that reason, the *READY* input of the DMAC must be controlled by the FDC in order to insert WAIT states until the next data byte can be read. This is the purpose of the D flip-flop in Fig. 7.47.

The timing diagram in Fig. 7.48 will help explain the process. When DRQ first goes high, the DMA request is passed on to the CPU. We will assume that the block transfer mode has been programmed, and thus, the full sector of data will have to be written before the microprocessor is again given control of its buses. The falling edge of $\overline{IOW}$ output by the DMAC resets DRQ, and the disk drive writes the data byte (requiring 16 μs). The flip-flop is used to extend DRQ beyond the end of $\overline{IOW}$, preventing a WAIT-state request until the data byte has been transferred.

The rising edge of $\overline{IOW}$ (or $\overline{IOR}$ for a read operation) enables the flip-flop (which now follows DRQ), and a logic 0 is applied to the READY input of the DMAC. The DMAC samples this input during S3 and inserts WAIT states until READY again goes high. This occurs when the data byte has been written and the data register is again empty (DRQ = 1).

Although using the DMAC's READY input is an effective way of synchronizing the disk drive to the DMAC for block mode transfers, this technique may not always be the best choice. Assuming 0.8 μs for the data transfer and a worst-case response time to the DMA

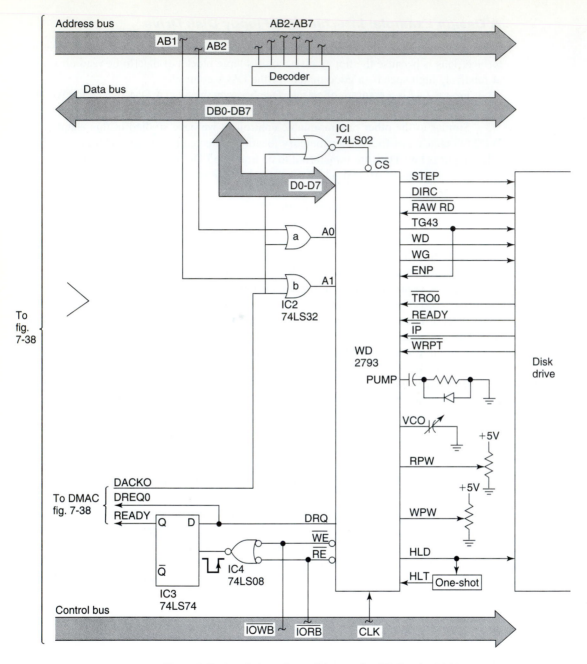

Figure 7.47 Interfacing a floppy disk controller (FDC) using DMA.

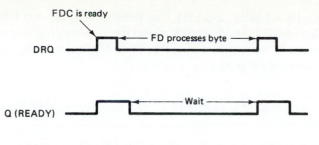

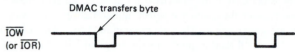

Figure 7.48 DRQ is extended to the rising edge of $\overline{IOW}$ and used as the READY input to the DMAC. WAIT states are inserted until DRQ again returns high.

```
;INITIALIZATION ROUTINE FOR THE FDC IN FIG. 7-47
;
;THIS ROUTINE WILL WRITE 1K BYTES TO THE DISK WHEN
;THE FDC DRQ OUTPUT GOES HIGH.
;
;THE PROGRAM FOLLOWS THE FLOW CHART IN FIG. 7-45
;
OUT     0FDH            ;MASTER CLEAR
MVI     A,04            ;DISABLE DMAC UNTIL PROGRAMMED
OUT     0F8H            ;COMMAND REGISTER
;
;PROGRAM MODE REGISTER FOR CHANNEL 0, READ MODE,
;AUTOINITIALIZATION, ADDRESS INCREMENT, BLOCK MODE
;
MVI     A,98H           ;MODE WORD CHANNEL 0
OUT     0FBH            ;MODE REGISTER
;
;UNMASK CHANNEL 0 (AFTER MASTER CLEAR)
;
MVI     A,0             ;CLEAR CHANNEL 0 MASK
OUT     0FAH            ;MASK REGISTER
;
;PROGRAM CHANNEL 0 MEMORY ADDRESS AND WORD COUNT
;
MVI     A,0             ;LOW ORDER ADDRESS
OUT     0F0H            ;CHANNEL 0
MVI     A,80H           ;HIGH ORDER ADDRESS
OUT     0F0H            ;CHANNEL 0
MVI     A,0FFH          ;LOW ORDER WORD COUNT
OUT     0F1H            ;CHANNEL 0
MVI     A,3FH           ;HIGH ORDER WORD COUNT
OUT     0F1H            ;CHANNEL 0
;
;PROGRAM COMMAND REGISTER FOR DREQ AND DACK
;SENSE, LATE WRITE, FIXED PRIORITY, NORMAL TIMING,
;AND ENABLE CONTROLLER
;
MVI     A,80H           ;COMMAND WORD
OUT     0F8H            ;COMMAND REGISTER
;
;NORMALLY THE MICROPROCESSOR WOULD NOW SEND A "WRITE
;SECTOR" COMMAND TO THE FDC AND IT WOULD RESPOND BY
;RAISING DRQ INITIATIING THE 1K BYTE TRANSFER.
```

Figure 7.49 Initialization routine for Example 7.19.

request of 3.5 μs (7 T states with a 2-MHz clock), 11.7 μs remains until the next DRQ pulse from the disk drive. If byte mode (instead of block mode) transfers are programmed, one or two CPU instructions can be performed during this "WAIT" time, resulting in a more efficient use of the resources of the processor.

Example 7.19

Write the initialization routine required to transfer 1K of data from address 8000H to the drive interface in Fig. 7.47.

Solution. Following the steps outlined in the flowchart in Fig. 7.45, we set a master clear and then program the mode register for channel 0 select, autoinitialize, block mode, and write transfers. The address and word count registers are programmed next. After clearing the mask bit for channel 0, the command register programs the sense of DREQ and DACK to match the WD2793, and initialization is complete. The program is given in Fig. 7.49.

SELF-REVIEW 7.5

7.5.1 What two signals are used by the 8080 and 8085 microprocessors to accept and acknowledge DMA cycles?

7.5.2 Why must the CPU put its buses in a tristate condition during DMA cycles?

7.5.3 When a peripheral is ready for a DMA transfer to begin, it activates one of the four _____ inputs of the 8237A.

7.5.4 How many different I/O ports does the 8237A occupy?

7.5.5 How does the 8237A learn the source and destination memory addresses and the number of bytes involved in a DMA transfer?

7.6 BUFFERING THE DMA CONTROLLER

Introduction

In Chapter 4, we learned that the microprocessor is ill equipped to drive the loads presented by the memory and I/O devices. Bus buffers were required to supply the necessary current. It should come as no surprise, then, that the peripheral controller chips we have been studying in the current chapter will also require buffers. And if DMA is to be accommodated, bidirectional buffers will be necessary on all three buses.

In this section, we:

* Show how to provide bus buffers for a DMA controller.
* Show how to control the direction of a bidirectional bus buffer when a DMA controller is used.

Bidirectional Buffers

When a DMA controller is to be interfaced, the control, data, and address bus lines must all be bidirectional. This is because during DMA cycles the DMAC will be driving the buses, but during non-DMA cycles the processor will be driving the buses.

Figure 7.50 illustrates the bus buffering required for a general I/O module that includes a DMA controller. Bidirectional bus buffers, used on all three sets of bus lines, are enabled by the signal MODULE SELECT + DMA. This signal is obtained from an address decoder and the DMA acknowledge signal. It will go low when any support device in the I/O module is selected or whenever a DMA operation is occurring.

The direction of the data bus buffer is controlled by DMA WRITE + CPU READ. This signal is active whenever the CPU performs a read operation or the DMAC performs a write operation. If the signal is inactive, the buffers default to the write mode, presenting their inputs to the system data bus lines.

The last control signal is DMA. This signal is active for DMA read or write cycles and is used to turn the control and address bus lines around (that is, make them outputs onto the bus) when DMA cycles are performed.

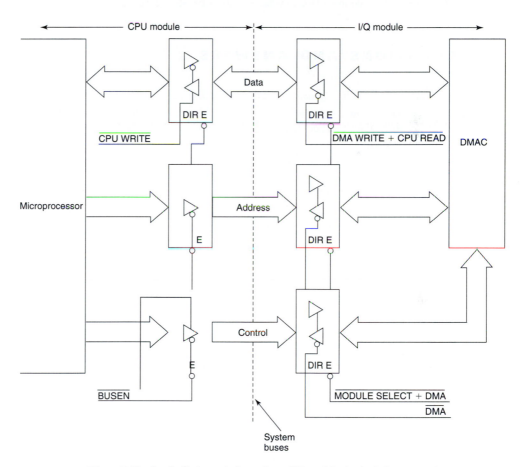

Figure 7.50 Bus buffering techniques for an I/O module that includes a DMAC.

Of course, when DMA is not implemented, the control and address buffers can be unidirectional and left permanently enabled. In small systems, no buffering is required, and the control, address, and data bus lines can be connected directly to the CPU. In this case, the CPU and DMAC will control the direction of the bus lines "automatically." Chapter 4 provides guidelines for determining what is considered a "small system."

SELF-REVIEW 7.6

7.6.1 Why must the address and control bus buffers connected to a DMAC be bidirectional?

7.6.2 In Fig. 7.50, during a DMA cycle, we expect $\overline{\text{BUSEN}}$ to be _____ .

QUESTIONS AND ANSWERS

Q: *What is meant by a programmable I/O support device?*

A: These devices contain special-purpose I/O circuitry in a single chip. For example, the 8255A PPI contains three parallel I/O ports, each of which can be programmed to function as an input or output port.

Q: *What two components, when added to an 8085 processor, form a three-chip microcomputer system?*

A: The 8755A 2K-byte ROM with bit-programmable I/O and the 8185 1K-byte RAM.

Q: *List the major operating modes of the 8255A programmable peripheral interface.*

A: Simple I/O, strobed I/O with full handshaking, and bidirectional I/O. The last two modes support both polling and interrupts.

Q: *How is the 8255A programmed?*

A: A single byte must be written to the control port.

Q: *List the major operating modes of the 8254A programmable interval timer.*

A: Event counter, one-shot, divide-by-N counter, and hardware- or software-initiated strobe pulse generator.

Q: *How is the 8254 programmed?*

A: A single byte must be written to the control port for each counter, followed by 1 or 2 bytes to specify the initial count.

Q: *What is the purpose of the 8259A programmable interrupt controller?*

A: The controller is designed to enhance the limited interrupt capabilities of the 8080 processor by providing eight separate interrupt inputs. It can also be used as an interrupt support device for the 8088 and 8086 16-bit microprocessors.

Q: *How does the 8259A connect to the processor?*

A: The 8259A interfaces to the processor's data bus lines and drives the INTR input of the CPU. It allows as many as 64 separate interrupt requests to be prioritized and vectored to jump tables in the processor's memory space.

Q: *How is the 8259A programmed?*

A: Two to four initialization control words (ICWs) must first be written, followed by three operation control words (OCWs).

Q: *How many I/O channels does the 8237A DMA controller support? What types of DMA transfers are possible?*

A: Four DMA channels are provided for memory-to-I/O, I/O-to-memory, and memory-to-memory DMA transfers.

Q: *How does the 8237A manage DMA transfers?*

A: The 8237A automatically takes care of incrementing (or decrementing) the memory address and testing the byte counter for a DMA transfer. This makes it useful for interfacing high-speed peripherals such as floppy and hard-disk drives that are too fast for interrupt-driven techniques.

Q: *How is the 8237A programmed?*

A: First a master clear command is given, followed by an operating mode command for each channel. Next, the mask register is written to define which channels will be allowed to process DMA requests. The current address and word count registers must then be specified for each channel. Finally, the chip is enabled by writing to the command register.

Q: *Are special bus buffers required when one interfaces a DMA controller?*

A: Because the DMAC must drive the buses during DMA cycles, but receive data off the bus during non-DMA cycles, bidirectional bus buffers are required on all three of the DMAC's buses (address, data, and control).

LAB PROJECTS

7.1. Study the schematic diagram of the microcomputer you are using to support this text or course, and see whether your computer uses an 8255A PPI. If so, answer the following questions about the interface:
  (a) Is the PPI I/O or memory mapped?
  (b) To what range of addresses is the chip mapped?
  (c) List the I/O devices (if any) connected to ports A, B, and C.

7.2. Write a program to access your computer's 8255A. For example, if a keypad and display are interfaced, write a program to read the keyboard and display the key's value. If a speaker is connected to one output bit, write a program to produce a tone. (Program 14 in Chapter 3 is an example of a computer music program.)

7.3. Using Fig. 7.51 as a guide, build the memory-mapped 8255A interface shown. Problems 7.12–15 suggest several control programs that can be written.

7.4. Construct the mode 0 8255A parallel-printer interface shown in Fig. 7.10. The program in Fig. 7.11 can be used to send (ASCII) data to the printer. By programming the 8255A for mode 1 and connecting INTRA to INTR of the CPU, the same interface can be used to control the printer in an interrupt-driven mode. This arrangement is shown in Fig. 7.16. A female DB-25 connector with long wires attached can be used to allow easy access to the printer signals.

7.5. Repeat Lab Project 7.1 for the 8254 PIT.

7.6. Using a circuit similar to Fig. 7.23, program one of the outputs of the 8254:
  (a) as a one-shot triggered by the gate input.
  (b) as a divide-by-N counter. Use a signal generator as the CLK input, and observe the output on an oscilloscope.

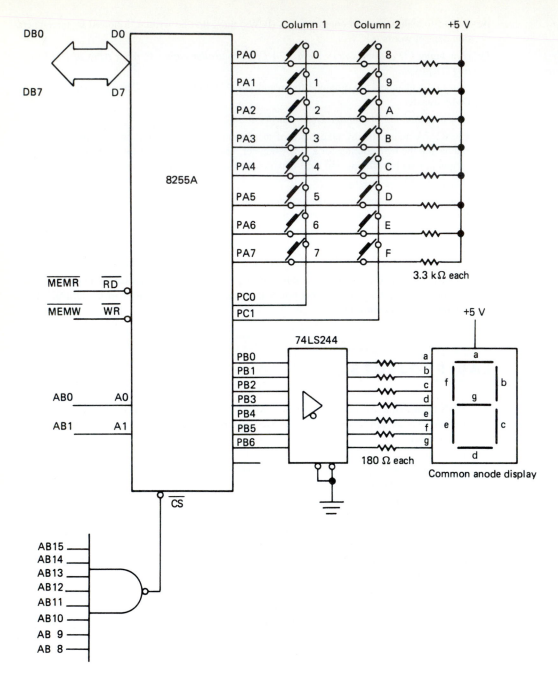

Figure 7.51 8255A interface for Lab Project 7.3 and Problems 7.12–15.

QUESTIONS AND PROBLEMS

Section 7.1

7.1. Write the instructions necessary to program the 8755A in Fig. 7.2 so that PA0–PA4 and PB0–PB6 are outputs and the remaining pins are inputs.

7.2. Suppose that IO/$\overline{\text{M}}$ and A10 are combined via an AND gate and the output is connected to the IO/$\overline{\text{M}}$ input of the 8755A in Fig. 7.2. Determine the resulting addresses of the four 8755A I/O ports.

7.3. Suppose that the three-chip 8085 computer in Fig. 7.4 has been built and that it is desired to test the two 8755A ports. Assuming that the two ports are wired in parallel, devise a test program that outputs data to port A and reads the data back from port B, branching to an error routine if the input and output do not agree.

7.4. Refer to the three-chip 8085 computer in Fig. 7.4, and show how to add a matrix of 16 key switches memory mapped to page FF of the 8085's memory space. (*Hint:* Review Fig. 6.8.)

7.5. Refer to the three-chip 8085 computer in Fig. 7.4, and show how to add two decoded seven-segment displays to port B.

7.6. Draw a memory and I/O map for the 8085 computer in Fig. 7.4, including the keypad and LED displays described in Problems 7.4 and 7.5.

Section 7.2

7.7. Determine the control byte required for each of the following 8255A configurations:
(a) Set PC5 using the bit set/reset mode.
(b) Mode 0: port A = input, port B = output, PC7–PC4 = output, PC3–PC0 = input.
(c) Port A = mode 1 output, port B = mode 1 input, and PC4 and PC5 = inputs.
(d) Port A is bidirectional, port B = mode 0 output, and PC0–2 = inputs.

7.8. The following program is written to control the 8255A in Fig. 7.6:

```
SET    MVI    A,07H
       OUT    0F3H
       CALL   WAIT      ;0.5-ms time delay
       MVI    A,06H
       OUT    0F3H
       CALL   WAIT      ;0.5-ms delay
       JMP    SET
```

What does this program do?

*7.9. A technician is testing the 8255A interface in Fig. 7.6 and has wired ports A and B in parallel. The test program in Fig. 7.52 is run, but constantly jumps to the error routine. What do you think is wrong?

7.10. Answer the following questions about the 8255A keyboard interface and control program in Figs. 7.8 and 7.9:
(a) To read only column 1, PC6 must be _____ and PC7 must be _____ .
(b) If only key 6 is held down, what is the value of register A after the KREAD subroutine returns?
(c) If keys 4, 7, and 8 are all held down simultaneously, which key value will be encoded?

```
          MVI    A,82H    ;A = output and B = input

          OUT    F2H      ;port C

          MVI    A,0      ;starting pattern

LOOP      MOV    B,A      ;save in B

          OUT    FOH      ;output to A

          IN     F1H      ;read back on B

          CMP    B        ;same ?

          JNZ    ERROR    ;if not then error

          INR    A        ;next pattern

          JNZ    LOOP     ;done?

          RET
```

Figure 7.52   8255A test program for Problem 7.9.

7.11. Explain how the parallel-printer interface in Fig. 7.10 generates the printer $\overline{\text{STROBE}}$ pulse without using a one-shot.

7.12. Refer to the 8255A interface in Fig. 7.51 to answer the following questions:
  (a) Specify the value of the required control byte. Assume mode 0 operation.
  (b) Is the PPI memory or I/O mapped?
  (c) Specify the range of port addresses to which the PPI chip will respond.
  (d) To read any of the keys 0–7, PC0 must be _____ and PCI must be _____ .
  (e) What hex byte must be output to port B to cause the number 5 to appear in the seven-segment display?

7.13. Write a subroutine to read the key matrix in Fig. 7.51 and return with the key value (0–F) in register A, bits 0–3.

7.14. Write a subroutine that reads the low 4 bits of the accumulator and displays the results as a hex number in the seven-segment display shown in Fig. 7.51. (*Hint:* Use A as the index into a 16-byte seven-segment code table.)

7.15. Combine the two subroutines from Problems 7.13 and 7.14 to write a program that reads the key matrix and displays the last key pressed in the display.

*7.16. Suppose that the seven-segment display in Fig. 7.51 is always dark, even when the test program in Problem 7.14 is run. Which of the following problems could account for this symptom?
  (a) One of the keys in the keyboard is stuck closed.
  (b) The outputs of the 74LS244 are stuck low.
  (c) The tristate enable inputs of the 74LS244 are open.
  (d) The 3.3K resistors have accidentally been replaced with 33K resistors.

7.17. Answer the following questions about the 8255A interrupt-driven printer interface in Fig. 7.16:
  (a) How does the printer "know" when data are available to be read?
  (b) What signal causes the $\overline{\text{STROBE}}$ pulse to terminate?
  (c) How does the CPU "know" when to write another byte of data to the 8255A?

```
             MVI    A,30H          ;set counter mode

             OUT    F3H

             MVI    A,00           ;load time delay parameter

             OUT    F0H

             MVI    A,80H

             OUT    F0H

      WAIT   MVI    A,E2           ;poll the counter

             OUT    F3H

             IN     F0H

             RAL

             JNC    WAIT           ;wait until done

             RET
```

Figure 7.53   Program for Problem 7.19.

Section 7.3

7.18. Specify the 8254 control words required to do the following:
  (a) set program counter 1 for mode 5, BCD, 16-bit count.
  (b) latch the status of counter 0.
  (c) latch the count of counters 0 and 1.

7.19. Assume the port addresses in Fig. 7.23. The following questions refer to the 8254 time-delay subroutine in Fig. 7.53:
  (a) Which of the 8254 counters is being used?
  (b) What is the counter mode?
  (c) Why is it necessary to *poll* the counter?
  (d) If the clock input is 2 MHz, what is the time delay produced by this program?

7.20. What changes are needed in the frequency counter program in Fig. 7.27 to allow a maximum frequency of 99,990 Hz with 10-Hz resolution?

7.21. Suppose that the CLK2 input of the 8254 in Fig. 7.23 is connected to the 2-MHz system clock signal. Write the program required to produce a 1-KHz 50% duty-cycle square wave at OUT2. Assume that GATE2 is wired high.

7.22. Study the 8254 interface in Fig. 7.54. Specify the port addresses of the three counters and the control port.

7.23. Because partial decoding is used, the 8254 interface in Fig. 7.54 responds to a *range* of addresses. Calculate the total number of addresses in this range.

7.24. Suppose that counter 0 of the 8254 in Fig. 7.54 is to be used as a hardware-triggered one-shot. Design the hardware and write the software to produce a 10-s pulse. Assume a 2-MHz system clock as the time base. (*Hint:* Use counter 1 to frequency divide the 2-MHz signal for counter 0.)

7.25. Design the hardware and write the software to convert the 8254 into a digital stopwatch with .01-s resolution. Your design should provide a run/stop switch and accumulate times to 99.99 s.

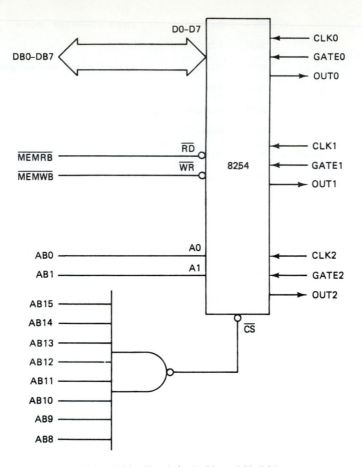

Figure 7.54 Circuit for Problems 7.22–7.24.

Section 7.4

7.26. Suppose that a PIC programmed for the *fully nested mode* is servicing an interrupt on IR5. If an interrupt occurs on IR6, will the IR5 service routine be interrupted? Does the 8085 allow lower priority interrupts to interrupt higher priority service routines that are in progress?

7.27. Write the initialization routine to program the PIC in Fig. 7.29 for the following conditions:
  (a) Jump table on page 8000H
  (b) Four-byte interval
  (c) Rising-edge trigger
  (d) Interrupts 0 and 1 masked
  (e) Rotating equal priority

7.28. Suppose that the PIC described in Problem 7.27 currently has the following interrupt priority structure:

lowest								highest
4	3	2	1	0	7	6	5	4

If the IR3 service routine is in progress, can IR5 interrupt this routine? Sketch the new priority structure after IR3 and IR5 have been serviced.

7.29. An interrupt service routine written for the PIC in Fig. 7.29 ends with the following instruction sequence:

```
MVI   A,E2H
OUT   F0H
RET
```

How does the PIC interpret these instructions?

7.30. Using the port assignments shown in Fig. 7.29, write the instruction sequences required to do each of the following:
(a) read the interrupt mask register.
(b) read the in-service register.
(c) set the special mask mode.

7.31. If eight interrupts occur simultaneously and the PIC is programmed for equal rotating priority, in the worst case, how long might one device have to wait for service?

Section 7.5

7.32. When doing a memory-to-I/O DMA transfer, the 8237A will simultaneously activate the _____ and _____ control bus signals.

7.33. What is the purpose of the $\overline{\text{BUSEN}}$ signal in the 8080 and 8085 CPU modules shown in Figs. 4.25 and 4.26?

7.34. Indicate the logic level (high or low) for each of the signals listed in the following table, for idle and active 8237A modes.

Signal	Idle mode	Active mode
HRQ		
HLDA		
AEN		
DREQn		
DACKn		
ADSTB		

7.35. One channel of the 8237A is required for I/O-to-memory and memory-to-I/O DMA transfers. However, memory-to-memory DMA transfers require two channels. Explain.

7.36. Calculate the time required to fill 100 bytes of RAM using the DMA interface in Fig. 7.38 and the control program in Fig. 7.46. Assume noncompressed timing and a 200-ns 8237A clock period. Compare the time against the 8080/85 block-fill program of Fig. 3.13, Program 7. Assume a 2-MHz 8080 or 3-MHz 8085 CPU.

7.37. What byte should be written to the 8237A mode register if it is desired to transfer 16K bytes of data from memory to a disk drive using channel 2? Enable autoinitialization and select address increment.

Section 7.6

7.38. Figure 7.55 shows an 8255A interface with a bidirectional data bus buffer.
What signals should be connected to DIR and $\overline{\text{E}}$ to properly control this buffer?

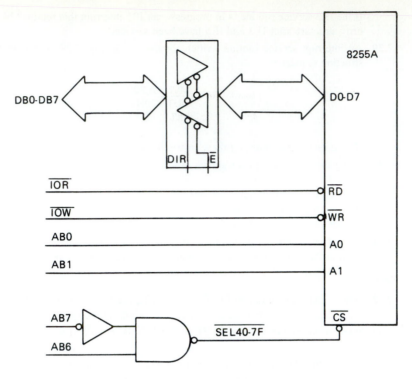

Figure 7.55 Circuit for Problem 7.39.

*7.39. A technician designing the 8255A interface in Fig. 7.55 connects $\overline{E}$ to ground and DIR to $\overline{IOR}$. She finds that the computer appears to power on properly, but the keyboard now produces "odd" characters. What do you think is wrong?

SELF-REVIEW ANSWERS

7.1.1. 2K, 2

7.1.2. 0FH

7.2.1. three, one

7.2.2. bit 7 (1 → mode set, 0 → bit set/reset)

7.2.3. 8BH

7.2.4. mode 1

7.2.5. Set or reset individual bits of port C, and mask or enable interrupts on the mode 1 and 2 INTR outputs.

7.2.6. bidirectional

7.3.1. three

7.3.2. standard, counter latch, read-back

7.3.3. mode 3

7.3.4. BCD

7.4.1. eight

7.4.2. CALL

7.4.3. The ICWs specify hardware parameters: vector address and trigger. The OCWs specify the software arbitration modes and masks.

7.4.4. rotating equal priority

7.4.5. IR3

7.5.1. HOLD and HLDA

7.5.2. To avoid bus contention with the DMAC.

7.5.3. DREQ

7.5.4. 16

7.5.5. This information must be programmed into the appropriate DMAC registers before the transfer begins.

7.6.1. When the DMAC is being programmed, address and control signals are output to the DMAC. During DMA cycles, the DMAC outputs these signals.

7.6.2 inactive

8

SPECIAL-PURPOSE SUPPORT DEVICES: THE Z-80 FAMILY

OUTLINE

OBJECTIVES

After completing this chapter, you should be able to:

- Describe each of the Z-80 PIO operating modes and specify the software control word for each.
- Show how to use the Z-80 PIO to construct a six-digit multiplexed seven-segment LED display.
- Compare the Z-80 CTC timer and counter modes and specify the control words for each.
- Program the Z-80 CTC to function as a one-shot.
- Describe the DMA sequence for the Z-80 DMA in byte, burst, and continuous modes.
- Explain how to access and program the read/write registers of the Z-80 DMA.

OVERVIEW

Like the 8080 and 8085, the Z-80 microprocessor is supported by a number of special peripheral support devices. (See Table 8.1.) These chips are designed to eliminate the discrete logic parts that would normally be required to construct serial and parallel I/O parts, direct memory access interfaces, modem interfaces, and circuits to count or time events.

The parts are available in two forms: as individual functions (the Z-80 PIO, the Z-80 DMA, the Z-80 CTC, and the Z-80 SIO) or as complete integrated systems. The Z84C90, for example, integrates the PIO, CTC, and SIO in a single package. The Z84015 is essentially a *computer on a chip,* incorporating a Z-80 processor along with the PIO, CTC, and SIO functions.

The most powerful feature of the peripheral controllers is that they are *programmable* by the CPU. By writing to special control ports within the device, the "personality" of the part can be changed "on the fly." The controllers also support the Z-80 "daisy-chain" priority structure and can be programmed to output any desired vector during INTA.

Because the Z-80 CPU module can be made to look exactly like an 8080, all of the 8080 support devices covered in Chapter 7, including the 8255A, 8254, 8259A, and 8237A, can be interfaced to the Z-80. Of these devices, the 8255A programmable peripheral interface, or PPI, would be the most useful. The PPI is similar to the Z-80 PIO, but offers three I/O ports. The 8259A programmable interrupt controller can be interfaced to the Z-80, but doing so would not be logical because the Z-80 processor already has similar interrupt capabilities.

The 8085 support devices covered in Chapter 7 cannot be interfaced to the Z-80 without considerable external logic, due to the multiplexed data bus of the 8085.

The Z-80 support devices to be discussed in this chapter include the Z-80 PIO, the Z-80 CTC, and the Z-80 DMA, which require decoding of IORQ, RD, and M1 to generate IOR, IOW, RESET, and INTA. For this reason, there are parts not (normally) compatible with the 8080 or 8085. In addition, they take advantage of the Z-80's mode 2 interrupts not supported by the 8080 or 8085.

TABLE 8.1 Peripheral Support Devices for Z-80 Microprocessor

Part number	Description
Z8410/C10	Direct memory access (DMA) controller
Z8420/C20	Parallel input/output (PIO) controller
Z8430/C30	Counter/timer circuit (CTC)
Z8440/C40	Serial input/output (SIO) controller
Z8470	Dual asynchronous receiver/transmitter (DART)
Z84C90	Serial/parallel/counter/timer (KIO). Integrates in one chip the functions of the PIO, CTC, and SIO, including an onboard crystal oscillator.
Z84015/C15	Intelligent peripheral controller (IPC). Integrates in one chip the functions of the Z-80 CPU, plus PIO, CTC, SIO, watch dog timer (WDT), and clock generator controller (CGC).

8.1 THE Z8420 PARALLEL INPUT/OUTPUT CONTROLLER

Introduction

The Z8420 (usually called the Z-80 PIO) provides two 8-bit input/output ports, each supported by two handshaking signals, labeled $\overline{STB}$ (strobe) and RDY (ready). The four operating modes of the PIO are defined and compared with the operating modes of the 8255A in Table 8.2. The two parts are comparable, except that the PIO has a bit-programmable mode that is not supported by the 8255A. The 8255A also has three I/O ports, compared with the PIO's two.

In this section, we:

- Describe each of the Z-80 PIO operating modes and specify the software control word for each.
- Show how to use the Z-80 PIO to construct a six-digit multiplexed seven-segment LED display.

Pinout diagram.   Figure 8.1 provides a pinout diagram of the PIO. Note that three pins are devoted to interrupt control: $\overline{INT}$, interrupt enable in (IEI), and interrupt enable out (IEO). $\overline{INT}$ connects directly to the $\overline{INT}$ input of the Z-80, and IEI and IEO are used when several PIOs (or other support devices) are connected in a daisy-chain priority interrupt structure. To use this feature, the PIO must be programmed for a (Z-80) mode 2 interrupt vector.

Interfacing the Z-80 PIO

Figure 8.2 illustrates an interface between the Z-80 microprocessor and the Z-80 PIO. Note that the PIO is directly compatible with the Z-80 control signals (and therefore does not require the control bus decoding shown in the Z-80 CPU module in Fig. 4.27).

Another interesting feature is the omission of the $\overline{WR}$ control signal. Because of a limited number of package pins, Zilog has chosen to have the PIO internally decode $\overline{IORQ}$, $\overline{M1}$, and $\overline{RD}$. From these three signals, five processor activities are decoded, as shown in Table 8.3. The $\overline{WR}$ signal is not required, because $\overline{IOW}$ can be assumed when $\overline{IORQ}$ is active, $\overline{M1}$ inactive, and $\overline{RD}$ high.

TABLE 8.2   Operating Modes of the Z-80 PIO

Mode	Function	8255A mode
0	8-bit output port with two handshaking signals	1
1	8-bit input port with two handshaking signals	1
2	Bidirectional data port with four handshaking signals[a]	2
3	Bit-programmable input/output port	None[b]

[a]Port A is the bidirectional port; port B must be programmed for mode 3.

[b]Similar to 8255A mode 0, but each PIO pin can be individually programmed.

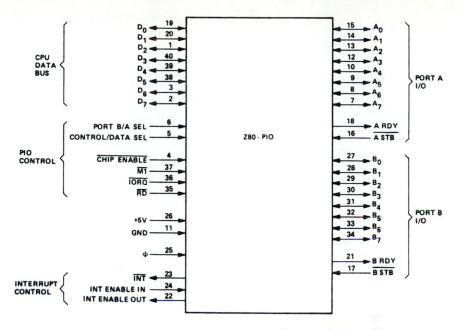

Figure 8.1   Pin definitions for the Z-80 PIO. (Courtesy of Zilog, Inc.)

The $\overline{\text{INTA}}$ decoding is standard, as the Z-80 does not output an $\overline{\text{INTA}}$ signal. The instruction fetch decoding is required so that the RETI op code can be detected and the daisy-chain IEO output pin reset. (See Chapter 6 for a detailed discussion of the Z-80's daisy-chain interrupt capabilities.)

The designers ran out of pins when it came time to provide a reset. By holding $\overline{\text{IORQ}}$ and $\overline{\text{RD}}$ inactive and applying 0 V to $\overline{\text{M1}}$, the reset function can be accomplished. The PIO also performs a power-on reset.

To the programmer, the PIO appears to be four I/O ports. (Memory mapping is not allowed.) Table 8.4 specifies the four port addresses for the circuit in Fig. 8.2. AB0, connected to $\text{C}/\overline{\text{D}}$, controls the selection of the control port or data port. AB1, connected to $\text{B}/\overline{\text{A}}$, determines which of the two ports, A or B, will be selected.

IEI is shown connected to +5 V in Fig. 8.2. The daisy-chain priority structure allows an interrupt request only if IEI is a logic 1. When the request occurs, IEO is forced low. By connecting IEO to the next-*lowest*-priority IEI input, lower priority devices are prevented from interrupting higher priority service routines. Figure 8.3 illustrates typical IEI and IEO connections when several PIO chips are involved.

The Z-80 acknowledges an interrupt request by outputting $\overline{\text{IORQ}}$ and $\overline{\text{M1}}$ low. The active PIO responds by placing its 7-bit interrupt vector onto the data bus at this time. Control is then transferred to the address stored in the memory location formed by register I (the high-order address) and the 7-bit vector from the PIO.

The interrupt service routine is expected to terminate with an $\overline{\text{RETI}}$ instruction. The PIO detects the op code for this instruction and resets its IEO output, allowing lower priority devices access to the Z-80.

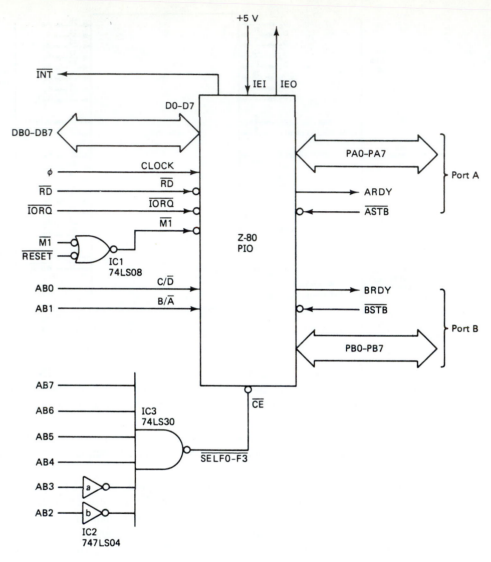

Figure 8.2 Interfacing the Z-80 PIO to the three-bus system architecture of the Z-80 microprocessor.

Programming the Z-80 PIO

Each PIO port is programmed by writing a control word (or words) to the corresponding control port. There are four basic control words:

1. Mode control word
2. Interrupt control word
3. Interrupt disable control word
4. Interrupt vector control word

TABLE 8.3 Internal PIO Control Bus Decoding

$\overline{IORQ}$	$\overline{RD}$	$\overline{M1}$	Internally decoded to:
0	0	0	Inactive
0	0	1	$\overline{IOR}$
0	1	0	$\overline{INTA}$
0	1	1	$\overline{IOW}$
1	0	0	Instruction fetch
1	0	1	Inactive
1	1	0	Reset
1	1	1	Inactive

Table 8.5 illustrates the bit assignments for each of these control words. Although each word is written to the same address, the PIO examines bits 0–3 to determine which control word is being written. For example, if bits 0–3 are 1111, the mode control word is specified.

Note that in two cases—the mode control word and the interrupt control word—a 2-byte sequence may be required. If the mode control word selects mode 3, a second write will be required to define each pin as an input or an output.

When the interrupt control word is selected, the PIO will generate an interrupt when a certain condition occurs on the port data pins (programmed as mode 3 inputs). In this case a mask word can be written, masking some of the input pins from consideration.

Example 8.1

Program port B of the PIO in Fig. 8.2 for mode 3 such that an interrupt will be generated if bit 0, 1, 4, *OR* 7 is high. Program bits 2, 3, and 6 as outputs and bits 0, 1, 4, 5, and 7 as inputs.

Solution. The program is given in Fig. 8.4. It begins by programming port B for mode 3 and then specifying the input/output pin combinations. Next, the interrupt control word is written, followed by a mask word for bits 0, 1, 4, and 7 (the only bits to be considered).

When interrupts are to be used, the (Z-80) mode 2 interrupt vector must be programmed into the PIO. This is the purpose of the interrupt vector control word.

TABLE 8.4 Port Definitions and Addresses for the Z-80 PIO Interface in Fig. 8.2

AB1 (B/$\overline{A}$)	AB0 (C/$\overline{D}$)	Figure 8.2 port address	Register selection
0	0	F0	Port A data
0	1	F1	Port A control
1	0	F2	Port B data
1	1	F3	Port B control

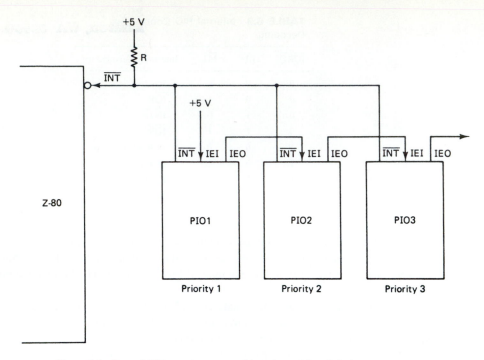

Figure 8.3   Several PIOs can be connected by using a daisy-chain interrupt structure.

Example 8.2

Assume that the Z-80 maintains a jump table at memory address FC80H. Write the code required to enable an interrupt at PIO port B to vector to this address.

Solution.   The program is as follows:

```
IM      2           ;MODE 2 INTERRUPTS
LD      A,0FCH      ;HIGH-ORDER ADDRESS
LD      I,A         ;COPY TO REGISTER I
LD      A,80H       ;LOW-ORDER ADDRESS
OUT     (0F3H),A    ;PORT B INTERRUPT VECTOR
```

The address of the ISR for port B should be stored in FC80 and FC81. Note that one page of RAM can accommodate 64 PIOs.

In some cases, it might be desirable to be able to disable interrupts for the PIO without changing the interrupt control word. This is the purpose of the interrupt disable control word. Writing 03H to the desired port disables interrupts; 83H enables interrupts.

Finally, note that when the PIO is reset, both the port A and port B mask registers are set (masking all port data bits), the port data bus lines are set to a high impedance, ARDY and BRDY are low, and mode 1 is automatically selected. In addition, interrupts are disabled for both ports, but the vector address registers are not affected. Both port data registers are reset.

TABLE 8.5 Four Control Words are Used to Specify the Operating Conditions of the Z-80 PIO

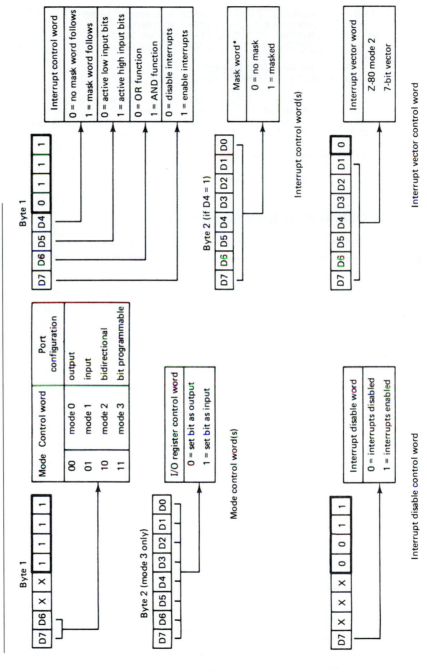

Byte 1

D7	D6	X	1	1	1	1

Mode	Control word	Port configuration
00	mode 0	output
01	mode 1	input
10	mode 2	bidirectional
11	mode 3	bit programmable

Byte 2 (mode 3 only)

D7	D6	D5	D4	D3	D2	D1	D0

I/O register control word
0 = set bit as output
1 = set bit as input

Mode control word(s)

Byte 1

D7	D6	D5	D4	0	1	1	1

Interrupt control word
0 = no mask word follows
1 = mask word follows
0 = active low input bits
1 = active high input bits
0 = OR function
1 = AND function
0 = disable interrupts
1 = enable interrupts

Byte 2 (if D4 = 1)

D7	D6	D5	D4	D3	D2	D1	D0

Mask word*
0 = no mask
1 = masked

Interrupt control word(s)

D7	X	X	X	0	0	1	1

Interrupt disable word
0 = interrupts disabled
1 = interrupts enabled

Interrupt disable control word

D7	D6	D5	D4	D3	D2	D1	0

Interrupt vector word
Z-80 mode 2
7-bit vector

Interrupt vector control word

*The nonmasked pins must be defined as mode 3 inputs.

413

```
;PROGRAM TO DEMONSTRATE Z-80 PIO PROGRAMMING
;
;PORT 3 IS PROGRAMMED FOR MODE 3 SUCH THAT AN
;INTERRUPT IS REQUESTED IF BITS 0,1,4 OR 7 ARE HIGH.
;
LD       A,OCFH          ;MODE 3 CONTROL WORD
OUT      (OF3H),A        ;PORT B CONTROL
LD       A,OB3H          ;I/O BIT SELECTION
OUT      (OF3H),A        ;PORT B CONTROL
;
;PORT B IS NOW CONFIGURED
;NOW SPECIFY INTERRUPT CONDITIONS
;
LD       A,OB7           ;INTERRUPT CONTROL WORD
OUT      (OF3H),A        ;PORT B CONTROL
LD       A,6CH           ;MASK WORD FOR BITS 0,1,4 AND 7
OUT      (OF3H),A        ;PORT B CONTROL
;
;INITIALIZATION IS COMPLETE
```

Figure 8.4   Program for Example 8.1.

Mode 0: Output Port with Handshake

Figure 8.5 illustrates the timing relationships among READY, $\overline{\text{STROBE}}$, and $\overline{\text{INT}}$ when a data port is programmed for mode 0 output. Because the PIO does not have a $\overline{\text{WR}}$ input, a pseudowrite signal ($\overline{\text{WR}}*$) is derived from $\overline{\text{RD}}$ and $\overline{\text{IORQ}}$.

When data are written to the PIO in mode 0, the READY line is driven high on the first falling edge of the clock after the trailing edge of $\overline{\text{WR}}*$. This is an indication to the peripheral that data is available to be read. The PIO takes no further action.

The peripheral, upon "seeing" READY high, accepts the data and applies a $\overline{\text{STROBE}}$ pulse, indicating to the PIO that the data has been received. Following the trailing edge of $\overline{\text{STROBE}}$, and assuming that interrupts are enabled, the PIO will force $\overline{\text{INT}}$ low, requesting an interrupt from the Z-80. The READY line will also be reset on the first falling edge of ϕ after $\overline{\text{STROBE}}$. In most cases, the interrupt service routine will respond by writing a new data byte to the PIO.

Example 8.3

Explain the output obtained if the PIO's READY output is connected to the $\overline{\text{STROBE}}$ input as shown in Fig. 8.6(a).

Solution.   The timing is shown in Fig. 8.6(b). Before the CPU initiates a write cycle, the READY output will hold the $\overline{\text{STROBE}}$ input low. READY will be forced high on the first falling edge of ϕ after $\overline{\text{WR}}*$. But because READY is reset by the rising edge of $\overline{\text{STROBE}}$, it

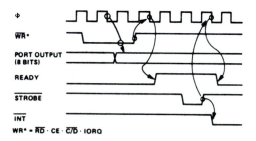

Figure 8.5   Mode 0 Z-80 PIO output timing. (Courtesy of Zilog, Inc.)

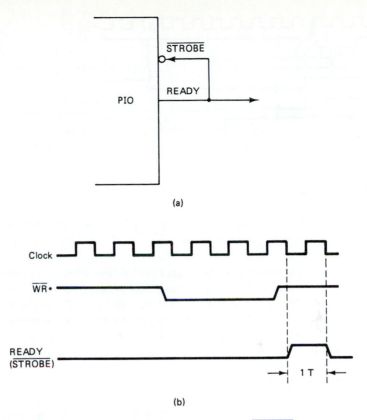

(a)

(b)

Figure 8.6 (a) Connecting the PIO's READY output to its $\overline{\text{STROBE}}$ input produces an active high pulse (b) for one clock period.

returns low on the falling edge of the next clock pulse. The result is an active-high pulse with a duration of one clock period.

Some peripherals require a $\overline{\text{STROBE}}$ pulse rather than a level-sensitive trigger achieved with the conventional PIO timing. In these cases, the $\overline{\text{STROBE}}$ pulse is used by the peripheral to latch the data output by the PIO. However, the peripheral will usually require the PIO to monitor some form of a BUSY/READY or ACK signal to synchronize the data transfers (and complete the "handshake"). This is where PIO mode 1 comes in.

Mode 1: Input Port with Handshake

Figure 8.7 illustrates the timing relationships among $\overline{\text{STROBE}}$, READY, and $\overline{\text{INT}}$ when a data port is programmed for mode 1 input. The transfer begins with the peripheral monitoring the READY output of the PIO. If this output is high, the PIO is indicating that its input buffer is READY to receive a new data byte.

Detecting READY high, the peripheral strobes the PIO, causing the data byte to be latched and the READY line to be reset, in order to prevent the peripheral from writing another data byte before the CPU has had a chance to read the last one. Assuming that the

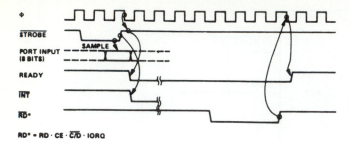

Figure 8.7 Mode 1 Z-80 PIO input timing. (Courtesy of Zilog, Inc.)

$RD* = RD \cdot CE \cdot \overline{C/D} \cdot IORQ$

PIO interrupts are enabled, the $\overline{STROBE}$ signal also initiates $\overline{INT}$, requesting an interrupt from the Z-80.

The interrupt service routine responds by reading the data byte from the PIO. The rising edge of $\overline{RD*}$ (another pseudocontrol signal) causes READY to return high, and a new data byte can be written to the PIO.

Note how the PIO mode 1 input port differs from a conventional input port discussed in Chapter 6. In the latter case, data were presented to the CPU via eight tristate buffers. The data had to be held stable until the CPU enabled the buffers and read the data. With the PIO in mode 1, the peripheral can latch its data into the PIO even though the CPU has not yet read the data byte. Eventually, when READY returns high, the peripheral "knows" that the data have been read, and another data byte can be input.

It is possible to use the PIO in mode 0 or mode 1 for *unconditional* I/O transfers (comparable to the 8255A's mode 0). For mode 0 (outputs), data written by the CPU will always be latched by the PIO independently of STROBE and READY. Ignoring these two lines and disabling interrupts results in a simple 8-bit output port.

When programmed for mode 1 (inputs), input data can be permanently enabled into the PIO by holding the $\overline{STROBE}$ input low. The result is a simple 8-bit input port. As we will see, mode 3 can also be used for this purpose and offers the versatility of programmed input or output for each pin.

Using the Z-80 PIO to Interface a Parallel Printer

Because of its built-in handshake logic and interrupt capabilities, the PIO is a natural choice for interfacing a parallel printer. Consider the circuit shown in Fig. 8.8. Port A of the PIO is programmed for mode 0 and is used to output the data to the printer. READY and $\overline{ASTB}$ (port A STROBE) are connected together so that the PIO "automatically" generates a one-clock-period STROBE signal. The inverter is required to change the sense to active low.

Two signals are available from the printer for handshaking: the level-sensitive $\overline{BUSY/READY}$ and the strobe signal $\overline{ACK}$. If polling were to be used, $\overline{BUSY/READY}$ would be the logical choice. However, when interrupts are involved, $\overline{ACK}$ will work best. In this example, an interrupt-driven scheme will be used.

When the data byte output by the PIO has been accepted and printed, the printer responds by pulsing $\overline{ACK}$. If port B is programmed for mode 1 input and $\overline{ACK}$ is connected to $\overline{BSTB}$ through inverter IC1B, the falling edge of $\overline{ACK}$ (rising edge of $\overline{BSTB}$)

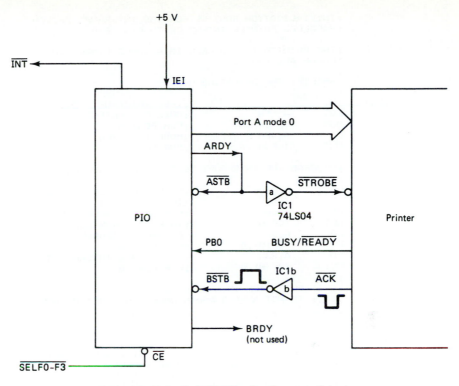

Figure 8.8 Using the Z-80 PIO to interface a parallel printer.

will generate an interrupt request. The ISR can respond by fetching a new data byte and outputting it to port A. Note that interrupts for port A should be disabled.

PB0 (bit 0 of port B) is used to monitor the BUSY/READY flag of the printer. This is done to prevent the system from "hanging up" if the printer should be off-line. Note that the printer ACK signal holds BSTB low, allowing PB0 to monitor the BUSY/READY flag.

Example 8.4

Write the initialization routine required for the interrupt-driven parallel-printer interface in Fig. 8.8. Assume that the ISR address is stored in memory locations E000H and E001H.

Solution. The program is shown in Fig. 8.9. Z-80 interrupt mode 2 is specified, and then port A is programmed for mode 0 and port B for mode 1. Register I is loaded with E0H, the high-order interrupt vector address, while the 7-bit interrupt vector for port B is programmed for 00. Interrupts are disabled for port A, but enabled for port B. This will allow the printer's ACK signal to initiate the interrupt request.

Initialization of the PIO is now complete and need not be specified again unless a restart should occur. The system monitor can execute a CALL to address PRINT whenever data is to be output to the printer. Assuming that the B register holds the number of bytes to be printed, the PRINT routine writes this byte to address (NUMB). Next, the BUSY/READY status of the printer is polled to make sure that the printer is on-line. If it is not, the message

```
              ;INITIALIZATION ROUTINE FOR THE INTERRUPT DRIVEN
              ;PARALLEL PRINTER INTERFACE IN FIG. 8-8.
              ;
              ;THE PRINTER ISR ADDRESS IS ASSUMED STORED IN
              ;E000H AND E001H.
              ;
              ;SPECIFY THE OPERATING MODES
              ;
INIT    IM      2                       ;Z-80 INTERRUPT MODE 2
        LD      A,0FH                   ;MODE 0 - OUTPUT
        OUT     (0F1H),A                ;FOR PORT A
        LD      A,4FH                   ;MODE 1 - INPUT
        OUT     (0F3H),A                ;FOR PORT B
        ;
        ;PROGRAM THE INTERRUPT VECTORS AND ENABLES
        ;
        LD      A,0E0H                  ;HIGH ORDER JUMP TABLE ADDRESS
        LD      I,A                     ;TO REGISTER I
        LD      A,00                    ;PORT B INTERRUPT VECTOR
        OUT     (0F3H),A                ;TO PORT B CONTROL
        LD      A,3                     ;DISABLE INTERRUPTS
        OUT     (0F1H),A                ;FOR PORT A
        LD      A,83H                   ;BUT ENABLE INTERRUPTS
        OUT     (0F3H),A                ;FOR PORT B
        ;
        ;INITIALIZATION IS NOW COMPLETE
        ;INIT IS NOT NEEDED AGAIN UNLESS A RESET OCCURS
        ;
        RET


              ;AFTER CALLING INIT A CALL TO PRINT WILL START THE
              ;PRINTING SEQUENCE BY LOADING (NUMB) WITH THE NUMBER
              ;OF BYTES TO BE OUTPUT, TESTING TO BE SURE THE PRINTER IS
              ;ON LINE, ENABLING INTERRUPTS AND BRANCHING TO THE PRINT
              ;ISR
              ;
PRINT   LD      A,B                     ;GET NUMBER OF BYTES
        LD      (NUMB),A                ;STORE IT IN (NUMB)
        ;
        ;NOW MAKE SURE PRINTER IS ON LINE
        ;
        IN      A,(0F2H)                ;READ PRINTER BUSY/READY
        RRA                             ;MOVE TO CARRY
        JP      C,MSG                   ;PRINT "PRINTER OFF LINE"
        ;
        ;PRINTER IS READY
        ;
        EI                              ;ENABLE INTERRUPTS
        CALL    ISR                     ;GO TO THE PRINT ROUTINE
        ;
        ;PRINT IS NOT NEEDED AGAIN UNTIL THE BUFFER IS EMPTY
        ;
        RET                             ;NORMAL PROCESSING RESUMES
```

Figure 8.9   Program for Example 8.4.

"Printer off-line" is output. Interrupts can now be enabled and a CALL to the printer ISR executed to begin the sequence.

Note that after the initial CALL, data transfers will occur "automatically" under interrupt control, and PRINT need not be called again. The printer ISR would look as shown in Fig. 6.22, with DPORT defined as port F0H. The RET instruction in this routine should be changed to RETI.

One word of caution about the printer interface in Fig. 8.8: The strobe signal generated by connecting ARDY and $\overline{\text{ASTB}}$ may be too short for some printers. For example, with a 4-MHz Z-80 processor, the pulse width will be 250 ns, yet a common printer specification is 0.5 μs minimum. The solution is a software strobe or an external one-shot triggered by ARDY.

Mode 2: Bidirectional I/O with Handshake

When mode 2 is selected, port A becomes a *bidirectional* data port supported by all four handshaking signals, and port B must be programmed for mode 3. The timing relationships are shown in Fig. 8.10. As can be seen from studying this figure, mode 2 timing is a combination of mode 0 and mode 1 timing. The only difference is that data is not output onto the bidirectional bus until $\overline{\text{ASTB}}$ is brought low. The remainder of the time the bus is in a tristate condition. This is done to prevent bus contention problems.

The general rule for mode 2 is "Strobe data off the bus only when ARDY is high, and gate data onto the bus only when BRDY is high."

Figure 8.11 illustrates an application for this mode. PIO1 is assumed to be interfaced to one computer system and PIO2 to a second. By programming both PIOs for mode 2, data can be transferred between the two computers. One PIO will be programmed as a transmitter and the other as a receiver. Note that the electrical connections are symmetric, so that either PIO can function as a transmitter or a receiver, depending on which way data is to flow.

In Fig. 8.11, PIO1 is assumed to be the transmitter and PIO2 the receiver. The flowcharts describe the actions required of the PIOs under program control. The transmitter initiates the transfer. If BRDY2 is high, the input buffer of PIO2 is empty and ready to receive a data byte. By using PB7 to *poll* BRDY2, a data byte is written to PIO1, causing its ARDY1 output to go high.

No further action is taken by PIO1 until PIO2 generates a (software) $\overline{\text{STROBE}}$ signal on PB1. This $\overline{\text{STROBE}}$ gates data onto the bidirectional bus lines, and the rising edge causes PIO2 to latch the data byte. BRDY2 now goes low, indicating that the data byte has been accepted by PIO2, but not yet read by CPU2. The PB1 strobe also resets ARDY1, indicating that the PIO1 transmitter buffer is empty.

When the data byte is read, BRDY2 returns high, indicating that PIO2 is again ready for data, and the cycle repeats.

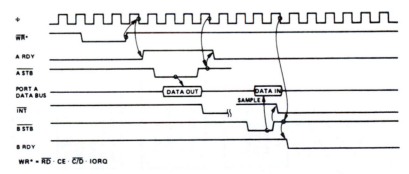

Figure 8.10   Mode 2 Z-80 PIO bidirectional timing. (Courtesy of Zilog, Inc.)

Sec. 8.1   The Z8420 Parallel Input/Output Controller   **419**

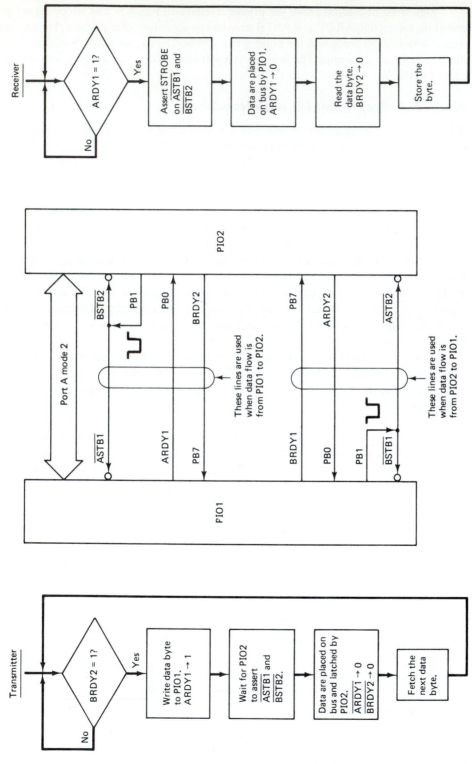

Figure 8.11 Two PIOs can be used to allow communications between two different computers.

Mode 3: Bit-Defined I/O

When the PIO is programmed for mode 3, each of the eight pins of the data port can be individually assigned as an input or an output. The handshaking lines are not used in this mode. Note from the mode 3 control word in Table 8.5 that 2 bytes are required. The first is used to specify mode 3 and the second to indicate the input/output definitions.

Mode 3 can be very useful when more control signals are required than are afforded by STROBE and READY. For example, in the preceding section PB0 and PB7 were programmed as polled inputs supporting the bidirectional data port. PB1 in that circuit was programmed as an output (used to generate the STROBE pulse).

Example 8.1 illustrated another feature of mode 3: An interrupt can be requested based on a logical OR or AND of the unmasked bits of this port. One application could be a control program required to poll bit 0, but generate an interrupt (alarm) if bits 0 AND 1 AND 4 should all be low. (See Problem 8.4.)

Because no handshaking signals are involved, mode 3 is similar to the 8255A's mode 0. In fact, if all of the bits of one port are programmed the same, the two modes are identical.

A Design Example: Mode 3 Control of a Multiplexed LED Display

Chapters 6 and 7 discussed two methods for interfacing a matrix keyboard to a microcomputer system. (See Sections 6.2 and 7.2.) In such systems, a seven-segment display is often used as an output device. In interfacing this type of display, two problems must be solved:

1. Decode the BCD or hex-encoded binary digits to seven-segment code.
2. Provide a driver circuit capable of handling the LED currents required.

Problem 1 can be solved by using a BCD-to-seven-segment or hex-to-seven-segment decoder. Problem 2 is solved by selecting a buffer or driver circuit capable of sinking or sourcing the LED currents.

Although this hardware approach works fine when only one or two displays are to be interfaced, it becomes very cumbersome when several digits of display are needed. For example, if a six-digit display is desired, you will require six displays, six decoders, and six drivers. Eighteen IC sockets and numerous connections will be needed.

A better approach is to let the microprocessor do the decoding and *multiplex* the displays. Figure 8.12 illustrates this technique for a six-digit display controlled by a Z-80 PIO. Looking at the inset to the figure, note that each display has all of its cathodes connected together (called a "common-cathode display"). Grounding this common pin while applying $+1.5$ V to any of the pins *a* through *g* will light the appropriate segment.

The interface shown in the figure has the segment pins from each display connected in parallel and driven by IC1 and IC2, each a common-cathode *segment driver.* IC6, a common-cathode *digit driver,* is used to sink the segment currents. Figure 8.13 provides a description of these two devices.

The "trick" to making this circuit work is the software. Port A of the PIO is used to turn on one of the digits by forcing the selected digit line low. For example, if 04H is written to port F0 of the PIO (port A) and 6DH is written to port F2 (port B), digit 2 will light

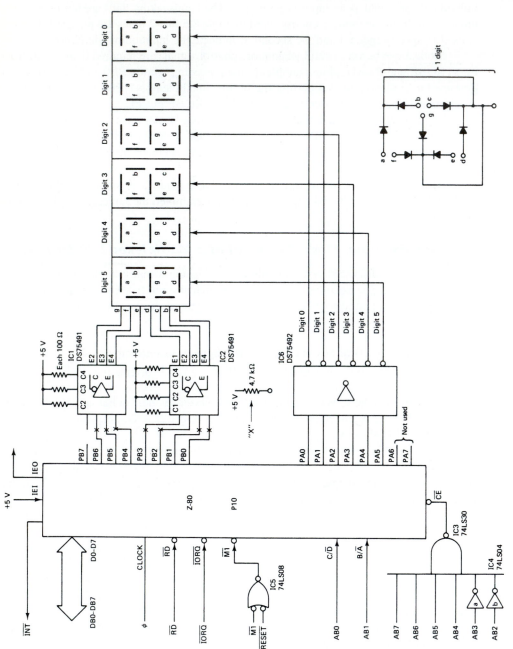

Figure 8.12 Interfacing a six-digit multiplexed display to the Z-80 PIO.

DS75491 MOS-to-LED Quad Segment Driver
DS75492 MOS-to-LED Hex Digit Driver

General Description

The DS75491 and DS75492 are interface circuits designed to be used in conjunction with MOS integrated circuits and common-cathode LED's in serially addressed multi-digit displays. The number of drivers required for this time-multiplexed system is minimized as a result of the segment-address-and-digit-scan method of LED drive.

Features

- 50 mA source or sink capability per driver (DS75491)
- 250 mA sink capability per driver (DS75492)
- MOS compatability (low input current)
- Low standby power
- High-gain Darlington circuits

Schematic and Connection Diagrams

DS75491 (each driver)

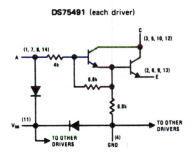

DS75492 (each driver)

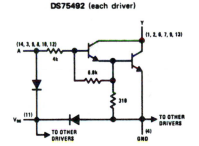

DS75491 Dual-In-Line Package

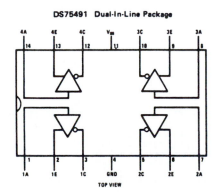

DS75492 Dual-In-Line Package

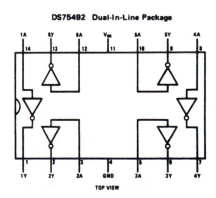

Figure 8.13   Segment and digit drivers for the six-digit display in Fig. 8.12. (Courtesy of National Semiconductor Corporation.)

423

up and display a 5. If the software turns on each digit in sequence for a short time and can do this quickly enough, your eyes will be "fooled" into thinking that all six displays are on at once, even though only one digit is on at a time.

What have we gained by this multiplexing scheme? For one thing, only one set of drivers is required (instead of one set per display). Also, the decoder has been eliminated. And because this function is now accomplished with software, special characters (such as P, L, U, etc.) can be output in addition to the numerals 0–9 and letters A–F obtained with hardware decoders. (This idea was presented in Lab Project 3.10.)

Example 8.5

Write a subroutine called SCAN that will scan and display the contents of a display buffer in memory called DSBF. Use the multiplexed display in Fig. 8.12.

```
;                    SCAN

;A SOFTWARE DRIVER FOR THE MULTIPLEXED DISPLAY
;        PIO INTERFACE IN FIG. 8-12.
;
;SCAN IS A SUBROUTINE THAT DISPLAYS THE CONTENTS
;OF THE SIX BYTE DISPLAY BUFFER (DSBF).
;(DSBF) = RIGHTMOST DIGIT (#0).
;(DSBF+5) = LEFTMOST DIGIT (#5).
;
;NOTE: TO PREVENT THE DISPLAY FROM FLICKERING
;SCAN SHOULD BE CALLED AT LEAST ONCE EVERY 5-10 MS.
;
DIGT   EQU     0F0H        ;THIS IS THE DIGIT DRIVER PORT
SEGM   EQU     0F2H        ;THIS IS THE SEGMENT DRIVER PORT
DSBF   EQU     0000        ;CHOOSE A SUITABLE LOCATION
MS     EQU     0000        ;THIS SHOULD BE THE ADDRESS OF
                           ;A 1 MS SUBROUTINE
;
;BEGIN BY MAKING THE ROUTINE TRANSPARENT AND
;INITIALIZING SEVERAL REGISTERS.
;
SCAN   PUSH    AF          ;
       PUSH    HL          ;
       PUSH    BC          ;
       PUSH    DE          ;
;
       LD      HL,DSBF     ;THIS IS THE DISPLAY BUFFER
       LD      A,1         ;DIGIT CODE
       LD      B,6         ;DIGIT COUNTER
       LD      C,SEGM      ;SEGMENT PORT
;
;CALL HXSG TO CONVERT THE HEX DIGIT IN (HL) TO
;A SEVEN-SEGMENT CODE.  RETURN WITH THE CODE IN D.
;
NXD    CALL    HXSG        ;CONVERT TO SEVEN-SEGMENT
       OUT     (C),D       ;OUT TO SEGMENT PORT
       OUT     (DIGT),A    ;TURN ON ONE DISPLAY
       CALL    MS          ;1 MS DELAY SUBROUTINE
       RLA                 ;PREPARE FOR NEXT DIGIT
       INC     HL          ;ADVANCE POINTER
       DJNZ    NXD         ;DO FOR ALL 6 DIGITS
;
;TURN OFF ALL OF THE DISPLAYS AND RESTORE THE REGISTERS
;
       SUB     A           ;CLEAR ACCUMULATOR
       OUT     (DIGT),A    ;ALL DISPLAYS OFF
       OUT     (C),A       ;ALL SEGMENTS OFF
```

Figure 8.14   Z-80 control subroutine for the multiplexed display interface in Fig. 8.12.

Solution.   The program will require two routines:

1. *HXSG.* This subroutine is passed the offset address (in register pair HL) of the hex digit to be converted to seven-segment code. It will return with the seven-segment encoded byte in register D.

2. *SCAN.* This subroutine will point HL at the display buffer and call HXSG. It will then output the contents of the D register to the segment driver (port B of the PIO) and turn on digit 0 for 1 ms. The process is repeated until all six digits have been converted and displayed.

The Z-80 program is shown in Fig. 8.14; we assume that the PIO has been programmed with ports A and B specified as mode 3 output ports.

So that SCAN can be called at any time, it begins by saving all CPU registers used. Several registers are then initialized and HL is pointed at the display buffer. HXSG is then called and the seven-segment code for the hex digit in the buffer looked up in a table. Note how the hex digit's value is used to form the *address offset* into this table. (For example, if HL = 4810 and the hex digit is 07, location 4817 will contain the seven-segment code for a 7.)

```
        POP     DE              ;
        POP     BC              ;
        POP     HL              ;
        POP     AF              ;
        RET
        ;
        ;                         HXSG
        ;THIS SUBROUTINE LOOKS UP THE SEVEN-SEGMENT CODE FOR
        ;THE HEX DIGIT IN BITS 0-3 OF (HL).   THE RESULT IS
        ;RETURNED IN REGISTER D.
        ;
HXSG    PUSH    AF              ;DO NOT CHANGE SCAN REGISTERS
        PUSH    HL              ;
        LD      A,(HL)          ;GET THE HEX DIGIT
        LD      HL,CTBL         ;POINT AT CODE TABLE
        AND     OFH             ;MAKE SURE BITS 4-7 ARE 0
        ADD     A,L             ;FORM AN OFFSET
        LD      L,A             ;INTO THE TABLE
        LD      D,(HL)          ;RETRIEVE THE CODE TO D
        POP     HL              ;RESTORE
        POP     AF              ;
        RET
        ;
        ;THESE ARE THE SEVEN-SEGMENT CODES
        ;
CTBL    DEFB    3FH             ;0
        DEFB    06H             ;1
        DEFB    5BH             ;2
        DEFB    4FH             ;3
        DEFB    66H             ;4
        DEFB    6DH             ;5
        DEFB    7DH             ;6
        DEFB    07H             ;7
        DEFB    7FH             ;8
        DEFB    67H             ;9
        DEFB    77H             ;A
        DEFB    7CH             ;B
        DEFB    39H             ;C
        DEFB    5EH             ;D
        DEFB    79H             ;E
        DEFB    71H             ;F
```

Figure 8.14   (*Continued*)

Returning to SCAN, the code is output to the segment driver and digit 0 is turned on for 1 ms. Register A is rotated left to prepare to turn on the next digit. The buffer pointer is advanced and DJNZ is used to test whether all six digits have been output.

In actual use, the main software must be sure to include a CALL SCAN instruction in all program loops to ensure that the display is continually "refreshed." Failure to perform this call at least once every 5 to 10 ms will cause the display to flicker (and, of course, go dark if SCAN is not called at all). To write data to the display, the display buffer should be written to. For example, to show a 5 in digit 4, use the following code:

```
LD      A,05
LD      (DSBF+4),A
```

Electrical Characteristics of the Ports

The specification for the data ports is 2 mA for I_{OL} and 1.5 mA for I_{OH}. This means that one standard TTL load or five LSTTL loads can be driven safely at each pin. In addition, port B can supply up to 1.5 mA at 1.5 V. This means that Darlington transistors can be driven and used to control high current loads such as mechanical or solid-state relays.

Three versions of the PIO, each with a different speed, are the 4-MHz Z0842004 PIO, the 6-MHz Z0842006 and Z84C2006 PIO, and the 8-MHz Z84C2008 PIO.

SELF-REVIEW 8.1

8.1.1. Which PIO operating mode should be selected for an I/O interface that requires 12 input bits and 4 output bits?

8.1.2. The daisy-chain priority structure used by Z-80 peripherals requires that output IEO be connected to the IEI input of the next _____ priority peripheral.

8.1.3. The PIO can be programmed to generate an interrupt based on a logical _____ or _____ condition of the unmasked mode 3 input bits.

8.1.4. When the PIO is operated in mode 0 or mode 1, what signal is used by the peripheral to indicate that the output data have been accepted or input data written?

8.1.5. What is the advantage of using a multiplexed LED display?

8.2 THE Z8430 COUNTER/TIMER CIRCUIT

Introduction

The Z8430 counter/timer (or simply Z-80 CTC) is commonly used in Z-80 microcomputer systems for the generation of accurate time delays. In software, this is typically done by forming counting loops that accumulate the time delay as the product of X passes through a loop Y T-states long.

Programming the microprocessor to count backward from one million to zero may be one method of generating a time delay, but it hardly qualifies as an efficient use of the resources of the processor! The CTC, on the other hand, is designed specifically for just such a task.

The Z-80 CTC can be programmed by the Z-80 to operate as a *counter* or a *timer.* As a counter, it decrements an internal 8-bit counter each time an external clock signal (applied to CLK/TRG) makes an active transition. When the count passes from 1 to 0, the ZC/TO output pulses high for 1.5 system clock periods. At the same time, if the CTC is enabled, an interrupt request will be generated. And, like the PIO, the CTC is capable of supplying a (Z-80) mode 2 interrupt vector to the Z-80 during $\overline{INTA}$.

When the Z-80 CTC is programmed as a timer, the 8-bit counter is decremented once for every 16 (or 256) system clock pulses. In this mode, the CLK/TRG input becomes a programmable trigger initiating the timer. A timing interval as short as 16 system clock states can be detected (1.6 μs with the 10 MHz Z84C3010).

The main features of the Z-80 CTC are as follows:

1. Four individual programmable channels.
2. Three channels with ZC/TO outputs.
3. Each counter capable of being read by the CPU at any time.
4. Selection of counter or timer mode for each channel.
5. Programmable active trigger edge.
6. Standard Z-80 type interface with daisy-chain priority structure.

If you are comparing the Z-80 CTC with the Intel 8254, the main differences are as follows:

1. The 8254 has only three channels.
2. The 8254 counters are all 16 bits wide.
3. The 8254 can be programmed to generate various waveshapes (strobes, pulses, and square waves).

In this section, we:

- Compare the Z-80 CTC timer and counter modes and specify the control words for each.
- Program the Z-80 CTC to function as a one-shot.

Interfacing the Z-80 CTC

Pin functions and pin numbers for the Z-80 CTC are shown in Fig. 8.15. Figure 8.16 illustrates typical connections when the Z-80 CTC is interfaced to a Z-80 microprocessor. Like the PIO, the CTC decodes $\overline{M1}$, $\overline{IORQ}$, and $\overline{RD}$ to identify the $\overline{IOW}$, $\overline{IOR}$, $\overline{INTA}$, and M1 machine cycles. This was shown previously in Table 8.3; note that, unlike the PIO, the CTC has a separate RESET input.

The CTC appears to the programmer as four I/O ports defined by the two channel-select pins CS0 and CS1. However, only when the chip enable ($\overline{CE}$) input is low can the microprocessor access the CTC, and the address decoder connected to this pin determines

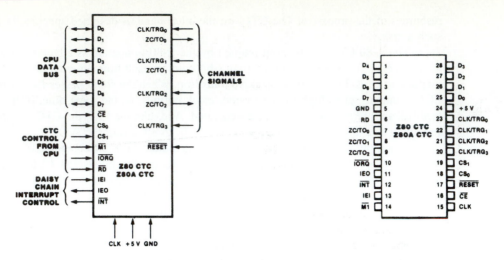

Figure 8.15 Pin functions and numbers for the Z-80 CTC. (Courtesy of Zilog, Inc.)

the specific port addresses. Table 8.6 summarizes the I/O read and write operations that are possible with the CTC. Note that the channel control lines ZC/TO and CLK/TRG cannot be read.

Three of the CTC pins are dedicated to the daisy-chain interrupt structure. The technique used is identical to that discussed previously regarding the PIO. (See Fig. 8.3.) Any number of compatible devices can be added to the daisy chain. Chips farthest from the CPU have the lowest priority.

Simultaneous interrupt requests within the CTC will be arbitrated such that channel 0 has the highest priority and channel 3 the lowest. In programming the interrupt vector, only bits 3–7 of channel 0 need to be specified, as the CTC automatically inserts bits 1 and 2. (Recall that bit 0 must be 0.)

Programming the Z-80 CTC: Counter Mode

The main difference between the counter mode and the timer mode is the source of the clock signal. When programmed as a counter, the CTC counts clock pulses applied to the CLK/TRG input. When programmed as a timer, the CTC counts *system* clock pulses.

Figure 8.17 is a flowchart of the operation of the Z-80 CTC in the counter mode. Two control words must be written. The first identifies the counter mode and the second is called the *time constant*. This 8-bit value will be loaded into the counting register and used as the base when decrementing begins. The remaining operations in the flowchart occur without CPU intervention and continue indefinitely until a reset or new control word is written.

After the two control words are written, the first active transition at the CLK/TRG input (programmable as either a rising or falling edge) will cause the counter to be decremented by 1. This is shown in Fig. 8.18. Note that the CLK/TRG transition must occur 210 ns before the rising edge of ϕ (for the 4MHz CTC). If this condition is not met, the

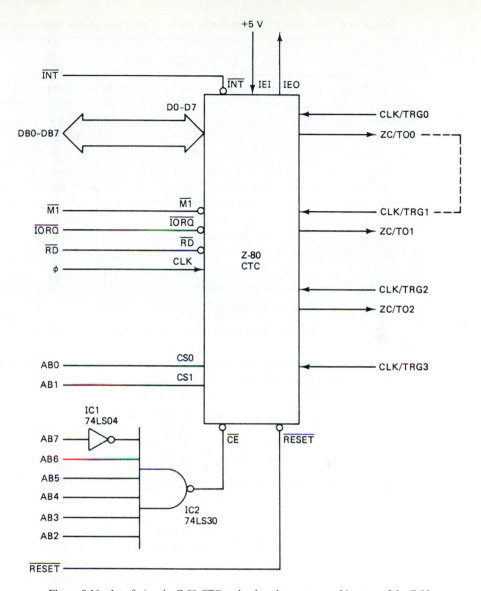

Figure 8.16 Interfacing the Z-80 CTC to the three-bus system architecture of the Z-80 microprocessor. The dashed line indicates how two counters can be cascaded to achieve larger counts. (See Example 8.7.)

counter will not be decremented until the next rising edge of ϕ. The CLK/TRG must also have a minimum pulse width of 200 ns, and the trigger period must be at least twice the clock period.

When the Nth CLK/TRG pulse finally occurs, the ZC/TO output will pulse high for 1.5 periods of the ϕ clock. INT will also become active at this time if interrupts have been enabled. The base count is then automatically reloaded into the counter and the cycle repeated indefinitely.

TABLE 8.6 The Z-80 CTC Appears to be Four I/O Ports to the Microprocessor

Figure 8.16 port address	CS1	CS0	M1	IORQ	RD	Function
7C	0	0	1	0	0	Read channel 0 counter
	0	0	1	0	1	Write channel 0 control word
7D	0	1	1	0	0	Read channel 1 counter
	0	1	1	0	1	Write channel 1 control word
7E	0	1	1	0	0	Read channel 2 counter
	0	1	1	0	1	Write channel 2 control word
7F	1	1	1	0	0	Read channel 3 counter
	1	1	1	0	1	Write channel 3 control word

In programming a counter (by writing to the desired channel port address), three types of control words are possible. (See Fig. 8.19.) Initially, the CTC control logic examines bit 0 of the control word. If this bit is a 0, the *interrupt vector* is assumed; If the bit is a 1, the *channel control word* is indicated. The interrupt vector need only be written to channel 0; the CTC automatically determines the address for the other channels, as shown in the figure.

Example 8.6

Assume that the address for the channel 0 ISR is stored in locations D8C0H and D8C1H. Write the interrupt initialization routine required for the Z-80 CTC interface in Fig. 8.16. What locations will store the ISRs for channels 1–3?

Solution. The program to initialize the CTC is as follows:

```
LD    A,0D8H     ;HIGH-ORDER ADDRESS
LD    I,A        ;TO REGISTER I
IM    2          ;INTERRUPT MODE 2
LD    A,0C0H     ;LOW-ORDER ADDRESS
OUT   (7CH),A    ;TO CTC CHANNEL 0
```

The other CTC channels will automatically be programmed for address D8C2H (channel 1), D8C4H (channel 2), and D8C6H (channel 3).

When bit 0 of the control word is a 1, the channel control word is indicated. Several characteristics of the CTC can then be specified, as Fig. 8.19 illustrates. Note that the prescaler value (16 or 256) and timer trigger are "don't cares" for the counter mode.

When bit 2 of the channel control word is a 1, the CTC is alerted to interpret the next channel write as a time-constant byte.

Example 8.7

Program the Z-80 CTC in Fig. 8.16 to count 1000 rising edges of the signal applied to a CLK/TRG input, generate an interrupt request, and repeat the cycle.

Solution. With an 8-bit counter, 256 clock edges can be counted. Therefore, for this application, two counters will have to be cascaded; that is, the ZC/TO output of one will be connected to the CLK/TRG input of another. This configuration is shown in Fig. 8.16 with

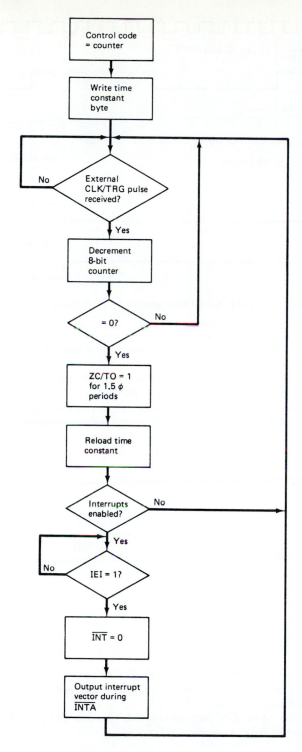

Figure 8.17 Flowchart of operations when the Z-80 CTC is programmed in the counter mode.

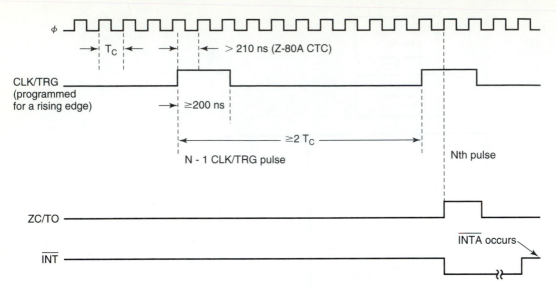

Figure 8.18 Z-80 CTC timing diagram when operated in counter mode.

a dashed line between ZC/TO0 and CLK/TRG1. The choice of channels 0 and 1 is arbitrary.

What time-constant value should we program for the channel 0 and 1 counters? If cascading resulted in a true 16-bit counter, the answer would be 03E8H (1000_{10}). However, when channel 0 passes through 0, it will be reloaded with its base count, not zero. The result is that we will decrement the channel 1 counter once each time the channel 0 counter is decremented to zero. If channel 0 is loaded with N0 and channel 1 with N1, the total clocks required to make both counters go to 0 (and the ZC/TO1 output pulse high) is N0 × N1. In this example, we will choose N0 = 10 and N1 = 100.

The control word for each channel is found as follows:

	Channel 0	Channel 1
Interrupts	0 (disabled)	1 (enabled)
Mode	1 (counter)	1
Prescale	X	X
CLK/TRG edge	1 (rising)	1
Timer trigger	X	X
Time constant	1 (to follow)	1
Reset	0 (normal)	0
Control/vector	1 (control word)	1

The result is 01X1X101 for channel 0 and 11X1X101 for channel 1. Note that just interrupts for channel 1 are enabled. This is because only when the channel 1 counter passes through 0 will 1000 clock edges have occurred.

Figure 8.20 is a copy of the Z-80 program required. Locations D8C2H and D8C3H should be loaded with the desired ISR address.

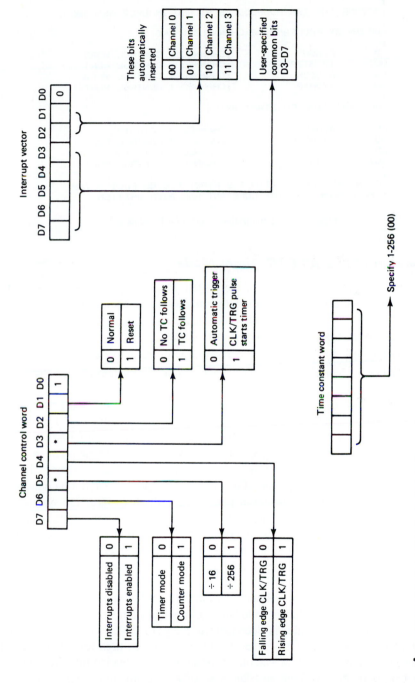

Figure 8.19 Three forms of the CTC control word are possible. The channel control word and time constant need to be written to each channel's port address. The interrupt vector should be written to channel 0 only.

433

```
;PROGRAM TO INITIALIZE THE Z-80 CTC IN FIG. 8-16 TO
;CAUSE AN INTERRUPT REQUEST EVERY 1000 RISING EDGES
;OF THE SIGNAL APPLIED TO CLK/TRG0.
;
;ASSUME THE ISR ADDRESS IS STORED IN D8C2 AND D8C3.
;
;BEGIN BY PROGRAMMING CHANNELS 0 AND 1
;
LD        A,55H          ;CHANNEL 0 CONTROL WORD
OUT       (7CH),A        ;CHANNEL 0 CONTROL PORT
LD        A,0D5H         ;CHANNEL 1 CONTROL WORD
OUT       (7DH)A         ;CHANNEL 1 CONTROL PORT
;
;NOW THE TIME CONSTANT BYTES
;
LD        A,0AH          ;CHANNEL 0 GETS 10
OUT       (7CH),A        ;CHANNEL 0 CONTROL PORT
LD        A,64H          ;CHANNEL 1 GETS 100
OUT       (7DH),A        ;CHANNEL 1 CONTROL PORT
;
;COUNTING BEGINS WITH THE FIRST RISING EDGE AFTER
;THE CHANNEL 0 TIME CONSTANT HAS BEEN WRITTEN
```

Figure 8.20   Initialization program for Example 8.7.

Programming the Z-80 CTC: Timer Mode

Figure 8.21 illustrates the operation of the Z-80 CTC when programmed in the timer mode. There are three differences between this mode and the counter mode:

1. The clock source is ϕ and not an external signal.
2. The timing period is initiated via software or with the active edge of CLK/TRG.
3. The counter is decremented once after each 16 or 256 system clock pulses.

The timer mode is intended for accurate timing applications that use the system clock as the time base. The counter mode can also be used in this way (by connecting CLK/TRG to ϕ), but is best suited for counting pulses arriving at the CLK/TRG input.

Note that in the timer mode some initial counts cannot be obtained. For example, to time for 64 system clock periods, a time constant of 4 with a prescale factor of 16 should be selected. However, a timing period of 65 system clock periods cannot be obtained, because the prescaler requires that the timing period be a multiple of 16 or 256 system clocks.

A timing diagram for this mode is shown in Fig. 8.22. The timer is initiated by the active edge of CLK/TRG (in this case the rising edge). Note that 210 ns of lead time (for the 4 MHz CTC) is required between the active edge of the trigger and the rising edge of ϕ. If this condition is met, the timer will begin with the rising edge of the *second* clock pulse.

It is also possible to start the timer from software. In this case, the timer begins with the second rising edge immediately following the time-constant write machine cycle.

In either case, the counter is decremented every 16 or 256 system clock pulses. When the count passes from 1 to 0, the ZC/TO output pulses high for 1.5 periods of ϕ, and if enabled, INT is forced low. The time constant is now reloaded into the counter and the cycle repeats (that is, without an additional software command or CLK/TRG pulse). A reset command should be used to stop the timer.

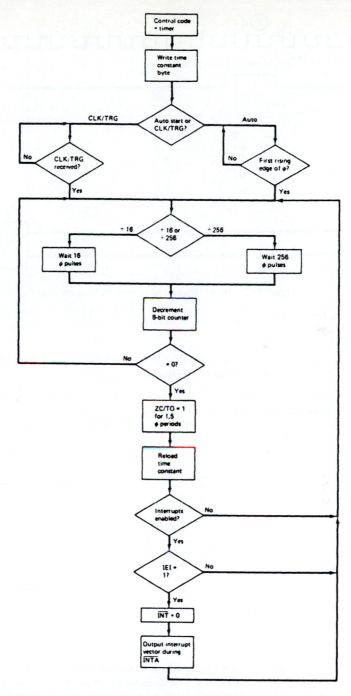

Figure 8.21 Flowchart of operations when the Z-80 CTC is programmed in the timer mode.

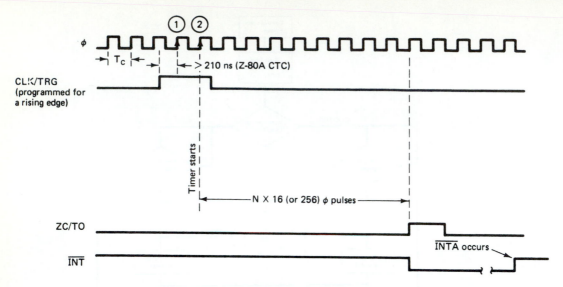

Figure 8.22 Timing diagram when the CTC is operated in the timer mode.

Example 8.8

Design the hardware and write the software to utilize the Z-80 CTC as a one-shot. Applying an active-low pulse to the CLK/TRG input should produce a 3.6-s active-high pulse.

Solution. The Z-80 CTC has no provision for controlling the shape or pulse width of the ZC/TO output (as does the 8254 PIT). Instead, the Z-80 CTC is restricted to 1.5 system clock periods, or 375 ns, with a 4-MHz clock. This problem can be overcome by adding an external flip-flop as shown in Fig. 8.23. Pushing the button sets the flip-flop and starts the timer. When ZC/TO occurs, the flip-flop is clocked and the pulse terminated.

Unfortunately, 3.6 s is too long a period for one timer alone. For example, if the time constant is 256 and the prescaler is also set to 256, 65,536 clock periods will occur before ZC/TO0 goes high. At 4 MHz, this is 0.016384 s, too short to be used for the one-shot. However, if the ZC/TO0 output is used as the clock signal for channel 1, programmed as a counter, the 3.6-s time delay can be realized.

The "trick" now is to select time-constant values, N0 and N1, for CT0 and CT1 such that either

$$N0 \times N1 \times 256 = \frac{4,000,000}{1/3.6} = 14,400,000$$

or

$$N0 \times N1 \times 16 = 14,400,000$$

In either case, N0 and N1 are restricted to integers between 1 and 256. There are no solutions if the prescaler $= 16$, but if a prescale factor of 256 is chosen, then N0 $= 250$ and N1 $= 225$ will work. (Try it! Then do Problem 8.21 to see how I found these values.)

Using N0 $= 250$ and N1 $= 225$, we can write the program in Fig. 8.24. Note that once programmed, the circuit runs independent of the CPU.

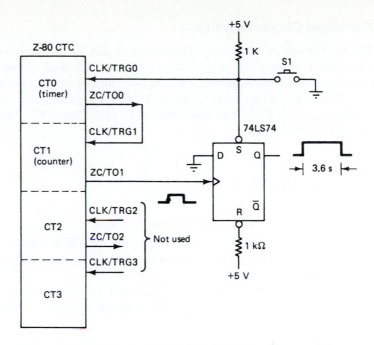

Figure 8.23   This circuit allows the Z-80 CTC to function as a one-shot.

```
;THIS PROGRAM CONVERTS THE Z-80 CTC AND HARDWARE
;SHOWN IN FIG. 8-23 TO A ONE-SHOT.  THE PULSE WIDTH
;IS FOUND AS
;               PW = (NO x N1 x P)/F
;
;NO AND N1 ARE THE TIME CONSTANTS FOR COUNTERS O AND 1,
;P IS THE PRESCALE FACTOR AND F IS THE SYSTEM CLOCK
;FREQUENCY.
;
;IN THIS EXAMPLE NO=250, N1=225, P=256 AND F= 4 MHZ.
;THE PULSE WIDTH IS 3.6 S.
;
LD      A,2DH           ;CHANNEL O IS A TIMER, P=256
OUT     (O7CH),A        ;CHANNEL O CONTROL WORD
LD      A,55H           ;CHANNEL 1 IS A COUNTER
OUT     (O7DH),A        ;CHANNEL 1 CONTROL WORD
;
;THE NEXT TWO WRITES SPECIFY THE TIME CONSTANTS
;
LD      A,OFAH          ;NO=250
OUT     (O7CH),A        ;CHANNEL O TIME CONSTANT
LD      A,OE1H          ;N1=225
OUT     (O7DH),A        ;CHANNEL 1 TIME CONSTANT
;
;THE CTC NOW RUNS INDEPENDENT OF THE CPU
;PRESSING THE SWITCH WILL PRODUCE A 3.6 S PULSE
```

Figure 8.24   Control program for the one-shot circuit in Fig. 8.23. The pulse width is 3.6 s, assuming a 4-MHz system clock.

Sec. 8.2   The Z8430 Counter/Timer Circuit   **437**

Electrical Characteristics

The ZC/TO outputs have drive capabilities of 2 mA in the low state and 1.6 μA in the high state. Thus, they can safely drive one standard TTL load or five LSTTL loads. Each output is also capable of driving a Darlington transistor pair, sourcing 1.5 mA at 1.5 V.

There are four versions of the CTC, each with a different speed: the Z0843004 (4 MHz), the Z0843006 and Z84C3006 (6.17 MHz), the Z84C3008 (8 MHz), and the Z84C3010 (10 MHz).

SELF-REVIEW 8.2

8.2.1. What are the two operating modes of the Z-80 CTC?

8.2.2. What clock source is used as the time base when the CTC is operated in the counter mode?

8.2.3. In the counter mode, one channel of the CTC can count as many as _____ external pulses.

8.2.4. When the Z-80 CTC is used in the timer mode, each count represents _____ or _____ system clock pulses, depending on the prescale factor.

8.3 THE Z8410 DIRECT MEMORY ACCESS CONTROLLER

Introduction

Nearly all input/output interfacing is concerned with the transfer of data between system memory and the I/O devices. As we have seen, three techniques are commonly used to accomplish this transfer:

1. Programmed I/O
2. Interrupt-driven I/O
3. Direct memory access

Programmed I/O (also called polling) and interrupts both utilize the microprocessor to control the data transfer. As a result, the data transfer rate is relatively slow, due to the software overhead involved in setting up data pointers and byte counters and testing for the end-of-block condition.

The direct memory access, or DMA, technique replaces this software with hardware. A special DMA controller, or *DMAC,* manages the data transfer after receiving source and destination addresses from the processor. The advantage of this technique is that DMA transfers can occur at speeds approaching the access time of the memory. The disadvantage is that the CPU must suspend all operations while the DMAC controls the system buses. This means that interrupts will not be recognized and CPU-refreshed dynamic memories will not be refreshed.

Because the DMAC takes the place of the microprocessor during a DMA transfer, it must be compatible with the control signals of the processor. In the case of the Z-80, a special DMA processor called the *Z-80 DMA* is available from Zilog. This device is fully compatible with all control signals generated by the Z-80 and possesses the following features:

1. Four-MB/s DMA transfers using two clock cycle simultaneous transfers (8 MHz Z-80 DMA)
2. One channel with 16-bit source and destination addresses
3. Transfer and/or search modes with byte masking
4. Byte, burst, and continuous DMA modes
5. Software- or hardware-initiated DMA requests
6. Direct Z-80 compatibility, including programmable mode 2 interrupt vector and daisy-chain priority structure
7. I/O-to-I/O, I/O-to-memory, memory-to-I/O, and memory-to-memory DMA transfers

In this section, we:

- Describe the DMA sequence for the Z-80 DMA in byte, burst, and continuous modes.
- Explain how to access and program the read/write registers of the Z-80 DMA.

Interfacing the Z-80 DMA

Pin functions and numbers for the Z-80 DMA are shown in Fig. 8.25. The most important characteristic to note is that all three system buses can be output by the DMA with exactly the same timing as generated by the Z-80 processor. Because of this, the memory and I/O can be accessed by the DMA without these devices "knowing" that the CPU is not in control.

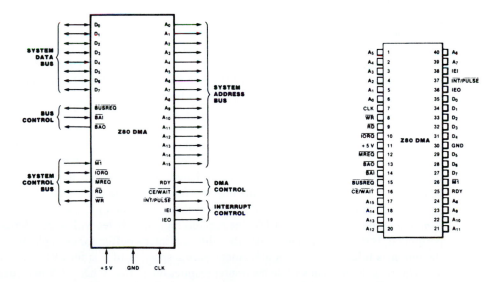

Figure 8.25 Pin functions and numbers for the Z-80 DMA. (Courtesy of Zilog, Inc.)

Observe that $\overline{\text{IORQ}}$, $\overline{\text{RD}}$, and $\overline{\text{WR}}$ are also input signals. This enables the DMA to be accessed by the Z-80 as a single I/O port. M1 and $\overline{\text{IORQ}}$ allow recognition of the Z-80 INTA condition ($\overline{\text{IORQ}} \cdot \text{M1}$) and detection of the RETI instruction.

Figure 8.26 illustrates how the Z-80 DMA is interfaced to the Z-80 microprocessor. For non-DMA operations ($\overline{\text{BUSAKB}} = 1$), the $\overline{\text{CE/WAIT}}$ input acts as a normal *chip enable* and is driven by the address decoder IC1. In this example, port FFH is decoded. When DMA is active, the I/O device can request *WAIT* states by pulling the DMA's $\overline{\text{CE/WAIT}}$ line low; the timing is identical to Z-80 WAIT state timing discussed in Chapter 4.

The DMA cycle is initiated by the DMA output signal $\overline{\text{BUSRQ}}$. The CPU responds with $\overline{\text{BUSAKB}}$ and places all of its buses in a tristate condition. In larger systems, $\overline{\text{BUSAKB}}$ is also used to tristate the bus buffers (See Fig. 4.27.) In Fig. 8.26, this means that all three system buses to the left of the diagram become open circuits. The Z-80 DMA now controls these bus lines.

Two inputs are provided to synchronize the DMA to the speed of the peripheral: $\overline{\text{WAIT}}$ and RDY. $\overline{\text{WAIT}}$ functions as a normal WAIT-state request input, as discussed previously. The RDY input can be connected to the peripheral's BUSY/READY status output. Only when RDY is high can DMA transfers take place.

Finally, the $\overline{\text{BAI}}$ and $\overline{\text{BAO}}$ bus acknowledge input and output are used to connect several DMA devices together in a daisy chain, similar to the standard Z-80 daisy-chain interrupt structure. $\overline{\text{BAO}}$, connected to $\overline{\text{BAI}}$ of the next-highest-priority DMA, is output high when its $\overline{\text{BAI}}$ input is low, preventing lower priority DMAs from generating a $\overline{\text{BUSRQ}}$.

Typical DMA Transfer

Figure 8.27 is a flowchart of the operation of the Z-80 DMA when programmed for the *burst* mode. Before the DMA transfer takes place, control codes must be written to the DMA's I/O port, selecting the operating mode, number of bytes to transfer, and source and destination addresses.

The transfer sequence begins when the peripheral's READY flag becomes active. The DMA can be programmed to *interrupt on RDY;* the interrupt service routine then starts the DMA by writing a DMA enable command word, or else it begins the transfer as soon as READY is active. The flowchart shows both choices.

In either case, the DMA asserts $\overline{\text{BUSRQ}}$ and the processor responds (within one machine cycle) with $\overline{\text{BUSAK}}$, relinquishing control of the system buses to the DMA. The data byte is then fetched from memory, brought into the DMA, and written to the I/O port. This is called "sequential" DMA—a read followed by a write. Next, the byte counter is incremented and compared with the block length. If more data is to be transferred, the RDY line is again sampled, and if the line is found active, the cycle repeats.

Recall from the discussion in Chapter 6 that this mode of DMA is called *burst,* or *demand,* DMA. As long as the RDY line remains high, data bytes will be transferred to the peripheral. Burst DMA is appropriate for filling a printer's buffer, for example. In this case, the buffer is filled by the DMA at memory access speed until it is full (RDY = inactive). The DMA cycle then ends while the printer empties the buffer. When RDY becomes active again, another DMA transfer begins.

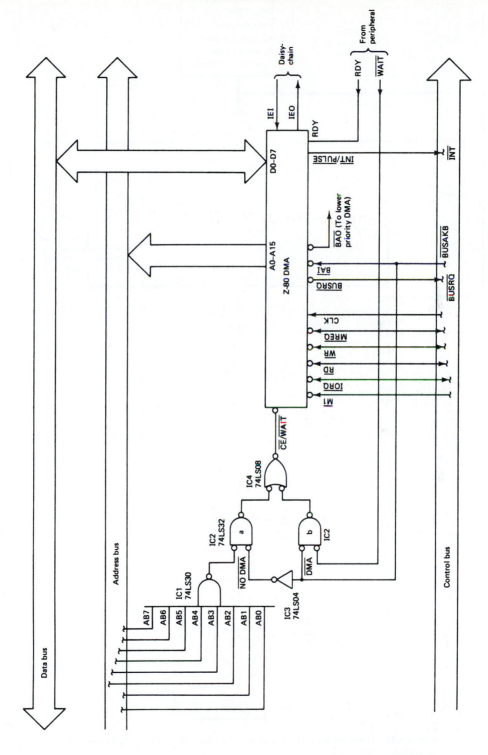

Figure 8.26 Interfacing the Z-80 DMA to the three-bus system architecture of the Z-80 micro-processor. The RDY and WAIT inputs are used to synchronize the DMA to the I/O device.

441

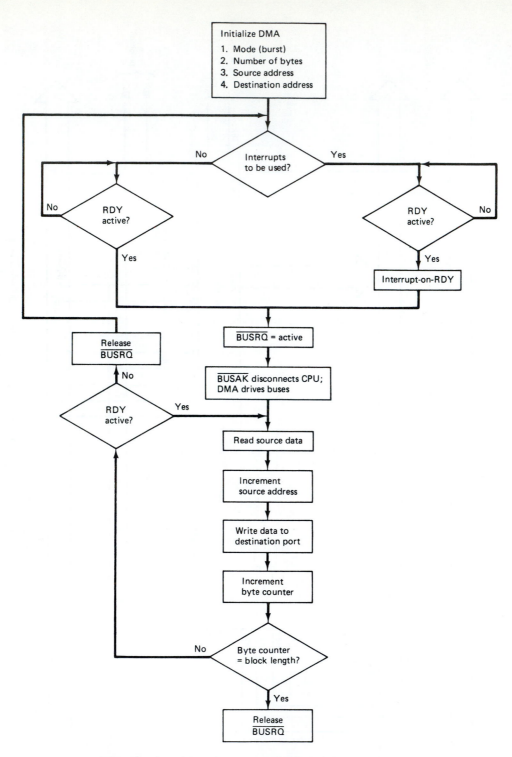

Figure 8.27 Flowchart of the DMA sequence when the Z-80 DMA is programmed for the burst mode.

The Z-80 DMA can also be programmed to operate in a *continuous*, or *block*, mode. The only difference is that after transferring a byte, if the RDY input is found inactive, the DMA idles, waiting for the RDY condition. The buses are not released to the processor until the entire block has been transferred.

A third mode, called *byte-*, or *single*-mode, DMA can also be programmed. In this mode a single byte is transferred, after which control of the buses is relinquished to the CPU—even if RDY remains active. In the latter case, one machine cycle will always be executed before the DMA again takes control of the buses for the next transfer.

Response Time and Transfer Rate

As pointed out in Fig. 8.27, there are two ways that a DMA transfer can be requested. Both involve the RDY input. If the *interrupt on RDY* option is selected, an interrupt will be generated when RDY becomes active. The interrupt service routine can then enable the DMA, and the transfer sequence will begin. Because of the interrupt response time and software overhead involved, this will be the slowest means of responding to RDY.

The other technique is to enable the DMA *before* RDY becomes active. In this case, the DMA sequence will occur within one machine cycle (plus one T-state) after RDY becomes active. In the worst case this will require 11 T-states, or 2.75 μs, with a 4-MHz clock.

The transfer rate, on the other hand, refers to how fast data can be transferred to the I/O device. Using standard Z-80 timing and a sequential DMA technique (read a byte and then write a byte), we find that four clock cycles are required for each operation, or eight clock cycles per transfer. At 4 MHz, this corresponds to 0.5 MB/s.

A unique feature of the Z-80 DMA is that the number of clock periods per read or write cycle can be programmed as two, three, or four. Therefore, the maximum transfer rate is obtained by programming two clock periods per cycle, or four clock periods per transfer. In this case, the transfer rate becomes 1 MB/s.

The fastest transfer speed of all is obtained if *simultaneous* DMA transfers are allowed. In this technique, the $\overline{\text{MEMR}}$ and $\overline{\text{IOW}}$ (or $\overline{\text{MEMW}}$ and $\overline{\text{IOR}}$) control bus signals are active simultaneously. Data are fetched from memory and written directly to the I/O device. This is the (only) technique used by Intel's 8237A DMAC and is illustrated in Fig. 7.39. The Z-80 DMA can also support the technique, but external hardware is required.

When simultaneous DMA transfers are used and the option of two clock periods per operation is programmed, the Z-80 DMA can transfer 1 byte every two clock periods. The transfer rate becomes 2 MB/s with a 4-MHz clock (4 MB/s with an 8 MHz clock).

Of course, the memory devices and peripheral must be capable of keeping up with the DMA transfer rate. For memory, this is not a problem: Even with only two clock periods per transfer, the memory has nearly 500 ns to fetch and output the data byte. This is quite slow by today's standards, according to which memory access times are commonly less than 100 ns.

For many peripherals, however, a data rate of 2 MB/s (or even 1 MB/s) will be too fast. In this case, the RDY line can be used to synchronize the peripheral and DMA. Another option is to use the WAIT input to cause WAIT states while the I/O device processes the data byte.

The type of interfacing technique to use—polling, interrupts, or DMA—must be considered carefully. And even if DMA is selected, the type of DMA transfer to use—byte, burst, or continuous—must also be given careful consideration if maximum utilization of the resources of the processor is to be achieved.

Example 8.9

Determine, from an efficiency standpoint, which interfacing technique to use—polling, interrupts, or DMA—to interface a $3\frac{1}{2}''$ high-density disk drive. Assume a Z-80A microprocessor.

Solution. A $3\frac{1}{2}''$ high-density disk drive reads and writes data at a rate of 500,000 bit/s. This corresponds to a new byte every 16 μs. Let us examine each interfacing technique for feasibility:

1. *Polling.* A programmed I/O technique would require a program similar to that shown in Fig. 6.14. Although developed for a parallel printer, the program is easily adapted to the READY flag of the floppy disk drive. In Example 6.6, the transfer period of this routine was shown to be 12.75 μs with a Z-80A. Therefore, the technique will work, although the processor will be dedicated to this single task.

2. *Interrupts.* If interrupts are used, the READY output of the floppy disk drive is utilized to generate the interrupt request. Control then branches to a special interrupt service routine (ISR) in which a data byte is output to the disk drive. In principle, the processor is now free to perform some other task, as opposed to polling the READY flag repeatedly, as is done in the programmed solution. However, Fig. 8.28 illustrates that the interrupt service routine alone will require 49 T-states. The response time will require an additional 20–43 T-states. (See Table 6.6.) This is 23 μs (the worst case)—too slow to keep up with the drive.

3. *DMA.* If the Z-80 DMA is used and READY is utilized to start the transfer sequence (that is, no interrupt on ready), 11 T-states (the worst case) will elapse before the transfer, and 8 more T-states will be required, assuming a sequential transfer with standard Z-80 timing. Therefore, 19 T-states, or 4.75 μs, will be required. Certainly, the DMA technique is fast enough.

The choice of DMA mode still remains. If the continuous, or block, mode is selected, the DMA (and microprocessor) will idle for 11.25 μs (16 μs–4.75 μs) until the READY flag is again set. Although this technique will work, it is analogous to polling and does not utilize the full resources of the processor.

```
        ;EXAMPLE OF A Z-80 INTERRUPT SERVICE ROUTINE FOR
        ;TRANSFERRING DATA TO A FAST PERIPHERAL.
        ;
        ;THE ALTERNATE REGISTERS ARE USED TO SAVE THE
        ;ENVIRONMENT AND SPEED UP THE HOUSEKEEPING.
        ;
        ;T STATES ARE SHOWN ALONG THE RIGHT MARGIN.
        ;
ISR     EXX                     ;GET TRANSFER PARAMETERS        [4]
        OUTI                    ;TRANSFER A BYTE, BUMP COUNTER [16]
        JR      Z,DONE          ;TEST FOR END OF DATA           [7]
        EXX                     ;IF NOT THEN SAVE PARAMETERS    [4]
        EI                      ;REENABLE INTERRUPTS            [4]
        RETI                    ;RETURN CONTROL                [14]
        ;
        ;TOTAL T STATES IS 49 OR 12.25 MICROSECONDS AT 4 MHZ
```

Figure 8.28 Sample Z-80 ISR for Example 8.9.

The burst mode would be a better choice. After transferring the byte and finding the READY low, DMAC will release control of the system buses and the processor will be given 11.25 μs to work on some other task. (One or two instructions could be executed per transfer.) Programming the DMA for byte mode would work equally well.

Read/Write Registers

Although the Z-80 DMA appears to the programmer to be only one input and one output port, in fact it contains 21 writable registers and readable registers. Figure 8.29 lists the write registers, referred to as WR0 through WR6. Examining WR0, note that two ports, A and B, are defined. One of these is chosen as the *source* port and the other becomes the *destination* port. For example, programming WR0 bit 2 to a 1 defines port A as the source and port B as the destination. Subsequent programming then allows you to define specific addresses for ports A and B.

Example 8.10

Assume that DMA is to be used to transfer data from memory beginning at location D800H to an output port. If 1000H bytes are to be transferred, write the Z-80 program required to program WR0. Assume that the circuit in Fig. 8.26 is used.

Solution. WR0 actually consists of five registers. Bits 3 through 6, if set, specify that subsequent write cycles should be interpreted as the port A starting address and block length: To program this mode, the following codes should be written to WR0.

1. 01111101 (7D) A → B transfer, address and block length to follow
2. 00000000 (00) Port A starting address (low byte)
3. 11011000 (D8) Port A starting address (high byte)
4. 11111111 (FF) Block length (low byte)
5. 00001111 (0F) Block length (high byte)

Note: One more byte is transferred than is specified. The initialization program can take advantage of the Z-80's *OTIR* instruction:

```
        LD    C,0FFH      ;C HOLDS DMA PORT ADDRESS
        LD    B,05H       ;5 BYTES TO PROGRAM
        LD    HL,CODES    ;POINT HL AT CODES
        OTIR              ;PROGRAM THE BYTES
    DB  CODES   7DH,00,0D8H,0FFH,0FH
```

The following is a brief description of each of the writable registers.

WR0   Port A address, transfer or search, and source/destination definitions.

WR1   Port A controls. Note that timing can be shortened from the Z-80 standard four clock cycles per operation to two or three cycles per operation.

WR2   Port B controls.

WR3   Specifies the match byte when programmed for the search mode. The mask byte allows certain bits of the match byte to be masked (not considered).

WR4   Port B address and DMA mode. Also interrupt control, including the Z-80 mode 2 interrupt vector.

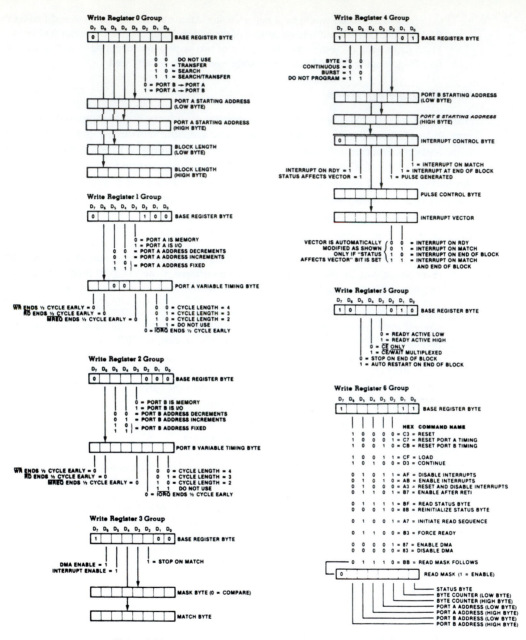

Figure 8.29 Z-80 DMA write register bit functions. (Courtesy of Zilog, Inc.)

WR5 When the end-of-block condition occurs, the DMA can be programmed to reload the starting address automatically and begin again.

WR6 Sixteen different commands can be given to the DMA. (See Fig. 8.30 for a description of each.) Example 8.11 will show how these commands are used in a typical initialization routine.

WR6 code (hex)	Command	Action/Comment
C3	Reset	Do at power on
C7	Reset port A timing	Standard Z-80 timing
CB	Reset port B timing	Standard Z-80 timing
CF	Load	Load source address register (specified by WR0) and clear byte counter; load destination address register (specified by WR4) during the first count to the destination address
D3	Continue	Clear byte counter and continue DMA
AF	Disable interrupts	Simulate $\overline{INTA}$ for non Z-80 CPUs
AB	Enable interrupts	Do only at power on or with non Z-80 CPUs to simulate RETI
A3	Reset and disable interrupts	This and the AB control word simulate the RETI instruction for non Z-80 CPUs
B7	Enable after RETI	Use when interrupt-on-RDY is selected to allow subsequent interrupt requests
BF	Read status byte	Next I/O read will be status byte
8B	Reinitialize status byte	Reinitialize (set) the match-found and end-of-block status flags
A7	Initialize read sequence	Next I/O read will be first low order read register designated by read mask
B3	Force ready	Takes the place of external READY signal for memory-memory transfers
87	Enable DMA	If RDY is active, DMA will begin immediately with $\overline{BUSRQ}$
83	Disable DMA	Prevent DMA from requesting bus even if RDY = active
BB	Read mask follows	A 0 bit masks that read register; 2-byte command

Figure 8.30 In writing to the Z-80 DMA write register 6 (WR6), 16 different commands can be specified.

The seven read registers are labeled RR0 through RR6, and their descriptions are provided in Fig. 8.31. These registers should not be read until one of two special read commands has been given (see Fig. 8.30):

1. *Read status byte:* This command causes the next CPU read operation to return the DMA status byte (the contents of the first register in the RR0 group).
2. *Initiate read sequence*: This command causes the next CPU read operation to return the contents of the first unmasked read register, beginning with RR0. For example, if the *Read mask follows* command specifies the mask word 00011001 (see WR6 in Fig. 8.29), the read registers will be read in the following order:

RR0   Status byte
RR3   Port A address counter (low byte)
RR4   Port A address counter (high byte)

Programming the Z-80 DMA

All registers of the Z-80 DMA must be programmed at power-on; none come up in a predictable state. Table 8.7 is the recommended initialization sequence. In the worst case, 35 bytes will be required. Note that the *Reset* command is given six times. This is done to

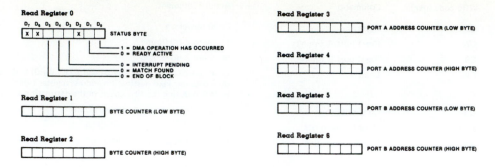

Read Register 0

D₇ D₆ D₅ D₄ D₃ D₂ D₁ D₀

| x | x | | | | x | | |

STATUS BYTE

1 = DMA OPERATION HAS OCCURRED
0 = READY ACTIVE
0 = INTERRUPT PENDING
0 = MATCH FOUND
0 = END OF BLOCK

Read Register 1

BYTE COUNTER (LOW BYTE)

Read Register 2

BYTE COUNTER (HIGH BYTE)

Read Register 3

PORT A ADDRESS COUNTER (LOW BYTE)

Read Register 4

PORT A ADDRESS COUNTER (HIGH BYTE)

Read Register 5

PORT B ADDRESS COUNTER (LOW BYTE)

Read Register 6

PORT B ADDRESS COUNTER (HIGH BYTE)

Figure 8.31 Z-80 DMA read register bit functions. (Courtesy of Zilog, Inc.)

guarantee a reset in the event that you are in the middle of a 5-byte write to WR4. (The DMA would interpret the resets as addresses.) All WR6 commands disable the DMA, except *Enable DMA,* which should be the last command programmed. In this way, if RDY is active, the DMA transfer can begin immediately.

Example 8.11

Assuming the circuit in Fig. 8.26, program the Z-80 DMA for burst mode and to transfer 1000H bytes beginning at address D800H to output port 05. Initiate the transfer with an interrupt request when the RDY input goes *low,* and generate a second interrupt at the end of the block. Determine addresses on page F8H to store the ISR jump vectors for the end-of-block and interrupt-on-RDY conditions.

TABLE 8.7 Initialization Sequence for the Z-80 DMA

Initialization/reinitialization sequence	Maximum number of bytes for Z-80 CPU
DISABLE DMA command	1
RESET command (multiple)	6
WR0 control bytes	5
WR1 control bytes	2
WR2 control bytes	2
WR3 control bytes	3
WR4 control bytes	5
WR5 control bytes	1
RESET PORT A TIMING command	1
RESET PORT B TIMING command	1
LOAD command	1
REINITIALIZE STATUS BYTE command	1
READ MASK FOLLOWS command	1
Read mask control byte	1
INITIATE READ SEQUENCE command	1
FORCE READY command	1
ENABLE INTERRUPTS command	1
ENABLE DMA command	1
	35

Source: Zilog, Incorporated.

Line	Register	Code	Action/Comment
1	WR6	83	Disable DMA
2	WR6	C3	Reset (do 6 times)
3	WR0	79	Port B → A*, transfer no search
4	WR0	00	Port A address (lower)
5	WR0	D8	Port A address (upper)
6	WR0	FF	Block length (less 1, lower)
7	WR0	0F	Block length (upper)
8	WR1	14	Standard timing, address increments Port A is memory
9	WR2	28	Standard timing, address fixed, Port B is I/O
			Skip WR3 — no match required
10	WR4	D5	Burst mode, interrupt control byte follows, no upper address, Port B lower address follows
11	WR4	05	Port B lower address
12	WR4	72	Interrupt control byte: interrupt vector follows, interrupt on end of block and RDY, status affects vector
13	WR4	E0	Interrupt vector
14	WR5	82	No auto restart, no WAIT states, RDY active low
			Skip reset port A, B timing — reset already does this
15	WR6	CF	LOAD* — load source (port B) address registers and clear byte counter
16	WR0	05	Port A → B*, transfer no search
17	WR6	CF	LOAD* — load source (port A) address register
18	WR6	8B	Reinitialize status byte
19	WR6	BB	Read mask follows
20	WR6	3F	Mask port B high address
21	WR6	A7	Reinitialize read sequence — next read will be RR0
			Skip force ready — I/O port supplies RDY input
22	WR6	AB	Enable interrupts
23	WR6	87	Enable DMA — this command should be given in the ISR

*Refer to the text to explain these steps.

Figure 8.32 Programming codes for Example 8.11.

Solution. The programming codes required are listed in Fig. 8.32 and follow the recommended sequence given in Table 8.7. Note in line 3 that port B (the I/O port) is temporarily assigned as the source. This is because the LOAD command loads a *fixed address* to a source port, not a destination port. In line 9, port B is indicated as a fixed address, and in line 15, the address is loaded from the address register to the address counter (where it is used as the DMA address). Line 16 redefines port A as the source and line 17 loads this address. In this way, port B is defined as a fixed address and the destination port.

The interrupt control register is written in line 12. The *interrupt-on-RDY* and *interrupt-on-end-of-block* conditions are enabled with bits 1 and 6. By making bit 5 a 1, the interrupt vector will automatically be altered for these two conditions. (Status affects a vector.) Bit 4 of the interrupt control byte indicates that the interrupt vector follows, and this is given in line 13. With E0H arbitrarily selected as the base, the *interrupt-on-RDY* condition will vector to F8E0H, and the *interrupt-on-end-of-block* condition will vector to F8E4H. (See WR4 in Fig. 8.29.)

The programming codes end by enabling interrupts, but not the DMA. Now, as soon as RDY goes low, control is transferred to the ISR whose address is stored in F8E0. Presumably, this routine enables the DMA, and a burst transfer occurs until RDY goes inactive. The DMA releases control of the buses and normal processing resumes. When the peripheral is ready for new data (RDY = 0), the DMA requests control of the buses and the transfer continues. Eventually, the entire block will be transferred and an interrupt generated (interrupt on end of block), vectoring to the ISR whose address is stored in F8E4H. This routine can define a new block or end the DMA.

The program to support the codes in Fig. 8.32 is very similar to the program given in Example 8.10, except that mode 2 interrupts should be specified and the I register loaded.

SELF-REVIEW 8.3

8.3.1. The Z-80 DMA performs sequential DMA cycles. What does this mean?

8.3.2. What are the two ways of requesting that a DMA transfer begin?

8.3.3. Which Z-80 DMA mode—byte, burst, or continuous—does not relinquish control of the system buses until all bytes have been transferred?

8.3.4. The DMA programming sequence should begin with a disable DMA command. This is accomplished by writing _____ to register _____.

8.4 PERIPHERAL CONTROLLER BUS BUFFERING TECHNIQUES

When using the special family support devices, one must pay careful attention to the bus buffers. The techniques required are the same, whether the Z-80 family or the 8080/85 family of devices is being considered. Section 7.6 provides details on the techniques required.

QUESTIONS AND ANSWERS

Q: *Are the Z-80 support devices compatible with the 8080/8085 processors and vice versa?*

A: No. Although the 8080/8085 support devices can be used with a Z-80 CPU, the Z-80 devices require signals not present with an 8080/8085 processor.

Q: *Describe the I/O ports available with the Z-80 PIO.*

A: Two 8-bit programmable input/output ports are provided, each with two handshaking signals.

Q: *What are the four operating modes of the Z-80 PIO?*

A: Mode 0: Output port with handshaking. Mode 1: input port with handshaking. Mode 2: bidirectional I/O port. Mode 3: bit-programmable I/O port.

Q: *How do the Z-80 peripheral controller chips support interrupts?*

A: A daisy-chain priority structure is implemented using Z-80 mode 2 interrupts.

Q: *What are the basic features of the Z-80 CTC?*

A: Four 8-bit counter/timer channels are provided.

Q: *How does the Z-80 CTC operate in counter mode?*

A: The CTC will decrement an 8-bit counter with each external clock pulse. When a 0 count occurs, an interrupt can be requested, and the ZC/T0 output will pulse high for 1.5 clock periods.

Q: *How does the Z-80 CTC operate in timer mode?*

A: Timer mode is the same as counter mode, except that the counter is decremented once for every 16 or 256 system clock pulses.

Q: *What type of DMA cycle does the Z-80 DMA perform? What is the transfer rate?*

A: The Z-80 DMA performs sequential DMA transfers. (Read a byte into the DMAC, and write the byte to the destination.) The transfer rate is 1 MB/s.

Q: *How many channels are provided by the Z-80 DMA?*

A: One channel, with separately programmable 16-bit source and destination addresses.

Q: *What DMA transfer modes are supported by the Z-80 DMA?*

A: Byte-, burst-, and block-mode transfers can be programmed. In addition, a maskable match byte can be specified in search mode.

LAB PROJECTS

8.1. Study the schematic diagram of the microcomputer you are using to support this text or course, and see whether your computer uses a Z-80 PIO. If so, answer the following questions about the interface:

    (a) To what range of addresses is the chip mapped?

    (b) List the I/O devices (if any) connected to ports A and B.

    (c) List the operating modes for ports A and B.

8.2. Write a program to access your computer's PIO chip. For example, if a keypad and display are interfaced, write a program to read the keyboard and display the key's value. If a speaker is connected to one output bit, write a program to produce a tone. (Program 14 in Chapter 3 is an example of a computer music program.)

8.3. Using Fig. 8.33 as a guide, build the PIO matrix keyboard interface shown. Problems 8.8 and 8.9 outline the necessary control software.

8.4. Construct the mode 0 and mode 1 PIO parallel-printer interface shown in Fig. 8.8. The program in Fig. 8.9 can be used to send (ASCII) data to the printer. A female DB-25 connector with long wires attached can be employed to bring the printer signals to a breadboard.

8.5. Repeat Lab Project 8.1 for the Z-80 CTC.

8.6. Using a circuit similar to Fig. 8.16, program the Z-80 CTC.

    (a) as a one-shot triggered by the CLK/TRG input. (See Problems 8.19–8.21.)

    (b) as a divide-by-N counter. Use a signal generator as the CLK input, and observe the output on an oscilloscope. (See Problems 8.17 and 8.21.)

QUESTIONS AND PROBLEMS

Section 8.1

    8.1. The Z-80 port B control register is accessed when $C/\overline{D}$ is _____ and $B/\overline{A}$ is _____.

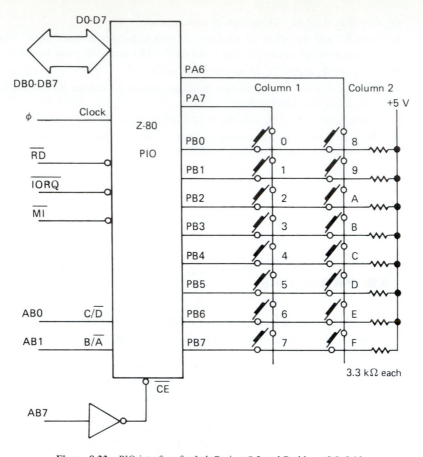

Figure 8.33 PIO interface for Lab Project 8.3 and Problems 8.8–8.10.

8.2. The Z-80 PIO and CTC do not use the CPU's $\overline{WR}$ signal. How is an I/O write cycle detected by these chips?

8.3. Write a program like that of Example 8.2 for the Z-80 PIO interface in Fig. 8.2. Have your program enable mode 2 interrupts on port A, assuming a jump table at address C840H.

8.4. Refer to the Z-80 PIO interface in Fig. 8.2. Write a program that will cause the PIO to generate an interrupt when bits PA0, PA1, and PA4, each programmed as an input, are all low. Program the remaining bits of port A as outputs.

8.5. The program in Fig. 8.34 is written to control the PIO interface in Fig. 8.2. Answer the following questions about this program:
  (a) Which port—A or B—is being programmed?
  (b) What PIO mode is being programmed?
  (c) Under what conditions will an interrupt be generated?
  (d) What is the interrupt vector address?

8.6. Assume the hardware interface in Fig. 8.2, and specify the PIO programming sequence required for the following configuration:
  (a) Port A = mode 3, all bits active-high inputs.
  (b) Port B = mode 0.

```
           IM      2

           LD      A,80H

           LD      I,A

INIT       LD      HL,CODES

           LD      B,5

           LD      C,F3H

           OTIR

CODES      DEFB    CFH, F0H, B7H, 3FH, 6EH      Figure 8.34   Program for Problem 8.5.
```

(c) Port A low-order interrupt vector = 00.

(d) Port B interrupts disabled.

(e) Port A interrupt request to occur only if PA1, PA2, or PA7 is high.

8.7. Suppose that port A of the Z-80 PIO interface in Fig. 8.2 is used to control an industrial process with bit definitions as shown in Fig. 8.35. Bits 0, 2, and 3 are active-high inputs, while bits 5 and 7 are active-high alarm outputs. Write two subroutines to supervise control of this process. Subroutine 1 should initialize the PIO, turn on the power, and, after a 10-s delay, turn on the heaters. Subroutine 2 should be called as an ISR if OVFLW or HIGH TEMP occurs. If an OVFLW condition occurs, cause the process to halt; if HIGH TEMP occurs, power down the system.

8.8. Figure 8.33 shows a 16-key switch matrix interfaced to a Z-80 PIO. This circuit is similar to the memory-mapped interface in Fig. 6.8 of Chapter 6. Answer the following questions about this interface:

(a) What *range* of I/O addresses does the PIO occupy?

(b) To read only column 1, PA6 must be _____ and PA7 must be _____.

(c) If only key 6 is held down, what hex code will be read from PIO port B?

8.9. Write the software to control the keyboard interface in Fig. 8.33. Your program should have the following subroutines:

(a) INIT: Program the PIO chip so that port A is an output and port B an input. Any active-low input on port B should cause an interrupt to location 8000H.

(b) START: Program PA6 and PA7 low to enable both columns. Check to make sure that no keys are down (KREAD subroutine), and then enable interrupts.

(c) KREAD: Read port B and set flags. (A nonzero result means that a key is down in the active column.)

(d) ISR: When any key is pressed, control vectors here. This routine should call KREAD and encode the key pressed in register A.

*8.10. In Fig. 8.33, suppose that key 5 is stuck closed. What would the *symptom* of this problem be, assuming the control software described in Problem 8.9?

D7	D6	D5	D4	D3	D2	D1	D0
OVFLW	X	HIGH TEMP	X	POWER ON	HEATERS ON	X	HALT PROCESS

Figure 8.35   PIO port A bit definitions for Problem 8.7.

8.11. Sketch a timing diagram for the PIO printer interface and control program shown in Figs. 8.8 and 8.9, respectively. Your diagram should include ARDY/ASTB, STROBE, BUSY/READY, $\overline{ACK}$, BSTB, and $\overline{INT}$.

*8.12. Suppose the PIO printer interface in Fig. 8.8 malfunctions in such a way that the PB0 input is always high. Which of the following would be symptoms of this problem?
   (a) The printer would miss characters because the CPU would be outputting data faster than the data could be printed.
   (b) The message "PRINTER OFF-LINE" would be output each time the printer was accessed.
   (c) Bus contention could occur each time the CPU attempted to read from the PIO chip.

8.13. What codes must be output to ports A and B in the PIO-controlled multiplexed display in Fig. 8.12 to cause the letter "F" to appear in the digit 2 position?

*8.14. If the digit 4 and digit 5 pins of IC6 in the multiplexed display in Fig. 8.12 were accidentally shorted together, what would the symptom of this problem be? Assume that the software in Fig. 8.14 is used to control the interface.

*8.15. In Fig. 8.12, suppose that the digit 0 output of IC6 is stuck low. What would the *symptom* of this problem be?

8.16. Write a program for the multiplexed display in Fig. 8.12 that will cause the message "CPU UP" to appear in the six displays.

Section 8.2

8.17. A Z-80 CTC is interfaced to a 4-MHz Z-80 microprocessor. A 2-MHz square-wave signal is connected to the CLK/TRG0 input of the CTC.
   (a) When the CTC is operated in the counter mode, what is the maximum time delay that can be programmed between successive ZC/TO0 output pulses?
   (b) Repeat (a) for the timer mode.
   (c) Repeat (a) if channels 0, 1, and 2 are cascaded and the output is taken at ZC/TO2.

8.18. Suppose the CTC in Example 8.7 is programmed with the following time constants: channel 0 = E8H and channel 1 = 03H. How many clock edges will occur between ZC/TO1 output pulses?

8.19. Assuming the I/O ports shown in Fig. 8.16, write a program to initialize the CTC as follows:
   (a) Channel 0 timer mode, time constant = F9H, interrupts enabled, falling = edge trigger, prescale = 256.
   (b) Channel 1 counter mode, time constant = B3H, interrupts enabled, rising-edge trigger.

8.20. Calculate the width of the one-shot pulse produced by the CTC circuit in Fig. 8.23 when it is programmed as described in Problem 8.19. Assume the system clock frequency is 4 MHz.

8.21. Write a BASIC program to find all possible time-constant combinations of N0 and N1 that solve the equation

$$N0 \times N1 \times P = N$$

where N0 and N1 are integers between 1 and 256; P is a prescale factor, either 16 or 256; and N is an integer describing the Z-80 CTC as a divide-by-N counter with channel 0 a timer, and channel 1 a counter, wired in cascade.

8.22. Calculate the frequency and duty cycle of output Q in Fig. 8.36. Assume channel 0 of the CTC is programmed as a timer with prescale factor = 16, time constant = 125, and an automatic trigger.

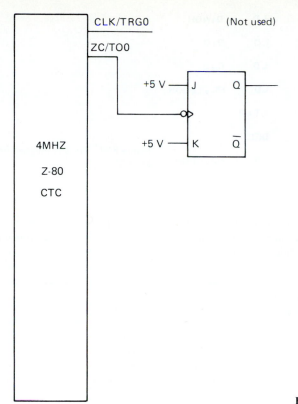

CLK/TRG0   (Not used)

ZC/TO0

+5 V ── J   Q

+5 V ── K $\overline{Q}$

4MHZ

Z-80

CTC

Figure 8.36   CTC circuit for Problem 8.22.

8.23. Sketch a circuit diagram to interface a Z-80 PIO at I/O ports 40–43H and a Z-80 CTC at ports 44–47H using full decoding. Connect the daisy-chain interrupts such that the PIO has the highest priority.

Section 8.3

8.24. Which are faster, sequential or simultaneous DMA transfers? Why?

8.25. State the logic condition—active or inactive—of the Z-80 DMA RDY and $\overline{\text{WAIT}}$ inputs in order for a DMA transfer to take place.

8.26. With a cycle length of 4, calculate the length of time required by a Z-80 DMA to transfer a 16K-byte file to an I/O device, assuming a 4-MHz clock and sequential DMA.

8.27. The program in Fig. 8.37 uses the Z-80 OTIR instruction to transfer a block of data from memory to an I/O device. (In effect, this is a DMA transfer using the Z-80 as the controller.) Answer the following questions about this program:
  (a) What is the I/O port address?
  (b) What is the starting memory location?
  (c) How many bytes will be transferred?
  (d) Calculate the data transfer rate, assuming a 4-MHz clock.
  (e) How long will it take to transfer the entire block?

```
             LD      D,40H

             LD      B,0

             LD      C,5

             LD      HL,1000H

   LOOP      OTIR

             DEC     D

             JR      NZ,LOOP
```

Figure 8.37 Transfer program for Problem 8.27.

8.28. Suppose a 16K-byte DMA transfer is to take place from I/O port 07H to memory beginning at address A000H and using the Z-80 DMA. For each of the following, determine the specified bytes for the conditions listed:

	Register	No. of bytes to program	Condition
(a)	WR0	4	A $\rightarrow$ B transfer
(b)	WR1	1	Normal timing, four cycles
(c)	WR2	1	Normal timing, four cycles
(d)	WR4	5	Interrupt on RDY and end of block, burst, vector address 8040H
(e)	WR5	1	Active-high RDY, $\overline{CE}/\overline{WAIT}$ multiplexed, stop on end of block
(f)	WR6	1	Disable DMA

8.29. Calculate the worst-case 4-MHz Z-80A response (the time from RDY active until the first instruction of the service routine) for each of the following:

(a) Polling:

```
        LOOP      IN      A,(C)
                  RRA
                  JR      NC,LOOP
        ;service routine begins here
```

(b) The peripheral's READY flag is used to generate a mode 2 interrupt.

(c) The peripheral's READY flag is used to initiate a Z-80 DMA transfer (with no interrupts).

Section 8.4

8.30. Suppose the data bus of the Z-80 PIO in Fig. 8.2 is buffered with a bidirectional bus buffer. (See, for example, Fig. 7.50) What signals should be used to control the DIR and $\overline{E}$ inputs of the buffer?

SELF-REVIEW ANSWERS

8.1.1. mode 3

8.1.2. lowest

8.1.3. AND, OR

8.1.4. $\overline{\text{STROBE}}$

8.1.5. Only one decoder/driver is required.

8.2.1. counter and timer

8.2.2. external clock applied to CLK/TRG input

8.2.3. 256

8.2.4. 16, 256

8.3.1. Data is read into the DMA and then written to the destination.

8.3.2. (1) When RDY becomes active, begin the DMA transfer. This requires the DMA to be enabled ahead of time. (2) Enable the DMA after RDY becomes active (via an interrupt).

8.3.3. continuous

8.3.4. 83H, WR6

9

SERIAL I/O TECHNIQUES

OUTLINE

9.1 Asynchronous Serial Communications

9.2 Synchronous Serial Communications

9.3 Error Detection and Correction

9.4 The Intel 8251A USART

9.5 The Zilog Z-80 SIO and Z-80 DART

9.6 Remote Control Applications for Asynchronous Serial Data

9.7 Serial Data Interface Standards

9.8 Telecommunications

OBJECTIVES

After completing this chapter, you should be able to:

- Explain the role of start and stop bits in asynchronous serial communications.
- Identify the function of the universal asynchronous receiver/transmitter (UART) in a serial interface.
- Explain how serial data can be transmitted in synchronous form without start and stop bits.
- Show the difference between synchronous data frames in bisync and SDLC formats.

- Show how parity, checksums, and CRC are used to detect transmission errors in digital systems.
- Explain how the Hamming code can be used to detect and correct transmission errors in digital systems.
- Show how to interface the 8251A USART to the three-bus system architecture of the 8080/8085 processors.
- Explain how to program the 8251A USART for asynchronous or synchronous data communications.
- Show how to interface the Z-80 SIO to the three-bus system architecture of the Z-80 processor.
- Explain how to program the Z-80 SIO for asynchronous or synchronous data communications.
- Show how two UARTs can be interfaced to allow a remote-control application.
- Explain how the MC14469 can be used to construct a network of addressable UARTs.
- Describe the electrical characteristics of the RS-232 serial interface standard and show how to construct a TTL-compatible interface.
- Identify and describe the function of the signals that make up the RS-232 standard.
- Identify common national and international standards for modems.
- Show how the AT command set is used to control the functions of a modem.

OVERVIEW

All microcomputer input/output falls under one of two broad categories: *serial* or *parallel*. A parallel port is the more natural for the 8080, 8085, and Z-80, because such ports are designed for 8-bit parallel data transfers. All of their registers are 8 bits wide (or multiples of 8 bits), and the data bus is optimized for the handling of parallel data. Because of these features, data bytes can be transferred at very high speeds. For example, the Z-80 *OTIR* instruction can transfer data to a parallel port at over 190,000 bytes per second.

However, the parallel port is not without its drawbacks. In most cases, the high transfer speed requires some form of handshaking logic to synchronize the data transfer. In the case of a printer, the following are required:

1. One 8-bit parallel output port
2. One 1-bit input port to monitor BUSY/$\overline{\text{READY}}$
3. A device select pulse for the $\overline{\text{STROBE}}$ signal

This means (at least) that an 11-conductor cable will be required. The parallel port also tends to become *hardware specific,* with the result that a parallel port on one computer may not be compatible with a parallel port on another. (For example, the $\overline{\text{STROBE}}$ signals might not match, or one port might use the $\overline{\text{ACK}}$ signal and the other a BUSY/$\overline{\text{READY}}$ signal.)

A *serial* I/O port transmits each data byte bit by bit. The immediate advantage of this technique is that only two conductors are required—the signal wire and ground—three wires if *full-duplex* operation (simultaneous transmission and reception) is allowed.

Of course, we must decide how long each bit will persist and what the order of the bits will be. These "rules" are referred to as the *serial communications protocol*. As you might imagine, several different protocols have been developed over the years.

The obvious penalty with a serial I/O port is a significant reduction in the data transfer rate. The most popular serial standard, *EIA RS-232*, restricts the data rate to less than 2000 bytes per second and cable lengths to less than 50 ft. Newer (and faster) standards have been proposed, but have not (yet) gained the RS-232's popularity.

Despite this disadvantage, serial communications—and the RS-232 standard in particular—have become widely accepted. One of the reasons is the definition by the EIA committee of a "standard" serial port. By defining the protocol (right down to the pinning of the connector), users can be sure of compatibility between their equipment and an RS-232 serial port.

Another powerful feature of serialized data is that such data can easily be converted to audio tones and transmitted over the switched telephone network. This is done with a *modem* and allows communications between computer equipment thousands of miles apart.

In this chapter, we study *synchronous* and *asynchronous* serial I/O ports and the Intel 8251 USART and Zilog Z-80 SIO. These chips are used to convert data from parallel to serial form and vice versa. Common error detection and correction techniques are also discussed. The chapter concludes with an introduction to the prevailing modem standards used in the telecommunications field.

9.1 ASYNCHRONOUS SERIAL COMMUNICATIONS

Introduction

One of the most common applications of a serial I/O port is the interface of a keyboard on a video display terminal (VDT). In this circuit, each keystroke generates a 7-bit ASCII code that is converted to bit-by-bit serial form and then transmitted to a computer over a two- or three-conductor cable. Because even the fastest typist cannot exceed data rates of 60 to 100 words per minute, these rates are a good match for the (relatively) slow transmission rate of the serial port.

Note an important characteristic of this interface: At some times the serial port will be required to transfer data at 10 to 20 characters per second, but at other times the data rate may be only 1 or 2 characters per second. Indeed, most of the time the keyboard is not in use and the data rate is zero. Because of this erratic data rate, an *asynchronous* communications protocol must be established.

In this section, we:

- Explain the role of start and stop bits in asynchronous serial communications.
- Identify the function of the universal asynchronous receiver/transmitter (UART) in a serial interface.

Start Bits, Stop Bits, and the Baud Rate

The accepted technique for asynchronous serial communications is to hold the serial output line at a logic 1 level (called a *mark*) until data is to be transmitted. Each character is

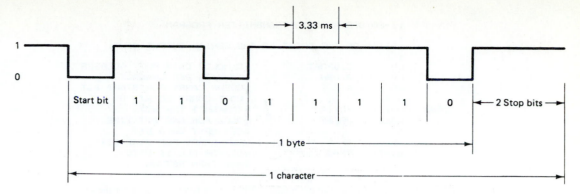

Figure 9.1 Standard asynchronous serial data format. The data byte is framed between the start bit and two stop bits. In this example, the data byte is 7BH.

required to begin with a logic 0 (called a *space*). This character is called the *start bit* and is used to synchronize the transmitter and receiver. Figure 9.1 illustrates how the data byte 7BH would look when transmitted in the asynchronous serial format. The data is sent least significant bit first and framed between a start bit (always a 0) and one or two stop bits (always a 1).

The start and stop bits carry no information, but are required because of the asynchronous nature of the data. The data rate can be expressed as bits per second (bps) or characters per second (cps). The term "bits per second" is also called the *baud rate*.*

Example 9.1

Calculate the baud rate and character rate for the serial data shown in Fig. 9.1.

Solution. Because one bit persists for 3.33 ms, the bps rate is 1/3.33 ms = 300 bps, or 300 baud. Because there are 11 bits per character, it will require 11 × 3.33 ms = 36.63 ms to transmit the entire byte. The character rate is therefore 1/36.63 ms = 27.3 cps.

Example 9.2

A VDT has 80 characters per line and 24 lines. At 300 baud, how long will it take to fill the screen of this terminal?

Solution. The total number of characters required is 80 × 24 = 1920. The total time is thus

$$\frac{1920 \text{ characters}}{27.3 \text{ cps}} = 70.3 \text{ s}$$

(*Note:* A *memory-mapped* video display could fill this screen in less than 1 s, reflecting the difference between writing to memory and writing to the serial port.)

Generating and Recovering Asynchronous Serial Data

All microprocessors are capable of generating serial data without special hardware. For example, consider the Z-80 program in Fig. 9.2. Suppose that bit 0 of the DPORT is used

---

Baud rate actually refers to *signal events* per second. This is often the same as bits/s—but not always, as shown later in the chapter.

```
;Z-80 SERIAL DATA TRANSMITTER PROGRAM
;
;BIT 0 OF THE DPORT IS THE SERIAL OUTPUT LINE.
;
        LD      C,DPORT         ;C HOLDS DATA PORT ADDRESS
        LD      B,0BH           ;11 BITS PER CHARACTER
        AND     A               ;CLEAR CARRY FOR START BIT
        RLA                     ;MOVE CARRY TO BIT 0
TRAN    OUT     (C),A           ;TRANSMIT THE BIT
        CALL    DELAY           ;HOLD FOR ONE BIT TIME
        RRA                     ;GET NEXT DATA BIT
        SCF                     ;SET CARRY FOR STOP BIT
        DJNZ    TRAN            ;DO FOR ALL 11 BITS
        RET                     ;AND THEN RETURN
```

Figure 9.2 Z-80 serial transmitter program. Bit 0 of the DPORT is used for the serial output line.

as the serial output pin. Each bit to be transmitted is rotated to the bit 0 position of the accumulator and output. The DELAY subroutine determines the baud rate.

The 8085 microprocessor even has two pins—serial output data (*SOD*) and serial input data (*SID*) devoted specifically to this task. Hence, in this case, an external data port is not required. (See Problem 9.7.)

Recovering serial data requires a more complex program, but again, no special hardware is needed. Fig. 9.3 flowcharts the process, assuming that a 1-bit input port is used. The program begins by waiting for the one-to-zero transition of the start bit. Once this is found, the middle of the bit is located by waiting one-half bit time. If the input bit is still 0, a valid start bit is assumed, and the program then waits for one additional bit time (thus sampling in the middle of all subsequent bits).

As each bit is read, it is rotated right—through the carry—and after eight reads the entire byte has been recovered. The ninth read should return the first stop bit, but if this bit is low, a *framing* error is indicated. If the stop bit is high, the data byte can be saved, and the program begins searching for the next start bit.

Our discussion has thus far implied that the receiver and transmitter data rates are exactly matched. But is this necessary? Can we tolerate slight differences? For example, with the use of software timing loops, it is unlikely that the DELAY subroutine in two different computers will be *exactly* the same.

Figure 9.4 illustrates the results of trying to recover data that are too fast or too slow for the receiver. In either case, note how the error *accumulates*. If sampling is done in the middle of the bit time, the maximum allowable error will cause the ninth bit to be shifted 1/2 bit time to the right or left. If all bits are shifted equally (because of a data rate mismatch), the amount of error in one bit will be 1/2 bit time $\div$ 9 = 1/18 bit time. This means that the rates for received and transmitted data must match within 5.6%.

This is an interesting result. You might have guessed that the data rates had to match exactly. That would be true if there were no start or stop bits. But because of these bits, synchronization need only be held from the beginning of one start bit to the beginning of the first stop bit. The technique *self-synchronizes* itself after each character. Of course, the price we pay for self-synchronization is that each data byte must be increased in length by 3 bits, or 37.5% (25% with only one stop bit). If these bits were not required, the character rate calculated in Example 9.2 would rise to 37.5 cps, and the VDT screen could be filled in 52 s instead of 70 s.

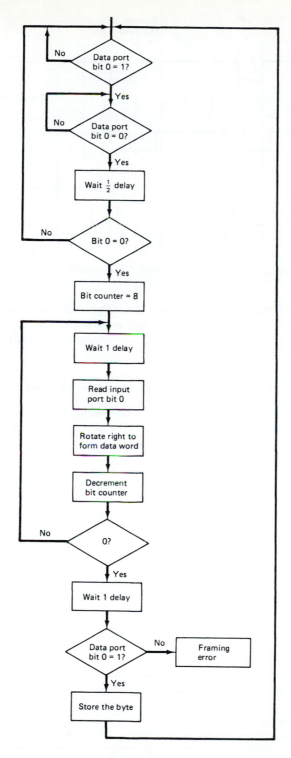

Figure 9.3 Flowchart of the process required to recover asynchronous serial data.

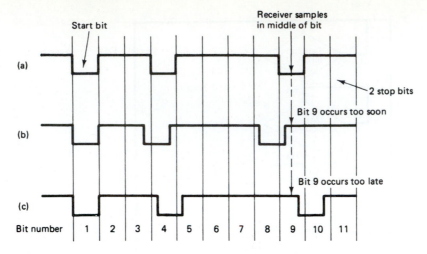

Figure 9.4 (a) Data transmitted at the proper rate; (b) the data rate is too fast; (c) the data rate is too slow.

In some cases, a logic 1 might be delayed more than a logic 0 (or vice versa) when passing through the transmission medium. This can lead to individual bit errors rather than framing errors. Because of that possibility, the rule of thumb is to try to match the rates for receiving and transmitting data to 1% or less.

Standard Asynchronous Serial Communications Protocols

As mentioned previously, protocols define certain rules that should be followed to help standardize the communications technique. An example is the adoption of a 0 start bit and logic 1 stop bits. Certain baud rates have also become standard and are listed in Table 9.1.

TABLE 9.1 Common Data Rates for Serial Data Communications

75	
110	These first three rates are now obsolete. They were used with early teletype equipment.
150	
300	Early modems operated at 300 baud.
600	
1200	
2400	
4800	
9600	
14,400	This is a popular modem data rate. Referred to as "14.4."
19,200	
28,800	For several years this was the top-of-the-line speed for modems.
33,600	Some 28.8 modems can be upgraded to operate at this speed.
38,400	
57,600	The current maximum data rate for modems.
115,200	28.8 modems can exchange data with the PC at this rate.

In setting up a serial port, several parameters must be specified, the most common of which are as follows:

1. Data bits per character, usually five to eight
2. Stop bits, one or two
3. Parity bit, used to detect single-bit errors, may be specified as odd or even or no parity (see Section 9.3)
4. Baud rate (see Table 9.1 for standard frequencies)

As an example, the old (and venerable) ASR-33 teletype (TTY) requires seven data bits, two stop bits, (3) even parity, and (4) 110 baud.

The UART

Although serial data can be received and transmitted via software, programs that are able to adapt to the various protocols can become very long and tedious, tying up the processor in timing loops, shuffling data bits, and, in general, requiring time that might otherwise be spent more efficiently. For this reason, the semiconductor companies long ago designed the single-chip *universal asynchronous receiver/transmitter,* or UART.

Figure 9.5 is the block diagram of a common second-generation part, the General Instruments AY-5-1013. This chip provides a separate and independent transmitter and receiver of serial data. The two clock inputs (labeled *16X CLOCK*) determine the baud rate and should be chosen 16 times higher than the intended data rate. For example, if the transmitter should operate at 300 baud, the transmitter clock pin should receive a 4800-Hz square wave.

By dividing each bit time into 16 periods, the UART is more accurately able to locate the center of each data bit. Some UARTs allow the clock to be 32 or 64 times the data rate.

Note that because of the separate receiver and transmitter circuits, full-duplex operation—that is, simultaneous transmission and reception—can occur. This would be particularly difficult to accomplish with the "software UART" discussed earlier.

I called the AY-5-1013 a *second-generation* part because it combines the receiver and transmitter functions in a single chip. However, unlike third-generation parts, all of its control functions must be hardwired. That is, they are not directly programmable by the microprocessor. The following functions can be selected:

1. *Data word (DW1, DW2)*: allows 5 to 8 bits per data word
2. *Parity select (PS)*: odd or even parity
3. *Stop bits (SB)*: 1 or 2
4. *No parity (NP)*: no parity bit

In addition to these control functions, three status bits can be monitored:

1. *Transmitter buffer empty (TBE)*: transmitter is ready for a new character
2. *Receiver data ready (RDR)*: receiver has a character to be read
3. *End of transmission (EOT)*: no character is being transmitted

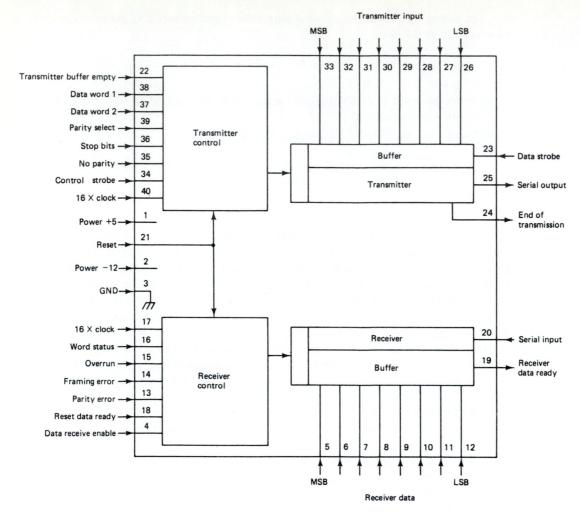

Figure 9.5 The AY-5-1013 UART. A separate transmitter and receiver are provided. Control functions are hardwired.

Three other signals are provided to indicate error conditions:

1. *Framing error* (*FE*): stop bit not received
2. *Parity error* (*PE*): received word's parity is incorrect
3. *Overrun* (*OR*) *error:* new received character has overwritten the preceding one

Figure 9.6 illustrates how the AY-5-1013 can be interfaced to the three-bus system architecture of any of the CPU modules discussed in Chapter 4. To understand this circuit, consider the sequence of events as one character is transmitted and received.

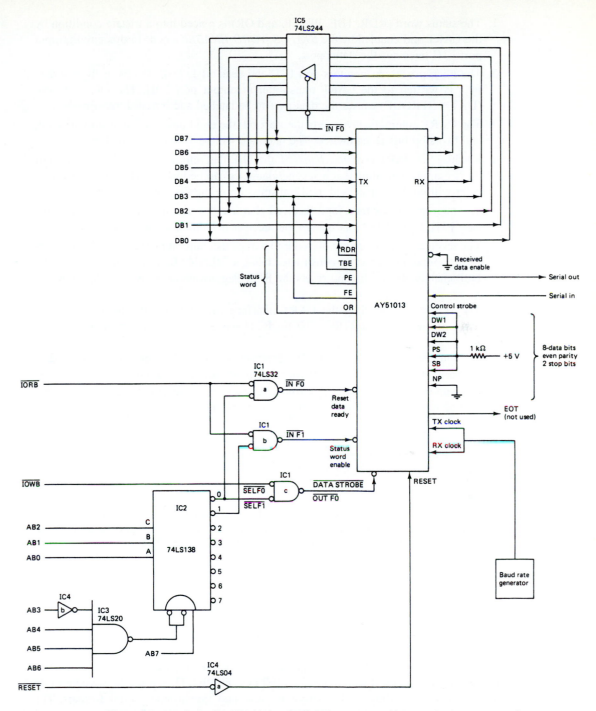

Figure 9.6 Interfacing the AY-5-1013 to the three-bus system architecture. One output port and two input ports are required.

1. The status word (RDR, TBE, PE, FE, and OR) is placed into a tristate condition by the UART and enabled by the *STATUS WORD ENABLE* input. In this circuit, input port F1H becomes the status port.

2. The microprocessor monitors port F1H and tests bit 1, TBE. If TBE is high, a data byte is written to the UART transmitter at output port F0H. The OUT F0 DSP (DATA STROBE) causes the data byte to be latched and initiates transmission.

3. The UART automatically inserts the start bit, the eight data bits, an even-parity bit, and two stop bits as hardwired. The data rate will be 1/16 of the clock rate.

4. Because the UART is *double buffered,* the TBE flag returns high as soon as the start bit is output, indicating that a second character can be loaded. (However, this character will not be transmitted until transmission of the first one is complete.)

5. The microprocessor tests for a received character by reading the status port, in this case F1H. If the RDR flag is high the receiver is holding a data byte.

6. The receiver outputs are not placed into a tristate condition by the AY-5-1013; therefore, an input port must be constructed using a 74LS244 buffer. Note that the $\overline{\text{IN F0}}$ DSP enables this buffer and resets the RDR flag, avoiding an overrun condition.

The software controlling the UART interface can also test the three error flags while waiting for TBE and RDR to be ready. However, in many cases these lines are ignored.

The interesting feature of the UART interface is that, to the microprocessor, the data transfer appears to be parallel. The microprocessor simply writes a byte to the transmitter (parallel) output port and reads a byte from the receiver (parallel) input port. The UART takes care of serializing the data, inserting start, stop, and parity bits, and controlling the data rate.

Usually, the UART is controlled with a simple polling routine, but interrupts and DMAs can also be used. Either of the latter two might be a good choice due to the (relatively) long period between ready signals.

Example 9.3

Consider again Program 9 in Chapter 3. This is a simple serial communications test program that causes the UART to transmit to itself. (Serial out must be connected to serial in.) What changes should be made to the program to adapt it to the circuit of Fig. 9.6?

Solution. The following equates should be changed:

```
SPORT    EQU   0F1H
DPORT    EQU   0F0H
TMSK     EQU   2
RMSK     EQU   1
```

Third-generation UARTs are programmable by the microprocessor in a manner similar to the techniques used with the 8255A PPI or Z-80 PIO. They are also more versatile than the AY-5-1013, allowing both asynchronous and synchronous serial formats. The Intel 8251A USART and Zilog Z-80 SIO circuits are discussed in detail in Sections 9.4 and 9.5.

SELF-REVIEW 9.1

9.1.1 Asynchronous serial data is framed between a _____ bit and one or more _____ bits.

9.1.2 The serial data rate in bits per second is often called the _____ rate.

9.1.3 The _____ is an integrated circuit designed to transmit and receive asynchronous serial data.

9.2 SYNCHRONOUS SERIAL COMMUNICATIONS

Introduction

The start and stop bits of asynchronous serial communications represent wasted overhead bits that reduce the overall character rate no matter what the baud rate. Even adding a parity bit can reduce the transfer rate by 10%.

But giving up the start and stop bits will require some means of synchronizing the data. How will we know when the data starts and when to sample the data?

In this section, we:

- Explain how serial data can be transmitted in synchronous form without start and stop bits.
- Show the difference between synchronous data frames in bisync and SDLC formats.

Bisync Protocol

Because there is no start bit, a special *sync* character is required in all synchronous serial formats. This character tells the receiver that data is about to follow. This requires the UART to have a special "hunt" or "search" mode so that the sync character can be found.

Because there is no stop bit, a clock signal usually accompanies the synchronous data to maintain synchronization. When synchronous serial data is to be transmitted over the telephone network, it is not possible to provide a separate clock channel. Instead, in this case, a special *synchronous modem* is used that encodes the data and clock into a single signal. The receiving modem separates the data and clock signals.

Another difference compared to asynchronous serial is that the clock rate is the same as the baud rate. (That is, a 1X clock is used.)

In the *bisync* protocol, several special (ASCII) characters are used to control the data transfer, as shown in Table 9.2. Figure 9.7 illustrates one "frame" of a synchronous message. Just as asynchronous data is framed between start and stop bits, synchronous data is framed between special control codes. In the figure, two sync characters are output, followed by *STX*—start of text. Next, the data bytes follow. This block may consist of 100 or more data bytes or may simply be other control codes. *ETX* signifies the end of text. *BCC* is a block check character for error detection. (See Section 9.3.) *PAD* is the character that is output when no data is being transmitted and corresponds to the "mark" output in asynchronous serial transmission.

TABLE 9.2 Special Characters Used in the Bisync Synchronous Serial Protocol

Character	ASCII code	Description
SYNC	16	Sync character
PAD	FF	End-of-frame pad
DLE	10	Data link escape
ENQ	05	Enquiry
SOH	01	Start of header
STX	02	Start of text
ITB	0F	End of intermediate transmission block
ETB	17	End of transmission block
ETX	03	End of text

Of course, the bisync protocol is simply a set of rules that everyone has agreed to follow. It is not necessarily any better or worse than some other set of rules.

Example 9.4

Calculate the percentage of "wasted" bits incurred in using the bisync protocol compared with eight-data-bit, two-stop-bit, one-parity-bit asynchronous serial transmission. Assume that the data block size is 100 bytes.

Solution. The overhead required for the asynchronous character is 50% (4 extra bits for each byte). The bisync protocol requires six extra bytes (assuming a 16-bit BCC) for the 100-byte block. The overhead is 6%.

The consequences of the reduced overhead should be clear: For a given baud rate, synchronous data will have a considerably higher character rate.

Another not-so-obvious advantage of synchronous data is due to the UART clock rate being the same as the data rate. (That is, the multiplier is 1, not 16.) This means that for a given UART maximum operating frequency, the synchronous baud rate can be 16 times higher than the asynchronous rate.

Serial Data Link Control

This format was developed by IBM for use with the company's Systems Network Architecture (SNA) communications package. Figure 9.8 illustrates one frame of data using this protocol, which is similar to bisync, but is not byte oriented.

The serial data link control (SDLC) receiver searches for the beginning flag (01111110) as its sync character. An 8-bit address field follows, allowing each frame to be addressed to a particular station among a network of stations. Next is an 8-bit control field with special control characters identified by a sequence of six or more logic 1's.

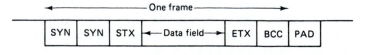

Figure 9.7   One frame of a synchronous message using the bisync protocol.

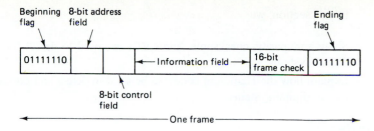

Figure 9.8 One frame of a synchronous message using the SDLC protocol.

The information field can be of any format. (That is, it does not have to consist of an integral number of bytes.) The transmitter will automatically insert 0's in this field if five or more logic 1's should appear in sequence. This will avoid inadvertent control characters appearing in the information field. The receiver automatically deletes these 0's.

The 16-bit frame check is used for error detection, similarly to the way the BCC character is used in bisync. The frame ends with the ending flag.

SDLC is actually a subset of HDLC (high-level data link control), which is an international synchronous communications protocol. As with bisync, SDLC is simply a set of rules that have been agreed on for the transfer of serial data.

SELF-REVIEW 9.2

9.2.1 How does the transmission of synchronous serial data differ from that of asynchronous serial data?

9.2.2 The bisync serial protocol is _____ oriented, but the SDLC protocol format is _____ oriented.

9.3 ERROR DETECTION AND CORRECTION

Introduction

Whenever data is transmitted between two points, it is important to be sure of the integrity of the data. This is true whether the data path is a 2000-mile telephone connection or a 2-inch trace on a PC board.

Errors can be handled in one of two ways:

1. *Error detection* using parity, checksums, or cyclic redundancy characters (CRCs). If an error is detected, the receiver requests retransmission.
2. *Error correction* using the Hamming (or modified Hamming) codes. The most common forms detect multiple-bit errors and correct single-bit errors.

In this section, we:

- Show how parity, checksums, and CRCs are used to detect transmission errors in digital systems.
- Explain how the Hamming code can be used to detect and correct transmission errors in digital systems.

Parity

Perhaps the simplest scheme for detecting single-bit errors is to add a parity bit to each data byte transmitted. This *redundant checking bit* is chosen to make the total number of bits (including the parity bit) in the word odd or even.

Example 9.5

The following data bytes are ASCII characters encoded with an even-parity bit in the MSB position: D1,36,E5. Which of these bytes, if any, are in error?

Solution. Convert each byte to binary:

$$D1 = 11010001$$
$$36 = 00110110$$
$$E5 = 11100101$$

Inspecting each byte, we see that only E5 has an odd number of 1's and must therefore be in error. The actual bit that is erroneous, however, is unknown.

All UARTs are designed to implement parity automatically. When an error is detected, the parity error (PE) flag is set. The receiver can then request another transmission if desired. Note that the UART takes no other action than to set its PE flag.

The inherent assumption behind parity is that a multiple-bit error is unlikely. In Example 9.5, if the data byte D1 were received as D2, the parity would still be correct, but two bits would be in error. It can be shown* that adding a parity bit improves the data integrity by a factor of 357. This is quite an improvement for the price of an extra bit!

The use of parity is not restricted to serial communications channels. Indeed, the contents of RAM in many microcomputer systems today is protected by a ninth bit—the parity bit. Each time the CPU writes to memory, the value of this bit is computed. When the byte (together with parity bit) is read back, the parity is checked. If an error is detected, the machine is halted.

Checksums

The main disadvantage of parity is that an extra bit is required for each data byte. This reduces the character rate (as do the asynchronous start and stop bits) and requires additional space or memory cells when data is to be stored. A 64K memory will require 64K parity bits. When parity bits are used with secondary memory devices such as disk drives and magnetic tape units, valuable storage space is taken up by the parity bits.

---

*William I. Fletcher, *An Engineering Approach to Digital Design* (Englewood Cliffs, N.J.: Prentice-Hall, Inc., 1980), p. 47.

For this reason, the *checksum* has become popular in transferring blocks of data. The checksum is a byte usually sent as the last byte in a block of data. The receiver calculates the checksum on the block of data received (including the checksum). If an error is detected, the transmitter is instructed to retransmit the block.

The advantage of checksums is much less overhead compared with that used by parity. For example, for a 256-byte block, 1 byte, or ~4% is devoted to error checking. If parity is used, 256 extra bits, or 32 extra bytes, are required—12.5% of the block size.

There is another good reason for using the checksum: Errors introduced when data blocks are transmitted over the telephone network tend to occur in "bursts." For example, a lightning strike or a noisy switch may garble the received data for several milliseconds, causing multiple-bit errors to occur. Because the checksum character is characteristic of the entire block of data, it is more likely to detect these errors than the simpler parity scheme is.

How is the checksum calculated? The byte needs to be representative of the entire data block. One way of doing this is to sum all of the bytes in the block. Any carries that are generated are ignored. The resulting byte is then complemented and incremented by 1. (That is, the two's *complement* is formed.) The last two steps are done to make it easier for the receiver to test the checksum byte.

Example 9.6

Calculate the checksum byte for the four hex data bytes 10, 23, 45, and 04.

Solution.   The sum is calculated first:

$$
\begin{array}{r}
10 \\
23 \\
45 \\
\underline{04} \\
7C
\end{array}
$$

Inverting 7C and adding 1, we have

$$\overline{01111100} + 1 = 10000011 + 1 = 10000100 = 84H$$

Example 9.7

Suppose that the following data bytes are received and the last byte is the checksum character: 10,23,45,04,84. Has the data been received correctly?

Solution.   The receiver need only add the five data bytes:

$$
\begin{array}{r}
10 \\
23 \\
45 \\
04 \\
\underline{84} \\
1\quad 00
\end{array}
$$

Because the carry is discarded, the result is 00. The data has been received correctly.

You should now be able to see why the two's complement of the sum is formed. In this way, the receiver need only add all the bytes and test for a zero result. You should also be able to see that the checksum is not perfect: If the data byte 45H in Example 9.7

changed to 44H and the byte 04H to 05H, the checksum would be the same. However, the likelihood of a multiple-bit error that does not affect the checksum is very small.

Cyclic Redundancy Checks

The *cyclic redundancy check* (CRC) technique, like the checksum method, is used to detect errors in a block of data. The technique is commonly used in reading and writing data to a floppy disk and to ensure data integrity in programmable ROMs. It is universally used for detecting errors in synchronous data communications.

Unlike the checksum, the CRC method is not byte oriented. Instead, the data block is thought of as a "stream" of serial data bits. The bits in this n-bit block are considered the coefficients of a *characteristic polynomial* (usually referred to as $M(X)$—"M of X"). $M(X)$ has the form

$$M(X) = b_n + b_{n-1}X + b_{n-2}X^2 + \cdots + b_1X^{n-1} + b_0X^n$$

where b_0 is the least significant bit (LSB) and b_n is the most significant bit (MSB).

Example 9.8

Calculate the data polynomial $M(X)$ for the 16-bit data stream 26F0H.

Solution.   First visualize this data in binary form:

$$0\,0\,1\,0 \qquad 0\,1\,1\,0 \qquad 1\,1\,1\,1 \qquad 0\,0\,0\,0$$

Now write the data as

$$M(X) = 0 + 0X^1 + 1X^2 + 0X^3 + 0X^4 + 1X^5 + 1X^6 + 0X^7$$
$$+ 1X^8 + 1X^9 + 1X^{10} + 1X^{11} + 0X^{12} + 0X^{13} + 0X^{14} + 0X^{15}$$

and eliminate the terms whose coefficient is zero:

$$M(X) = X^2 + X^5 + X^6 + X^8 + X^9 + X^{10} + X^{11} \tag{9.1}$$

Equation (9.1) is a unique polynomial representing the data in the 16-bit block. If one bit were to change, the polynomial would also change. The CRC bytes are found by applying the equation

$$\frac{M(X) \times X^n}{G(X)} = Q(X) + R(X) \tag{9.2}$$

In this equation, $G(X)$ is called the *generator polynomial.* For the bisync protocol,

$$G(X) = X^{16} + X^{15} + X^2 + 1 \tag{9.3}$$

The SDLC protocol uses

$$G(X) = X^{16} + X^{12} + X^5 + 1 \tag{9.4}$$

When the division in Eq. (9.2) is performed, the result will be a *quotient $Q(X)$* and a *remainder $R(X)$.* The CRC technique consists of calculating $R(X)$ for the data stream and then *appending* the result to the data block. When $R(X)$ is again calculated by the receiver, the result should be zero. Note that because $G(X)$ is of order (power)

16, the remainder, $R(X)$, cannot be of order higher than 15 and is thus represented by 2 bytes (no matter what the block length itself).

Example 9.9

Using the bisync generator polynomial, calculate the CRC bytes for the data block 26F0H.

Solution. Figure 9.9 shows the arithmetic. The remainder is

$$R(X) = X^{15} + X^{13} + X^9 + X^8 + X^6 + X^4 + X^3 + X + 1$$

Expressed in binary, $R(X)$ becomes (recalling that the coefficient of the highest power becomes the LSB)

$$1101 \quad 1010 \quad 1100 \quad 0101 = DAC5H$$

If the two bytes DAC5H are appended to the 26F0H data stream, the received CRC calculation should result in $R(X) = 0$, indicating that no errors have been detected. In practice, the CRC bytes can be generated by hardware or software. The division operations can be performed by a shift register and exclusive-OR gates.

Although the CRC bytes can be calculated with software, more and more of the peripheral controller circuits are performing this function onboard. In this way, the CRC generation and checking become transparent to the user.

The Hamming Code

In 1950, an article entitled "Error Detecting and Error Correcting Codes" appeared in the *Bell System Technical Journal*. In this article, mathematician Richard Hamming described a technique that not only detected transmission errors, but also *corrected* those errors. The resulting Hamming codes have become the basis for all error-correcting schemes in use today.

This seemingly impossible task is done by performing multiple parity checks on each data word. The additional bits are transmitted together with the data word. Figure 9.10 illustrates the technique for an 8-bit word. Four parity bits (labeled P0 through P3 in the figure) are required.

Note that each parity bit checks a different set of bits and each bit is included in at least two of the parity checks. In this example, the data byte D6H would be transmitted as the 12-bit number 4D6H.

Figure 9.11 shows how the received word is tested. Four parity bits are again generated, but this time include the four check bits generated by the transmitter. For example, the low-order check bit is found by calculating the odd parity of data bits 0, 1, 2, 6, and 8.

To illustrate the technique, bit 7 in Fig. 9.11 is assumed to be in error and has become a 0. The four parity bits generated are referred to as the *error code*. Table 9.3 explains the significance of each of the 16 possible error codes. An error code of 0000 indicates that no error was detected.

In this example, the error code is 1110 and data bit 7 has been correctly identified as the errant bit. If the true Hamming code is used, the error code should identify the actual bit position that is in error. Because of this, the technique is referred to as a *modified Hamming code*.

$$\frac{M(X)\,X^{16}}{G(X)} = \frac{X^{27} + X^{26} + X^{25} + X^{24} + X^{22} + X^{21} + X^{18}}{X^{16} + X^{15} + X^2 + 1} =$$

$$
\begin{array}{l}
\phantom{X^{16}+X^{15}+X^2+1\,\big|\;} X^{11} + X^9 \qquad\quad + X^6 \qquad\qquad\qquad\qquad + X^2 + X + 1 \\[4pt]
X^{16} + X^{15} + X^2 + 1 \;\big|\; X^{27} + X^{26} + X^{25} + X^{24} + X^{22} + X^{21} + X^{18} \\[2pt]
\phantom{X^{16} + X^{15} + X^2 + 1 \;\big|\;} X^{27} + X^{26} \hspace{5.5cm} + X^{13} + X^{11} \\[2pt]
\hline
\phantom{X^{16} + X^{15} + X^2 + 1 \;\big|\;} X^{25} + X^{24} + X^{22} + X^{21} + X^{18} \hspace{1.5cm} + X^{13} + X^{11} \\[2pt]
\phantom{X^{16} + X^{15} + X^2 + 1 \;\big|\;} X^{25} + X^{24} \hspace{5.5cm} + X^{11} + X^9 \\[2pt]
\hline
\phantom{X^{16} + X^{15} + X^2 + 1 \;\big|\;\;\;\;\;\;} X^{22} + X^{21} + X^{18} \hspace{1.5cm} + X^{13} \qquad + X^9 \\[2pt]
\phantom{X^{16} + X^{15} + X^2 + 1 \;\big|\;\;\;\;\;\;} X^{22} + X^{21} \hspace{4.5cm} + X^8 + X^6 \\[2pt]
\hline
\phantom{X^{16} + X^{15} + X^2 + 1 \;\big|\;\;\;\;\;\;\;\;\;\;\;\;} X^{18} \hspace{1.5cm} + X^{13} \qquad + X^9 + X^8 + X^6 \\[2pt]
\phantom{X^{16} + X^{15} + X^2 + 1 \;\big|\;\;\;\;\;\;\;\;\;\;\;\;} X^{18} + X^{17} \hspace{4cm} + X^4 \qquad + X^2 \\[2pt]
\hline
\phantom{X^{16} + X^{15} + X^2 + 1 \;\big|\;\;\;\;\;\;\;\;\;\;\;\;\;\;\;\;\;\;} X^{17} \hspace{0.7cm} + X^{13} \qquad + X^9 + X^8 + X^6 + X^4 \qquad + X^2 \\[2pt]
\phantom{X^{16} + X^{15} + X^2 + 1 \;\big|\;\;\;\;\;\;\;\;\;\;\;\;\;\;\;\;\;\;} X^{17} + X^{16} \hspace{3.5cm} + X^3 \qquad\quad + X \\[2pt]
\hline
\phantom{X^{16} + X^{15} + X^2 + 1 \;\big|\;} X^{16} + X^{13} \qquad + X^9 + X^8 + X^6 + X^4 + X^3 + X^2 + X \\[2pt]
\phantom{X^{16} + X^{15} + X^2 + 1 \;\big|\;} X^{16} + X^{15} \hspace{4cm} + X^2 \qquad\quad + 1 \\[2pt]
\hline
\phantom{X^{16} + X^{15} + X^2 + 1 \;\big|\;\;\;\;\;} R(X) = X^{15} + X^{13} \qquad + X^9 + X^8 + X^6 + X^4 + X^3 \qquad\quad + X + 1
\end{array}
$$

Figure 9.9 Generating the CRC bytes from the bisync data stream 26F0H.

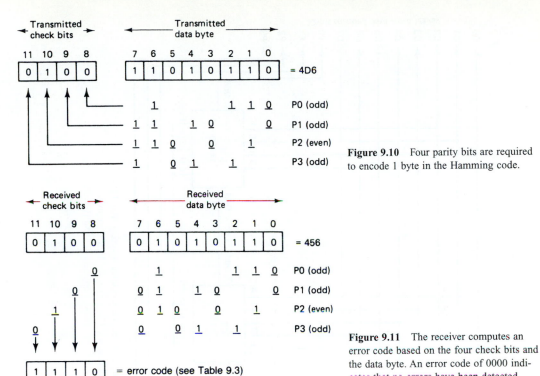

Figure 9.10 Four parity bits are required to encode 1 byte in the Hamming code.

Figure 9.11 The receiver computes an error code based on the four check bits and the data byte. An error code of 0000 indicates that no errors have been detected.

TABLE 9.3 Error Codes for the 8-Bit Modified Hamming Code Technique in Fig. 9.11

Error code	Bit in error
0000	No error detected
0001	Check bit 0
0010	Check bit 1
0011	Data bit 0
0100	Check bit 2[a]
0101	Data bit 1
0110	Data bit 3
0111	Data bit 6
1000	Check bit 3
1001	Data bit 2
1010	Data bit 4
1011	All data and parity bits set to 0
1100	Data bit 5
1101	Multibit error
1110	Data bit 7
1111	Multibit error

[a]All data and parity bits are set to a 1.

Sec. 9.3   Error Detection and Correction

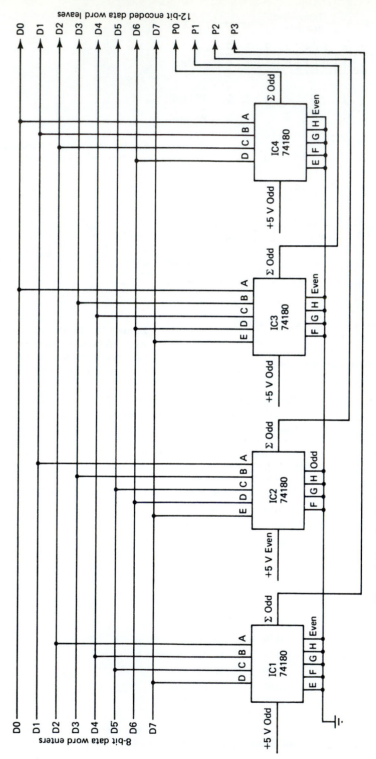

Figure 9.12 The check bits of the modified Hamming code can be generated by using four 74180 parity generators/checkers. (Redrawn from "Error Checking and Correcting for Your Computer," by Gregory J. Walker, appearing in the May 1980 issue of *BYTE* magazine. Copyright © 1980 Byte Publications, Inc. Used with the permission of Byte Publications, Inc.)

478

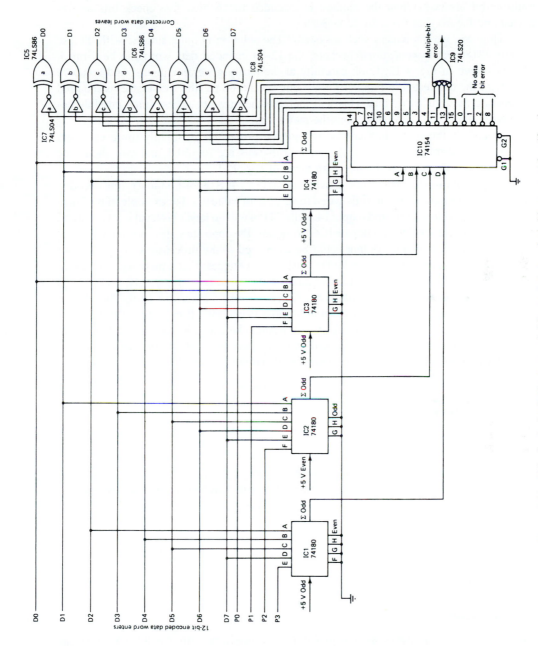

Figure 9.13 This circuit checks the error code bits, corrects any single-bit errors, and notifies the processor of any multiple-bit errors. (Redrawn from "Error Checking and Correcting for Your Computer," by Gregory J. Walker, appearing in the May 1980 issue of *BYTE* magazine. Copyright © 1980 Byte Publications, Inc. Used with the permission of Byte Publications, Inc.)

Although four additional bits represent a 50% storage penalty, the technique will detect and correct all single-bit errors and reportedly detect an average of 97% of all multiple-bit errors.* When the method is extended to 16 bits, five check bits are required and the overhead is reduced to 32%.

How can we implement such a system? The solution is quite simple: with the use of four 74180 parity generators/checkers, the 12-bit encoded data word can be formed. This is shown in Fig. 9.12. Look carefully at the parity generator inputs, and compare them with the bits tested in Fig. 9.10. With this circuit, 68 ns (the worst case) is required to generate the four parity bits. This will increase the memory access time, possibly necessitating high-speed RAMs to store the parity bits.

Decoding the parity bits and correcting the proper bit is slightly more complex. Figure 9.13 illustrates the circuit. Again, four 74180s are required, and you should be able to see that the bits tested agree with those of Fig. 9.11.

The resulting 4-bit error code is used to enable a 74LS154 4-line-to-16-line decoder. The output of this circuit is carefully wired to agree with Table 9.3. For example, if bit 7 is in error, the error code is 1110, and output 14 of the 74154 will go low. This level is inverted and causes the output of exclusive-OR gate IC6d to assume the opposite state (correcting the bit).

The *multiple-bit-error* output could be connected to the processor's interrupt input and cause the processor to refetch the last data byte or suggest that a memory test be run.

A considerably more elaborate version of the circuits in Figs. 9.12 and 9.13 is manufactured by Intel as the 8206 *Error Detection and Correction Unit.* This device will handle 16-bit data words and generate up to 8 check bits. It is designed to be interfaced between the microprocessor and system RAM. The check bits are generated during memory write operations and are checked and corrected during memory read operations. The total time to detect and correct all single-bit errors is 67 ns.

SELF-REVIEW 9.3

9.3.1 When 1 bit of a byte changes, the _____ of that byte must also change.

9.3.2 True or False? The byte C5H has even parity.

9.3.3 What is the advantage of the checksum method of error detection versus single-byte parity?

9.3.4 The CRC method of error detection is similar to the checksum, but is _____ oriented.

9.3.5 The Hamming code uses _____ parity bits to encode 1 byte of data.

9.4 THE INTEL 8251A USART

Introduction

Intel supports its family of 8- and 16-bit microprocessors with the 8251A *universal synchronous/asynchronous receiver/transmitter* (USART). A third-generation part, the

---

*George J. Walker, "Error Checking and Correcting for Your Computer," *BYTE,* Volume 5, No. 5 (1980), p. 260.

8251A can be programmed by the microprocessor for synchronous or asynchronous serial communications. Also under program control are the number of bits per data word, the number of stop bits, and the choice of parity.

When the 8251A is operated in the synchronous mode, each frame is preceded by one or two sync characters as specified. These characters will automatically be inserted by the transmitter and searched for by the receiver in the "hunt" mode.

All status signals can be monitored via an internal 8-bit input port. Flags for parity error, framing error, and overrun error are also provided.

The 8251A is an improved version of the 8251, the most significant difference being an increase in the asynchronous baud rate from 9600 to 19,200.

In this section, we:

- Show how to interface the 8251A USART to the three-bus system architecture of the 8080/8085 processors.
- Explain how to program the 8251A USART for asynchronous or synchronous data communications.

Interfacing the 8251A

A block diagram and pin description for the 8251A are provided in Fig. 9.14. Figure 9.15 illustrates a typical I/O-mapped interface. As with all Intel programmable I/O devices, the $\overline{CS}$ input must be low for the device to be selected. Normally, this function is controlled by an address decoder, as shown in the figure.

The $C/\overline{D}$ input selects the control functions or data functions of the USART, as indicated in the control logic truth table in Table 9.4. In Fig. 9.15, ports 70H and 71H have been selected arbitrarily.

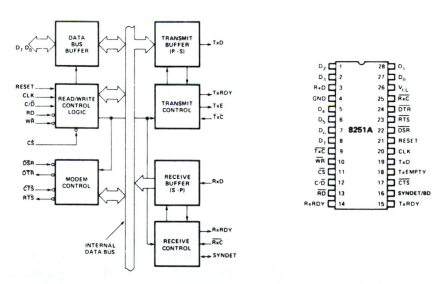

Figure 9.14 Block diagram and pin description for the Intel 8251A USART. (Courtesy of Intel Corporation.)

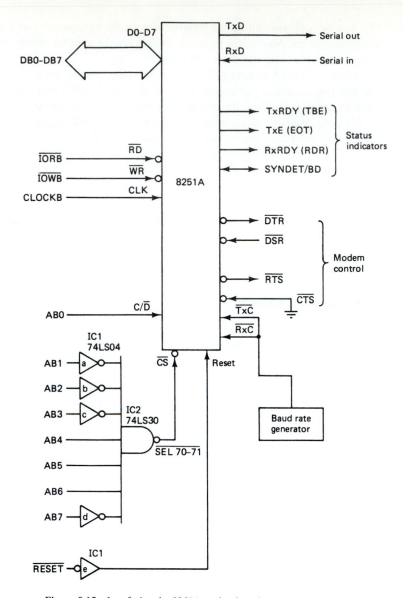

Figure 9.15 Interfacing the 8251A to the three-bus system architecture.

The CLK input is not related to the baud rate clocks, but is required for internal timing. It must have a frequency at least 30 times higher than the data rate. For 19,200 baud, this is 576 kHz. Usually, CLK is connected to $\phi 2$ of the 8080/85 system clock.

Figure 9.15 shows the two baud rate clock inputs, T×C and R×C, connected together. The connection will cause the receiver and transmitter to operate at the same baud rate, as is usually desired. Under program control, the clocks can be chosen to operate at 1, 16, or 64 times the data rate.

TABLE 9.4 8251A Control Logic Truth Table

C/$\overline{\text{D}}$	$\overline{\text{RD}}$	$\overline{\text{WR}}$	Figure 9.15 port address	Function
0	0	1	70H	Read data word
0	1	0	70H	Write data word
1	0	1	71H	Read status word
1	1	0	71H	Write status word

Example 9.10

What frequency is required for a baud rate of 1200 using a 16× clock signal? What is the baud rate if 64× is selected?

Solution. For 1200 baud, the clock frequency must be 16 × 1200 = 19,200 Hz. If the USART is programmed for 64× operation, the baud rate becomes 19,200/64 = 300 baud.

The block marked "baud rate generator" in Fig. 9.15 can be implemented in one of three ways:

1. *TTL oscillator.* This type of circuit requires three 74LS04 inverters and a crystal. Chapter 4 demonstrated its use as a microprocessor system clock generator. Although a very simple solution, its main disadvantage is that the frequency cannot be changed without changing the crystal time base.

2. *PIT oscillator.* The 8254 PIT was discussed in Chapter 7 and provides an elegant solution to the baud rate clock problem—elegant because different baud rates can be *programmed* by changing the initial count in a PIT register programmed as a square-wave generator (mode 3). (See Problems 9.24 and 9.25 for an interesting application of this idea.)

3. *External baud rate generator.* The Motorola MC14411 shown in Fig. 9.16 provides 14 different baud rate clocks that can be jumped to the USART clock inputs. Note that the clock outputs can be programmed as 1×, 8×, 16×, or 64× the desired baud rate.

Note in Fig. 9.15 that the 8251A supplies four status signals for external control. All of these can also be monitored internally via the status port. The more familiar names (discussed in Section 9.1) are shown in parentheses. T×E indicates that the transmitter's buffer is empty and that no characters are being transmitted. This signal can be used to "turn the line around" for half-duplex operations. (Half duplex is discussed in Section 9.7.)

T×RDY and R×RDY indicate a ready condition for the transmitter and receiver. These signals could be used to request an interrupt or initiate a DMA transfer. They can also be tested by polling the internal status port.

SYNDET/BD is a signal that goes high when the sync character has been detected during operation in the synchronous mode. Note that this pin can also be programmed as an input. In that case, it is used to provide the sync signal externally.

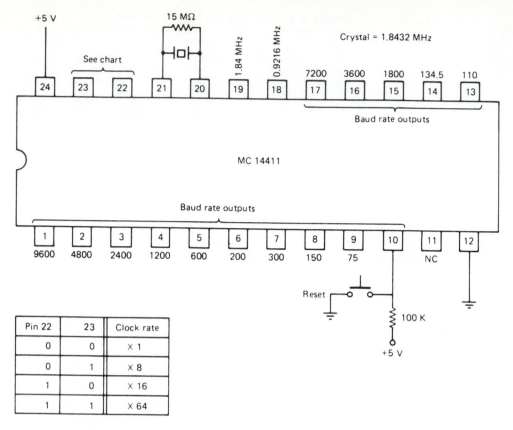

Pin 22	23	Clock rate
0	0	× 1
0	1	× 8
1	0	× 16
1	1	× 64

Figure 9.16 The MC14411 supplies 14 different baud rate clock signals. (From J. Uffenbeck, *Hardware Interfacing with the Apple II Plus,* Prentice-Hall, Inc., Englewood Cliffs, NJ, 1983.)

In the asynchronous mode, SYNDET/BD is an output that goes high to indicate a "break" condition. The break character is a constant logic 0, usually sent by the receiver to the transmitter to suspend transmission (perhaps due to an error condition).

Four modem-control signals are also provided: $\overline{DTR}$ and $\overline{RTS}$, both outputs, and $\overline{DSR}$ and $\overline{CTS}$, both inputs. These signals are intended for handshaking applications and will be discussed in detail in Section 9.7. Note now, however, that $\overline{CTS}$ must be low to enable the transmitter function of the 8251A. The $\overline{DSR}$ input is general purpose in nature and can be monitored via the status word.

Programming the 8251A: Asynchronous Mode

In programming the 8251A, the following sequence must be adhered to:

1. Reset (either internal or external)
2. Mode instruction (specify the asynchronous mode)
3. Command instruction

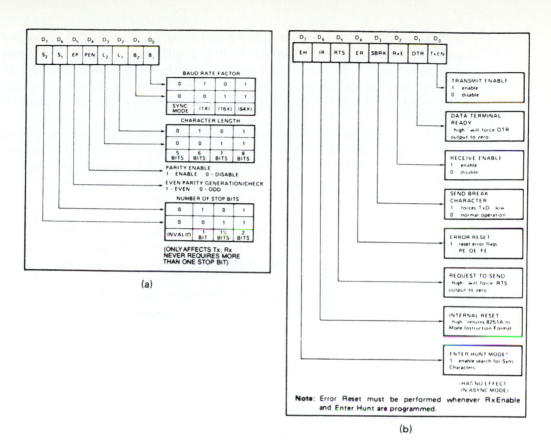

Figure 9.17 (a) Asynchronous mode instruction format; (b) synchronous or asynchronous command instruction format. (Courtesy of Intel Corporation.)

Figure 9.17 describes the form of the mode and command instructions. A reset command must be used to start the initialization sequence. The command that follows, and only that command, will be interpreted as a mode instruction. After the mode instruction has been written, all further writes will be interpreted as command instructions. *The only way to return to the mode instruction is to apply a reset pulse or write a command word with bit 6 high.*

Example 9.11

Write the initialization routine required to program the 8251A USART in Fig. 9.15 for asynchronous transmission with seven data bits, two stop bits, and odd parity. Select a 16× clock and program $\overline{DTR}$ and $\overline{RTS}$ active.

Solution. The program is as follows:

```
MVI    A,40H      ;RESET
OUT    71H        ;COMMAND INSTRUCTION
MVI    A,0DAH     ;7 DATA, 2 STOP, ODD PARITY, 16×
OUT    71H        ;MODE INSTRUCTION
MVI    A,37H      ;RTS,ERROR RESET,DTR, ENABLE
OUT    71H        ;COMMAND INSTRUCTION
```

Although the 8251A is often used in a polled mode, interrupts and DMA can also be employed. In an interrupt environment, T×RDY and R×RDY can be used to initiate the interrupt request. If this is done, the T×RDY output pin can be masked by making the CTS input high or by giving the transmit enable inactive command (command instruction bit 0 = 0). If DMA is used, T×RDY is connected to the DREQ input (of the 8237).

DMA and interrupts are often associated with high-speed data transfers and would seem incompatible with the slow data rates usually associated with serial I/O techniques. However, there are good reasons for using DMA or interrupts to control a serial port.

The inherently slow data rate of the serial port means that polling will be very wasteful of the resources of the microprocessor. Through the use of interrupts or DMA, data can be transferred to the port only when such transfer is needed, thereby allowing the processor considerable time between data transfers. For example, assuming a 10-bit character and a baud rate of 1200, more than 8300 μs is available between transmissions of each character. Note that if DMA is used, the byte transfer mode should be selected.

When polling is used, the status register should be read and the appropriate bits tested. Figure 9.18 indicates the bit assignments for this register.

Example 9.12

Write a subroutine that outputs the contents of a print buffer to the 8251A interface in Fig. 9.15. The buffer begins at location BUF and terminates with a carriage return.

Solution.   The program is given in Fig. 9.19. The T×RDY flag is polled and a data byte fetched from the buffer each time this flag is found high. After outputting the byte to the USART data port, the byte is compared against the ASCII code for a carriage return, and when a match is found, the subroutine returns.

Programming the 8251A: Synchronous Mode

The synchronous mode programming sequence consists of the following control port writes:

1. Reset (either internal or external)
2. Mode instruction (specify the synchronous mode and the number of sync characters)
3. One or two sync characters
4. Command instruction

As with the asynchronous mode, the mode instruction can be written only immediately after a reset. Following this instruction, the USART expects one or two sync characters. The next (and all subsequent) writes will be interpreted as command instructions.

Figure 9.20 indicates the format for the mode instruction when the USART is operated in the synchronous mode. The command instruction format does not change and was given in Fig. 9.17(b).

After programming the USART for the synchronous mode, the serial output line will be high (marking) until CTS goes low. At that time, the contents of the transmitter buffer will be serialized and output. Normally, this will be one or two sync characters.

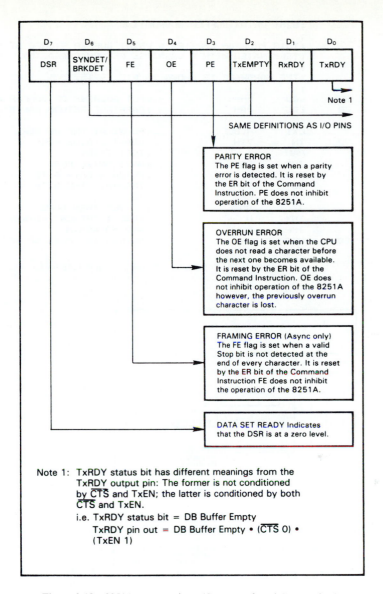

Figure 9.18 8251A status register. (Courtesy of Intel Corporation.)

Polling T×RDY, the processor can now output the data to be transmitted. If the transmitter's buffer becomes empty at any time, the SYNC characters will automatically be inserted. (See Fig. 9.21.) Note that one bit is transmitted for each pulse of the baud rate clock. (That is, the 16× and 64× clock options do not apply in the synchronous mode.)

When the 8251A is receiving data, the command instruction should specify "enter hunt mode." The USART will then test the incoming data after each bit is received for a match with the sync character. When a match is found, SYNDET/BD will go high, indicating character synchronization. Data can now be read by polling R×RDY.

```
;8251 PRINT BUFFER SUBROUTINE
;
;THIS PROGRAM EMPTIES A PRINT BUFFER STORED AT BUF
;TERMINATED WITH A CARRIAGE RETURN CHARACTER.
;
;THE HARDWARE IS SHOWN IN FIG. 9-15.
;
BUF      EQU     nnnn            ;PUT ADDRESS OF BUFFER HERE
CR       EQU     OAH             ;CARRIAGE RETURN MARKS BUFFER END
;
         LXI     H,BUF           ;POINT AT THE BUFFER
POLL     IN      71H             ;USART STATUS PORT
         RAR                     ;TEST TXRDY
         JNC     POLL            ;WAIT UNTIL READY
         MOV     A,M             ;FETCH A DATA BYTE
         OUT     70H             ;TRANSMIT THE BYTE
         CPI     CR              ;IS IT CR?
         JZ      DONE            ;IF YES THEN DONE
         INX     H               ;ELSE INCREMENT POINTER
         JMP     POLL            ;AND DO AGAIN
DONE     RET                     ;BUFFER IS EMPTY SO RETURN
```

Figure 9.19 Print buffer subroutine using polling for Ex. 9.12.

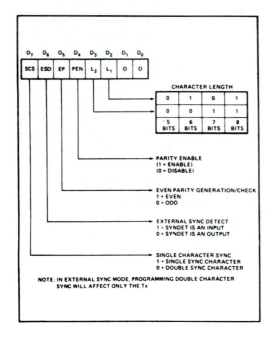

Figure 9.20 Synchronous mode instruction format. The command instruction format is the same as Fig. 9.17(b). (Courtesy of Intel Corporation.)

SELF-REVIEW 9.4

9.4.1 To the microprocessor, the 8251A appears to be _____ I/O ports.

9.4.2 List three different ways of developing a baud rate clock signal.

9.4.3 The _____ signal indicates that the USART is holding a byte of received data.

9.4.4 What is the function of the USART when operated in *hunt* mode?

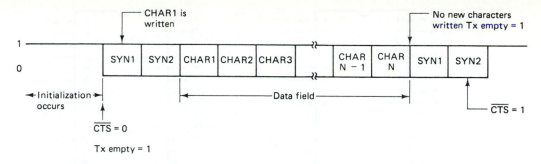

Figure 9.21 Synchronous data format when the 8251A is programmed for two sync characters.

9.5 THE ZILOG Z-80 SIO AND Z-80 DART

Introduction

For serial communications, the Z-80 is supported by the *Z-80 serial input/output controller (SIO)* and the *Z-80 dual asynchronous receiver/transmitter (DART)*. Both devices provide two separate and independent serial communications channels. This means that one channel can be programmed to communicate with a 19,200-baud VDT while the other is interfaced to a modem at 300 baud, for example.

The SIO has both asynchronous and synchronous capabilities, including compatibility with the bisync, SDLC, and HDLC synchronous protocols. Automatic CRC checking and generation are also provided in this mode. For asynchronous-mode-only applications, the Z-80 DART should be selected. This device has all of the SIO's asynchronous capabilities and is pin compatible with the Z-80 SIO/0 version of the SIO.

As with other Z-80 support devices, all control functions of the SIO and DART are programmable by the microprocessor. Several status registers are provided that allow monitoring of all important UART flags and error conditions. Also supported is the Z-80 mode 2 interrupt scheme (the standard technique for all Zilog peripheral controllers), including the daisy-chain priority structure.

Clock multipliers of $\times 1$, $\times 16$, $\times 32$, and $\times 64$ are programmable, and data rates up to one-fifth of the system clock frequency are possible. A Z-80A SIO with a 4-MHz clock can operate at 800K bps in the synchronous mode and as high as 50K baud in the asynchronous mode ($\times 16$ clock).

In this section, we:

- Show how to interface the Z-80 SIO to the three-bus system architecture of the Z-80 processor.
- Explain how to program the Z-80 SIO for asynchronous or synchronous data communications.

Comparing the SIO with the DART

Figure 9.22 shows the pin assignments for the three versions of the SIO and the single version of the DART. As mentioned, the DART pinning is identical to the SIO/0 option,

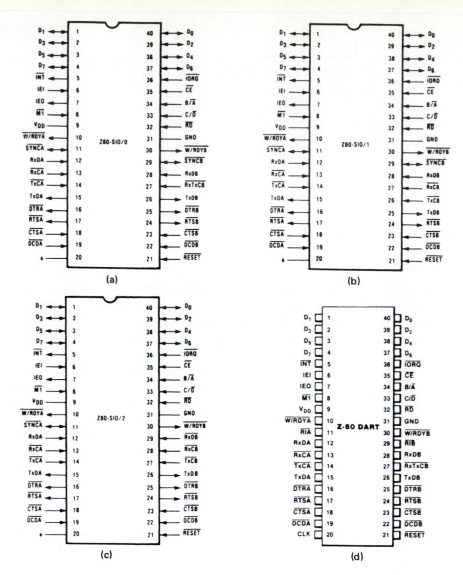

Figure 9.22 (a)–(c) Pin assignments for the three versions of the Z-80 SIO; (d) single version of the Z-80 DART. The SIO/0 and DART have identical pin assignments. (Courtesy of Zilog, Inc.)

except that pins 11 and 29 are labeled $\overline{\text{SYNCA}}$ and $\overline{\text{SYNCB}}$ on the SIO and $\overline{\text{RIA}}$ and $\overline{\text{RIB}}$ on the DART. In the asynchronous mode (the only mode of operation for the DART), these pins are general-purpose inputs that have no special function. Indeed, they could be connected to a ring indicator signal from a modem (hence the DART signal names).

When the SIO is operated in the synchronous mode the $\overline{\text{SYNCA}}$ and $\overline{\text{SYNCB}}$ signals indicate reception of valid sync characters. More details on the SYNC pins will be provided later in this section.

The differences between the three versions of the SIO are as follows:

1. The SIO/0 channel B receiver and transmitter have a common clock pin.
2. The SIO/1 lacks the $\overline{\text{DTRB}}$ signal.
3. The SIO/2 lacks the $\overline{\text{SYNCB}}$ signal.

These differences mean that channel B of the SIO/0 and the DART have a common transmitter and receiver clock, but that channel A can have separate clocks. The discussion that follows examines the Z-80 SIO/0, but all comments regarding asynchronous operation apply equally to the Z-80 DART.

Interfacing the Z-80 SIO

Interfacing the Z-80 SIO to the Z-80 microprocessor is straightforward, as illustrated in Fig. 9.23. All control signals are directly compatible with the Z-80. Internally, the SIO decodes IORQ, M1, and RD to generate IOR, IOW, and INTA. (See Table 8.3.) All communications between the Z-80 and the SIO are done using the bidirectional data bus, and to the processor, the SIO appears to be four parallel I/O ports.

The B/A input selects channel A or B, and the C/D input determines whether the control or data registers will be examined. The CE input must be low for all I/O read or write operations with the processor. (It need not be low when transmitting or receiving data.) Table 9.5 lists specific port addresses based on the address decoding in Fig. 9.23.

For variety, a more elaborate address decoder than is required is shown. This circuit generates three additional chip-enable signals that could be used with additional SIO chips or other peripheral controllers, such as the Z-80 PIO or CTC. If this is done, the IEI and IEO daisy-chain controls should be used to establish interrupt priorities. In Fig. 9.23, the SIO is given the highest priority by wiring its IEI input to +5 V.

Examining the serial interfaces, we find that two channels are provided, labeled Channel A and Channel B. Note that each furnishes separate serial in and out lines and has independent clock inputs. The SIO/0 option shown has the channel B receiver and transmitter pins internally connected.

As mentioned in Section 9.4, the baud rate can be controlled by changing the clock multiplier ($\times 16$, $\times 32$, $\times 64$) without changing the baud rate clock frequency. The baud rate generator itself can be a crystal-controlled TTL oscillator, a Z-80 CTC programmed for a specific baud rate, or a special baud rate generator IC such as the Motorola MC14411.

Four modem control signals are provided for each channel: two inputs and two outputs. These are used to establish a handshaking protocol between the serial peripheral and the SIO. (More details will be given in Section 9.7.) Note that the signals are identical to those provided on the Intel 8251A, except that $\overline{\text{DSR}}$ is replaced with $\overline{\text{DCD}}$ on the SIO.

If the auto enables function is selected, $\overline{\text{DCD}}$ and $\overline{\text{CTS}}$ become the receiver and transmitter enables, respectively. If disabled, they function as general-purpose inputs.

Each channel of the SIO/0 also has two special-purpose control signals:

1. $\overline{\text{SYNC}}$ can be programmed to be an input or output signal when the SIO is operated in the synchronous mode. As an output, $\overline{\text{SYNC}}$ indicates that valid sync characters

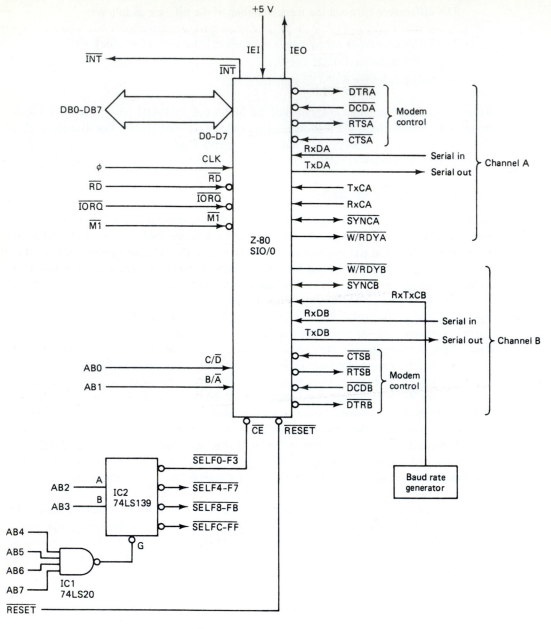

Figure 9.23 Interfacing the Z-80 SIO to the three-bus system architecture of the Z-80 micro-processor.

TABLE 9.5 Port Addresses for the Z-80 Interface in Fig. 9.23

$\overline{B/A}$	$\overline{C/D}$	$\overline{IORQ}$	$\overline{RD}$	Figure 9.23 port address	Function	
0	0	0	0	F0H	Data read	
0	0	0	1	F0H	Data write	Channel
0	1	0	0	F1H	Status read	A
0	1	0	1	F1H	Control write	
1	0	0	0	F2H	Data read	
1	0	0	1	F2H	Data write	Channel
1	1	0	0	F3H	Status read	B
1	1	0	1	F3H	Control write	

are being received and could be used by non-Z-80 processors to initiate an interrupt request. As an input, $\overline{SYNC}$ allows an external signal to indicate synchronization and cause the SIO to begin capturing the synchronous data.

In the asynchronous mode, $\overline{SYNC}$ is a general-purpose input that can be monitored via a status register. A typical application is to detect the ring signal output by a modem.

2. $\overline{W/RDY}$ is an output that can be programmed as an open-drain *WAIT* request signal. It is used for block transfers to synchronize the data rate between the SIO and a DMA controller or the processor. $\overline{W/RDY}$ can also be programmed as a RDY signal compatible with the Z-80 DMA RDY input.

Programming the Z-80 SIO: Asynchronous Mode

Figures 9.24 and 9.25 describe the read and write registers, respectively, of the Z-80 SIO. These are usually referred to as RR0–RR2 (read registers 0 through 2) and WR0–WR7 (write registers 0 through 7). Registers WR2 and RR2 can be accessed only when $B/\overline{A} = 1$. This does not mean that the interrupt vector can be specified only for channel B; rather, the interrupt vector is common to channels A and B and therefore need not be specified for both.

All other registers are duplicated for channel A and channel B. Note that WR6 and WR7 control the synchronous mode of operation exclusively and are not available in the Z-80 DART. In general, all bits dedicated to the synchronous mode are "do nothing" bits for the DART.

You may be wondering how eight write registers and three read registers can be accessed through one control port. The trick is to use WR0 as a *pointer register.* For example, by specifying D2–D0 as 010, RR2 will be accessed with the next control port read operation, and WR2 will be written to with the next control port write.

As with all programmable I/O devices, an initialization sequence must be followed before the device can be used. Figure 9.26 shows the suggested sequence for the SIO. As can be seen, WR0 must repeatedly be programmed to point to the desired register.

READ REGISTER 0

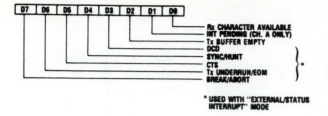

Rx CHARACTER AVAILABLE
INT PENDING (CH. A ONLY)
Tx BUFFER EMPTY
DCD
SYNC/HUNT
CTS
Tx UNDERRUN/EOM
BREAK/ABORT

* USED WITH "EXTERNAL/STATUS INTERRUPT" MODE

READ REGISTER 1 †

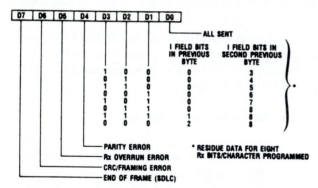

ALL SENT

I FIELD BITS IN PREVIOUS BYTE | I FIELD BITS IN SECOND PREVIOUS BYTE

PARITY ERROR
Rx OVERRUN ERROR
CRC/FRAMING ERROR
END OF FRAME (SDLC)

* RESIDUE DATA FOR EIGHT Rx BITS/CHARACTER PROGRAMMED

† USED WITH SPECIAL RECEIVE CONDITION MODE

READ REGISTER 2

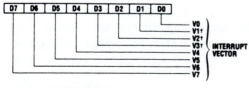

V0
V1†
V2†
V3†   INTERRUPT
V4   VECTOR
V5
V6
V7

†VARIABLE IF "STATUS AFFECTS VECTOR" IS PROGRAMMED

Figure 9.24 Z-80 SIO read register bit functions. (Courtesy of Zilog, Inc.)

WRITE REGISTER 0

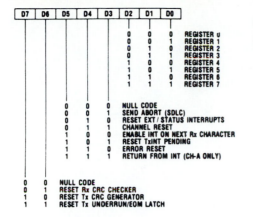

| D7 | D6 | D5 | D4 | D3 | D2 | D1 | D0 |

```
              0  0  0   REGISTER 0
              0  0  1   REGISTER 1
              0  1  0   REGISTER 2
              0  1  1   REGISTER 3
              1  0  0   REGISTER 4
              1  0  1   REGISTER 5
              1  1  0   REGISTER 6
              1  1  1   REGISTER 7

     0  0  0   NULL CODE
     0  0  1   SEND ABORT (SDLC)
     0  1  0   RESET EXT / STATUS INTERRUPTS
     0  1  1   CHANNEL RESET
     1  0  0   ENABLE INT ON NEXT Rx CHARACTER
     1  0  1   RESET TxINT PENDING
     1  1  0   ERROR RESET
     1  1  1   RETURN FROM INT (CH-A ONLY)

0  0   NULL CODE
0  1   RESET Rx CRC CHECKER
1  0   RESET Tx CRC GENERATOR
1  1   RESET Tx UNDERRUN/EOM LATCH
```

WRITE REGISTER 1

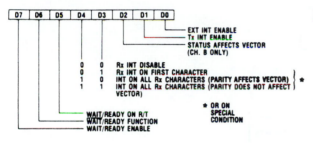

| D7 | D6 | D5 | D4 | D3 | D2 | D1 | D0 |

```
                    EXT INT ENABLE
                    Tx INT ENABLE
                    STATUS AFFECTS VECTOR
                    (CH. B ONLY)

     0  0   Rx INT DISABLE
     0  1   Rx INT ON FIRST CHARACTER
     1  0   INT ON ALL Rx CHARACTERS (PARITY AFFECTS VECTOR) }  *
     1  1   INT ON ALL Rx CHARACTERS (PARITY DOES NOT AFFECT }
             VECTOR)
                                        * OR ON
                                          SPECIAL
                                          CONDITION
     WAIT/READY ON R/T
     WAIT/READY FUNCTION
     WAIT/READY ENABLE
```

WRITE REGISTER 2 (CHANNEL B ONLY)

| D7 | D6 | D5 | D4 | D3 | D2 | D1 | D0 |

```
     V0
     V1
     V2
     V3   INTERRUPT
     V4   VECTOR
     V5
     V6
     V7
```

WRITER REGISTER 3

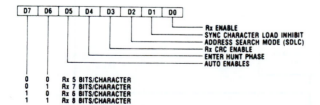

| D7 | D6 | D5 | D4 | D3 | D2 | D1 | D0 |

```
                    Rx ENABLE
                    SYNC CHARACTER LOAD INHIBIT
                    ADDRESS SEARCH MODE (SDLC)
                    Rx CRC ENABLE
                    ENTER HUNT PHASE
                    AUTO ENABLES

0  0   Rx 5 BITS/CHARACTER
0  1   Rx 7 BITS/CHARACTER
1  0   Rx 6 BITS/CHARACTER
1  1   Rx 8 BITS/CHARACTER
```

WRITE REGISTER 4

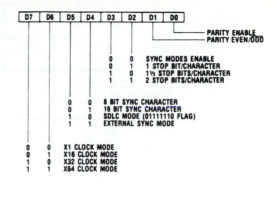

| D7 | D6 | D5 | D4 | D3 | D2 | D1 | D0 |

```
                                   PARITY ENABLE
                                   PARITY EVEN/ODD

              0  0   SYNC MODES ENABLE
              0  1   1 STOP BIT/CHARACTER
              1  0   1½ STOP BITS/CHARACTER
              1  1   2 STOP BITS/CHARACTER

        0  0   8 BIT SYNC CHARACTER
        0  1   16 BIT SYNC CHARACTER
        1  0   SDLC MODE (01111110 FLAG)
        1  1   EXTERNAL SYNC MODE

0  0   X1 CLOCK MODE
0  1   X16 CLOCK MODE
1  0   X32 CLOCK MODE
1  1   X64 CLOCK MODE
```

WRITE REGISTER 5

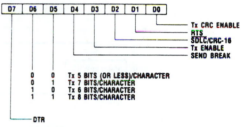

| D7 | D6 | D5 | D4 | D3 | D2 | D1 | D0 |

```
                    Tx CRC ENABLE
                    RTS
                    SDLC/CRC-16
                    Tx ENABLE
                    SEND BREAK

     0  0   Tx 5 BITS (OR LESS)/CHARACTER
     0  1   Tx 7 BITS/CHARACTER
     1  0   Tx 6 BITS/CHARACTER
     1  1   Tx 8 BITS/CHARACTER

     DTR
```

WRITE REGISTER 6

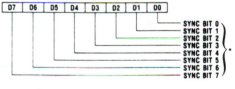

| D7 | D6 | D5 | D4 | D3 | D2 | D1 | D0 |

```
                    SYNC BIT 0
                    SYNC BIT 1
                    SYNC BIT 2
                    SYNC BIT 3  } *
                    SYNC BIT 4
                    SYNC BIT 5
                    SYNC BIT 6
                    SYNC BIT 7
```

*ALSO SDLC ADDRESS FIELD

WRITE REGISTER 7

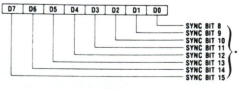

| D7 | D6 | D5 | D4 | D3 | D2 | D1 | D0 |

```
                    SYNC BIT 8
                    SYNC BIT 9
                    SYNC BIT 10
                    SYNC BIT 11  } *
                    SYNC BIT 12
                    SYNC BIT 13
                    SYNC BIT 14
                    SYNC BIT 15
```

*FOR SDLC IT MUST BE PROGRAMMED
TO "01111110" FOR FLAG RECOGNITION

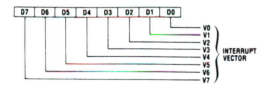

Figure 9.25 Z-80 SIO write register bit functions. Registers 6 and 7 are not available in the Z-80 DART. (Courtesy of Zilog, Inc.)

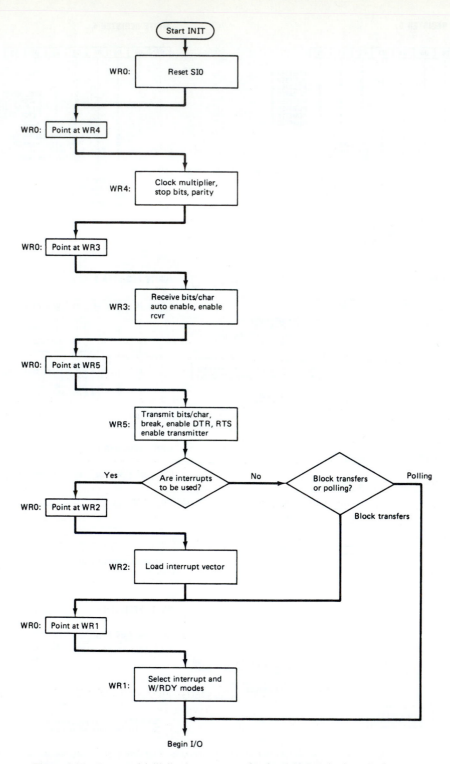

Figure 9.26 Suggested initialization sequence for the Z-80 SIO in the asynchronous mode.

The SIO can be controlled using any of the familiar I/O techniques:

1. Polling
2. Interrupts
3. DMA

The particular scheme used affects the last steps of the initialization sequence. As an illustration, consider the following example, which will program the SIO for simple polling.

Example 9.13

Determine the codes and write the program required to initialize channel B of the Z-80 SIO interface in Fig. 9.23 for asynchronous polled transfers. Use eight data bits per character, odd parity, one stop bit, and a 64× clock multiplier. Disable the auto enables function.

Solution. Figure 9.27(a) lists the required sequence of codes. Figure 9.27(b) is the Z-80 control program that puts the OTIR instruction to good use.

	Register	Binary Code Required	Hex	Explanation
1.	WR0	00 011 000	18	Channel reset command sent to WR0.
2.	WR0	00 010 100	14	Reset status/interrupts and point at WR4. *
3.	WR4	11 XX 01 01	C5	64X clock, 1 stop bit, odd parity (trans and rcvr).
4.	WR0	00 010 011	13	Point to WR3.
5.	WR3	11 000001	C1	8 bits/char, $\overline{DCD}$ and $\overline{CTS}$ disable (auto enables disable), rcvr enable.
6.	WR0	00 010 101	15	Point to WR5.
7.	WR5	0 11 01000	68	No DTR or RTS, 8 bits/char, no break, trans enable.

*When any of the external lines $\overline{DCD}$, $\overline{CTS}$ or a Break condition occurs, the status bits of RR0 are latched. These bits should be reset during initialization. It is just as easy to do this with each write to WR0 and no harm is done. This is done in this example.

(a)

```
;Z-80 SIO ASYNCHRONOUS INITIALIZATION ROUTINE
;
;THIS PROGRAM INITIALIZES THE Z-80 SIO FOR 1 STOP
;BIT, ODD PARITY, 8 DATA BITS AND 64X CLOCK MODE.
;ALL MODEM CONTROL SIGNALS ARE DISABLED.
;
INSIO   LD      C,0F3H          ;CHANNEL B CONTROL PORT
        LD      B,7             ;7 BYTES TO PROGRAM
        LD      HL,CODES        ;POINT HL AT CODE TABLE
        OTIR                    ;OUTPUT THE CONTROL CODES
;
;I/O CAN BEGIN HERE
;
CODES   DB      18H,14H,0C5H    ;THESE ARE THE INITIALIZATION
        DB      13H,0C1H,15H    ;CODES
        DB      68H
```

(b)

Figure 9.27 (a) Control codes required for Example 9.13; (b) Z-80 initialization routine.

Controlling the Z-80 SIO in the Asynchronous Mode

Polling. The simplest way to use the SIO (although not the most efficient) is with polling. Example 9.13 illustrates the initialization required. Once the SIO is initialized, receiving and transmitting programs must be written. Flowcharts for these programs are provided in Fig. 9.28.

Referring to the read register definitions in Fig. 9.24, we see that bit 0 of RR0 is the receive data ready flag. When this bit is high, one to three data bytes are available to be read. (The SIO has a three-character buffer.) If bit 0 is not high, the $\overline{\text{DCD}}$ bit can be tested (this line is usually used by a modem to indicate that it has a valid carrier from the distant station) or the break condition can be tested. The break character is a continuous logic 0 level and is used to interrupt the transmitter.

When bit 0 goes high, RR1 should be read and its contents saved. As indicated in Fig. 9.24, this register stores the error conditions. Next, the data character itself should be read and, after RR1 is tested for errors, stored in a buffer. If errors did occur, retransmission can be requested. Note that RR1 *latches* the error bits, so that unless they are reset, they will still be there on the next read. An output write to WR0 with D5–D3 = 110 accomplishes latching. Because the error bits are latched, it may be desirable to read a *block* of characters and then test for an error. This technique would be more appropriate when interrupts are used, as it would allow the processor maximum time between character reads.

Example 9.14

Assuming that the initialization routine in Fig. 9.27(b) has been executed, write a subroutine that polls the Z-80 SIO in Fig. 9.23 and returns with the received character in register A. If an error has occurred (e.g., a parity, overrun, or framing error), return with the Z flag reset and all error bits reset. Assume that the modem control lines and the break character are not used.

Solution. The program is shown in Fig. 9.29 and follows the receiver flowchart in Fig. 9.28(a).

(*Note:* See Problem 9.29 for the corresponding polled transmitter program.)

Interrupts. The flowchart in Fig. 9.26 indicates that WR2 and WR1 must also be initialized when the SIO is used with interrupts. WR2 holds the base interrupt vector for both of channels A and B. The SIO can be programmed to output this vector for all interrupt conditions or to output up to eight variations of the vector corresponding to different status conditions. Bit D2 of WR1 for channel B controls the selection.

Assuming that this bit is set, Table 9.6 lists the conditions tested and the resulting modifications to the interrupt vector. "External/status change" refers to the modem input control signals $\overline{\text{DCD}}$ and $\overline{\text{CTS}}$, and the $\overline{\text{SYNC}}$ pin programmed as an input.

WR1 controls the interrupt mode. Using this register, you control the source of the interrupts (receiver, transmitter, or special receive conditions) and whether to generate an interrupt on all received characters or just the first. You can also program parity errors to alter the interrupt vector if you desire.

Example 9.15

Modify the initialization codes given for the program in Example 9.13 to allow interrupt-driven I/O instead of polled I/O. Choose the codes such that all interrupts have their own

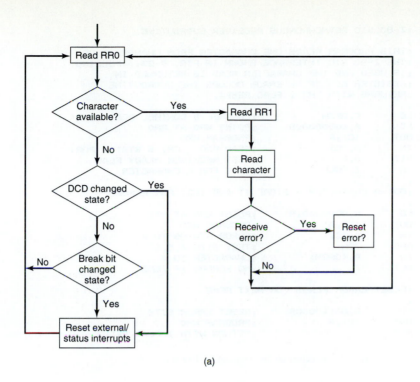

(a)

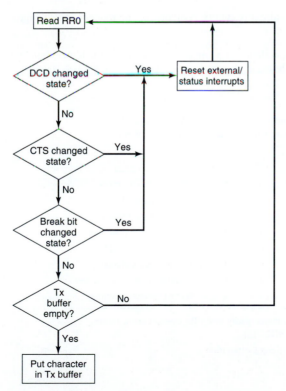

(b)

Figure 9.28 Z-80 SIO flowcharts for asynchronous mode polling: (a) receiver; (b) transmitter.

```
;Z-80 SIO ASYNCHRONOUS RECEIVER SUBROUTINE
;
;THIS PROGRAM READS ONE CHARACTER FROM CHANNEL B OF
;THE Z-80 SIO INTERFACE SHOWN IN FIG. 9-23.   POLLING
;IS USED AND THE CHARACTER READ IS RETURNED IN
;REGISTER A.   IF AN ERROR OCCURS THE SUBROUTINE
;RETURNS WITH THE Z FLAG RESET.
;
        LD      C,OF3H          ;CHANNEL B CONTROL PORT ADDR
        LD      A,00000000B     ;POINT WRO AT RRO
        OUT     (C),A           ;PROGRAM WRO
POLL    IN      A,(C)           ;READ RRO - CH. B STATUS PORT
        BIT     O,A             ;TEST RECEIVER READY FLAG
        JR      Z,POLL          ;WAIT FOR A CHARACTER
;
;GOT A CHARACTER - STORE IT AND TEST FOR ERRORS
;
        LD      A,00000001B     ;POINT WRO AT RR1
        OUT     (C),A           ;PROGRAM WRO
        IN      A,(C)           ;ERROR STATUS TO A
        AND     70H             ;TEST BITS 4,5,6
        IN      A,(OF2H)        ;CHARACTER TO A
        RET     Z               ;NO ERRORS IF ZERO
;
;RESET ERROR FLAGS FOR NEXT READ
;
        LD      B,00110000B     ;RESET ERROR BITS
        OUT     (C),B           ;PROGRAM WRO
        RET                     ;RETURN WITH Z FLAG RESET
```

Figure 9.29   Receiver polling program for Example 9.14.

address. The jump table base address is 1080H. Assume that the modem control signals are not used.

Solution.   The seven codes specified in Example 9.13 need not be changed, but four new codes will have to be added. These are shown in Fig. 9.30(a). Figure 9.30(b) shows the Z-80 program required.

TABLE 9.6   Effect on the Interrupt Vector Due to Enabling the Status Effects Vector, Bit D2 of WR1

	V_3	V_2	V_1	
Channel B	0	0	0	Transmit buffer empty
	0	0	1	External/status change
	0	1	0	Receive character available
	0	1	1	Special receive condition[a]
Channel A	1	0	0	Transmit buffer empty
	1	0	1	External/status change
	1	1	0	Receive character available
	1	1	1	Special receive condition[a]

[a]Special receive conditions: parity error, Rx overrun error, framing error, end of frame (SDLC).

Source: Courtesy of Zilog Corporation.

Register	Binary Code Required	Hex	Explanation
8. WR0	00 010 010	12	Point to WR2.
9. WR2	10000000	80	Interrupt vector.
10. WR0	00 010 001	11	Point to WR1.
11. WR1	XXX 10 110	16	Interrupt on all rcvd char, status affects vector, trans interrupts enabled, external interrupts (the modem control signals) disabled.

(a)

```
;Z-80 SIO ASYNCHRONOUS INITIALIZATION ROUTINE
;             (WITH INTERRUPTS)
;
;THIS PROGRAM IS SIMILAR TO FIG. 9-27(B) BUT INCLUDES
;INITIALIZATION FOR A Z-80 MODE 2 INTERRUPT VECTOR.
;
        IM      2              ;MODE 2 INTERRUPTS
        LD      A,10H          ;HIGH ORDER JUMP TABLE ADDRESS
        LD      I,A            ;TO REGISTER I
;
;THE REMAINDER IS THE SAME AS FIG. 9-27(B)
;
        LD      C,0F3H         ;CHANNEL B CONTROL PORT
        LD      B,0BH          ;11 BYTES TO PROGRAM
        LD      HL,CODES       ;POINT HL AT CODE TABLE
        OTIR                   ;OUTPUT THE CODES
        EI                     ;ENABLE INTERRUPTS
;
;I/O CAN BEGIN HERE
;
CODES   DB      18H,14H,0C5H   ;THESE ARE THE INITIALIZATION
        DB      13H,C1H,15H    ;CODES
        DB      68H,12H,80H
        DB      11H,16H
```

(b)

Figure 9.30 (a) Additional control codes required when initializing the Z-80 SIO for interrupts; (b) initialization program for Example 9.15.

Example 9.16

Specify jump table addresses for the interrupt sources initialized in Example 9.15.

Solution. Refer to Table 9.6 and use a base address of 1080H:

1080	Channel B transmitter buffer empty
1082	Not enabled
1084	Channel B receive character available
1086	Channel B parity, overrun, or framing error

(*Note:* The four addresses for channel A are not enabled.)

Using the SIO with the initialization program given in Fig. 9.30(b), we would have to locate the transmitter, receiver, and error routines at the addresses stored in the jump table shown in Example 9.16.

Block transfer mode.   At first, the thought of transferring data to or from the SIO in blocks does not seem logical. However, what is intended is to have the SIO facilitate a block transfer without direct CPU intervention. Certainly, the transfer of individual bytes will occur (relatively) slowly, but if it is implemented properly, the CPU will be free to perform other tasks while the block is being transferred.

Block transfers are more commonly done in the synchronous mode, but can be done asynchronously as well. Two methods are possible:

1. *DMA controlled.*   A Z-80 DMA can be programmed for byte-mode transfers and the $\overline{\text{W/RDY}}$ output of the SIO programmed as a RDY signal to synchronize the transfer. In this way, the transfer of data to the SIO will occur very rapidly and will allow the CPU considerable time for other processing between each byte.

2. *Z-80 block transfer instructions.*   The Z-80 has several block transfer instructions that should be capable of keeping up with even the fastest SIO baud rates. The SIO $\overline{\text{W/RDY}}$ output can be programmed to request WAIT states automatically and thereby synchronize the SIO and Z-80 CPU. Of course, this technique does not allow the processor to perform other tasks simultaneously, but does eliminate the need for polling and provides the highest transfer rate possible without going to the Z-80 DMA.

Control of the $\overline{\text{W/RDY}}$ pin is via bits 5–7 of WR1, as summarized in Fig. 9.31. Regardless of the block transfer technique, the SIO would normally be programmed to interrupt the processor on the first character received, after which the block would be completely transferred.

Using the Z-80 SIO in the Synchronous Mode

As mentioned earlier in this chapter, synchronous communications involve more than deleting the start and stop bits of asynchronous serial data: The receiving and transmitting stations must strictly adhere to a *protocol* governing the form of the data transfer.

	If $D_7 = 0$	
	And $D_6 = 1$	And $D_6 = 0$
	$\overline{\text{READY}}$ is High	$\overline{\text{WAIT}}$ is floating

	If $D_7 = 1$		
	And $D_5 = 0$		And $D_5 = 1$
$\overline{\text{READY}}$	Is High when transmit buffer is full.	$\overline{\text{READY}}$	Is High when receive buffer is empty.
$\overline{\text{WAIT}}$	Is Low when transmit buffer is full and an SIO data port is selected.	$\overline{\text{WAIT}}$	Is Low when receive buffer is empty and an SIO data port is selected.
$\overline{\text{READY}}$	Is Low when transmit buffer is empty.	$\overline{\text{READY}}$	Is Low when receive buffer is full.
$\overline{\text{WAIT}}$	Is floating when transmit buffer is empty.	$\overline{\text{WAIT}}$	Is floating when receive buffer is full.

Figure 9.31   The $\overline{\text{W/RDY}}$ output is controlled by bits 5–7 of WR1. (Courtesy of Zilog, Inc.)

The Z-80 SIO supports four such protocols:

1. Monosync
2. Bisync
3. External sync
4. SDLC

The first three protocols are character oriented, which means that the data field is made up of fixed-length characters (8 bits, for example). Figure 9.7 illustrated one frame of a bisync message. Monosync is identical, except only one sync character is used. External sync allows an external signal (applied to the $\overline{\text{SYNC}}$ input) to start the transmission without using the sync characters.

When the SIO is used in the synchronous mode, WR3–WR5 control the various options. Figure 9.32 indicates the bit selections for monosync, bisync, external sync, and the SDLC mode. Bits 4 and 5 of WR4 select one of these four modes. Of course, in the synchronous mode the clock multiplier must be specified as ×1. (Bits 6 and 7 of WR4 = 00.)

When the SIO is operated as a transmitter, the sync bytes are written to WR6 and WR7. The SIO will automatically insert these bytes at the start of a message and whenever the transmitter buffer becomes empty. At the completion of the message, the SIO will automatically send the CRC (or BCC) bytes if the transmitter CRC has been enabled (bit 0 of WR5).

In the receive mode, the sync characters (to be searched for) should also be loaded into WR6 and WR7. Then, when enabled, the receiver will be in the *hunt* mode. Assuming that the sync characters match, the receiver can be programmed to interrupt on the first character, and the following characters can then be read using polling, interrupts, or block transfers (synchronized with $\overline{\text{W/RDY}}$).

If the SDLC protocol is selected, the operation of the SIO is similar. Figure 9.33 illustrates the bit definitions for WR3–WR5. Recall that SDLC is bit oriented with the

	BIT 7	BIT 6	BIT 5	BIT 4	BIT 3	BIT 2	BIT 1	BIT 0
WR3	00 = Rx 5 BITS/CHAR 10 = Rx 6 BITS/CHAR 01 = Rx 7 BITS/CHAR 11 = Rx 8 BITS/CHAR		AUTO ENABLES	ENTER HUNT MODE	Rx CRC ENABLE	0	SYNC CHAR LOAD INHIBIT	RX ENABLE
WR4	0	0	00 = 8-BIT SYNC CHAR 01 = 16-BIT SYNC CHAR 10 = SDLC MODE 11 = EXT SYNC MODE		0 SELECTS SYNC MODES	0	EVEN/$\overline{\text{ODD}}$ PARITY	PARITY ENABLE
WR5	DTR	00 = Tx 5 BITS (OR LESS)/CHAR 10 = Tx 6 BITS/CHAR 01 = Tx 7 BITS/CHAR 11 = Tx 8 BITS/CHAR		SEND BREAK	Tx ENABLE	1 SELECTS CRC-16	RTS	Tx CRC ENABLE

Figure 9.32 WR3–WR5 control operation of the Z-80 SIO operated in the synchronous mode. (Courtesy of Zilog, Inc.)

	BIT 7	BIT 6	BIT 5	BIT 4	BIT 3	BIT 2	BIT 1	BIT 0
WR3	00 = Rx 5 BITS/CHAR 10 = Rx 6 BITS/CHAR 01 = Rx 7 BITS/CHAR 11 = Rx 8 BITS/CHAR		AUTO ENABLES	ENTER HUNT MODE (IF INCOMING DATA NOT NEEDED)	Rx CRC ENABLE	ADDRESS SEARCH MODE	0	Rx ENABLE
WR4	0	0	1 0 SELECTS SDLC MODE		0	0	0	0
WR5	DTR		00 = Tx 5 BITS (OR LESS)/CHAR 10 = Tx 6 BITS/CHAR 01 = Tx 7 BITS/CHAR 11 = Tx 8 BITS/CHAR	0	Tx ENABLE	0 SELECTS SDLC CRC	RTS	Tx CRC ENABLE

Figure 9.33 Bit designations for WR3–WR5 when the SIO is operated with the SDLC synchronous serial protocol. (Courtesy of Zilog, Inc.)

information field-framed between a beginning flag, an 8-bit address field, an 8-bit control field, and an ending field. (See Fig. 9.8.)

When the transmitter is initialized, the SIO will automatically supply the beginning flag (01111110), but the address byte and control byte must be written by the CPU. The information field follows. Any occurrence of five or more consecutive logic 1's will cause the SIO to insert a 0 automatically, to prevent the field from being interpreted as a control code. At the completion of the message, the CRC bytes will again be automatically inserted by the SIO.

In the SDLC receive mode, WR6 holds the address field and WR7 the flag character. The receiver will then be in the *hunt* mode until the first flag is received. If WR3 bit 2 is set, the receiver then enters the address search mode, and if an address match is found, the data transfer begins. Control is again via polling, interrupts, or block transfers. Any 0's inserted into the data stream by the transmitter will be deleted by the receiver.

SELF-REVIEW 9.5

9.5.1 In effect, the Z-80 SIO and DART include _____ separate USARTs in one package.

9.5.2 The Z-80 SIO includes _____ write registers and _____ read registers.

9.5.3 List three different ways of interfacing the Z-80 SIO to the processor.

9.5.4 With only one control port, how can the eight separate write registers of the Z-80 SIO be accessed?

9.5.5 The _____ _____ _____ flag should be monitored to determine when the Z-80 SIO is ready to accept a new character to be transmitted.

9.5.6 Which write registers control the function of the Z-80 SIO in synchronous mode?

9.6 REMOTE-CONTROL APPLICATIONS FOR ASYNCHRONOUS SERIAL DATA

Introduction

Perhaps the principal advantage of serial communications is the simplicity of the data path: Only a two- or three-conductor cable is required for many applications. Because of this, we should not restrict the serial data link to computer peripherals such as printers, VDTs, and modems.

In this section, we:

- Show how two modems can be interfaced to allow a remote-control application.
- Explain how the MC14469 can be used to construct a network of addressable UARTS.

A Remote Solar-Heating System

Figure 9.34 illustrates how a microcomputer and two UARTs can be used to control a remote solar-heating system. The transmit channel of the remote UART is used to relay

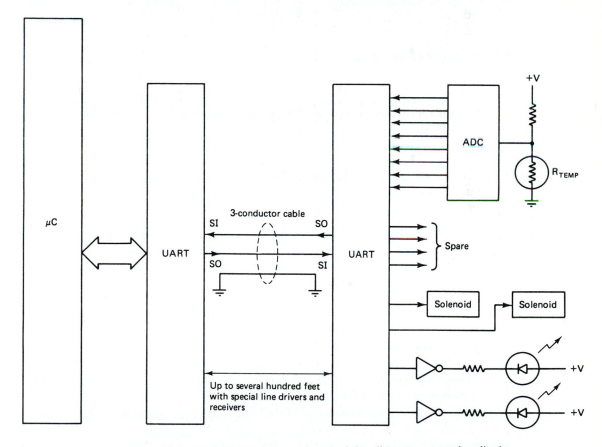

Figure 9.34 Serial data techniques can be extended to allow remote-control applications.

temperature information about the system. It uses an *analog-to-digital converter* to convert the temperature-sensitive voltage developed across the thermistor to an 8-bit digital word.

The receiver channel of the same UART is used to control the water flow by means of two solenoid-actuated valves. Provision has also been made for status indicators at the remote site with two LEDs. Four outputs remain available and can be used for other miscellaneous control functions.

The most interesting feature of the circuit is the fact that only a three-conductor cable is required at the remote site. Depending on the baud rate and voltages used on this cable, the distance between computer and remote site can be several thousand feet. In fact, if a transmitting and receiving *modem* are used, the computer could "call" the solar-heating station from several thousand miles away and monitor and control its status.

Another possibility is to construct a network of *addressable* UARTs, all connected in parallel with the transmission line. When the particular UART that is selected sees its address, it responds, while all others remain in the standby mode. The Motorola MC14469 is an *addressable asynchronous receiver/transmitter* (AART) designed exactly for this purpose. A 7-bit address code can be hardwired, allowing up to 128 such devices in the network. Clock generation is simplified by the inclusion of an onboard oscillator requiring only an external crystal.

SELF-REVIEW 9.6

9.6.1 With the use of only a _____ conductor cable and two UARTs, _____ input and _____ output lines can be controlled by a microcomputer.

9.6.2 What is meant by an *addressable* UART?

9.7 THE EIA RS-232 SERIAL INTERFACE STANDARD

Introduction

RS-232 is by far the most popular serial interface standard. First published in 1969, it was intended to describe the interface between a computer terminal and a modem. In RS-232 jargon, the terminal is referred to as *data terminal equipment* (DTE) and the modem as *data communications equipment* (DCE).*

The RS-232 specifications limit the data rate to 19,200 bps with a 50-foot cable. In practice, much longer cables can be accommodated, but at lower data rates. RS-232 is a voltage standard with typical logic levels of -12 V for a logic 1 and $+12$ V for a logic 0.

In this section, we will:

- Describe the electrical characteristics of the RS-232 serial interface standard and show how to construct a TTL-compatible interface.
- Identify and describe the function of the signals that make up the RS-232 standard.

---

*The RS-232 standard has gone through several revisions. The current level is RS-232E.

Electrical Characteristics of RS-232

Figure 9.35 compares the logic level specifications of RS-232 with those of standard TTL. As mentioned earlier in the text, standard TTL uses positive logic and provides 0.4 V of noise immunity. RS-232 is quite different: It uses *negative logic* with typical output levels of +12 V. The higher voltages are necessary to ensure reliable operation with long cables. A 2-V noise immunity specification allows the cables to be routed through noisy environments that would be a problem for TTL.

In order to interface RS-232 with TTL, special line drivers and receivers are required. [See Fig. 9.36(a).] The MC1488 accepts TTL-level inputs and provides RS-232 output levels. The MC1489 does the opposite, converting the RS-232 levels on the transmission line to TTL levels for the receiving UART. Because of these drivers and receivers, the negative-logic aspect of RS-232 is transparent to the user.

Figure 9.37 shows an RS-232 *transceiver* manufactured by Maxim Integrated Products. The device offers two RS-232 drivers and receivers in one package (thus the term *transceiver*). In addition, it features an onboard "charge pump" that can generate the +12 V directly from the +5 V supply. This single chip thus replaces the two chips shown in Fig. 9.36(a) and negates the need to construct separate +12 V power supplies.

One of the requirements of the RS-232 standard is that the transition time from one logic level to the other must not exceed 4% of one bit time. Hence, at 19,200 baud, the transition time must be less than $.04 \times 1/19,200 = 2.1$ μs. This in turn imposes a limit on the length of cable that can be driven. The longer the cable, the greater the capacitive load on the driver and the slower the transition time. At 19,200 baud, the maximum cable length is restricted to 50 ft.

RS-422A and RS423A

One of the reasons that RS-232 is restricted to relatively short cable lengths is that the drivers and receivers are *unbalanced,* or *single ended.* This means the input and output signals are referenced to a common ground. [See Fig. 9.36(a).] Because it is likely that the receiving and transmitting nodes will be at different ground potentials, a current will flow in the common ground-wire connection. The resulting voltage (IR) drop in this conductor then reduces the 2.0 V of noise immunity. The unbalanced nature of the driver and receiver thus becomes another limiting factor in the length of cable that can be used.

Figures 9.36(b) and (c) illustrate two new electrical interface standards: RS-423A and RS-422A. RS-422A uses a *differential* transmitter and receiver, eliminating the common ground wire. The receiver detects the *difference* between its two inputs as positive or negative. RS-423A is similar, but uses a single-ended driver with a differential receiver. Again, no common ground path exists. Figures 9.38(a) and (b) compare the logic level specifications for these two standards.

Because of its differential design, RS-422A can tolerate a much smaller transition region than RS-232 can. This in turn allows a much higher data rate. For example, with RS-422A, 100,000 bps is possible with a 4000-ft cable.

The EIA would like to see the electronics industry move to the newer RS-422A standard. However, as you can see by comparing RS-232 in Fig. 9.35(b) with RS-422A in Fig. 9.38(a), the two are not compatible. This incompatibility is one of the reasons that RS-423A was developed. An RS-423A driver produces voltages within the RS-232

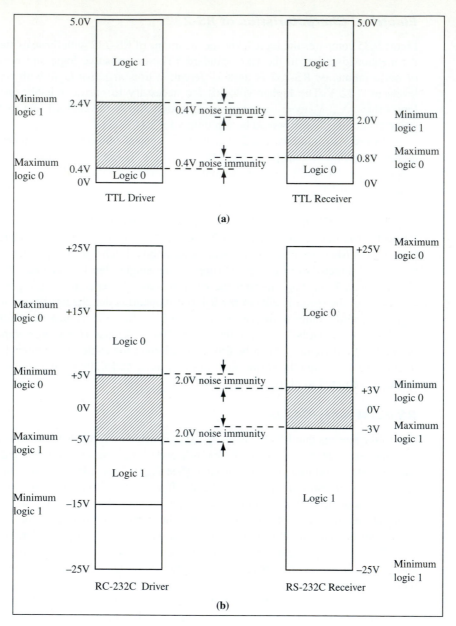

Figure 9.35   Comparing the logic-level specifications of (a) standard TTL, and (b) RS-232. The RS-232 standard uses negative logic (true=low).

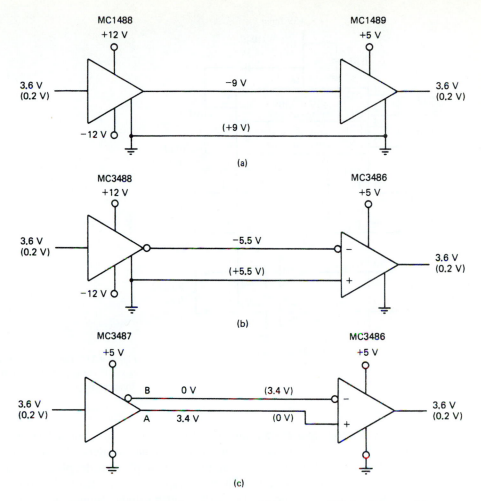

Figure 9.36 Line drivers and receivers are available to convert TTL levels to any of the three standards: (a) RS-232; (b) RS-423A; (c) RS-422A.

specifications. In addition, its receiver will correctly convert RS-232 levels to TTL. Thus, RS-423A establishes a sort of interim standard between RS-422A and RS-232. Table 9.7 compares important electrical characteristics of the three standards discussed.

RS-232 Signal Descriptions and Mechanical Interface

Table 9.8 lists the names of the signals and the source and destination for the 25 pins of the RS-232 interface standard. The data pins are grouped into a primary and a secondary channel. The latter is seldom used, but does allow a path for confirmation or interruption of the data flow.

The six control pins establish a protocol between the modem (DCE) and terminal (DTE). (The operation of these pins is explained in detail later in the section.) The remaining signals are less frequently used and support a secondary data channel, synchronous

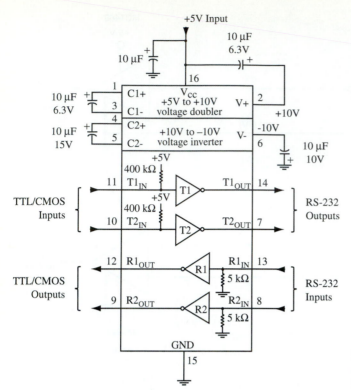

Figure 9.37 The MAX232 RS-232 transceiver. (Courtesy of Maxim Integrated Products, Inc.)

modems (requiring separate transmit and receive clock signals), and a data-rate-select pin for dual-rate modems. Note that the (names of the) signals are defined from the DTE's point of view. This is very important. For example, if we simply consider pin 2 to be transmitted data, then we could easily end up with two transmitters connected to the same pin. Fortunately, the standard allows any two pins to be shorted without damage, but the interface will certainly not work.

Example 9.17

Show the minimum connections required to interface a microcomputer serial port wired as a DTE to a serial printer wired as a DCE.

Solution. As shown in Fig. 9.39, a straight-through cable can be used. Three signals are required: transmitted data, received data, and signal ground. Technically, protective ground, pin 1, should also be used to help eliminate the ground loop problem mentioned earlier. However, the connections shown in the figure are very common.*

Two different connectors are in popular use with RS-232. (See Fig. 9.40.) The 25-pin male and female connectors are referred to as DB-25P (for plug) and DB-25S (for socket),

---

*The connections described in this example do not include *handshaking logic,* the absence of which may cause the printer's buffer to overflow at higher data rates. Later in this section we show an example that uses handshaking to avoid this problem.

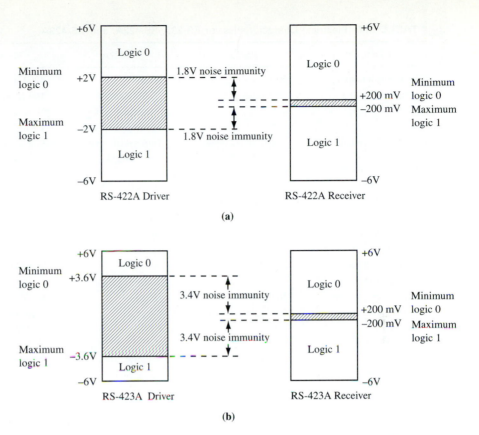

Figure 9.38   Comparing the logic-level specifications of (a) RS-422A, and (b) RS-423A.

respectively. Because these connectors are relatively large and many of the 25 pins are not used, manufacturers have taken to providing a subset of the standard that uses 9-pin male and female connectors. Table 9.9 compares the pinouts for the two connectors. Adapters are available to convert 9-pin connectors to 25-pin and vice versa.

Caution is required when spotting 9- or 25-pin connectors on the rear of a computer, however. The parallel port on a PC also uses a DB25 connector, and CGA/EGA video cards (now nearly obsolete) use 9-pin connectors. No confusion should arise, however, as the 9- and 25-pin connectors used by the PC's serial ports are male while the printer and video cards use female connectors.

RS-232 Data Exchange Protocol

When RS-232 was developed, six active-low (+12 V in RS-232) signals were defined to control the transfer of data between a terminal (DTE) and a modem (DCE). The definitions of each of these signals are as follows:

1. *Data carrier detect* ($\overline{\text{DCD}}$): This signal is output by the DCE and indicates that the modem has detected a valid carrier from a remote site.

Sec. 9.7   The EIA RS-232 Serial Interface Standard   **511**

TABLE 9.7 Electrical Characteristics for RS-232, RS-422A, and RS-423A

Parameter	RS-232	RS-422A	RS-423A
Line length (max.)	50 ft	4000 ft	4000 ft
Frequency (max.)	20 Kbaud/50 ft	10 Mbaud/40 ft	100 Kbaud/30 ft
		1 Mbaud/400 ft	10 Kbaud/300 ft
		100 Kbaud/4000 ft	1 Kbaud/4000 ft
Mode of operation	Single-ended input and output	Differential input and output	Single-ended output, differential input
Driver logic levels			
"0"	> +5 to +15 V	> +2 to +5 V	> +3.6 to +6 V
"1"	< −5 to −15 V	< −2 to −5 V	< −3.6 to −6 V
Noise immunity	2.0 V	1.8 V	3.4 V
Number of receivers allowed on one line	1	10	10
Input impedance	3–7 kΩ and 2500 pF	> 4 KΩ	> 4 kΩ
Output impedance	—	< 100 Ω balanced	< 50 Ω
Short circuit current	500 mA	150 mA	150 mA
Output slew rate	30 V/µs maximum	—	Controls provided
Receiver input voltage range	±15 V	±7 V	±12 V
Maximum voltage applied to driver output	±25 V	−0.25 to +6 V	±6 V

2. *Data terminal ready* ($\overline{\text{DTR}}$): This signal is output by the DTE to indicate that it is present and ready for communications. $\overline{\text{DTR}}$ can be used to switch on a modem.

3. *Data set ready* ($\overline{\text{DSR}}$): This signal is output by the DCE in response to $\overline{\text{DTR}}$ and indicates that the DCE is on and connected to the communications channel.

4. *Request to send* ($\overline{\text{RTS}}$): This signal is output by the DTE to indicate that it is ready to transmit data.

5. *Clear to send* ($\overline{\text{CTS}}$): This signal is output by the DCE and acknowledges $\overline{\text{RTS}}$. CTS indicates that the DCE is ready for transmission.

6. *Ring* ($\overline{\text{RI}}$): This signal is output by the DCE (modem) and is active in synchronism with the telephone ring signal.

Figure 9.41 shows the typical cabling required between a PC and modem. Note that either the standard 25-pin or newer 9-pin connectors can be used. The pin numbers shown are for the 25-pin connector.

Let us now consider the handshaking that goes on between a PC wired as a DTE and a modem wired as a DCE. We will examine two cases: placing a call to a remote site and receiving a call from a remote site.

Placing a call. Figure 9.42 is a flowchart of the sequence involved in placing a call. Typically, a communications program (PROCOM, TERMINAL, etc.) is used to place the

TABLE 9.8 Signal Designations for the RS-232C Serial Interface Standard

Pin	Signal name	Data		Control	
		From DTE to DCE	To DTE from DCE	From DTE to DCE	To DTE from DCE
1	Protective ground				
2	Transmitted data	X			
3	Received data		X		
4	Request to send ($\overline{\text{RTS}}$)			X	
5	Clear to send ($\overline{\text{CTS}}$)				X
6	Data set ready ($\overline{\text{DSR}}$)				X
7	Signal ground				
8	Data carrier detect ($\overline{\text{DCD}}$)				X
9/10	Reserved for data set testing				
11	Unassigned				
12	Secondary data carrier detect				X
13	Secondary clear to send				X
14	Secondary transmitted data	X			
15	Transmit signal element timing				X
16	Secondary received data		X		
17	Receive signal element timing				X
18	Unassigned				
19	Secondary request to send			X	
20	Data terminal ready ($\overline{\text{DTR}}$)			X	
21	Signal-quality detector (indicates probability of error)				X
22	Ring indicator				X
23	Data signal rate select (allows selection of two different baud rates)				X
24	Transmit signal element timing			X	
25	Unassigned				

call. When this program starts, it causes $\overline{\text{DTR}}$ to become active. If the modem is present and turned on, it responds with $\overline{\text{DSR}}$, establishing the PC-to-modem connection.

The communications program now sends commands to the modem to take the phone off the hook and dial the remote computer.* When this computer "answers the phone," it places a high-pitched tone (the carrier) on the line, causing the $\overline{\text{DCD}}$ signal to become active. The PC and remote computer are now connected.

To begin the actual transfer of data, the PC makes $\overline{\text{RTS}}$ active and then waits for the modem to respond with $\overline{\text{CTS}}$. Data is then output to the modem (and transmitted to the

---

*Usually this is done using a standard set of commands developed by the Hayes Corporation. The commands are collectively known as the *AT command set* because each command is prefaced with the letters AT (for *attention*). The command to take the phone off the hook, for example, is ATH1. (Section 9.8 describes modems and the Hayes commands in more detail.)

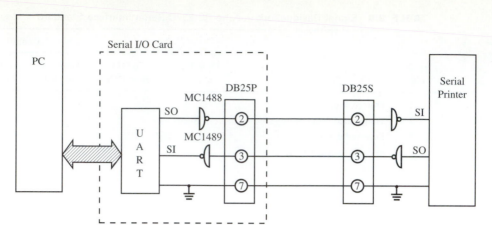

Figure 9.39 Interfacing a serial printer wired as a DCE to a PC wired as a DTE.

remote computer) as long as $\overline{CTS}$ remains active. Note that the carrier must be maintained during this transfer, or the connection will be lost.

In effect, $\overline{DTR}$ and $\overline{DSR}$ *"handshake" the connection* between the PC and modem, while $\overline{RTS}$ and $\overline{CTS}$ *"handshake" the transfer of data* between the PC and modem.

Receiving a call. Figure 9.43 is a flowchart of the sequence involved in receiving an incoming call. The only difference compared to Fig. 9.42 is that the PC does not begin the $\overline{DTR}/\overline{DSR}$ handshaking until the phone is detected to be ringing (via $\overline{RI}$). Thus, the

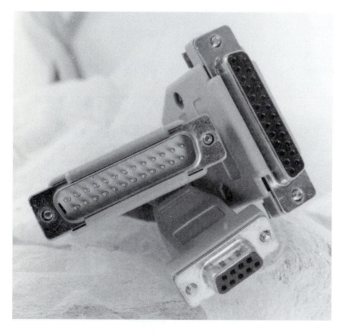

Figure 9.40 Both DB25 and DB9 connectors are in common use with RS-232 ports.

TABLE 9.9 DB-9 and DB-25
RS-232 Pin Designations

Signal Name	DB-9	DB-25
DCD	1	8
RxD	2	3
TxD	3	2
DTR	4	20
GND	5	7
DSR	6	6
RTS	7	4
CTS	8	5
RI	9	22

remote computer initiates the connection. The remainder of the sequence follows the protocol in Fig. 9.42.

When the transfer of data is complete and the connection is to be broken, each computer (local and remote) sends the on-hook command (ATH0 in the Hayes command set) to the modem. This "hangs up" the phone and causes the carrier signal to be terminated. The connection then ends.

Interfacing Nonmodem Peripherals

Although originally intended to describe the interface between a modem and a terminal, RS-232 is commonly used to interface printers, plotters, and other serial devices to PCs. Indeed, it is common practice to transfer files between a desktop and laptop computer

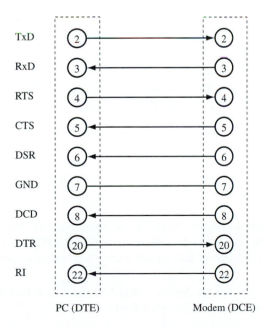

TxD · RxD · RTS · CTS · DSR · GND · DCD · DTR · RI

PC (DTE)   Modem (DCE)

Figure 9.41 Interfacing a PC and a modem using RS-232. A nine-conductor cable is required.

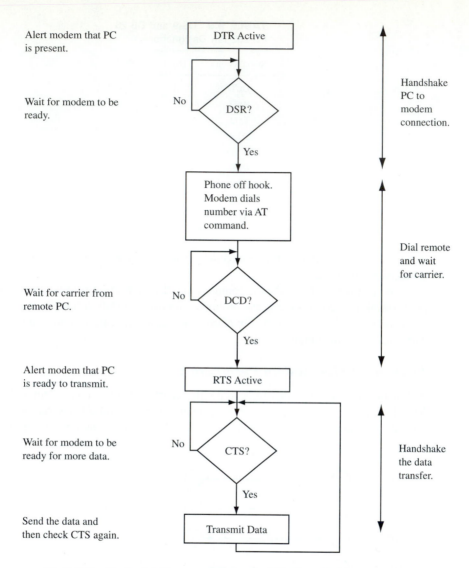

Alert modem that PC is present.	DTR Active	
Wait for modem to be ready.	No ← DSR?	Handshake PC to modem connection.
	↓ Yes	
	Phone off hook. Modem dials number via AT command.	
Wait for carrier from remote PC.	No ← DCD?	Dial remote and wait for carrier.
	↓ Yes	
Alert modem that PC is ready to transmit.	RTS Active	
Wait for modem to be ready for more data.	No ← CTS?	Handshake the data transfer.
	↓ Yes	
Send the data and then check CTS again.	Transmit Data	

Figure 9.42   The handshaking sequence between a PC and a modem for an outgoing call.

using each computer's COM (serial) port. In constructing these interfaces, two problems must be overcome:

1. *The proper cable wiring must be determined.* If the serial ports of both devices are wired as DTEs (as is the case when one interfaces a desktop PC to a laptop computer), each will attempt to transmit data on pin 2 and receive data on pin 3. Clearly, this will not work.
2. *A handshaking protocol for the data transfer must be established.* Two methods are common: one involves software and the other hardware.

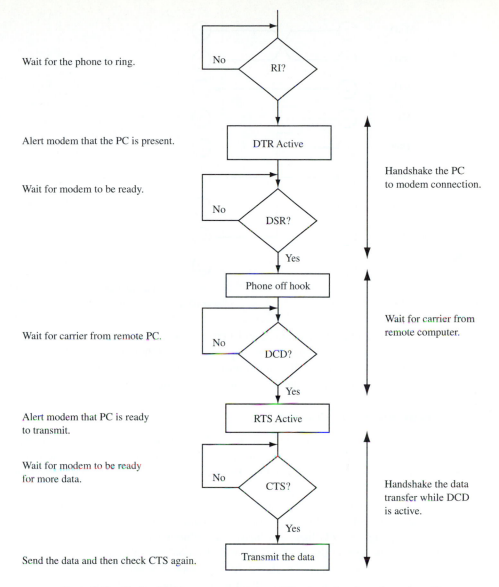

Wait for the phone to ring.

Alert modem that the PC is present.

Wait for modem to be ready.

Wait for carrier from remote PC.

Alert modem that PC is ready
to transmit.

Wait for modem to be ready
for more data.

Send the data and then check CTS again.

Handshake the PC
to modem connection.

Wait for carrier from
remote computer.

Handshake the data
transfer while DCD
is active.

Figure 9.43   The handshaking sequence between a PC and a modem for an incoming call.

Determining the proper cable wiring.   Printers and plotters are often wired as DTEs and therefore require a special cable when they are interfaced to a PC (which is also a DTE). As an example, consider the interface shown in Fig. 9.44 between a Hewlett Packard plotter and a PC running OrCAD Schematic Design Tools software. Because the computer and plotter are both DTEs, pins 2 and 3 must be "crossed." In addition, pin 20 of the plotter ($\overline{DTR}$) is connected to pins 5 and 6 ($\overline{CTS}$ and $\overline{DSR}$, respectively) of the PC. (The latter connections provide *hardware handshaking* and are explained further in the next section.)

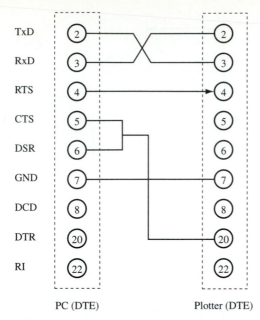

TxD 2
RxD 3
RTS 4
CTS 5
DSR 6
GND 7
DCD 8
DTR 20
RI 22

PC (DTE)   Plotter (DTE)

Figure 9.44 A null-modem cable is re-quired when connecting a DTE and DCE.

An RS-232 cable with pins 2 and 3 crossed as in Fig. 9.44 is often referred to as a *null modem*. That is, the cabling must be adapted to the fact that there is no DCE (modem) in the connection. Many other null-modem wiring schemes are in common use. It is important, therefore, to locate the proper wiring diagram for the device you are trying to interface.*

Hardware Handshaking

The need for handshaking signals with a serial data port may not be immediately obvious. Normally, the microcomputer is synchronized to the *character rate* of the UART by testing the latter's transmitter-ready flag. The flaw in this technique is that the *readiness* of the data receiver is not being tested.

For example, in interfacing a plotter, a command may be given that requires a new pen to be selected. While the new pen is being mounted, data will be lost unless the plotter notifies the PC that it is busy. But without handshaking, the transmitter has no way of knowing that the plotter is busy, and it continues to output data.

The interface example shown in Fig. 9.44 supports *hardware handshaking*. The plotter uses pin 20 (normally, DTR in a modem interface) to supply its BUSY/READY status. The OrCAD software then tests this signal via pins 5 and 6 (normally reserved for CTS and DSR in a modem interface) and transmits data only when these pins are low (indicating that the plotter is ready for more data).

Now here is where things can get "sticky." Another CAD program might expect the BUSY/READY status to be supplied on pin 8 (DCD) instead of pins 5 and 6. In that case, you could have a situation in which the plotter works with one program, but not another.

---

*When all else fails, *breakout boxes* are available that allow pins on one side of the RS-232 interface to be jumpered to pins on the other side. In this way, the proper cabling can be determined experimentally. The process can be frustrating, however, as each manufacturer seems to have come up with its own "standard."

This would lead you to suspect a software problem, but the cable would actually be at fault. You might then end up having to maintain a stock of cables to support different programs! Of course, this kind of situation is to be expected, since RS-232 was designed to support a terminal-to-modem connection—everything else violates the standard.

Software Handshaking

If the serial device being interfaced can transmit as well as receive data, *software handshaking* may be possible. In this scheme, the I/O device can request that data transmission be halted by sending the ASCII character 13H (X-OFF, or control-S) to the PC. Transmission resumes when the character 11H (X-ON, or control-Q) is received. The advantage of the technique is that it eliminates the need for the handshaking wires. The disadvantage is that the UART may have one or two characters stored in its buffer when X-OFF is received. These characters will still be transmitted and thus may be lost.

Another technique is to use the ETX/ACK characters, which provide a block-oriented protocol. After a block of data has been sent, it is terminated with 03H (ETX, or end of transmission). Further transmissions are inhibited until 06H (ACK, or acknowledge) is received from the I/O device. This technique is suitable for peripherals with data buffers that can be filled as fast as the UART can output data.

Note, however, that in order to use either of the two foregoing techniques, the peripheral must be designed to support the protocol and the PC driver to recognize it.

8251A USART and Z-80 SIO RS-232 Support

Both the 8251A USART and the Z-80 SIO provide for direct connections to the modem control signals. (See Figs. 9.15 and 9.23.) Consider first the 8251A. The $\overline{\text{RTS}}$ and $\overline{\text{DTR}}$ outputs of the USART can be set or reset by writing to the command register. The $\overline{\text{DSR}}$ input can be monitored as bit 7 of the status port. The $\overline{\text{CTS}}$ input, however, cannot be read, as the USART uses this line as a transmitter enable. Only when $\overline{\text{CTS}}$ is low is the transmitter enabled for sending serial data.

The Z-80 SIO RTS and DTR modem outputs can be set or reset by writing to WR5 of the appropriate channel. The SIO modem inputs are $\overline{\text{DSR}}$ and $\overline{\text{CTS}}$. These can be used in two ways: If auto enables are selected (i.e., if bit 5 of WR3 is set), $\overline{\text{DCD}}$ and $\overline{\text{CTS}}$ act as enables for the receiver and transmitter, respectively; if bit 5 of WR3 is reset, $\overline{\text{DCD}}$ and $\overline{\text{CTS}}$ can simply be monitored as bits 3 and 5 of RR0.

Example 9.18

Suppose that a serial printer connects its BUSY/$\overline{\text{READY}}$ status signal to $\overline{\text{DSR}}$ of the 8251A interface in Fig. 9.15 or to $\overline{\text{DCDB}}$ of the Z-80 SIO interface in Fig. 9.23. Write the 8080/85 and Z-80 polled subroutines required to transmit data to the printer with handshake control. Assume that initialization has been completed.

Solution. Figure 9.45(a) is the 8080/85 solution and Fig. 9.45(b) the Z-80 solution. Both programs poll the printer's status (via $\overline{\text{DSR}}$ or $\overline{\text{DCDB}}$) before loading the transmitter's buffer with a character. In this way, the printer receives a character only when it is ready.

(*Note:* A printer is classified as a DTE and therefore should use $\overline{\text{DTR}}$ and $\overline{\text{RTS}}$ as status outputs. However, both the 8251A and Z-80 SIO output $\overline{\text{DTR}}$ and $\overline{\text{RTS}}$, and therefore, these devices are also DTEs! The problem is solved by using the $\overline{\text{DSR}}$ (or DCD) pin to carry the BUSY/$\overline{\text{READY}}$ flag.)

```
                    ;8251A POLLED TRANSMITTER SUBROUTINE
                    ;    (WITH DSR HANDSHAKING)
                    ;
                    ;THIS SUBROUTINE OUTPUTS THE DATA BYTE IN REGISTER B TO
                    ;A SERIAL PRINTER INTERFACED TO THE 8251 SHOWN IN
                    ;FIG. 9.15.  THE BUSY/READY FLAG OF THE PRINTER IS
                    ;ASSUMED TO BE CONNECTED TO THE RS-232D SIGNAL DSR.
                    ;
                    ;ASSUME THE 8251 HAS BEEN INITIALIZED
                    ;
                    ;BEGIN BY TESTING THE PRINTER'S BUSY/READY STATUS
                    ;
        WDSR    IN      71H             ;READ 8251 STATUS PORT
                RAL                     ;DSR TO CARRY
                JNC     WDSR            ;WAIT FOR PRINTER
                    ;
                    ;PRINTER IS READY - TEST TXRDY
                    ;
        WTXRDY  IN      71H             ;READ 8251 STATUS PORT
                ANI     02H             ;TXRDY IS IN BIT 1
                JZ      WTXRDY          ;WAIT FOR TXRDY
                    ;
                    ;PRINTER AND 8251 ARE READY - TRANSMIT THE BYTE
                    ;
                MOV     A,B             ;FETCH THE CHARACTER
                OUT     70H             ;8251 DATA PORT
                RET                     ;DONE
                                (a)

                    ;Z-80 SIO POLLED TRANSMITTER SUBROUTINE
                    ;         (WITH DCD HANDSHAKING)
                    ;
                    ;THIS SUBROUTINE OUTPUTS THE DATA BYTE IN REGISTER B TO
                    ;A SERIAL PRINTER INTERFACED TO THE Z-80 SIO SHOWN IN
                    ;FIG. 9.23.  THE BUSY/READY FLAG OF THE PRINTER IS
                    ;ASSUMED TO BE CONNECTED TO THE RS-232D SIGNAL DCD.
                    ;
                    ;ASSUME THE SIO HAS BEEN INITIALIZED AND CHANNEL B IS
                    ;USED FOR THE INTERFACE
                    ;
                    ;BEGIN BY RESETTING EXTERNAL STATUS (REMEMBER THE SIO
                    ;LATCHES ITS MODEM AND ERROR STATUS BITS)
                    ;
                LD      C,0F3H          ;CHANNEL B CONTROL PORT
                LD      A,00010000B     ;POINT WR0 AT RR0 AND RESET STATUS
                OUT     (C),A           ;PROGRAM WR0
                    ;
                    ;NOW TEST THE PRINTER'S BUSY/READY STATUS
                    ;
        WDCD    IN      A,(C)           ;READ RR0
                BIT     3,A             ;TEST DCD
                JR      NZ,WDCD         ;WAIT FOR PRINTER
                    ;
                    ;PRINTER IS READY - TEST TX BUFFER EMPTY
                    ;
        WTXB    IN      A,(C)           ;READ RR0
                BIT     2,A             ;TEST TX BUFFER
                JR      Z,WTXB          ;WAIT UNTIL READY
                    ;
                    ;PRINTER AND SIO ARE READY - TRANSMIT THE BYTE
                    ;
                LD      C,0F2H          ;CHANNEL B DATA PORT
                OUT     (C),B           ;OUTPUT THE BYTE
                RET                     ;DONE
                                (b)
```

Figure 9.45   (a) 8080/85 solution to Example 9.18; (b) Z-80 solution to the same problem.

SELF-REVIEW 9.7

9.7.1 Standard TTL provides a noise immunity of _____ volts. RS-232 provides _____ volts of noise immunity.

9.7.2 Because it uses a _____ transmitter and receiver, RS-422A offers much higher data rates than RS-232.

9.7.3 Give an example of a device that is considered (a) a DTE; (b) a DCE.

9.7.4 PCs typically use _____ or _____ pin *male/female* (pick one) serial connectors.

9.7.5 Which local modem control signal indicates that the remote computer has placed its carrier on the line?

9.7.6 When waiting for a call from a remote computer, how does the PC know when to take the phone off-hook?

9.7.7 When is a null-modem cable required?

9.7.8 The X-OFF/X-ON protocol is an example of _____ handshaking.

9.8 TELECOMMUNICATIONS

Introduction

The switched-telephone network was originally designed to handle analog (voice) communications with a maximum frequency of 3 KHz. However, computer users today routinely transfer data over this network with effective throughputs greater than 50,000 bps. The key component to facilitate this process is the *modem*.

In this section, we will:

- Identify common national and international modem standards.
- Show how the AT command set is used to control the functions of a modem.

Modems

Modems allow computer users to communicate with each other over long distances using the existing telephone network. The reason for using a modem may not be obvious, however. Indeed, why not simply place the serial data to be transmitted directly on the telephone wires?

To answer this question, consider the fact that the DC voltage levels used by a computer—typically 0 V and 5 V—require a metallic (wire) path between the two telephones. At best, such a connection occurs only in the *local area* covered by the central office. If loading coils (transformers) are used in the local loop, the DC levels cannot even be transmitted that far.

In addition, because the telephone network has been optimized for *voice transmissions,* a narrow 300- to 3300-Hz transmission bandwidth exists. (See Fig. 9.46.) A digital signal with submicrosecond rise and fall times exhibits frequency components well into the tens of megahertz. The result of attempting to pass such signals through this low-pass filter (the telephone network) would be a signal unrecognizable as a logic 1 or 0.

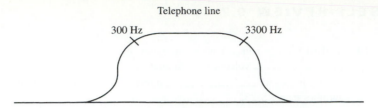

Telephone line

300 Hz   3300 Hz

Figure 9.46 The switched telephone network has an upper bandwidth limit of just 3300 Hz.

For this reason, the modem—short for *modulator/demodulator*—was invented. When transmitting data, the modem emits a carrier frequency that is modulated in some way in synchronism with the input serial data. The receiving modem demodulates the information riding on the carrier signal and converts it back to standard logic levels. The "trick" is to find a modulation scheme that packs as much information as possible into the carrier wave. With current technology, data throughput rates greater than 100 Kbps are possible—quite an accomplishment considering the 3300-Hz bandwidth of the telephone network!

Early modems were connected to the telephone network using an *acoustic coupler.* This device was required because the phone company did not allow users to connect wires directly to their system. Since 1976, however, direct connections have been allowed if a registered protective circuit is included in the modem. Nearly all modems today come with standard RJ-11 phone jacks. As shown in Fig. 9.47, a short cable can then be used to connect the modem to the standard wall interface.

Figure 9.48 shows a typical direct-connect interface circuit. The modulated data is applied and received via the RCVA and TXA signals, respectively. Op amp A1 is used to amplify the transmitted signal, which is then coupled to the phone line via an isolation transformer. This same transformer tap is used to retrieve the incoming signal, which is then amplified by op amp A2.*

The SN75472 relay driver allows the modem to apply an off-hook signal that in turn allows automatic dialing.** (We discuss this feature further when the Hayes AT command set is covered later in the chapter.) The ring detection circuit uses an optoisolator and LM393 voltage comparator to convert the high-voltage (typically 135 V RMS) ring signal into an active-low TTL signal.

Types of Modulation

Several modulation methods have been used for impressing the serial data output by a UART onto the carrier wave produced by a modem. The following is a brief description of the most common techniques.

---

*Careful study shows that op amp A2 amplifies the received signal by 2, but the transmitted signal by 0, thus preventing the receiver from receiving its own transmitted signal.

**Pulse dialing is used in this example. Most modems also support tone dialing via a dual-tone, multiple-frequency (DTMF) circuit.

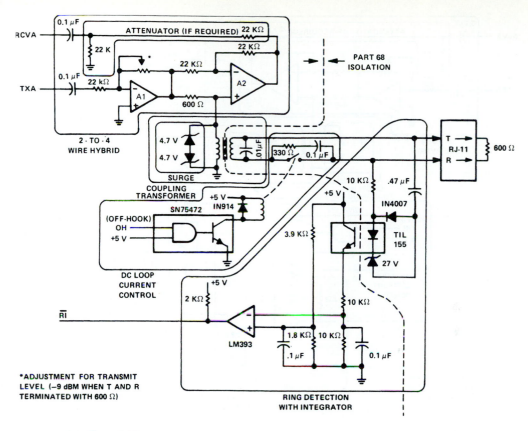

Figure 9.47 Most modems include an RJ-11 connector to allow the device to be directly connected to the telephone lines.

Amplitude modulation (AM). This technique is illustrated in Fig. 9.49(a). The *amplitude* of the carrier signal follows the binary data—present for a logic 1 and absent for a logic 0. Some modems transmit several different amplitude levels.

Frequency modulation (FM). This technique is shown in Fig. 9.49(b). The *frequency* of the carrier signal is shifted high for a logic 1 and low for a logic 0. In addition to its use in modems, FM is also utilized to transmit digital data via radio. In the latter case, the transmitter is said to be "keyed" each time it is turned on. The term *frequency shift keying* (FSK) is thus applied. Modems using this modulation scheme are often described as FSK modems.

Phase modulation (PM). A third technique for modulating the carrier wave is shown in Fig. 9.49(c). In this scheme, each time the logic state changes, the *phase angle* of the carrier changes. In the example illustrated, the phase change is 180°. Like FSK modems, devices that use this modulation technique are described as phase shift keying (PSK) modems. PSK modems need not be limited to 180° changes in phase. In fact, current modems encode data by means of eight or more different phase angles.

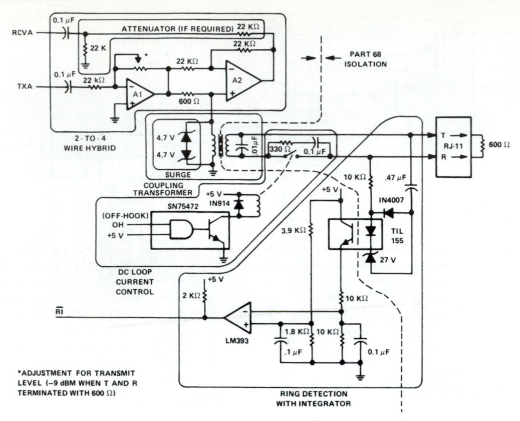

Figure 9.48 Example of a direct-connect interface circuit for a modem. The telephone connection is made via the RJ-11 connector. The analog input and output of the modem is attached via the RCVA and TXA connections.

Baud Rate vs. Data Rate

Much confusion surrounds these two terms. The baud rate of a modem is the number of *signal events* per second, where a signal event is a change in amplitude, frequency, or phase of the modem's carrier signal. The data rate of a modem is the number of bits transmitted per second.

In Fig. 9.49, each time a signal event occurs, a new data bit is transmitted. Thus, the baud rate and data rate are the same. But consider a modem that transmits four different amplitude levels (or four different phase changes). In this case, we could associate two bits with each unique amplitude level (or phase level) as follows:

Amplitude level	Bit pattern
0	00
1	01
2	10
3	11

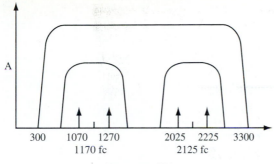

A

300	1070 1270	2025 2225	3300
	1170 fc	2125 fc	

Frequency (Hz)

Specifications and channel assignments for the full-duplex 300 bps asynchronous Bell 103/113 modem are shown in this illustration. The Bell 103 modem can transmit and receive the low or high band. The ability to switch modes has been termed "originate and answer." The Bell 113A/D operates only in the originate mode; the Bell 113B/C operates only in the answer mode.

Specifications

Data:
  Serial, binary, asynchronous, full duplex
Data transfer rate:
  0 to 300 bps
Modulation:
  Frequency shift-keyed (FSK) FM
Frequency assignment:

	Originating end	Answering end
Transmit	1070 Hz space	2025 Hz space
	1270 Hz mark	2225 Hz mark
Receive	2025 Hz space	1070 Hz space
	2225 Hz mark	1270 Hz mark

Transmit level:
  0 to −12 dBm
Receive level:
  0 to −50 dBm simultaneous with adjacent channel transmitter at as much as 0 dBm

Figure 9.49   The output carrier produced by a modem can be modulated using
(a) amplitude modulation;
(b) frequency modulation; or
(c) phase modulation.

If we transmit these changes in amplitude level at a rate of 600 baud (i.e., 600 amplitude changes per second), the actual data rate (in bits per second) will be 600 baud × 2 bits/baud = 1200 bps.

In Fig. 9.50, we show a "constellation pattern" for a modem that transmits two different amplitude levels and eight different phase angles. Altogether, 16 different amplitude–phase angle combinations are possible. (Note the 16 different arrowheads.) Now, because 4 bits exactly define 16 combinations, a *baud rate* of 600 allows a *data rate* of 2400 bps.

Modern modems typically transmit several different phase angle and amplitude levels. With these modems, the data rate and baud rate are not equal.

Communications Standards

Standards are important for compatibility reasons. The ASCII code developed by the American National Standards Institute, for example, ensures that computer text files can be transferred between different types and makes of computer equipment. The EIA RS-232 standard discussed in Section 9.7 provides a standard serial port for the attachment of modems and other data communications equipment.

Until its breakup in 1984, the telephone industry in the United States was controlled by the Bell System. As a result, the Bell System originally supplied all modems that could be attached to the telephone network. By the time other vendors were allowed to sell communications products, a large base of telephone company devices existed. For

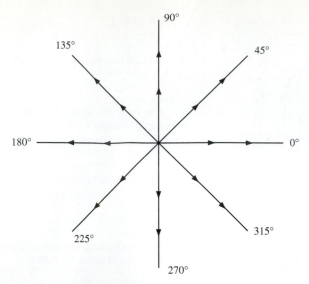

Figure 9.50 Constellation pattern showing two different amplitude levels and eight different phase angles.

their products to be compatible with these devices, vendors followed the protocols established by the Bell System products.

Most modern modems follow a set of international standards developed by the International Telecommunications Union (ITU), a specialized agency of the United Nations. The ITU has in turn formed a committee that deals with technical issues and the development of data communications standards. The group is referred to as the Consultive Committee for International Telephone and Telegraph (CCITT). The standards developed by the CCITT are written as V.xx (pronounced "V dot xx").

The following paragraphs provide a brief description of the most common types of modem.

Bell 103 (300-bps FSK).   This is a full-duplex (simultaneous reception and transmission) modem. It uses FSK with two different sets of frequencies—one for the originating modem (the one that placed the call) and another for the answering modem (the one receiving the call). The frequency assignments are shown in Fig. 9.51.

Full-duplex operation is possible because the originating modem transmits using the low set of frequencies and receives using the high set of frequencies. The answering modem uses the opposite sets. Because one signal event—the transmission of a high or low frequency—corresponds to one data bit, the data and baud rates are the same.

V.21 (200-bps FSK).   This is the international standard similar to that of the Bell 103 modem. However, because it uses a different set of frequencies, V.21 is incompatible with that standard. Notice also that it is limited to a lower data rate.

V.23 (1200-bps FSK).   Modems that follow this standard are designed to operate at 1200 bps using half-duplex. (Only one modem may transmit at a time.) V.23 uses FSK with 1300 Hz representing a mark and 2100 Hz a space. As with Bell 103 modems, the data rate and baud rate are the same. A low-speed (75 bps) reverse channel is also provided using 390 Hz for a mark and 450 Hz for a space.

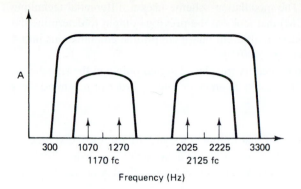

Specifications

Data:

Serial, binary, asynchronous, full duplex

Data transfer rate:

0 to 300 bps

Modulation:

Frequency shift-keyed (FSK) FM

Frequency assignment:

	Originating end	Answering end
Transmit	1070 Hz space 1270 Hz mark	2025 Hz space 2225 Hz mark
Receive	2025 Hz space 2225 Hz mark	1070 Hz space 1270 Hz mark

Transmit level:

0 to −12 dBm

Receive level:

0 to −50 dBm simultaneous with adjacent channel transmitter at as much as 0 dBm

Specifications and channel assignments for the full-duplex 300-bps asynchronous Bell 103/113 modem are shown in this illustration. The Bell 103 modem can transmit and receive the low or high band. The ability to switch modes has been termed "originate and answer." The Bell 113A/D operates only in the originate mode; the Bell 113B/C operates only in the answer mode.

Figure 9.51 Specifications for the Bell 103 300-bps full-duplex modem standard. (Courtesy of Racal Vadic.)

Bell 212A (1200-bps DPSK). This modem uses PSK with four different phase angles. Thus, two data bits (dibits) can be transmitted with each phase change. The resulting modulation scheme is called DPSK. Bell 212A modems operate at 600 baud, but with 2 bits per baud, the actual data rate is 1200 bps.

V.22 (1200-bps DPSK). This modem standard is similar to that of the Bell 212A, but uses a different phase angle assignment for each dibit. In addition, whereas Bell 212A modems are compatible with the Bell 103 standard (300 bps), V.22 modems use two-phase PSK to operate at 600 bps for the device's lower data rate.

V.22bis* (2400-bps QAM). Modems that follow this standard operate in full duplex at 600 baud, but encode 4 bits into each signal event. This is done by transmitting 16 different phase–amplitude combinations. The result is called *quadrature amplitude modulation* (QAM). At 600 baud, the data rate becomes 2400 bps (4 × 600).

Bell 208 and V.27 (4800-bps PSK). These modems operate in half-duplex at 1600 baud. Eight different phase angle combinations allow three data bits (tribits) to be encoded in each baud. The resulting data rate is therefore 4800 bps (3 × 1600). Because the phase angle assignments for the two modems are different, they are incompatible with each other.

V.32 (9600-bps TCM). This standard defines a full-duplex modem that operates at 2400 baud. Because the transmitting and receiving frequencies are the same, a sophisticated

---

*The term *bis* means *second* in Latin. In data communications standards, it is applied to indicate a second version of an existing standard.

echo-canceling circuit is required. The modulation scheme uses a differential technique called *trellis-coded modulation* (TCM) that looks at the previous output to determine the new output. Like QAM, TCM encodes 16 different phase–amplitude combinations into 4 bits. The data rate is thus 9600 bps (4 × 2400).

TCM also permits the modem to identify misplaced signal points in the signal constellation and correct these errors. This results in an error rate an order of magnitude less than that of modems without TCM.

V.32bis (14,400-bps TCM).   Modems that follow this standard also use TCM, but encode six data bits per baud. With a baud rate of 2400, the data rate of the modem becomes 14,400 bps (6 × 2400). Like V.32 modems, V.32bis provides full-duplex operation via an echo cancellation circuit.

V.34 (28,800-bps TCM).   V.34 modems use the full bandwidth of the telephone network to operate at 3200 baud. TCM is again employed and in this standard encodes nine data bits per baud. The resulting data rate is 28,800 bps (9 × 3200).

When V.34 modems first connect, they *"negotiate"* for a compatible data rate. If the phone line conditions permit, both modems will operate at 28,800 bps. If not, the modems will fall back to a lower data rate (26,400 bps, 24,000 bps, or 21,600 bps).

The V.34 standard also provides an optional specification for asymmetric transmitting and receiving speeds. For example, a connection might support a transmitting speed of 28,800 bps, but a receiving speed of 26,400 bps. Without split speed, the connection would be restricted to the slower 26,400-bps rate.

Most V.34 modems now support two even faster data rates: 31,200 bps and 33,600 bps. These devices are then referred to as 33.6 modems. The higher connection speeds can be achieved only under the best of conditions, however.

V.90 (56,000-bps digital).   In a typical modem connection, the PC's digital data is converted to analog form by the modem and then transmitted to the phone company's central office (co). At the co, the data is converted back to digital form and then routed to the destination co. At that point, the data is again converted to analog form for passage over the local subscriber line to the destination modem. Finally, this modem converts the data back to digital form for processing by the destination PC. Four analog-to-digital/digital-to-analog conversions are required—eight for full-duplex operation.

All of these conversions add noise to the signal and limit the maximum data rate to about 35,000 bps. V.90 is an (almost) all-digital scheme. Data in the local loop is still transmitted in analog form. However, once the data arrives at the co, it is converted to digital form and then remains digital all the way to its destination. The destination site thus requires an all-digital modem.

V.90 modems work by synchronizing themselves to the 8000-Hz data-sampling rate of the co's analog-to-digital converter. In this scheme, 128 different voltage levels (7 bits) are allowed. At 8000 Hz, a data rate of 56,000 bps (7 × 8000) is theoretically possible. In practice, however, this data rate cannot be achieved, for two reasons. First, FCC rules limit the amount of power that can be placed on the phone line—128 different voltage levels may not be possible. This restriction reduces the number of bits encoded with each sample. Second, the quality of the local subscriber's phone line (and distance from the co) may not support the higher data rate. For these reasons, most users report connection speeds of 50,000 bps or less.

One final point to note is that V.90 was designed to provide high-speed Internet connections—but in the *download* direction only. Uploads occur at the V.34 rate of 28.8K to 33.6K bps.

Data compression modems

Data compression involves finding a more efficient way of coding and then transmitting a block of data. Two methods are in common use: MNP Classes 5 and 7 and V.42bis.

MNP class 5 and class 7. Microcom Corporation developed a series of networking protocols that are referred to as Microcom Networking Protocols (MNPs). Two of the protocols deal specifically with data compression. MNP Class 5 uses a real-time adaptive algorithm for compressing individual characters.* Typical compression ratios vary between 1.3:1 and 2:1.

MNP Class 7 provides an enhanced data compression algorithm and can achieve data compression ratios up to 3:1.

V.42bis is becoming the preferred standard for data compression. Unlike the MNP protocols, it operates on a *string* of characters using the hardware-based Ziv-Lempel algorithms. Compression ratios as high as 4:1 can be achieved.

When interfacing modems that employ data compression, the DTE must supply uncompressed data to the modem at a higher rate than the modem can send the compressed data over the phone lines. For example, a V.34 modem employing V.42bis data compression could achieve a data throughput of 115,200 bps (28,800 bps $\times$ 4). In this case, the line speed of the modem (the DCE speed) is 28,800 bps, but the DTE speed (PC-to-modem data rate) is 115,200 bps. It is important, therefore, to check the DTE speed setting in the communications software.

Error-Detecting and -Correcting Modems

When data and program files are transmitted via modem, it is imperative that the data be received without error. Imagine misplacing a decimal point in transferring money from your savings account to your checking account! Or consider downloading an EXE file. One incorrect bit could make the processor incorrectly interpret an instruction or a jump address, causing your system to crash.

Although error detection can be done by the processor in software, the task is increasingly being performed by the modem in real time. Typically, the originating modem groups the data to be transmitted into blocks of characters. A mathematical calculation is then performed on each block, creating a checksum byte that is then appended to the

---

*Using the ASCII code, the protocol assigns a unique 7-bit code to all text characters, independent of their frequency of use. Character-oriented data compression schemes assign shorter codes to frequently occurring characters (vowels, for example) and longer codes to characters that are infrequently used. Adaptive codes continuously adjust themselves to provide maximum data throughput.

block. The receiving modem computes the checksum on the received data. If the characters match, the data block is assumed to be error free. If not, an error signal is sent to the transmitting modem, and the block is retransmitted.

Two error detection schemes are in popular use with modems: MNP Class 2–4 and V42. Although the two are similar, MNP Class 2–4 is designed only for modems that support MNP. V.42 was designed specifically to support V.42bis modems.

Synchronous Transmission

In Section 9.1, we learned that asynchronous serial data are transmitted framed between a start bit and a stop bit. This means that 10 bits are required to transmit a single 8-bit byte. MNP Class 3 and V.42 modems strip the start and stop bits received from the serial port and communicate *synchronously*. The result is a data throughput increase of about 10%. For example, a V.34 (28,800 bps) modem will achieve a throughput of 32,000 to 33,000 bps.

The AT Command Set

Most modems today are considered to be *"smart modems"* if they respond to commands from the Hayes AT command set. These commands were first offered by Hayes Microcomputer Products when the company began manufacturing its line of Hayes Smartmodems. Each command is preceded by the letters *AT,* for "attention." Typically, the commands are issued via a communications program set up to access the COM port to which the modem is connected.

Figure 9.52 shows an example using Hyper Terminal, the communications program in Windows. The sequence begins with the "at" command. The modem responds with "OK," verifying the connection between the PC and modem.

Next, the command "atdt7984620" is given. This command instructs the modem to dial the number 798-4620 using tone dialing. After a short delay, the modem establishes a connection and then *leaves the command mode.* The user is now connected to the remote computer (an Internet provider in this example) for access verification (user name and password). After entering point-to-point protocol (ppp) mode the Internet connection is established (indicated by the odd sequence of characters seen scrolling across the screen). The user now types "+++" to force the modem to *return to command mode.* The modem again responds with "OK." The user hangs up the phone with the command "ath0". The carrier from the remote computer is lost and the modem returns off line.

Table 9.10 provides information on several commands in the AT command set. You should consult your modem manual for a complete list of commands that your modem will execute.

The S Registers

Modems store configuration and status information in a series of registers referred to as the S registers. On a U.S. Robotics modem, this information can be displayed with the command "ATS$." Individual registers can be examined with the command "ATSn?" where n is the register number. For example, the command "ATS0=5" tells the modem to answer the phone after five rings. Table 9.11 lists the function of the first 12 S registers of a US Robotics modem. (In all, 38 registers are defined for this particular modem.)

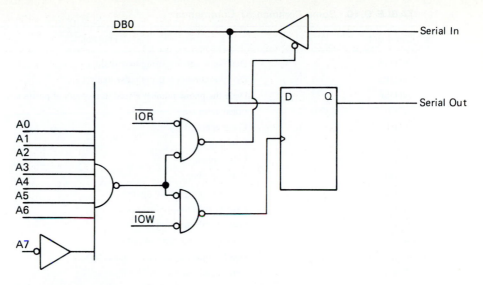

Figure 9.52 Typical AT command sequence when connecting a PC to a remote computer (in this example an Internet provider).

Modem Initialization String

Some communications programs require that an initialization string be sent to the modem to set initial conditions. For example, one such string might be the following:

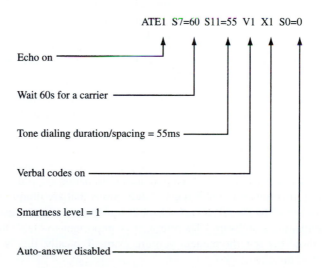

TABLE 9.10 Some Common AT Commands

Command	Function
ATDTn	Dial the number n using tone dialing
ATDPn	Dial the number n using pulse dialing
ATDSn	Dials the phone number stored in memory at position n ($n = 0-3$)*
ATE0	Local echo on
ATE1	Local echo off
ATF0	Half duplex
ATF1	Full duplex
ATH0	Hang up phone
ATH1	Go off hook (pick up phone)
ATI0	Display modem product code
ATI3	Display call duration
ATI4	Display current modem settings
ATI6	Display link diagnostics (connect speed)
ATK0	Return call duration at I3
ATK1	Return actual time at I3[†]
ATM0	Speaker always off
ATM1	Speaker on until carrier established
ATM2	Speaker always on
ATO	Return on line after command execution (see $+++$)
ATSr=n	Set S register r to the value n
ATSr?	Display the contents of S register r
ATS$	Display the contents of all S registers
ATV0	Return result codes in numbers
ATV1	Return result codes in words
ATXn	Set the result code displayed
ATZ	Reset modem
A/	Reexecute last issued command
A>	Reexecute last issued command continuously
+++	Go to command mode

*Phone numbers are stored with the command AT&Zn = s ($n = 0-3$ and s is the phone number)

[†]Set clock using ATI3 = HH:MM:SS K1

Today, many modems can be initialized with the string "AT&F1", which loads the factory configuration and enables hardware flow control. The command "AT&F2" loads the factory configuration and enables software flow control.

The AT command set has become a *de facto* standard. That is, it is in such common use that it has become a standard. Having said this, we must note that a caution is in order: As new modems are developed, new commands are added to the AT command set, resulting in commands and S register definitions that are unique to a particular modem.

Fortunately, the AT command set is *transparent* to most users. (It is built into their communications software.) Therefore, it is important to "tell" the communications program about the specific modem you are using. Typically, this is accomplished when the modem is installed.

TABLE 9.11 S Registers 0 through 12 and Their Defaults*

Register	Range/Value	Default	Function
S0	0–255 rings	1	Number of rings to auto-answer
S1	0–255 rings	0	Counts incoming rings
S2	0–255 ASCII	43	Escape character
S3	0–127 ASCII	13	Carriage return character
S4	0–127 ASCII	10	Line feed character
S5	0–255 ASCII	8	Backspace character
S6	2–255	2	Dial tone time before blind dialing
S7	1–255	60	Remote carrier wait time
S8	0–255	2	Comma pause time in dialing
S9	1–255 × .1s	6	Carrier detect response time
S10	1–255 × .1s	7	Delay between carrier loss and hang up
S11	50–255 ms	70	Tone duration and spacing for DTMF dialing
S12	0 255 × 20 ms	50	Escape code guard time

*Default values shown are for a US Robotics Sportster.

SELF-REVIEW 9.8

9.8.1 The commercial telephone network has an upper bandwidth limit of _____ Hz.

9.8.2 _____ is a modem modulation method in which a logic 1 is transmitted as a high frequency and a logic 0 as a low frequency.

9.8.3 The baud rate of a modem is measured in signal events per second. What is a signal event?

9.8.4 A 600-baud modem using PSK with eight different phase combinations has a data rate of _____ bps.

9.8.5 What is the baud rate for a V.32 modem? What is the data rate?

9.8.6 The DTE speed of a 28.8 modem using V.32bis data compression should be set to _____ bps.

9.8.7 How do you "hang up the phone" using an AT command?

9.8.8 What is the AT command to tell the modem to answer the phone on the tenth ring?

QUESTIONS AND ANSWERS

Q: *What is meant by serial data transmission?*

A: The transmission of digital data one bit at a time.

Q: *What is the difference between the baud rate and the data rate for a serial transmission channel?*

A. The baud rate is the number of signal events (amplitude, phase, or frequency changes) per second. The data rate is the equivalent number of data bits transmitted per second. With some modems, one baud can represent several bits. For example, V.34 modems encode 9 bits per baud. Operating at 3200 baud, these modems have a data rate of 28,800 bps (9 × 3200).

Q: *What are two basic methods for transmitting serial data?*

A: Asynchronous with start and stop bits, and synchronous with special sync characters identifying the start and end of data.

Q: *What is a UART?*

A: Universal asynchronous receivers/transmitters, UARTs are integrated circuits designed to convert parallel data to serial form and vice versa.

Q: *Which UARTs are commonly used with the 8080, 8085, and Z-80 processors?*

A: The Intel 82521A USART is designed to support the 8080 and 8085. Zilog supports the Z-80 with its Z-80 SIO and Z-80 DART chips. The 8251A provides a single channel, while the SIO and DART provide dual channels.

Q: *What are some common error-detecting and -correcting schemes?*

A: Parity, checksum, and cyclic redundancy checks are commonly used to detect data errors. The Hamming code uses multiple parity bits to detect and correct data errors.

Q: *What is the advantage of using a serial data channel to control a remote device?*

A: Only a three-conductor cable is required. Alternatively, via a modem, control can be extended to thousands of miles.

Q: *What is RS-232?*

A: RS-232 is a data communications standard defining the interface between data terminal equipment (typically a PC) and data communications equipment (a modem). The standard defines data signals, flow control signals, connector pinouts, cable lengths, and data rates.

Q: *What is a modem?*

A: A modulator–demodulator, or modem, converts binary square waves into modulated sine waves that can be passed over the switched-telephone network.

Q: *What are three common modem modulation schemes?*

A: Frequency modulation, amplitude modulation, and phase modulation.

Q: *What are AT commands?*

A: AT commands are commands sent to a modem by a PC. Preceded by the letters "AT," these commands instruct the modem to take the phone off or on the hook, dial a number, and set other communications parameters.

LAB PROJECTS

9.1. Study the schematic diagram of the microcomputer you are using to support this text or course. If your computer includes a serial port, answer the following questions about that port:*
  (a) What chip is used to implement the UART function?
  (b) Determine the addresses of the control, status, and data input and output ports of your computer's UART.
  (c) Locate the baud rate generator circuit. What baud rates are supported?
  (d) Check to see whether the serial port is RS-232 compatible.
  (e) Is the port wired as a DCE or a DTE?
  (f) Which modem-control signals are supported?

9.2. Write a program that will cause your serial port to continually transmit the same character. Monitoring the serial output with an oscilloscope, switch the time base out of calibration and

---

*On some computers a *software UART* is used via 1 bit of an I/O port. (See Fig. 9.53 and Problems 9.4 through 9.7.) The 8085 microprocessor has this feature built in via its SID and SOD input and output pins. (See Problem 9.8.)

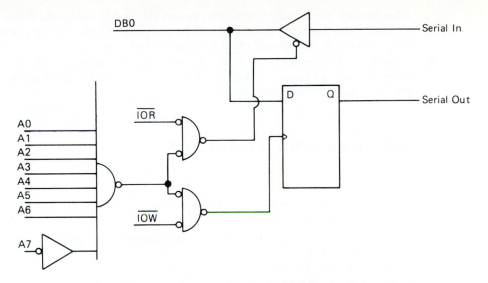

Figure 9.53 Circuit for Lab Project 9.1 and Problems 9.4 through 9.7.

adjust it so that one division equals one bit time. Sketch the output waveform. (See Problems 9.1 and 9.5.)*

9.3. Repeat Lab Project 9.2, but try the following changes:
 (a) Add an even parity bit.
 (b) Add an odd parity bit.
 (c) Switch to higher and lower baud rates.

9.4. Try interfacing two computers via their serial ports. One machine should be programmed as a transmitter and the other as a receiver. (See Problems 9.4 through 9.8).

9.5. Two PC's can be interfaced via their serial ports if a *null*-modem cable is used. The following diagram shows two DTE's connected by such a cable:

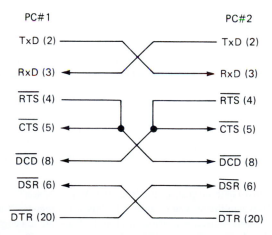

---

*Early IBM PCs and compatibles came with a BASIC program called COMM. This program can be used to access the PC's serial port if your trainer does not have one. Alternatively, any data communications program (Hyperterminal, PROCOM, etc.) can be used.

After you have wired a null-modem cable, connect the two PC's and use the BASIC program COMM to have them "talk" to each other. See if you can send a file from one machine to another. Experiment with the baud rate and communications parameters.

9.6. Using the cable described in Lab Project 9.5 and a communications program, link two computers together and practice sending files between them. Several different protocols can be used: ASCII, X-modem, Kermit, etc.

QUESTIONS AND PROBLEMS

Section 9.1

9.1. Sketch the output waveform of a UART transmitting the 7-bit ASCII letter "B" with even parity and 2 stop bits at 1200 baud.

9.2. Answer the following questions about the 7-data-bit-with-parity, 2-stop-bit serial waveform shown in Fig. 9.54:
(a) Calculate the baud rate.
(b) Is even or odd parity being used?
(c) Interpreted in ASCII, what is the character being sent?

9.3. Serial data can be saved on a cassette recorder if the data are converted to audio form. One standard uses 8 cycles of a 2400-Hz sine wave for a logic 1 and 4 cycles of a 1200-Hz sine wave for a logic 0.
(a) What is the equivalent baud rate of this standard?
(b) Using eight data bits, one stop bit, and no parity, how long would it take to store a 16K-byte file?

9.4. The circuit in Fig. 9.53 can be used to transmit and receive serial data. Answer the following questions about this circuit:
(a) What is the port address of the receiver and transmitter?
(b) What prevents the flip-flop from storing the incoming serial data?
(c) Why is it important that the flip-flop be *rising-edge* triggered?

9.5. The following program can be used to transmit serial data using the interface shown in Fig. 9.53 (see Fig. 9.2 for the Z-80 equivalent program):

```
        MOV    B,0BH     ;11 bits per character
        ANA    A         ;Clear carry flag
        RAL              ;Move carry to bit 0
TRAN    OUT    DPORT     ;Transmit the bit
        CALL   DELAY     ;Hold for one bit time
        RAR              ;Next bit
        STC              ;Set carry for stop bit
        DCR    B         ;Bump bit counter
        JNZ    TRAN      ;Do for all 11 bits
        RET
```

(a) What is the purpose of the RAL (RLA) instruction?
(b) How can the program transmit 11 bits when register A is only 8 bits wide?
(c) Assume register A is loaded with 69H. What are the contents of register A and the carry flag the first time the OUT instruction is executed?
(d) In (c), what are the contents of register A and the carry flag after all 11 bits have been transmitted?

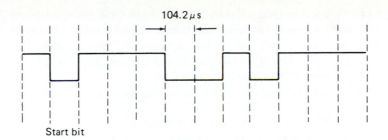

104.2 μs

Start bit

Figure 9.54 Serial waveform for Problem 9.2.

9.6. Write an 8080/85 or Z-80 program that calls the serial transmitter described in Problem 9.5 and transmits the 4K block of memory beginning at address A000H.

9.7. Write the matching 8080/85 or Z-80 serial-data receiver program for the interface in Fig. 9.53. Use the flowchart in Fig. 9.3 as a guide.

9.8. Using the 8085's SID and SOD lines, write serial transmitter and receiver programs similar to Figs. 9.2 and 9.3. Refer to Fig. 6.20 for the SID/SOD bit definitions.

9.9. Write a subroutine that polls the RDR flag of the UART interface shown in Fig. 9.6 and returns with the received character in register A. Register B should hold an error code as follows:

        00   → no error

        01   → parity error

        02   → framing error

        03   → overrun

*9.10. Suppose two computers are connected via a serial data link. Inadvertently, one user has set her baud rate to 300 and the other user has set his to 600. Which of the following would be symptoms of this problem?
(a) At the 300-baud terminal, you would see each character repeated twice.
(b) Each system's UART would report *framing errors*.
(c) The data displayed on each system's screen would be "garbage."
(d) Each terminal would receive the characters correctly, but the UARTs would report parity errors.

Section 9.2

9.11. Calculate the time required to transmit an 8K-byte file at 1200 bps using the bisync synchronous serial protocol. Assume 256-byte data fields. Compare the result with the time required for asynchronous serial transmission with eight data bits, two stop bits, and even parity.

Section 9.3

9.12. For the following bytes, (a) calculate the checksum, and (b) if all bytes are encoded with odd parity, determine which byte(s) are in error:

        A7H, 09H, 6EH, C2H

9.13. Write a subroutine that adds an even parity bit (in bit position 7) to the 7-bit character passed it in register C. Return the encoded byte in register C.

9.14. Write a subroutine to generate the checksum for a 256-byte block of data whose starting address is passed in the HL pair. Return with the checksum byte in register A.

9.15. Write a subroutine that tests the checksum of a 256-byte block of data whose starting address is passed in the HL pair. Return with the zero flag set if there is no error. The checksum byte is passed in register C.

9.16. Suppose the data byte A5H is to be transmitted using the Hamming code described in Section 9.3.
  (a) What is the 12-bit word to be transmitted?
  (b) What is the error code if this byte is received as 3ADH?

9.17. A certain 8-bit computer uses the Hamming code described in Section 9.3. If the code B27H is received, what is the (corrected) data byte?

9.18. If the 12-bit number B27H is input by the error-correcting and -detecting circuit of Fig. 9.13, determine the logic levels at the following points:
  (a) 74154 A–D inputs
  (b) 74154 0–15 outputs
  (c) 74LS20 output
  (d) IC7 and 8 outputs
  (e) 74LS86 outputs D0–D7

9.19. Calculate the worst-case time required to detect and correct a single-bit error using the circuit in Fig. 9.13. (*Hint:* Look up each chip's propagation delay time in a TTL data book.)

Section 9.4

9.20. Write the 8080/85 initialization routine required to program the 8251A USART in Fig. 9.15 for the following features:
  (a) 16× clock
  (b) eight data bits
  (c) even parity
  (d) one stop bit
  (e) $\overline{\text{DTR}}$ and $\overline{\text{RTS}}$ active

9.21. Assuming the USART has been programmed as described in Problem 9.20, what is the baud rate if the transmitter and receiver clock frequencies are both 307.2 KHz?

9.22. Describe the contents of the 8251A status register when programmed for the asynchronous mode and the following conditions apply:
  (a) No errors are detected.
  (b) The receiver has a character to be read.
  (c) The transmitter is outputting a character and is not ready for new data.
  (d) The break character has not been received.
  (e) $\overline{\text{DSR}} = 0$.

9.23. Suppose the print buffer subroutine in Fig. 9.19 is used to send data from one computer to another via a serial data link. Write the corresponding receiver subroutine such that the received character is returned in register B. Ignore the error flags, and assume that the hardware interface in Fig. 9.15 applies.

9.24. In this problem, you are to design an interface to the three-bus architecture of the 8080/85 with the following features:
  (a) 8255A mapped to I/O ports C0–C3H.
  (b) 8254 mapped to I/O ports C4–C7H.
  (c) 8251A mapped to I/O ports C8–C9H.

(d) Wire the 8254 so that it can be used as a baud rate generator for the 8251A. Use a 1.8432-MHz time base.

(e) Wire a three-switch DIP switch to PC0–PC2 of the 8255A.

9.25. Assume a 16× clock, and write a control program for the interface described in Problem 9.24 that allows the switch to select eight different baud rates as listed in the following table:

Switch value	Baud rate
0	110
1	300
2	600
3	1200
4	2400
5	4800
6	9600
7	19,200

Section 9.5

9.26. Using the Z-80 SIO initialization routine in Fig. 9.27(b), determine the new codes to program for the following configuration:

(a) 16× clock

(b) seven data bits

(c) no parity

(d) one stop bit

(e) receiver enabled by $\overline{DCD}$, transmitter by $\overline{CTS}$

(f) DTR and RTS active

(d) 1 stop bit

(e) receiver enabled by $\overline{DCD}$, transmitter by $\overline{CTS}$

(f) DTR and RTS active

9.27. Assuming that the SIO has been programmed as described in Problem 9.26, what is the baud rate if the transmitter and receiver clock frequencies are both 38.4 KHz?

9.28. Answer the following questions about the Z-80 SIO interface in Fig. 9.23 and receiver subroutine in Fig. 9.29:

(a) Which channel of the SIO is being used?

(b) What is the port address corresponding to WR0?

(c) From which port should the incoming character be read?

(d) How does the *calling* routine know if a parity, overrun, or framing error has occurred?

9.29. Write a subroutine to serially transmit the character passed in register A using channel B of the Z-80 SIO interface shown in Fig. 9.23. Assume that the $\overline{DCD}$ and $\overline{CTS}$ inputs are permanently enabled and that no break is used.

9.30. In this problem, you are to design an interface to the three-bus architecture of the Z-80 with the following features:

(a) Z-80 PIO mapped to I/O ports C0–C3H.

(b) Z-80 CTC mapped to I/O ports C4–C7H.

(c) Z-80 SIO mapped to I/O ports C8–CBH.

(d) Wire the CTC so that it can be used as a baud rate generator for the SIO. Use a 1.8432-MHz time base.

(e) Wire a three-switch DIP switch to PA0–PA2 of the PIO.

9.31. Write a control program for the interface described in Problem 9.30 that allows the switch to select eight different baud rates as listed in the table in Problem 9.25. Assume a 16× clock.

Section 9.6

9.32. At first it would seem that an 8-bit UART would be limited to monitoring or controlling the on/off status of eight I/O devices. What is wrong with this logic? What are the actual limits?

Section 9.7

9.33. When a serial port is not transmitting data ("marking"), its output is a logic 1. According to the RS-232 standard, what voltage level would you expect to measure for this condition?

*9.34. A technician is troubleshooting an RS-232 interface. Spotting a 25-pin connector, his first job is to determine whether the connector is wired as a DTE or a DCE. The technician says, "That's easy. I'll just measure the voltage on pin 2." Is this correct? Explain.

9.35. Suppose two computers are to be wired together to exchange data via their RS-232 serial ports. If both machines are wired as DTEs, how should the cable be wired? Assume that only DTR and DSR are used for handshaking.

9.36. Which two modem-control signals are used to handshake the PC-to-modem connection (not the data transfer)?

9.37. Explain how the four modem-control signals of the 8251A USART or the Z-80 SIO should be connected to the BUSY/READY and STROBE handshaking signals of a serial printer.

9.38. Explain how the X-ON/X-OFF protocol can be used to synchronize the flow of data between two serial ports.

Section 9.8

9.39. Explain the following statement: For full-duplex operation, an answering modem and an originating modem are required.

*9.40. When a modem is operating in half-duplex mode, only one station can transmit at a time. Because of this, a terminal set for half duplex displays the operator's keystrokes as they are typed. However, when set for full duplex, the terminal expects the distant station to "echo" the keystrokes back. Assume you are troubleshooting such a system and find that each keystroke is repeated *twice* on the CRT screen. What do you think is wrong?

9.41. Determine the *data rate* for a 600-baud modem using
  (a) FSK
  (b) PSK (di-bits)
  (c) QAM (quad bits)

9.42. QAM is a modem modulation method that varies the _____ and _____ of the carrier signal.

9.43. Calculate the baud rate required to achieve a 9600-bps data rate with 4 bits per baud.

9.44. With V.42bis, the throughput of a modem can be as much as _____ times the modem's specified data rate.

9.45. Give an example of an AT command that verifies that your communications software is on-line with your modem. What response from the modem do you predict?

9.46. The OH input to the dc loop current control circuit in Fig. 9.48 can be used to implement a computer-controlled automatic dialing circuit. Figure 9.55 illustrates the timing required to dial the two-digit sequence consisting of a "4" followed by a "3." Write a subroutine that pulses the OH line in Fig. 9.55 the appropriate number of times and with the proper inter-digital timing to facilitate a computer-controlled automatic dialer. Assume that the digit to be dialed is passed to the subroutine in register A and that the OH input is connected to DTR of the 8251A interface in Fig. 9.15.

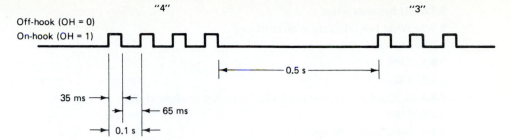

Figure 9.55 Telephone pulse timing required to dial the two-digit sequence consisting of a "4" followed by a "3."

ANSWERS TO SELF-REVIEW QUESTIONS

9.1.1. start, stop

9.1.2. baud

9.1.3. UART

9.2.1. The transmission of synchronous serial data does not use start and stop bits.

9.2.2. byte, bit

9.3.1. parity

9.3.2. True

9.3.3. The checksum requires less overhead and is more likely to detect burst errors.

9.3.4. bit

9.3.5. four

9.4.1. two (two input ports and two output ports)

9.4.2. TTL oscillator, 8254 PIT oscillator, baud rate generator chip (MC14411, for example)

9.4.3. R×RDY

9.4.4. The USART can be programmed to hunt for a special sync character indicating the start of synchronous serial data.

9.5.1. two

9.5.2. eight, three

9.5.3. polling, interrupts, DMA

9.5.4. Write to WR0 and specify the register to be accessed.

9.5.5. transmitter-buffer-empty

9.5.6. WR3–WR5

9.6.1. three-, eight, eight

9.6.2. A UART that can be programmed to recognize a specific address. For all other addresses, the chip operates in standby mode.

9.7.1. 0.4, 2.0

9.7.2. differential

9.7.3. (a) PC, (b) modem

9.7.4. 9-, 25-, male

9.7.5. $\overline{\text{DCD}}$

9.7.6. $\overline{\text{RI}}$ becomes active.

9.7.7. When two DTEs are to be interfaced

9.7.8. software

9.8.1. 3300

9.8.2. FSK

9.8.3. A signal event is one amplitude, frequency, or phase change.

9.8.4. 1800

9.8.5. 2400 baud, 9600 bps

9.8.6. 115.2K

9.8.7. With ATH0

9.8.8. ATS0=10

10

FLOPPY- AND HARD-DISK DRIVES

OUTLINE

OBJECTIVES

After completing this chapter, you should be able to:

- Explain how magnetic flux transitions are used to store digital data on a magnetic disk.
- Compare the media used for floppy- and hard-disk drives.
- Describe the components of a floppy-disk drive.
- Describe the components of a hard-disk drive.
- Show how to calculate the storage capacity of a drive on the basis of its physical or logical geometry.
- Explain how DOS's FAT file system stores files using data clusters.

- Explain how a serial data pattern can be converted to flux transitions for storage on a magnetic disk.
- Compare the flux transition rates and disk storage capacities of the FM, MFM, and RLL 2,7 magnetic-disk-encoding schemes.
- Describe the electrical interface associated with a floppy-disk drive.
- Compare ATA/IDE and SCSI, the two most common hard-disk drive interface technology standards.

OVERVIEW

In Chapter 5, we spent a considerable amount of time studying RAM and ROM memory technologies. This type of memory, called *main memory,* is interfaced to the microprocessor in such a way that each memory location has its own unique address. Using its address, data, and control buses, the microprocessor is then able to repeatedly fetch and execute program instructions stored in main memory.

Some computers can get by with a single program stored in one or more ROM chips. Microcomputer-controlled appliances like VCRs, dishwashers, and microwave ovens are good examples. Desktop computers, on the other hand, usually have a large amount of RAM into which applications programs are loaded via a disk drive.

Disk drives are referred to as *secondary* storage devices. Their purpose is twofold: to back up data that is stored in RAM, but that will be lost when power is removed, and to provide a means of quickly loading new applications programs into RAM. Two types of disk drives are in common use: *floppy-* and *hard-,* or *fixed-*disk, drives.

In this chapter, we will study the technology behind these two types of drives. We begin by learning how binary data can be stored on a magnetic disk. The components of a typical drive are then explained. It is here that the differences between a floppy- and hard-disk drive will become clear. Next, common disk drive terminology, such as *tracks, sectors, cylinders,* and *clusters,* are explained. The popular data-encoding techniques—MFM and RLL—are also discussed. The chapter concludes with a discussion of the disk drive interface, identifying the industry standard interfaces that are used to mate the disk drive electronics to the disk controller.

10.1 STORING DATA ON A MAGNETIC DISK

Introduction

Although floppy-disk drives and hard-disk drives are quite different as far as data rates and storage capacities are concerned, the data-recording technique used by the two drives is the same. Data to be written must first be converted to serial form. The data bits are then written by applying pulses of current to a read/write head positioned over the surface of a spinning magnetic disk.

In this section, we:

- Explain how magnetic flux transitions are used to store digital data on a magnetic disk.
- Compare the media used for floppy- and hard-disk drives.

Flux Transitions

As shown in Fig. 10.1, the read/write head of a floppy or hard disk is actually an *electro-magnet*. When a pulse of current is applied to the head, the surface of the disk directly under the head becomes magnetized. Depending on the direction of the applied current, the flux lines produced will be oriented left to right or right to left.

Note that each time a set of north or south poles faces each other, the flux lines must reverse. Data is written to the disk by defining a *bit cell* within which a logic 1 or 0 is written. In the single-density encoding scheme, a flux transition in the middle of the bit cell is interpreted as a logic 1, the absence of this transition as a logic 0. Each time a flux transition is to occur, the *direction* of the current through the read/write head must be reversed.*

In the playback, or read, mode, the head acts as a magnetic pickup. Each time a flux transition occurs, a small voltage is induced in the head. (Recall Faraday's law: $v = N \, d\phi/dt$). *In this way, the original waveform can be recovered.*

The Medium

The magnetic disk upon which the data is stored is called the *medium*. Floppy disks use a Mylar disk coated with iron oxide, a magnetic compound. Because of the flexibility of the Mylar disk, the term "floppy" has been applied. Hard drives use a rigid disk often made of aluminum coated with a thin film-plated magnetic medium. This creates a much thinner and smoother surface compared with that of floppy disks.

---

*Be careful not to interpret each flux transition as a logic 1. Because of the need to maintain synchronization with the data, *clock* pulses are embedded within the data stream. Thus, some flux transitions may represent data, others the synchronizing clock pulses. This scheme is explained in more detail in Section 10.4.

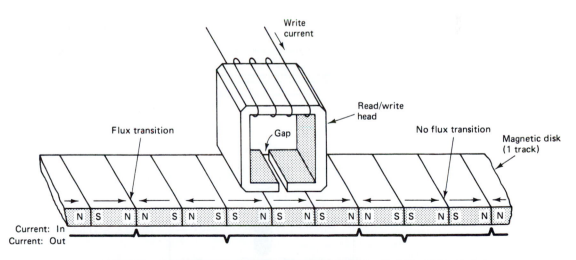

Figure 10.1 The read/write head of a floppy- or hard-disk drive. Each time the current reverses, a flux transition is recorded.

Figure 10.2 shows two types of floppy disks. The principal difference is the size of the disk: 3½″ or 5 ¼″. Both types consist of a Mylar disk enclosed in a protective jacket. Read/write head access to the disk is provided via an opening in the jacket, as shown. Surprisingly, the 3½″ disks actually store more data than the 5¼″ disks, and for this reason the larger disks are now nearly obsolete.

Floppy-disk drives use a technique called *contact recording* in which the read/write head rests on the surface of the disk. The potential frictional losses limit floppy drives to relatively low rotational speeds (300 or 360 RPM).

Hard-disk drives rotate at 3600 to 10,000 RPM. This high speed allows the heads to "float" on a cushion of air a few millionths of an inch above the disk's surface. However, the extremely close tolerance also requires the disk to be enclosed in a sealed container to protect it from the environment. (A typical human hair is .003 inch in diameter—several thousand times greater than the "flying height" of the hard-disk drive's read/write head).

Floppy disks are double sided, meaning that data can be stored on both sides of the disk. Hard disks typically employ several platters arranged one on top of another in a stack. Because of their higher rotational speed, hard-disk drives provide much higher storage capacities and data rates than do floppy-disk drives.

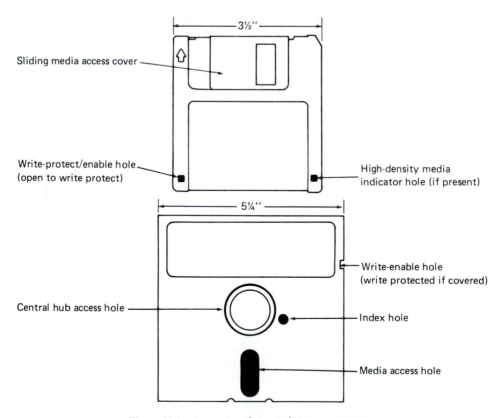

Figure 10.2   Comparing 3½″ and 5¼″ floppy diskettes.

10.1.1 Data to be stored on a magnetic disk must first be converted to _____ form.

10.1.2 The read/write head of a disk drive functions as a(n) _____.

10.1.3 A logic 1 is written to a magnetic disk by causing a _____ _____ to occur within a bit cell.

10.1.4 True or false? Unlike the mechanism of a floppy-disk drive, the read/write heads of a hard-disk drive do not normally contact the surface of the disk.

10.2 THE COMPONENTS OF A DISK DRIVE

Introduction

Floppy- and hard-disk drives are similar in that each uses a rotating magnetic disk with the data accessed via an electromagnetic read/write head. However, the components of a floppy-disk drive are quite different from those of a hard-disk drive.

In this section, we:

- Describe the components of a floppy-disk drive.
- Describe the components of a hard-disk drive.

Floppy-Disk Drives

Figure 10.3 highlights the major components of a floppy-disk drive. The disk is rotated by the *spindle motor* at 360 RPM (300 RPM for a low-density 5¼" drive). Unlike the mechanism of hard-disk drives, the spindle motor runs only when the disk is being accessed.

A second motor called the *stepper motor* is used to move the read/write head linearly across the surface of the spinning disk. The resolution of this motor determines the number of tracks—concentric circles—within which data is stored. A single voltage pulse applied to the stepper motor moves the head in or out by one track. Typical drives have 40 or 80 tracks per disk side.

The *read/write* head is actually three heads in one. This configuration is shown in Fig. 10.4(a). The data head is in the center, with *tunnel erase* heads mounted on each side. The purpose of the latter is to clear the intertrack region of any flux transitions [Fig. 10.4(b)]. Nearly all disk drives today are *double sided.* This means that data can be written to both sides of the disk. Of course, such drives require two read/write heads, with the disk sandwiched between the two.

Although not shown in Fig. 10.3, every floppy-disk drive also includes a *logic board.* This printed circuit board contains the circuitry needed to translate the flux transitions into valid logic levels. Also included are circuits for controlling the various motors and sensors within the drive. Section 10.5 discusses the disk-drive/computer interface.

Hard-Disk Drives

In Fig. 10.5, we show the major components of a typical hard-disk drive. Early versions of these drives had an 8" *form factor* (that is, the internal disk has an 8" diameter). The

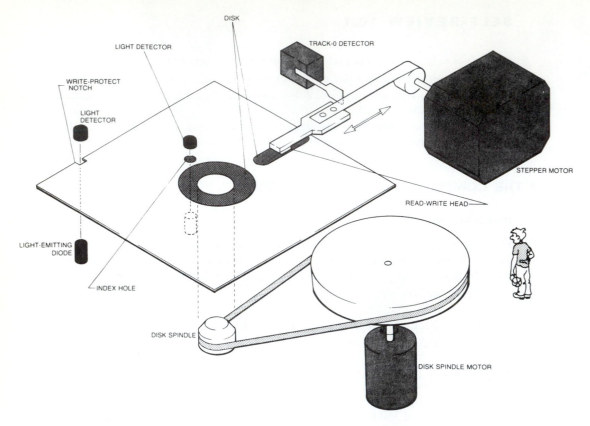

Figure 10.3 Mechanical design of a floppy-disk drive. The spindle motor rotates the disk, and a stepper motor is used to position the read/write head over the desired data track. (Courtesy of Reason Redacting.)

IBM PC/XT was one of the first personal computers to include a hard-disk drive—one with a 5¼″ form factor. The XT could store 10 MB of information.

In the ensuing years, hard-disk drive capacities have grown larger and larger, with ever-smaller form factors. Today we have laptop computers with 2-GB (2000-MB) matchbox-sized hard-disk drives (1.8″ form factor). Desktop computers typically use 3½″ drives with 4–10-GB capacities.

As mentioned previously, hard-disk drives normally have several rigid platters referred to as the *disk stack assembly*. (See Fig. 10.5.) Each platter requires a separate read/write head, and all the heads are moved across the surface of the disks in unison by the *head actuator arm.* That is, all heads are positioned over the same track at any given time.*

The spindle motor rotates the disk stack assembly at a constant speed. Because the data rate of the drive is directly related to its RPM rating, manufacturers are continually pushing to offer drives with ever-higher RPM ratings. Early hard-disk drives operated at

---

*In the next section, we define this collection of tracks to be a *cylinder.* Thus, a disk with 3000 tracks has 3000 cylinders.

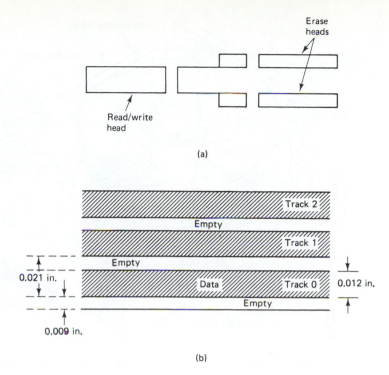

Figure 10.4 (a) Read/write head with tunnel erase; (b) the path written by the head as the disk rotates. The dimensions shown are typical for a low-density 5¼″ drive.

3600 RPM, but modern drives operate at 7200 RPM, with some drives rated as high as 10,000 RPM.

Unlike floppy-disk drives, which use a stepper motor to position the heads over the desired track, hard-disk drives use a *servomotor*. In one version of this scheme, one disk surface is dedicated to storing track position information. If it is desired to move the heads to track 1239, the heads slide smoothly out to this position, getting information from the dedicated surface. This information is fed back to the controller electronics, which direct the servomotor to readjust the position of the heads accordingly.

Early hard-disk drives used a single ferrite block for the read/write head. Later drives used *composite heads, metal-in-gap heads,* and, finally, *thin-film heads.* The latter were actually integrated circuits and provided bit densities as high as 200 million bits per square inch. Typical drives could store 500–800 MB of information.

To break the 1-GB barrier, a new type of head was required. The result was the *magnetoresistive* (*MR*) head, which can support bit densities as high as 2 billion bits per square inch. MR technology is based on a special material whose electrical resistance changes in the presence of a magnetic field. Unfortunately, the mechanism cannot be used for writing data, and a conventional thin-film inductive write element must be deposited alongside the MR strip for this purpose.

The extremely high bit densities of modern hard drives result in very weak pickup signals from the magnetic disks. It is the job of the disk controller electronics to amplify

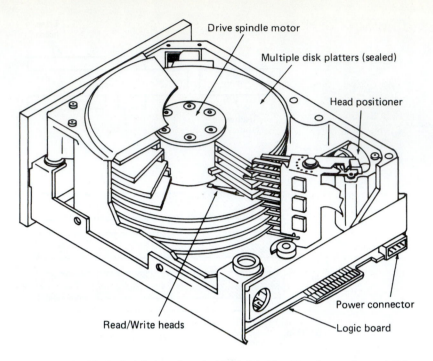

Figure 10.5 Mechanical design of a typical hard-disk drive. Note the use of several disk platters.

these (analog) signals and convert them to digital form. Typically, the controller has four components:

1. A digital signal processor (DSP) to convert the analog signals to digital.
2. Spindle and head actuator motor controllers.
3. Interface electronics to communicate with the system processor.
4. A microprocessor and related memory to oversee all drive operations.

SELF-REVIEW 10.2

10.2.1 List the two types of motors used in a floppy-disk drive.

10.2.2 Desktop computers today typically use hard-disk drives with a _____ form factor.

10.2.3 True or false? A hard-disk drive with three platters will have six read/write heads.

10.2.4 In a hard-disk drive, the _____ _____ _____ is controlled by a closed-loop servomotor.

10.2.5 For precise positioning of the read/write heads, hard-disk drives use _____ motor-controlled positioners.

10.2.6 Hard-disk drives with capacities greater than 1 GB typically use _____ read heads.

10.3 COMMON DISK DRIVE SPECIFICATIONS

Introduction

The rotating disk of a hard- or floppy-disk drive causes the data to be stored in circular tracks. The head actuator arm then sweeps out numerous tracks as it moves across the surface of the disk. It is up to the disk operating system to manage these tracks in some way so that data can be efficiently stored and quickly retrieved.

In this section, we:

- Show how to calculate the storage capacity of a drive on the basis of its physical or logical geometry.
- Explain how DOS's FAT file system stores files using data clusters.

Sectors

As the read/write head of a floppy- or hard-disk drive is stepped in and out across the surface of a disk, concentric data circles—*tracks*—are defined. These are shown in Fig. 10.4. To allocate space efficiently within these tracks, the *disk operating system* (DOS) divides these tracks further into *sectors*. This arrangement is shown in Fig. 10.6.

Under Microsoft's MS-DOS, five different floppy-disk formats have become standard. Table 10.1 lists the important parameters for these formats.

Example 10.1

Calculate the total number of sectors and storage capacity for a high-density $3\frac{1}{2}''$ floppy-disk drive.

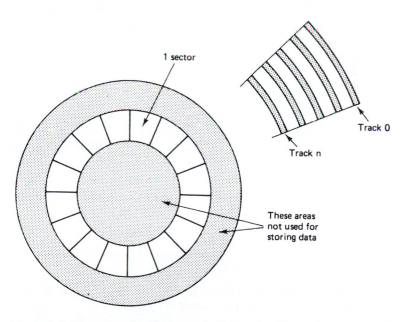

Figure 10.6 The surface of the disk is organized into tracks with several sectors per track.

TABLE 10.1 Floppy-Disk Drive Formats

Drive size	5¼"	5¼"	3½"	3½"	3
Density	low	high	low	high	very high
Tracks per side	40	80	80	80	80
Sides	2	2	2	2	2
Sectors per track	9	15	9	18	36
Bytes per sector	512	512	512	512	512
Total sectors	720	2400	1440	2880	5760
Total capacity	360K[a]	1200K	720K	1440K	2880K

[a]1K = 1024 bytes

Solution. The total number of sectors is

$$\text{Sectors} = \frac{\text{sectors}}{\text{tracks}} \times \frac{\text{tracks}}{\text{side}} \times \text{no. of sides}$$

$$= 18 \quad \times 80 \quad \times 2 = 2880 \text{ sectors}$$

The total disk capacity is then

$$\text{Disk capacity} = \text{total sectors} \times \frac{\text{bytes}}{\text{sector}}$$

$$= 2880 \quad \times 512 = 1,474,560 \text{ bytes}$$
$$= 1440K \ (1K = 1024 \text{ bytes})$$

Comparing the five types of drive in Table 10.1, we note that 3½" drives are able to store more data than their 5¼" counterparts. The smaller drives are actually storing data at a higher *bit density* (bits/in). This is an indication of the improved technology present in these drives.

Cylinders

The term *cylinder* is often applied in describing the capacity of a hard-disk drive. A cylinder is defined as all of the tracks under the read/write heads at a given time—in effect, a *three-dimensional area* that traces out the shape of a cylinder. Figure 10.7 is an illustration of a hard-disk drive with three disk platters. As is evident, with three disks there are *six* disk surfaces and therefore six read/write heads (heads 0 through 5). Cylinder 0 is defined to be the outermost track (on all three surfaces), with higher numbers associated with the inner tracks. The numbers of cylinders associated with a drive is therefore the same as the number of tracks per disk side.

Less frequently, the term *cylinders* is applied to floppy disks.

Example 10.2

Calculate the total number of cylinders for a 3½" high-density floppy-disk drive. How many bytes are stored per cylinder?

Solution. Referring to Table 10.1, we see that a 3½" drive has 80 tracks per side. Thus, this disk stores 80 cylinders. The capacity of 1 cylinder is

18 sectors/track × 2 tracks/cylinder × 512 bytes/sector = 18,432 bytes/cylinder (18 KB)

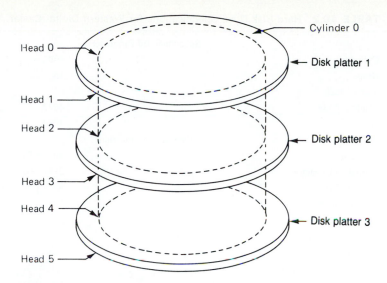

Head 0

Head 1

Head 2

Head 3

Head 4

Head 5

Cylinder 0

Disk platter 1

Disk platter 2

Disk platter 3

Figure 10.7 A cylinder encompasses all tracks under the read/write heads at a given time. In this example, there are three platters and therefore six tracks per cylinder.

Logical Geometry vs. Physical Geometry

In recent years, hard-disk drive manufacturers have taken advantage of the fact that the outermost cylinders of a disk have a greater storage capacity than the innermost cylinders. (The perimeter grows with increasing radius.) Accordingly, these drives have a *variable* number of sectors per track. In one scheme, the disk is divided into two *zones:* an inner zone and an outer zone. The outer zone may store 35 sectors per track, while the inner zone stores just 17 sectors per track.

The "trick" that allows this arrangement to work is to use an *intelligent disk controller.* Consider the specifications shown in Table 10.2 for a Western Digital Caviar AC12100. The recommended parameters—those given to DOS via the CMOS setup software—indicate a fixed geometry of 4092 cylinders, 16 heads, and 63 sectors per track. However, the physical specifications indicate just two disk surfaces (and two heads). How can this arrangement work?

When the Western Digital drive is accessed by DOS, its built-in controller translates the fixed (logical) geometry into the actual values for heads, cylinders, and sectors. The process is completely hidden from the user. In Section 10.5, we discuss these intelligent disk controllers in more detail.

Example 10.3

Calculate the total storage capacity and the size of one cylinder of a Western Digital AC12100. Use the drive's logical specifications.

Solution.   The capacity of the drive is

4092 tracks/side $\times$ 16 sides $\times$ 63 sectors/track $\times$ 512 bytes/sector =

$$2,111,864,832 \text{ bytes} = 2.1 \text{ GB}$$

The capacity of one cylinder is

16 tracks/cylinder $\times$ 63 sectors/track $\times$ 512 bytes/sector = 516,096 bytes/cylinder

TABLE 10.2 Hard-Disk Drive Specifications for Western Digital Caviar AC12100

Recommended Parameters

Cylinders	4092
Heads	16
Sector Track	63
Landing Zone	4092
WPC	4092

Physical Specifications

Interface	40-pin EIDE
Formatted Capacity	2111 MB
Actuator Type	Rotary Voice Coil
Number of Disks	1
Data Surfaces	2
Number of Heads	2
Bytes Per Sector	512
User Sectors Per Drive	4,124,736
Servo Type	Embedded
Recording Method	GCR 8, 9-PRML
ECC	Reed Solomon
Head Park	Automatic

Performance Specifications

Average Seek Read	9.5 ms
Track to Track	2.0 ms
Full Stroke Seek	19 ms
Average Latency	5.5 ms
Rotational Speed	5400 RPM
Data Transfer Rate:	
	16.6 MB/s (burst Mode 4 PIO)
Buffer to Host	16.6 MB/s (burst Mode 2 DMA)
	33.3 MB/s (Mode 2 Ultra DMA)
Media to Buffer	68 Mbits/s min
	131 Mbits/s max
Read Cache	Adaptive
Write Cache	Yes
Buffer	256K DRAM
Interleave	1:1
Spindle Start Times:	
From Power-on to Drive Ready	11s typical, 18s max
From Power-on to Rotational Speed	7s typical, 15s max
Start/Stop Cycles	40,000 min
Master/Slave support	Yes
LBA Support	Yes
IORDY Support	Yes
Error Rate: Non-recoverable	<1 in 10^{13} bits read

TABLE 10.3 Hard-Disk Drive
Partition Size and Corresponding
Cluster Size

Partition size	Cluster size
2 GB	32 KB
<1 GB	16 KB
<512 MB	8 KB
<256 MB	4 KB
<128 MB	2 KB

Clusters

DOS uses the file allocation table (FAT) file system to store data to floppies and hard disks. In order to do this job as efficiently as possible, the FAT allocates storage space in *clusters,* with several (consecutive) disk sectors per cluster. In general, the larger the drive, the larger is the cluster size. (See Table 10.3.)

The advantage of clustering is to make it easier for DOS to keep track of files and speed up disk access. Consider using a 2-GB hard-disk drive to store a 20-KB file. Without clustering, DOS would break this file into 40 sectors and store it in various locations on the disk, depending on the available space. That is, the file would become *fragmented.* When it came time to read this file back, the read/write head would have to move back and forth across the disk surface to pick up the fragmented pieces of the file. Obviously, this would affect the performance of the system.

Now suppose that the same file is saved using a 32-KB cluster size. When DOS stores the file, it searches for an open cluster—in this example, 64 consecutive sectors. Because the cluster size is greater than the file size, fragmenting is avoided. Indeed, 24 additional sectors remain before this file will have to be broken into a second cluster.

The drawback to clustering is wasted disk space. In the previous example, a file of just 10 bytes will be saved using one cluster and thus actually take up 32 KB of disk space. This indicates that clustering can be inefficient if many small files are to be stored.

By definition, floppy disks are limited to storing relatively small files. For these disks, DOS allocates space with just one sector per cluster for high-density drives and two sectors per cluster for low-density drives.

High- and Low-Level Formatting

Before a floppy or hard disk can be used to store data, it must be formatted. This is a software process in which each sector on the disk is prepared so that it can be referenced by DOS and included in the FAT.

The low-level format. The low-level format creates the individual tracks and sectors. In addition, the surface of the disk may be scanned to ensure that each track is capable of storing data.

With floppy-disk drives, low- and high-level formatting are accomplished via the single DOS command FORMAT. With hard-disk drives, however, low-level formatting is accomplished at the factory. In this way, the low-level formatting actually defines the translation tables stored by the drive's onboard controller.

The high-level format.   High-level formatting finishes the formatting process by creating the boot sector (a sector that contains code responsible for starting up the computer), the root directory, and two copies of the FAT. The typical command is

FORMAT C:/s

which will high-level format drive C (the hard drive) and copy the system files to the hard disk.

SELF-REVIEW 10.3

10.3.1 Data is stored on a floppy or hard disk in concentric tracks, with each track further divided into _____.

10.3.2 One cylinder corresponds to all _____ under the read/write heads at a given time.

10.3.3 What is the difference between a hard drive's logical geometry and its physical geometry?

10.3.4 A certain hard drive is logically organized as 16 heads, 63 sectors per track, and 2048 tracks per side. (a) How many cylinders does this drive store? (b) Calculate the total storage capacity of the drive in bytes.

10.3.5 What is the advantage of organizing the data on a disk into clusters?

10.3.6 The process of defining the individual tracks and sectors on a hard-disk drive is accomplished via a _____-level format.

10.4 DATA-ENCODING TECHNIQUES

Introduction

In Section 10.1, we learned that data is stored on a floppy or hard disk as a series of *flux transitions*. Over the years, several different encoding schemes have been developed that utilize these flux transitions to store data.

In this section, we:

- Explain how a serial data pattern can be converted to flux transitions for storage on a magnetic disk.
- Compare the flux transition rates and disk storage capacities of the FM, MFM, and RLL 2,7 magnetic-disk-encoding schemes.

Single Density

When data are encoded in single-density format, there is one clock pulse written for each data bit. Figure 10.8 provides an example. At the top, the data pattern is shown as it would

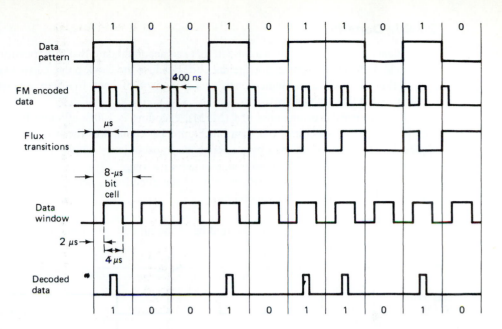

Figure 10.8 Single-density encoding. Each bit cell begins with a clock pulse, and two flux transitions (maximum) are required per cell.

appear after having been converted from parallel to serial form. Each bit persists for a period of time called the *bit cell*. For example, a low-density 5¼" disk drive has a data rate of 125,000 bits/s, which requires a bit cell 8 μs wide.

The rules for single-density encoding are as follows:

1. Begin each bit cell with a clock pulse.
2. If a logic 1 is to be stored, write a pulse in the middle of the bit cell. If a logic 0 is to be stored, do not write any pulse.

If you compare the data pattern in Fig. 10.8 with the encoded data, you should be able to see how the rules for single-density data are applied. Note that each clock or data pulse becomes a *flux transition* when it is written to the disk.

Single-density encoding is also called frequency modulation (FM) encoding, because a string of logic 1's will produce a different frequency than a string of logic 0's. That is, the data is encoded by *modulating* a carrier frequency.

FM encoding is said to be *self-clocking,* because the clock signal can be derived from the bit stream. Self-clocking is important because it is tolerant of slight variations in motor speed, as are likely to occur in moving a disk from one drive to another.

When the IBM-PC was first introduced, it used single-sided, single-density encoding. This allowed a 5¼" disk to store 160 KB of data. Today, single-density encoding is considered obsolete and has been replaced by double-density and RLL encoding.

Double Density

Single-density encoding requires a bit cell that can accommodate two flux transitions: one for the clock pulse and another for the data bit. Because the clock pulse carries no useful information about the data, single-density encoding is inefficient. In effect, it wastes 50% of the possible flux transitions.

Double-density, or *modified* FM (MFM), encoding is 100% efficient because only one flux transition is required per data bit. Figure 10.9 compares the two encoding techniques. In Fig. 10.9(a), the data byte is encoded in accordance with the rules for single-density data. The resulting 8-bit data stream is 64 μs long.

In Fig. 10.9(b), the same data byte has been encoded in accordance with the following rules for double-density encoding:

1. Write a logic 1 as a pulse in the middle of the bit cell, as with single-density data.

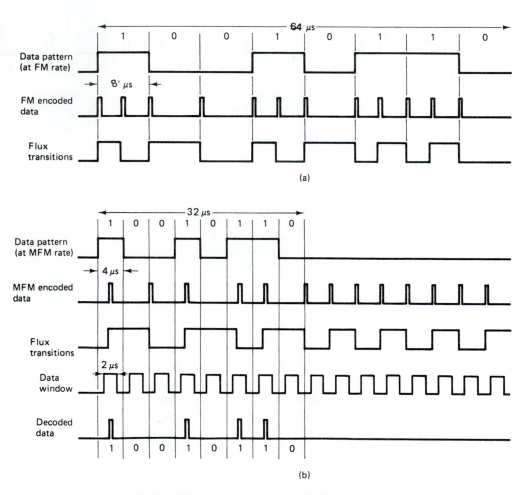

Figure 10.9 (a) Single-density encoding is compared with (b) double-density encoding. The latter requires only one flux change per data bit.

2. Write a logic 0 as a pulse at the beginning of the bit cell (in the clock position), except if the logic 0 would be preceded by a logic 1. In that case, no pulse is written.

Studying the MFM data pattern in Fig. 10.9(b), we can note the following:

1. There is one flux transition (maximum) per data bit.
2. The maximum rate of change of flux transitions is the same as for FM data.
3. The bit cell is one-half the single-density cell size, allowing two bits to be stored per single-density cell.
4. Because two bits are written in the time required for one single-density bit, the data rate for MFM is twice that of FM.

The MFM encoding process is really a software "trick." By eliminating the clock pulses associated with FM data, it is able to pack two data bits in the space previously required for one. No hardware changes are required of the disk drive. A drive used for writing single-density data can be used for double-density data as well. And because the flux transition rate is the same, special disks are not required.

Run-Length Limited (RLL)

FM-encoded data requires a minimum of one pulse per bit cell (when storing a logic 0) and a maximum of two (when storing a logic 1). This means that FM data is limited to a minimum of 0 missing pulses and a maximum of 1. We could describe this as run-length limited with a minimum run length of 0 and maximum run length of 1, or *RLL 0,1*. The term *run length* thus refers to the number of missing pulses.

Studying the MFM waveforms in Fig. 10.9(b), you can see a minimum run length of 1 (between two consecutive logic 1's or 0's) and a maximum of 3 (in storing the data pattern 101). MFM can thus be described as RLL 1,3.

Many hard drives today are using RLL 2,7, an encoding scheme that has a minimum run length of 2 and a maximum of 7. The rules for RLL 2,7 are shown in Table 10.4. Note that the data bits are not encoded individually, but rather as a *group*. Thus, the data pattern 00 is encoded as a single pulse followed by three missing pulses. Studying this table, you can see that there will always be at least two missing pulses, but no more than seven, no matter what the data pattern.

Figure 10.10 compares FM- and RLL 2,7-encoded data. Note that three RLL data bits can be encoded in the space for one FM data bit. For example, the data pattern 101 is stored as one pulse, two spaces, one pulse, and, again, two spaces. Notice, however, that the pulse-to-pulse spacing is the same as that of the FM-encoded data.

When a hard-disk drive is RLL encoded, it can store three times as much data as the equivalent FM drive and one and one-half times as much data as the equivalent MFM drive.

Example 10.5

A certain hard drive has been formatted to 100 MB using FM encoding. Determine the storage capacity of this drive when it is formatted using (a) MFM; (b) RLL 2,7.

Solution. When the drive is formatted using MFM, its capacity doubles to 200 MB. The same drive formatted with RLL 2,7 has a capacity of 300 MB.

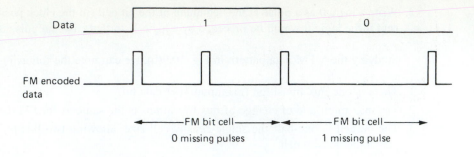

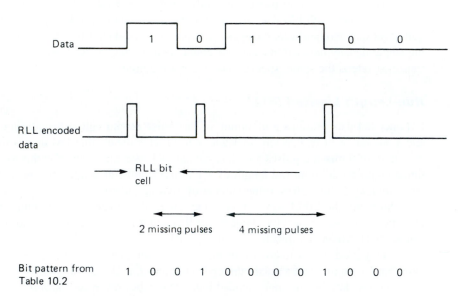

Figure 10.10 Comparing the FM- and RLL 2,7-encoding schemes. Three RLL data bits can be stored in the space required by one FM data bit.

TABLE 10.4 Rules for RLL 2,7 Encoding

Data bit group	RLL 2,7 encoding*
0 0	1 0 0 0
0 1	0 1 0 0
1 0 0	0 0 1 0 0 0
1 0 1	1 0 0 1 0 0
1 1 0 0	0 0 0 0 1 0 0 0
1 1 0 1	0 0 1 0 0 1 0 0
1 1 1	0 0 0 1 0 0

*A 1 indicates a data pulse, a 0 the absence of a pulse.

At one time, special controllers were necessary to use RLL-encoded drives. Today, with the disk controller incorporated into the drive itself, the encoding is transparent to the user and no special controller is required.

SELF-REVIEW 10.4

10.4.1 What is meant by the term "bit cell"?

10.4.2 True or False? The flux transition rate using RLL 2,7 is three times higher than that for FM encoding.

10.4.3 In MFM encoding, a maximum of _____ missing pulses is allowed. RLL 2,7 allows as many as _____ missing pulses.

10.5 THE DISK DRIVE INTERFACE

Introduction

Floppy-disk drives and hard-disk drives are connected to a computer via a cable and an interface adapter. Because the interface has been standardized, computer users can easily add to or upgrade their existing disk drives without concern about compatibility problems.

In this section, we:

- Describe the electrical interface associated with a floppy-disk drive.
- Compare ATA/IDE and SCSI, the two most common hard-disk drive interface technology standards.

Floppy-Disk Drives

The floppy disk drive interface consists of three parts:

1. Read, write, and control logic circuits, mounted on a card (the *logic board*) on the disk drive.
2. Data and power cables.
3. Disk drive controller interface board.

The disk drive logic board is a combination of digital and analog circuits. It converts the serial data from the computer into pulses of current that are applied to the read/write head. In the playback mode, the flux transitions are detected and converted into voltage pulses.

It is the job of the floppy-disk controller (FDC) to encode and decode these pulses. (All floppy-disk drives uses MFM encoding.) As you might imagine, special floppy-disk formatter/controller LSI chips are available for this purpose. The typical chip used with the IBM-PC family of computers is the NEC765, which will accept 15 different commands, such as *format a track, read a track, write data, restore to track 0,* etc. These high-level commands make the FDC software much easier to write, as the "nitty gritty" details are handled by the controller chip.

All five types of floppy-disk drives described in this chapter use the same electrical interface, known as the *SA-450*. This interface, invented by Shugart Associates in the 1970s, uses a 34-pin data cable between the disk drive and disk controller and a 4-pin power cable (+12 V, +5 V, and 2 ground pins).*

Perhaps the most important feature of the SA-450 interface is that any manufacturer's compatible drive can be plugged into any other manufacturer's compatible disk controller card. Be careful with high-density drives, however: Because they read and write data at a 500-kHz rate (low-density drives operate at 250 kHz or 300 kHz), high-density FDCs will be incompatible with low-density drives.

Hard-Disk Drives

There are two popular hard-disk drive interface specifications: ATA/IDE and SCSI.

ATA/IDE.   A key task for the hard-disk controller is to convert the digital data received from the processor into an analog signal that the drive's read/write heads can use to cause changes in magnetic flux on the disk surface. First-generation (ST-506/412) hard drives performed this conversion on an external adapter card known as the *hard-drive controller* (*HDC*). The analog signals were transmitted to the drive via a 12″–18″ 20-conductor data cable and a 34-conductor control cable. In this scheme, the drive itself is *unintelligent* and contains only the electronics to control the motors and access the read/write heads.

There are two disadvantages to this interface. First, because the data signals must travel through a (relatively) long cable, data rates are limited. Typical drives operate at 625,000 bits/s (.625 Mb/s).** Second, the hard drive and the HDC must be *matched,* because the controller defines the encoding scheme. For example, a drive formatted with RLL 2,7 cannot be read with a controller that uses MFM.

In 1984, Compaq initiated development of the *Intelligent Drive Electronics* (IDE) interface. In this scheme, all of the electronics for controlling the drive and processing the analog flux transition signals are moved to the drive itself. A controller card—now called the *host adapter*—is still required, but it simply contains buffers to bring the system board bus signals to the drive.† A 40-conductor interface cable is required, limited to 18″ in length. Data transfer rates as high as 1 MB/s can be achieved.

In 1989, several new high-level commands were added to the original IDE command set, and the interface was established as an industry standard, renamed *AT attachment* (ATA), where *AT* refers to the AT system bus made popular in the IBM AT computer.

Most IDE hard drives today utilize *enhanced IDE* (EIDE) technology, also called *Fast ATA*. This is an extension to IDE that allows a primary and secondary channel, each supporting a master and a slave drive (four drives all together). In addition, non-hard-drive peripherals (IDE CD-ROM drives for example) are supported. The data transfer rate with EIDE is increased to a theoretical maximum of 16.6 MB/s. Finally, the specification defines how large hard drives are to be addressed. (Earlier, some older computers could not recognize drives larger than 528 MB).

---

*Most 3½″ drives use +5-V motors and require only a two-conductor powercable: +5 V and ground.

**ATA/IDE drives operate as fast as 33 MB/s.

†Today, most computers have the IDE host adapter built into the system board. A separate adapter card is not required.

TABLE 10.5 Hard-Disk Drive Specifications for Western Digital Caviar AC34000

Recommended Parameters	
Cylinders	7752
Heads	16
Sectors per Track	63
Landing Zone	7752
WPC	7752
Physical Specifications	
Interface	40-pin EIDE
Formatted Capacity	4001 MB
Type of Actuator	Rotary Voice Coil
Number of Disks	3
Data Surfaces	6
Number of Heads	6
Bytes per Sector	512
User Sectors per Drive	7,814,016
Type of Servo	Embedded
Recording Method	GCR 8,9-PRML
ECC	Reed Solomon
Head Park	Automatic

Recently, some manufacturers have been announcing IDE drives with a burst transfer rate of 33 MB/s. The technology is referred to as *Ultra ATA*.

SCSI. SCSI ("scuzzy") is the acronym for *small-computer system interface*. Unlike IDE, SCSI is not specifically a hard-drive interface; instead, it defines a bus standard to which all types of I/O devices—floppy and hard drives, scanners, mice, plotters, etc.—can be interfaced.

In a typical implementation, a SCSI host adapter is installed in the computer, which can then control seven other SCSI adapter cards, each connected to some type of I/O device.* If you want to install a SCSI hard drive, you first install the SCSI host adapter card. This card is then connected—via cables—to a hard drive that has an embedded SCSI controller.

The principal advantage of SCSI vs. ATA/IDE is the former's ability to support multiple I/O devices at the same time. For example, because the SCSI host is itself a processor, the system processor can instruct the host to perform a system backup and then proceed to perform other tasks. The SCSI host then manages the backup, controlling the SCSI hard drive and tape units without further CPU intervention.

Standard (8-bit) SCSI supports an asynchronous data transfer rate of 3 MB/s and a synchronous rate of 10 MB/s. A 50-conductor cable is required. Wide SCSI provides support for 16- and 32-bit data bus widths using a 68-conductor cable and can operate as fast as 80 MB/s.

SELF-REVIEW 10.5

10.5.1 The electrical interface used with floppy-disk drives is called _____ . It uses a _____ -conductor data cable.

---

*Newer versions of SCSI support up to 15 separate I/O devices.

10.5.2 The two electrical interfaces commonly used with hard-disk drives are _____ and _____ .

10.5.3 The EIDE interface supports a maximum data transfer rate of _____ MB/s.

QUESTIONS AND ANSWERS

Q: *What are two common secondary storage devices for computers?*

A: Floppy-disk drives and hard-disk drives. Floppy-disk drives use removable magnetic media available in $5\frac{1}{4}''$ and $3\frac{1}{2}''$ formats. Hard-disk drives use nonremovable magnetic disks mounted in a sealed chamber.

Q: *How is data stored on a floppy- or hard-disk drive?*

A: As the disk spins beneath the drive's read/write head, pulses of current cause tiny flux transitions to be stored. These transitions are used to represent a logic 1; the absence of a transition stores a logic 0.

Q: *How fast does the disk spin in a floppy-disk drive and a hard-disk drive?*

A: Low-density $5\frac{1}{4}''$ floppy-disk drives operate at 300 RPM; all other floppy-disk drives operate at 360 RPM. Hard-disk drives typically spin at 3600–7200 RPM, with some drives as fast as 10,000 RPM.

Q: *Why do hard-disk drives store more data than floppy-disk drives?*

A: In a floppy-disk drive, the read/write head contacts the disk. In a hard-disk drive, the heads "float" on a cushion of air microinches above the disk's surface. As a result, hard-disk drives spin 20 or more times faster than floppy-disk drives and store a correspondingly greater amount of data per disk revolution. In addition, the sealed chamber of a hard-disk drive allows finer track-to-track spacing, thus permitting more tracks per disk side. Finally, hard-disk drives typically have several (double-sided) disk platters in the same package, compared with the single (double-sided) surface of a floppy disk.

Q: *What is a cylinder?*

A: All of the heads in a floppy- or hard-disk drive move together in unison. The collection of these simultaneously selected tracks is called a cylinder. In a floppy-disk drive with 80 tracks per side, there will be 80 cylinders consisting of the top and bottom tracks on each side of the disk. In a hard-disk drive with three platters, 1 cylinder will comprise six tracks.

Q: *What is a cluster?*

A: DOS allocates disk space by grouping contiguous disk sectors into clusters and then assigning these to files as necessary. The size of one cluster varies with the drive. For example, a 2-GB hard-disk drive uses 32 KB per cluster (64 sectors), while high-density floppy-disk drives have just 512 bytes (1 sector) per cluster. Clustering represents a trade-off between storage efficiency and file fragmenting.

Q: *What is the difference between a high- and low-level format?*

A: The low-level format defines the individual tracks and sectors on the disk. The high-level format writes the boot sector and file directory and sets up the file allocation table (FAT).

Q: *Why does data need to be stored on a disk in coded form? What codes are commonly used?*

A: Data is stored on a magnetic disk serially in synchronous form, without start and stop bits. Coding involves embedding clock pulses within the data to help identify each bit cell. The two most common encoding schemes are MFM and RLL.

Q: *How are disk drives connected to a computer?*

A: Floppy-disk drives use a 34-conductor cable connected to a disk controller card known as the SA-450 interface, an industry standard. Hard-disk drives are connected using one of two standards: ATA/IDE or SCSI. ATA/IDE supports two channels with two drives per channel via a 40-conductor cable. SCSI supports as many as 15 different I/O devices via a 50- or 68-conductor cable connected to an intelligent host adapter.

QUESTIONS AND PROBLEMS

Section 10.1

10.1. List two reasons more data can be stored on a hard disk than on a floppy disk.

10.2. Each time the current through a drive's read/write head reverses, a _____ _____ is recorded on the disk.

Section 10.2

10.3. Compare the times required for one revolution of a disk at each of the following speeds:
  (a) 360 RPM
  (b) 3600 RPM
  (c) 7200 RPM
  (d) 10,000 RPM

*__**10.4.**__ You are troubleshooting a floppy-disk drive and note that the disk does not spin when it is accessed. Which drive motor would you suspect to be the problem?

10.5. Low-density $5\frac{1}{4}''$ floppy-disk drives have 40 tracks per side and 48 tracks per inch.
  (a) If the inside track has a radius of 1.542 in, calculate the radius of the *outside* track.
  (b) Using the result of part (a), calculate the amount of area on the $5\frac{1}{4}''$ disk used for storing data.
  (c) Compare the area calculated in part (b) with the total area of the disk.

10.6. Floppy- and hard-disk drives typically use two motors. Compare the corresponding motors in the two drives. In what ways are they similar? In what ways are they different?

10.7. List four different functions of a hard-disk drive's controller.

Section 10.3

10.8. A certain hard-disk drive has four heads and 1224 cylinders. How many tracks per disk side does this drive have?

10.9. If the hard-disk drive in Problem 10.8 is formatted with 63 sectors per track, how many sectors does the drive have?

10.10. Calculate the total storage capacity of the drive in Problem 10.8 and 10.9.

10.11. Refer to the hard-disk specifications in Table 10.5.
  (a) To the operating system this drive appears to have _____ disks.
  (b) Physically this drive has _____ disks.
  (c) The total storage capacity of the drive is:

10.12. A high-density $3\frac{1}{2}''$ floppy disk stores 1440K bytes. Express this capacity in bytes and MB.

10.13. The defect map accompanying a hard-disk drive indicates that cylinder 347, head 3, is bad. If the drive is formatted with 17 sectors per track, how many bytes correspond to this defect?

10.14. Suppose you have created a short data file of only 10 bytes. When the directory command is given, DOS reports that the file is actually 1024 bytes long. Explain.

10.15. Why does a hard-disk drive formatted with 34 sectors per track have a data transfer rate twice that of a drive formatted with 17 sectors per track? Assume that both drives operate at the same RPM rate.

10.16. True or false? The maximum flux transition rate for MFM-encoded data is the same as that for FM-encoded data.

10.17. For each of the encoding techniques FM, MFM, and RLL 2,7, determine the minimum and maximum number of missing pulses allowed in the data stream.

10.18. Suppose that, with RLL 2,7, the following pattern is received (with 0 representing a missing pulse and 1 a data pulse): 1001000010001000. What is the value of the byte being transmitted?

Section 10.5

10.19. For each of the following types of drive specify the number of conductors in the standard data cable:
  (a) 3.5″ high-density floppy
  (b) ATA/IDE
  (c) Standard SCSI

SELF-REVIEW ANSWERS

10.1.1. serial

10.1.2. electromagnet

10.1.3. flux transition

10.1.4. True

10.2.1. spindle motor and read/write head stepper motor

10.2.2. $3\frac{1}{2}$″

10.2.3. True

10.2.4. head actuator arm

10.2.5. servo

10.2.6. magnetoresistive

10.3.1. sectors

10.3.2. tracks

10.3.3. A drive's physical geometry corresponds to the actual (physical) number of heads, cylinders, and sectors per track. With many drives these numbers vary, depending on the zone on the disk. A drive's logical geometry defines a fixed geometry that can be used by DOS to access the drive regardless of the zone.

10.3.4. (a) 2048; (b) 1,056,964,608 (1 GB)

10.3.5. Faster access of files (less fragmenting) and fewer storage units per file.

10.3.6. low

10.4.1. A timing window corresponding to the time allocated to one data bit.

10.4.2. False. The flux transition rates are the same.

10.4.3. three, seven

10.5.1. SA-450, 34

10.5.2. ATA/IDE, SCSI

10.5.3. 16.6

11

MICROCOMPUTER CONTROL APPLICATIONS AND TROUBLESHOOTING TECHNIQUES

OUTLINE

OBJECTIVES

After completing this chapter, you should be able to:

- Show how to construct an analog voltage comparator circuit using the LM393.
- Show how to wire the LM334 constant-current source to provide a voltage signal whose amplitude corresponds to the temperature in degrees Kelvin.
- Show how logic gates can be used to drive and control electromechanical relays.
- Identify the components, and explain the operation, of a solid-state relay.
- Explain the operation of a digital-to-analog converter based on the R-2R resistor ladder network.

- Write an 8080/8085 program for synthesizing a sine wave using the MC1408 8-bit DAC interfaced to an 8255A PPI chip.
- Compare flash, feedback, and dual-slope analog-to-digital converters.
- Show how to interface the eight-channel ADC0809 ADC to the three-bus system architecture.
- Explain the operation of common microcomputer troubleshooting tools, including the multimeter, logic probe, oscilloscope, signature analyzer, and logic analyzer.
- Develop a strategy for troubleshooting a microcomputer system.

OVERVIEW

In this book, we have studied several aspects of microcomputer input/output, including the following:

> Serial and parallel data ports
>
> Software control techniques
>
> Special-purpose programmable I/O controllers

But believe it or not, one point has not been discussed: What do we do with all of the I/O pins our interfaces have provided? For example, adding an 8255A PPI chip provides the microcomputer with 24 programmable I/O pins. Presumably, we can use these to control or monitor the "outside world"—but how, exactly?

Perhaps we are building a microprocessor-controlled vending machine and need to detect the closing of a switch and then turn on a relay. Can the PPI drive the relay directly, and how do we test whether the switch is closed? Figure 11.1 illustrates the problem in general terms. The microcomputer "lives and breathes" TTL voltage levels, but the same can hardly be said for most real-world sensors and controllers. Some form of converter is required between the microprocessor and the real world. Such a converter can generally be considered to fit into one of two categories:

1. Converters to monitor or control the real-world device's on/off status
2. Converters that change the computer's digital signals to analog signals compatible with the real-world device

An example of the first kind of converter would be a circuit that allowed a microcomputer to turn a 120-V ac light on or off. An example of the second kind would be a circuit that allowed the computer to output 47.9 V (or any other voltage within some range) to a light, controlling its brilliance.

In this chapter, we study the microprocessor as a *controller* and learn how it can be made compatible with the (non-TTL) real world.

But now imagine that you have designed and built a microcomputer controller, perhaps to monitor and control the functions of a solar-heating system. You have interfaced sensors for measuring the inside and outside water temperatures, sensors for monitoring the level of water in the holding tank, and solenoids for controlling the water flow. A com-

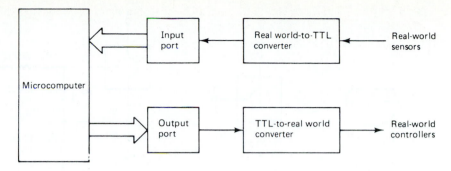

Figure 11.1 Interfacing a microcomputer to the real world.

plex controller program has been written and stored in an EPROM. Finally, the moment of truth arrives: Power is applied to the circuit. What happens? Unless you are very lucky, probably nothing.

But what could be wrong? Is it a hardware problem, or is there a bug in the software? Unfortunately, there are no easy answers. The microprocessor, while providing the designer with an extremely powerful design tool, can also be the source of much anguish and frustration. A simple wiring error such as crossing the A0 and A1 address lines will stop the processor dead in its tracks—and without any obvious clues.

The last section of this chapter deals with microprocessor *troubleshooting techniques*—from a discussion of the logical steps to follow in approaching a "dead" computer to an examination of the tools required for the task and how to use them.

11.1 DETECTING THE PRESENCE OF AN ANALOG SIGNAL: THE COMPARATOR

In many control applications, it is not necessary to know the exact value of an analog signal. For example, a warning may need to be sounded if the temperature in a freezer is *too high* or the temperature in a room is *too cold*. In these cases, a "TEMPERATURE TOO HIGH" or "TEMPERATURE TOO COLD" digital signal will suffice; the exact temperature is unimportant.

In this section, we:

- Show how to construct an analog voltage comparator circuit using the LM393.
- Show how to wire the LM334 constant-current source to provide a voltage signal whose amplitude corresponds to the temperature in degrees Kelvin.

Figure 11.2 shows the LM334 three-terminal current source, which produces an output current that is directly proportional to temperature in degrees Kelvin. (The Kelvin temperature scale is 273 degrees higher than the Celsius scale.) At 72°F (22°C), $V_{OUT} = (22° + 273°) \times 10$ mV/°K $= 2.95$ V.

Using the LM334, we could design a computer interface that warns when the temperature is too high or too low.

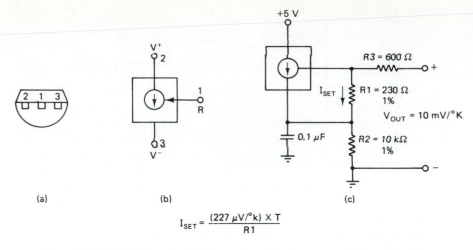

(a)　　　　　　(b)　　　　　　(c)

$$I_{SET} = \frac{(227\ \mu V/^{\circ}k) \times T}{R1}$$

Figure 11.2　LM334 three-terminal temperature-dependent source: (a) the package outline; (b) the schematic symbol; (c) a typical application.

Example 11.1

Suppose that the LM334 is to be used to indicate a "temperature too high" condition. What
output voltage is produced by a temperature of 100°F or higher?

Solution.　The conversion is

$$^{\circ}K = \left[(100^{\circ} - 32^{\circ}) \times \frac{5}{9}\right] + 273^{\circ} = 311^{\circ}$$

Therefore, a voltage of 3.11 V or more corresponds to 100°F or higher.

Of course, now we need a circuit that can be set to detect a voltage of 3.11 V or
higher. Such a circuit can be built using an *analog comparator.* A data sheet for the National Semiconductor LM393 dual comparator is shown in Fig. 11.3. Similar to a digital
comparator, the LM393 compares the voltages applied to its (+) and (−) inputs and produces the following results: If $V(+) > V(-)$, then V_{OUT} = open circuit, but if $V(+) <
V(-)$, then V_{OUT} = 0 V. By pulling the output to +5 V through a resistor, TTL compati-
bility can be achieved.

Example 11.2

Design an interface to a microcomputer input port using the LM334 temperature sensor and
the LM393 analog comparator. A logic 1 input should indicate a temperature > 100°F.

Solution.　Figure 11.4 shows the circuit. The 10-kΩ potentiometer is adjusted to produce
3.11 V at the (−) input, and if the LM334 output should ever exceed this value, the comparator output will become an open circuit and be pulled to a logic 1 by the 10-kΩ resistor R4.

The analog comparator is very useful for detecting a voltage level and converting the information into a TTL-compatible logic 1 or 0. It can be used to monitor a
number of real-world sensors, such as photocells, strain gauges, thermistors, and other

LM193/LM293/LM393, LM193A/LM293A/LM393A, LM2903
Low Power Low Offset Voltage Dual Comparators

General Description

The LM193 series consists of two independent precision voltage comparators with an offset voltage specification as low as 2.0 mV max for two comparators which were designed specifically to operate from a single power supply over a wide range of voltages. Operation from split power supplies is also possible and the low power supply current drain is independent of the magnitude of the power supply voltage. These comparators also have a unique characteristic in that the input common-mode voltage range includes ground, even though *operated from a single power supply voltage.*

Application areas include limit comparators, simple analog to digital converters; pulse, squarewave and time delay generators; wide range VCO; MOS clock timers; multivibrators and high voltage digital logic gates. The LM193 series was designed to directly interface with TTL and CMOS. When operated from both plus and minus power supplies, the LM193 series will directly interface with MOS logic where their low power drain is a distinct advantage over standard comparators.

Advantages

- High precision comparators
- Reduced V_{OS} drift over temperature

- Eliminates need for dual supplies
- Allows sensing near ground
- Compatible with all forms of logic
- Power drain suitable for battery operation

Features

- Wide single supply
  Voltage range   2.0 V_{DC} to 36 V_{DC}
  or dual supplies   ±1.0 V_{DC} to ±18 V_{DC}
- Very low supply current drain (0.8 mA)—independent of supply voltage (1.0 mW/comparator at 5.0 V_{DC})
- Low input biasing current   25 nA
- Low input offset current   ±5 nA
  and maximum offset voltage   ±3 mV
- Input common-mode voltage range includes ground
- *Differential input voltage range equal to the power supply voltage*
- Low output   250 mV at 4 mA
  saturation voltage
- Output voltage compatible with TTL, DTL, ECL, MOS and CMOS logic systems

Schematic and Connection Diagrams

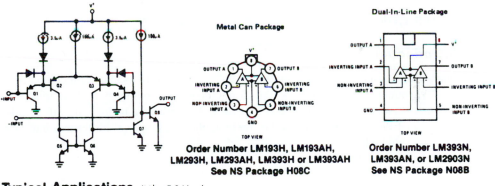

Metal Can Package

OUTPUT A 1   7 OUTPUT B
INVERTING INPUT A 2   6 INVERTING INPUT B
NON-INVERTING INPUT A 3   5 NON-INVERTING INPUT B
GND 4
TOP VIEW

**Order Number LM193H, LM193AH, LM293H, LM293AH, LM393H or LM393AH
See NS Package H08C**

Dual-In-Line Package

OUTPUT A   V⁺
INVERTING INPUT A   OUTPUT B
NON-INVERTING INPUT A   INVERTING INPUT B
GND   NON-INVERTING INPUT B
TOP VIEW

**Order Number LM393N, LM393AN, or LM2903N
See NS Package N08B**

Typical Applications   (V⁺ = 5.0 V_{DC})

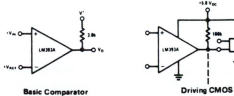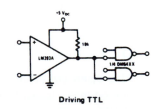

Basic Comparator   **Driving CMOS**   **Driving TTL**

Figure 11.3   LM393 voltage comparator. (Courtesy of National Semiconductor Corporation.)

571

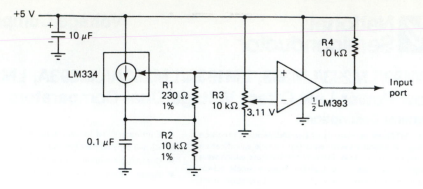

Figure 11.4 This circuit will produce a logic 1 output whenever the LM334 temperature exceeds 100°F. The 10-kΩ potentiometer allows the switching threshold of the comparator to be varied.

transducers (devices that convert a physical phenomenon to an analog voltage). The LM393 is particularly useful, as it will allow up to a 36-V differential between its (+) and (−) inputs.

SELF-REVIEW 11.1

11.1.1 The LM334 produces an output _____ that is directly proportional to _____.

11.1.2 State the input conditions on V(+) and V(−) required to cause the output of the LM393 to be (a) an open circuit; (b) a short circuit to ground.

11.2 ON/OFF CONTROL OF ANALOG PERIPHERALS

Introduction

Many real-world peripherals require high voltages and currents that are incompatible with the TTL output capabilities of a typical microcomputer output port. Examples are 5-V, 100-mA dc relays; 120-V ac solenoids; 12-V, 2-A indicator lamps; and 20- to 30-V dc pulses for EPROM programmers. For these applications, special buffer and interface circuits are required.

In this section, we:

- Show how logic gates can be used to drive and control electromechanical relays.
- Identify the components, and explain the operation, of a solid-state relay.

DC Control

The open-collector buffer. When the control voltage and current requirements are not too high, standard 7400-family TTL open-collector buffers can be used. We first discussed the open-collector gate in Chapter 4, where its capability to perform the "wired-

TABLE 11.1 Buffer and Interface Gates with Open-Collector Outputs

Description	High-level output voltage	Low-level output current	Typical delay time	Typical power per gate	Type of device and package −55°C to 125°C		Type of device and package 0°C to 70°C	
					Device	Package	Device	Package
Hex Buffers/Drivers	30 V	40 mA	13 ns	21 mW	SN5407	J, W	SN7407	J, N
	30 V	30 mA	13 ns	21 mW				
	15 V	40 mA	13 ns	21 mW	SN5417	J, W	SN7417	J, N
	15 V	30 mA	13 ns	21 mW				
Hex Inverter Buffers/Drivers	30 V	40 mA	12.5 ns	26 mW	SN5406	J, W	SN7406	J, N
	30 V	30 mA	12.5 ns	26 mW				
	15 V	40 mA	12.5 ns	26 mW	SN5416	J, W	SN7416	J, N
	15 V	30 mA	12.5 ns	26 mW				
Quadruple Two-Input Positive-NAND Buffers	15 V	16 mA	13.5 ns	10 mW	SN5426	J	SN7426	J, N
	15 V	8 mA	16 ns	2 mW	SN54LS26	J, W	SN74LS26	J, N
	15 V	4 mA	16 ns	2 mW				
	5.5 V	60 mA	6.5 ns	41 mW	SN54S38	J, W	SN74S38	J, N
	5.5 V	48 mA	12.5 ns	24.4 mW	SN5438	J, W	SN7438	J, N
	5.5 V	24 mA	19 ns	4.3 mW	SN54LS38	J, W	SN74LS38	J, N
	5.5 V	12 mA	19 ns	4.3 mW				
Quadruple Two-Input Positive-NOR Buffers	5.5 V	48 mA	11 ns	28 mW	SN5433	J, W	SN7433	J, N
	5.5 V	24 mA	19 ns	5.45 mW	SN54LS33	J, W	SN74LS33	J, N
	5.5 V	12 mA	19 ns	5.45 mW				

Source: Courtesy of Texas Instruments, Inc.

OR" function was taken advantage of. In this section, we are more interested in the buffer's ability to pull the output to levels other than +5 V.

Table 11.1 lists the capabilities of the 7400 family of open-collector buffers. Note that voltages as high as 30 V can be switched. Also, remember that in the low state the buffer must be capable of *sinking* current from the controlled device and its pull-up resistor. This current can be as high as 60 mA with the 74S38.

Figure 11.5 illustrates several typical control applications for open-collector buffers. Note that in all cases the buffer is required to sink the *on* current of the controlled device and to withstand the power supply voltage in the *off* state. The clamp diode in the relay driver circuit is needed to protect the buffer's output transistor when the relay is turned off. The sudden reduction to zero of current in the relay coil causes a *back emf* to be developed as the magnetic field in the relay coil collapses [$V_L = L(di/dt)$]. The diode clamps the output pin to +12 V. When larger currents must be switched, buffers may be paralleled as shown in the lamp-driver interface in Fig. 11.5(c).

The 75400 family of peripheral drivers. Table 11.2 lists the current and voltage capabilities of the SN75400 family of peripheral drivers with logic gates, and Fig.

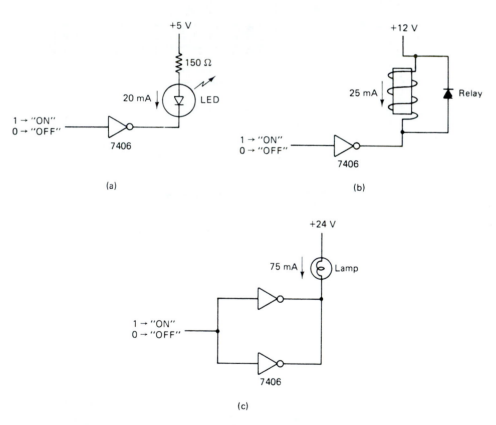

(a)

(b)

(c)

Figure 11.5 Typical control applications for the open-collector buffer gate: (a) LED driver; (b) relay driver; (c) lamp driver.

TABLE 11.2 SN75400 Family of Peripheral Devices

Drivers with Logic Gates

Military Temperature Range ($-55°C$ to $125°C$)

Switching Voltage	Maximum Recommended Output Current	Drivers Per Package	Internal Clamp Diodes	Logic Gate Function				Package Options
				AND	NAND	OR	NOR	
20 V	300 mA	2	—	SN55450B				J
				SN55451B	SN55452B	SN55453B	SN55454B	JG
30 V	300 mA	2	—	SN55460				J
				SN55461	SN55462	SN55463	SN55464	JG
55 V	300 mA	2	—	SN55470				J
				SN55471	SN55472	SN55473	SN55474	JG

Commercial Temperature Range ($0°C$ to $70°C$)

Switching Voltage	Maximum Recommended Output Current	Drivers Per Package	Internal Clamp Diodes	Logic Gate Function				Package Options
				AND	NAND	OR	NOR	
15 V	300 mA	2	—	SN75430				J, N
				SN75431	SN75432	SN75433	SN75434	JG, P
20 V	100 mA	2	—			SN75441		J, N
	300 mA	2	—	SN75450B				J, N
				SN75451B	SN75452B	SN75453B	SN75454B	JG, P
30 V	300 mA	2	—	SN75460				J, N
			—	SN75461	SN75462	SN75463	SN75464	JG, P
	500 mA	2	—	SN75401	SN75402	SN75403	SN75404	NE
35 V	500 mA	4	YES		SN75437			NE
55 V	300 mA	2	—	SN75470				J, N
				SN75471	SN75472	SN75473	SN75474	JG, P
			YES	SN75476	SN75477	SN75478	SN75479	JG, P
	350 mA	2	YES	SN75446	SN75447	SN75448	SN75449	JG, P
	500 mA	2	—	SN75411	SN75412	SN75413	SN75414	NE
			YES	SN75416	SN75417	SN75418	SN75419	NE

Source: Courtesy of Texas Instruments, Inc.

11.6 shows the pinouts for the 75416 series. All of these devices are open-collector buffers, but with considerably higher current capabilities than the standard TTL buffers. Even higher current devices are available in the ULN series (not shown in Table 11.2). These buffers use *Darlington* output transistors to achieve output sink currents as high as 1.5 A.

The 75416 series of drivers shown in Fig. 11.6 include all four logic functions and are characterized for applications to 500 mA. Clamp diodes for transient suppression for driving inductive loads (relays) are built into the package. Note that six pins in each package are used as a heat sink and ground.

Sec. 11.2   On/Off Control of Analog Peripherals

- Characterized for Use to 500 mA
- No Output Latch-Up at 55 V (After Conducting 500 mA)
- High-Voltage Outputs (100 V Typical)
- High-Speed Switching
- Output Clamp Diodes for Transient Suppression (500 mA, 70 V)
- TTL- or MOS-Compatible Diode-Clamped Inputs
- P-N-P Inputs Reduce Input Current
- Standard Supply Voltage
- Suitable for Hammer-Driver Applications
- Available in the 14-Pin NE Package
- 2-Watt Power Dissipation Capability

description

Series 75416 dual peripheral drivers are designed for use in systems that require high output voltage, high current, and fast switching times. The SN75416, SN75417, SN75418, and SN75419 provide AND , NAND, OR, and NOR functions respectively. The devices have diode-clamped inputs as well as high-current, high-voltage inductive clamp diodes on the outputs. Each device has a 2-watt power dissipation capability.

Series 75416 drivers are characterized for operation from 0°C to 70°C.

schematics of inputs and outputs

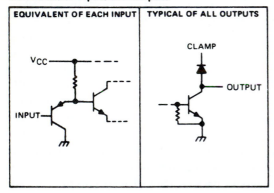

EQUIVALENT OF EACH INPUT	TYPICAL OF ALL OUTPUTS

SN75416

**FUNCTION TABLE
(EACH AND DRIVER)**

INPUTS		OUTPUT
A	S	Y
L	L	L
L	H	L
H	L	L
H	H	H

H = high level
L = low level

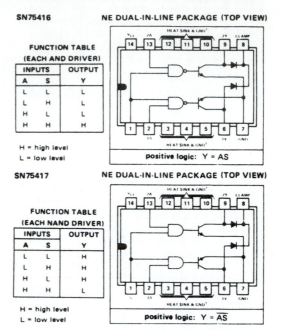

NE DUAL-IN-LINE PACKAGE (TOP VIEW)

positive logic: Y = AS

SN75417

**FUNCTION TABLE
(EACH NAND DRIVER)**

INPUTS		OUTPUT
A	S	Y
L	L	H
L	H	H
H	L	H
H	H	L

H = high level
L = low level

NE DUAL-IN-LINE PACKAGE (TOP VIEW)

positive logic: Y = $\overline{AS}$

SN75418

**FUNCTION TABLE
(EACH OR DRIVER)**

INPUTS		OUTPUT
A	S	Y
L	L	L
L	H	H
H	L	H
H	H	H

H = high level
L = low level

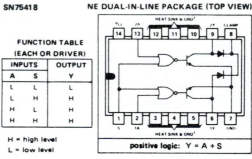

NE DUAL-IN-LINE PACKAGE (TOP VIEW)

positive logic: Y = A + S

SN75419

**FUNCTION TABLE
(EACH NOR DRIVER)**

INPUTS		OUTPUT
A	S	Y
L	L	H
L	H	L
H	L	L
H	H	L

H = high level
L = low level

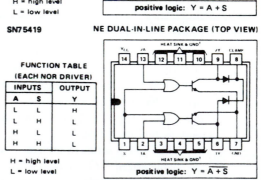

NE DUAL-IN-LINE PACKAGE (TOP VIEW)

positive logic: Y = $\overline{A + S}$

†Heat-sink pins are internally connected to pin 7.

Figure 11.6 SN75416 series of peripheral drivers. (Courtesy of Texas Instruments.)

Variations on the 75416 series include the following:

1. Eight-pin packages for lower current devices (SN75476–479)
2. Eight-pin packages for devices without clamp diodes and no common gate pins (SN75451B–454B)

One application for these drivers is to control high-current lamps. Initially, this would seem to be a trivial problem. However, because a lamp's "cold" resistance can be as much as 10 times less than its "hot" resistance, care must be taken to avoid an initial inrush of current that could destroy the driver.

Figure 11.7(a) illustrates an application for the SN75452B as a lamp driver with warm-up circuit. A graph of current versus time is shown in Fig. 11.7(b). Note that both gates in the 75452B are used in this design. When the input control is first applied, only Q1 is on, as the 500-μF capacitor holds the AND gate inputs low and Q2 off. The surge of current is limited by the 18-Ω resistor. Now, as the capacitor charges, Q2 turns on and the load current is shifted to Q2. During this time, the lamp filament is heating up, with its resistance increasing. The effect is to limit the initial surge to a safe value, protecting the lamp and driver.

AC Control

Logic gates are, of course, restricted to processing DC signals. Control applications, however, often require the on and off switching of AC signals—the power mains, for example. For these applications, *relays* are commonly used.

Electromechanical relays.   The electromechanical relay (EMR) has been the workhorse of the control industry for many years. By providing sets of switched contacts, both ac and dc devices can be controlled. Several circuits can be switched simultaneously with

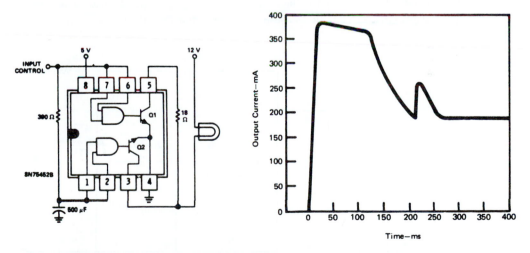

Figure 11.7   (a) Using the SN75452B as a lamp driver; (b) lamp current versus time. The surge current is limited to less than 400 mA. (Courtesy of Texas Instruments.)

the use of parallel sets of contacts. The contacts are usually described as *normally open* (N.O.) or *normally closed* (N.C.).

Depending on the control current, relays can be driven directly by a TTL gate [see Fig. 11.5(b)] or with a special peripheral driver (see Fig. 11.6). Some low-current relays are even available in DIP packages and can be plugged into standard IC sockets.

Disadvantages of the EMR include the device's finite lifetime, corrosion of the contacts, arcing, contact bounce, and slow operation.

Hybrid solid-state relays.   The solid-state relay (SSR) was developed to solve the problems associated with the EMR. Two types of SSR are popular: *isolated* and *nonisolated*. Figure 11.8 shows an example of a nonisolated SSR. A peripheral driver is used to control the flow of current through a diode bridge. When the driver is on, current passes through the bridge and develops a voltage across the 0.1-μF capacitor. When this voltage reaches a trigger threshold, the 2N4992 asymmetrical trigger (AST) "fires" the TRIAC, causing a nearly short circuit to appear between its MT1 and MT2 terminals. Because the TRIAC will conduct in both directions, MT1 and MT2 resemble the normally open contacts on a conventional EMR.

Among the advantages to this type of relay are that it has no moving parts, no contact bounce, fast operation (usually < 1 μs to activate), TTL level compatibility, and logic gate control.

Once fired, the TRIAC will remain on until its load current falls below a small "holding" value. This means that when the control signal is removed, the ac load will not be turned off until the next zero-crossing of the line voltage. This action is ideal for ac control applications, because it eliminates transients that would be produced by an abrupt turnoff. It also eliminates the arcing problem that is associated with EMRs. Of course, this same feature makes the SSR totally unsatisfactory for controlling dc devices. (Why?)

There are two main disadvantages to this circuit. The first is a problem that plagues all solid-state devices: High-voltage transients can destroy the TRIAC. The nonisolated SSR is especially susceptible because it is connected directly to the main lines, where

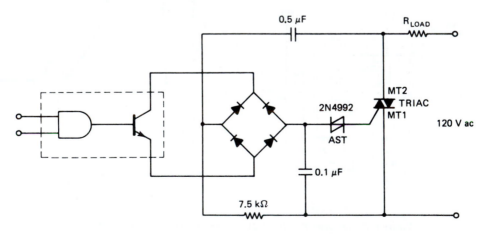

Figure 11.8   Nonisolated hybrid solid-state relay.

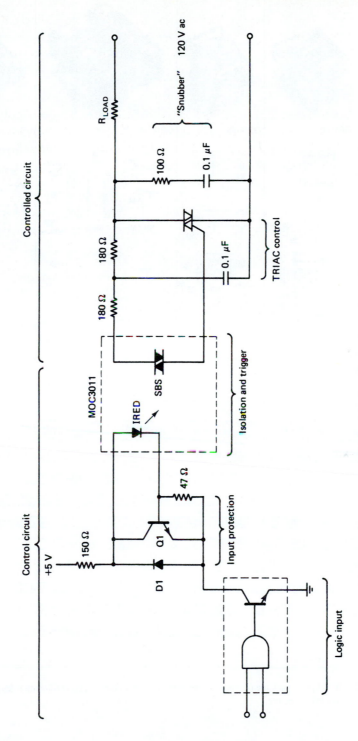

Figure 11.9 Isolated hybrid solid-state relay. The control and controlled circuits are separated by the infrared light path.

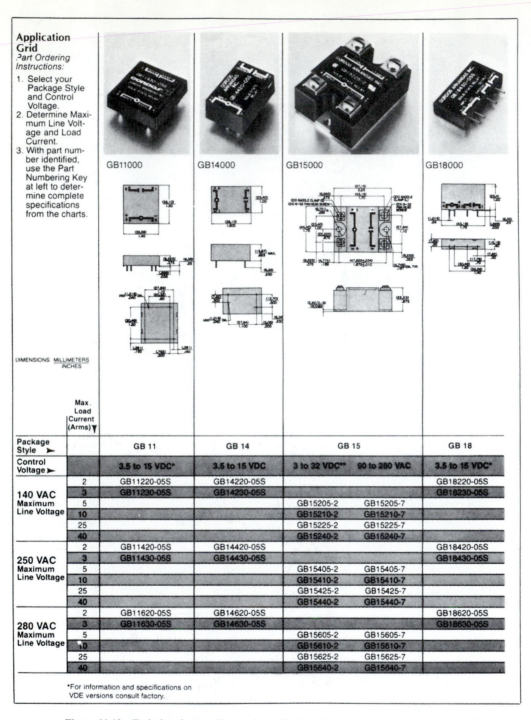

Application Grid

Part Ordering Instructions:

1. Select your Package Style and Control Voltage.
2. Determine Maximum Line Voltage and Load Current.
3. With part number identified, use the Part Numbering Key at left to determine complete specifications from the charts.

GB11000 GB14000 GB15000 GB18000

DIMENSIONS MILLIMETERS / INCHES

Max. Load Current (Arms)	GB 11 3.5 to 15 VDC*	GB 14 3.5 to 15 VDC	GB 15 3 to 32 VDC**	GB 15 90 to 280 VAC	GB 18 3.5 to 15 VDC*
140 VAC Maximum Line Voltage					
2	GB11220-05S	GB14220-05S			GB18220-05S
3	GB11230-05S	GB14230-05S			GB18230-05S
5			GB15205-2	GB15205-7	
10			GB15210-2	GB15210-7	
25			GB15225-2	GB15225-7	
40			GB15240-2	GB15240-7	
250 VAC Maximum Line Voltage					
2	GB11420-05S	GB14420-05S			GB18420-05S
3	GB11430-05S	GB14430-05S			GB18430-05S
5			GB15405-2	GB15405-7	
10			GB15410-2	GB15410-7	
25			GB15425-2	GB15425-7	
40			GB15440-2	GB15440-7	
280 VAC Maximum Line Voltage					
2	GB11620-05S	GB14620-05S			GB18620-05S
3	GB11630-05S	GB14630-05S			GB18630-05S
5			GB15605-2	GB15605-7	
10			GB15610-2	GB15610-7	
25			GB15625-2	GB15625-7	
40			GB15640-2	GB15640-7	

*For information and specifications on VDE versions consult factory.

Figure 11.10 Typical package outlines and specifications for commercial solid-state relays. (Courtesy of Gordos Arkansas, Inc.)

these transients are initiated. The second problem is the lack of isolation between the control circuit (the peripheral driver) and the 120-V ac mains. If a component—say, one of the diodes—should fail, it might become a short circuit, passing 120 V ac to the peripheral driver. Obviously not intended for 120 V ac, the peripheral driver could then be destroyed and pass the ac on to the output port of the computer and on to the data bus and memory, and so on.

Figure 11.9 shows an improved SSR that includes a "snubber circuit" for suppressing transients on the line and that uses an *optocoupler* to isolate the control circuit from the controlled circuit. The digital input is also protected against excessive currents and reverse voltages by D1 and Q1.

The peripheral driver allows logic gate control of the relay and is used to sink the *on* current of the infrared-emitting diode (IRED). The Motorola MOC3011 is an optically triggered silicon bilateral switch (SBS). This device provides 7500 V minimum isolation between the SBS and IRED. The only path between control and controlled circuit is through the light emitted by the IRED.

The SBS is used like the AST to trigger the TRIAC into conduction. For low current and voltages less than 250 V, the SBS can be used by itself to control the ac load. The *RC* "snubber" suppresses high-frequency transients that can damage the TRIAC or trigger it into conduction.

Commercial solid-state relays.   Rather than having to build your own SSR, several types are available with all components encapsulated in one package. These devices usually have four terminals: two for the output contacts and two for the control circuit. Figure 11.10 shows the Gordos Arkansas GB series of zero-voltage turn-on SSRs. The GB1500 devices are rated to switch currents as high as 40 A.

Generally, two types of commercial SSRs can be purchased: *zero-cross switching* or *random switching*. Zero-cross switching relays do not switch on until the first zero-crossing of the line voltage after the control signal is applied. Random-switching relays switch on immediately after receipt of the control signal.

The zero-crossing technique is desirable for driving incandescent lamps, due to the inrush of current when power is first applied. If this current is not limited, it can easily burn out the switching device in the SSR. On the other hand, zero-crossing relays are reputed to be the worst case for switching inductive loads (motors, for example). This is due to large transient currents set up when the motor is first turned on. Application Note SSR 110, prepared by Gordos Arkansas, Inc., explains this problem in detail and shows that optimum switching for an inductive load should occur at the 90° point of the input sinusoid.

SELF-REVIEW 11.2

11.2.1 What is the maximum high-level output voltage for the 7406 open-collector buffer?

11.2.2 What is the purpose of the clamp diodes in the 75416 series of peripheral drivers?

11.2.3 Why is the bridge circuit required in the SSR circuit shown in Fig. 11.8?

11.2.4 Commercial solid-state relays may be _____ switching or _____ switching.

11.3 INTERFACING A DIGITAL-TO-ANALOG CONVERTER

Introduction

The peripheral drivers and open-collector buffers discussed in Section 11.2 allow a microcomputer to provide on/off control of a peripheral. But what if the application requires the microcomputer to output a sine wave or a complex waveform such as speech or music? In this case, some means of converting digital bits and bytes to a continuous analog signal must be found.

In this section, we:

- Explain the operation of a digital-to-analog converter based on the R-2R resistor ladder network.
- Write an 8080/8085 program for synthesizing a sine wave using the MC1408 8-bit DAC interfaced to an 8255A PPI chip.

The Digital-to-Analog Conversion Process

Figure 11.11 illustrates the major components required in a digital-to-analog converter system. The latch stores the digital word that is output by the computer and presents it to the *digital-to-analog converter* (DAC). This circuit, using a stable reference voltage or current, converts the binary data to an analog current. Finally, a current-to-voltage converter changes this current to a unipolar or bipolar voltage.

Of course, to truly be an analog signal, the output voltage must be capable of assuming any value between 0 V and some full-scale value. If the DAC in Fig. 11.11 has 10 V full scale and receives 8-bit input words, it can output 256 values between 0 and 10 V. Figure 11.12 shows the result (not drawn to scale) of programming the DAC to generate a sine wave.

Examining Fig. 11.12, we can list two properties of an "ideal" DAC:

1. Infinitely small step size
2. Instantaneous conversion time

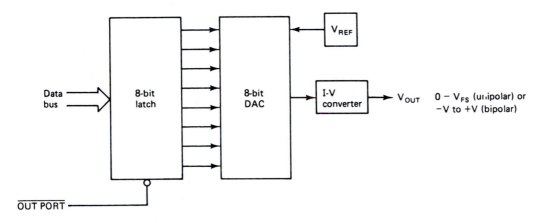

Figure 11.11 Digital-to-analog converter system.

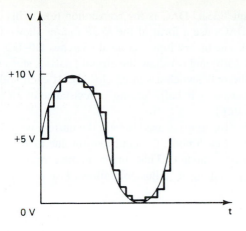

Figure 11.12 Using a DAC to generate a sine wave. The finite step size and conversion time cause a staircase-shaped output waveform.

Example 11.3

Calculate the step size of the 8-bit DAC shown in Fig. 11.11, assuming that full-scale output is 10.0 V. Calculate the output voltage when the binary input is 3CH.

Solution. The step size is found by dividing the full-scale output voltage by the number of steps:

$$\text{step size} = V_{FS}/2^n = 10 \text{ V}/256 = 0.0390625 \text{ V}$$

When the input is 3CH (60_{10}), 60 steps are indicated and V_{OUT} must be 60×0.0390625 V $= 2.34375$ V. Another way to express this is 60/256 of full scale, or $60/256 \times 10$ V $= 2.34375$ V.

How many bits do you think are required for the "ideal" DAC? It should be obvious that the more bits a DAC inputs, the smaller is its step size. As the step size shrinks to zero, the number of input bits must increase to infinity. Unfortunately, a DAC with an infinite number of input bits would require a package with an infinite number of pins!

Example 11.4

What is the maximum output voltage of the 8-bit DAC in Fig. 11.11 if $V_{FS} = 10.0$ V?

Solution. Strangely enough, it is *not* 10 V! Consider why. When the most significant bit is turned on, 5.0 V is output ($V_{FS}/2$), the next bit adds half of this, or 2.5 V ($V_{FS}/4$), the next bit 1.25 V ($V_{FS}/8$), the next bit 0.625 V ($V_{FS}/16$), and so on. Each bit adds half of the preceding bit's contribution. An infinite number of bits will be required to reach full scale. So what will the maximum output be? The maximum input is FFH, and this produces an output of $255/256 \times 10$ V $= 9.960375$ V. The general rule is that the maximum output will always be one step less than full scale.

The step size of a DAC is referred to as its *resolution*. An 8-bit DAC with 10 V full scale has a resolution of 39.1 mV. A 12-bit DAC has a 2.4-mV resolution. The accuracy of a DAC is usually expressed as a percentage. Most DACs are specified as accurate to $\pm 1/2$ LSB (least significant bit). For an 8-bit DAC, this means 1 part in 512, or $\pm 0.19\%$. The 12-bit DAC is accurate to 1 part in 8192 and has an accuracy of $\pm 0.012\%$.

The other property of an "ideal" DAC is the conversion time. This depends on the conversion technique. Most DACs use a form of the *R-2R ladder* shown in the switched voltage DAC in Fig. 11.13(a). The binary inputs control switches D0–D2, connected to a voltage reference. Figures 11.13(b) and (c) show the circuit analysis steps in realizing the contribution due to bit D0 (the only switch assumed closed). At each node in the ladder (A, B, or C), the current splits exactly in half, "seeing" a resistance of $2R$ to ground in either direction. [See Fig. 11.13(c).]

The operational amplifier (op amp) is used to sum the current contributions of each bit. Because the current splits at each node, the contribution due to D0 is reduced to $I/2$ at node A, $I/4$ at node B, and $I/8$ at node C. This current is then forced through the feedback resistor to develop V_{OUT}. Making R_F adjustable allows V_{FS} to be set to any desired

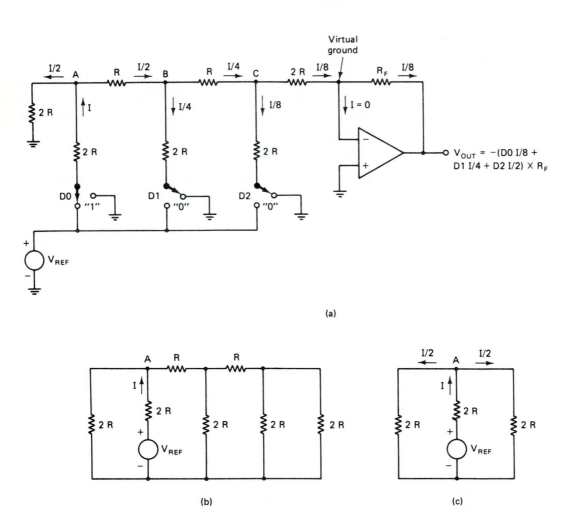

Figure 11.13 (a) Switched voltage R-2R DAC; (b) equivalent circuit at node A when only switch D0 is closed; (c) at each node, the current splits exactly in half.

value within the saturation limits of the op amp. Applying superposition, we obtain, for the output voltage,

$$V_{OUT} = -\left[\left(D0 \times \frac{I}{8}\right) + \left(D1 \times \frac{I}{4}\right) + \left(D2 \times \frac{I}{2}\right)\right] \times R_F$$

Although other techniques for digital-to-analog conversion have been developed (see Problem 11.12), the R-2R ladder is used in the majority of DACs today. Because only two different resistor values are required, it lends itself well to integrated techniques.

Figure 11.14 shows a switched-current DAC similar to that found in the Motorola MC1408 8-bit DAC. A reference current is injected into the ladder, splitting by exactly one-half at each node. Because the switch connects each leg of the ladder to virtual ground (through the op amp) or actual ground, the current in each leg of the ladder is constant and independent of the digital input. This increases the speed of conversion, because the junction capacitances of the resistors need not be continually charged and discharged.

The effect of the conversion time can be seen in Fig. 11.12 by the flat part of the step in the output waveform. If the sinusoid changes too fast, the DAC output will have to change by more than one step to keep up, causing a herky-jerky output. Eventually, the resemblance to a sine wave will be lost entirely. Because the output voltage "settles" to a particular value, the conversion time is usually called the *settling time* on most DAC data sheets. Values typically range from 100 ns to more than 1.5 μs.

Interfacing the MC1408 DAC

The MC1408 is an 8-bit DAC that is popular because of its simplicity and low cost. Motorola manufactures three versions, labeled the 1408L8, 1408L7, and 1408L6, with 8-, 7-, and 6-bit accuracies, respectively. A microcomputer interface using one output port of the 8255A PPI is shown in Fig. 11.15.

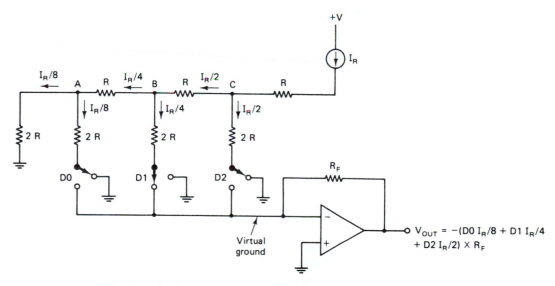

Figure 11.14 Switched-current DAC. The current in each leg is constant and independent of the digital input.

Sec. 11.3   Interfacing a Digital-to-Analog Converter

585

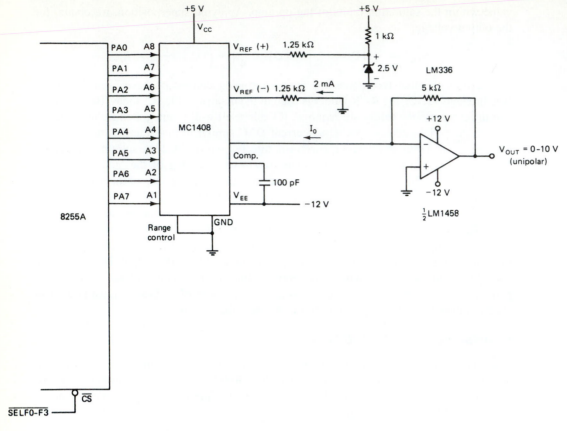

Figure 11.15 The MC1408 8-bit DAC can be interfaced to a microcomputer with an 8-bit output port. In this example, one port of the 8255A PPI is used.

Comparing Fig. 11.15 with Fig. 11.11, we see that an LM336 precision zener diode is used to establish a 2-mA reference current. The output of the DAC is a current, which is converted to a voltage by the op amp. The output voltage is given by

$$V_{\text{OUT}} = 2 \text{ mA} \times \frac{\text{binary input}}{256} \times 5 \text{ k}\Omega$$

Because the full-scale output current is 2 mA, the full-scale output voltage is 10 V. The MC1408 has a 300-ns typical settling time.

Example 11.5

Write an 8080/85 program to synthesize the 1-kHz sine wave shown in Fig. 11.16. Use 12 samples per period.

Solution. The DAC must produce a new output voltage every 1 ms/12 = 83.3 μs. The value of the voltage to output can be found from

$$V_{\text{OUT}} = 5 \text{ V} + 3 \text{ V} \sin \theta, \qquad \text{where } \theta = 0°, 30°, 60°, \text{ etc.}$$

These values are shown in the table in Fig. 11.16.

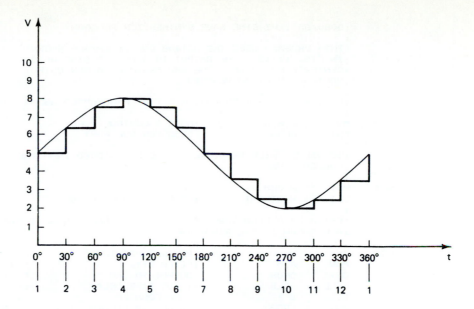

θ (deg)	$\sin \theta$	V_{OUT}	Hex code
0	0	5 V	80
30	0.5	6.5 V	A6
60	0.866	7.6 V	C3
90	1.0	8 V	CD
120	0.866	7.6 V	C3
150	0.5	6.5 V	A6
180	0	5 V	80
210	−0.5	3.5 V	5A
240	−0.866	2.4 V	3D
270	−1.0	2 V	33
300	−0.866	2.4 V	3D
330	−0.5	3.5 V	5A

Figure 11.16 One-kHz sine wave to be synthesized in Example 11.5. Twelve samples are output per cycle, distributed every 30°.

Figure 11.17 is the 8080/85 program. It begins by programming port A of the 8255A as a simple output port. Register B counts the bytes to be output per cycle. The HL pair is used as a pointer into the sine wave data table. After each value is output, it is held for 83 μs (27 μs in the program loop and 56 μs in the HOLD subroutine).

The sine wave produced by the program in Example 11.5 will be rather crude because there are few samples per cycle. By increasing the number of samples, the output can be made to resemble the desired sine wave more closely. Of course, the time delay in the loop will ultimately limit the number of samples per cycle.

A number of interesting applications are suggested by the program in Fig. 11.17. For example, a complex waveform displayed on an oscilloscope could be photographed and then

```
;8080/85 1KHZ SINE WAVE SYNTHESIZER PROGRAM
;
;THIS PROGRAM USES THE MC1408 DAC INTERFACE SHOWN
;IN FIG. 11-15.   THE OUTPUT IS A 6V P-P SINE WAVE
;CENTERED ON 5V DC.   THE DAC PRODUCES A NEW OUTPUT
;VOLTAGE EVERY 30 DEGREES.
;
;PORT A OF THE 8255 MUST FIRST BE PROGRAMMED AS AN OUPUT
;
        MVI     A,80H           ;MODE O CONTROL WORD
        OUT     OF3H            ;8255 CONTROL PORT
        ;
        ;12 VALUES WILL BE OUTPUT PER CYCLE STORED IN A TABLE
        ;CALLED SINE
        ;
NEW     MVI     B,OCH           ;COUNTER
        LXI     H,SINE-1        ;POINT AT TABLE LESS 1
        ;
        ;FETCH DATA FROM TABLE AND OUTPUT TO DAC.  8085 T STATES
        ;ARE SHOWN IN THE RIGHT MARGIN.
        ;
LOOP    INX     H               ;ADVANCE POINTER        [6]
        MOV     A,M             ;FETCH BYTE             [7]
        OUT     OFOH            ;OUTPUT TO DAC          [10]
        CALL    HOLD            ;1 KHZ TIME DELAY       [18]
        DCR     B               ;BUMP COUNTER           [4]
        JNZ     LOOP            ;DO ALL 12 VALUES       [7/10]
        JMP     NEW             ;THEN BEGIN A NEW CYCLE [10]
        ;
        ;TOTAL T STATES FOR ONE LOOP IS 55 OR 27.5 MICROSECONDS
        ;WITH A 2 MHZ CLOCK.   THE HOLD SUBROUTINE THUS REQUIRES
        ;83.3 MICROSECONDS (1000 MICROSECONDS / 12 SAMPLES) -
        ;27.5 MICROSECONDS = 55.8 MICROSECONDS OR 112 T STATES.
        ;
HOLD    MVI     C,7             ;STANDARD DELAY ROUTINE [7]
WAIT    DCR     C               ;                       [4]
        JNZ     WAIT            ;                       [7/10]
        RET                     ;                       [10]
        ;
        ;DATA VALUES FOR THE DAC - SEE FIG. 11-16.
        ;
SINE    DB      80H,OA6H,OC3H
        DB      OCDH,OC3H,OA6H
        DB      80H,5AH,3DH
        DB      33H,3DH,5AH
        END
```

Figure 11.17 8080/85 program to control the DAC in Fig. 11.15 and synthesize a 1-kHz 6-V p-p sine wave.

duplicated by storing the proper values in a table. Outputting these codes to the DAC should reproduce the original waveshape. In this way, patterns of speech could be synthesized.

A Touch-Tone™ dialer could similarly be implemented by storing values for each numeral in a code table. This application is particularly interesting because the tones used are actually two different frequencies summed together. Rather than doing this summing with an analog circuit, the computer can add values from two different tables, synthesizing the waveshape directly.

Interfacing the DAC1200

When the resolution of an 8-bit DAC is insufficient, a 10- or 12-bit DAC can be selected. An example of such a DAC is the National Semiconductor DAC 1200 shown in

National Semiconductor

DAC1200, DAC1201 12-Bit Digital-to-Analog Converters

General Description

The DAC1200 series of D/A converters is a family of precision low-cost converter building blocks intended to fulfill a wide range of industrial and military D/A applications. These devices are complete functional blocks requiring only application of power for operation. The design combines a precision 12-bit weighted current source (12 current switches and 12-bit thin-film resistor network), a rapid-settling operational amplifier, and 10.24V buffered reference.

Input coding is complementary binary. In all instances, a logic "low" ($\leqslant$ 0.8V) turns a given bit ON, and a logic "high" ($\geqslant$ 2.0V) turns the bit OFF. Output format may be programmed for bipolar ($\pm$10V) or unipolar (0 to 10V) operation using internally supplied thin-film resistor pin strap options. Current mode operation is also available from 0 to 2 mA.

The entire series is available in hermetically sealed 24-lead DIP.

Features

- Circuit completely self-contained
- Both current and voltage-mode outputs
- Standard power supplies: $\pm$15V and +5V
- Internal buffered reference: 10.24V
- 0 to 2 mA, $\pm$10V or 0 to 10V output by strapping internal resistors; other scales by external resistors
- $\pm$1/2 LSB linearity
- Fast settling time: 1.5 μs in current mode
  2.5 μs in voltage mode
- High slew rate: 15 V/μs
- TTL and CMOS compatible complementary binary input logic
- 12 bit linearity
- Standard 0.6" 24-pin DIP package

Block and Connection Diagrams

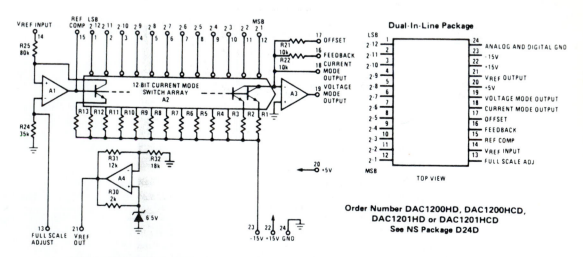

Figure 11.18 Description and block diagram of the National Semiconductor DAC1200. (Courtesy of National Semiconductor Corporation.)

589

Fig. 11.18. This device is unique because, in addition to providing 12 bits of resolution, it contains an internal reference and a current-to-voltage converter. The only external support required is a latch for the data bits.

Of course, we do have one problem. How do you interface a 12-bit DAC to an 8-bit microprocessor? The answer is—very carefully! Actually, the problem is not as difficult as it might seem. Figure 11.19 shows a method using port A and the lower portion of port C of an 8255A PPI. The control program outputs the low 8 bits of the 12-bit data to port A and the high 4 bits to port C (lower). A second buffer is required between the PPI and the DAC to prevent a glitch from being generated as the DAC first receives the low 8 bits and then the high 4 bits.

An OUT F4 command loads the two 74LS374s with the PPI data and transfers the data as one 12-bit word to the DAC. The price we pay for the *double buffering* is the additional time required to fetch the extra 4 bits, output them to port C, and then clock the 74LS374 buffers.

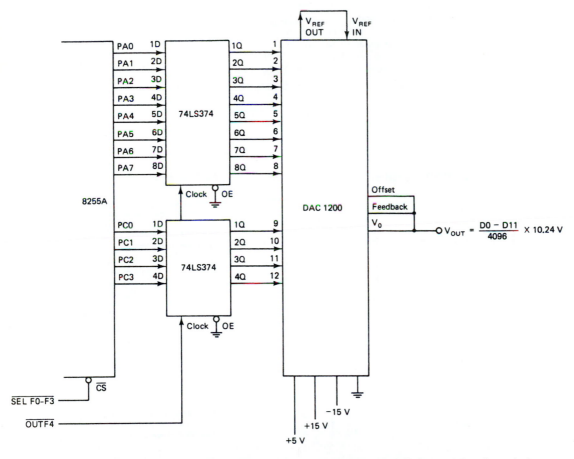

Figure 11.19 Interfacing the DAC1200 to the 8255. A "double-buffering" technique is required to prevent glitches (momentary voltage spikes) in the DAC output.

With ± 15-V power supplies, the full-scale output voltage is 10.24 V (set by the internal reference). Note that the feedback resistors for controlling V_{FS} are provided internally at pins 16 and 17 and need only be connected to the V_{OUT} pin. The step size is found to be $V_{FS}/2^n = 10.24$ V/4096 = 2.5 mV. With the use of the internal current-to-voltage converter, the settling time is 2.5 μs.

Example 11.6

Write an 8080/85 subroutine to transfer the 12 bits of data stored in two sequential memory locations to the DAC interface in Fig. 11.19. Assume that the address of the first byte is passed in the HL pair.

Solution. The program is as follows:

```
MOV     A,M     ;GET LOW BYTE
OUT     0F0H    ;OUTPUT TO PORT A
INX     H       ;POINT TO HIGH 4 BITS
MOV     A,M     ;MOVE TO A
OUT     0F2H    ;OUTPUT TO PORT C
OUT     0F4H    ;LOAD LATCHES AND TRANSFER TO DAC
RET
```

The interface in Fig. 11.19 is truly remarkable: It provides microcomputer control of an output voltage from 0 V to 10.24 V with 4096 steps of 2.5 mV each! No external components are required, except for ± 15-V power sources.

SELF-REVIEW 11.3

11.3.1 A certain 8-bit DAC has a full-scale voltage rating of 10.0 V. What is the step size for this DAC?

11.3.2 Because only two different resistor values are required, the _____ _____ is the most popular form of DAC.

11.3.3 By storing output samples in a _____ , a microcomputer interfaced to a DAC can synthesize any analog waveform.

11.3.4 A 12-bit DAC has a full-scale rating of 5.00 V. What is the 12-bit code that must be applied to this DAC to produce a 4.00-V output?

11.4 INTERFACING AN ANALOG-TO-DIGITAL CONVERTER

Introduction

The analog comparator is useful for detecting when some analog threshold level has been exceeded. However, in many cases it is desirable to know the *exact* voltage, the *exact* temperature, or the *exact* pressure sensed by a transducer. Consider an interface designed to measure the temperature of a room every five minutes for 24 hours. This would require 288 data samples. Using conventional analog techniques, all of the data could be recorded by hand, or a chart recorder could be employed. In either case, analysis of the data will require going back through selected data points.

Now assume that an interval timer is programmed to interrupt a microprocessor once every five minutes and request that an analog-to-digital converter sample its temperature sensor. The data point read can be stored in memory or on magnetic disk. The data can then be analyzed by writing an appropriate program. In fact, the data can even be analyzed upon input if desired.

In this section, we:

- Compare flash, feedback, and dual-slope analog-to-digital converters.
- Show how to interface the eight-channel ADC0809 ADC to the three-bus system architecture.

The Analog-to-Digital Conversion Process

The analog-to-digital converter (ADC) is actually just one part of what is called a *data acquisition system*. (See Fig. 11.20.) Because the amplitude of the analog signal output by many transducers is usually quite small, amplification is required before the signal can be converted to digital form. The amplifier should have a high input resistance so that the signal being measured is not affected by the data acquisition system.

After amplification, the signal is passed through a filter to reject any noise or other undesirable signals that may be present. The resulting amplified and filtered signal is applied to one of the inputs of an analog *multiplexer*. This circuit behaves like a rotary switch, routing the selected input signal on to the ADC. The technique allows the data acquisition system to monitor several analog signals at once.

If the signal is changing rapidly, a *sample-and-hold* circuit can be used to temporarily hold a sample of the analog signal long enough for the ADC to convert it to digital form. A set of tristate buffers is provided so that the digital output can be gated directly onto the microprocessor data bus.

Depending on the design, all of the components in Fig. 11.20 may be integrated into a single chip, or you may have to build the system out of several chips.

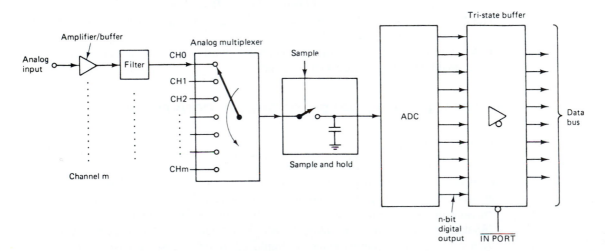

Figure 11.20 Multichannel data acquisition system.

For the moment, let us turn our attention to the ADC. In many cases, this circuit and the tristate buffers are sufficient to form a useful data acquisition system. Unlike the DAC, in which the conversion process is fairly standard for all types, there are three popular techniques for converting analog signals to digital form: *open-loop, feedback,* and *integrating* converters.

The open-loop flash converter.   Figure 11.21 illustrates a flash converter for 2 bits. This converter is so named because it converts its analog input to a digital output after propagation delay times through the analog comparators and logic gates (in a "flash"). The circuit is open loop because there is no feedback between input and output. As with a logic gate, the output appears within a propagation delay period after the input is applied.

Note that a separate comparator is required for each voltage step possible. For 2 bits, there are three voltage levels (not counting 0), and in general, $2^n - 1$ comparators are required for an n-bit converter. The logic gate array is needed to produce standard 1–2–4–8 binary code from the nonstandard output of the comparators. The advantage of this type of ADC is a very high-speed operation. For example, TRW manufactures an 8-bit flash ADC called the *TDC1018.* This converter can operate at speeds up to 125 million conversions per second. It is emitter-coupled logic (*ECL*)-compatible and intended for high-resolution graphics displays used in image processing.

The obvious disadvantage of the flash converter is that the number of comparators double for each additional bit. Although only 255 comparators are required for an 8-bit ADC, 4095 comparators are required for a 12-bit converter. For this reason, flash converters are usually expensive and are reserved for specialized applications.

Feedback converters.   Feedback ADCs are considerably slower, but much less costly, than flash converters. Figure 11.22 shows how the MC1408 interface described in Section 11.3 is modified to become an ADC interface. The only (hardware) addition is an

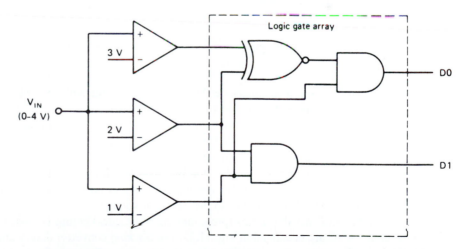

Figure 11.21   Flash converter. Three comparators are used to detect the three possible voltage steps: 1 V, 2 V, and 3 V. The logic gates convert the comparator outputs to standard binary code. (From J. Uffenbeck, *Hardware Interfacing with the Apple II Plus,* Prentice-Hall, Inc., Englewood Cliffs, NJ, 1983.)

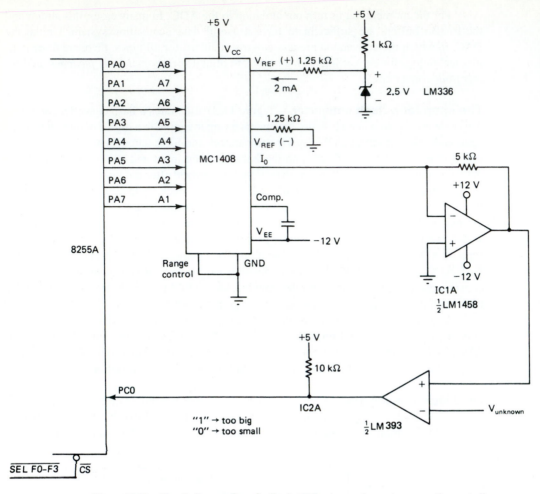

Figure 11.22 Circuit diagram for a feedback ADC using a microprocessor as the controller.

analog comparator used to compare the MC1408 DAC output with the unknown analog input voltage. What makes this circuit work is the software.

The conversion process is begun by outputting a value to port A of the 8255A. (Call this "guess 1.") The MC1408 and LM1458 convert the guess to a voltage, which is then compared with the unknown input voltage by IC2A. If "guess 1" is too small, the comparator output will be low; if "guess 1" too big, the comparator output will be high. By monitoring PC0, the control program can adjust its guess up or down until the binary code output to the DAC corresponds to the unknown voltage.

Flowcharts of two algorithms (programming techniques) commonly used to control the feedback ADC are presented in Fig. 11.23. The *tracking* converter diagrammed in Fig. 11.23(a) simply increments or decrements a counter, using the comparator output to tell it which way to go. Figure 11.24 shows the output of the LM1458 (IC1A) in Fig. 11.22 as it attempts to track the input signal. The program begins by guessing that the input is

$V_{FS}/2$ and, because this is too low, slowly ramps up until it locks on the input signal. Now, as the input slowly changes, the converter tracks the changes, faithfully reproducing the input signal.

However, note what happens when the input makes a sudden change. The tracking converter falls out of lock and does not regain a lock until the signal returns to a more constant level. Thus, we see that the tracking converter is good for tracking slowly changing signals (say, temperature levels over a long period), but is inadequate for signals that make rapid transitions (say, music or speech waveforms).

We can imagine a worst-case scenario for the tracking ADC in which the input makes a sudden transition from V_{FS} to near 0 V. The control program will begin decrementing the output code to the DAC, but could require as many as 256 cycles before a lock is again found. Assuming that approximately 25 μs is required to test the comparator output at PC0 and output a new code, 256×25 μs $= 6.4$ ms will be required to regain a lock.

The trouble with the tracking converter is that the algorithm used to control it is too simpleminded. A "smarter" approach is taken in the *successive approximations* flowchart in Fig. 11.23(b). This technique requires only eight cycles to converge on the unknown voltage. It begins by turning on bit 7, the most significant bit, and outputs this value (80H) to the DAC. If the comparator output goes high, the value was too big, and bit 7 should then be reset. If the comparator output is low, bit 7 is left on.

The cycle now repeats, working on bit 6 (but keeping bit 7 on or off, as determined previously). After eight cycles, all 8 bits will have been tested and the DAC output will be within one least significant bit (LSB) of the unknown input voltage.

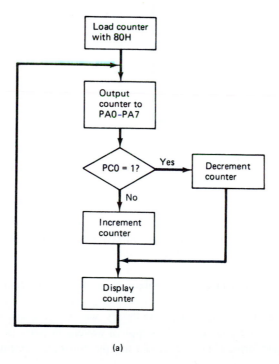

(a)

Figure 11.23 Flowcharts for the (a) tracking ADC and (b) successive approximations ADC.

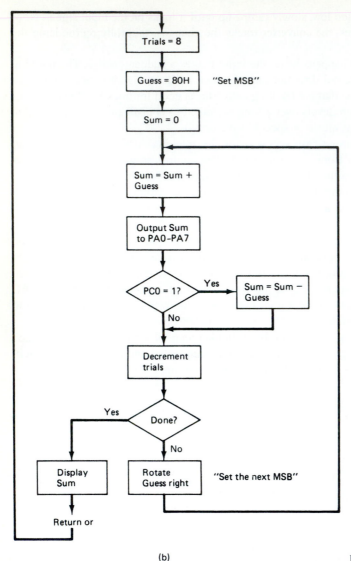

Trials = 8

Guess = 80H   "Set MSB"

Sum = 0

Sum = Sum + Guess

Output Sum to PA0-PA7

PC0 = 1?   —Yes→   **Sum = Sum − Guess**

No

Decrement trials

Done?   Yes

No

Display Sum

Rotate Guess right   "Set the next MSB"

Return or

(b)

Figure 11.23   *(Continued)*

Examining Fig. 11.24, you can see that the successive approximations converter does not try to follow the input signal. Instead, the software begins a conversion cycle, and eight cycles later the conversion has ended. The ability of this converter to return an accurate representation of the input voltage depends on the speed of conversion. If the input changes too rapidly, the converter can be "fooled," as shown in the second sample in Fig. 11.24.

Without getting too deep into communications theory, we can note that there is a *sampling theorem* which states that you need only sample a waveform twice per cycle to be able to reproduce that waveform. Thus, we should not put too much emphasis on a

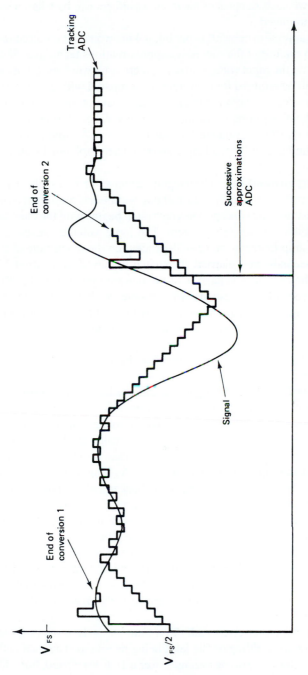

Figure 11.24 A tracking ADC follows a slowly changing input signal, but falls out of lock when the input makes rapid transitions. A successive approximations ADC does not try to follow the input signal, but converges on the digital code after eight cycles.

converter's ability to track a waveform, but rather, we should stress its ability to return an accurate sample of that waveform. If the input signal does change rapidly, a sample-and-hold circuit can be used to hold the sample constant until the conversion is complete. As long as at least two such samples of the input waveform can be taken per cycle, the wave-shape can be reproduced.

Assuming approximately 50 μs per bit, 0.4 ms would be required to converge on the input signal with the use of the successive approximations technique. Note that this value does not depend on the input voltage. (That is, there is no worst case.) In general, for *n* bits, *n* conversions will be required for convergence (compared with 2^n for the tracking design).

Finally, observe that both the tracking and the successive approximations converter can be built without requiring a microprocessor controller. A special *successive approximations register* (SAR) is available for that technique. A simple up–down counter can also be used to implement the tracking converter. (See Problem 11.16.)

The integrating converter. The integrating converter, or, as it is more often called, the *dual-slope* converter, is commonly used in digital voltmeters, multimeters, and panel meters. Figure 11.25 illustrates the concept. The conversion begins with the electronic switch in the T1 position and the counter reset to zero. The input voltage causes the capacitor connected to the op amp to charge at a rate dependent on the magnitude of the input voltage.

After T1 seconds have elapsed, the switch is moved to position T2 by the control logic. Because the reference voltage is of the opposite polarity to V_{in}, the capacitor now discharges. The control logic also starts the counter at this time. When the capacitor has fully discharged, the comparator output level switches and the counter is halted. The value in the counter is directly proportional to the input voltage:

$$V_{in} = \frac{T2}{T1} \times V_{REF}$$

As shown in Fig. 11.25, the higher the input voltage, the greater is the charge stored on the capacitor during T1. During T2 this voltage is discharged, but at a *constant rate* that is dependent on V_{REF}. This means that larger voltages will require more time to discharge and the preceding equation can be used to calculate V_{in}. The technique is analogous to measuring the quantity of water in a bucket by measuring the time it takes to empty the bucket through a fixed-diameter hose. As long as the time to fill the bucket is kept constant, the longer it takes to empty the bucket and the more water in the bucket.

Dual-slope converters are quite slow, requiring anywhere from 1 to 200 ms for one conversion. For this reason, they are most often used in digital panel meters—faster conversion times could not be noted by the human eye. The main advantages of the technique are its simplicity (which translates into low cost) and its relative immunity to noise. Because the sampling period (T1) is so long, it is a good assumption that any noise that is present will add to the signal as much as it subtracts. This means that the voltage stored on the capacitor at the end of T1 seconds represents the *average* value of the input signal over that interval.

Some dual-slope converters make T1 a multiple of 16.6 ms (1/60 Hz), thus averaging out any 60-Hz noise riding on the level being measured. The data collected by a flash or feedback converter can also be averaged over a 16.6-ms period, but additional software is required. Data from the dual-slope converter is averaged in real time.

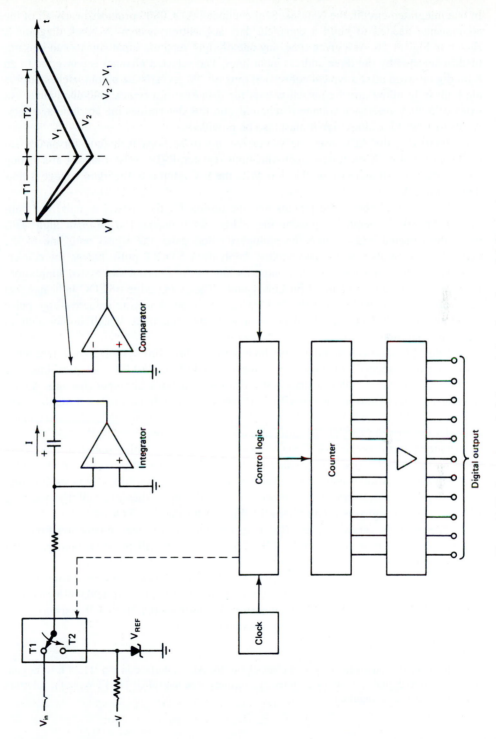

Figure 11.25 Integrating, or dual-slope, technique for analog-to-digital conversion.

Interfacing the ADC0809 Eight-Channel ADC

In one integrated circuit, the National Semiconductor ADC0809 provides nearly all of the components needed to build a complete data acquisition system. A block diagram is shown in Fig. 11.26. At a given time, any one of eight separate input signals can be sampled as selected by the three address input lines. The selected channel is converted to an 8-bit digital word after a typical conversion time of 100 μs. Tristate output latches/buffers are built in to allow direct connection with the data bus of a typical microcomputer. An external 5.00-V reference voltage is required, and this determines the absolute accuracy. A 10- to 1280-kHz clock signal must also be provided.

Internally, the ADC uses the *successive approximations* technique for analog-to-digital conversion. A successive approximations register, R-2R resistor ladder, and analog comparators are all included on the chip. With the 5-V reference, the input voltage is limited to 0 to 5 V.

Figure 11.27 shows the pinouts and the timing for the control signals. The conversion process is begun by pulsing the address latch enable (ALE) input high. This loads the selected address into the multiplexer and gates the signal onto one of the eight-channel inputs into the comparator. Applying a START pulse begins the conversion. The end-of-conversion (EOC) output is low as the internal successive approximations register accumulates the 8-bit binary code. The rising edge of EOC indicates that the conversion is complete and the data byte can be read. Applying an active-high pulse to output enable (OE) places the data on the eight data bus lines, which are normally in a tristate condition.

The ADC0809 can be interfaced directly to the three-bus system architecture without the need for special I/O chips such as the 8255A PPI or Z-80 PIO. A typical interface is shown in Fig. 11.28. Address lines AB0–AB2 select one of eight input channels. An I/O write instruction to any port address 30–37H (corresponding to channels 0 through 7) will generate a START and ALE pulse, beginning the conversion for the selected channel. Note that no data are actually transferred with this instruction.

Once the conversion has begun, the EOC output can be either polled or used as an interrupt to the processor. The interface in Fig. 11.28 uses the latter approach. The rising edge of EOC, indicating that data is available, clocks the D flip-flop, setting its Q output and requesting an interrupt. The processor acknowledges the interrupt by asserting INTAB, and this signal is used to reset the flip-flop for the next EOC.

The interrupt service routine (ISR) must execute an I/O read instruction from any of the eight input port addresses 30–37H. This instruction will pulse OE and place the data byte onto the data bus.

A simple TTL oscillator is sufficient for the clock signal. Using the values in Fig. 11.28, we obtain, for the clock frequency, approximately 500 kHz. An LM336-5 precision zener diode is used for the 5.00-V reference. The additional diodes and resistors compensate for voltage drifts in the LM336 with temperature.

Example 11.7

Suppose that an analog signal on channel 3 of the ADC interface in Fig. 11.28 is to be converted to digital and the result stored in a memory location called TEMP. Write the interrupt service routine required.

National Semiconductor

ADC0808, ADC0809 8-Bit μP Compatible A/D Converters With 8-Channel Multiplexer

General Description

The ADC0808, ADC0809 data acquisition component is a monolithic CMOS device with an 8-bit analog-to-digital converter, 8-channel multiplexer and microprocessor compatible control logic. The 8-bit A/D converter uses successive approximation as the conversion technique. The converter features a high impedance chopper stabilized comparator, a 256R voltage divider with analog switch tree and a successive approximation register. The 8-channel multiplexer can directly access any of 8-single-ended analog signals.

The device eliminates the need for external zero and full-scale adjustments. Easy interfacing to microprocessors is provided by the latched and decoded multiplexer address inputs and latched TTL TRI-STATE® outputs.

The design of the ADC0808, ADC0809 has been optimized by incorporating the most desirable aspects of several A/D conversion techniques. The ADC0808, ADC0809 offers high speed, high accuracy, minimal temperature dependence, excellent long-term accuracy and repeatability, and consumes minimal power. These features make this device ideally suited to applications from process and machine control to consumer and automotive applications. For 16-channel multiplexer with common output (sample/hold port) see ADC0816 data sheet. (See AN-247 for more information.)

Features

- Resolution — 8-bits
- Total unadjusted error — ± 1/2 LSB and ± 1 LSB
- No missing codes
- Conversion time — 100 μs
- Single supply — 5 V_{DC}
- Operates ratiometrically or with 5 V_{DC} or analog span adjusted voltage reference
- 8-channel multiplexer with latched control logic
- Easy interface to all microprocessors, or operates "stand alone"
- Outputs meet T^2L voltage level specifications
- 0V to 5V analog input voltage range with single 5V supply
- No zero or full-scale adjust required
- Standard hermetic or molded 28-pin DIP package
- Temperature range — 40°C to + 85°C or − 55°C to + 125°C
- Low power consumption — 15 mW
- Latched TRI-STATE® output

Block Diagram

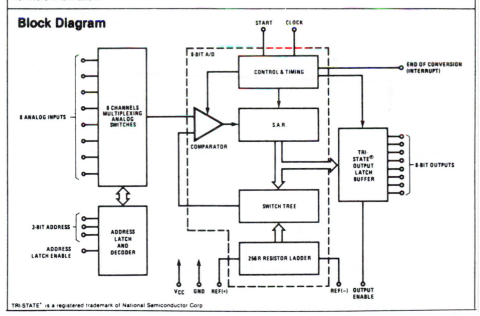

TRI-STATE® is a registered trademark of National Semiconductor Corp

Figure 11.26 Features and block diagram of the National Semiconductor ADC0809 eight-channel ADC. (Courtesy of National Semiconductor Corporation and Prentice Hall, Inc.)

Connection Diagram

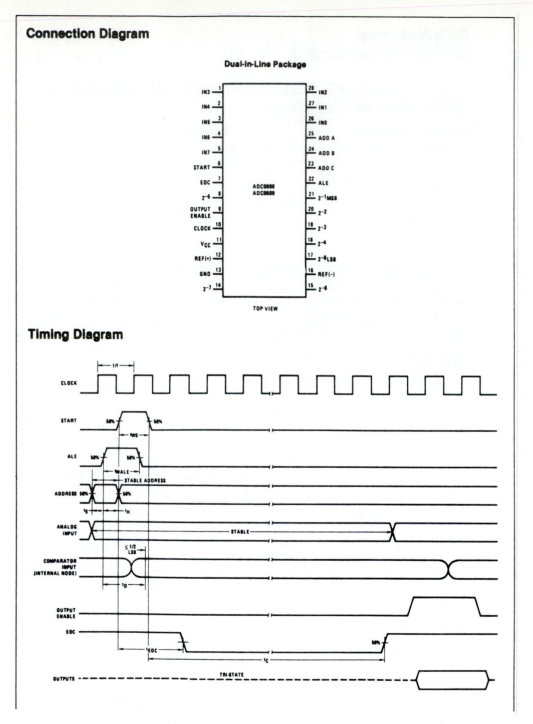

Figure 11.27 Connection diagram and timing relationships of the ADC0809 control signals. (Courtesy of National Semiconductor Corporation and Prentice Hall, Inc.)

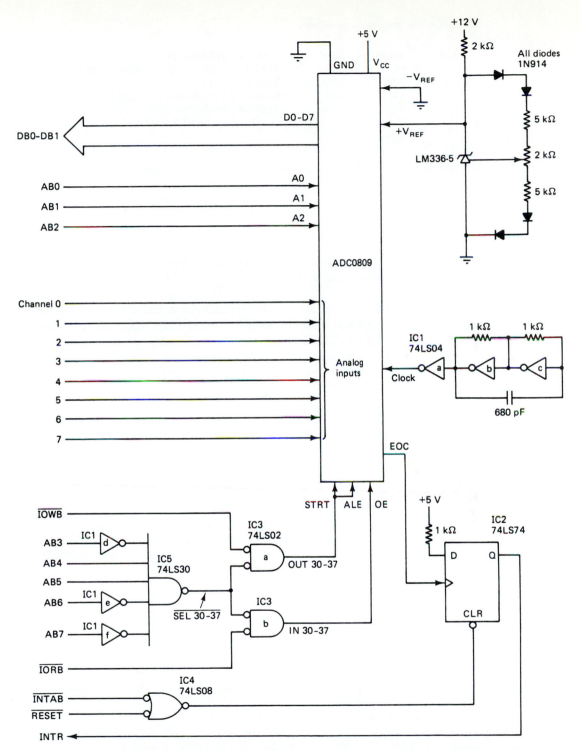

Figure 11.28 Interfacing the ADC0809 to the three-bus system architecture. Eight input and eight output ports are required. This circuit uses an interrupt-driven technique to control data transfers.

Solution. The program is as follows:

```
ISR     PUSH    PSW     ;MAKE TRANSPARENT
        IN      30H     ;READ DATA BYTE—ANY ADDRESS 30–37H
        STA     TEMP    ;STORE RESULT
        OUT     33H     ;START CONVERSION FOR NEXT CYCLE
        POP     PSW     ;RESTORE ENVIRONMENT
        EI              ;ENABLE FOR NEXT EOC PULSE
        RET
```

The main program can execute the following code to start the process:

```
OUT     33H     ;START CONVERSION FOR CHANNEL 3
EI              ;ENABLE INTERRUPT STRUCTURE
```

The processor can now perform some other task. Every 100 μs, it will be interrupted to perform the ISR. The most recent value of the analog input on channel 3 can be found by reading the contents of memory location TEMP.

One disadvantage to using the 8080/85 I/O instructions in this example is that the port address is fixed. If a different channel is to be converted, a new ISR must be written. This is not a problem with the Z-80 microprocessor; the port address can be passed in register C and an *OUT (C),r* instruction used. If the interface is changed to become memory mapped, the 8080 and 8085 can pass the port address in a register pair.

Example 11.8

Suppose that an LM334 temperature sensor (see Section 11.1) is connected to channel 3 and the ISR in Example 11.7 executed. If memory location TEMP contains 9CH, what is the temperature of the sensor?

Solution. $9CH = 156_{10}$, and thus, $V_{in} = 156/256 \times 5.0\ V = 3.05\ V$. This corresponds to $305°K = 32°C = 90°F$.

(*Note:* Machine code to convert 9CH to 90°F could be written by storing the possible temperatures in a table, with the hex code found in TEMP used as an *index* into the table. Alternatively, a program written in BASIC could easily *calculate* the temperature directly from the number stored in TEMP.)

SELF-REVIEW 11.4

11.4.1 List the three types of common analog-to-digital converters (ADCs).

11.4.2 Feedback converters can be controlled by a _____ or _____ _____ technique.

11.4.3 Which type of ADC is often used in digital voltmeters?

11.4.4 The ADC0809 is an _____ bit ADC with _____ separate analog inputs.

11.5 TROUBLESHOOTING TECHNIQUES

Introduction

It would be nice if a microcomputer system could be designed, constructed, and used without having to spend long hours tracking down bad connections, design errors, and software bugs. It would also be nice if we did not have to pay taxes. But both being inevitable, it is probably wise to prepare for the eventuality and become familiar with basic microcomputer troubleshooting techniques. As Murphy* has said, *"Anything that can go wrong, will."*

When faced with any troubleshooting problem, the goal is to isolate the problem area. Which part of the system is working and which parts are not? A good starting point is to determine whether the problem is due to a *hardware* failure or a *software* bug. For example, a "new" computer being booted up for the first time may appear "dead" if a wrong code has been programmed into its bootstrap PROM. Several hours could easily be spent looking for an apparent hardware problem that is not there.

Separating hardware from software problems can result in a lot of "finger pointing" if the hardware designer and programmer have too much confidence in their work. I can remember thinking that I surely had a bad microprocessor chip when my first machine language programs caused the system to "crash" repeatedly.

In new systems, test PROMs from similar systems should be used so that the software is known to be good. If this is not possible, a very simple test PROM should be programmed that will cause an unmistakable pattern to appear on the system buses.

An example of the "wrong way" of developing system software would be to try to write a complete disk operating system (DOS) without first testing the disk primitives, such as "load the head," "locate track 00," and "read or write a sector of data." Because the program would have to be so complex, it would be very difficult to isolate any problems to hardware or software.

When software problems are indicated, special aids are available. Among these aids are debuggers that allow instructions to be *traced* in a single-step mode, displaying all CPU registers after each instruction.

Another software debugging tool, called the *breakpoint,* is a special instruction inserted into a program to cause control to be transferred to a routine that displays the contents of all microprocessor registers at the time of the breakpoint. This strategy is similar to the trace technique, but allows known good sections of the program to be executed at normal speeds. Because they occupy only 1 byte of memory, the RST instructions are usually used for breakpoints in 8080/85 and Z-80 microcomputer systems. The DDT program included with CP/M supports the insertion (and automatic deletion) of breakpoints in 8080/85 programs.

When hardware problems are indicated, several tools also are available for locating the fault. The most common of these are the following:

1. Multimeter
2. Logic probe

---

*Well-known pessimist.

3. Oscilloscope
4. Signature analyzer
5. Logic analyzer

In this section, we:

- Explain the operation of common microcomputer troubleshooting tools, including the multimeter, logic probe, oscilloscope, signature analyzer, and logic analyzer.
- Develop a strategy for troubleshooting a microcomputer system.

Hardware Troubleshooting Tools

Multimeter. Each connection in a new microcomputer system should be tested for *continuity* before any of the ICs are placed in their sockets and power is applied. The ohms function of the multimeter can be used for this purpose. Some of the newer meters emit a beep to indicate continuity and help make the task less tedious. Each connection should be checked off against a wiring list or schematic diagram of the system.

When it has been determined that all connections are correct, the power supply voltages should be measured by using the voltmeter function of the meter. This measurement is performed at the power source terminals *and* at the power pins of each IC socket. (You do not want +12 V going to all of the TTL chips!)

Logic probe. In troubleshooting a digital system, a logic probe is useful for two measurements:

1. To check for valid logic levels.
2. To detect pulses.

In bringing up a new system, a logic probe can be used to verify that the system clock is running. Note, however, that you will be unable to verify the actual voltage levels of the clock or its exact frequency.

A logic probe is most effective if the processor can be *single-stepped.* In Chapter 4, we saw circuits that permitted single-stepping by forcing the processor to execute one machine cycle and then enter a *WAIT* state. In this state, all data, address, and control bus signals are "frozen" and can readily be tested with a logic probe.

Example 11.9

Figure 11.29 shows a schematic diagram of a simple Z-80 microcomputer system with 2K RAM, 2K EPROM, and 24 I/O lines. The memory map is also shown. (Note that the 8255A is memory mapped.) Write the code for a simple Z-80 test EPROM that could be executed in the single-step mode to verify the basic operation of the system.

Solution. Because the system is so simple, the test PROM might do best to exercise the address decoding and read/write logic. One possibility would be to perform a memory read from each of the three devices (2716, 6116, and 8255A), a memory write to the RAM, and, finally, a memory read from an address not decoded. Figure 11.30(a) shows one such program.

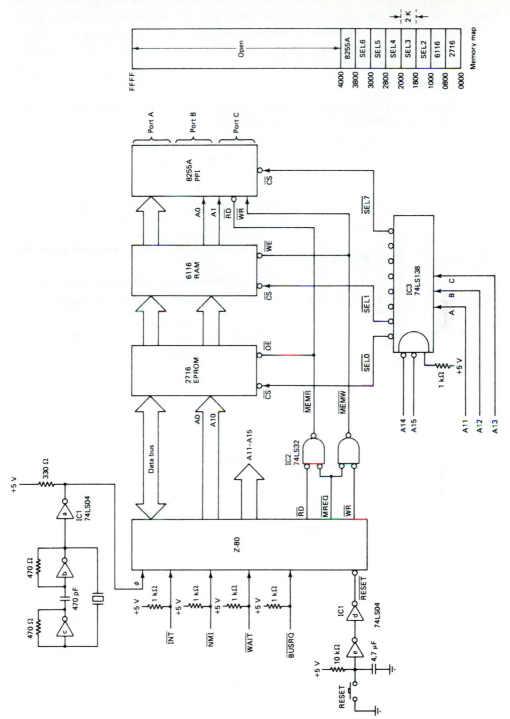

Figure 11.29 Simple Z-80-based microcomputer system used to illustrate troubleshooting techniques.

607

Figure 11.30(b) shows the hex codes for the test PROM as they would be stored, starting at location 0 of the 2716 EPROM. Pushing RESET should start the program. The MEMR and MEMW lines should be pulsing from high to low (the logic probe will show this as a steady logic 1 with the pulse indicator flashing), and the SEL0, SEL1, and SEL7 decoder outputs should also be pulsing.

Example 11.10

Sketch a machine-cycle timing diagram for the program in Fig. 11.30(a). Indicate the contents of the address and data buses for each cycle.

Solution.   The diagram is shown in Fig. 11.31. Note that the addresses have been chosen to allow each address and data bus line to be tested for a logic 1 and logic 0 condition.

Without a single-step circuit, the contents of the buses in Fig. 11.29 will appear only as pulse indications on the logic probe. This will prove that none of the data or ad-

```
                                            Lifeboat Assoc. Z80 Assembler Page 0001
ADDR    CODE       STMT SOURCE STATEMENT

                   0001          ;Z-80 TEST PROGRAM FOR THE HARDWARE IN FIG.11-29
                   0002          ;
>0000              0003          ORG    0000         ;RESET WILL START PROGRAM
                   0004          ;
'0000   3AFF07     0005 LOOP     LD     A,(07FFH)    ;GENERATE SEL0 AND MEMR
'0003   3AFF0F     0006          LD     A,(0FFFH)    ;GENERATE SEL1 AND MEMR
'0006   3A0038     0007          LD     A,(3800H)    ;GENERATE SEL7 AND MEMR
'0009   32FF0F     0008          LD     (0FFFH),A    ;GENERATE SEL1 AND MEMW
'000C   3AFFFF     0009          LD     A,(0FFFFH)   ;ALL SELECTS SHOULD BE HIGH
'000F   C30000'    0010          JP     LOOP         ;NOW SINGLE-STEP WHILE LOOPING

ERRORS=0000
```

(a)

PROM ADDRESS	DATA
0000	3A
0001	FF
0002	07
0003	3A
0004	FF
0005	0F
0006	3A
0007	00
0008	38
0009	32
000A	FF
000B	0F
000C	3A
000D	FF
000E	FF
000F	C3
0010	00
0011	00

(b)

Figure 11.30   (a) Test EPROM program for the Z-80 system in Fig. 11.29; (b) the EPROM hex codes.

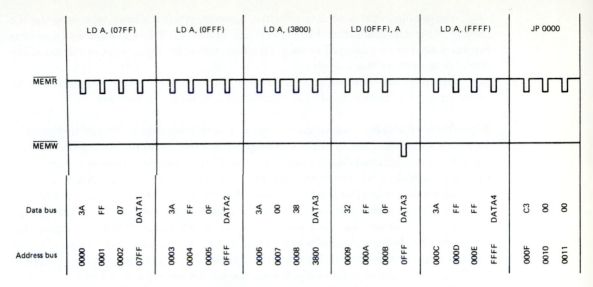

Figure 11.31 Machine-cycle timing diagram for the test program in Fig. 11.30(a).

dress lines are "stuck" high or low, but is not as conclusive a result as could be found by stepping the processor through each machine cycle shown in Fig. 11.31.

A single-step circuit is not shown in Fig. 11.31, but was presented in Fig. 4.31 for the Z-80. With this circuit, the following steps should be undertaken:

1. With the single-step switch in the RUN position, start the program running by pushing the RESET switch.
2. Switch to the single-step position.
3. Find your "place" in the program by monitoring $\overline{\text{MEMW}}$ with the logic probe. $\overline{\text{MEMW}}$ will go low only once for each loop through the program.
4. Having found the memory-write machine cycle, trace the program by pushing the STEP switch, examining the buses with the logic probe and verifying the addresses and data for each cycle.
5. The memory read cycle from address FFFF should cause all of the decoder outputs to be high. (This is the only cycle for which that will occur).

Assuming that this program runs correctly, more elaborate programs can now be written that read and write data to the RAM and program the 8255A for simple I/O operations. If these programs check out, the system can be declared functional and you can begin writing the application programs.

Oscilloscope. Compared with the logic probe, the oscilloscope lets you "see" the logic pulses. Problems such as marginal voltage levels and excessive ringing can readily be spotted. The main advantage in using the oscilloscope lies in its ability to compare the timing between two signals (assuming a dual trace). If SEL1 must go low during $\overline{\text{MEMW}}$ low, the oscilloscope can show the exact relationship between these two signals.

The oscilloscope is not too effective, however, when it comes to monitoring the content of the data and address bus lines. This is because all 8 data bus and all 16 address bus lines need to be examined at once. (For that matter, the logic probe is not too effective at reading these buses either.)

Generally, the oscilloscope is used when the timing between two signals must be observed or when the electrical characteristics of a signal are in question.

Signature analyzer. Signature analysis is a troubleshooting technique developed by Hewlett-Packard specifically for microcomputer systems. A signature analyzer is used much like a conventional digital voltmeter by touching a probe to various nodes in the circuit. At each node, a "characteristic signature" is displayed—a four-digit number made up of the numerals 0–9 and (for clarity) the letters A, C, F, H, P, or U. Comparing the measured signature against a predetermined value on a schematic diagram (much as voltages are recorded on an analog schematic), a technician can quickly isolate defective components.

The basis of the technique is to note that at any circuit node a serial stream of pulses will be observed over time. If this stream is repetitive, a CRC character can be generated that is representative of the data block. (See Section 9.3 for a discussion of CRC.)

The signature analyzer has three inputs: START, STOP, and CLOCK. START and STOP are signals used to tell the analyzer when to begin and end the CRC calculation. The rising or falling edge of the CLOCK signal is used to cause the analyzer to sample the logic level at the circuit node.

For signature analysis to be most effective, the signature at each node in the circuit must be known (before the system needs troubleshooting!). This feature is best designed in by the manufacturer, who can then identify a logical sequence to follow when an incorrect signature is found. However, in a known good microcomputer system, signature analysis can be used by recording the signatures at important nodes. Note that it will be important to document the program that is utilized to produce this signature, as well as the definitions of the CLOCK, START, and STOP signals.

Realistically, few users will take the time to record signatures on functioning equipment. Determining the important nodes to be tested and developing test programs that exercise these nodes requires a knowledge of the system unique to the manufacturer. For these reasons, signature analysis tends to be restricted to equipment that supports the technique by design.

Logic analyzer. The logic analyzer is the most sophisticated (and most expensive) tool available for troubleshooting the microcomputer. It has anywhere from 8 to over 40 input channels. Unlike an oscilloscope, the logic analyzer does not display its input signals in real time. Instead, it stores this information in a semiconductor memory, usually allowing 16 to 1024 words of storage. (That is, a 40-channel analyzer would have storage capabilities for 1024 40-bit words.)

The stored data can be displayed as a conventional voltage waveform (without rise and fall times) by using the *timing mode*. It can also be displayed as binary, octal, hex, ASCII, or disassembled mnemonics in the *state mode*. Recalling the logic probe example, we essentially performed a state-mode analysis. However, it was necessary to single-step the processor manually to collect and then record the data on paper to reconstruct the data and address bytes.

Figure 11.32(a) shows an example of the display produced by a Hewlett-Packard model 1630 logic analyzer when the device is operated in the timing mode. Note that each channel can be assigned a label, making analysis of the display much simpler. The sample period is similar to the horizontal sweep rate of a conventional oscilloscope and controls the resolution of the data stored.

Figure 11.32(b) illustrates the display produced when the logic analyzer is operated in the state mode. Again, labels have been used to simplify interpretation. Note that in this case ADDR represents 16 input channels, DATA represents 8 input channels, and STAT represents 4 input channels. The operator has chosen to display the data in a hex format.

A very powerful feature of most logic analyzers is the ability to *trigger* data collection on a particular data word. Using this feature, you can, for example, specify data col-

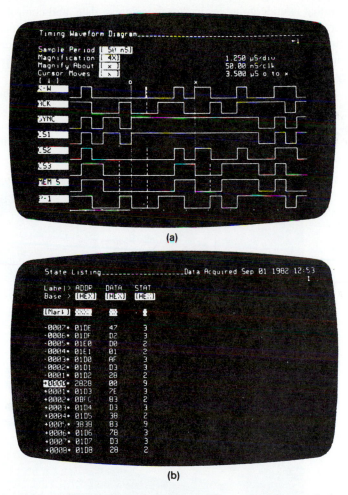

(a)

(b)

Figure 11.32   (a) In the timing mode, voltage waveforms versus time are displayed by the logic analyzer. An internal clock determines the sampling period. (b) In the state mode, data can be displayed in binary, octal, hex, ASCII, or disassembled mnemonic form. In this example, 28 channels are used. (Courtesy of Hewlett-Packard.)

lection to begin when $\overline{\text{MEMR}}$ is low, the address bus contains 2800H, and the data bus contains 3EH. In addition, data can be collected in either a pre- or posttrigger mode. This feature can be seen in Fig. 11.32(b), where the trigger word is highlighted in reverse video (ADDR = 2828). Seven data samples are shown before the trigger word and eight samples after the trigger word.

The logic analyzer is itself a microcomputer system programmable by a front-panel keyboard. The operation of the analyzer is simplified due to various control menus placed on the screen by the instrument. Figure 11.33 shows the calculatorlike front panel of the Hewlett-Packard model 1630. Note that the roll keys allow the data on the screen to be scrolled up or down so that all of the stored data can be examined by the operator.

The most difficult part about using a logic analyzer is the setup. For example, the state display in Fig. 11.32(b) requires that 28 probes be connected to the microcomputer system that is undergoing testing for the address, data, and control bus signals. Next, the proper operating mode must be selected via the front panel. Of particular importance is the clock signal. In the timing mode, this is usually an internally generated signal that determines when to sample the input data. The HP 1630 will allow clock samples as fast as every 20 ns or as slow as one each millisecond.

Selecting a 20-ns sample period might be a good choice when one is looking for close timing problems, but doing so will restrict the timing period to 1024 samples $\times$ 0.02 μs/sample = 20.48 μs. Depending on the microprocessor's clock frequency, this may not be enough time to see more than two or three complete instructions. On the other

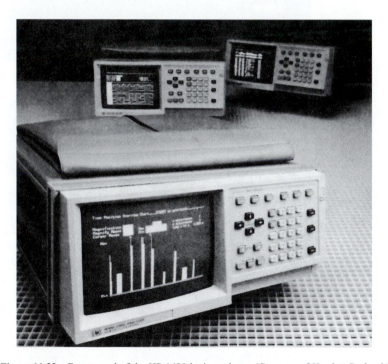

Figure 11.33 Front panel of the HP 1630 logic analyzer. (Courtesy of Hewlett-Packard.)

hand, selecting a 1-ms sample period will store 1.024 s of data, possibly resulting in waveforms so compressed as to be unreadable.

In the state mode the clock signal is supplied externally, because it is desirable to take the data samples synchronously with a particular clock signal. Two examples will help illustrate.

Example 11.11

Describe the connections required to set up a logic analyzer in the state mode to the Z-80 system shown in Fig. 11.29. Assuming that the test EPROM used to obtain the machine-cycle timing diagram in Fig. 11.31 is used, explain the resulting state display.

Solution. Using the labels ADDR, DATA, and STAT (where STAT = $\overline{\text{MEMR}}$ and $\overline{\text{MEMW}}$, in that order) the display is shown in Fig. 11.34. We assume that a trigger word of ADDR = 0000 has been selected (although with the roll feature of the HP 1630, this is not essential). Note that the clock must be connected to $\overline{\text{MREQ}}$ (and programmed for a rising-edge trigger) so that data samples are recorded for both memory read and memory write cycles. Note also that the data is essentially identical to the data shown in Fig. 11.31 (but has been found a lot more quickly!).

Example 11.12

If the clock input to the logic analyzer is changed from $\overline{\text{MREQ}}$ to $\overline{\text{MEMW}}$ in Fig. 11.29, what will the state display become?

ADDR	DATA	STAT ($\overline{\text{MEMR}}$ $\overline{\text{MEMW}}$)
0000	3A	1
0001	FF	1
0002	07	1
07FF	DATA1*	1
0003	3A	1
0004	FF	1
0005	0F	1
0FFF	DATA2	1
0006	3A	1
0007	00	1
0008	38	1
3800	DATA3	1
0009	32	1
000A	FF	1
000B	0F	1
0FFF	DATA3	2
000C	3A	1
000D	FF	1
000E	FF	1
FFFF	DATA4	1
000F	C3	1
0010	00	1
0011	00	1
0000	3A	1
⋮	⋮	⋮

Figure 11.34 Logic analyzer display in the state mode for the test program in Fig. 11.30(a). $\overline{\text{MREQ}}$ is used as the clock source. STAT = 1 (01–memory read) or 2 (10–memory write).

ADDR	DATA	STAT (MEMR MEMW)
0FFF	DATA3	2
0FFF	DATA3	2
0FFF	DATA3	2
.	.	.
.	.	.
.	.	.

Figure 11.35 Changing the logic analyzer clock from MREQ to MEMW results in only one data sample per program loop.

Solution. The display is shown in Fig. 11.35. There is only one memory write cycle per loop through the program, and this occurs when the LDA (0FFF),A instruction is executed. The address bus contains 0FFF, and the data bus contains the data byte read in the preceding instruction.

Summary

Before you attempt to troubleshoot a microcomputer system, be sure that you understand its operation. Get a copy of the system monitor in PROM. Make sure that you are familiar with the system memory map. Although a number of sophisticated troubleshooting tools are available, you must understand the system to make effective use of these tools. Often, test PROMs will have to be programmed to exercise selected portions of the hardware. A little luck won't hurt either!

SELF-REVIEW 11.5

11.5.1 In troubleshooting a microcomputer system, the first task is to isolate the problem to _____ or _____.

11.5.2 Explain the role of a test ROM in booting up a computer for the first time.

11.5.3 What is the difference between the state and timing modes as applied to a logic analyzer?

QUESTIONS AND ANSWERS

Q: *How can a microcomputer monitor the on/off state of a sensor?*

A: A voltage comparator can be used. When the sensor signal rises above a certain level, the output of the comparator switches high (+5 V). When the sensor signal is below the designated level, its output is 0 V.

Q: *Can standard TTL gates be used to turn analog peripherals on and off?*

A: Yes, provided that the peripheral is dc controlled. Special open-collector gates are available with voltage breakdown ratings greater than 50 V and current capacities as high as 500 mA.

Q: *How can a microcomputer be used to control an ac peripheral?*

A: Electromechanical or solid-state relays (SSRs) can be used. SSRs offer the advantages of fast switching speed, no moving parts, and isolation from the switched circuit.

Q: *How is a digital-to-analog converter (DAC) built?*

A: Most DACs use the R-2R ladder network, a circuit requiring only two different resistor values and designed such that the source current divides in half at each active circuit node. An op amp is utilized to sum the resulting current and convert it to a voltage.

Q: *How is an analog-to-digital (ADC) converter built?*

A: Three techniques are common: flash converters based on multiple voltage comparators, feedback converters that feed "best guess" information to a DAC in a feedback loop, and dual-slope converters based on the time required by the analog signal to charge a reference capacitor.

Q: *What is a data acquisition system?*

A: An ADC system with a microprocessor-compatible interface capable of amplifying, storing, and converting an analog signal to digital form. In many cases, the entire system is integrated on a single chip with several analog input channels.

Q: *How do you troubleshoot a new microcomputer system?*

A: One method is to program a ROM with a simple test program. Then, by using a single-step circuit, the signals on the buses can be monitored to verify that the processor is correctly fetching instructions from memory. When the system passes this test, more elaborate test programs can be written and applied.

Q: *What is a logic analyzer?*

A: A sophisticated microcomputer troubleshooting tool that allows all three buses of the computer to be monitored simultaneously.

LAB PROJECTS

11.1. Light-activated relay:
  (a) Using one bit of an available input port, construct the photocell input circuit shown in Fig. 11.36. Adjust the potentiometer so that the output switches reliably when covered and uncovered by your thumb. (See Problem 11.2.)
  (b) Using one bit of an available output port, construct a relay control circuit. Fig 11.5(b) shows an example of a circuit using an open-collector buffer. Fig. 11.37 shows another method that does not require an output port. (See Problems 11.6 and 11.7.)
  (c) Write a program to activate the relay when the photocell is covered for one or two seconds. Have the relay stay on until the next time the cell is similarly covered.*

---

*Conventional push-button switches will wear out, especially when exposed to heavy use. The circuit in Fig. 11.36 can be employed to replace such switches. If the photocell is mounted behind a piece of glass, it will still be accessible, but should have an unlimited life.

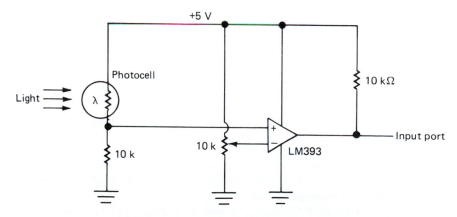

Figure 11.36   Photocell interface for Lab Project 11.1 and Problem 11.2.

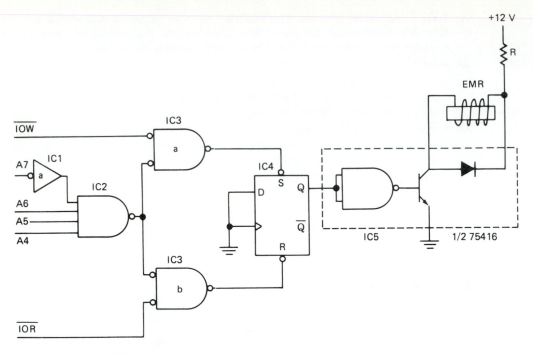

Figure 11.37   Relay driver circuit for Lab Project 11.1 and Problems 11.6–7.

11.2. Computer-controlled lamp dimmer:
    (a) Construct the solid-state relay circuit shown in Fig. 11.9 by utilizing an MOC3011. Use a 12-V ac signal for the source and a 12-V incandescent lamp as the load. An open-collector buffer can be substituted for the 75416 relay driver. Connect the input of this buffer to one bit of an available output port. Test to be sure that you can turn the lamp on and off via software.
    (b) Use a comparator like the LM393 to generate a 60-Hz TTL-compatible square wave from a 6-V or 12-V ac transformer. Connect this signal to one bit of an available input port.
    (c) Write a program to detect zero-crossings of the line voltage (rising or falling edges of the 60-Hz square wave), enter a time delay, and then activate the SSR, turning on the lamp for the remainder of the half-cycle. The brilliance of the bulb can be controlled by selecting different time delays. Be sure to observe the waveforms across the lamp, TRIAC, 60-Hz square wave, and computer output port using an oscilloscope.

11.3. Synthesizing a sine wave:
    (a) Construct a DAC interface like that shown in Fig. 11.15.
    (b) Write a program to cause the output to ramp from 0 V to 10 V and back down again, repeating. Observe this waveform on an oscilloscope. Measure the step size.
    (c) Using a program similar to that of Fig. 11.17, write a program to synthesize a 1-kHz sine wave. Try adding more samples to produce a "cleaner" waveform.
    (d) Connect the op-amp output to an LM386 driving a loudspeaker. Modify your program from part (c) to emulate a European police siren as described in Problem 11.14.

11.4. Digital voltmeter/thermometer:
    (a) Modify the DAC circuit described in Lab Project 11.3 to become a feedback ADC. (See Fig. 11.22.)

(b) Write a program to control the interface following the tracking or successive approximations flowchart given in Figs. 11.23(a) and (b), respectively. Have your program output the hex value of the result to the displays on your computer.

(c) Modify the program from part (b) to display the *decimal* value of the input voltage. (The easiest way to do this is to set up a data table.) Check your interface with a conventional digital voltmeter.

(d) Monitoring the voltage across an LM334 (see Fig. 11.2), convert your voltmeter into a digital thermometer. (Again, a data table may be the easiest way to do this.)

QUESTIONS AND PROBLEMS

Section 11.1

11.1. True or false? The output of the LM393 in Fig. 11.36 will be +5 V whenever the voltage applied to its V(+) input exceeds the voltage applied to its V(−) input.

11.2. Suppose that the resistance of the photocell in Fig. 11.36 varies from 1 kΩ in bright daylight to 1 MΩ in darkness. At dusk, the cell's resistance is 10 kΩ. To what resistance value should the 10-kΩ port be adjusted to cause the circuit's output to be low from dusk to daylight?

Section 11.2

***11.3.** Study the driver circuits in Fig. 11.38, and identify the design error in each.

11.4. One bit of a microcomputer output port is to be used to control a 24-V dc mechanical relay. The pull-in current of the relay is 35 mA. Sketch the schematic diagram of a circuit that uses a TTL open-collector buffer to interface this relay and microcomputer.

11.5. Using the graph of I versus time in Fig. 11.7(b), calculate the "cold" and "hot" resistance of the incandescent lamp.

11.6. Answer the following questions about the EMR interface shown in Fig. 11.37.
(a) To turn on the relay, the flip-flop must be _____.
(b) If the relay has a pull-in current of 150 mA and the coil is rated at 9 V, calculate the value of the series-dropping resistor R.
(c) What is the range of I/O addresses to which this circuit will respond?
(d) Give an example of an instruction that will turn the relay on.

***11.7.** Which of the following could cause the relay in Fig. 11.37 to be "stuck" on?
(a) A solder splash has shorted the output of IC3a to ground.
(b) The collector–emitter junction of the driver transistor in IC5 is shorted.
(c) The series-dropping resistor has burned out, becoming an open circuit.

11.8. What is the purpose of the bridge rectifier in the hybrid SSR of Fig. 11.8?

11.9. Answer the following questions about the SSR in Fig. 11.9:
(a) What logic condition is required to turn the relay on?
(b) Assuming that the IRED drops 3.0 V, calculate the current through the IRED.
(c) Explain how Q1 and D1 protect the IRED. If Q1 comes on when its V_{BE} = 0.6 V, what is the maximum current that can be forced through the IRED?

Section 11.3

11.10. Calculate the smallest output voltage for an 8-bit and a 12-bit DAC, each with V_{FS} = 10.0 V.

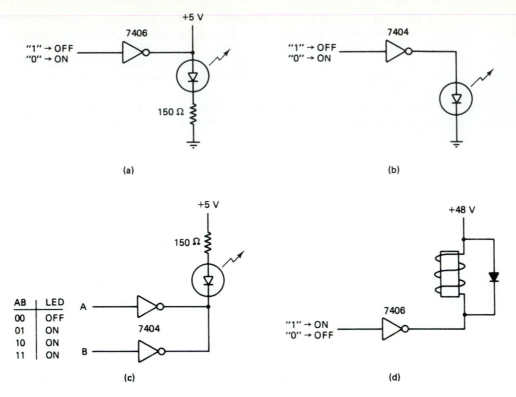

Figure 11.38 TTL control circuits for Problem 11.3.

11.11. Calculate all currents and the output voltage for the R-2R DAC in Fig. 11.13 if D2 D1 D0 = 101. Assume that V_{REF} = 3.0 V, R = 1 kΩ, and R_F = 8 kΩ. (*Hint:* Find I0 and I2, and then use superposition.)

11.12. Calculate the output voltage of the *weighted-resistor DAC* in Fig. 11.39, assuming that V_R = 1 V and D3 D2 D1 D0 = 0101. Why do you think the R-2R DAC is preferable?

11.13. Answer the following questions about the MC1408 PPI interface in Fig. 11.15:
  (a) What is the purpose of the LM336.
  (b) What is the function of the op amp?
  (c) What is the maximum output voltage for the circuit as shown?

11.14. Write a program to synthesize a European police siren with an 8-bit DAC. Your program should produce 1 s of a 1-kHz tone and then 1 s of a 500-Hz tone, repeating. Use the program in Fig. 11.17 as a subroutine.

Section 11.4

11.15. Compare the worst-case conversion time for an 8-bit tracking ADC and an 8-bit successive approximations ADC. Assume 25 μs of conversion time per bit.

11.16. Sketch the schematic diagram of an 8-bit ADC using an 8-bit DAC, up–down counter, and analog comparator. Indicate where the analog input is applied and the digital output retrieved.

11.17. Refer to the feedback ADC in Fig. 11.22. If the analog input voltage is 6.25 V and the digital output is 9EH, determine the logic level on the output of the analog comparator.

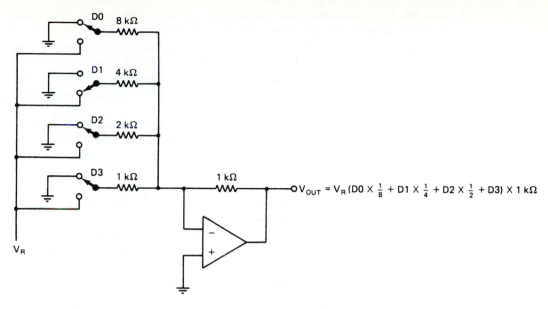

$V_{OUT} = V_R (D0 \times \frac{1}{8} + D1 \times \frac{1}{4} + D2 \times \frac{1}{2} + D3) \times 1\ k\Omega$

Figure 11.39   Weighted-resistor DAC for Problem 11.12.

11.18. Write a program to convert the feedback ADC in Fig. 11.22 into a tracking ADC as per the flowchart in Fig. 11.23(a).

11.19. Write a program to convert the feedback ADC in Fig. 11.22 into a successive approximations ADC as per the flowchart in Fig. 11.23(b).

*11.20. Suppose that a tracking routine has been written for the ADC circuit in Fig. 11.22. In testing the circuit, you find that the program continually converges on FFH, regardless of the analog input voltage. Which of the following could be a cause of this problem?
   (a) The output of the LM393 is "stuck" high.
   (b) The reference current is set too high.
   (c) The output of the LM1458 is shorted to ground.

11.21. Answer the following questions about the ADC0809 interface in Fig. 11.28:
   (a) What is the I/O port address of the analog input to channel 5?
   (b) Give an example of a command that will cause a conversion to begin for channel 5.
   (c) What signal indicates to the microprocessor that the conversion for channel 5 has been completed?
   (d) Give an example of a command that can be used to read the converted data for channel 5.

Section 11.5

11.22. Answer the following questions about the microcomputer system shown in Fig. 11.29:
   (a) How much ROM does this system have?
   (b) How much RAM does this system have?
   (c) What is the *range* of port addresses to which the 8255A will respond?
   (d) Each of the $\overline{SEL}$ outputs of the 74LS138 is active for _____ consecutive bytes.

*11.23. Suppose that, with the test program of Fig. 11.30 running, you are checking the microcomputer system of Fig. 11.29. You find $\overline{MEMR}$ to be pulsing, but $\overline{MEMW}$ appears to be stuck low. List at least three possible causes of this problem. What action would you take to prove or disprove each hypothesis? Assume that all chips are socketed.

*11.24. Suppose you are tracing the test program in Fig. 11.30(a). Watching the address bus, you see 0000, 0001, 0002, and then 07FFH. Is this sequence correct? Explain.

*11.25. Suppose that the A15 and A14 address lines in the microcomputer system shown in Fig. 11.29 have become shorted. Will the test program in Fig. 11.30(a) detect this problem? Explain.

*11.26. Suppose that a microcomputer system you have been using for several months suddenly goes "dead." The system uses a machine language monitor in PROM, a hex keypad, and seven-segment LED displays. In its "dead" state, the system will not respond to the keypad, and although the displays are lit, they do not change. What steps and tools would you use to troubleshoot this problem?

*11.27. If the "dead" system described in Problem 11.26 is being booted up for the very *first* time, how would you modify your troubleshooting procedure?

11.28. Write a simple test program for the 8255A in Fig. 11.29. Have your software program the 8255A for mode 0, with each port programmed to follow a binary count sequence. A logic probe can then be used to verify the correct operation of the device.

11.29. What *mode*—timing or state—should be selected to cause a logic analyzer to display the MEMR and MEMW waveforms shown in Fig. 11.31?

*11.30. You have connected a logic analyzer to an 8080/85 or Z-80 microcomputer. Using the state mode, you program the analyzer to begin collecting data after a system reset (address bus = 0000). Explain the following data:

ADDR	DATA	STAT	$(\overline{\text{MEMR}}\ \overline{\text{MEMW}})$
0000	FF		1
274E	00		2
274D	01		2
000F	FF		1
274C	00		2
274B	01		2
000F	FF		1

What do you think is wrong with this system?

SELF-REVIEW ANSWERS

11.1.1. current, temperature

11.1.2. $V(+) > V(-)$, $V(-) > V(+)$

11.2.1. 30 V

11.2.2. When the 75416 is used to drive a relay, the diodes protect the output transistor from the inductive voltage spike created when the current in the relay coil collapses.

11.2.3. To steer the current through the transistor from collector to emitter regardless of the polarity of the ac signal.

11.2.4. zero-cross, random

11.3.1. 39 mV

11.3.2. R-2R ladder

11.3.3. Table

11.3.4. 1100 1100 1101

11.4.1. Open loop; feedback; and integrating, or dual slope

11.4.2. tracking, successive approximations

11.4.3. dual slope

11.4.4. 8, 8

11.5.1. hardware, software

11.5.2. The test ROM can put a known pattern on the buses, allowing the basic pieces of the system (address decoders, buffers, control logic gating) to be easily tested.

11.5.3. Timing mode: Data is displayed as voltage waveforms. State mode: Data is displayed as the hex, ASCII, or instruction mnemonic equivalents.

12

INTRODUCTION TO THE 8086
16-BIT MICROPROCESSOR

OUTLINE

OBJECTIVES

After completing this chapter, you should be able to:

- Explain the operation of the 8086 CPU, including that of the bus interface and execution units.
- Describe the function of the various 8086 processor pins.
- Sketch a drawing of a CPU module for the 8086 when operated in minimum mode.
- Sketch a drawing of a CPU module for the 8086 when operated in maximum mode.
- Draw a programming model for the 8086 processor, showing the data, pointer, index, and control register groups.

- Use the 8086's segmented memory model and explain the difference between a physical memory address and a logical memory address.
- List and briefly describe the various 8086 processor instruction groups.
- Write a simple 8086 program to fill a block of memory.
- Show how to interface a 32K-byte memory to the 8086.
- Show how to interface the 8255A PPI chip to the 8086.
- Compare the various processors in the 80x86 family, including the 8088, 80286, 80386, 80486, Pentium, Pentium Pro, and Pentium II.
- Explain what is meant by the term *superscaler processor*.

OVERVIEW

"Just when you think you understand the picture, the picture changes." This was the key line in an advertisement that ran on television several years ago. Anyone who has studied electronics soon learns this (sad?) lesson. It took only two years for the 8-bit microprocessor to replace the early 4-bit chips. Now we have 16-bit, 32-bit, and even 64-bit microprocessors. Clock speeds have gone from 1 or 2 MHz to over 400 MHz today. By the time you sit down and study one chip, it has been rendered obsolete by another!

Or has it? Although this book is written around the 8080, 8085, and Z-80 chips in particular, what we have really been studying is *microprocessor technology*. What is a RAM chip, what is a ROM, and how do we connect these parts to a microprocessor? How do we interface a parallel printer, monitor a temperature sensor, or control a mechanical relay? What if your software doesn't run as expected? How do you go about troubleshooting it? This is what microprocessor technology is all about.

As you read this chapter and study the 16-bit 8086 microprocessor, you will find that all of the concepts studied in the previous chapters still apply. The memory and I/O interfaces still require address decoders and buffers. Output ports are still built from latches, input ports from tristate gates.

The main difference is the *width* of the data bus. Sixteen bits of data can now be fetched from memory instead of 8. The internal registers are also 16 bits wide. This allows more data to be manipulated at a given time. The result is faster program execution.

Electrically, the 8086 appears similar to the 8085. It uses a multiplexed address/data bus and an 8085-like set of control signals—ALE, M/IO, RD, WR, and INTA. Twenty address lines are provided. This means that the 8086 can access as much as 1 MB of memory.

The 8086 is a good 16-bit chip to study. Its 8-bit "cousin," the 8088, was used by IBM in its PC and XT computers. In addition, the more powerful 80286, 80386, 80486 and Pentium microprocessors are all *object-code compatible*. This means that programs written for the 8086 can be run on these processors without change, making the 8086 a good stepping-off point.

In this chapter, we will first develop a CPU module for the 8086, learning about the support chips required. The programming model is presented next. Here you will learn about the internal registers available to the programmer. The instruction set is then surveyed, and two examples of a program to fill a block of memory are presented.

The software sections are followed by discussions on memory and I/O interfacing. Included is an 8255A interface that provides three 16-bit input–output ports. The chapter concludes with a brief description of the other chips available in the 8086 family. These include the 8-bit 8088, the 16-bit 80286, the 32-bit 80386 and 80486, and the 64-bit Pentium processors.

12.1 8086 HARDWARE DETAILS AND BASIC SYSTEM TIMING

Introduction

We began this book with a description of the stored-program digital computer, which works by storing program instructions in a separate memory unit from which the CPU fetches commands arranged in a logical sequence. The process is called "fetch and execute."

The 16-bit 8086 still follows this basic principle. Where it differs from most 8-bit microprocessors is that it assigns two separate processors to the job. These processors are called the *execution unit* (EU) and the *bus interface unit* (BIU). Figure 12.1 illustrates this dual organization in a block diagram.

The BIU fetches instructions from memory and transfers data between the EU general registers and the outside world. The EU decodes the instructions and executes them.

In this section, we:

- Explain the operation of the 8086 CPU, including that of the bus interface and execution units.
- Describe the function of the various 8086 processor pins.

The Queue

A unique feature of the 8086 is the use of an *instruction prefetch queue*. This is a 6-byte (4-byte in the 8088) first-in, first-out storage area in the BIU used to save instructions that are pending execution in the EU. Because the queue will normally hold the next instruction to be executed, the fetch and execute phases of the classic stored-program computer can *overlap*. While the EU is executing one instruction, the BIU can be fetching another, ensuring that the queue will always be full and that no time will have to be spent waiting for an instruction fetch. This technique of allowing the fetch and execute cycles to overlap is also called *pipelining*.

It is interesting to note that the 8086 and 8088 differ only in their BIUs: The 8088's BIU is 16 bits wide, the 8086's 8 bits wide. Not only does this technique decrease instruction execution times; it simplifies the task of redesigning the 8086 into an 8088—only the BIU need be redesigned.

The Min and Max Modes

The names of the signals for the 40-pin 8086 are given in Fig. 12.2. In order to maintain a 40-pin package and still provide 20 address lines, 16 data bus lines, and several control and status signals, nearly every pin of the 8086 is time *multiplexed*. This is a scheme in which a pin carries one type of signal during one period and a different signal during another.

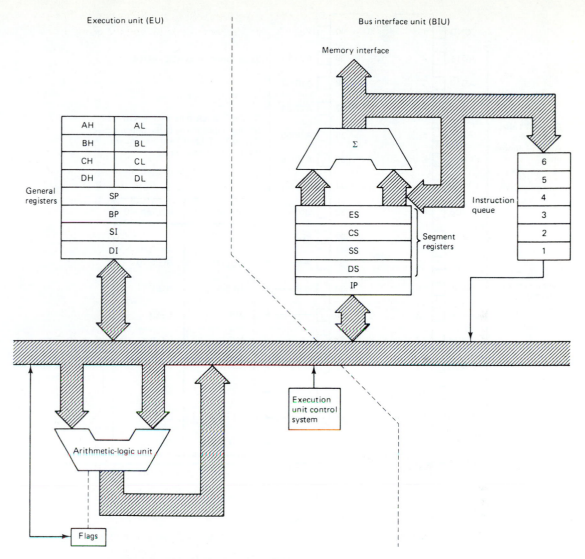

Execution unit (EU)　　　　　　　　　Bus interface unit (BIU)

Memory interface

General registers: AH AL / BH BL / CH CL / DH DL / SP / BP / SI / DI

Σ

ES / CS / SS / DS / IP — Segment registers

Instruction queue: 6 5 4 3 2 1

Execution unit control system

Arithmetic-logic unit

Flags

Figure 12.1 Block diagram of the 8086 microprocessor. The chip is made up of two processors: the execution unit (EU) and the bus interface unit (BIU).

Consider first the data/address bus. These lines are labeled AD0–AD15 and A16/S3–A19/S6. As with the 8085, AD0–AD15 and A16–A19 hold a valid address when pin 25, the address latch enable (ALE), is high. When ALE is low, these lines carry the 16 data bus lines and status information on S3–S6.

A second group of multiplexed pins is controlled by the MN/$\overline{\text{MX}}$ input. When this pin is high, the *min mode* is selected, and pins 24 through 31 take on the control signal definitions shown under the column MN/$\overline{\text{MX}}$ = 1 in Fig. 12.2. When operated in the min mode, the 8086 presents a control bus similar to that of the 8085 and requires only an address latch and clock generator to form a CPU module. (See Section 12.2.)

Sec. 12.1　　8086 Hardware Details and Basic System Timing　　　**625**

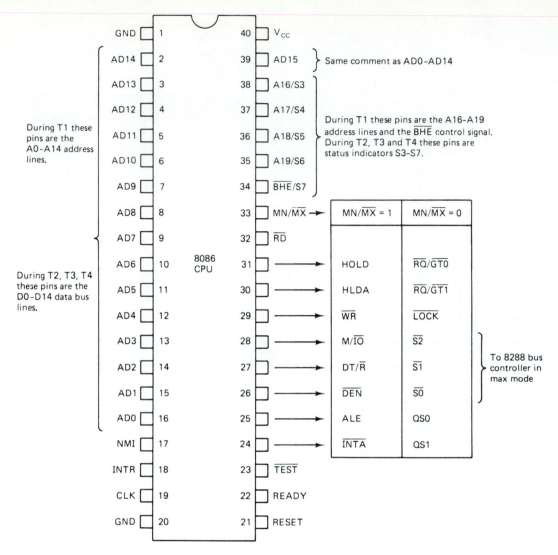

Figure 12.2 Pin definitions for the 8086 microprocessor. The control signals on pins 24 through 31 change, depending on the mode of operation of the processor.

When MN/$\overline{\text{MX}}$ is low, the *max mode* of operation is selected. This mode is intended for more complex applications in which the 8086 is supported by the 8087 numeric data processor and the 8089 I/O processor. The control signals on pins 24–31 change to become those shown under the column MN/$\overline{\text{MX}}$ = 0 in Fig. 12.2. In this mode, a special bus controller (the 8288) is required to develop the memory and I/O control bus signals. (See Section 12.2.)

One of the philosophical changes Intel has made in developing its family of 16-bit microprocessors is to share the processing among several specialized *coprocessors*. These are optional processors that can be used to speed up mathematical and I/O processing. In simpler (min mode) systems, coprocessors can be omitted.

Memory Organization

As mentioned, the 8086 (and 8088) has a 20-bit address bus. This allows the processor to access 2^{20}, or 1,048,576, memory locations. But what is a memory location for a 16-bit microprocessor? Is it a 16-bit word or an 8-bit byte?

Figures 12.3(a) and (b) illustrate the two common ways of organizing the memory space of a 16-bit microprocessor. Both memories store 1,048,576 bytes (1 MB). The difference is that the organization in Fig. 12.3(a) can be accessed as a byte or a word, while the organization in Fig. 12.3(b) must be accessed as a 16-bit word only. The 8086 uses the technique in Fig. 12.3(a).

Operation codes for the 8086 are all 8 bits in length, with the second through fifth bytes specifying the operand. Several instructions are only a single byte in length. Thus, it is logical for the 8086 to be able to access its memory as a byte or a word.

There are actually three types of memory cycles:

1. Word access on AD0–AD15
2. Even-addressed byte access on AD0–AD7
3. Odd-addressed byte access on AD8–AD15

Table 12.1 helps explain how the 8086 identifies which type of memory access it is performing. The bus high enable ($\overline{\text{BHE}}$) control bus signal—multiplexed with the S7 status signal—must be latched when ALE is high. The latched signal is then combined with A0 to determine the type of memory access. Be sure that you understand the consequences of this encoding. The A0 address line no longer connects to the memory devices. Instead, it is combined with $\overline{\text{BHE}}$ to generate an ODD BYTE SEL and EVEN BYTE SEL pair of control signals. This concept should become clearer when we study memory and I/O interfacing in Section 12.5.

From a speed standpoint, it is most advantageous for the 8086 to access the memory as 16-bit words. In this way, one memory cycle brings two bytes into the BIU via AD0–AD15. However, referring to Table 12.1, we see that this can happen only when A0 is low. (That is, the word must be stored at an *even address.*) If a 16-bit word is stored beginning at an *odd address,* two memory cycles will be required to fetch both bytes. This is illustrated in Fig. 12.3(c).

The BIU handles the job of determining the type of memory access automatically, and the programmer need not be concerned, except to be aware that four extra clock states are required for words stored at odd addresses. Indeed, the 8088 suffers this speed penalty with every memory access, because its data bus is only 8 bits wide.

A memory with a 20-bit address will also cause us to "rethink" our memory-map nomenclature. Figure 12.4 shows such a map, divided into 16 "64K pages." Note that five hex digits are required to describe any one address. This is a convenient way of drawing the map because the most significant hex digit increments by 1 with each new (64K) page.

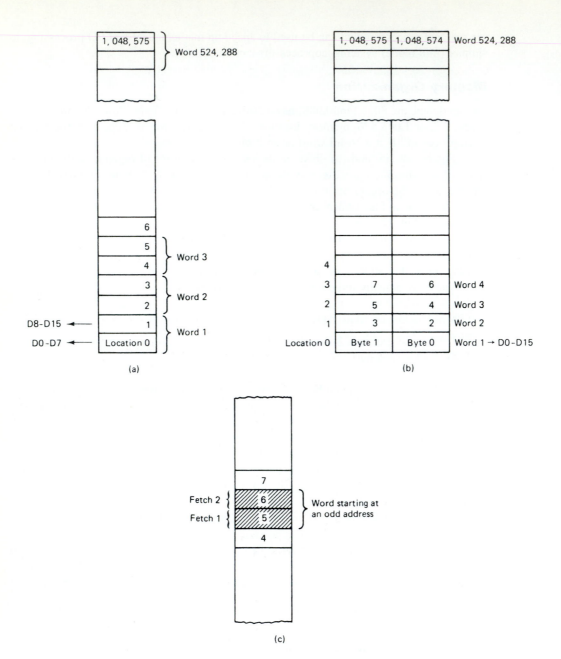

Figure 12.3 (a) and (b) Two methods of organizing a 16-bit memory; (c) a 16-bit word is stored at an odd address, causing the 8086 to perform two fetches to retrieve the full word.

TABLE 12.1 8086 Memory Access Encoding

$\overline{BHE}$	A0	Action
0	0	Access 16-bit word
0	1	Access odd byte to D8–D15
1	0	Access even byte to D0–D7
1	1	No action

Basic System Timing

Figure 12.5 illustrates 8086 system timing. Each machine cycle consists of four T states (plus any WAIT states if requested). All read or write cycles begin with an ALE pulse, which should be used to latch AD0–AD19 for a memory address, AD0–AD15 for an I/O address, and $\overline{BHE}$ to determine whether a word or byte is to be accessed.

In the max-mode status, signals $\overline{S0}$, $\overline{S1}$, and $\overline{S2}$ are decoded by the 8288 bus controller to provide the I/O and memory control signals. The eight possible "status words" are listed in Table 12.2. Note that the control bus output by the 8288 is similar to that of the 8080.

In the min-mode, $M/\overline{IO}$ can be combined with $\overline{RD}$ and $\overline{WR}$ to decode memory and I/O operations. The result is a control bus nearly identical to that of the 8085.

The 8086 (and 8088) provide two signals for controlling data bus buffers: data transmit/receive (DT/$\overline{R}$) and data enable ($\overline{DEN}$). $\overline{DEN}$, which is low whenever the processor is using its data bus, can be used to enable a set of bidirectional bus buffers. DT/$\overline{R}$ is

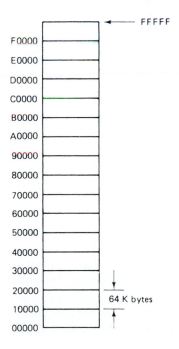

Figure 12.4 Memory map for the 1 MB of memory accessible by 8086 and 8088 microprocessors. Sixteen pages of 64K bytes each are provided.

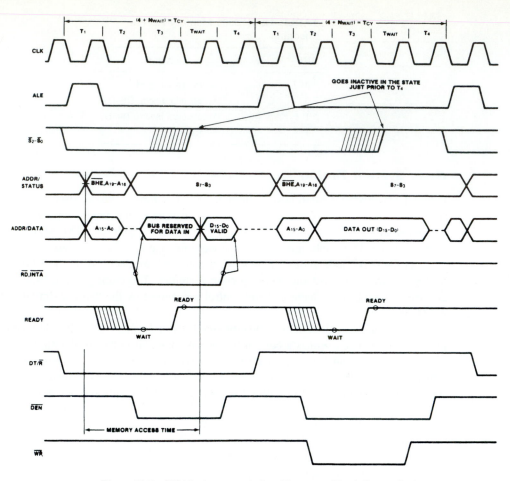

Figure 12.5 8086 basic system timing. (Courtesy of Intel Corporation.)

normally used to control the *direction* of data through the buffers. When DT/$\overline{\text{R}}$ is low, the buffers should be enabled to input data off the system data bus lines.

The status signals S3–S7 are multiplexed with A16–A19 and $\overline{\text{BHE}}$; they hold valid status information when ALE is low. The S3 and S4 status outputs indicate which segment register (see Section 12.3) is in use for the current bus cycle. S5 reflects the status of the internal-interrupts-enabled flag bit, S6 = 0, and S7 is a spare status bit.

The remaining min-mode control bus signals have functions similar to their counterparts in the 8080 and 8085. This group includes HOLD, HLDA, and $\overline{\text{INTA}}$.

In the max mode, $\overline{\text{RQ}}/\overline{\text{GT0}}$ and $\overline{\text{RQ}}/\overline{\text{GT1}}$ are intended for use with the 8087 numeric data processor. These lines are bidirectional and allow the coprocessor to request control of the buses when it must access system memory. The 8086 grants control of the buses by pulsing the lines for one clock cycle. The $\overline{\text{LOCK}}$ signal is also intended for the 8087 coprocessor. When active, it indicates that the 8087 should not attempt to gain control of the system buses. The $\overline{\text{LOCK}}$ signal is used by the 8086 when updating information in mem-

TABLE 12.2 8288 Status Words Based on the $\overline{S0}$, $\overline{S1}$, and $\overline{S2}$ Max-Mode Status Signals

$\overline{S2}$	$\overline{S1}$	$\overline{S0}$	Processor state	8288 active output
0	0	0	Interrupt acknowledge	$\overline{\text{INTA}}$
0	0	1	Read I/O port	$\overline{\text{IORC}}$
0	1	0	Write I/O port	$\overline{\text{IOWC}}$ (also advanced $\overline{\text{IOWC}}$)
0	1	1	Halt	None
1	0	0	Code access	$\overline{\text{MRDC}}$
1	0	1	Read memory	$\overline{\text{MRDC}}$
1	1	0	Write memory	$\overline{\text{MWTC}}$ (also advanced $\overline{\text{MWTC}}$)
1	1	1	Passive	None

ory that the 8087 will in turn be processing. It is used in conjunction with the *LOCK* instruction.

QS0 and QS1 are status signals that are also intended for the 8087. They are used by the 8087 to synchronize its queue with that of the 8086.

The $\overline{\text{TEST}}$ input can be monitored in software (with the *WAIT* instruction). If this line is found high, the 8086 will idle until $\overline{\text{TEST}} = 0$. Like QS0 and QS1, $\overline{\text{TEST}}$ is intended for the 8087. When the 8086 needs a result from the 8087, it can execute a *WAIT* instruction to ensure that the calculation has been completed by the 8087 before continuing.

The READY input provides a means of synchronizing the processor to slow memories, as does the same signal on the 8080 and 8085. RESET forces the 8086 to fetch its next instruction from memory location FFFF0H. Normally, a jump instruction would be stored here, transferring control to the main program.

There are two interrupt inputs, labeled INTR and NMI. INTR can be masked by resetting the interrupt-enable flag bit. The NMI input is nonmaskable. Like the 8080 INTR input, the interrupting device must supply an 8-bit "type" number during $\overline{\text{INTA}}$. The 8086 multiplies this number by 4 and fetches a 4-byte jump address from the resulting location (and the next three consecutive bytes) as the location of the interrupt service routine. The first 1K of memory is reserved for interrupt jump addresses corresponding to the 256 possible "type" numbers. The NMI input automatically retrieves its ISR address from locations 00008H–0000BH.

Example 12.1

An interrupting device gates 03 onto AD0–AD7 when $\overline{\text{INTA}}$ is low. Where should the interrupt jump address be located in memory?

Solution. The address is $3 \times 4 = 12 = 0$CH. The jump address should be stored in 0000CH–0000FH.

(*Note:* Section 12.3 will explain the segment registers and show how 4 bytes can be combined to form the 20-bit physical address.)

Interrupt requests can also be initiated via software, and this technique is discussed in Section 12.4.

Special Support Chips

Because of the dual and specialized nature of many of the 8086 signals, Intel has developed several support devices designed to simplify the task of building an 8086 microcomputer system. Figure 12.6 identifies these chips by function and part number.

The 8086 requires an external clock signal, a function provided by the 8284 clock generator. The 8286 is an octal data transceiver similar to the 74LS245. The 8282 is an octal latch specifically designed to demultiplex the address/data bus of the 8086 and is similar to the 74LS373. Note that three latches are required for the 20-bit address bus. The 8288 bus controller, required in all max-mode designs, decodes $\overline{S0}$, $\overline{S1}$, and $\overline{S2}$ to provide the system control bus.

Also shown in Fig. 12.6 are the optional coprocessors designed to enhance system throughput. The 8087 numeric data processor (NDP) executes special instructions prefixed by an *ESCAPE* command. These instructions include exponential, logarithmic, and trignometric math functions. The 8087 can speed up the calculation of these functions by a factor of 100 or more. For example, a square-root routine written for the 8086 will require 19,600 μs with a 5-MHz 8086, but only 36 μs with a 5-MHz 8087 NDP!

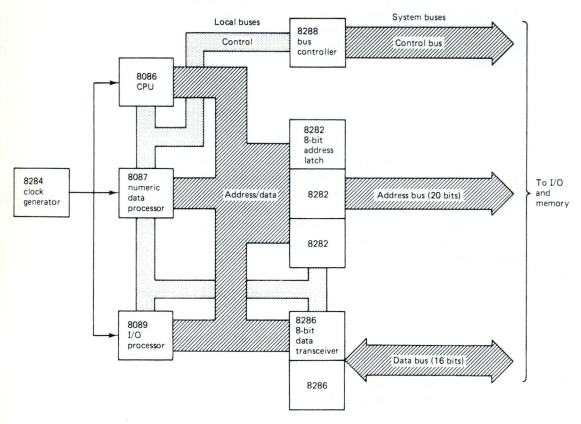

Figure 12.6 The 8086 is supported by several ICs designed to interface with the specialized local buses of the processor.

The 8089 has two dedicated I/O channels that can function independently of the 8086 processor. The 8089 can be operated as a DMA controller or as a programmable peripheral controller device. What separates the 8089 from other peripheral controllers is its own built-in instruction set, which allows it to transfer data to or from the processor's I/O and memory.

In conclusion, we can say that the 8086 still follows the principles set down in Chapter 1 for a stored-program computer. However, it allows the basic fetch and execute cycles to be overlapped through the use of two separate processors, called the EU and BIU. Externally, the three-bus system architecture is still followed, but is broken into a specialized set of *local* buses and a conventional set of *system* buses. This configuration is shown in Fig. 12.6.

SELF-REVIEW 12.1

12.1.1 The 8086 is divided into two separate processors called the _____ and the _____.

12.1.2 When used with the 8087 numeric coprocessor, the 8086 should be operated in the _____ mode.

12.1.3 List the three types of 8086 memory read/write cycles.

12.1.4 Each 8086 machine cycle requires _____ T states.

12.2 MIN- AND MAX-MODE CPU MODULES FOR THE 8086

Introduction

The CPU module has been consistently emphasized throughout the book. It is this module that provides all bus signals to the microcomputer system. The CPU must develop the system clock signal, provide a means for resetting the processor, allow interrupts and DMA activities, and, for the special case of the 8086 (and 8088), demultiplex the address and data bus lines. Bus buffering must be incorporated to allow for reliable system expansion without loading problems.

In this section, we:

- Sketch a drawing of a CPU module for the 8086 when operated in minimum mode.
- Sketch a drawing of a CPU module for the 8086 when operated in maximum mode.

The Min Mode

The min and max modes of the 8086 are sufficiently different that the designer must choose one operating mode and design the system to that mode. Figure 12.7 shows a CPU module based on the min mode of operation. In this mode, the 8086 develops its own set of control bus signals (without the 8288) and provides a bus interface very similar to that of the 8085.

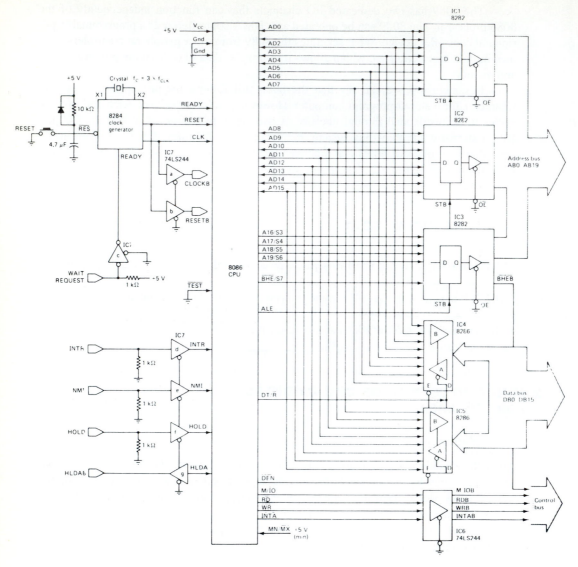

Figure 12.7 Min-mode 8086 CPU module.

Consider the following points about this circuit:

1. The 8284 is used to develop the system clock signal. The clock frequency generated will be one-third of the external crystal frequency. The clock signal itself has a 30% duty cycle and switches between 0 and 4.5 V. The 8284 also accepts *WAIT* requests via the READY input and synchronizes these to the system clock. The RESET circuit functions similarly to the way those described in Chapter 4 function and provides for a power-on reset function.

TABLE 12.3 Electrical Specifications of the 8286 and 74LS245 Octal Transceivers

	8286	74LS245
I_{OL}	32 mA at 0.45 V	12 mA at 0.4 V
I_{OH}	5 mA at 2.4 V	3 mA at 2.4 V
I_{IL}	0.2 mA	0.2 mA
I_{IH}	50 μA	20 μA

2. The 20-bit address is demultiplexed with three 8282 octal latches. ALE is used to strobe data into the latches, and data are stored with the falling edge of this signal. Note that $\overline{BHE}$ is also latched by ALE.

3. The data bus is buffered by two 8286 octal transceivers. As mentioned before, $\overline{DEN}$ and DT/$\overline{R}$ are output by the processor specifically for the purpose of controlling these buffers.

4. The control bus signals are identical to those of the 8085 (except that M/$\overline{IOB}$ must be inverted) and are buffered with one 74LS244.

5. The INTR, NMI, and HOLD inputs are active high and therefore are held low with 1-kΩ resistors. The HLDA output is buffered and is available for DMA applications.

The control bus could be decoded to provide an "8080-like" control bus if desired. (This was, in fact, done for the 8085 CPU module in Fig. 4.26.) Another option is to include the decoding as part of the address-decoding logic associated with the memory or I/O interface.

Table 12.3 compares the 8286's electrical capabilities with those of the more familiar 74LS245. If we allow a V_{OL} of 0.45 V, the 8286 exceeds the specifications of the 74LS245 in all categories except for I_{IH}.

Table 12.4 provides a similar comparison between the 8282's octal latch and that of the 74LS373. Again, if the higher V_{OL} level is acceptable, the 8282 exceeds the capabilities of the 74LS373.

The Max Mode

Figure 12.8 illustrates a CPU module for the 8086 when operated in the max mode. The clock, data bus, and address bus connections do not change from those of the min-mode diagram in Fig. 12.7. However, the former control bus signals, ALE, DT/$\overline{R}$, $\overline{DEN}$, M/$\overline{IO}$,

TABLE 12.4 Electrical Specifications of the 8282 and 74LS373 Octal Latches

	8282	74LS373
I_{OL}	32 mA at 0.45 V	12 mA at 0.4 V
I_{OH}	5 mA at 2.4 V	2.6 mA at 2.4 V

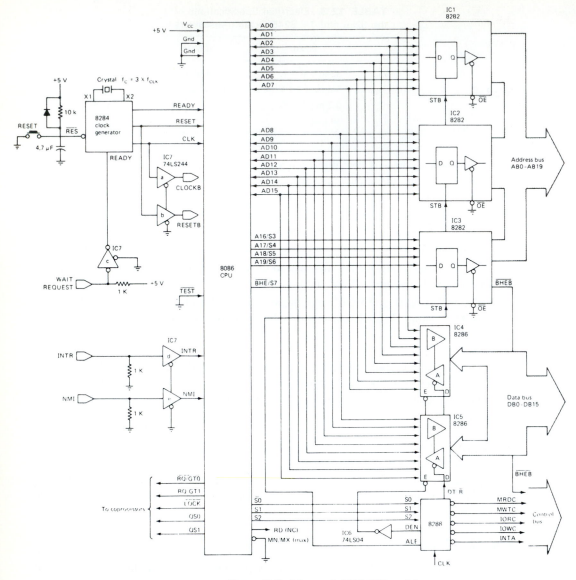

Figure 12.8 Max-mode 8086 CPU module.

$\overline{WR}$, and $\overline{INTA}$, plus the HOLD and HLDA pins, all have new names. (See pins 24 through 31 in Fig. 12.2.) Five of these eight signals—$\overline{RQ}/\overline{GT0}$, $\overline{RQ}/\overline{GT1}$, $\overline{LOCK}$, QS0, and QS1—become special control signals for the 8087 and 8089 coprocessors.

The remaining three signals are now called $\overline{S0}$, $\overline{S1}$, and $\overline{S2}$ and are decoded by the 8288 to provide the new max-mode control bus $\overline{MRDC}$, $\overline{MWTC}$, $\overline{IORC}$, $\overline{IOWC}$, and $\overline{INTA}$. Note that these are in an "8080-like" form. The 8288 also generates the buffer control signals lost when the max mode was selected. These include DT/$\overline{R}$, DEN, and ALE. Observe that the 8288 outputs DEN, not $\overline{DEN}$.

The HOLD and HLDA signals appear to be lost. Actually, they are renamed $\overline{RQ}/\overline{GT0}$ and $\overline{RQ}/\overline{GT1}$ (request/grant). Other local-bus masters (such as the 8089 I/O processor) can request (and be granted) control of the local bus via these two pins.

SELF-REVIEW 12.2

12.2.1 What is the purpose of the 8284 in an 8086 microcomputer system?

12.2.2 What signal is provided by the 8086 to demultiplex the address/data bus?

12.2.3 What two signals are used by the 8086 to control the data bus buffers?

12.2.4 In which 8086 operating mode—min or max—is the 8288 bus controller required?

12.3 A PROGRAMMING MODEL FOR THE 8086

Introduction

As an 8086 programmer, you are less interested in the electrical interface required between the 8086 and its support chips and more interested in the size and number of registers and how the instruction set is used to manipulate data within these registers.

In this section, we:

- Draw a programming model for the 8086 processor, showing the data, pointer, index, and control register groups.
- Use the 8086's segmented memory model and explain the difference between a physical memory address and a logical memory address.

Internal Register Array

One view of the internal architecture of the 8086 has been presented in Fig. 12.1. In this model, the 8086 is broken into two processors, called the EU and BIU. Note that each processor has a set of registers. In the BIU, these are called the *segment registers* and will be discussed in detail in the next subsection. The registers of the EU form the *programming model*. Figure 12.9 provides a closer look.

Perhaps one of the most interesting features of the 8086 register array is that it is not too different from the 8080/85 set of registers, shown shaded in the figure, with their names enclosed in parentheses. The following are main differences between the two sets of registers:

1. The 8086 accumulator is 16 bits wide.
2. The 8086 has two 16-bit index registers and a 16-bit pointer register that are not present in the 8080/85.
3. The 8086 flag word is 16 bits wide.

Because of the 8086's ability to manipulate bytes as well as 16-bit words, the four data registers (AX, BX, CX, and DX) can be read as a word or a high or low byte. For ex-

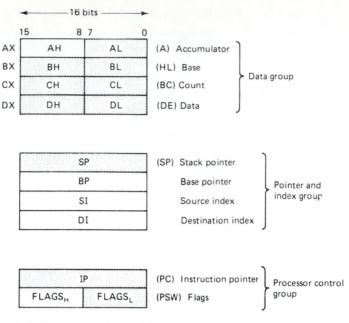

Figure 12.9 8086 programming model. The shaded registers are the 8080/85 equivalents.

ample, CH represents the 8 high-order bits of 16-bit register CX. Similarly, CL represents the low 8 bits of this register.

The stack pointer register performs the same function as it does in the 8080/85. A new addition is register BP, which can be used as a second stack pointer. This is useful for passing parameters to a subroutine on the stack. Register BP can point at the parameters without disturbing the stack pointer itself (and the subroutine return address).

Registers SI and DI are used as pointers for the indirect and indexed addressing modes. For example, a typical instruction might move the data byte pointed at by the source index (SI) to the memory location pointed at by the destination index (DI).

The 8080/85's program counter is called the *instruction pointer* (IP) in the 8086. It points to the next instruction or operand to be brought into the prefetch queue.

A unique feature of the 8086 is that many of its instructions require that specific registers be used. The use of the SI and DI registers as source and destination pointers, respectively, has already been mentioned. Table 12.5 indicates the assignments for all of the registers. Until we examine the instruction set, these definitions may not be too meaningful, but the point to note is that the programmer is not always free to use any register he or she wishes in developing an 8086 program.

The 8086 flag word is shown in Fig. 12.10. To simplify the conversion of 8080/85 programs to the 8086, the low 8 bits of the flag word are identical to those of the 8080/85. Three of the four new flag bits are actually *control* flags. When the TF flag is set, the 8086 operates in single-step mode, branching to the address stored in 00004–00007 after each instruction. The program at this address can be a routine to display the contents of the various registers to aid in software debugging.

TABLE 12.5   General Registers with Dedicated Uses

Register	Dedicated operation
AX	Word multiply, word divide, word I/O
AL	Byte multiply, byte divide, byte I/O, translate, decimal arithmetic
AH	Byte multiply, byte divide
BX	Translate
CX	String operations, loops
CL	Variable shift and rotate
DX	Word multiply, word divide, indirect I/O
SP	Stack operations
SI	String operations
DI	String operations

The IF flag, when set, enables interrupts on the INTR input. The DF flag is used with string or block instructions. When DF is set, the memory pointer is decremented after each transfer; when DS is reset, the pointer is incremented.

Overflow is a new status flag. When set, it represents an error condition indicating that a mathematical operation has caused the sign bit to change.

Segment Registers

Although Fig. 12.4 shows the 1-MB address space of the 8086 as a linear sequence of 8-bit memory locations, the memory is not actually used in this way. Instead, only four 64K pages, or *segments,* are active at any given time. This arrangement is shown in Fig. 12.11. The four segment registers of the BIU are used as pointers to location 0 of each of four segments, called the *code, data, stack,* and *extra* segments.

With a segmented memory, the 8086 can devote the code segment to the program op codes, the data segment to program data, and the stack segment to the stack, keeping a fourth segment as an extra one.

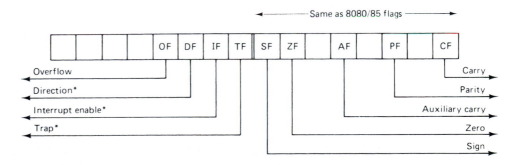

*These three flags can be set or reset to control the operation of the processor. The remaining flags are status indicators.

Figure 12.10   8086 flag word.

Sec. 12.3   **A Programming Model for the 8086**

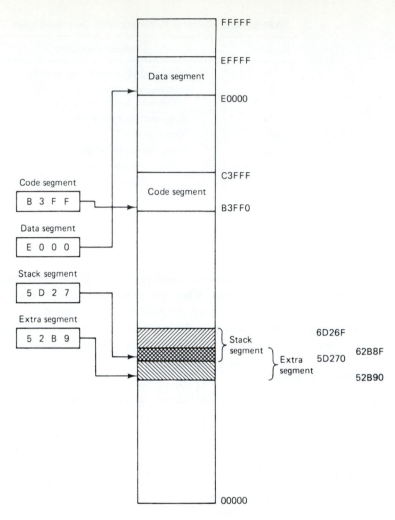

Figure 12.11 The full 1 MB of 8086 memory space is accessed in 64K-byte segments. Only four segments, determined by the segment registers in the BIU, are active at a given time.

The segment registers also allow the 16-bit EU registers to be used as memory pointers, even though the memory address is 20 bits long. The "trick" is to force the low 4 bits of the segment address to be 0. Thus, in Fig. 12.11, the code segment register contains B3FF, but should be interpreted as pointing to address B3FF0. Similarly, the extra segment register points to 52B90.

Example 12.2

Referring to Fig. 12.11, calculate the starting and ending addresses of the stack segment of memory.

Solution. We form the 20-bit address by appending four 0's to the stack segment register. The starting address is then 5D270. The last address can be found by adding FFFFH (that is, 64K). We have

$$\begin{array}{r} 5D270 \\ +\,0FFFF \\ \hline 6D26F \end{array}$$

The four 64K segments can be located anywhere within the 1-MB memory space of the 8086, but must begin at an address that is divisible by 16. (That is, the low 4 bits must be 0.) As Fig. 12.11 illustrates, the segments can be disjoint, partially overlapping, fully overlapping, or in any other order.

Because of the memory segmenting, there are two types of memory address associated with each program: the *logical address* and the *physical address*. The logical address ranges from 0 to 65535 (FFFFH) and corresponds to the 64K locations within one segment. In developing small programs, these are the only addresses that the programmer need worry about.

The physical address corresponds to the actual address output by the 8086 on the AD0–AD19 address lines. This address is formed by combining the logical address as an *offset* to the base segment address.

Example 12.3

If register SI = 0005H, what memory location will be accessed as the string source? Use the segment definitions shown in Fig. 12.11.

Solution. String operations work on data in the data segment. To calculate the string address, add the contents of register SI to the contents of the data segment register with four appended 0's:

$$\begin{array}{r} \text{DS} \rightarrow \text{E0000} \\ +\ \ 0005 \\ \hline \text{E0005} \end{array}$$

The byte will be fetched from physical address E0005H.

Once the segment registers have been loaded, the programmer need not be concerned with the physical address. In Example 12.3, the source of data is simply thought of as offset by 0005 locations from the start of the data segment (wherever that is in the physical address space).

Instruction fetches work in a similar manner. If register IP contains 2600, then, using the contents of the code segment register in Fig. 12.11, we see that the next fetch will come from

$$\begin{array}{r} \text{CS} \rightarrow \text{B3FF0} \\ +\ \ 2600 \\ \hline \text{B65F0} \end{array}$$

One of the advantages of the logical address concept is that programs can be dynamically relocated to run anywhere within the 1-MB address space of the processor. This is because *the logical address is always the same, no matter what the physical address*. This setup also is advantageous when one works with large data files with similar information: A whole new set of data can be operated on with the same program simply by changing the contents of the data segment register to the address of the new data file.

Just as all of the general registers have dedicated uses, depending on the instruction being executed (see Table 12.5), each type of physical memory reference has a dedicated segment register. The default segment assignments are shown in Table 12.6. For example, all instruction fetches use the code segment (CS), with the offset supplied by register IP. String sources are accessed from the data segment (DS), with register SI supplying the offset. String destinations are accessed with ES as the segment address and DI as the offset. Note that the segment register for some types of memory references can be changed from the default setting obtained at power-on.

Let us summarize what we know about the 8086's segmented memory:

1. The physical address is 20 bits long.
2. The logical address is 16 bits long.
3. The physical address is formed by adding the logical address as an offset to the segment address (with four appended 0's).
4. The segment address must begin at an address that is a multiple of 16.
5. The segment address will vary, depending on the segment register to be used.

In the remainder of this chapter, the term "offset" will mean the logical address within a particular 64K segment.

Addressing Modes

The 8086 expands on the four addressing modes of the 8080/85 (and six of the Z-80), to include the nine modes listed in Table 12.7. The table indicates where the data to be manipulated are obtained from or written to and which registers are involved. Also shown is a sample 8086 mnemonic and a symbolic interpretation of the instruction. For example, in the immediate addressing mode, the instruction MOV AX,1000H loads the AX register with the 16-bit word 1000H.

The first four addressing modes should be familiar from their 8080/85 and Z-80 equivalents. The *register indirect* mode is similar to the 8080/85's use of the HL pair, but the SI, DI, BX, or BP registers can be utilized. Instructions using the indexed addressing mode must supply a displacement in addition to the offset in the SI or DI pointer registers.

TABLE 12.6 Default Memory Segment Assignments for Each Type of Memory Reference

Type of memory reference	Default segment	Alternative segment	Offset (logical address)
Instruction fetch	CS	None	IP
Stack operation	SS	None	SP
Variable	DS	CS, ES, SS	Effective address
String (source)	DS	CS, ES, SS	SI
String (destination)	ES	None	DI
BP used as base register	SS	CS, ES, SS	Effective address

TABLE 12.7 Addressing Modes of the 8086 Microprocessor

Mode	Physical memory location	Examples (using MOV)	
		Mnemonic	Symbolic
Immediate	Within instruction + code segment	MOV AX,1000H	$10 \rightarrow$ AH $00 \rightarrow$ AL
Register	In register + code segment	MOV BX,DX	DL $\rightarrow$ BL DH $\rightarrow$ BH
Direct	Address + segment	MOV 8000H,BX	BL $\rightarrow$ (8000) BH $\rightarrow$ (8001)
Register indirect	SI + segment DI + segment BX + segment BP + segment	MOV CX,(BX)	(BX) $\rightarrow$ CL
Indexed	SI + displacement + segment DI + displacement + segment	MOV AL,(SI)+6	(SI+6) $\rightarrow$ AL
Relative	Displacement + IP + code segment	JMP target	Displacement + IP $\rightarrow$ IP
Based	BX + displacement + segment BP + displacement + segment	MOV (BX)+6,AL	AL $\rightarrow$ (BX + 6)
Based and indexed	BX + SI + segment BX + DI + segment BP + SI + segment BP + DI + segment	MOV DX,(BX+DI)	(BX+DI) $\rightarrow$ DL (BX+DI+1) $\rightarrow$ DH
Based and indexed with displacement	BX + SI + displ. + segment BX + DI + displ. + segment BP + SI + displ. + segment BP + DI + displ. + segment	MOV (BX+DI)+5,DX	DL $\rightarrow$ (BX+DI+5) DH $\rightarrow$ (BX+DI+6)

Notes:

1. All operands are of the form *destination, source.*

2. Parentheses indicate the contents of memory addressed by the operand.

3. In all cases, the operand specifies an offset that must be added to the contents of the proper segment register to form the physical address.

4. Table 12.6 indicates the default segment register to be used, depending on the type of memory reference.

The *relative* addressing mode is used with the transfer instructions to transfer control ahead of or behind the present location of the instruction pointer. This feature allows position-independent code within a given segment. Both the relative and indexed addressing modes are also supported by the Z-80.

The 8086 has three new addressing modes not available with the 8080/85 or Z-80. The *based mode* is similar to the indexed mode, but uses the BX or BP registers plus a displacement to locate the data. The *based-and-indexed mode* (without displacement) forms the offset by adding the contents of BX or BP to the contents of SI or DI. The offset is then combined with the contents of the segment register to form the physical address. The *based-and-indexed-with-displacement mode* is similar to the based-and-indexed mode, but allows the instruction to supply a displacement as well.

12.3.1 Explain the difference between 8086 registers AH, AL, and AX.

12.3.2 In which 8086 memory segment are the instruction codes stored?

12.3.3 Explain the difference between a logical address and a physical address.

12.3.4 The instruction MOV AX,(BP)+6 uses the _____ addressing mode and copies the word pointed to by register BP + 6 in the _____ segment to register AX.

12.4 PROGRAMMING THE 8086

Introduction

The mnemonics used in Table 12.7 give an indication of the form and complexity of the 8086 instruction set. The mnemonics themselves are similar to those of the 8080/85, but are more general purpose. For example, the 8086 *MOV* op code replaces such 8080/85 op-codes as *LXI, LDA, STA, MVI,* and *STAX.* This makes it simpler to form the desired instruction (somewhat like the Z-80 instruction set).

Because the 8080/85 registers can be considered a subset of the 8086 register set, it is possible to convert 8080/85 programs to run on the 8086 using a *translator*—i.e., a program that accepts 8080/85 assembly code and outputs 8086 assembly code. The resulting programs are not as efficient as, and require more memory than, an 8086 program designed specifically for the purpose. However, the translator offers a quick way of upgrading large numbers of 8080/85 programs to the more powerful 8086.

Among the new operations possible with the 8086 that were not available with the 8080/85 are the following:

1. Byte and word multiplication and division instructions
2. Block moves and comparisons
3. Byte translations
4. Software interrupts
5. Program loop instructions (for example, loop until zero)
6. Multiprocessor or coprocessor coordination
7. Nondestructive bit testing

Because of the large number of instructions and addressing modes (there are over 1000 different variations of the 8086 instruction set), hand assembly of 8086 programs is extremely tedious. Serious work should be attempted only with an editor and 8086 assembler.

In this section, we:

• List and briefly describe the various 8086 processor instruction groups.
• Write a simple 8086 program to fill a block of memory.

Data Transfer Group

Table 12.8 lists the form of the instructions in the data transfer group. In general, each instruction could use any of the addressing modes listed in Table 12.7 (except relative

TABLE 12.8 Data Transfer Group of Instructions

General mnemonic	Sample	Description of operation
MOV dest,source	MOV DS,AX	Put a copy of AX in DS
PUSH source	PUSH BX	Push BX onto top of stack
POP dest	POP ES	Pop top of stack into ES
PUSHF	Same[a]	Push flags onto top of stack
POPF	Same[a]	Pop top of stack into flag register
XCHG op1,op2	XCHG AL,BL	Exchange contents of AL and BL
LAHF	Same[a]	Copy 8080/85 flags into AH
SAHF	Same[a]	Copy AH into the 8080/85 flags
IN acc,port	IN AL,DX (indirect)	Input a byte to AL from the port whose address is in DX
OUT port,acc	OUT 27H,AX (direct)	Output AX to ports 27H and 28H
LEA dest,source	LEA DX,TABLE	Load DX with the address of TABLE
LDS dest,source	LDS DX,TABLE	Load DX with (TABLE) and (TABLE+1) Load DS with (TABLE+2) and (TABLE+3)
LES dest,source	LES CX,TABLE	Load CX with (TABLE) and (TABLE+1) Load ES with (TABLE+2) and (TABLE+3)
XLAT	XLAT TABLE	AL is replaced with (BX+AL)

[a]Use the general mnemonic.

addressing). The MOV instructions allow 8- or 16-bit data to be moved between registers or between memory and the CPU registers. Note that the segment registers are loaded in this way.

The XCHG command is similar to the 8080/85 instruction XCHG, but can be used to exchange 8- or 16-bit registers or an 8-bit register with a memory location.

LAHF and SAHF allow the 8086 to access the 8080/85 flag word directly, assisting in the conversion of these programs to the 8086.

The 8086, like the 8080/85, has only two I/O instructions. However, these instructions may be used in two ways. In the *direct* mode, the I/O instructions are similar to those of the 8080/85, inputting or outputting 8- or 16-bit data from register AL or AX to the 8-bit port or consecutive ports whose address is carried by AD0–AD7. In the *indirect* mode, register DX is used to hold a 16-bit port address, and data may again be 8 or 16 bits wide. This mode can accommodate up to 65,536 unique I/O ports. Data is still required to flow through the accumulator, however. A significant advantage of the indirect mode is that the port address can be changed by the program [unlike the situation with the 8080/85, but similar to the Z-80's OUT (C),r].

There are three load commands that can be used to fill CPU registers with the addresses or contents of memory locations. LDS and LES are 32-bit load operations, filling the ES or DS segment registers and a general register. LEA loads the destination operand with the *address* of the source operand.

The XLAT instruction uses register AL as an 8-bit offset pointer into a table with base address in BX. The byte that is found replaces the byte in register AL.

Arithmetic Group

Table 12.9 summarizes the arithmetic group of instructions. Addition and subtraction (with and without a carry or borrow) are similar to the 8080/85 addition and subtraction instructions, but work on 8- or 16-bit data. Note that the accumulator does not have to be used as the destination or source of data.

The INC and DEC instructions are also similar to their counterparts in the 8080/85. Because the 16-bit increments (or decrements) affect all flags, 16-bit counters can easily be tested for 0 (unlike the 8080/85's INX or DCX instructions).

TABLE 12.9 Arithmetic Group of Instructions

General mnemonic	Sample	Description of operation
ADD dest, source	ADD DX,BX	Replace DX with DX + BX
ADC dest,source	ADC DX,BX	Replace DX with DX+BX+CF
SUB dest,source	SUB CX,1000H	Replace CX with CX−1000H
SBB dest,source	SBB CX,1000H	Replace CX with CX−1000H−CF
INC dest	INC DI	Replace DI with DI+1 (flags affected)
DEC dest	DEC CL	Replace CL with CL−1
NEG dest	NEG AX	Replace AX with the two's complement of AX; set OF if AX = 8000H or 0080H
CMP dest,source	CMP AX,BX	Set flag based on AX−BX
MUL source	MUL BX	Unsigned multiply—BX times AX; store the result in DX and AX
IMUL source	IMUL BX	Signed multiply—BX times AX; store the result in DX and AX
DIV source	DIV BX	Unsigned division—DX,AX by BX; store the result in AX and the remainder in DX
IDIV source	IDIV BX	Signed division—DX,AX by BX; store the result in AX and the remainder in DX
CBW	Same[a]	Convert signed AL byte to signed AX word
CWD	Same[a]	Convert signed word in AX to signed double word in AX,DX
DAA	Same[a]	Adjust AL after the addition of two packed BCD numbers
DAS	Same[a]	Adjust AL after the subtraction of two packed BCD numbers
AAA	Same[a]	Adjust AL after the addition of two unpacked BCD numbers
AAS	Same[a]	Adjust AL after the subtraction of two unpacked BCD numbers
AAM	Same[a]	Adjust AX after the multiplication of two unpacked BCD numbers
AAD	Same[a]	Adjust AX after the division of two unpacked BCD numbers

[a]Use the general mnemonic.

The multiplication and division instructions require specific registers for one of the operands and the result, as shown in Fig. 12.12. Either signed or unsigned operations are possible on 8- or 16-bit data. It is interesting to note that a 5-MHz 8086 8-bit multiplication will require approximately 16 μs. The Z-80 8-bit multiplication routine developed as Program 5 in Chapter 3 requires approximately 100 μs (at 4 MHz).

The CBW and CWD instructions are used with the multiplication and division instructions to extend signed bytes into words and signed words into double words, maintaining the proper sign.

The decimal adjust instructions are used after addition and subtraction instructions to ensure that register AL contains a valid BCD number.

The ASCII adjustment instructions work with unpacked BCD numbers (one digit per byte). These instructions are used after any of the four mathematical operations to adjust the accumulator to an unpacked BCD number with the most significant four bits as zeros.

Bit Manipulation Group

This group includes the logical NOT, AND, OR, and XOR instructions, as shown in Table 12.10. The operations are performed bit by bit and can specify 8- or 16-bit operands. As with the mathematical operations, neither the source nor the destination need be the accumulator.

The TEST instruction is a nondestructive AND that sets the flags on the basis of the result.

The shift instructions shift the contents of a register or memory location, but without wraparound. The rotate instructions are circular, and the carry flag can be included. A unique feature of these instructions is that the number of rotations or shifts can be programmed in register CL, allowing up to 255 shifts or rotations with one instruction.

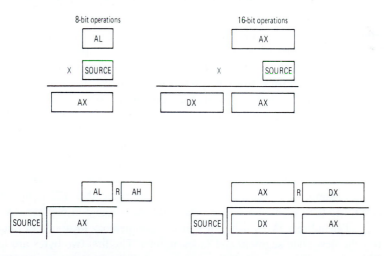

Figure 12.12   The multiplication and division instructions require one of the operands and the result to be in dedicated registers.

TABLE 12.10 Bit Manipulation Group of Instructions

General mnemonic	Sample	Description of operation
NOT dest	NOT BX	Replace BX with $\overline{\text{BX}}$
AND dest,source	AND BX,CX	Replace BX with the bit-by-bit result of BX·CX
OR dest,source	OR DL,80H	Replace DL with the bit-by-bit result of DL+80H
XOR dest,source	XOR SI,SI	Replace SI with the bit-by-bit result of SI + SI (in this case, clear SI)
TEST dest,source	TEST BX, 8000H	AND BX bit by bit with 8000H and set the flags accordingly—BX does not change
SHR dest,count	SHR AX	Shift AX logically right CX times—zeros are shifted in on the left
SAR dest,count	SAR BX	Shift BX arithmetic right CX times—bits equal to the original high-order bit are shifted in on the left
SHL/SAL dest,count	SHL BL	Shift BL left CX times—zeros are shifted in on the right
ROR dest,count	ROR DX	Rotate DX right CX times
RCR dest,count	RCR AH	Rotate AH right through the carry CX times
ROL dest,count	ROL (BX)	Rotate (BX) left CX times
RCL dest,count	RCL BX	Rotate BX left through the carry CX times

Transfer Group

The 8086 fetches instructions from memory using CS as the segment register and IP as the offset. The transfer group of instructions allows these two registers to be changed under program control. Table 12.11 lists the instructions in this group.

Two types of JMP instruction are possible. In the *direct* mode, the instruction supplies the JMP address. In the *indirect* mode, a general register holds the address. Direct-mode JMPs can be *short, near,* or *far.* Short JMPs supply an 8-bit displacement that is added to register IP to form the new address. This allows transfers up to 127 bytes ahead or 128 bytes backward from the present value of IP.

Near JMPs supply a 16-bit displacement, allowing a transfer up to +32,767 bytes or −32,768 bytes relative to register IP.

Far JMPs are a third type of direct JMP, requiring five instruction bytes: one for the op code, two for the new value of IP, and two for the new value of CS. This is the only (direct) JMP that allows you to move to a new code segment.

Indirect JMPs can be near or far. A near indirect JMP uses one of the general registers to supply a 16-bit offset. Thus, the mnemonic JMP BX is interpreted as "Transfer control to the instruction whose offset address is found in register BX."

Far indirect JMPs use four consecutive memory locations (a double word) to identify the new code segment and index pointer. The first two bytes are loaded into register IP, the second two into the CS register.

TABLE 12.11 Transfer Group of Instructions

General mnemonic	Sample	Description of operation
JMP JMPS, JMPF target	Same[a]	Transfer control to the address specified by target (short, near, or far jump)
Jcond target	JNZ target	IFZF = 0, transfer control to the address specified by target (short jump only)
LOOP target	Same[a]	Decrement CX and transfer control to the address specified by target if CX ≠ 0; else continue (short jump only)
LOOPE/LOOPZ target	Same[a]	Decrement CX and transfer control to the address specified by target if CX ≠ 0 and ZF is set (short jump only)
LOOPNE/LOOPNZ target	Same[a]	Decrement CX and transfer control to the address specified by target if CX ≠ 0 and ZF is reset
JCXZ target	Same[a]	If CX = 0, transfer control to the address specified by target
CALL, CALLF target	Same[a]	Push IP (and CS for a far CALL) onto the stack, and transfer control to the address specified by target (near or far CALL only)
RET, RETF optional value	RET 4	POP the top of the stack into IP (and CS for a far CALL), and add 4 to SP
INT type	INT 1	Transfer control to the address stored in 1 × 4 = 00004 through 00007; push IP and the flags onto the stack
INTO	Same[a]	If the OF flag is set, transfer control to the address stored in 00010 through 00013
IRET	Same[a]	POP the top of the stack into the flags, IP, and CS

[a]Use the general mnemonic.

A number of conditional JMPs can also be specified, as indicated in Table 12.12. Note that all of these instructions are *short direct* jumps and that most instructions have two mnemonics saying the same thing—for example, "Jump if greater than" or "Jump if not less than or equal to."

Similar to the Z-80 instruction DJNZ, the LOOP instruction transfers control to the target address until register CX is 0. The conditional loop instructions transfer control if CX ≠ 0 and the specified condition is met.

The JCXZ instruction should be used before a LOOP command when the contents of CX are unknown. If this is not done and CX = 0, 65,536 loops could occur until the instruction is completed.

The CALL instruction can be near (within the current segment) or far (outside the current segment). It can also be direct (address in an instruction) or indirect (address in a register). The far version requires that 4 bytes be pushed onto the stack, saving register IP and CS. The RET instruction must also be near or far, so that the data on the stack is handled correctly. RET instructions can specify an optional number, for instance, as in RET5. This value is added to register SP after CS and IP are popped to form the stack address. RET allows parameters to be passed onto the stack and then discarded after the subroutine has been executed.

TABLE 12.12 Conditional-Transfer Group of Instructions

Mnemonic	Condition
Signed operations	
JG/JNLE	Greater/not less or equal ((SF + OF) + ZF) = 0
JGE/JNL	Greater or equal/not less (SF + OF) = 0
JL/JNGE	Less/not greater or equal (SF + OF) = 1
JLE/JNG	Less or equal/not greater ((SF + OF) + ZF) = 1
JO	Overflow (OF = 1)
JS	Sign (SF = 1)
JNO	Not overflow (OF = 0)
JNS	Not sign (SF = 0)
Unsigned operations	
JA/JNBE	Above/not below or equal (CF + ZF) = 0
JAE/JNB	Above or equal/not below (CF = 0)
JB/JNAE	Below/not above or equal (CF = 1)
JBE/JNA	Below or equal/not above (CF + ZF) = 1
Either	
JC	Carry (CF = 1)
JE/JZ	Equal/zero (ZF = 1)
JP/JPE	Parity/parity even (PF = 1)
JNC	Not carry (CF = 0)
JNE/JNZ	Not equal/not zero (ZF = 0)
JNP/JPO	Not parity/parity odd (PF = 0)

Interrupts

The 8086 has three sources of interrupts:

1. Hardware
2. Software
3. The processor

Regardless of the source, all interrupts must furnish an 8-bit type number. This number is multiplied by 4 by the 8086 to determine the interrupt service routine (ISR) address from a 1K-byte table beginning at address 00000. Figure 12.13 shows this interrupt-pointer table. Note that each entry in the table is 4 bytes long to accommodate a new instruction pointer and a new code segment.

Hardware-initiated interrupts can be maskable, like INTR, or nonmaskable, like NMI. Maskable interrupts supply an 8-bit type number during INTA and can be masked by resetting the IF bit in the flag register. Nonmaskable interrupts automatically generate a type 2 interrupt. (That is, the address of the ISR is assumed to be stored in locations 00008–0000B.) This interrupt cannot be masked.

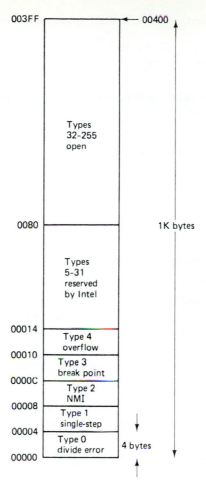

Figure 12.13 The interrupt-pointer table reserves 4 bytes of memory for each of 256 type numbers. Note that some of the type numbers are reserved for future use by Intel Corp.

Software interrupts are given with the *INT type* instruction, causing control to be transferred to the address stored in the appropriate table entry. INTO is a special software interrupt instruction that will cause a type 4 interrupt if an overflow condition exists; if not, control proceeds to the next instruction.

The 8086 will generate a type 0 interrupt if a divide error occurs (such as division by 0 or a result too large for the destination register). If the TF flag is set, the 8086 will generate a type 1 interrupt after each instruction. This can be used for debugging purposes.

The op code for a type 3 interrupt is a single byte, allowing this special software interrupt to be used as a "break point." In practice, you would place an INT 3 instruction at a test point in your program, causing control to transfer to a routine in which the CPU registers could be examined. The process is then repeated, moving the break point farther into the program until all bugs have been found.

Regardless of the source of the interrupt, the processor will push the 16-bit flag word, the CS segment register, and register IP onto the stack when the interrupt occurs.

Because the flags are included, the special IRET instruction must be used to terminate the ISR.

String Group

Table 12.13 lists the instructions in the string, or block, group. Three basic operations are possible:

1. Move a byte or a word from one location to another.
2. Compare a byte or a word in one memory location with that in another.
3. Scan and compare the contents of memory with the contents of the accumulator.

Instructions in this group use the following registers for dedicated functions:

1. DS and SI for the physical source address
2. ES and DI for the physical destination address
3. CX as a repetition counter
4. The accumulator for the value to be scanned, the destination for load operations, and the source for store operations

The REP prefix in front of MOVSB/MOVSW, LODSB/LODSW, or STOSB/STOSW will cause the instruction to repeat until CX = 0. The direction flag (DF) deter-

TABLE 12.13 String Group of Instructions

General mnemonic	Sample	Description of operation
MOVSB/MOVSW	MOVSB	Move the byte or word pointed at by SI and DS to the memory location pointed at by DI and ES. Increment SI and DI if DF = 0, else decrement these registers.
CMPSB/CMPSW	CMPSW	Compare the byte or word pointed at by SI and DS to the word pointed at by DI and ES. Increment SI and DI if DF = 0, else decrement these registers.
SCASB/SCASW	SCASB	Compare AL or AX with the contents of the memory location pointed at by DI and ES. Increment DI if DF = 0, else decrement DI.
LODSB/LODSW	LODSW	Load the sequential bytes or words pointed at by SI and DS to AX. Increment SI if DF = 0, else decrement SI.
STOSB/STOSW	STOSB	Store AL or AX at the memory location pointed at by DI and ES. Increment DI if DF = 0, else decrement DI.
REP	REP MOVSW	Repeat MOVSW until CX = 0
REPE/REPZ	REPZ CMPSW	Repeat CMPSW until CX = 0 or the memory locations do not compare
REPNE/REPNZ	REPNZ SCASB	Repeat SCASB until CX = 0 or a match is found

mines whether the pointer registers are incremented or decremented. Using prefix REP, entire blocks of data can be moved with a single instruction.

REPE and REPNE can be used with CPMSB/CMPSW and SCASB/SCASW and will cause the instruction to repeat until CX = 0 or a match is or is not found. When the loop terminates, the flags can be tested to determine whether a match was found.

Processor Control Group

The processor control instructions are shown in Table 12.14. These instructions primarily allow various flags to be set or reset.

The ESC and LOCK instructions are used with the 8087 NDP coprocessor. Commands intended for the 8087 are prefixed by an ESC, alerting the 8087 to read the next instruction. In the meantime, the 8086 goes on to the instructions that follow. When the 8087 result is needed by the 8086, it executes a WAIT instruction, idling until its $\overline{\text{TEST}}$ input, driven by the 8087, is found low, indicating that the result is ready. The NDP stores the result in memory by requesting control of the buses (via $\overline{\text{RQ}}/\overline{\text{GT0}}$) and performing a direct memory access.

Any instruction preceded by LOCK has total control of the system buses during its activities. This prevents the 8089 or 8087 processors from reading or writing data to a block of RAM that the 8086 is updating.

An Example: Two 8086 Block Fill Programs

So that we might gain some appreciation of how the 8086 is programmed, we will develop two 8086 programs for filling a block of memory with a constant. This operation might be required to initialize a block of memory or clear a memory-mapped video screen.

TABLE 12.14 Processor Control Group of Instructions

General mnemonic	Description of operation
STC	Set carry flag
CLC	Clear carry flag
CMC	Complement carry flag
STD	Set direction flag
CLD	Clear direction flag
STI	Set interrupt-enable flag
CLI	Clear interrupt-enable flag
HLT	Halt until interrupted or reset
WAIT	Idle until the $\overline{\text{TEST}}$ input = 0
ESC	Escape to external processor
LOCK	Lock buses during next instruction
NOP	No operation

The block fill problem was first solved with the 8080/85 and Z-80 as Program 7 in Chapter 3. The 8080/85 solution appears in Fig. 3.13 and the Z-80 solution in Fig. 3.14. The objective of the program is to fill a block of memory (up to 64K bytes) with a special character. The starting address of the block is assumed to be stored in a memory location called *START*. The number of bytes in the block is stored in another memory location, called *BYTES*. The byte to be written is stored in a third memory location, called *FILL*.

Figure 12.14 shows how the memory is assumed to be organized for the problem. The physical addresses of the segments do not matter; however, the block to be filled is assumed to be within the data segment. The DI register will be used as the destination pointer. This presents a problem because DI is normally the offset for the ES segment. (See Table 12.6.) The problem can easily be overcome by making ES = DS.

Figure 12.15(a) shows version 1 of the 8086 block fill program. The PUSH DS, POP ES sequence makes ES = DS for the reasons just mentioned. Next, AL, CX, and DI are loaded with the program variables. The contents of AL are then written to the desti-

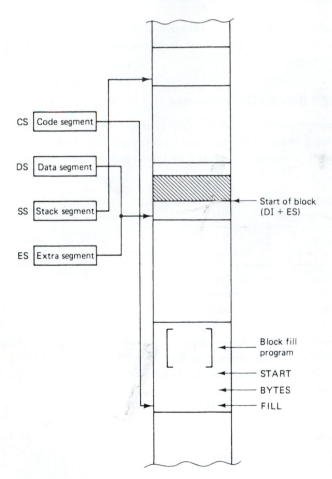

Figure 12.14 Memory usage for the 8086 block fill programs in Fig. 12.15.

```
;8086 BLOCK FILL PROGRAM - VERSION 1
;
;THE BLOCK TO BE FILLED IS CONTAINED WITHIN
;THE DATA SEGMENT
;
        PUSH    DS                  ;ES IS THE DESTINATION SEGMENT
        POP     ES                  ;EQUATE IT WITH DS
        ;
        MOV     AL,FILL             ;AL HOLDS THE CHARACTER
        MOV     CX,BYTES            ;CX IS THE BYTE COUNTER
        MOV     DI,START            ;DI HOLDS THE BLOCK ADDRESS
        ;
AGAIN   MOV     (DI),AL             ;WRITE BYTE
        INC     DI                  ;ADVANCE MEMORY POINTER
        LOOP    AGAIN               ;CONTINUE UNTIL CX=0
        HLT
        ;
START   DW      NNNN                ;PUT STARTING ADDRESS HERE
BYTES   DW      NNNN                ;PUT NUMBER OF BYTES HERE
FILL    DB      NN                  ;PUT FILL CHARACTER HERE
                        (a)


;8086 BLOCK FILL PROGRAM - VERSION 2
;
        PUSH    DS                  ;AGAIN ES MUST BE
        POP     ES                  ;EQUATED TO DS
        ;
        MOV     AL,FILL             ;AL HOLDS THE CHARACTER
        MOV     CX,BYTES            ;CX IS THE BYTE COUNTER
        MOV     DI,START            ;DI HOLDS THE BLOCK ADDRESS
        ;
        CLD                         ;DIRECTION = INCREMENT
        REP STOSB                   ;WRITE BYTE, INCREMENT DI,
                                    ;DECREMENT CX, REPEAT UNTIL
                                    ;CX=0
        HLT
        ;
START   DW      NNNN                ;PUT STARTING ADDRESS HERE
BYTES   DW      NNNN                ;PUT NUMBER OF BYTES HERE
FILL    DB      NN                  ;PUT FILL CHARACTER HERE
                        (b)
```

Figure 12.15 (a) Version 1 of the 8086 block fill program, using the LOOP instruction; (b) version 2, using the REP and STOSB instructions.

nation address, DI is incremented, and the LOOP instruction is used to decrement the counter (CX) automatically and transfer control back to location AGAIN until all bytes have been written.

Figure 12.15(b) is version 2 of the same program, which is essentially the same as version 1, but uses the STOSB instruction and the REP prefix to automatically write the byte, decrement the CX counter, and increment the DI pointer until CX = 0.

Comparing the four versions of this program, we see that the 8080/85 routine requires 14 instructions, the Z-80 requires 7, version 1 for the 8086 requires 9, and version 2 requires 8.

The 8086 does not compare as well as we might think it should. This is due to the instructions that are required to get the segment registers pointing to the right locations, load the dedicated registers for the LOOP and STOSB instructions, and, finally, fill the block.

SELF-REVIEW 12.4

12.4.1 The indirect I/O instructions use register _____ to hold a 16-bit I/O port address.

12.4.2 Which CPU registers store the result of the instruction MUL BX?

12.4.3 Which type of jump instruction is required to transfer control to a program in a different code segment?

12.4.4 What is a software interrupt?

12.5 8086 MEMORY AND I/O INTERFACING

Introduction

Although the 8086 has a 16-bit data bus, it is capable of accessing memory (and its I/O devices) as bytes or words. The A0 address line and $\overline{BHE}$ control signal define the type of access that will occur, as was shown in Table 12.1.

In this section, we:

- Show how to interface a 32K-byte memory to the 8086.
- Show how to interface the 8255A PPI chip to the 8086.

Interfacing a 32K-Byte Memory

Figure 12.16 illustrates a 32K-byte memory using 16K × 1 static RAM chips. The memory is organized as two banks of 16K bytes. RAMs 0–7 supply the even-addressed byte and RAMs 8–15 supply the odd-addressed byte. By selecting both banks simultaneously, a 16-bit word can be read.

Example 12.4

For what range of addresses will the signal $\overline{\text{MEM SEL}}$ in Fig. 12.16 be active?

Solution. The address decoder consists of IC1 and IC2 and tests address lines AB15–AB19. These lines must all be low for $\overline{\text{MEM SEL}}$ to be active. The range of addresses is thus

$$0000\ 0XXX\ XXXX\ XXXX\ XXXX$$

or 00000H–07FFFH. This corresponds to the low 32K bytes of the first 64K segment in the 1-MB address space.

The $\overline{\text{MEM SEL}}$ signal is combined with AB0 and $\overline{BHE}$ to form the even- and odd-byte-select signals. This arrangement is consistent with the decoding of A0 and $\overline{BHE}$ in Table 12.1. Note that because of the even/odd bank arrangement, each bank stores every other byte. For example, the even bank stores bytes 0, 2, 4, 6, . . . , 32,764, 32,766.

The 2167 RAMs have separate data-in and -out pins and the 74LS244 buffers (IC4–7) convert these lines into a bidirectional bus. Note that the buffers must also be separated into an even bank and an odd bank and can be enabled only if the address matches and a memory read or memory write cycle is taking place. (This feature ensures that the memory interface is not enabled by an I/O address.)

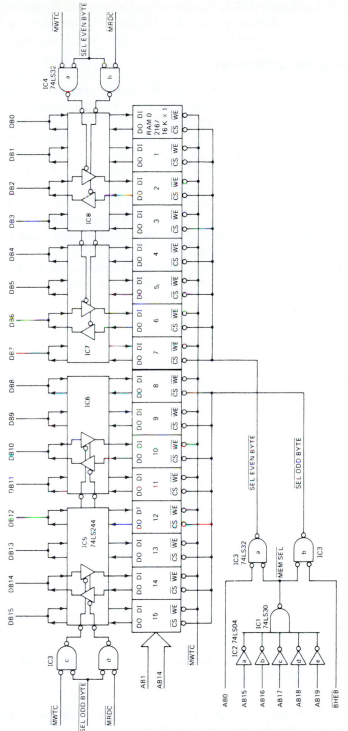

Figure 12.16 Max-mode 32K-byte 8086 memory module.

Although not shown, all of the control and address bus signals are assumed to be buffered as they enter the memory module. The control signals shown are for a max-mode system, but the module could be redesigned for a min mode if desired.

Interfacing the 8255A PPI

The 8086 I/O operations may transfer 8- or 16-bit data quantities. The particular instruction used determines the number of bits to be input or output. Again, A0 and $\overline{\text{BHE}}$ are utilized to determine the byte or word selected.

Because of the byte input/output capability, all of the 8080/85 support devices discussed in Chapter 7 can be used with the 8086. This is an important point; there is no need to redesign the PPI, PIT, or USART to accommodate the 16-bit 8086. By exchanging bytes with these devices, they can be used directly.

Figure 12.17 shows an I/O interface between the 8086 max-mode CPU module and two 8255As. This design will allow 16 bits of data to be exchanged between an I/O device and the 8086. Be sure to note, however, that a single 8255A could also be interfaced if 8-bit I/O operations were sufficient.

The port decoding is similar to the memory interface in the last section, using AB0 and $\overline{\text{BHE}}$ to select an even set of ports and an odd set of ports. IC1 and IC2 determine the specific port address.

Example 12.5

Determine the 8255A port addresses in Fig. 12.17 for *direct* I/O instructions and for *indirect* I/O instructions.

Solution. The direct I/O instructions supply an 8-bit fixed address as part of the instruction on AB0–AB7. The decoding in Fig. 12.17 will cause $\overline{\text{PORT SEL}}$ to be active over the range. Thus,

$$\text{AB7–AB0} = 00000\text{XXX} = 00\text{H} - 07\text{H}$$

IC3 combines the $\overline{\text{PORT SEL}}$ signal with AB0 and $\overline{\text{BHE}}$ to produce $\overline{\text{EVEN PORT SEL}}$ and $\overline{\text{ODD PORT SEL}}$. There will be four combinations of each of these signals, because they do not include AB1 and AB2. For example, $\overline{\text{EVEN PORT SEL}}$ will be active if the direct port address is 0, 2, 4, or 6. Similarly, $\overline{\text{ODD PORT SEL}}$ will be active if the direct port address is 1, 3, 5, or 7.

Because AB1 and AB2 are used to select one of four ports within the 8255, the four combinations of the $\overline{\text{EVEN PORT SEL}}$ and $\overline{\text{ODD PORT SEL}}$ signals correspond to ports A, B, and C and the control port of the 8255A. This is shown more clearly in Table 12.15.

When indirect I/O instructions are given, register DX is used to hold a 16-bit port address. Because AB8–AB15 are not decoded in Fig. 12.17, this circuit is only *partially decoded* for indirect I/O instructions. This means that, in addition to ports 0–7, ports 0100H–0107H, 0200H–0207H, . . . , FF00H–FF07H will all respond to indirect I/O instructions.

Normally, both 8255As would be programmed identically, allowing 16-bit data transfers with the I/O device.

Example 12.6

Write the 8086 initialization routine required to program both 8255As in Fig. 12.17 for mode 0 with port A an output and ports B and C inputs.

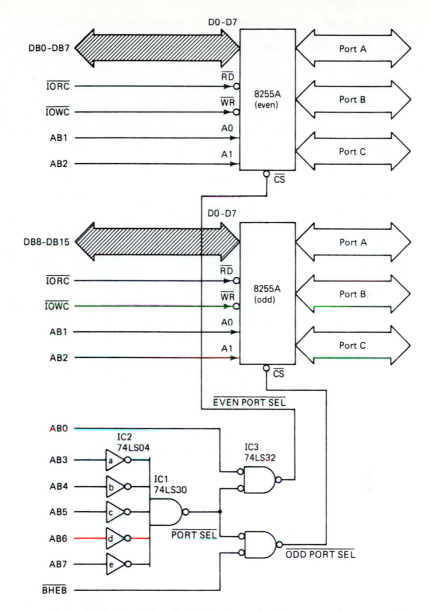

Figure 12.17 Interfacing the 8255A PPI to the 8086 max-mode CPU module. Two 8255As are required for 16-bit I/O operations.

Solution. The direct or indirect mode can be employed. By using register AX, both PPI chips can be programmed simultaneously. The program is as follows:

```
MOV     DX,0006H        ;DX POINTS TO THE EVEN CONTROL PORT
MOV     AX,8B8BH        ;CONTROL WORD DUPLICATED IN AL AND AH
OUT     DX,AX           ;WRITE AL TO EVEN PPI AND AH TO ODD PPI
```

TABLE 12.15 8255 Port Addresses for the Interface in Fig. 12.17

AB7–AB3	AB2	AB1	AB0	BHE	Port	Description	Comment
00000	0	0	0	1	0	Port A	Even port on
00000	0	1	0	1	2	Port B	DB0–DB7
00000	1	0	0	1	4	Port C	
00000	1	1	0	1	6	Control port	
00000	0	0	1	0	1	Port A	Odd port on
00000	0	1	1	0	3	Port B	DB8–DB15
00000	1	0	1	0	5	Port C	
00000	1	1	1	0	7	Control port	
00000	0	0	0	0	0 and 1	Port A	Even port
00000	0	1	0	0	2 and 3	Port B	on DB0–DB7
00000	1	0	0	0	4 and 5	Port C	and odd port
00000	1	1	0	0	6 and 7	Control port	on DB8–DB15

Note that when the OUT DX,AX instruction is executed, AB0 and $\overline{\text{BHE}}$ will both be low, enabling the control port of both 8255As simultaneously.

Example 12.7

Write an 8086 program to input a byte from port B of the even PPI chip and output this byte to port A of the odd PPI chip in Fig. 12.17.

Solution.　The program is very simple:

```
IN   AL,02    ;READ PORT B OF THE EVEN PPI
OUT  01,AL    ;WRITE THE BYTE TO PORT A OF THE ODD PPI
```

Note that the contents of AL are automatically put on AD8–AD15 for the odd port address.

SELF-REVIEW 12.5

12.5.1　What signals are provided by the 8086 to allow selection of the even and odd memory banks?

12.5.2　Will the 8086 operate successfully with only an even or only an odd bank of memory?

12.5.3　Is it necessary to interface 8-bit I/O chips like the 8255A in pairs, so that even and odd I/O ports are provided?

12.6 THE 80x86 FAMILY OF MICROPROCESSORS

Introduction

As mentioned in the overview of this chapter, the 8086 is a "stepping-off" point. Behind, it leaves the 8-bit 8080 and 8085 microprocessors: ahead, it leads the way to the more powerful 80286, the 32-bit 80386 and 80486, and the 64-bit Pentium processors.

In this section, we:

- Compare the various processors in the 80x86 family, including the 8088, 80286, 80386, 80486, Pentium, Pentium Pro, and Pentium II.
- Explain what is meant by the term *superscaler processor*.

The 8088

In 1979, when Intel first introduced the 8086, the microcomputer industry had not yet standardized a particular CPU. The CP/M operating system was popular on S-100 machines, the Apple II Plus was becoming a standard in the education market, and Tandy was announcing an improved version of its TRS-80 computer based on the Z-80. There didn't seem to be a place for the new 16-bit chip.

Someone at Intel then came up with a clever idea: Why not design an *8-bit* version of the 8086? Externally, it would have an 8-bit data bus, appearing very similar to the 8085 electrically. But internally, it would be an 8086. That is, all of the CPU registers would be 16 bits wide, and the chip would execute the complete instruction set of the 8086. Thus was born the 8088 microprocessor.

You might wonder, "Why an 8-bit 8086?" One advantage of the 8-bit data bus is the fact that memory can be added 8 bits at a time, instead of 16, as is required by the even/odd memory bank arrangement of the 8086. With 64K memory chips selling for $10–$20 apiece at the time, this was a significant consideration.

Figure 12.18 compares the pinouts for the 8088 and 8086. The two chips are identical, except for the following features:

1. Address lines A8–A15 are not multiplexed on the 8088.
2. The 8088 data bus is just 8 bits wide (AD0–AD7).
3. There is no need for the $\overline{\text{BHE}}$ signal on the 8088; it is replaced by SS0, a status signal.
4. M/$\overline{\text{IO}}$ of the 8086 is changed to IO/$\overline{\text{M}}$ on the 8088 (for compatibility with the 8085).

When operated in the min mode, the bus structure of the 8088 is identical to that of the 8085. Because of this, all of the 8085 peripherals, such as the 8755A 16K EPROM with I/O and the 8155 2K RAM with timer and parallel I/O, are directly compatible with the 8088. This feature allows a min-mode 8088 microcomputer system to be built with only a few ICs.

The 8088's bus timing is essentially the same as that of the 8086, except that four additional T states are required when fetching 16-bit operands. This causes the 8088 to be somewhat slower than the 8086. Both processors are object code compatible, so programs written for one chip will run without changes on the other.

In 1981, IBM selected the 8088 as the CPU chip for its new family of PCs. And, as they say, the rest is history.

The 80286

The 80286 is a more powerful version of the 8086 and was used by IBM in its advanced technology (AT) computer in 1984. Like the 8086, the 80286 has a 16-bit data bus, but its

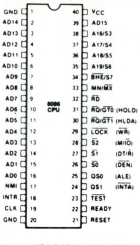

GND	1	40	Vcc
AD14	2	39	AD15
AD13	3	38	A16/S3
AD12	4	37	A17/S4
AD11	5	36	A18/S5
AD10	6	35	A19/S6
AD9	7	34	$\overline{BHE}$/S7
AD8	8	33	MN/$\overline{MX}$
AD7	9	32	$\overline{RD}$
AD6	10	31	$\overline{RQ}/\overline{GT0}$ (HOLD)
AD5	11	30	$\overline{RQ}/\overline{GT1}$ (HLDA)
AD4	12	29	$\overline{LOCK}$ ($\overline{WR}$)
AD3	13	28	$\overline{S2}$ (M/$\overline{IO}$)
AD2	14	27	$\overline{S1}$ (DT/$\overline{R}$)
AD1	15	26	$\overline{S0}$ ($\overline{DEN}$)
AD0	16	25	QS0 (ALE)
NMI	17	24	QS1 ($\overline{INTA}$)
INTR	18	23	$\overline{TEST}$
CLK	19	22	READY
GND	20	21	RESET

8086 CPU

40 LEAD

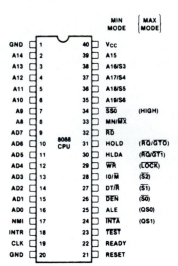

		MIN MODE	MAX MODE
GND	1	40	Vcc
A14	2	39	A15
A13	3	38	A16/S3
A12	4	37	A17/S4
A11	5	36	A18/S5
A10	6	35	A19/S6
A9	7	34	$\overline{SS0}$ (HIGH)
A8	8	33	MN/$\overline{MX}$
AD7	9	32	$\overline{RD}$
AD6	10	31	HOLD ($\overline{RQ}/\overline{GT0}$)
AD5	11	30	HLDA ($\overline{RQ}/\overline{GT1}$)
AD4	12	29	$\overline{WR}$ ($\overline{LOCK}$)
AD3	13	28	IO/$\overline{M}$ ($\overline{S2}$)
AD2	14	27	DT/$\overline{R}$ ($\overline{S1}$)
AD1	15	26	$\overline{DEN}$ ($\overline{S0}$)
AD0	16	25	ALE (QS0)
NMI	17	24	$\overline{INTA}$ (QS1)
INTR	18	23	$\overline{TEST}$
CLK	19	22	READY
GND	20	21	RESET

8088 CPU

Figure 12.18   8086 and 8088 microprocessor pinouts. (Courtesy of Intel Corporation.)

address bus has been expanded to 24 bits. Two programming modes are provided: *real mode* and *protected mode*. When first powered on, the 80286 (or, simply, *286*) comes up in real mode. In this mode, the chip functions exactly like an 8086. That is, any 8086 program can be run on a real-mode 286 without change. In real mode, the 286 uses only its 20 least significant address lines, so that the memory space is limited to 1 MB, just like that of the 8086.

Intel designed the 286 to be software compatible with the 8086. Thus, all of the existing software designed to run on the 8086 and 8088 processors will run on the 286 without change. Sixteen new instructions were added, but these were all intended for managing the protected mode of the processor. When the 286 is operated in real mode, the only significant difference between it and the 8086 is that most of the 286 instructions execute faster due to a redesigned processor and a higher maximum clock speed (6 or 8 MHz).

When switched to protected mode, the 286 supports a *multiprogram* environment, by giving each program a predetermined amount of memory. In this scheme, programs no longer have physical addresses, but rather, are addressed via a segment selector. On the 286, this allows a program to "see" as much as 16 MB of memory. Protected mode is so called because several programs can be loaded into memory at once (each in its own segment), but protected from each other. That is, a program running in one segment cannot read data from or write data to another segment.

When the 80286 was designed, it was decided that once switched to protected mode, the chip should not be able to switch back to real mode. This arrangement was to prevent a clever programmer from accessing data in another segment by switching the chip back and forth between the two modes. Ironically, it turned out to be a *fatal flaw,* as the MS-DOS operating system (the dominant operating system for the 286) requires that all programs be run in 8086 mode (real mode). As a result, most, if not all, 286 chips are operated in real mode and thus function only as fast 8086s.

The 80386

When Intel announced the 80386 (the 386) microprocessor in 1985, the company made a commitment that through the year 2000, each successive generation of microprocessors would remain compatible with this chip. The 386 represents a major redesign of the older 8086 and 80286 processors. The data bus width and internal processor registers are all 32 bits wide, as is the address bus, thus allowing the chip to access 4 GB (4096 MB) of physical memory.

Like the 286, the 386 supports two different operating modes: *real address mode* and *protected virtual address mode* (protected mode, for short). Real address mode is identical to the 80286's real mode and limits the processor to 1 MB of memory. In effect, the 386 becomes a (very) fast 8086 processor. This is the mode used by MS-DOS.*

The true power of the 386 is revealed when it is switched to protected mode. In this mode, the onboard memory management unit (MMU) manages the 4 GB of memory in a way similar to that of the Protected Mode 286. That is, tasks are given a segment of memory in which to run, governed by a descriptor register that defines the segment base address, the segment limit, and the *attributes* for that particular segment (execute code, program data, read-only, etc.). The segment can be as large as 4 GB or as small as a single byte. In addition, via a technique called *paging,* 4-KB pages can be swapped in and out of memory (using a hard-disk drive) to allow a task to have a *virtual memory space* as large as 64 terabytes (64 million megabytes!).

The protected-mode features of the 386 can be taken advantage of only by an operating system that is aware of these features. Common examples are Microsoft Windows, IBM's OS/2, and Unix. Windows and OS/2 use another protected-mode feature of the 386

---

*You might wonder why DOS would force the 386 to operate in such a limited mode. The answer is *compatibility:* If DOS were written to require the 386's protected mode, all users of 80286 and 8086 machines would be left out.

called *virtual 8086 mode*. This mode is similar to real mode, except that multiple 8086 machines can be run simultaneously, protected from each other. Windows uses the technique to launch multiple DOS programs, each in its own window.

The 386 requires just two clock pulses per (memory read or write) bus cycle and is available with clock speeds as high as 40 MHz. Because of this, an external memory *cache* is required to prevent the processor from entering long wait cycles while data is read from or written to (slow) conventional main memory.

The instruction set of the 386 is again 100% compatible with the older processors in the family (the 8086, 8088, and 80286). Fourteen new instructions have been added and several others have been modified. For example, data can now be moved between the internal processor registers 8, 16, or 32 bits at a time. And, of course, all of the mathematical operations now support 32-bit operands.

The 80386SX

Just as the 8088 helped designers make the transition from 8-bit to 16-bit microprocessors, the 80386SX is designed to ease the transition from 16- to 32-bit microprocessors. This is done by providing a 16-bit external data bus width and reducing the address bus to 24 bits. In all other ways, the 386SX is identical to the 386 (now called the 386DX to differentiate the two chips).

The 80486DX

In 1989, IBM's PC was seven years old, and the Intel microprocessor architecture (8086, 80286, 80386) was solidly entrenched as the de facto standard. Accordingly, Intel realized that new processors in the family would have to maintain compatibility with past generations of processors. The 80486 therefore represents a more polished and refined 386. Only six new instructions were added, intended primarily for use by operating system software, not applications programs. The data bus, address bus, and internal registers all remain 32 bits wide. The core of the chip has been redesigned using RISC concepts, thereby allowing frequently used instructions to execute in a single clock cycle. Chips with clock speeds as high as 50 MHz are available. A new five-stage execution pipeline allows portions of five instructions to be executing at once.

The 486 is also highly integrated. Included onboard is an 8K memory cache and a floating-point processor that is the equivalent of the (external) 80387 coprocessor chip popular in 386 systems. The result is a processor that operates about twice as fast as a 386 for any given clock speed. That is, a 20-MHz 486 performs essentially the same as a 40-MHz 386.

The 80486SX

Based on its numerical designation, you might expect the 486SX to be a 16-bit version of the 486DX. However, that is not the case. Instead, Intel has designated this chip for low-end applications that do not require a coprocessor. Therefore, that function has been disabled. In addition, clock speeds for the 486SX are limited to 33 MHz.

The 80486DX2 and DX4

As microprocessor system clock speeds have increased, the job of designing a compatible microcomputer around these chips has become increasingly difficult. A 50-MHz clock signal, for example, provides only 20 ns between clock "ticks." This means that the time required for a signal to travel from point A to point B on the system board becomes significant (about 6″ per nanosecond). A buffer that introduces 5–10 ns of delay may cause the entire system to shut down.

Once again, a new way of thinking was required. The result was a new breed of microprocessors that operate with an *internal* clock rate that is twice (in the DX2) or three times (in the DX4) the *external* clock rate. This permits the computer system board to be designed using less expensive components, while still allowing the processor to operate at its maximum data rate (internally). Of course, operations that require access to data outside of the processor will have to be slowed down to the system-board rate. The internal cache of the 486 helps offset this loss so that a DX2 chip achieves about 80% of the performance of an equivalent DX chip.

DX2 and DX4 chips are usually described in terms of their internal clock rate. Thus, the description "486DX2 66" is interpreted to mean a 486 microprocessor with an internal clock rate of 66 MHz and an external clock rate of 33 MHz. A DX4-100 with the same external clock operates internally at 100 MHz.

The Pentium

One method of increasing the complexity of an integrated circuit is simply to *scale* the chip down. For example, if every line etched into the silicon die could be shrunk in half, the same circuit could be built in one-fourth the area. The evolution of dynamic memory chips (DRAMs) follows this rule exactly. The original IBM PC used 16K DRAMs. These were soon replaced with 64K chips, then 256K chips, and now 1M, 4M, 16M, and even 64 M chips.

The "trick," of course, is being able to improve processing skills sufficiently to allow this scaling to continue. In 1969, the minimum feature size (the smallest detail that can be etched into a chip) was 10 microns (10×10^{-6} meter). By 1997, this had shrunk to 0.25 micron—40 times smaller!*

The Pentium uses a *superscaler* architecture. This means that the chip's capabilities go beyond those achieved simply by scaling down its size. In particular, the Pentium is the first microprocessor in the Intel family to support *two* instruction pipelines, each with its own arithmetic–logic unit, address generation circuitry, and data cache interface. The result is a processor that can actually execute two different instructions simultaneously.

Like the 486, the Pentium incorporates an onboard cache and a floating-point processor. However, to avoid bottlenecks when the processor accesses program instruc-

---

*In 1965, Gordon Moore, one of the founders of Intel, was graphing chip complexity vs. time. He noticed that the number of integrated components doubled every two years. Moore then boldly predicted that this doubling would continue indefinitely. Remarkably, his prediction—now referred to as Moore's law—has held up for more than 30 years.

tions and data, separate 8K code and data caches are provided. The 486's coprocessor has been completely redesigned and now includes an eight-stage instruction pipeline. In addition, many of the floating-point functions have been optimized. As a result, the Pentium achieves 5 to 10 times the floating-point performance of the 486.

The internal architecture of the Pentium, as presented to the programmer, remains compatible with the 386 and 486. That is, all registers are 32 bits wide, as is the address bus. The external data bus, however, has been expanded to 64 bits to allow higher data transfer rates.* Six new instructions have been added, but again, these are primarily for use by the operating system, not the applications programmer. In all other ways, the Pentium remains compatible with the 386 and 486.

Performance tests have shown the Pentium to be about twice as fast as the 486 at any given clock speed. The entry-level P66 for example, operates at 66 MHz and provides twice the performance of the 486DX2 66.

The Pentium MMX

In 1996, Intel began delivering versions of the Pentium with *multimedia extensions* (MMXs). These processors have three architectural enhancements over non-MMX processors (now renamed Pentium Classic):

1. Fifty-seven instructions have been added, specifically designed for multimedia (audio, video, and graphical data) applications. Like DSPs, many of these instructions have been optimized for repetitive operations.
2. A process called single-instruction multiple data (SIMD) allows the same function to be performed on multiple pieces of data. Because multimedia applications often require large blocks of data to be manipulated, SIMD provides a significant enhancement of performance.
3. The internal cache size has been extended from 16K to 32K, increasing the likelihood that program instructions and data will be stored in the cache.

For general applications, benchmark tests show a 10–20-percent improvement over the Pentium Classic, increasing to nearly 70 percent when *multimedia-specific* applications are considered. Chips with (internal) clock speeds as high as 233 MHz are available.

Applications of MMX processors include decompression of audio and video files. Indeed, software video players may become a reality. Some vendors are replacing conventional modems and sound cards with MMX-driven software equivalents.

The Pentium Pro

Perhaps the most striking feature of the Pentium Pro is the package itself. As shown in Fig. 12.19, the Pro consists of two separate silicon dies. The largest is the processor; fabricated with 0.35 micron design rules, it incorporates 5.5 million transistors. The smaller die beside it is a 256-KB *level-two cache*. Oddly enough, the cache has three times as

---

*Note that this approach is *opposite* to that taken with the 8088 and 80386SX: These chips have external data buses smaller than the internal register sizes.

Figure 12.19 The P6 is two chips in one. The larger die is the processor, the smaller a 256-KB level-two cache. (Courtesy of Intel Corporation)

many transistors as the processor (15.5 million), but because of its uniformity, less silicon area is required. Versions of the Pentium Pro with a 512-KB, and a 1-MB cache are also available.

The Pentium Pro retains all of the architectural features of the Pentium that preceded it. That is, internally, all registers are 32 bits, while the external data bus is 64 bits wide. Four additional address lines have been added, allowing 64 GB of physical memory to be accessed. From a software point of view, the Pentium Pro remains 100% compatible with the previous generation of 80x86 processors. Three new processor instructions have been added, as well as two new floating-point-unit instructions.

The most touted feature of the Pentium Pro is what Intel calls *dynamic execution.* This new approach to processing software instructions that reduces idle processor time to an absolute minimum. Dynamic execution consists of the following three techniques:

Multiple branch prediction. Conventional processors "blindly" fetch instructions without regard to program branches. If a conditional jump instruction is fetched, subsequent instructions may have to be discarded if the jump is taken. Using a technique called *multiple branch prediction,* the Pentium Pro can look as far as 30 instructions ahead to anticipate program branches.

Data flow analysis. Using this technique, the Pentium Pro looks at upcoming software instructions and determines whether they are available for processing, depending on other instructions. The Pentium Pro then determines the optimal sequence for processing and begins executing the instructions.

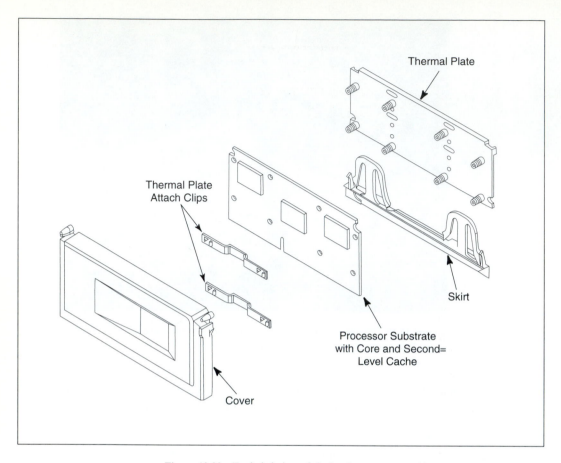

Figure 12.20 Exploded view of single-edge contact cartridge.

Speculative execution.   This technique allows the Pentium Pro to execute instructions in a different order from which they entered the processor. Such "out-of-order" execution allows the Pentium Pro processor to execute instructions in an efficient manner. The results of the executed instructions are stored as speculative until their final status can be determined.

Like the Pentium processor before it, the Pentium Pro is superscaler. However, whereas the Pentium was able to execute only two instructions per clock cycle, the Pentium Pro, with three instruction decoders, can execute *three* instructions simultaneously.

The onboard (level-one) 8-KB data and instruction cache of the Pentium was described previously. Most microcomputer systems also have an *external* cache of 64 KB to 512 KB. The Pentium Pro incorporates a level-two cache *onboard*. This feature simplifies system board design, requires less space, and, because the processor and cache are wired in the same package, allows the CPU core to communicate with the cache at full (core) speed.

The 133-MHz version of the Pentium Pro provides twice the performance of a 66-MHz Pentium and four times that of a 486 DX2 66. Compared with a 100-MHz Pentium,

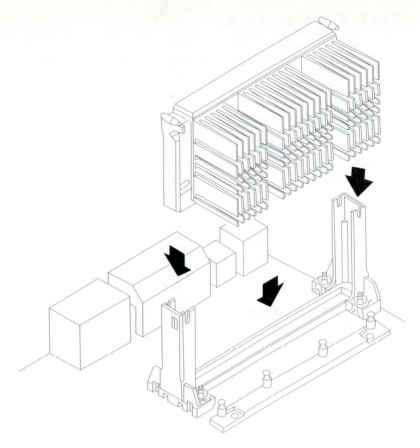

Figure 12.21 Installing the SEC cartridge into the retention mechanism.

the Pentium Pro offers a 70% performance boost. Chips with internal clock speeds as high as 200 MHz are available.

The Pentium II

The newest member of the 80x86 family is the Pentium II. First made available in 1997, it is basically a Pentium Pro with MMX technology, repackaged in a new, single-edge contact (SEC) cartridge. (See Fig. 12.20.) As the figure shows, the processor is mounted on a ceramic substrate along with a level-two cache. The entire assembly is then encased in a plastic cartridge. Figure 12.21 shows how the cartridge (and heat sink) are inserted into the system board connector (referred to as the "Slot 1" connector).

The Pentium II is made with 0.25-micron technology, allowing clock speeds of 300 to 450 MHz. System bus frequencies as high as 100 MHz are supported. The lower clock speeds will support a 66-MHz system bus frequency. The level-two cache, which operates at half the speed of the processor, stores 512 KB and has its own 64-bit dedicated bus. The level-one cache has been increased from 16 KB in the Pentium Pro to 32 KB in the Pentium II.

SELF-REVIEW 12.6

12.6.1 Which of the following processors have 16-bit internal data registers?
    (a) 8086
    (b) 8088
    (c) 80286
    (d) 80386
    (e) 80386SX
    (f) 80486DX

12.6.2 The 386 introduced a new protected-mode feature called _____ _____ mode that allows multiple 8086 programs to run and be protected from each other.

12.6.3 To speed up memory accesses, the 386 uses an external _____. On the 486 and Pentium processors, the _____ is internal.

12.6.4 The Pentium can execute _____ instructions simultaneously. The Pentium Pro and Pentium II can execute _____ instructions simultaneously.

QUESTIONS AND ANSWERS

Q: *What two units make up the 8086 processor?*

A: The bus interface unit (BIU) and the execution unit (EU).

Q: *Do 80x86 processors still follow the basic fetch-and-execute principle of the stored-program computer?*

A: Yes; however, with a prefetch queue and separate bus interface and execution units, the two phases can overlap, increasing processing throughput.

Q: *What is the address bus width of the 8086 processor? How much memory can it access?*

A: With a 20-bit memory bus, the 8086 can access 1 MB of memory.

Q: *What is the purpose of the 8087 numeric data processor?*

A: The 8087 is designed to support the 8086 and perform high-level mathematical functions at very high speed. Beginning with the 486, this function has been built into the processor.

Q: *What is the difference between the min and max mode as applied to the 8086 and 8088 processors?*

A: When wired for min mode, these processors support an 8085-like control bus. In max mode, the 8288 bus controller is required to generate control bus signals. Max mode is required when using the 8087 coprocessor.

Q: *How many different I/O ports can the 8086 access?*

A: Two different methods are supported. For direct I/O operations, the instruction supplies an 8-bit port address as part of the instruction. The processor is thus limited to 256 ports. With indirect I/O, register DX holds the port address, and 64K ports can therefore be accessed.

Q: *What is the address bus width of the 386, 486, and Pentium processors. How much memory can these chips access?*

A: All of these chips support a 32-bit memory bus. This allows 4 GB of memory to be accessed. The Pentium Pro and Pentium II can access 64 GB of memory due to their 36-bit address buses.

Q: *What is the difference between real mode and protected mode?*

A: In real mode, the processor "looks like" an 8086 processor. Protected tasks are not supported and the memory space is restricted to 1 MB. In protected mode, multiple tasks can run at the same time, with all protected from each other. The full memory space of the processor is available. The 8086 and 8088 processors support real mode only. The other processors support both modes.

Q: *The 80x86 processors use segmented memory. What does this mean?*

A: These processors divide the memory space into several segments, with each segment designated to store program code, data, or information about the stack. The 8086 and 8088 have four such segments, limited to 64 KB each. The 386 and later processors have six segments, with each as large as 4 GB.

Q: *How do the data bus widths of the 386 and 486 compare with that of the Pentium processors?*

A: The 386 and 486 each have a 32-bit data bus width with 32-bit internal data registers. The Pentium processors have a 64-bit data bus width, but internally the data registers remain 32 bits.

Q: *What is MMX technology?*

A: The term "MMX technology" refers to a set of instructions built into the Pentium MMX and Pentium II processors. These instructions are specifically designed to enhance the processing of multimedia data (audio and video). Because the instructions are hard-wired into the CPU, the performance of these systems is greatly enhanced.

LAB PROJECTS

12.1. If you have access to a computer from the 8086 family, answer the following questions about your system:
  (a) Which microprocessor chip is used?
  (b) What is the system clock frequency?
  (c) How much total DRAM does your system have?
  (d) How much total ROM?
  (e) Does your system have cache memory? How much?
  (f) Make a list of all of the I/O ports in your computer.

12.2. Sketch a *memory map* of your computer, identifying the RAM and ROM blocks. Identify the size of any "open" areas.

12.3. * Start DEBUG, and type "R" at the "–" prompt. You should see a display of all the 8086 CPU registers and flags. The instruction pointed to by register IP will also be shown. Type "A100" to begin assembling instruction mnemonics at logical address 0100H. Enter the following program:

```
0100    MOV    AX,0000
0103    MOV    CX,8000
0106    DEC    AX
0107    MOV    BX,AX
0109    LOOP   0106
010B    INT    3
```

12.4. With the program in Lab Project 12.3 loaded, give the command "U100 LC" to unassemble (U) the program beginning at address 100H with a length (L) of 12 (0CH) bytes.

Note: The MS-DOS operating system includes the utility DEBUG.COM. This program can be used to enter 8086 instruction mnemonics into memory. The resulting program can then be traced or run at full speed. All of the CPU registers can be examined and modified.

(a) Examine the program listing. Note that DEBUG has determined the hexadecimal object code for each instruction.

(b) For another view of the program, type "D100 LC." This command will display (D) 12 bytes of memory, beginning at address 100H. Note that the display is shown in hex and its ASCII equivalent.

12.5. There are several ways of running and testing the program in Lab 12.3.

(a) Press the "T" key for a trace. The first instruction will execute, and DEBUG will then display the contents of all CPU registers. Repeatedly pressing "T" will cause one instruction at a time to execute.

(b) Type "G=100" to run the program at full speed, beginning at address 100H. In this example the program will stop at the INT 3 (break-point) instruction, displaying the contents of all CPU registers. (Note that CX has been counted down to 0.)

(c) Type "G=100 109" to run the program at full speed, beginning at address 100H but halting at address 109H.

(d) Type "RIP" to examine register (R) IP. Enter the value 0100 to point this register to the beginning of the program. Now type "G" to run the program at full speed, starting at the address in register IP.

12.6. If you have written a program with DEBUG, you can save it with the N and W commands.

(a) Type "N TEST" to name the program TEST.

(b) The number of bytes to be written must be stored in the 32-bit register pair BX:CX. In this example, 12 bytes must be written. Use "RBX" to set BX to 0 and RCX to make CX=000CH.

(c) Type "W" to write the (12-byte) file to the disk.

12.7. A saved file can be retrieved by loading it when DEBUG is first started. Type "DEBUG TEST" to start DEBUG and load the file TEST.

QUESTIONS AND PROBLEMS

Section 12.1

12.1. What is the advantage of having the fetch and execute cycles of a microcomputer *overlap*? What makes this possible in an 8086 CPU?

12.2. If you intend to use the 8087 numeric coprocessor, then the 8086 must be wired for the _____ mode.

12.3. The following logic levels or their hex equivalents are observed on the buses of an 8086 microprocessor during an instruction cycle:

    address bus: D8000H

    data bus: 1234H

    control bus: $M/\overline{IO} = 1$, $\overline{RD} = 1$, $\overline{WR} = 0$, $\overline{BHE} = 0$

(a) Does the instruction produce a byte or word access?

(b) From memory or an I/O device?

(c) Read or write cycle?

12.4. Describe the contents of the address data, and control buses (see Problem 12.3 for an example) if the 8086 is reading the byte 73H from memory location 80001H.

12.5. The 8086 can access 1 MB of memory. How many 64K *pages* is this?

*12.6. Planning to add 64 KB of memory to an 8086 computer system, you purchase eight 64-KB DRAM chips. Unfortunately, your idea will not work. Explain why.

12.7. If an interrupt-driven peripheral gates the type number 9AH onto the data bus during $\overline{\text{INTA}}$, from which group of memory locations will the address of the ISR be fetched?

Section 12.2

12.8. Refer to the min-mode 8086 CPU module in Fig. 12.7. Suppose the 8086 is performing a memory write cycle, and determine the logic level of the following control signals during the T3 clock cycle:
   (a) DT/$\overline{\text{R}}$
   (b) $\overline{\text{DEN}}$
   (c) ALE
   (d) M/$\overline{\text{IO}}$
   (e) $\overline{\text{RD}}$
   (f) $\overline{\text{WR}}$

*12.9. Refer to the max-mode 8086 CPU module in Fig. 12.8. Suppose the $\overline{\text{OE}}$ inputs of the three 8282 chips are inadvertently tied to $+5$ V instead of ground. How would this affect the operation of the CPU module?

Section 12.3

12.10. How do the 8086's four pointer and index registers differ from the chip's four data registers?

12.11. Assume that register CS contains 2700H and register IP contains 0300H. Calculate the *logical* and *physical* addresses pointed to by register IP.

12.12. Sketch a diagram similar to Fig. 12.11 showing the starting and ending physical addresses for each 8086 memory segment if CS contains 1000H, DS contains 8800H, SS contains 57F0H, and ES contains 5FFFH.

12.13. Using the segment assignments given in Problem 12.12, calculate the physical address of the memory operand in each of the following 8086 instructions:
   (a) MOV (0200H),AH
   (b) MOV (BP),AH   (assume BP contains A800H)
   (c) MOV (SI)+6,AH   (assume SI contains C010H)
   (d) JMP 089EH   (089E is the target address)

12.14. Determine the addressing mode for each of the instructions in Problem 12.13.

12.15. True or false? Because each of the four 8086 memory segments is 64K bytes in length, a minimum of 256K of memory (64K $\times$ 4) is required in an 8086-based computer.

Section 12.4

12.16. Write an 8086 program to load register BX with B370H, register DL with the contents of memory location D800H in the data segment, and SI with a copy of the data in register AX. Identify the addressing mode of each instruction you use.

12.17. What is wrong with each of the following 8086 instructions?
   (a) MOV BL,AX
   (b) MOV DX,FE000H
   (c) INC (AX)
   (d) IN AX,8000H

12.18. What is the I/O port address of the 8086 program shown in Fig. 12.22?

12.19. Under what condition will the 8086 program in Fig. 12.22 escape the loop?

12.20. Determine the contents of AX after each of the following programs has been run:

(a) MOV	AL,80H	(b) MOV	AX,C879H
MOV	BL,63H	MOV	BL,D9H
MUL	BL	DIV	BL

```
                    ; INPUT TEST PROGRAM
                    ;
                    MOV          DX,00C3H
        INPUT       IN           AL,DX
                    TEST         AL,40H
                    JNE          INPUT
                    ;
                    ;PROGRAM CONTINUES
```

Figure 12.22 Program for Problems 12.18 and 12.19.

12.21. Answer the following questions about the block move program shown in Fig. 12.23.

  (a) What value is loaded into the DS and ES segment registers?

  (b) Register SI points to the block starting address in the data segment. What is this (logical) address?

  (c) Register DI points to the block destination address in the extra segment. What is this (logical) address?

  (d) Register CX is the byte/word counter. How many words are transferred by this program?

12.22. The program shown in Fig. 12.24 functions as a time delay routine. The program is made up of an inner loop and an outer loop.

  (a) How many times are the instructions in the inner loop executed for each pass through the other loop?

  (b) How many times will the LOOP instruction be executed?

  (c) Calculate the total number of times the instructions in the inner loop are executed.

12.23. Code the 8-bit addition problem, Program 1 (see Fig. 3.1), for the 8086.

12.24. Code the 32-bit addition problem, Program 3 (see Fig. 3.4), for the 8086.

Section 12.5

12.25. Answer the following questions about the 8086 memory interface in Fig. 12.16:

  (a) How many total bytes does this interface provide?

  (b) Which RAM chip among RAM0–RAM15 stores bit 5 of the byte at location 06A83H?

  (c) MWTC is connected in common to all the RAM chips. If a write cycle to the even bank occurs, what prevents data from also being written to the odd bank?

  (d) Which memory bank—even, odd, or both—will be accessed for the instruction MOV AL,0005H?

*12.26. Suppose the 8086 memory interface in Fig. 12.16 has been wired incorrectly. In particular, the data bus connections—DB0 and DB1—are interchanged. What would the symptom of this problem be?

12.27. Show how to expand the 8086 memory in Fig. 12.16 to 64K bytes using additional 2167 SRAMs. Map your design to cover the address range 00000–0FFFFH.

12.28. True or false? All 8086 I/O instructions use register AX and input or output 16 bits of data.

```
                 ;BLOCK MOVE PROGRAM
                 ;
                 MOV          AX,8000H
                 MOV          DS,AX
                 MOV          ES,AX
                 MOV          SI,SOURCE
                 MOV          DI,DEST
                 MOV          CX,0080H
                 CLD
                 REP MOVSW
                 HLT
        SOURCE   DW           1000H
        DEST     DW           0C000H
```

Figure 12.23 Program for Problem 12.21.

```
                MOV        CX,8000H

        OUTER   MOV        BX,0

        INNER   INC        BX

                JNZ        INNER

                LOOP       OUTER

                RET
```

Figure 12.24   Program for Problem 12.22.

12.29. Give an example of an 8086 instruction to input data from port C of the odd 8255A in Fig. 12.17.

12.30. Give an example of an 8086 instruction to output data to 16-bit port B of the 8255A in Fig. 12.17.

12.31. Sketch a circuit diagram showing an 8254 PIT interfaced to a max-mode 8086. Map the PIT to cover even port addresses from 08H to 0EH.

Section 12.6

12.32. List all 80x86 processors that have a data bus width different from their internal data register size.

12.33. True or false? Any program written for the 8086 will also run on the 8088 without requiring any changes.

12.34. Intel microprocessors organize their memory into 8-bit-wide banks. The 16-bit 80286, for example, requires two such banks. Typically, these banks are built using 1-MB or 4-MB (single in-line memory modules (SIMMs). For each of the following processors, determine the *minimum* number of 1-MB SIMMs required, the resulting amount of memory, and the maximum amount of memory possible. The figures for the 80286 are given as an example. (Assume byte-wide SIMMs).

Microprocessor	Minimum number of SIMMs	Total memory capacity for these SIMMs (at 1 MB each)	Maximum memory capacity for this processor
80286	2	2 MB	16 MB
80386DX			
80386SX			
8046DX			
Pentium			

12.35. Explain why each of the following microprocessor features affect (or do not affect) the processing rate of the chip:
(a) clock frequency,
(b) data bus width,
(c) address bus width,
(d) internal cache memory,
(e) coprocessor (internal or external).

12.36. Beginning with the 386, the 80x86 processors supported three different operating modes. List these modes and give a brief explanation of each.

12.37. For each of the following, indicate whether the feature is the same or different for the Pentium and Pentium Pro processors. If the feature is different, explain the difference.

Feature	Same/different	Explanation if different
Data bus width		
Address bus width		
General-purpose registers		
Execution of simultaneous instructions		
Cache		
Instruction set		
Package		
Dynamic execution		

SELF-REVIEW ANSWERS

12.1.1. BIU, EU

12.1.2. max

12.1.3. even-byte, odd-byte, and 16-bit-word access

12.1.4. 4

12.2.1. The 8284 generates the clock signal.

12.2.2. ALE

12.2.3. $\overline{DEN}$ and DT/$\overline{R}$

12.2.4. max

12.3.1. AX is the 16-bit accumulator. The high-order 8 bits can be accessed as register AH and the low-order 8 bits as register AL.

12.3.2. the code segment

12.3.3. The logical address is the 16-bit offset (0–64K) within a segment. The physical address is the 20-bit address output by the 8086.

12.3.4. based, stack

12.4.1. DX

12.4.2. DX:AX

12.4.3. far jump

12.4.4. an interrupt initiated by the instruction INT n, where n is the type number.

12.5.1. A0 and $\overline{BHE}$

12.5.2. No. Both even and odd banks must be present.

12.5.3. Even and odd banks are required only for interfacing memory.

12.6.1. (a), (b), (c)

12.6.2. virtual 8086

12.6.3. cache, cache

12.6.4. two, three

ANSWERS TO ODD-NUMBERED PROBLEMS

Chapter 1

1.1. The address bus holds the I/O or memory address that data—via the data bus—is to be sent to or received from. The control bus identifies the direction—into or out of the processor—data is to be moved. The control bus also identifies whether the data is for memory or an I/O device.

1.3. Control bus: S1 = memory, S2 = write, S3 = memory; address bus: 16; data bus: 26

1.5. (a) 6
   (b) 10
   (c) 2
   (d) 9
   (e) 5
   (f) 4
   (g) 3
   (h) 7
   (i) 8
   (j) 11
   (k) 1

1.7. Microcontroller

1.9. It doubles

1.11. (a) 1011, 13H
   (b) 0110 0011, 63H

(c) 1110 1100 1000, EC8H

(d) 1110 0001 0001 1101, E11DH

1.13. (a) 1110 1001

(b) 1001 1010

(c) 1000 0000

(d) 0010 1111

1.15. 3CH + 92H corresponds to 60 + 146 = 206 (1100 1110). However, 92H corresponds to −110 when interpreted as a signed binary number. The addition is then 60 + −110 = −50 which equals 1100 1110 in signed binary—the same result obtained above.

1.17. After looking up the program codes on a reference sheet, they are transferred (by hand) to a programming sheet.

1.19. Assembly language runs fastest.

1.21. Hint: When low, the EI input enables the chip.

1.23. 32K = 32,768

1.25. 13FFH

1.27. 33H; "3", INX SP

1.29. M1: memory read (op-code fetch); M2: memory read (port address); M3: I/O read

1.31. 8

1.33. Change location 0001 from 32H to 26H

1.35. 37 T states (18.5 μs)

Chapter 2

2.1. High, 10

2.3. The 8085 and Z-80 status information is not multiplexed.

2.5. Input read and output write

2.7. Nine pulses on $\overline{\text{MEMR}}$

2.9.

Machine cycle	$\overline{\text{RD}}$	$\overline{\text{WR}}$	IO/$\overline{\text{M}}$	S0	S1
memory read	0	1	0	0	1
I/O write	1	0	1	1	0

2.11.

	M1	M2	M3	M4
MVI A,10H	Instruction fetch S0=1 S1=1	Memory Read S0=0 S1=1		
ADD B	Instruction fetch S0=1 S1=1			

2.13. The $\overline{\text{M1}}$ signal is active.

2.15. True

2.17. Use a 74LS374 with A0–A6 wired to the data inputs of the latch. Clock the latch with the inverted $\overline{\text{RFSH}}$ signal.

2.19. A = 7BH

2.21. Hint: C9H = −55 in signed binary

2.23. The Z-80 has the same general purpose register set as the 8080 and 8085, but two sets. The Z-80 also has two index registers (IX and IY) not present in the 8080 and 8085.

2.25. A = 7BH

2.27. **(a)** 04H

2.29. After executing the instruction if A = 0 bit 6 of A is 0, if A does not equal 0, bit 6 is 1.

2.31. 07FDH

2.33. **(a)** S = 0; Z = 0; H = 1; P/V = 0; CY = 0

2.35. OR 20H

2.37. 07FDH

2.39. 0701H

2.41. 0711H

2.43.

0600	MVI	B,3CH
0602	IN	03H
0604	RAL	
0605	JNC	0602H
0608	ANA	B
0609	OUT	05H
060B	HLT	

Chapter 3

3.1. Change the LXI H,0700H instruction to LXI H,0C000H.

3.3. The very first addition adds the LSDs together with the carry. The carry must be zero for this addition.

3.5. 16FFH; 2BH

3.7. 7.8 KHz and 0.6 Hz

3.9. F420H

3.11. Change BLINE EQU 16 to BLINE EQU 1

3.13. 1

3.15. Change the LD IX,0700H to LD IX,0D780H.

3.17. F4H = -12

3.19. CF34H

3.21. 16,777,215

3.23. 256 byte memory transfer from A000H–A0FFH to 0100H–01FFH.

3.25. Change the JR Z,CIN to JR NZ,CIN.

3.27. The RLA and JR Z,TEST2 instructions are incorrect.

3.29. $\frac{1}{2} \times 1/342 = 32 \times E \times \frac{1}{4}$ MHz; E = 183 = B7H

3.31. A = DDH

Chapter 4

4.1. Yes

4.3. 4

4.5. The RESET input forces the CPU to begin executing instructions from a specific address. By mapping a ROM to this address, control of the computer can be assured when a RESET occurs.

4.7. Produce a RESET signal with fast rise and fall times.

4.9. 0.7V high, 0.3V low

4.11. 2.6V high, 0.4V low

4.13. Reflections at the end of the bus line.

4.15. $\overline{OUT} = \overline{A} + \overline{B} + \overline{C}$

4.17.

4.19. 261 Ohms < R < 3291 Ohms

4.21. For the 1 0 case: B = output; A = input

4.23. **(b)** Bi-directional data bus buffer

4.25. Change the port address to something other than 3FH.

4.27. False

4.29. set, low

4.31. Switch debouncer

4.33. The single-step switch would have no effect.

4.35. Prevents data bus contention when the jump-on-reset circuit is being accessed.

4.37. Rewire the 3B input of IC6 and the 1B input of IC7.

Chapter 5

5.1. **(b)** secondary storage

5.3. true

5.5. rising edge

5.7. $t_{DW} = 265$ ns

5.9. $t_{RD} = 120$ ns; $t_{ACC} = 190$ ns; $t_{CA} = 20$ ns; $t_{DW} = 130$ ns; $t_{AW} = 395$ ns

5.11.

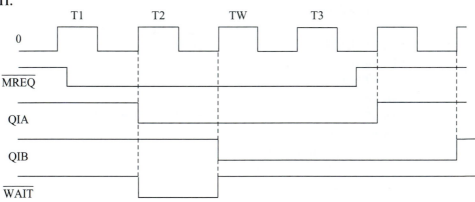

5.13. The CPU would continually execute wait states.

5.15. Yes if stack memory and other temporary storage are not required.

5.17. BFFFH

5.19.

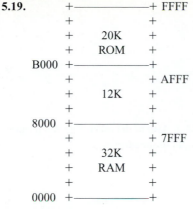

```
        +————————————+ FFFF
        +            +
        +    20K     +
        +    ROM     +
 B000   +————————————+
        +            + AFFF
        +    12K     +
        +            +
 8000   +————————————+
        +            + 7FFF
        +    32K     +
        +    RAM     +
        +            +
 0000   +————————————+
```

5.21. 11011

5.23. (b) and (d)

5.25. 8 chips

5.27. Jumper pin 21 to $\overline{WE}$ (6116) or +5V (2716 read) or +25V (2716 program)

5.29. Invert AB14 before connecting to IC1A.

5.31. 2732A: 0000-0FFFH and 8000-8FFFH

5.33. 260 ns

5.35. Use eight 2716 EPROM chips with the chip enable inputs driven by the 74LS138 outputs. Address lines A11-A13 connect to the ABC inputs of the decoder. Use A14 and A15 to enable the decoder.

5.37. Use eight 2167 RAM chips with the chip select inputs driven by a NAND gate address decoder decoding address lines A14 and A15. Control the direction of the data bus buffers with the memory read and write control bus signals qualified with the chip select signal.

5.39.

H G F E	D C B A	DO3 (RAM3)	DO2 (ROM2)	DO1 (ROM1)
0 0 0 0	0 0 0 0	1	0	1
0 0 0 0	0 0 0 1	1	1	0
0 0 0 0	0 0 1 0	1	1	0
0 0 0 0	0 0 1 1	0	1	1
0 0 0 0	0 1 0 0	0	1	1
0 0 0 0	0 1 0 1	0	1	1
0 0 0 0	0 1 1 0	0	1	1

All remaining addresses store 111.

5.41. $\overline{ROM1} = \overline{A15}\ \overline{A14}\ \overline{A13}$

5.43. It appears that we are unable to write to the memory. Check IC4A for a write pulse and be sure buffers IC5 and IC6 are also receiving this pulse. Verify that the RAM chips are receiving the write pulse as well.

5.45. $\overline{RAS}$, data out

5.47. (b) 3

5.49. AB16

Chapter 6

6.1. Yes

6.3. MVI   A,3CH
OUT   27H
OUT   28H
HLT

6.5. False

6.7. Connect AB7–AB4 to one comparator, AB3–AB0 to the other. The A=B output of the low order comparator connects to the A=B input of the other.

6.9. (c)

6.11. (b), (c), (e)

6.13.

```
        ;8080/8085 version              ;Z-80 version
        LHLD    C800H                   LD    HL,C800H
LOOP    MOV     A,(HL)          LOOP    LD    A,(HL)
        ANI     03H                     AND   03H
        CPI     03H                     CP    03H
        JZ      LOOP                    JR    Z,LOOP
        JMP     READY                   JR    READY
```

6.15. 3

6.17.
```
BEGIN       OUT     0FFH
RESTART     MVI     B,6
            LXI     H,CODE
LOOP        PUSH    H
            CALL    KUP
            POP     H
            CMP     M
            JNZ     WAIT
            DCR     B
            JZ      OPEN
            INX     H
            JMP     LOOP
WAIT        ;1 minute wait routine goes here
            JMP     RESTART
OPEN        IN      0FFH
            CALL    KEY
            JMP     BEGIN
CODES       DB      n, n, n, n, n, n      ;six digit code
```

6.19. BUSY/$\overline{\text{READY}}$; peripheral; When high peripheral is busy and cannot accept data.

6.21. (b) port 0; (c) 1 bit input port to allow BUSY/$\overline{\text{READY}}$ to be polled

6.23. NUMB is a single byte number.

6.25. In the POLL loop change RAR to RAL

6.27. 117,647 bytes/sec

6.29. After a system reset, following a DI instruction, immediately after accepting an interrupt.

6.31. true

6.33. MVI   A, 00001110
      SIM
      EI

6.35. The interrupt must be held until acknowledged.

6.37. False

6.39. The NMI service routines need to terminate with an RETN instruction.

6.41. The RST 7.5 input is rising edge triggered.

6.43. The environment is being popped into the wrong registers.

6.45. Faster

Chapter 7

7.1. MVI A,00001111B
     OUT 0FEH   ;DDRA
     MVI A,01111111
     OUT 0FFH   ;DDRB

7.3.
               MVI A, 0FFH
               OUT 42H   ;DDRA
               MVI A,00
               OUT 43H   ;DDRB
               MVI B,0
     LOOP   MOV A,B
               OUT 40H
               IN   41H
               CMP B
               JNZ ERROR
               INR B
               JMP LOOP
               HLT

7.5. Wire two 7446/47 seven segment decoders to PB0-PB7.

7.7. (a) 0BH, (c) AEH

7.9. Control byte is written to the wrong port.

7.11. PC7 is set, reset, and set again via software.

7.13. The program is identical to Fig. 7.9 with the following changes:
    (**a**) OUT 0F2H becomes STA 0FF02H
    (**b**) The column access codes are 02H for COL1 and 01H for COL2
    (**c**) IN 0F1H becomes LDA 0FF00H
    (**d**) COL2 DB 7,8,9,A,B,C,D,E,F

7.15.
               MVI   A,90H   ;8255 init
               STA   0FF03H
     LOOP   CALL   READ
               CALL   DISPLAY
               JMP   LOOP

7.17. (**a**) $\overline{OBFA}$ goes low

7.19. (**a**) counter 0
     (**d**) 16.3845 ms

7.21.
```
MVI   A,1011X110B
OUT   0F3H
MVI   A,0D0H
OUT   0F2H
MVI   A,07H
OUT   0F2H
RET
```

7.23. 64

7.25. Use a debounced SPDT switch to generate a GATE2 signal (RUN) and an interrupt signal (STOP). Two software routines are then required. INIT must program counter 1 for mode 2 and divide by 2000. It must also program counter 2 for mode 0 BCD with an initial count of 9999H. The ISR will be called when the switch is returned to stop. It must read counter 0 and subtract the count from 9999 and display the result. It can then call INIT to reload counter 2 with 9999 and the watch will be ready for the next count.

7.27.
```
MVI   A,16H    ;ICW1
OUT   0F0H
MVI   A,80H    ;ICW2
OUT   0F1H
MVI   A,03H    ;OCW1
OUT   0F1H
MVI   A,0A0H   ;OCW2
OUT   0F0H
```

7.29. The PIC interprets E2H as OCW2 and assigns IR2 lowest priority.

7.31. The device may have to wait for the seven other interrupts to be serviced first.

7.33. When this signal is inactive all of the bus buffers become open circuits. This allows the DMAC to drive these lines without bus contention.

7.35. Memory to memory transfers cannot have $\overline{\text{MEMR}}$ and $\overline{\text{MEMW}}$ active simultaneously. Thus a byte must first be read, stored in the DMAC, and written to the new memory location.

7.37. 96H

7.39. Bus contention due to the buffer being permanently enabled.

Chapter 8

8.1. high, high

8.3.
```
IM    2
LD    A,C8H
LD    I,A
LD    A,40H
OUT   (0F1H),A
```

8.5. (a) port B
(b) mode 3
(c) PB6 or PB7 high

8.7.
```
SUB1   LD    HL,CODES   ;Point at INIT codes
       LD    B,5        ;Five codes to program
       LD    C,0F1H     ;Port A control
       OTIR             ;Program port A
       LD    A,08H      ;Power on
       OUT   (0F0H),A   ;Port A
```

	CALL	DELAY	;Wait 10s
	LD	A,0CH	;Heaters on
	OUT	(0F0H),A	;Port A
	RET		
CODES	DB	0CFH, 0F0H, 0B7H, 5FH, 0	

;(assume IM 2 has been set and register I loaded)

8.9.

INIT	LD	HL,CODES	;Point at INIT codes
	LD	B,2	;Two codes to program
	LD	C,81H	;Port A control
	OTIR		;Program port A
	LD	C,83H	;Port B control
	LD	B,4	;Four codes
	OTIR		;Program port B
	IM	2	;Mode 2 interrupts
	LD	A,80H	;High order address
	LD	I,A	
	RET		
CODES	DB	0CFH, 00, 0CFH, 0FFH, 87H, 00	
START	LD	A,3FH	;Both columns low
	OUT	(80H),A	;Port A
KDWN	CALL	KREAD	;Check keyboard
	JR	NZ,KDWN	;Wait for key up
	CALL	DELAY	;Debounce time
	EI		;Wait for key down
	RET		

8.11.

8.13. Port A = XX00 0100, port B = 71H

8.15. Digit 0 would probably display an 8 all the time

8.17. (a) 128μs

(b) 16,384s

(c) 4.19s

8.19. LD   A,0D5H

```
            OUT      (7DH),A
            LD       A,0ADH
            OUT      (7CH),A
            LD       A,0B3H
            OUT      (7DH),A
            LD       A,0F9H
            OUT      (7CH),A
```

8.21.
```
       10        I=1
       20        INPUT "WHAT IS THE PRESCALE FACTOR?";P
       30        INPUT "WHAT IS THE DESIRED MAX NUMBER?";N
       40        IF N<P*65536 THEN GOTO 60 ELSE PRINT "TOO BIG"
       50        GOTO 30
       60        FOR N0=1 TO 256
       70        FOR N1=1 TO 256
       80        M=P*N0*N1
       90        IF M<N THEN GOTO 150
       100       IF M=N THEN 120 ELSE N1=256
       110       GOTO 150
       120       PRINT I;". ";N0;" ";N1
       130       PRINT CHR$(7); INPUT A$
       140       I=I+1
       150       NEXT N1
       160       PRINT "PASS ";N0
       170       NEXT N0
       180       END
```

8.23. Wire the IEI input of the PIO to +5V and PIO IEO output to the IEI input of the CTC. Design an address decoder with a select output in the range 40H–47H. Combine this select signal with AB2 to select the PIO (AB2 = 0) or CTC (AB2 = 1).

8.25. RDY active, $\overline{WAIT}$ inactive

8.27. **(a)** port 5
      (c) 16,384 bytes
      (e) 86.016 ms

8.29. **(a)** 9.5μs
      (b) 10.75μs
      (c) 2.75μs

Chapter 9

9.1.

    0   0   1 0   0   0   0 1 0 1   1

9.3. **(a)** 300
      (b) 9 minutes and 6 seconds

9.5. **(a)** start bit
      (c) A=D2H
      (d) CF=1

9.7.
```
       STOP     CALL   READ      ;Read serial in
                JNC    STOP      ;Wait for stop bits
       START    CALL   READ
```

```
                    JC      START       ;Wait for start bit
                    CALL    DELAY1      ;Delay ½ bit time
                    CALL    READ
                    JC      STOP        ;Invalid start
                    MVI     B,8         ;Bit counter
            NXBT    CALL    DELAY       ;Wait one bit time
                    MOV     C,A         ;Save data word
                    CALL    READ
                    MOV     A,C         ;Recover data word
                    RAR                 ;Move in new bit
                    DCR     B           ;Bump bit counter
                    JNZ     NXBT        ;Do for 8 bits
                    MOV     C,A         ;Save byte in C
                    CALL    DELAY
                    CALL    READ
                    JNC     FE          ;Framing error
                    MOV     A,C         ;Put byte in A on return
                    RET
            READ    IN      0F0H        ;Input bit 0
                    RAR                 ;Move to carry
                    RET
9.9.                MVI     B,0
            LOOP    IN      0F1H
                    RAR
                    JNC     LOOP
                    ANI     0EH
                    JZ      DONE
                    MVI     B,1
                    CPI     02H
                    JZ      DONE
                    INR     B
                    CPI     04H
                    JZ      DONE
                    INR     B
            DONE    RET
9.11.   55.3s vs. 81.9s
9.13.               PUSH    PSW
                    MOV     A,C
                    ANI     7FH
                    JPE     DONE
                    ORI     80H
            DONE    MOV     C,A
                    POP     PSW
                    RET
9.15.               PUSH    B
                    MVI     B,0
                    SUB     A
            LOOP    ADD     M
                    INX     H
```

```
                    DCR     B
                    JNZ     LOOP
                    ADD     C
                    RET
```

9.17. 26H

9.19. 153 ns

9.21. 19,200

9.23.
```
        POLL        IN      71H
                    ANI     2
                    JZ      POLL
                    IN      70H
                    MOV     B,A
                    RET
```

9.25. ;Assume a 1.8432 MHz time base
```
                    MVI     A,81H       ;Port C lower = input
                    OUT     0C3H        ;PPI control port
                    MVI     A,36H       ;Counter 0 mode 3 binary
                    OUT     0C7H        ;PIT control port
                    IN      0C2H        ;Read switch value
                    ANI     0FH         ;Mask bits 4–7
                    LXI     H,BAUD      ;Point at baud rate table
                    MVI     B,0         ;Prepare to from offset in BC
                    ADD     A           ;Double the switch value
                    MOV     C,A         ;Offset now in BC
                    DAD     B           ;Add to HL
                    MOV     A,M         ;Get LSB of initial count
                    OUT     0C4H        ;Counter 0 LSB
                    INX     H           ;Point to next byte
                    MOV     A,M         ;Get MSB of initial count
                    OUT     0C4H        ;Counter 0 MSB
                    RET
        BAUD        DB                  ;Store the 16 bit initial counts here
```

9.27. 2400 baud

9.29.
```
                    LD      C,0F3H      ;Channel B control port
                    LD      B,0         ;Point WR0 at RR0
                    OUT     (C),B       ;Program WR0
        POLL        IN      B,(C)       ;Read RR0
                    BIT     2,B         ;Test TXBE
                    JR      Z,POLL      ;Wait until ready
                    OUT     (C),A       ;Output the byte
                    RET
```

9.31. Assume counters 0 and 1 of the CTC are programmed for the counter mode with a 1.8432 MHz clock input on CLK/TRG0 and ZC/TO0 connected to CLK/TRG1. ZC/TO)1 is used as the clock input to a toggle flip-flop providing a 50% duty cycle baud rate clock input.
```
                    LD      A,0CFH
                    OUT     0C1H
                    LD      A,0FFh
                    OUT     0C1H
```

```
                    LD    A,55H
                    OUT   0C4H
                    OUT   0C5H
                    IN    A,(0C0H)
                    AND   0FH
                    LD    HL,BAUD
                    LD    B,0
                    ADD   A,A
                    LD    C,A
                    ADD   HL,BC
                    LD    A,(HL)
                    OUT   0C4H
                    INC   H
                    LD    A,(HL)
                    OUT   0C5H
                    RET
            BAUD    DB    ;Put the time constant codes here
```

9.33. $-5V$ to $-15V$

9.35. 2 $\longrightarrow$ 3

3 $\longleftarrow$ 2

7 $\longrightarrow$ 7

6 $\longleftarrow$ 20

20 $\longrightarrow$ 6

9.37. 8251A: Connect BUSY/READY to $\overline{\text{DSR}}$ which then can be polled. Connect $\overline{\text{STROBE}}$ to $\overline{\text{DTR}}$ or $\overline{\text{RTS}}$ which then can be polled via a command instruction. $\overline{\text{CTS}}$ must be grounded to enable the USART transmitter.

SIO: The same connections can be used except BUSY/READY connects to $\overline{\text{DCD}}$ and the CTC input need not be grounded. Do not enable the auto enables function (WR3 bit 5 = 0).

9.39. Full duplex implies the ability to simultaneously transmit and receive. This requires two different sets of frequencies—originate and answer—by each modem.

9.41. **(a)** 600 bps

9.43. 2400

9.45. AT/OK

Chapter 10

10.1. More tracks/side

10.3. **(a)** 167 ms

(b) 16.7 ms

10.5. **(a)** 2.375 in

(b) 10.25 in^2

(c) Disk area = 21.65 in^2

10.7. Convert the analog signals to digital, control spindle and head actuator motors, communicate with the system processor, and oversee all drive operations.

10.9. 308,448

10.11. **(a)** 8

(b) 3

(c) 3,726 GB

Answers to Odd-Numbered Problems   **689**

10.13. 8704

10.15. One revolution of the disk supplies twice as much data.

10.17. FM: 0,1; MFM: 1,3; RLL 2,7: 2,7

10.19. **(a)** 34
   (b) 40
   (c) 50

Chapter 11

11.1. True

11.3. **(a)** Power supply shorted
   (c) Standard TTL cannot be wire-Ored

11.5. 14 and 62 ohms

11.7. **(b)**

11.9. **(b)** 10 mA
   (c) 12.8 mA

11.11. $V_{out} = -5V$

11.13. **(c)** V_{out} max = 9.96V

11.15. 6.4 ms and 0.2 ms

11.17. 6.172V

11.19.

START	LD	B,8	;Trials counter
	LD	D,80H	;Initial guess
	LD	C,0F0H	;DAC port address
	LD	A,0	;Sum = 0
LOOP	ADD	A,D	
	OUT	(C),A	
	LD	E,A	
	IN	A,(0F2H)	;Read comparator
	RRA		
	LD	A,E	
	JNC	SMALL	
	SUB	D	
SMALL	DJNZ	NXBT	
	INC	C	;Display port
	JR	START	
NXBT	RRC	D	
	JR	LOOP	

11.21. **(a)** 35H
   (b) OUT 35H or OUT (35H),A

11.23. The 6116 $\overline{WE}$ input or 8255 $\overline{WR}$ input is internally shorted to ground.

11.25. No

11.27. Because the computer has never been verified to run before, wiring errors may be present. Use a continuity checker to verify the wiring schematic.

11.29. timing

Chapter 12

12.1. Faster operating speed

12.3. (a) word access
   (c) read cycle

12.5. 16

12.7. 268H–26BH

12.9. Memory would be unable to receive its addresses.

12.11. 27300H

12.13. (a) 88200H
   (d) 1089EH

12.15. False

12.17. (a) Register sizes must match
   (c) AX cannot be used as a pointer

12.19. Bit 6 of port 00C3H must be low.

12.21. (a) 8000H
   (c) C000H

12.23.
```
ORG   0600H
MOV   SI,0700H     ;Point to first byte
MOV   AL,(SI)
INC   SI
ADD   AL,(SI)
INC   SI
MOV   (SI),AL
HLT
```

12.25. (a) 32K
   (c) $\overline{\text{SEL ODD BYTE}}$ holds the $\overline{\text{CS}}$ inputs inactive.

12.27. Wire the second bank of 16 2167 RAM chips in parallel with the first bank. Bank 0 is selected with SEL ODD0 and SEL EVEN0 (AB15 = 0) while bank 1 is selected with SEL ODD1 and SEL EVEN1 (AB15 = 1).

12.29. IN AL,05H

12.31. Design an address decoder (NAND gate) to detect the address 00001XX0 on AB7–AB0. Use this signal to enable the PIT. AB1 and AB2 (wired to A0 and A1 of the PIT) then select one of four ports in the PIT.

APPENDICES

APPENDIX A.1

Instruction		Code	Bytes	T States 8085A	T States 8080A	Machine Cycles
ACI	DATA	CE data	2	7	7	F R
ADC	REG	1000 1SSS	1	4	4	F
ADC	M	8E	1	7	7	F R
ADD	REG	1000 0SSS	1	4	4	F
ADD	M	86	1	7	7	F R
ADI	DATA	C6 data	2	7	7	F R
ANA	REG	1010 0SSS	1	4	4	F
ANA	M	A6	1	7	7	F R
ANI	DATA	E6 data	2	7	7	F R
CALL	LABEL	CD addr	3	18	17	S R R W W*
CC	LABEL	DC addr	3	9/18	11/17	S R•/S R R W W*
CM	LABEL	FC addr	3	9/18	11/17	S R•/S R R W W*
CMA		2F	1	4	4	F
CMC		3F	1	4	4	F
CMP	REG	1011 1SSS	1	4	4	F
CMP	M	BE	1	7	7	F R
CNC	LABEL	D4 addr	3	9/18	11/17	S R•/S R R W W*
CNZ	LABEL	C4 addr	3	9/18	11/17	S R•/S R R W W*
CP	LABEL	F4 addr	3	9/18	11/17	S R•/S R R W W*
CPE	LABEL	EC addr	3	9/18	11/17	S R•/S R R W W*
CPI	DATA	FE data	2	7	7	F R
CPO	LABEL	E4 addr	3	9/18	11/17	S R•/S R R W W*
CZ	LABEL	CC addr	3	9/18	11/17	S R•/S R R W W*
DAA		27	1	4	4	F
DAD	RP	00RP 1001	1	10	10	F B B
DCR	REG	00SS S101	1	4	5	F*
DCR	M	35	1	10	10	F R W
DCX	RP	00RP 1011	1	6	5	S*
DI		F3	1	4	4	F
EI		FB	1	4	4	F
HLT		76	1	5	7	F B
IN	PORT	DB data	2	10	10	F R I
INR	REG	00SS S100	1	4	5	F*
INR	M	34	1	10	10	F R W
INX	RP	00RP 0011	1	6	5	S*
JC	LABEL	DA addr	3	7/10	10	F R/F R R†
JM	LABEL	FA addr	3	7/10	10	F R/F R R†
JMP	LABEL	C3 addr	3	10	10	F R R
JNC	LABEL	D2 addr	3	7/10	10	F R/F R R†
JNZ	LABEL	C2 addr	3	7/10	10	F R/F R R†
JP	LABEL	F2 addr	3	7/10	10	F R/F R R†
JPE	LABEL	EA addr	3	7/10	10	F R/F R R†
JPO	LABEL	E2 addr	3	7/10	10	F R/F R R†
JZ	LABEL	CA addr	3	7/10	10	F R/F R R†
LDA	ADDR	3A addr	3	13	13	F R R R
LDAX	RP	000X 1010	1	7	7	F R
LHLD	ADDR	2A addr	3	16	16	F R R R R

Instruction		Code	Bytes	T States 8085A	T States 8080A	Machine Cycles
LXI	RP,DATA16	00RP 0001 data16	3	10	10	F R R
MOV	REG,REG	01DD DSSS	1	4	5	F*
MOV	M,REG	0111 0SSS	1	7	7	F W
MOV	REG,M	01DD D110	1	7	7	F R
MVI	REG,DATA	00DD D110 data	2	7	7	F R
MVI	M,DATA	36 data	2	10	10	F R W
NOP		00	1	4	4	F
ORA	REG	1011 0SSS	1	4	4	F
ORA	M	B6	1	7	7	F R
ORI	DATA	F6 data	2	7	7	F R
OUT	PORT	D3 data	2	10	10	F R O
PCHL		E9	1	6	5	S*
POP	RP	11RP 0001	1	10	10	F R R
PUSH	RP	11RP 0101	1	12	11	S W W*
RAL		17	1	4	4	F
RAR		1F	1	4	4	F
RC		D8	1	6/12	5/11	S/S R R*
RET		C9	1	10	10	F R R
RIM (8085A only)		20	1	4	–	F
RLC		07	1	4	4	F
RM		F8	1	6/12	5/11	S/S R R*
RNC		D0	1	6/12	5/11	S/S R R*
RNZ		C0	1	6/12	5/11	S/S R R*
RP		F0	1	6/12	5/11	S/S R R*
RPE		E8	1	6/12	5/11	S/S R R*
RPO		E0	1	6/12	5/11	S/S R R*
RRC		0F	1	4	4	F
RST	N	11XX X111	1	12	11	S W W*
RZ		C8	1	6/12	5/11	S/S R R*
SBB	REG	1001 1SSS	1	4	4	F
SBB	M	9E	1	7	7	F R
SBI	DATA	DE data	2	7	7	F R
SHLD	ADDR	22 addr	3	16	16	F R R W W
SIM (8085A only)		30	1	4	–	F
SPHL		F9	1	6	5	S*
STA	ADDR	32 addr	3	13	13	F R R W
STAX	RP	000X 0010	1	7	7	F W
STC		37	1	4	4	F
SUB	REG	1001 0SSS	1	4	4	F
SUB	M	96	1	7	7	F R
SUI	DATA	D6 data	2	7	7	F R
XCHG		EB	1	4	4	F
XRA	REG	1010 1SSS	1	4	4	F
XRA	M	AE	1	7	7	F R
XRI	DATA	EE data	2	7	7	F R
XTHL		E3	1	16	18	F R R W W

*All mnemonics copyrighted   Intel Corporation 1976.

Machine cycle types

F   Four clock period instr fetch
S   Six clock period instr fetch
R   Memory read
I   I/O read
W   Memory write
O   I/O write
B   Bus idle
X   Variable or optional binary digit

DDD   Binary digits identifying a destination register
SSS   Binary digits identifying a source register
RP   Register Pair   BC 00, HL 10 / DE 01, SP 11

B 000, C 001, D 010 Memory 110
E 011, H 100, L 101 A 111

* Five clock period instruction fetch with 8080A
† The longer machine cycle sequence applies regardless of condition evaluation with 8080A
• An extra READ cycle (R) will occur for this condition with 8080A

Appendix A.1   8080/85 Machine Cycle and T State Summary. (Courtesy of Intel Corporation.)

APPENDIX A.2

CONSTANT DEFINITION

0BDH / 1AH	Hex
105D / 105	Decimal
72O / 72Q	Octal
11011B / 00110B	Binary
'TEST' / 'A' 'B'	ASCII

OPERATORS

- (,)
- * , / , MOD, SHL, SHR
- + , -
- NOT
- AND
- OR, XOR

STANDARD SETS

A	SET	7
B	SET	0
C	SET	1
D	SET	2
E	SET	3
H	SET	4
L	SET	5
M	SET	6
SP	SET	6
PSW	SET	6

FLAG BYTE STACK FORMAT

7	6	5	4	3	2	1	0
S	Z	0	A	0	P	1	C

JUMP

C3	JMP		
C2	JNZ		
CA	JZ		
D2	JNC		
DA	JC		Adr
E2	JPO		
EA	JPE		
F2	JP		
FA	JM		
E9	PCHL		

CALL

CD	CALL	
C4	CNZ	
CC	CZ	
D4	CNC	
DC	CC	Adr
E4	CPO	
EC	CPE	
F4	CP	
FC	CM	

RETURN

C9	RET
C0	RNZ
C8	RZ
D0	RNC
D8	RC
E0	RPO
E8	RPE
F0	RP
F8	RM

RESTART

C7	RST	0
CF	RST	1
D7	RST	2
DF	RST	3
E7	RST	4
EF	RST	5
F7	RST	6
FF	RST	7

MOVE IMMEDIATE

06	MVI	B,
0E	MVI	C,
16	MVI	D,
1E	MVI	E,
26	MVI	H,	D8
2E	MVI	L,
36	MVI	M,
3E	MVI	A,

Acc IMMEDIATE*

C6	ADI	
CE	ACI	
D6	SUI	
DE	SBI	D8
E6	ANI	
EE	XRI	
F6	ORI	
FE	CPI	

LOAD IMMEDIATE

01	LXI	B,
11	LXI	D,	D16
21	LXI	H,
31	LXI	SP,

DOUBLE ADD†

09	DAD	B
19	DAD	D
29	DAD	H
39	DAD	SP

LOAD/STORE

0A	LDAX	B
1A	LDAX	D
2A	LHLD	Adr
3A	LDA	Adr
02	STAX	B
12	STAX	D
22	SHLD	Adr
32	STA	Adr

INCREMENT**

04	INR	B	03	INX	B
0C	INR	C	13	INX	D
14	INR	D	23	INX	H
1C	INR	E	33	INX	SP
24	INR	H			
2C	INR	L			
34	INR	M			
3C	INR	A			

DECREMENT**

05	DCR	B	0B	DCX	B
0D	DCR	C	1B	DCX	D
15	DCR	D	2B	DCX	H
1D	DCR	E	3B	DCX	SP
25	DCR	H			
2D	DCR	L			
35	DCR	M			
3D	DCR	A			

ROTATE†

07	RLC
0F	RRC
17	RAL
1F	RAR

CONTROL

00	NOP
76	HLT
F3	DI
FB	EI

MOVE

40	MOV	B,B
41	MOV	B,C
42	MOV	B,D
43	MOV	B,E
44	MOV	B,H
45	MOV	B,L
46	MOV	B,M
47	MOV	B,A
48	MOV	C,B
49	MOV	C,C
4A	MOV	C,D
4B	MOV	C,E
4C	MOV	C,H
4D	MOV	C,L
4E	MOV	C,M
4F	MOV	C,A
50	MOV	D,B
51	MOV	D,C
52	MOV	D,D
53	MOV	D,E
54	MOV	D,H
55	MOV	D,L
56	MOV	D,M
57	MOV	D,A

STACK OPS

C5	PUSH	B
D5	PUSH	D
E5	PUSH	H
F5	PUSH	PSW
C1	POP	B
D1	POP	D
E1	POP	H
F1	POP	PSW*
E3	XTHL	
F9	SPHL	

SPECIALS

EB	XCHG
27	DAA*
2F	CMA
37	STC†
3F	CMC†

INPUT/OUTPUT

D3	OUT	D8
DB	IN	

MOVE (cont)

58	MOV	E,B
59	MOV	E,C
5A	MOV	E,D
5B	MOV	E,E
5C	MOV	E,H
5D	MOV	E,L
5E	MOV	E,M
5F	MOV	E,A
60	MOV	H,B
61	MOV	H,C
62	MOV	H,D
63	MOV	H,E
64	MOV	H,H
65	MOV	H,L
66	MOV	H,M
67	MOV	H,A
68	MOV	L,B
69	MOV	L,C
6A	MOV	L,D
6B	MOV	L,E
6C	MOV	L,H
6D	MOV	L,L
6E	MOV	L,M
6F	MOV	L,A
70	MOV	M,B
71	MOV	M,C
72	MOV	M,D
73	MOV	M,E
74	MOV	M,H
75	MOV	M,L
77	MOV	M,A
78	MOV	A,B
79	MOV	A,C
7A	MOV	A,D
7B	MOV	A,E
7C	MOV	A,H
7D	MOV	A,L
7E	MOV	A,M
7F	MOV	A,A

ACCUMULATOR*

80	ADD	B	90	SUB	B	A0	ANA	B	
81	ADD	C	91	SUB	C	A1	ANA	C	
82	ADD	D	92	SUB	D	A2	ANA	D	
83	ADD	E	93	SUB	E	A3	ANA	E	
84	ADD	H	94	SUB	H	A4	ANA	H	
85	ADD	L	95	SUB	L	A5	ANA	L	
86	ADD	M	96	SUB	M	A6	ANA	M	
87	ADD	A	97	SUB	A	A7	ANA	A	
88	ADC	B	98	SBB	B	A8	XRA	B	
89	ADC	C	99	SBB	C	A9	XRA	C	
8A	ADC	D	9A	SBB	D	AA	XRA	D	
8B	ADC	E	9B	SBB	E	AB	XRA	E	
8C	ADC	H	9C	SBB	H	AC	XRA	H	
8D	ADC	L	9D	SBB	L	AD	XRA	L	
8E	ADC	M	9E	SBB	M	AE	XRA	M	
8F	ADC	A	9F	SBB	A	AF	XRA	A	

B0	ORA	B	B8	CMP	B
B1	ORA	C	B9	CMP	C
B2	ORA	D	BA	CMP	D
B3	ORA	E	BB	CMP	E
B4	ORA	H	BC	CMP	H
B5	ORA	L	BD	CMP	L
B6	ORA	M	BE	CMP	M
B7	ORA	A	BF	CMP	A

PSEUDO INSTRUCTION

ORG	Adr
END	
EQU	D16
SET	D16
DS	D16
DB	D8 [ ]
DW	D16 [ ]
IF	D16
ENDIF	
MACRO	[ ]
ENDM	

D8 = constant, or logical/arithmetic expression that evaluates to an 8 bit data quantity.

* = all Flags (C, Z, S, P, AC) affected

D16 = constant, or logical/arithmetic expression that evaluates to a 16 bit data quantity.

† = only CARRY affected

Adr = 16 bit address

** = all Flags except CARRY affected; (exception: INX & DCX affect no Flags)

Appendix A.2 8080/85 Hexadecimal Instruction Set Index. (Courtesy of Intel Corporation.)

Instruction Set

The Z80 microprocessor has one of the most powerful and versatile instruction sets available in any 8-bit microprocessor. It includes such unique operations as a block move for fast, efficient data transfers within memory or between memory and I/O. It also allows operations on any bit in any location in memory.

The following is a summary of the Z80 instruction set and shows the assembly language mnemonic, the operation, the flag status, and gives comments on each instruction. The *Z80 CPU Technical Manual* (03-0029-01) and *Assembly Language Programming Manual* (03-0002-01) contain significantly more details for programming use.

The instructions are divided into the following categories:

☐ 8-bit loads

☐ 16-bit loads

☐ Exchanges, block transfers, and searches

☐ 8-bit arithmetic and logic operations

☐ General-purpose arithmetic and CPU control

☐ 16-bit arithmetic operations

☐ Rotates and shifts

☐ Bit set, reset, and test operations

☐ Jumps

☐ Calls, returns, and restarts

☐ Input and output operations

A variety of addressing modes are implemented to permit efficient and fast data transfer between various registers, memory locations, and input/output devices. These addressing modes include:

☐ Immediate

☐ Immediate extended

☐ Modified page zero

☐ Relative

☐ Extended

☐ Indexed

☐ Register

☐ Register indirect

☐ Implied

☐ Bit

8-Bit Load Group

Mnemonic	Symbolic Operation	S	Z	H	P/V	N	C	Opcode 76 543 210	Hex	No.of Bytes	No.of M Cycles	No.of T States	Comments
LD r, r'	r ← r'	•	•	X	•	X	•	•	•	01 r r'		1	1	4	r, r' Reg.
LD r, n	r ← n	•	•	X	•	X	•	•	•	00 r 110 – n –		2	2	7	000 B
														001 C
LD r, (HL)	r ← (HL)	•	•	X	•	X	•	•	•	01 r 110		1	2	7	010 D
LD r, (IX + d)	r ← (IX + d)	•	•	X	•	X	•	•	•	11 011 101 01 r 101 – d –	DD	3	5	19	011 E 100 H
LD r, (IY + d)	r ← (IY + d)	•	•	X	•	X	•	•	•	11 111 101 01 r 110 – d –	FD	3	5	19	101 L 111 A
LD (HL), r	(HL) ← r	•	•	X	•	X	•	•	•	01 110 r		1	2	7	
LD (IX + d), r	(IX + d) ← r	•	•	X	•	X	•	•	•	11 011 101 01 110 r – d –	DD	3	5	19	
LD (IY + d), r	(IY + d) ← r	•	•	X	•	X	•	•	•	11 111 101 01 110 r – d –	FD	3	5	19	
LD (HL), n	(HL) ← n	•	•	X	•	X	•	•	•	00 110 110 – n –	36	2	3	10	
LD (IX + d), n	(IX + d) ← n	•	•	X	•	X	•	•	•	11 011 101 00 110 110 – d – – n –	DD 36	4	5	19	
LD (IY + d), n	(IY + d) ← n	•	•	X	•	X	•	•	•	11 111 101 00 110 110 – d – – n–	FD 36	4	5	19	
LD A, (BC)	A ← (BC)	•	•	X	•	X	•	•	•	00 001 010	0A	1	2	7	
LD A, (DE)	A ← (DE)	•	•	X	•	X	•	•	•	00 011 010	1A	1	2	7	
LD A, (nn)	A ← (nn)	•	•	X	•	X	•	•	•	00 111 010 – n – – n –	3A	3	4	13	
LD (BC), A	(BC) ← A	•	•	X	•	X	•	•	•	00 000 010	02	1	2	7	
LD (DE), A	(DE) ← A	•	•	X	•	X	•	•	•	00 010 010	12	1	2	7	
LD (nn), A	(nn) ← A	•	•	X	•	X	•	•	•	00 110 010 – n – – n –	32	3	4	13	
LD A, I	A ← I	↕	↕	X	0	X	IFF	0	•	11 101 101 01 010 111	ED 57	2	2	9	
LD A, R	A ← R	↕	↕	X	0	X	IFF	0	•	11 101 101 01 011 111	ED 5F	2	2	9	
LD I, A	I ← A	•	•	X	•	X	•	•	•	11 101 101 01 000 111	ED 47	2	2	9	
LD R, A	R ← A	•	•	X	•	X	•	•	•	11 101 101 01 001 111	ED 4F	2	2	9	

NOTES: r, r' means any of the registers A, B, C, D, E, H, L.
IFF the content of the interrupt enable flip-flop, (IFF) is copied into the P/V flag.

For an explanation of flag notation and symbols for mnemonic tables, see Symbolic Notation section following tables.

Appendix B.1 Z-80 Instruction Set Description. (Courtesy of Zilog, Inc.)

16-Bit Load Group

Mnemonic	Symbolic Operation	S	Z	H	P/V	N	C	Opcode 76 543 210 / Hex	No.of Bytes	No.of M Cycles	No.of T States	Comments
LD dd, nn	dd ← nn	•	•	X	•	X	•	•	•	00 dd0 001 ← n → ← n →	3	3	10	dd / Pair 00 BC 01 DE 10 HL 11 SP
LD IX, nn	IX ← nn	•	•	X	•	X	•	•	•	11 011 101 DD 00 100 001 21 ← n → ← n →	4	4	14	
LD IY, nn	IY ← nn	•	•	X	•	X	•	•	•	11 111 101 FD 00 100 001 21 ← n → ← n →	4	4	14	
LD HL, (nn)	H ← (nn + 1) L ← (nn)	•	•	X	•	X	•	•	•	00 101 010 2A ← n → ← n →	3	5	16	
LD dd, (nn)	dd$_H$ ← (nn + 1) dd$_L$ ← (nn)	•	•	X	•	X	•	•	•	11 101 101 ED 01 dd1 011 ← n → ← n →	4	6	20	
LD IX, (nn)	IX$_H$ ← (nn + 1) IX$_L$ ← (nn)	•	•	X	•	X	•	•	•	11 011 101 DD 00 101 010 2A ← n → ← n →	4	6	20	
LD IY, (nn)	IY$_H$ ← (nn + 1) IY$_L$ ← (nn)	•	•	X	•	X	•	•	•	11 111 101 FD 00 101 010 2A ← n → ← n →	4	6	20	
LD (nn), HL	(nn + 1) ← H (nn) ← L	•	•	X	•	X	•	•	•	00 100 010 22 ← n → ← n →	3	5	16	
LD (nn), dd	(nn + 1) ← dd$_H$ (nn) ← dd$_L$	•	•	X	•	X	•	•	•	11 101 101 ED 01 dd0 011 ← n → ← n →	4	6	20	
LD (nn), IX	(nn + 1) ← IX$_H$ (nn) ← IX$_L$	•	•	X	•	X	•	•	•	11 011 101 DD 00 100 010 22 ← n → ← n →	4	6	20	
LD (nn), IY	(nn + 1) ← IY$_H$ (nn) ← IY$_L$	•	•	X	•	X	•	•	•	11 111 101 FD 00 100 010 22 ← n → ← n →	4	6	20	
LD SP, HL	SP ← HL	•	•	X	•	X	•	•	•	11 111 001 F9	1	1	6	
LD SP, IX	SP ← IX	•	•	X	•	X	•	•	•	11 011 101 DD 11 111 001 F9	2	2	10	
LD SP, IY	SP ← IY	•	•	X	•	X	•	•	•	11 111 101 FD 11 111 001 F9	2	2	10	
PUSH qq	(SP − 2) ← qq$_L$ (SP − 1) ← qq$_H$ SP ← SP − 2	•	•	X	•	X	•	•	•	11 qq0 101	1	3	11	qq / Pair 00 BC 01 DE 10 HL 11 AF
PUSH IX	(SP − 2) ← IX$_L$ (SP − 1) ← IX$_H$ SP ← SP − 2	•	•	X	•	X	•	•	•	11 011 101 DD 11 100 101 E5	2	4	15	
PUSH IY	(SP − 2) ← IY$_L$ (SP − 1) ← IY$_H$ SP ← SP − 2	•	•	X	•	X	•	•	•	11 111 101 FD 11 100 101 E5	2	4	15	
POP qq	qq$_H$ ← (SP + 1) qq$_L$ ← (SP) SP ← SP + 2	•	•	X	•	X	•	•	•	11 qq0 001	1	3	10	
POP IX	IX$_H$ ← (SP + 1) IX$_L$ ← (SP) SP ← SP + 2	•	•	X	•	X	•	•	•	11 011 101 DD 11 100 001 E1	2	4	14	
POP IY	IY$_H$ ← (SP + 1) IY$_L$ ← (SP) SP ← SP + 2	•	•	X	•	X	•	•	•	11 111 101 FD 11 100 001 E1	2	4	14	

NOTES: dd is any of the register pairs BC, DE, HL, SP. (PAIR)$_H$, (PAIR)$_L$ refer to high order and low order eight bits of the register pair respectively.
qq is any of the register pairs AF, BC, DE, HL. e.g., BC$_L$ = C, AF$_H$ = A.

Exchange, Block Transfer, Block Search Groups

Mnemonic	Symbolic Operation	S	Z	H	P/V	N	C	Opcode 76 543 210 / Hex	No.of Bytes	No.of M Cycles	No.of T States	Comments
EX DE, HL	DE ← HL	•	•	X	•	X	•	•	•	11 101 011 EB	1	1	4	
EX AF, AF'	AF ← AF'	•	•	X	•	X	•	•	•	00 001 000 08	1	1	4	
EXX	BC ← BC' DE ← DE' HL ← HL'	•	•	X	•	X	•	•	•	11 011 001 D9	1	1	4	Register bank and auxiliary register bank exchange
EX (SP), HL	H ← (SP + 1) L ← (SP)	•	•	X	•	X	•	•	•	11 100 011 E3	1	5	19	
EX (SP), IX	IX$_H$ ← (SP + 1) IX$_L$ ← (SP)	•	•	X	•	X	•	•	•	11 011 101 DD 11 100 011 E3	2	6	23	
EX (SP), IY	IY$_H$ ← (SP + 1) IY$_L$ ← (SP)	•	•	X	•	X	•	•	•	11 111 101 FD 11 100 011 E3	2	6	23	
LDI	(DE) ← (HL) DE ← DE + 1 HL ← HL + 1 BC ← BC − 1	•	•	X	0	X	①	0	•	11 101 101 ED 10 100 000 A0	2	4	16	Load (HL) into (DE), increment the pointers and decrement the byte counter (BC)
LDIR	(DE) ← (HL) DE ← DE + 1 HL ← HL + 1 BC ← BC − 1 Repeat until BC = 0	•	•	X	0	X	0	0	•	11 101 101 ED 10 110 000 B0	2 2	5 4	21 16	If BC ≠ 0 If BC = 0

NOTE: ① P/V flag is 0 if the result of BC − 1 = 0, otherwise P/V = 1.

Exchange,
Block
Transfer,
Block Search
Groups
(Continued)

Mnemonic	Symbolic Operation	S	Z	Flags H		P/V	N	C	Opcode 76 543 210 Hex	No.of Bytes	No.of M Cycles	No.of T States	Comments
						①							
LDD	(DE) ← (HL) DE ← DE – 1 HL ← HL – 1 BC ← BC – 1	•	•	X	0	X	↕	0	•	11 101 101 ED 10 101 000 A8	2	4	16	
LDDR	(DE) ← (HL) DE ← DE – 1 HL ← HL – 1 BC ← BC – 1 Repeat until BC = 0	•	•	X	0	X	0	0	•	11 101 101 ED 10 111 000 B8	2 2	5 4	21 16	If BC ≠ 0 If BC = 0
			②			①							
CPI	A – (HL) HL ← HL + 1 BC ← BC – 1	↕	↕	X	↕	X	↕	1	•	11 101 101 ED 10 100 001 A1	2	4	16	
			②			①							
CPIR	A – (HL) HL ← HL + 1 BC ← BC – 1 Repeat until A = (HL) or BC = 0	↕	↕	X	↕	X	↕	1	•	11 101 101 ED 10 110 001 B1	2 2	5 4	21 16	If BC ≠ 0 and A ≠ (HL) If BC = 0 or A = (HL)
			②			①							
CPD	A – (HL) HL ← HL – 1 BC ← BC – 1	↕	↕	X	↕	X	↕	1	•	11 101 101 ED 10 101 001 A9	2	4	16	
			②			①							
CPDR	A – (HL) HL ← HL – 1 BC ← BC – 1 Repeat until A = (HL) or BC = 0	↕	↕	X	↕	X	↕	1	•	11 101 101 ED 10 111 001 B9	2 2	5 4	21 16	If BC ≠ 0 and A ≠ (HL) If BC = 0 or A = (HL)

NOTES: ① P/V flag is 0 if the result of BC – 1 = 0, otherwise P/V = 1.
② Z flag is 1 if A = (HL), otherwise Z = 0.

8-Bit Arithmetic and Logical Group

Mnemonic	Symbolic Operation	S	Z	Flags H		P/V	N	C	Opcode 76 543 210 Hex	No.of Bytes	No.of M Cycles	No.of T States	Comments
ADD A, r	A ← A + r	↕	↕	X	↕	X	V	0	↕	10 [000] r	1	1	4	r Reg.
ADD A, n	A ← A + n	↕	↕	X	↕	X	V	0	↕	11 [000] 110 ← n →	2	2	7	000 B 001 C 010 D
ADD A, (HL)	A ← A + (HL)	↕	↕	X	↕	X	V	0	↕	10 [000] 110	1	2	7	011 E
ADD A, (IX + d)	A ← A + (IX + d)	↕	↕	X	↕	X	V	0	↕	11 011 101 DD 10 [000] 110 ← d →	3	5	19	100 H 101 L 111 A
ADD A, (IY + d)	A ← A + (IY + d)	↕	↕	X	↕	X	V	0	↕	11 111 101 FD 10 [000] 110 ← d →	3	5	19	
ADC A, s	A ← A + s + CY	↕	↕	X	↕	X	V	0	↕	[001]				s is any of r, n, (HL), (IX + d), (IY + d) as shown for ADD instruction. The indicated bits replace the [000] in the ADD set above.
SUB s	A ← A – s	↕	↕	X	↕	X	V	1	↕	[010]				
SBC A, s	A ← A – s – CY	↕	↕	X	↕	X	V	1	↕	[011]				
AND s	A ← A ∧ s	↕	↕	X	1	X	P	0	0	[100]				
OR s	A ← A ∨ s	↕	↕	X	0	X	P	0	0	[110]				
XOR s	A ← A ● s	↕	↕	X	0	X	P	0	0	[101]				
CP s	A – s	↕	↕	X	↕	X	V	1	↕	[111]				
INC r	r ← r + 1	↕	↕	X	↕	X	V	0	•	00 r [100]	1	1	4	
INC (HL)	(HL) ← (HL) + 1	↕	↕	X	↕	X	V	0	•	00 110 [100]	1	3	11	
INC (IX + d)	(IX + d) ← (IX + d) + 1	↕	↕	X	↕	X	V	0	•	11 011 101 DD 00 110 [100] ← d →	3	6	23	
INC (IY + d)	(IY + d) ← (IY + d) + 1	↕	↕	X	↕	X	V	0	•	11 111 101 FD 00 110 [100] ← d →	3	6	23	
DEC m	m ← m – 1	↕	↕	X	↕	X	V	1	•	[101]				m is any of r, (HL), (IX + d), (IY + d) as shown for INC. DEC same format and states as INC. Replace [100] with [101] in opcode.

General-
Purpose
Arithmetic
and
CPU Control
Groups

Mnemonic	Symbolic Operation	Flags S	Z	H	P/V	N	C	Opcode 76 543 210	Hex	No.of Bytes	No.of M Cycles	No.of T States	Comments
DAA	Converts acc. content into packed BCD following add or subtract with packed BCD operands.	↕	↕	X	↕	X	P	•	↕	00 100 111	27	1	1	4	Decimal adjust accumulator.
CPL	A ← Ā	•	•	X	1	X	•	1	•	00 101 111	2F	1	1	4	Complement accumulator (one's complement).
NEG	A ← 0 − A	↕	↕	X	↕	X	V	1	↕	11 101 101 ED 01 000 100 44		2	2	8	Negate acc. (two's complement).
CCF	CY ← C̄Y	•	•	X	X	X	•	0	↕	00 111 111	3F	1	1	4	Complement carry flag.
SCF	CY ← 1	•	•	X	0	X	•	0	1	00 110 111	37	1	1	4	Set carry flag.
NOP	No operation	•	•	X	•	X	•	•	•	00 000 000	00	1	1	4	
HALT	CPU halted	•	•	X	•	X	•	•	•	01 110 110	76	1	1	4	
DI ★	IFF ← 0	•	•	X	•	X	•	•	•	11 110 011	F3	1	1	4	
EI ★	IFF ← 1	•	•	X	•	X	•	•	•	11 111 011	FB	1	1	4	
IM 0	Set interrupt mode 0	•	•	X	•	X	•	•	•	11 101 101 ED 01 000 110 46		2	2	8	
IM 1	Set interrupt mode 1	•	•	X	•	X	•	•	•	11 101 101 ED 01 010 110 56		2	2	8	
IM 2	Set interrupt mode 2	•	•	X	•	X	•	•	•	11 101 101 ED 01 011 110 5E		2	2	8	

NOTES: IFF indicates the interrupt enable flip-flop.
CY indicates the carry flip-flop.
★ indicates interrupts are not sampled at the end of EI or DI.

16-Bit Arithmetic Group

Mnemonic	Symbolic Operation	S	Z	H	P/V	N	C	Opcode 76 543 210	No.of Bytes	No.of M Cycles	No.of T States	Comments
ADD HL, ss	HL ← HL + ss	•	•	X	X	X	•	0	↕	00 ss1 001	1	3	11	ss Reg. 00 BC 01 DE 10 HL 11 SP
ADC HL, ss	HL ← HL + ss + CY	↕	↕	X	X	X	V	0	↕	11 101 101 ED 01 ss1 010	2	4	15	
SBC HL, ss	HL ← HL − ss − CY	↕	↕	X	X	X	V	1	↕	11 101 101 ED 01 ss0 010	2	4	15	
ADD IX, pp	IX ← IX + pp	•	•	X	X	X	•	0	↕	11 011 101 DD 01 pp1 001	2	4	15	pp Reg. 00 BC 01 DE 10 IX 11 SP
ADD IY, rr	IY ← IY + rr	•	•	X	X	X	•	0	↕	11 111 101 FD 00 rr1 001	2	4	15	rr Reg. 00 BC 01 DE 10 IY 11 SP
INC ss	ss ← ss + 1	•	•	X	•	X	•	•	•	00 ss0 011	1	1	6	
INC IX	IX ← IX + 1	•	•	X	•	X	•	•	•	11 011 101 DD 00 100 011 23	2	2	10	
INC IY	IY ← IY + 1	•	•	X	•	X	•	•	•	11 111 101 FD 00 100 011 23	2	2	10	
DEC ss	ss ← ss − 1	•	•	X	•	X	•	•	•	00 ss1 011	1	1	6	
DEC IX	IX ← IX − 1	•	•	X	•	X	•	•	•	11 011 101 DD 00 101 011 2B	2	2	10	
DEC IY	IY ← IY − 1	•	•	X	•	X	•	•	•	11 111 101 FD 00 101 011 2B	2	2	10	

NOTES: ss is any of the register pairs BC, DE, HL, SP.
pp is any of the register pairs BC, DE, IX, SP.
rr is any of the register pairs BC, DE, IY, SP.

Rotate and Shift Group

Mnemonic	Symbolic Operation	S	Z	H	P/V	N	C	Opcode 76 543 210	Hex	No.of Bytes	No.of M Cycles	No.of T States	Comments
RLCA		•	•	X	0	X	•	0	↕	00 000 111	07	1	1	4	Rotate left circular accumulator.
RLA		•	•	X	0	X	•	0	↕	00 010 111	17	1	1	4	Rotate left accumulator.
RRCA		•	•	X	0	X	•	0	↕	00 001 111	0F	1	1	4	Rotate right circular accumulator.
RRA		•	•	X	0	X	•	0	↕	00 011 111	1F	1	1	4	Rotate right accumulator.
RLC r		↕	↕	X	0	X	P	0	↕	11 001 011 CB 00 [000] r		2	2	8	Rotate left circular register r.
RLC (HL)		↕	↕	X	0	X	P	0	↕	11 001 011 CB 00 [000] 110		2	4	15	r Reg. 000 B 001 C 010 D 011 E 100 H 101 L 111 A
RLC (IX + d)	r,(HL),(IX + d),(IY + d)	↕	↕	X	0	X	P	0	↕	11 011 101 DD 11 001 011 CB − d − 00 [000] 110		4	6	23	
RLC (IY + d)		↕	↕	X	0	X	P	0	↕	11 111 101 FD 11 001 011 CB − d − 00 [000] 110		4	6	23	
RL m	m ← r,(HL),(IX + d),(IY + d)	↕	↕	X	0	X	P	0	↕	[010]					Instruction format and states are as shown for RLC's. To form new opcode replace [000] or RLC's with shown code.
RRC m	m ← r,(HL),(IX + d),(IY + d)	↕	↕	X	0	X	P	0	↕	[001]					

Rotate and Shift Group (Continued)

Mnemonic	Symbolic Operation	S	Z	H	P/V	N	C	Opcode 76 543 210	Hex	No. of Bytes	No. of M Cycles	No. of T States	Comments
RR m	[7→0]→[CY] loop; m = r,(HL),(IX + d),(IY + d)	↕	↕	X	0	X	P	0	↕	[011]				
SLA m	[CY]←[7←0]←0; m = r,(HL),(IX + d),(IY + d)	↕	↕	X	0	X	P	0	↕	[100]				
SRA m	[7→0]→[CY]; m = r,(HL),(IX + d),(IY + d)	↕	↕	X	0	X	P	0	↕	[101]				
SRL m	0→[7→0]→[CY]; m = r,(HL),(IX + d),(IY + d)	↕	↕	X	0	X	P	0	↕	[111]				
RLD	[7-4 3-0] A / [7-4 3-0] (HL)	↕	↕	X	0	X	P	0	•	11 101 101 / 01 101 111	ED / 6F	2	5	18	Rotate digit left and right between the accumulator and location (HL).
RRD	[7-4 3-0] A / [7-4 3-0] (HL)	↕	↕	X	0	X	P	0	•	11 101 101 / 01 100 111	ED / 67	2	5	18	The content of the upper half of the accumulator is unaffected.

Bit Set, Reset and Test Group

Mnemonic	Symbolic Operation	S	Z	H	P/V	N	C	Opcode 76 543 210	Hex	No. of Bytes	No. of M Cycles	No. of T States	Comments
BIT b, r	Z ← $\overline{r_b}$	X	↕	X	1	X	X	0	•	11 001 011 / 01 b r	CB	2	2	8	
BIT b, (HL)	Z ← $\overline{(HL)_b}$	X	↕	X	1	X	X	0	•	11 001 011 / 01 b 110	CB	2	3	12	
BIT b, (IX + d)_b	Z ← $\overline{(IX + d)_b}$	X	↕	X	1	X	X	0	•	11 011 101 / 11 001 011 / — d — / 01 b 110	DD / CB	4	5	20	
BIT b, (IY + d)_b	Z ← $\overline{(IY + d)_b}$	X	↕	X	1	X	X	0	•	11 111 101 / 11 001 011 / — d — / 01 b 110	FD / CB	4	5	20	
SET b, r	r_b ← 1	•	•	X	•	X	•	•	•	11 001 011 / [11] b r	CB	2	2	8	
SET b, (HL)	$(HL)_b$ ← 1	•	•	X	•	X	•	•	•	11 001 011 / [11] b 110	CB	2	4	15	
SET b, (IX + d)	$(IX + d)_b$ ← 1	•	•	X	•	X	•	•	•	11 011 101 / 11 001 011 / — d — / [11] b 110	DD / CB	4	6	23	
SET b, (IY + d)	$(IY + d)_b$ ← 1	•	•	X	•	X	•	•	•	11 111 101 / 11 001 011 / — d — / [11] b 110	FD / CB	4	6	23	
RES b, m	m_b ← 0; m = r, (HL), (IX + d), (IY + d)	•	•	X	•	X	•	•	•	[10]				To form new opcode replace [11] of SET b, s with [10]. Flags and time states for SET instruction.

r Reg.
- 000 B
- 001 C
- 010 D
- 011 E
- 100 H
- 101 L
- 111 A

b Bit Tested
- 000 0
- 001 1
- 010 2
- 011 3
- 100 4
- 101 5
- 110 6
- 111 7

NOTES: The notation m_b indicates bit b (0 to 7) or location m.

Jump Group

Mnemonic	Symbolic Operation	S	Z	H	P/V	N	C	Opcode 76 543 210	Hex	No. of Bytes	No. of M Cycles	No. of T States	Comments
JP nn	PC ← nn	•	•	X	•	X	•	•	•	11 000 011 / — n — / — n —	C3	3	3	10	
JP cc, nn	If condition cc is true PC ← nn, otherwise continue	•	•	X	•	X	•	•	•	11 cc 010 / — n — / — n —		3	3	10	
JR e	PC ← PC + e	•	•	X	•	X	•	•	•	00 011 000 / — e − 2 —	18	2	3	12	
JR C, e	If C = 0, continue; If C = 1, PC ← PC + e	•	•	X	•	X	•	•	•	00 111 000 / — e − 2 —	38	2 / 2	2 / 3	7 / 12	If condition not met. / If condition is met.
JR NC, e	If C = 1, continue; If C = 0, PC ← PC + e	•	•	X	•	X	•	•	•	00 110 000 / — e − 2 —	30	2 / 2	2 / 3	7 / 12	If condition not met. / If condition is met.
JP Z, e	If Z = 0, continue; If Z = 1, PC ← PC + e	•	•	X	•	X	•	•	•	00 101 000 / — e − 2 —	28	2 / 2	2 / 3	7 / 12	If condition not met. / If condition is met.
JR NZ, e	If Z = 1, continue; If Z = 0, PC ← PC + e	•	•	X	•	X	•	•	•	00 100 000 / — e − 2 —	20	2 / 2	2 / 3	7 / 12	If condition not met. / If condition is met.
JP (HL)	PC ← HL	•	•	X	•	X	•	•	•	11 101 001	E9	1	1	4	
JP (IX)	PC ← IX	•	•	X	•	X	•	•	•	11 011 101 / 11 101 001	DD / E9	2	2	8	

cc Condition
- 000 NZ non-zero
- 001 Z   zero
- 010 NC non-carry
- 011 C   carry
- 100 PO parity odd
- 101 PE parity even
- 110 P   sign positive
- 111 M   sign negative

Jump Group (Continued)

Mnemonic	Symbolic Operation	S	Z	H	P/V	N ②	C	Opcode 76 543 210 Hex	No. of Bytes	No. of M Cycles	No. of T States	Comments
JP (IY)	PC ← IY	•	•	X	•	X	•	•	11 111 101 FD 11 101 001 E9	2	2	8	
DJNZ, e	B ← B – 1 If B = 0, continue If B ≠ 0, PC ← PC + e	•	•	X	•	X	•	•	00 010 000 10 — e – 2 —	2 2	2 3	8 13	If B = 0. If B ≠ 0.

NOTES: e represents the extension in the relative addressing mode.
e is a signed two's complement number in the range < – 126, 129 >.
e – 2 in the opcode provides an effective address of pc + e as PC is incremented
by 2 prior to the addition of e.

Call and Return Group

Mnemonic	Symbolic Operation	S	Z	H	P/V	N ②	C	Opcode 76 543 210 Hex	No. of Bytes	No. of M Cycles	No. of T States	Comments
CALL nn	(SP – 1) ← PC$_H$ (SP – 2) ← PC$_L$ PC ← nn	•	•	X	•	X	•	•	11 001 101 CD — n — — n —	3	5	17	
CALL cc, nn	If condition cc is false continue, otherwise same as CALL nn	•	•	X	•	X	•	•	11 cc 100 — n — — n —	3 3	3 5	10 17	If cc is false. If cc is true.
RET	PC$_L$ ← (SP) PC$_H$ ← (SP + 1)	•	•	X	•	X	•	•	11 001 001 C9	1	3	10	
RET cc	If condition cc is false continue, otherwise same as RET	•	•	X	•	X	•	•	11 cc 000	1 1	1 3	5 11	If cc is false. If cc is true.
RETI	Return from interrupt	•	•	X	•	X	•	•	11 101 101 ED 01 001 101 4D	2	4	14	
RETN[1]	Return from non-maskable interrupt	•	•	X	•	X	•	•	11 101 101 ED 01 000 101 45	2	4	14	
RST p	(SP – 1) ← PC$_H$ (SP – 2) ← PC$_L$ PC$_H$ ← 0 PC$_L$ ← p	•	•	X	•	X	•	•	11 t 111	1	3	11	

cc	Condition	
000	NZ	non-zero
001	Z	zero
010	NC	non-carry
011	C	carry
100	PO	parity odd
101	PE	parity even
110	P	sign positive
111	M	sign negative

t	p
000	00H
001	08H
010	10H
011	18H
100	20H
101	28H
110	30H
111	38H

NOTE: [1]RETN loads IFF$_2$ → IFF$_1$

Input and Output Group

Mnemonic	Symbolic Operation	S	Z	H	P/V	N ②	C	Opcode 76 543 210 Hex	No. of Bytes	No. of M Cycles	No. of T States	Comments
IN A, (n)	A ← (n)	•	•	X	•	X	•	•	11 011 011 DB — n —	2	3	11	n to A$_0$ ~ A$_7$ Acc. to A$_8$ ~ A$_{15}$
IN r, (C)	r ← (C) if r = 110 only the flags will be affected	↕	↕	X	↕	X	P	0	11 101 101 ED 01 r 000	2	3	12	C to A$_0$ ~ A$_7$ B to A$_8$ ~ A$_{15}$
INI	(HL) ← (C) B ← B – 1 HL ← HL + 1	X	① ↕	X	X	X	X	↕	X	11 101 101 ED 10 100 010 A2	2	4	16	C to A$_0$ ~ A$_7$ B to A$_8$ ~ A$_{15}$
INIR	(HL) ← (C) B ← B – 1 HL ← HL + 1 Repeat until B = 0	X	1	X	X	X	X	↕	X	11 101 101 ED 10 110 010 B2	2 2	5 (If B≠0) 4 (If B = 0)	21 16	C to A$_0$ ~ A$_7$ B to A$_8$ ~ A$_{15}$
IND	(HL) ← (C) B ← B – 1 HL ← HL – 1	X	① ↕	X	X	X	X	↕	X	11 101 101 ED 10 101 010 AA	2	4	16	C to A$_0$ ~ A$_7$ B to A$_8$ ~ A$_{15}$
INDR	(HL) ← (C) B ← B – 1 HL ← HL – 1 Repeat until B = 0	X	1	X	X	X	X	↕	X	11 101 101 ED 10 111 010 BA	2 2	5 (If B≠0) 4 (If B = 0)	21 16	C to A$_0$ ~ A$_7$ B to A$_8$ ~ A$_{15}$
OUT (n), A	(n) ← A	•	•	X	•	X	•	↕	X	11 010 011 D3 — n —	2	3	11	n to A$_0$ ~ A$_7$ Acc. to A$_8$ ~ A$_{15}$
OUT (C), r	(C) ← r	•	•	X	•	X	•	↕	X	11 101 101 ED 01 r 001	2	3	12	C to A$_0$ ~ A$_7$ B to A$_8$ ~ A$_{15}$
OUTI	(C) ← (HL) B ← B – 1 HL ← HL + 1	X	① 1	X	X	X	X	↕	X	11 101 101 ED 10 100 011 A3	2	4	16	C to A$_0$ ~ A$_7$ B to A$_8$ ~ A$_{15}$
OTIR	(C) ← (HL) B ← B – 1 HL ← HL + 1 Repeat until B = 0	X	1	X	X	X	X	↕	X	11 101 101 ED 10 110 011 B3	2 2	5 (If B≠0) 4 (If B = 0)	21 16	C to A$_0$ ~ A$_7$ B to A$_8$ ~ A$_{15}$
OUTD	(C) ← (HL) B ← B – 1 HL ← HL – 1	X	① 1	X	X	X	X	↕	X	11 101 101 ED 10 101 011 AB	2	4	16	C to A$_0$ ~ A$_7$ B to A$_8$ ~ A$_{15}$

NOTE: ① If the result of B – 1 is zero the Z flag is set, otherwise it is reset.
② N Flag is 1 if data bit 7 is 1, otherwise N Flag is 0.

Input and Output Group (Continued)

Mnemonic	Symbolic Operation	S	Z	Flags H	P/V	N	C	Opcode 76 543 210	Hex	No.of Bytes	No.of M Cycles	No.of T States	Comments
OTDR	(C) ← (HL) B ← B - 1 HL ← HL - 1 Repeat until B = 0	X	1	X	X	X	1	X	11 101 101 10 111 011	ED	2 2	5 (If B ≠ 0) 4 (If B = 0)	21 16	C to A_0 ~ A_7 B to A_8 ~ A_{15}

Summary of Flag Operation

Instruction	D_7 S	Z	H	P/V	N	D_0 C	Comments
ADD A, s; ADC A, s	↑	↑	X	↑	X	V	0	↑	8-bit add or add with carry.
SUB s; SBC A, s; CP s; NEG	↑	↑	X	↑	X	V	1	↑	8-bit subtract, subtract with carry, compare and negate accumulator.
AND s	↑	↑	X	1	X	P	0	0	Logical operations.
OR s, XOR s	↑	↑	X	0	X	P	0	0	
INC s	↑	↑	X	↑	X	V	0	•	8-bit increment.
DEC s	↑	↑	X	↑	X	V	1	•	8-bit decrement.
ADD DD, ss	•	•	X	X	X	•	0	↑	16-bit add.
ADC HL, ss	↑	↑	X	X	X	V	0	↑	16-bit add with carry.
SBC HL, ss	↑	↑	X	X	X	V	1	↑	16-bit subtract with carry.
RLA, RLCA, RRA, RRCA	•	•	X	0	X	•	0	↑	Rotate accumulator.
RL m; RLC m; RR m; RRC m; SLA m; SRA m; SRL m	↑	↑	X	0	X	P	0	↑	Rotate and shift locations.
RLD; RRD	↑	↑	X	0	X	P	0	•	Rotate digit left and right.
DAA	↑	↑	X	↑	X	P	•	↑	Decimal adjust accumulator.
CPL	•	•	X	1	X	•	1	•	Complement accumulator.
SCF	•	•	X	0	X	•	0	1	Set carry.
CCF	•	•	X	X	X	•	0	↑	Complement carry.
IN r (C)	↑	↑	X	0	X	P	0	•	Input register indirect.
INI, IND, OUTI; OUTD	X	↑	X	X	X	X	1	•	Block input and output. Z = 0 if B ≠ 0 otherwise Z = 0.
INIR; INDR; OTIR; OTDR	X	1	X	X	X	X	1	•	
LDI; LDD	X	X	X	0	X	↑	0	•	Block transfer instructions. P/V = 1 if BC ≠ 0, otherwise P/V = 0.
LDIR; LDDR	X	X	X	0	X	0	0	•	
CPI; CPIR; CPD; CPDR	X	↑	X	X	X	↑	1	•	Block search instructions. Z = 1 if A = (HL), otherwise Z = 0. P/V = 1 if BC ≠ 0, otherwise P/V = 0.
LD A, I, LD A, R	↑	↑	X	0	X	IFF	0	•	The content of the interrupt enable flip-flop (IFF) is copied into the P/V flag.
BIT b, s	X	↑	X	1	X	X	0	•	The state of bit b of location s is copied into the Z flag.

Symbolic Notation

Symbol	Operation
S	Sign flag. S = 1 if the MSB of the result is 1.
Z	Zero flag. Z = 1 if the result of the operation is 0.
P/V	Parity or overflow flag. Parity (P) and overflow (V) share the same flag. Logical operations affect this flag with the parity of the result while arithmetic operations affect this flag with the overflow of the result. If P/V holds parity, P/V = 1 if the result of the operation is even, P/V = 0 if result is odd. If P/V holds overflow, P/V = 1 if the result of the operation produced an overflow.
H	Half-carry flag. H = 1 if the add or subtract operation produced a carry into or borrow from bit 4 of the accumulator.
N	Add/Subtract flag. N = 1 if the previous operation was a subtract.
H & N	H and N flags are used in conjunction with the decimal adjust instruction (DAA) to properly correct the result into packed BCD format following addition or subtraction using operands with packed BCD format.
C	Carry/Link flag. C = 1 if the operation produced a carry from the MSB of the operand or result.

Symbol	Operation
↑	The flag is affected according to the result of the operation.
•	The flag is unchanged by the operation.
0	The flag is reset by the operation.
1	The flag is set by the operation.
X	The flag is a "don't care."
V	P/V flag affected according to the overflow result of the operation.
P	P/V flag affected according to the parity result of the operation.
r	Any one of the CPU registers A, B, C, D, E, H, L.
s	Any 8-bit location for all the addressing modes allowed for the particular instruction.
ss	Any 16-bit location for all the addressing modes allowed for that instruction.
ii	Any one of the two index registers IX or IY.
R	Refresh counter.
n	8-bit value in range < 0, 255 >.
nn	16-bit value in range ≤ 0, 65535 >.

ABSOLUTE MAXIMUM RATINGS*

Temperature Under Bias . . . . 0°C to +70° C
Storage Temperature . . . . −65°C to +150°C
All Input or Output Voltages
 With Respect to V_{BB} . . . . −0.3V to +20V
V_{CC}, V_{DD} and V_{SS} With Respect to V_{BB} −0.3V to +20V
Power Dissipation 1.5W

NOTICE: Stresses above those listed under "Absolute Maximum Ratings" may cause permanent damage to the device. This is a stress rating only and functional operation of the device at these or any other conditions above those indicated in the operational sections of this specification is not implied. Exposure to absolute maximum rating conditions for extended periods may affect device reliability.

D.C. CHARACTERISTICS (T_A = 0°C to 70°C, V_{DD} = +12V ±5%, V_{CC} = +5V ±5%, V_{BB} = −5V ±5%, V_{SS} =0V; unless otherwise noted)

Symbol	Parameter	Min.	Typ.	Max.	Unit	Test Condition
V_{ILC}	Clock Input Low Voltage	$V_{SS}-1$		$V_{SS}+0.8$	V	
V_{IHC}	Clock Input High Voltage	9.0		$V_{DD}+1$	V	
V_{IL}	Input Low Voltage	$V_{SS}-1$		$V_{SS}+0.8$	V	
V_{IH}	Input High Voltage	3.3		$V_{CC}+1$	V	
V_{OL}	Output Low Voltage			0.45	V	I_{OL} = 1.9mA on all outputs, I_{OH} = −150μA.
V_{OH}	Output High Voltage	3.7			V	
$I_{DD(AV)}$	Avg. Power Supply Current (V_{DD})		40	70	mA	Operation T_{CY} = .48 μsec
$I_{CC(AV)}$	Avg. Power Supply Current (V_{CC})		60	80	mA	
$I_{BB(AV)}$	Avg. Power Supply Current (V_{BB})		.01	1	mA	
I_{IL}	Input Leakage			±10	μA	$V_{SS} \leq V_{IN} \leq V_{CC}$
I_{CL}	Clock Leakage			±10	μA	$V_{SS} \leq V_{CLOCK} \leq V_{DD}$
I_{DL} [2]	Data Bus Leakage in Input Mode			−100 / −2.0	μA / mA	$V_{SS} \leq V_{IN} \leq V_{SS}+0.8V$ / $V_{SS}+0.8V \leq V_{IN} \leq V_{CC}$
I_{FL}	Address and Data Bus Leakage During HOLD			+10 / −100	μA	$V_{ADDR/DATA} = V_{CC}$ / $V_{ADDR/DATA} = V_{SS}+0.45V$

CAPACITANCE (T_A = 25°C, V_{CC} = V_{DD} =V_{SS} = 0V, V_{BB} = −5V)

Symbol	Parameter	Typ.	Max.	Unit	Test Condition
C_ϕ	Clock Capacitance	17	25	pf	f_c = 1 MHz
C_{IN}	Input Capacitance	6	10	pf	Unmeasured Pins
C_{OUT}	Output Capacitance	10	20	pf	Returned to V_{SS}

NOTES:
1. The RESET signal must be active for a minimum of 3 clock cycles.
2. ΔI supply / ΔT_A = −0.45%/°C.

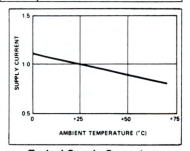

Typical Supply Current vs. Temperature, Normalized[3]

Appendix C.1 8080A Electrical Specifications. (Courtesy of Intel Corporation.)

A.C. CHARACTERISTICS (8080A) $(T_A = 0°C$ to $70°C$, $V_{DD} = +12V \pm 5\%$, $V_{CC} = +5V \pm 5\%$, $V_{BB} = -5V \pm 5\%$, $V_{SS} = 0V$; unless otherwise noted)

Symbol	Parameter	Min.	Max.	-1 Min.	-1 Max.	-2 Min.	-2 Max.	Unit	Test Condition
t_{CY}[3]	Clock Period	0.48	2.0	0.32	2.0	0.38	2.0	μsec	
t_r, t_f	Clock Rise and Fall Time	0	50	0	25	0	50	nsec	
$t_{\phi1}$	ϕ_1 Pulse Width	60		50		60		nsec	
$t_{\phi2}$	ϕ_2 Pulse Width	220		145		175		nsec	
t_{D1}	Delay ϕ_1 to ϕ_2	0		0		0		nsec	
t_{D2}	Delay ϕ_2 to ϕ_1	70		60		70		nsec	
t_{D3}	Delay ϕ_1 to ϕ_2 Leading Edges	80		60		70		nsec	
t_{DA}	Address Output Delay From ϕ_2		200		150		175	nsec	$C_L = 100$ pF
t_{DD}	Data Output Delay From ϕ_2		220		180		200	nsec	
t_{DC}	Signal Output Delay From ϕ_2 or ϕ_2 (SYNC, WR, WAIT, HLDA)		120		110		120	nsec	$C_L = 50$ pF
t_{DF}	DBIN Delay From ϕ_2	25	140	25	130	25	140	nsec	
t_{DI}[1]	Delay for Input Bus to Enter Input Mode		t_{DF}		t_{DF}		t_{DF}	nsec	
t_{DS1}	Data Setup Time During ϕ_1 and DBIN	30		10		20		nsec	
t_{DS2}	Data Setup Time to ϕ_2 During DBIN	150		120		130		nsec	
t_{DH}[1]	Data Holt time From ϕ_2 During DBIN	[1]		[1]		[1]		nsec	
t_{IE}	INTE Output Delay From ϕ_2		200		200		200	nsec	$C_L = 50$ pF
t_{RS}	READY Setup Time During ϕ_2	120		90		90		nsec	
t_{HS}	HOLD Setup Time to ϕ_2	140		120		120		nsec	
t_{IS}	INT Setup Time During ϕ_2	120		100		100		nsec	
t_H	Hold Time From ϕ_2 (READY, INT, HOLD)	0		0		0		nsec	
t_{FD}	Delay to Float During Hold (Address and Data Bus)		120		120		120	nsec	
t_{AW}	Address Stable Prior to WR	[5]		[5]		[5]		nsec	$C_L = 100$ pF: Address, Data $C_L = 50$ pF: WR, HLDA, DBIN
t_{DW}	Output Data Stable Prior to WR	[6]		[6]		[6]		nsec	
t_{WD}	Output Data Stable From WR	[7]		[7]		[7]		nsec	
t_{WA}	Address Stable From WR	[7]		[7]		[7]		nsec	
t_{HF}	HLDA to Float Delay	[8]		[8]		[8]		nsec	
t_{WF}	WR to Float Delay	[9]		[9]		[9]		nsec	
t_{AH}	Address Hold Time After DBIN During HLDA	−20		−20		−20		nsec	

A.C. TESTING LOAD CIRCUIT

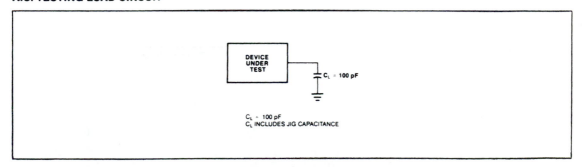

DEVICE UNDER TEST

$C_L = 100$ pF

$C_L = 100$ pF
C_L INCLUDES JIG CAPACITANCE

703

WAVEFORMS

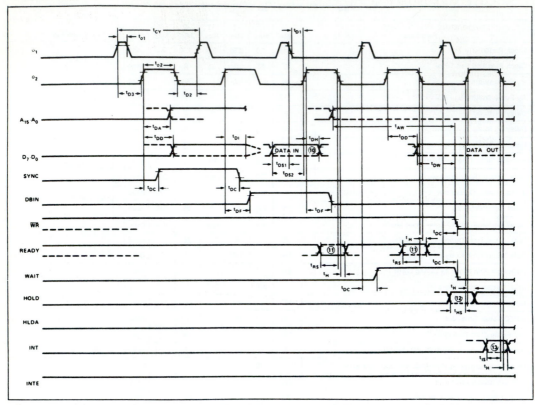

NOTE:
Timing measurements are made at the following reference voltages: CLOCK "1" = 8.0V,
"0" = 1.0V; INPUTS "1" = 3.3V, "0" = 0.8V; OUTPUTS "1" = 2.0V, "0" = 0.8V.

APPENDIX C.2

ABSOLUTE MAXIMUM RATINGS*

Ambient Temperature Under Bias .... 0°C to 70°C
Storage Temperature .... −65°C to +150°C
Voltage on Any Pin
  With Respect to Ground .... −0.5V to +7V
Power Dissipation .... 1.5 Watt

*NOTICE: Stresses above those listed under "Absolute Maximum Ratings" may cause permanent damage to the device. This is a stress rating only and functional operation of the device at these or any other conditions above those indicated in the operational sections of this specification is not implied. Exposure to absolute maximum rating conditions for extended periods may affect device reliability.

D.C. CHARACTERISTICS

8085AH, 8085AH-2: (T_A = 0°C to 70°C, V_{CC} = 5V ±10%, V_{SS} =0V; unless otherwise specified)*
8085AH-1: (T_A = 0°C to 70°C, V_{CC} = 5V ±5%, V_{SS} = 0V; unless otherwise specified)

Symbol	Parameter	Min.	Max.	Units	Test Conditions
V_{IL}	Input Low Voltage	−0.5	+0.8	V	
V_{IH}	Input High Voltage	2.0	V_{CC} +0.5	V	
V_{OL}	Output Low Voltage		0.45	V	I_{OL} = 2mA
V_{OH}	Output High Voltage	2.4		V	I_{OH} = −400μA
I_{CC}	Power Supply Current		135	mA	8085AH, 8085AH-2
			200	mA	8085AH-1 (Preliminary)
I_{IL}	Input Leakage		±10	μA	0 ≤ V_{IN} ≤ V_{CC}
I_{LO}	Output Leakage		±10	μA	0.45V ≤ V_{OUT} ≤ V_{CC}
V_{ILR}	Input Low Level, RESET	−0.5	+0.8	V	
V_{IHR}	Input High Level, RESET	2.4	V_{CC} +0.5	V	
V_{HY}	Hysteresis, RESET	0.25		V	

A.C. CHARACTERISTICS

8085AH, 8085AH-2: (T_A = 0°C to 70°C, V_{CC} = 5V ±10%, V_{SS} = OV)*
8085AH-1: (T_A = 0°C to 70°C, V_{CC} = 5V ±5%, V_{SS} = 0V)

Symbol	Parameter	8085AH[2] (Final) Min.	Max.	8085AH-2[2] (Final) Min.	Max.	8085AH-1 (Preliminary) Min.	Max.	Units
t_{CYC}	CLK Cycle Period	320	2000	200	2000	167	2000	ns
t_1	CLK Low Time (Standard CLK Loading)	80		40		20		ns
t_2	CLK High Time (Standard CLK Loading)	120		70		50		ns
t_r, t_f	CLK Rise and Fall Time		30		30		30	ns
t_{XKR}	X_1 Rising to CLK Rising	25	120	25	100	20	100	ns
t_{XKF}	X_1 Rising to CLK Falling	30	150	30	110	25	110	ns
t_{AC}	A_{8-15} Valid to Leading Edge of Control[1]	270		115		70		ns
t_{ACL}	A_{0-7} Valid to Leading Edge of Control	240		115		60		ns
t_{AD}	A_{0-15} Valid to Valid Data In		575		350		225	ns
t_{AFR}	Address Float After Leading Edge of READ (INTA)		0		0		0	ns
t_{AL}	A_{8-15} Valid Before Trailing Edge of ALE[1]	115		50		25		ns

*Note: For Extended Temperature EXPRESS use M8085AH Electricals Parameters.

Appendix C.2   8085AH Electrical Specifications. (Courtesy of Intel Corporation.)

A.C. CHARACTERISTICS (Continued)

Symbol	Parameter	8085AH[2] (Final)		8085AH-2[2] (Final)		8085AH-1 (Preliminary)		Units
		Min.	Max.	Min.	Max.	Min.	Max.	
t_{ALL}	A_{0-7} Valid Before Trailing Edge of ALE	90		50		25		ns
t_{ARY}	READY Valid from Address Valid		220		100		40	ns
t_{CA}	Address (A_{8-15}) Valid After Control	120		60		30		ns
t_{CC}	Width of Control Low ($\overline{RD}$, $\overline{WR}$, $\overline{INTA}$) Edge of ALE	400		230		150		ns
t_{CL}	Trailing Edge of Control to Leading Edge of ALE	50		25		0		ns
t_{DW}	Data Valid to Trailing Edge of $\overline{WRITE}$	420		230		140		ns
t_{HABE}	HLDA to Bus Enable		210		150		150	ns
t_{HABF}	Bus Float After HLDA		210		150		150	ns
t_{HACK}	HLDA Valid to Trailing Edge of CLK	110		40		0		ns
t_{HDH}	HOLD Hold Time	0		0		0		ns
t_{HDS}	HOLD Setup Time to Trailing Edge of CLK	170		120		120		ns
t_{INH}	INTR Hold Time	0		0		0		ns
t_{INS}	INTR, RST, and TRAP Setup Time to Falling Edge of CLK	160		150		150		ns
t_{LA}	Address Hold Time After ALE	100		50		20		ns
t_{LC}	Trailing Edge of ALE to Leading Edge of Control	130		60		25		ns
t_{LCK}	ALE Low During CLK High	100		50		15		ns
t_{LDR}	ALE to Valid Data During Read		460		270		175	ns
t_{LDW}	ALE to Valid Data During Write		200		120		110	ns
t_{LL}	ALE Width	140		80		50		ns
t_{LRY}	ALE to READY Stable		110		30		10	ns
t_{RAE}	Trailing Edge of $\overline{READ}$ to Re-Enabling of Address	150		90		50		ns
t_{RD}	$\overline{READ}$ (or $\overline{INTA}$) to Valid Data		300		150		75	ns
t_{RV}	Control Trailing Edge to Leading Edge of Next Control	400		220		160		ns
t_{RDH}	Data Hold Time After $\overline{READ}$ $\overline{INTA}$	0		0		0		ns
t_{RYH}	READY Hold Time	0		0		5		ns
t_{RYS}	READY Setup Time to Leading Edge of CLK	110		100		100		ns
t_{WD}	Data Valid After Trailing Edge of $\overline{WRITE}$	100		60		30		ns
t_{WDL}	LEADING Edge of $\overline{WRITE}$ to Data Valid		40		20		30	ns

WAVEFORMS

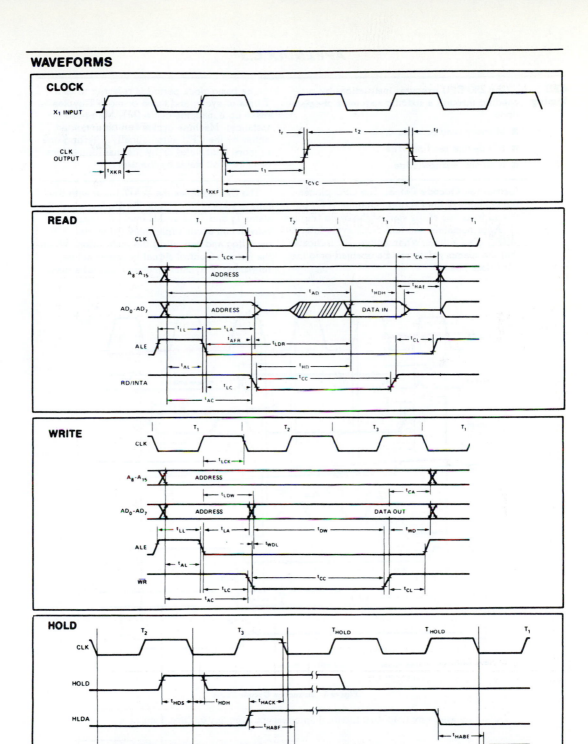

CPU Timing

The Z80 CPU executes instructions by proceeding through a specific sequence of operations:

- Memory read or write
- I/O device read or write
- Interrupt acknowledge

Instruction Opcode Fetch. The CPU places the contents of the Program Counter (PC) on the address bus at the start of the cycle (Figure 5). Approximately one-half clock cycle later, MREQ goes active. When active, RD indicates that the memory data can be enabled onto the CPU data bus.

The basic clock period is referred to as a T time or cycle, and three or more T cycles make up a machine cycle (M1, M2 or M3 for instance). Machine cycles can be extended either by the CPU automatically inserting one or more Wait states or by the insertion of one or more Wait states by the user.

The CPU samples the WAIT input with the falling edge of clock state T_2. During clock states T_3 and T_4 of an M1 cycle dynamic RAM refresh can occur while the CPU starts decoding and executing the instruction. When the Refresh Control signal becomes active, refreshing of dynamic memory can take place.

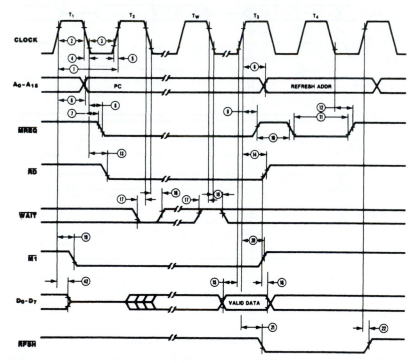

NOTE: T_W-Wait cycle added when necessary for slow ancilliary devices.

Figure 5. Instruction Opcode Fetch

Appendix C.3 Z-80 Electrical Specifications. (Courtesy of Zilog, Inc.)

Memory Read or Write Cycles. Figure 6 shows the timing of memory read or write cycles other than an opcode fetch ($\overline{\text{M1}}$) cycle. The $\overline{\text{MREQ}}$ and $\overline{\text{RD}}$ signals function exactly as in the fetch cycle. In a memory write cycle, $\overline{\text{MREQ}}$ also becomes active when the address bus is stable. The $\overline{\text{WR}}$ line is active when the data bus is stable, so that it can be used directly as an R/W pulse to most semiconductor memories.

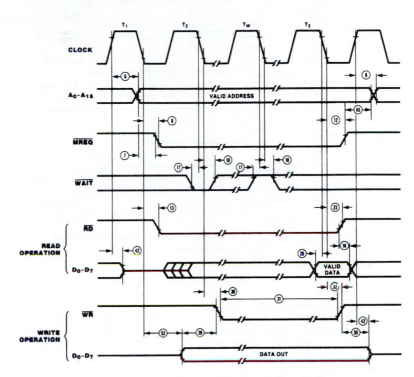

Figure 6. Memory Read or Write Cycles

CPU Timing (Continued)

Input or Output Cycles. Figure 7 shows the timing for an I/O read or I/O write operation. During I/O operations, the CPU automatically inserts a single Wait state (T_w). This extra Wait state allows sufficient time for an I/O port to decode the address from the port address lines.

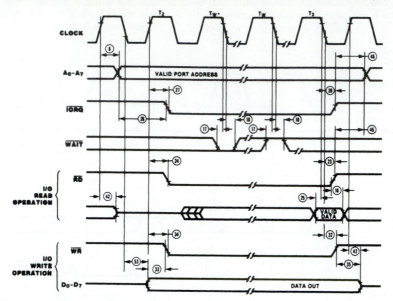

NOTE: T_{w^*} = One Wait cycle automatically inserted by CPU.

Figure 7. Input or Output Cycles

Interrupt Request/Acknowledge Cycle. The CPU samples the interrupt signal with the rising edge of the last clock cycle at the end of any instruction (Figure 8). When an interrupt is accepted, a special $\overline{M1}$ cycle is generated. During this $\overline{M1}$ cycle, $\overline{IORQ}$ becomes active (instead of $\overline{MREQ}$) to indicate that the interrupting device can place an 8-bit vector on the data bus. The CPU automatically adds two Wait states to this cycle.

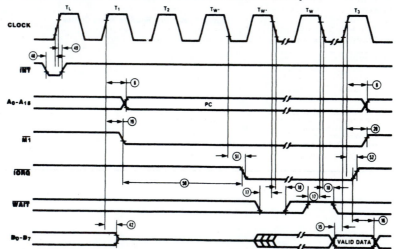

NOTE: 1) T_L = Last state of previous instruction.
2) Two Wait cycles automatically inserted by CPU(*).

Figure 8. Interrupt Request/Acknowledge Cycle

AC CHARACTERISTICS† (Z84C00/CMOS Z80 CPU)

$V_{cc}=5.0V \pm 10\%$, unless otherwise specified

No	Symbol	Parameter	Z84C0004**		Z84C0006		Z84C0008		Z84C0010		Z84C0020[1]		Unit	Note
			Min	Max	Min	Max	Min	Max	Min	Max	Min	Max		
1	TcC	Clock Cycle time	250*	DC	162*	DC	125*	DC	100*	DC	50*	DC	nS	
2	TwCh	Clock Pulse width (high)	110	DC	65	DC	55	DC	40	DC	20	DC	nS	
3	TwCl	Clock Pulse width (low)	110	DC	65	DC	55	DC	40	DC	20	DC	nS	
4	TfC	Clock Fall time		30		20		10		10		10	nS	
5	TrC	Clock Rise time		30		20		10		10		10	nS	
6	TdCr(A)	Address vaild from Clock Rise		110		90		80		65		57	nS	[2]
7	TdA(MREQf)	Address valid to /MREQ Fall	65*		35*		20*		5*		-15*		nS	
8	TdCf(MREQf)	Clock Fall to /MREQ Fall delay		85		70		60		55		40	nS	
9	TdCr(MREQr)	Clock Rise to /MREQ Rise delay		85		70		60		55		40	nS	
10	TwMREQh	/MREQ pulse width (High)	110*		65*		45**		30*		10*		nS	[3]
11	TwMREQl	/MREQ pulse width (low)	220*		132*		100*		75*		25*		nS	[3]
12	TdCf(MERQr)	Clock Fall to /MREQ Rise delay		85		70		60		55		40	nS	
13	TdCf(RDf)	Clock Fall to /RD Fall delay		95		80		70		65		40	nS	
14	TdCr(RDr)	Clock Rise to /RD Rise delay		85		70		60		55		40	nS	
15	TsD(Cr)	Data setup time to Clock Rise	35		30		30		25		12		nS	
16	ThD(RDr)	Data hold time after /RD Rise	0		0		0		0		0		nS	
17	TsWAIT(Cf)	/WAIT setup time to Clock Fall	70		60		50		20		7.5		nS	
18	ThWAIT(Cf)	/WAIT hold time after Clock Fall	10		10		10		10		10		nS	
19	TdCr(M1f)	Clock Rise to /M1 Fall delay		100		80		70		65		45	nS	
20	TdCr(M1r)	Clock Rise to /M1 Rise delay		100		80		70		65		45	nS	
21	TdCr(RFSHf)	Clock Rise to /RFSH Fall delay		130		110		95		80		60	nS	
22	TdCr(RFSHr)	Clock Rise to /RFSH Rise delay		120		100		85		80		60	nS	
23	TdCf(RDr)	Clock Fall to /RD Rise delay		85		70		60		55		40	nS	
24	TdCr(RDf)	Clock Rise to /RD Fall delay		85		70		60		55		40	nS	
25	TsD(Cf)	Data setup to Clock Fall during M2, M3, M4 or M5 cycles	50		40		30		25		12		nS	
26	TdA(IORQf)	Address stable prior to /IORQ Fall	180*		107*		75*		50*		0*		nS	
27	TdCr(IORQf)	Clock Rise to /IORQ Fall delay		75		65		55		50		40	nS	
28	TdCf(IORQr)	Clock Fall to /IORQ Rise delay		85		70		60		55		40	nS	
29	TdD(WRf)Mw	Data stable prior to /WR Fall	80*		22*		5*		40*		-10*		nS	
30	TdCf(WRf)	Clock Fall to /WR Fall delay		80		70		60		55		40	nS	
31	TwWR	/WR pulse width	220*		132*		100*		75*		25*		nS	
32	TdCf(WRr)	Clock Fall to /WR Rise delay		80		70		60		55		40	nS	
33	TdD(WRf)IO	Data stable prior to /WR Fall	-10*		-55*		-55*		-10*		-30*		nS	
34	TdCr(WRf)	Clock Rise to /WR Fall delay		65		60		60		50		40	nS	
35	TdWRr(D)	Data stable from /WR Rise	60*		30*		15*		10*		0*		nS	
36	TdCf(HALT)	Clock Fall to /HALT 'L' or 'H'		300		260		225		90		70	nS	
37	TwNMI	/NMI pulse width	80		60		60		60		60		nS	
38	TsBUSREQ (Cr)	/BUSREQ setup time to Clock Rise	50		50		40		30		15		nS	

* For clock periods other than the minimums shown, calculate parameters using the table on the following page.
  Calculated values above assumed TrC = TfC = 20 ns.
†Units in nanoseconds (ns)
†† For loading ≥ 50 pf. Decrease width by 10 ns for each additional 50 pf.

**4 MHz CMOS Z80 is obsoleted and replaced by 6 MHz

1-31

AC CHARACTERISTICS† (Z84C00/CMOS Z80 CPU; Continued)

V_{cc}=5.0V ± 10%, unless otherwise specified

No	Symbol	Parameter	Z84C0004** Min	Max	Z84C0006 Min	Max	Z84C0008 Min	Max	Z84C0010 Min	Max	Z84C0020[1] Min	Max	Unit	Note
39	ThBUSREQ (Cr)	/BUSREQ hold time after Clock Rise	10		10		10		10		10		nS	
40	TdCr (BUSACKf)	Clock Rise to /BASACK Fall delay		100		90		80		75		40	nS	
41	TdCf (BUSACKr)	Clock Fall to /BASACK Rise delay		100		90		80		75		40	nS	
42	TdCr(Dz)	Clock Rise to Data float delay		90		80		70		65		40	nS	
43	TdCr(CTz)	Clock Rise to Control Outputs Float Delay (/MREQ, /IORQ, /RD and /WR)		80		70		60		65		40	nS	
44	TdCr(Az)	Clock Rise to Address float delay		90		80		70		75		40	nS	
45	TdCTr(A)	Address Hold time from /MREQ, /IORQ, /RD or /WR	80*		35*		20*		20*		0*		nS	
46	TsRESET(Cr)	/RESET to Clock Rise setup time	60		60		45		40		15		nS	
47	ThRESET(Cr)	/RESET to Clock Rise Hold time	10		10		10		10		10		nS	
48	TsINTf(Cr)	/INT Fall to Clock Rise Setup Time	80		70		55		50		15		nS	
49	ThINTr(Cr)	/INT Rise to Clock Rise Hold Time	10		10		10		10		10		nS	
50	TdM1f (IORQf)	/M1 Fall to /IORQ Fall delay	565*		359*		270*		220*		100*		nS	
51	TdCf(IORQf)	/Clock Fall to /IORQ Fall delay		85		70		60		55		45	nS	
52	TdCf(IORQr)	Clock Rise to /IORQ Rise delay		85		70		60		55		45	nS	
53	TdCf(D)	Clock Fall to Data Valid delay		150		130		115		110		75	nS	

Notes:

* For Clock periods other than the minimum shown, calculate parameters using the following table.
Calculated values above assumed TrC = TfC = maximum.

** 4 MHz CMOS Z80 is obsoleted and replaced by 6 MHz

[1] Z84C0020 parameters are guuaranteed with 50pF load Capacitance.

[2] If Capacitive Load is other than 50pF, please use Figure 1. to calculate the value.

[3] Increasing delay by 10nS for each 50pF increase in loading, 200pF max for data lines, and 100pF for control lines.

FOOTNOTES TO AC CHARACTERISTICS

No	Symbol	Parameter	Z84C0004**	Z84C0006	Z84C0008	Z84C0010	Z84C0020
1	TcC	TwCh + TwCl + TrC + TfC					
7	TdA(MREQf)	TwCh + TfC	-65	-50	-45	-45	-45
10	TwMREQh	TwCh + TfC	-20	-20	-20	-20	-20
11	TwMREQl	TcC	-30	-30	-25	-25	-25
26	TdA(IORQf)	TcC	-70	-55	-50	-50	-50
29	TdD(WRf)	TcC	-170	-140	-120	-60	-60
31	TwWR	TcC	-30	-30	-25	-25	-25
33	TdD(WRf)	TwCl + TrC	-140	-140	-120	-60	-60
35	TdWRr(D)	TwCl + TrC	-70	-55	-50	-40	-25
45	TdCTr(A)	TwCl + TrC	-50	-50	-45	-30	-30
50	TdM1f(IORQf)	2TcC + TwCh + TfC	-65	-50	-45	-30	-30

AC Test Conditions: V_{IH} = 2.0 V V_{OH} = 1.5 V V_{IHC} = V_{CC} − 0.6 V   FLOAT = ± 0.5 V
V_{IL} = 0.8 V V_{OL} = 1.5 V V_{ILC} = 0.45 V

1-32

ABSOLUTE MAXIMUM RATINGS*

Temperature Under Bias .... −10°C to +80°C
Storage Temperature .... −65°C to +125°C
All Input or Output Voltages with
  Respect to Ground .... +7.0V to −0.6V
Voltage on Pin 24 with
  Respect to Ground .... +13.5V to −0.6V
V_{PP} Supply Voltage with Respect to
  Ground During Programming .... +22V to −0.6V

NOTICE: Stresses above those listed under "Absolute Maximum Ratings" may cause permanent damage to the device. This is a stress rating only and functional operation of the device at these or any other conditions above those indicated in the operational sections of this specification is not implied. Exposure to absolute maximum rating conditions for extended periods may affect device reliability.

D.C. AND A.C. OPERATING CONDITIONS DURING READ

	2764-2	2764	2764-3	2764-4	2764-25	2764-30	2764-45
Operating Temperature Range	0°C–70°C	0°C–70°C	0°C–70°C	0°C–70°C	0°C–70°C	0°C–70°C	0°C–70°C
V_{CC} Power Supply[1,2]	5V ± 5%	5V ± 5%	5V ± 5%	5V ± 5%	5V ± 10%	5V ± 10%	5V ± 10%
V_{PP} Voltage[2]	$V_{PP} = V_{CC}$	$V_{PP} = V_{CC}$	$V_{PP} = V_{CC}$	$V_{PP} = V_{CC}$	$V_{PP} = V_{CC}$	$V_{PP} = V_{CC}$	$V_{PP} = V_{CC}$

READ OPERATION

D.C. CHARACTERISTICS

Symbol	Parameter	Limits			Unit	Conditions
		Min	Typ[3]	Max		
I_{LI}	Input Load Current			10	μA	$V_{IN} = 5.5V$
I_{LO}	Output Leakage Current			10	μA	$V_{OUT} = 5.5V$
I_{PP1}[2]	V_{PP} Current Read			5	mA	$V_{PP} = 5.5V$
I_{CC1}[2]	V_{CC} Current Standby			40	mA	$\overline{CE} = V_{IH}$
I_{CC2}[2]	V_{CC} Current Active		70	100	mA	$\overline{CE} = \overline{OE} = V_{IL}$
V_{IL}	Input Low Voltage	−.1		+.8	V	
V_{IH}	Input High Voltage	2.0		$V_{CC}+1$	V	
V_{OL}	Output Low Voltage			.45	V	$I_{OL} = 2.1$ mA
V_{OH}	Output High Voltage	2.4			V	$I_{OH} = -400$ μA

A.C. CHARACTERISTICS

Symbol	Parameter	2764-2 Limits		2764-25 & 2764 Limits		2764-30 & 2764-3 Limits		2764-45 & 2764-4 Limits		Unit	Test Conditions
		Min	Max	Min	Max	Min	Max	Min	Max		
t_{ACC}	Address to Output Delay		200		250		300		450	ns	$\overline{CE} = \overline{OE} = V_{IL}$
t_{CE}	$\overline{CE}$ to Output Delay		200		250		300		450	ns	$\overline{OE} = V_{IL}$
t_{OE}	$\overline{OE}$ to Output Delay		75		100		120		150	ns	$\overline{CE} = V_{IL}$
t_{DF}[4]	$\overline{OE}$ High to Output Float	0	60	0	60	0	105	0	130	ns	$\overline{CE} = V_{IL}$
t_{OH}	Output Hold from Addresses, $\overline{CE}$ or $\overline{OE}$ Whichever Occurred First	0		0		0		0		ns	$\overline{CE} = \overline{OE} = V_{IL}$

NOTES:
1. V_{CC} must be applied simultaneously or before V_{PP} and removed simultaneously or after V_{PP}.
2. V_{PP} may be connected directly to V_{CC} except during programming. The supply current would then be the sum of I_{CC} and I_{PP1}.
3. Typical values are for $t_A = 25°C$ and nominal supply voltages.
4. This parameter is only sampled and is not 100% tested. Output Float is defined as the point where data is no longer driven — see timing diagram on page 4-21

Appendix D.1 Specifications for the 2764 EPROM. (Courtesy of Intel Corporation.)

CAPACITANCE ($T_A = 25°C$, $f = 1MHz$)

Symbol	Parameter	Typ.[1]	Max.	Unit	Conditions
C_{IN}[2]	Input Capacitance	4	6	pF	$V_{IN} = 0V$
C_{OUT}	Output Capacitance	8	12	pF	$V_{OUT} = 0V$

A.C. TESTING INPUT/OUTPUT WAVEFORM

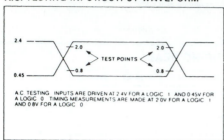

A.C. TESTING: INPUTS ARE DRIVEN AT 2.4V FOR A LOGIC 1 AND 0.45V FOR A LOGIC 0. TIMING MEASUREMENTS ARE MADE AT 2.0V FOR A LOGIC 1 AND 0.8V FOR A LOGIC 0

A.C. TESTING LOAD CIRCUIT

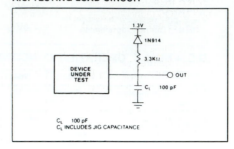

C_L 100 pF
C_L INCLUDES JIG CAPACITANCE

A.C. WAVEFORMS

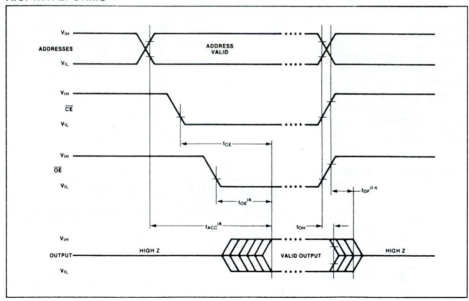

NOTES: 1. Typical values are for $T_A = 25°C$ and nominal supply voltages.
        2. This parameter is only sampled and is not 100% tested.
        3. $\overline{OE}$ may be delayed up to $t_{ACC} - t_{OE}$ after the falling edge of $\overline{CE}$ without impact on t_{ACC}.
        4. t_{DF} is specified from $\overline{OE}$ or $\overline{CE}$, whichever occurs first.

714

NEC
NEC Electronics U.S.A. Inc.
Microcomputer Division

μPD2167-2
μPD2167-3
16,384 x 1-BIT STATIC RAM

Description

The μPD2167 is a 16,384-word by 1-bit static MOS RAM. Using a scaled-NMOS technology, its design provides the easy-to-use features associated with non-clocked static memories.

The μPD2167 has a three-state output and offers a standby mode that features an 83% savings in power consumption. The μPD2167 requires a single +5 volt supply and is fully TTL-compatible. It features equal access and cycle times and, because of its fully static operation, it requires no external clocks or timing strobes. It is packaged in a standard 20-pin, 300 mil DIP.

Features

- 16384 x 1 organization
- Fully static memory — no clock or timing strobe required
- Equal access and cycle times
- Single +5v supply
- Automatic power-down
- Standard 20-pin DIP, 300 mil
- All inputs and output directly TTL-compatible
- Separate data input and output
- Three-state output
- Power dissipation: 180 mA max (active)
  30 mA max (standby)

	Access time	R/W Cycle time
μPD2167-2	70ns	70ns
μPD2167-3	55ns	55ns

Pin Configuration

Pin Names

A_0-A_{13}	Address Inputs
$\overline{WE}$	Write Enable
$\overline{CS}$	Chip Select
D_{IN}	Data Input
D_{OUT}	Data Output
V_{CC}	Power (+5v)
V_{SS}	Ground

Truth Table

$\overline{CS}$	$\overline{WE}$	Mode	Output	Power
H	X	not selected	High Z	Standby
L	L	write	High Z	Active
L	H	read	D_{OUT}	Active

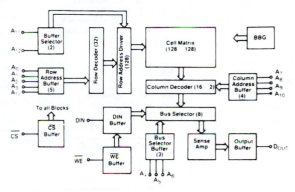

Absolute Maximum Ratings*

$T_a = 25°C$

Temperature under bias	−10°C to +85°C
Storage temperature	−65°C to +150°C
Voltage on any pin with respect to ground	−3.5v to +7v
D.C. output current	20mA
Power dissipation	1.2w

* Comment: Exposing the device to stresses above those listed in Absolute Maximum Ratings could cause permanent damage. The device is not meant to be operated under conditions outside the limits described in the operational sections of this specification. Exposure to absolute maximum rating conditions for extended periods may affect device reliability.

Capacitance
$T_a = 25°C$, f = 1.0 MHz

Parameter	Symbol	Max.	Unit	Conditions
Input Capacitance	C_{IN}	5	pF	$V_{IN} = 0V$
Output Capacitance	C_{OUT}	6	pF	$V_{OUT} = 0V$

This parameter is sampled and not 100% tested.

DC Characteristics
$T_a = 0°C$ to $+70°C$, $V_{CC} = +5v \pm 10\%$

Parameter	Sym	Min	Typ	Max	Unit	Test Conditions
Input load current all input pins	I_{LI}			10	μA	$V_{CC} = $ max, $V_{IN} = $ GND to V_{CC}
Output leakage current	I_{LO}		0.1	50	μA	$\overline{CS} = V_{IH}$, $V_{CC} = $ max, $V_{OUT} = $ GND to V_{CC}
Operating current	I_{CC}			170	mA	$T_A = 25°C$, $V_{CC} = $ max, $\overline{CS} = V_{IL}$,
				180	mA	$T_A = 0°C$, output open
Standby current	I_{SB}			30	mA	$V_{CC} = $ min to max, $\overline{CS} = V_{IH}$
Peak Power-On current	I_{PO}①		35	70	mA	$V_{CC} = $ GND to V_{CC} min. $\overline{CS} = $ Lower of V_{CC} or V_{IH} min.
Input low voltage	V_{IL}	−3.0		0.8	V	
Input high voltage	V_{IH}	2.0		6.0	V	
Output low voltage	V_{OL}			0.4	V	$I_{OL} = 8$ mA
Output high voltage	V_{OH}	2.4			V	$I_{OH} = -4$ mA
Output short circuit current	I_{OS1}		−150		mA	$V_{OUT} = $ GND
Output short circuit current	I_{OS2}		150		mA	$V_{OUT} = V_{CC}$

AC Characteristics
$T_a = 0°C$ to $+70°C$, $V_{CC} = +5V \pm 10\%$

Parameter	Symbol	μPD2167-3 min	typ	max	μPD2167-2 min	typ	max	Unit	Notes
Read Cycle									
Read cycle time	t_{RC}	55			70			ns	
Address access time	t_{AA}			55			70	ns	①
Chip select access time	t_{ACS}			55			70	ns	②
Output hold from address change	t_{OH}	5			5			ns	
Chip select to output in low Z	t_{LZ}	10			10			ns	
Chip deselect to output in high Z	t_{HZ}	0		40	0		40	ns	
Chip select to power up time	t_{PU}	0			0			ns	
Chip deselect to power down time	t_{PD}		30			30		ns	
Write Cycle									
Write cycle time	t_{WC}	55			70			ns	
Chip select to end of write	t_{CW}	45			55			ns	
Address valid to end of write	t_{AW}	45			55			ns	
Address setup time	t_{AS}	0			0			ns	
Write pulse	t_{WP}	35			40			ns	
Write recovery time	t_{WR}	10			15			ns	
Data valid to end of write	t_{DW}	25			30			ns	
Data hold time	t_{DH}	10			10			ns	
Write enabled to output in high Z	t_{WZ}	0		30	0		35	ns	
Output active from end of write	t_{OW}	0			0			ns	

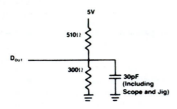

Figure 1 – Output Load

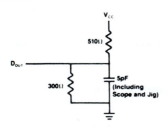

Figure 2 – Output Load for t_{HZ}, t_{LZ}, t_{WZ}, t_{OW}

Notes:
① $\overline{CS}$ valid prior to or coincident with address transition
② Address valid prior to or coincident with $\overline{CS}$ transition low

2164A FAMILY
65,536 × 1 BIT DYNAMIC RAM

	2164A-15	2164A-20
Maximum Access Time (ns)	150	200
Read, Write Cycle (ns)	260	330
Page Mode Read, Write Cycle (ns)	125	170

- HMOS-D III technology
- Low capacitance, fully TTL compatible inputs and outputs
- Single +5V supply, ±10% tolerance
- 128 refresh cycle/2 ms $\overline{RAS}$ only refresh
- Compatible with the 2118

- Extended page mode, read-modify-write and hidden refresh operation
- Inputs allow a −2.0V negative overshoot
- Industry standard 16-pin DIP
- Compatible with Intel's microprocessors and DRAM controllers

The 2164A is a 65,536 word by 1-bit N-channel MOS dynamic Random Access Memory fabricated with Intel's HMOS-D III technology for high system performance and reliability. The 2164A design incorporates high storage cell capacitance to provide wide internal device margins for reduced noise sensitivities and more reliable system operation. Moreover, high storage cell capacitance results in low soft error rates without the need for a die coat. HMOS-D III process employs the use of redundant elements.

The 2164A is optimized for high speed, high performance applications such as mainframe memory, buffer memory, microprocessor memory, peripheral storage and graphic terminals. For memory intensive microprocessor applications the 2164A is fully compatible with Intel's DRAM controllers and microprocessors to provide a complete DRAM system.

Multiplexing the 16 address bits into the 8 address input pins allows the 2164A to achieve high packing density. The 16 pin DIP provides for high system bit densities, and is compatible with widely available automated testing and insertion equipment. The two 8-bit TTL level address segments are latched into the 2164A by the two TTL clocks, Row Address Strobe ($\overline{RAS}$) and Column Address Strobe ($\overline{CAS}$). Non-critical timing requirements for the $\overline{RAS}$ and $\overline{CAS}$ clocks allow the use of the address multiplexing technique while maintaining high performance.

The non-latched, three state, TTL compatible data output is controlled by $\overline{CAS}$, independent of $\overline{RAS}$. After a valid read or read-modify-write cycle, data is held on the data output pin by holding $\overline{CAS}$ low. The data output is returned to a high impedance state, by returning $\overline{CAS}$ to a high state. Hidden refresh capability allows the device to maintain data at the output by holding $\overline{CAS}$ low while $\overline{RAS}$ is used to execute $\overline{RAS}$-only refresh cycles. Refreshing is accomplished by performing $\overline{RAS}$-only cycles, hidden refresh cycles, or normal read or write cycles on the 128 address combinations of addresses A_0 through A_6, during a 2 ms period.

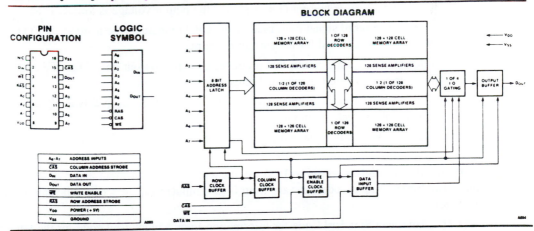

Appendix D.3   Specifications for the 2164A 64K DRAM. (Courtesy of Intel Corporation.)

GLOSSARY

Access time For a memory chip, the time from receipt of the memory address until valid data is output.

Accumulator Data register within the CPU. All 8080 and 8085 I/O instructions use this register.

Active high The signal is present (TRUE) when the output voltage is high.

Active low The signal is present (TRUE) when the output voltage is low.

Address bus The set of signal lines used by the CPU to indicate the memory or I/O port address that is to be accessed for the current machine cycle.

Address decoder A logic circuit that produces an active output only when the address applied to its inputs is within a specified range.

Addressing modes The list of methods by which a computer can specify a memory address. For example, direct and indirect.

Analog signal An electrical signal that may take on an infinite number of values over time.

ADC (analog-to-digital converter) A circuit with one analog input and n digital outputs. The binary output code can vary from 0 (OV input) to $2^n - 1$ (the full scale input voltage).

ASCII American Standard Code for Information Interchange, 7-bit code for the letters of the alphabet, numbers, punctuation symbols, and several control characters.

Assembler   A computer program that inputs instruction mnemonics (the source code) and outputs the binary equivalent (the object code).

Assembly language programming   A way of programming a computer using instruction mnemonics native to the particular CPU used. (*Example*: Z-80 assembly language programming.)

Asynchronous   A type of logic design in which the outputs change whenever the circuit inputs change. There is no synchronizing signal.

Asynchronous serial communications   A method of sending data serially with each character framed between a start and stop bit.

Baud rate   For serially transmitted data, the number of signal events per second (usually the same as the number of data bits per second, except for high speed modems which encode more than one bit per signal event).

Bi-directional bus   A type of bus over which data can flow in two directions. (*Example*: The data bus of a microprocessor.)

BCD (binary coded decimal)   A method of representing decimal numbers in binary with four bits for each decimal digit. (*Example*: 27 = 0010 0111.)

Bit   One binary digit.

Breakpoint   Software troubleshooting technique in which the program runs at full speed until the breakpoint is encountered. The CPU registers can then be examined, and the breakpoint moved further into the program.

Buffer   A type of logic circuit used to "clean up" a digital signal restoring the original logic 1 and logic 0 voltage levels and sharpening the pulse rise and fall times.

Bus   A collection of signal lines devoted to a common purpose.

Byte   8 bits.

CPU (central processing unit)   That portion of a digital computer that controls overall operation of the computer and in which all calculations and decisions are performed.

Checksum   An error detection scheme in which data is transmitted in blocks accompanied by a checking byte computed as the sum of the data bytes.

Chip   An integrated circuit.

Clock signal   The signal that specifies system timing for a synchronous logic circuit. The frequency of this signal thus determines the speed of that system.

CMOS (complementary metal-oxide semiconductor)   A type of digital circuit technology employing n- and p-channel field-effect transistors. CMOS circuits are best known for their low power consumption.

Control bus   The set of signal lines used by the CPU to indicate the current machine cycle type (memory or I/O) and direction (read or write).

CP/M (control program for microcomputers)   Popular disk operating system for microcomputers based on the 8080, 8085, and Z-80 8-bit microprocessors.

CRC (cyclic redundancy check)   Improved error detection scheme similar to the checksum but non-byte oriented.

Cylinder For a hard drive, all tracks under the read/write heads at a given time. The total number of cylinders is equal to the number of tracks on one disk surface.

Data bus The set of signal lines used to transfer data between the CPU and its memory unit and I/O devices.

DSP (device select pulse) Derived from the address and control buses, the DSP is a signal used to activate an input or output port.

DAC (digital-to-analog converter) A circuit with n binary inputs and one analog output. The output voltage can vary from 0 V to some full-scale value in 2^n discrete steps.

DMA (direct memory access) An I/O technique in which the CPU is disconnected from its buses and a special DMA controller. (DMAC) is used to directly route data between the I/O device and system memory.

DOS (disk operating system) A control program that manages the overall operation of a magnetic disk-based computer system.

DIP (dual in-line package) A type of through-hole IC package in which the leads are arranged in two parallel rows on each side of the case.

DRAM (dynamic RAM) A type of read/write semiconductor memory that uses a capacitor as the storage cell. DRAMs must be repeatedly refreshed or their data will be lost.

E²PROM (electrically erasable programmable ROM) A type of ROM that can be programmed and erased electrically without removing the chip from its socket.

Fanout A measure of the number of gate inputs another logic gate can drive without exceeding its I_{OL} or I_{OH} specifications.

Flags Internal microprocessor flip-flops whose outputs are set or reset depending on the result of the last computer instruction.

FM (frequency modulation) Single-density encoding scheme used by magnetic disks.

Full duplex Serial communications technique in which each modem can simultaneously transmit and receive data.

Half duplex Serial communications technique in which the receiver and transmitter share the signal line. When using half duplex, only one modem can transmit at a time.

Handshaking logic A digital interface in which the sender and receiver of data exchange BUSY/READY signals to synchronize the data transfer.

Hexadecimal A base-16 number system convenient with digital circuits because one hexadecimal digit exactly represents four binary bits.

I/O (input–output) device A device such as a printer or a keyboard through which a computer may input or output information.

I/O (input–output) port The electrical interface to which an I/O device is connected.

Interrupt See interrupt line.

Interrupt driven A computer interface that is controlled via interrupts.

Interrupt line   An input line monitored by the CPU. When this line is active, the current program is suspended and a special interrupt service routine (ISR) is run. Upon completion of the ISR, the interrupted program is resumed.

Interleave   Relative location of consecutive sectors on a magnetic disk. With an interleave of 3, consecutive sectors are located every third sector.

I_{OH} The high-level-output source current.

I_{OL} The low-level-output sink current.

K (kilo)   In binary 1024. (*Example*: A 64K byte memory [64KB]).

Label   A name given to a memory location.

Latch   Logic circuit made up of flip-flops and designed to store digital data. (*Example*: An 8-bit latch can be used as a microcomputer output port.)

Logic probe   A digital tester with LED indicators for a logic 0, a logic 1, and a pulsing condition.

Machine cycle   A computer operation in which an address is output and data transferred. (*Example*: A memory-read machine cycle.)

Mask   A software term used to describe a combination of bits chosen to force selected bits of the operand low thus hiding their effect.

M (mega)   In binary, 1,048,576. (*Example*: A 2 million byte/second data rate [2 MB/s].)

Memory   A digital circuit capable of storing a logic 1 or a logic 0.

Memory map   A drawing showing the type, size, and address location of the memory circuits in a computer.

Memory mapped I/O   An interfacing technique in which the I/O devices are wired to respond to memory addresses rather than I/O addresses.

Microcomputer   A digital computer system using a microprocessor chip as the CPU.

Microprocessor   An integrated circuit containing all of the logic of the central processing unit of a computer.

MS-DOS (Microsoft disk operating system)   Popular disk operating system for microcomputers based on the 8086 series of 16 and 32-bit microprocessors.

Mnemonic   Abbreviation for a computer instruction.

Modem (modulator/demodulator)   A device used to convert serial data into audio tones suitable for transmission over the telephone network.

MFM (modified FM)   Double-density encoding scheme used by magnetic disks.

Noise immunity   The ability of a logic circuit to reject and not respond to noise riding on its inputs, measured in volts.

Object code   The binary form of a computer program ready to run.

Op-code (operation code)   Mnemonic for a computer instruction specifying the type of operation that is to occur.

Open collector (or open drain)   A type of logic circuit in which the high output level corresponds to an open circuit. The outputs of such circuits are commonly wired together to perform the wired-OR function via an external pull-up resistor.

Operand   The memory location or CPU register to be accessed by the current instruction.

Parity   An error detection scheme in which a checking bit is added to each data character such that the total number of 1s in the character is always even (even parity) or always odd (odd parity).

Peripheral   An I/O device such as a keyboard or a printer.

Polling   An I/O technique in which the CPU continually checks the I/O device to see if it is ready. Also called programmed I/O.

Port   See I/O port.

Program counter   CPU register holding the address of the next instruction to be fetched and executed.

PROM (programmable read-only memory)   A type of ROM that can be programmed with the desired data. (*Example*: Mask- or fusible-link programmable.)

Propagation delay time   See switching time.

Protocol   A set of rules that have been developed to standardize the transmission of data between two systems.

RAM (random access memory)   Main memory that can be read from or written to by the CPU.

Read cycle   That portion of a computer instruction in which data is input to the CPU from memory or an I/O device.

ROM (read-only memory)   A type of memory from which the CPU can only read but not write; often used for "booting up" the computer.

Refresh   The process of recharging the bit cells in a DRAM.

Register   A set of flip-flops wired with a common clock line and used to store several bits of data.

RS-232D   Electronics Industries Associates (EIA) standard governing serial data transmission. Specified are logic 1 and 0 voltage levels, data rates, signal descriptions, and connector pinouts.

RLL (run length limited)   Encoding scheme used by magnetic disks. RLL-encoded disks achieve a 50% greater bit density and transfer rate than MFM encoded disks.

Schmitt trigger   A type of logic circuit that switches at two different input voltage levels depending if the input is high, going low, or low, going high. This property allows the circuit to reject noise and ringing on the input signal.

Sector   For a magnetic disk, a portion of a track used for storing data. (*Example*: A low-density MS-DOS-formatted 5¼″ floppy disk has nine sectors per track and 512 bytes per sector.)

Serial data transmission   A method of sending digital data one bit after the other on a single wire.

Signed binary number   A binary number in which the most significant bit, if set, represents a negative number.

Software   The instructions that form a computer program.

SSR (solid-state relay)   A semiconductor circuit equivalent to a mechanical relay but with no moving parts.

Source code   A form of a computer program in which the instructions are written in a high level form. (*Example*: Instruction mnemonics.)

Stack   A last-in first-out area of RAM set aside for storing temporary data via the PUSH and POP instructions. The stack is also used to store subroutine return addresses.

Start bit   With asynchronous serial data, a synchronizing bit, always a logic 0, identifying the start of a serial character.

SRAM (static RAM)   A type of read/write semiconductor memory that uses a flip-flop as the storage cell.

Stop bit   With asynchronous serial data, a synchronizing bit, always a logic 1, identifying the end of a serial character.

Subroutine   A program within a program that can be called whenever needed by the main program. Because subroutines can be used several times within the same program, their use helps minimize the total number of instructions required by that program.

Switching time   The time required for a logic circuit to switch from one logic state to the other—also called the propagation delay time.

Synchronous   A type of logic design in which all circuit outputs switch at the same instant synchronized to a common clock signal.

Synchronous serial communications   A method of sending data serially without start and stop bits.

T state   One period of the system clock signal.

Track   Circular path scanned by the read/write head of a magnetic disk. (*Example*: A 5¼″ MS-DOS-formatted floppy disk has 40 tracks per side.

TTL (transistor-transistor-logic)   A type of saturating digital circuit technology employing bipolar transistors; available as a complete catalog line of logic gates, flip-flops, and counters.

Tri-state   A type of logic circuit capable of producing three different output states: high-, low-, and open-circuit. The latter state is often referred to as the tri-state.

Truth table   For a digital circuit, the list of all possible inputs and the corresponding circuit outputs.

Two's complement   A method of representing negative numbers formed by complementing all bits in the byte or word and adding one.

V_{OH} The high level output voltage produced by a logic circuit.

V_{OL} The low level output voltage produced by a logic circuit.

UV EPROM (ultraviolet erasable programmable ROM) A type of ROM that can be electrically programmed, but erased via exposure to ultraviolet light.

UART (universal asynchronous receiver–transmitter) An IC used to transmit and receive serial data.

Wait state Extra T state added to an instruction to give the memory or I/O device additional time to respond with data.

Write cycle That portion of a computer instruction in which data is output from the CPU to memory or an I/O device.

INDEX

CPU module, 179; (illus.), 180
CPU specifications, 53–60; (illus.), 60
I/O support devices, (table), 326
I/O timing specifications, (table), 271
instruction set, 71–79
programming model, 68
single-stepping circuit, (illus.), 186, 187
three chip microcomputer system, 331–32; (illus.), 333
wait state generator, (illus.), 207
8204 DRAM controller, 251–52; (illus.), 253
8224 clock generator, 50, (illus.); 56, (illus.), 154
8228 system controller, 50, (illus.); 56, (illus.), 175
8237A programmable DMA controller, 375–78
  floppy disk interface example, 391–94
  programming, 382–90
  response time and transfer rate, 379–82
8251A universal synchronous/asynchronous receiver/transmitter (USART), 479–84
asynchronous mode programming, 484–86
  RS-232 support, 519–20
synchronous mode progamming, 486–88
8254A programmable interval timer (PIT), 353–63
  design example, 360–63
8255A programmable peripheral interface (PPI), 332–35
  bit set/reset mode, 339
  mode 0, 336–41
  mode 1, 341–48
  mode 2, 348–53
8259A programmable interrupt controller (PIC), 363–68
  programming, 368–74
8755A, 16K EPROM with I/O, 327–32
founders, 8–9
instruction set (table), 39, 71–79
programming model, 65–68; (illus.), 65
single-stepping circuit, 184; (illus.), 185, 186
wait state generator; (illus.), 206
Interrupts (*see also* Intel 8259A)
  8080, 8085, Z-80, 296–97; (table), 298, 299–303
  priorities, 306–9
  response time, (table), 303

summary, 309–11
transfer rate, 304–6
overview, (illus.), 295, 296

Jobs, Steve, 11

Keyboard, interface example, 282–86, 338–39
Kilby, Jack, 7

LED display, interface example, 421–26
Logic analyzer, 33
Logic gates, symbology, 176–77

Machine cycles (table); 5, (*see also* specific processor)
  I/O cycles, (illus.), 41
memory read and write cycles, (illus.), 40
  timing, 34–41; (illus.), 37
Machine language, 27–29
Magnetic tape, 201
Memory
  address decoders
    block, 235–36
    NAND gate, 232–35
    PAL, 242–44
    ROM, 240–42
  dump, program example, 120–22
  filling, program example, 112–16
  flash, 215–18
  map, 34; (illus.), 35, 209, 210
  overview of types, 198–201; (table), 201
  part numbers, 226; (table), 227
  read and write machine cycles, (illus.), 40, 202–5
    read cycle specifications for 8080, 8085 and Z-80 processors, (table), 204
    write cycle specifications for 8080, 8085 and Z-80 processors, (table), 205
  RAM
    applications, 208–9
    dynamic, 220–22; (illus.), 221
    EDO, 249
    interfacing, 251–55
    page mode, 247
    refresh, 249–51
    synchronous, 249
    timing, 247; (illus.) 248
    SIMMs, 222; (illus.), 223–25
    static, 218–20
      interfacing, 237–40